THE ECONOMICS OF SPORTS

Fifth Edition

THE ECONOMICS OF SPORTS

Michael A. Leeds
Temple University

Peter von Allmen
Skidmore College

Boston   Columbus   Indianapolis   New York   San Francisco   Upper Saddle River
Amsterdam   Cape Town   Dubai   London   Madrid   Milan   Munich   Paris   Montréal   Toronto
Delhi   Mexico City   São Paulo   Sydney   Hong Kong   Seoul   Singapore   Taipei   Tokyo

The Pearson Series in Economics

Abel/Bernanke/Croushore
*Macroeconomics**

Bade/Parkin
*Foundations of Economics**

Berck/Helfand
The Economics of the Environment

Bierman/Fernandez
Game Theory with Economic Applications

Blanchard
*Macroeconomics**

Blau/Ferber/Winkler
The Economics of Women, Men and Work

Boardman/Greenberg/Vining/ Weimer
Cost-Benefit Analysis

Boyer
Principles of Transportation Economics

Branson
Macroeconomic Theory and Policy

Brock/Adams
The Structure of American Industry

Bruce
Public Finance and the American Economy

Carlton/Perloff
Modern Industrial Organization

Case/Fair/Oster
*Principles of Economics**

Caves/Frankel/Jones
World Trade and Payments: An Introduction

Chapman
Environmental Economics: Theory, Application, and Policy

Cooter/Ulen
Law & Economics

Downs
An Economic Theory of Democracy

Ehrenberg/Smith
Modern Labor Economics

Farnham
Economics for Managers

Folland/Goodman/Stano
The Economics of Health and Health Care

Fort
Sports Economics

Froyen
Macroeconomics

Fusfeld
The Age of the Economist

Gerber
*International Economics**

González-Rivera
Forecasting for Economics and Business

Gordon
*Macroeconomics**

Greene
Econometric Analysis

Gregory
Essentials of Economics

Gregory/Stuart
Russian and Soviet Economic Performance and Structure

Hartwick/Olewiler
The Economics of Natural Resource Use

Heilbroner/Milberg
The Making of the Economic Society

Heyne/Boettke/Prychitko
The Economic Way of Thinking

Hoffman/Averett
Women and the Economy: Family, Work, and Pay

Holt
Markets, Games and Strategic Behavior

Hubbard/O'Brien
*Economics**
*Money, Banking, and the Financial System**

Hubbard/O'Brien/Rafferty
*Macroeconomics**

Hughes/Cain
American Economic History

Husted/Melvin
International Economics

Jehle/Reny
Advanced Microeconomic Theory

Johnson-Lans
A Health Economics Primer

Keat/Young
Managerial Economics

Klein
Mathematical Methods for Economics

Krugman/Obstfeld/Melitz
International Economics: Theory and Policy*

Laidler
The Demand for Money

Leeds/von Allmen
The Economics of Sports

Leeds/von Allmen/Schiming
Economics*

Lipsey/Ragan/Storer
Economics*

Lynn
Economic Development: Theory and Practice for a Divided World

Miller
Economics Today*
Understanding Modern Economics

Miller/Benjamin
The Economics of Macro Issues

Miller/Benjamin/North
The Economics of Public Issues

Mills/Hamilton
Urban Economics

Mishkin
The Economics of Money, Banking, and Financial Markets*
The Economics of Money, Banking, and Financial Markets, Business School Edition*
Macroeconomics: Policy and Practice*

Murray
Econometrics: A Modern Introduction

Nafziger
The Economics of Developing Countries

O'Sullivan/Sheffrin/Perez
Economics: Principles, Applications and Tools*

Parkin
Economics*

Perloff
Microeconomics*
Microeconomics: Theory and Applications with Calculus*

Phelps
Health Economics

Pindyck/Rubinfeld
Microeconomics*

Riddell/Shackelford/Stamos/ Schneider
Economics: A Tool for Critically Understanding Society

Ritter/Silber/Udell
Principles of Money, Banking & Financial Markets*

Roberts
The Choice: A Fable of Free Trade and Protection

Rohlf
Introduction to Economic Reasoning

Ruffin/Gregory
Principles of Economics

Sargent
Rational Expectations and Inflation

Sawyer/Sprinkle
International Economics

Scherer
Industry Structure, Strategy, and Public Policy

Schiller
The Economics of Poverty and Discrimination

Sherman
Market Regulation

Silberberg
Principles of Microeconomics

Stock/Watson
Introduction to Econometrics

Studenmund
Using Econometrics: A Practical Guide

Tietenberg/Lewis
Environmental and Natural Resource Economics
Environmental Economics and Policy

Todaro/Smith
Economic Development

Waldman
Microeconomics

Waldman/Jensen
Industrial Organization: Theory and Practice

Walters/Walters/Appel/Callahan/ Centanni/Maex/O'Neill
Econversations: Today's Students Discuss Today's Issues

Weil
Economic Growth

Williamson
Macroeconomics

Editor-in-Chief: Donna Battista
Acquisitions Editor: Noel Seibert
Editorial Assistant: Emily Brodeur
Director of Marketing: Maggie Moylan
Executive Marketing Manager: Lori DeShazo
Marketing Assistant: Kim Lovato
Senior Managing Editor: Nancy Fenton
Production Project Manager: Karen Carter
Production Manager: Maggie Brobeck
Manager, Central Design: Jayne Conte
Cover Designer: Suzanne Behnke
Cover Art: © S. Pytel/Shutterstock

Manager, Visual Research: Rachel Youdelman
Manager, Rights and Permissions: Michael Joyce
Media Director: Susan Schoenberg
Lead Media Project Manager: Melissa Honig
Full Service Project Management and Composition: George Jacob/Integra Software Services
Printer/Binder: Courier/Westford
Cover Printer: Lehigh Phoenix
Text Font: Palatino LT Std

Credits and acknowledgments borrowed from other sources and reproduced, with permission, in this textbook appear on the appropriate page within text or on page 423.

Library of Congress Cataloging-in-Publication Data
Leeds, Michael (Michael A.)
    The economics of sports/Michael A. Leeds, Peter von Allmen.— 5th ed.
        p. cm.
    ISBN-13: 978-0-13-302292-6
    ISBN-10: 0-13-302292-7
    1. Sports—Economic aspects.   I. Allmen, Peter von.   II. Title.
    GV716.L44 2013
    338.4'3796—dc23

                                    2012032292

10 9 8 7 6 5 4 3 2 1

ISBN-10:   0-13-302292-7
ISBN-13: 978-0-13-302292-6

For Daniel, Melanie, Dan, Tom, and Eric, who make everyday a treasure.

BRIEF CONTENTS

CONTENTS

PREFACE

As *The Economics of Sports* reaches its fifth edition, it is interesting for us to reflect back on the almost fifteen years since we began work on the first edition. When the first edition was published, the field was relatively new but rapidly growing. Undergraduate sports economics courses were popular, but not widely offered. Today, sports economics stands as a vital subdiscipline within applied microeconomics, with new and exciting research being produced by economists from around the world. Along with the increased research, the number of sports economics courses has grown as well. Throughout this process of growth and change, sports economics continues to serve as both a mirror and a lens, reflecting our broader culture and values, while at the same time bringing into focus such fundamental issues as fairness and the legitimacy of free markets. With the passing of each season, new events unfold in professional and amateur sports that deserve analysis and explanation. Finally, in the context of this book, sports economics remains a vital and interesting area of study for students of economics. Sports provides a seemingly endless set of examples from every area of microeconomics, giving students the opportunity to study public finance, industrial organization, and labor markets in a context that holds student interest like no other industry.

Over the many years that we have worked on this project, we have enjoyed continuous help and support from students and colleagues at colleges and universities across the United States and around the world. Our colleagues continue to offer encouragement, share classroom experiences, and suggest new and different coverage as the industry evolves. For all of this support and help, we are most grateful. And as we have said many times, we hope that our own enthusiasm, as well as the enthusiasm others have shared with us, is reflected in the text.

In recent years, many outstanding books that concentrate on specific sports or particular aspects of the economics of sports have been published. This text stands apart from the others in that it has the instruction of economic concepts as its central focus. We hope you find it useful and interesting.

NEW TO THIS EDITION

The fifth edition represents our most comprehensive revision and update of the text since the first edition appeared in 2001. In doing so, we have retained the features from previous editions that made learning about sports economics meaningful as well as enjoyable, while at the same time incorporating many recent events in the sports industry and the broader economy.

- We have introduced a new feature for the fifth edition: Sports and the Law. Though we discuss the important decisions that have shaped the sports industry throughout the text, we've chosen four specific cases that particularly highlight the profound impact of the law in this industry. You will find these features in Chapters 3, 4, 7, and 9.

- Chapter 2 now contains a full review of production theory in the context of team rosters as well as a review of the relationship between marginal product and marginal cost.
- Chapter 3 has been rearranged to highlight the differences between profit-maximization and win maximization as owner strategies. It also places greater emphasis on the role of the theory of clubs as an explanation for the recent turmoil in intercollegiate athletic conferences.
- We have supplemented our presentation of advanced profit-maximizing strategies with a discussion of dynamic ticket pricing, including a comparison to variable ticket pricing and ticket bundling.
- The most significant change for this edition is the reorganization of Chapters 6 and 7. Chapter 6 now covers the benefits of public support for stadiums and events such as the Olympics to owners, fans, and cities. Chapter 7 covers the economics of financing these facilities and events. While much of the discussion that users liked from previous editions has been retained, the new organization should lead to improved student understanding.
- Chapter 9 has been revised to provide a comprehensive explanation of the process and outcomes of the new collective bargaining agreements in the NBA and NFL.
- We have integrated Chapter 11 more fully into the rest of the book by emphasizing such concepts as profit-maximization and spillovers that appear elsewhere. This allows us to show more clearly how athletic departments resemble—and do not resemble—professional sports teams.

As with the previous editions, our goal for the fifth edition is to keep the text comprehensive yet accessible. The text is designed to serve as the foundation for undergraduate courses in sports economics. The nature of the subject matter makes this a unique challenge. Unlike area courses such as industrial organization or labor economics, which are self-contained fields in the broader area of economics, sports economics cuts across a wide array of economic disciplines. To deal with this problem, we have split the text into five parts, three of which are devoted to illustrating prominent areas of economics: industrial organization, public finance, and labor economics. We hope that this division provides students with an overview of much of economics and inspires them to pursue each field in its own right. Because we focus largely on professional sports in the first four parts of the book, we include a closing section devoted to amateur sports. This final part provides insights into theories related to the not-for-profit sector of the economy, such as the theory of bureaucracy. Each of the five parts of this text presents significant economic theory and recent evidence and research for that area of economics.

To make the text accessible, we assume that students have had one semester of microeconomics principles. Balancing accessibility against an economist's desire for theoretical rigor remains a challenge. In order to help the students understand the economics and to make the treatment more entertaining, we have included a generous component of sports history to place the events and economic theory in perspective.

INTENDED AUDIENCE

Economics of sports classes are taught at a variety of levels, ranging from undergraduate courses, with principles of economics as the only prerequisites, to the graduate level. This text is designed to offer a high level of flexibility to the instructor. All the material in the main body of the text should be accessible to students with a single semester of microeconomics principles. In order to enrich courses taught at a higher level, we have included appendices containing intermediate-level material at the end of several chapters. To ensure that all students begin the course with a common background, we provide a substantial review of principles-level material in Chapter 2. This material can either be covered explicitly with lecture support or left to the students to read on their own, as needed. For instructors interested in presenting the results of econometric research, Chapter 2 contains an appendix on the fundamentals of regression. In advanced undergraduate- and graduate-level courses, the text can serve as a foundation for common understanding of basic concepts.

ORGANIZATION OF THE TEXT AND COVERAGE OPTIONS

As stated previously, the text is divided into five parts. The first two chapters provide an introduction to sports economics, a review of principles-level tools, and an illustration of how economic principles apply to the sports industry. Chapters 3, 4, and 5 focus on the industrial organization of the sports industry. Here, we discuss the competitive landscape, the implications of monopoly power, profit-maximization, and competitive balance. Chapter 4 focuses specifically on issues of antitrust and regulation and discusses how they have impacted the formation, success, and, sometimes, the failure of leagues. Chapter 5 describes why leagues are concerned about competitive balance, how competitive balance is measured, and how leagues might attempt to alter the balance of competition in a league. Chapters 6 and 7 focus on public finance. In this portion of the text, students learn the benefits and costs of providing public support for stadiums and events, why teams seem to have so much power over municipalities and why municipalities fight so hard to keep the teams they have as well as court new ones. Chapters 8 through 10 focus on labor issues related to sports. Chapter 8 introduces the fundamental theories of labor markets, including human capital theory and tournament theory. Chapter 9 covers monopoly unions and monopsony, two labor market imperfections that profoundly impact the functioning of most sports labor markets. Chapter 10 discusses discrimination. Finally, Chapter 11 focuses on the economics of amateur sports, especially major collegiate sports. Because major college sports is really an industry itself, this chapter serves as a capstone to the text, incorporating the theories and concepts from many of the previous chapters.

ADDITIONAL RESOURCES

The text is accompanied by an online Instructor's Manual, updated for the fifth edition by George Diemer of Chestnut Hill College. We are pleased to provide PowerPoint slides, written by Eva Marikova Leeds of Moravian College that contain all figures and tables in the text as well as lecture notes for classroom presentation. We are also pleased to offer a Test Bank for the fifth edition of the text, written by, David Chaplin of Northwest Nazarene University which contains additional questions and suggested answers for further classroom or test use. The Instructor's Manual, PowerPoint slides, and Test Bank may be accessed via the Instructor's Resource Center at www.pearsonhighered.com/irc.

Students and instructors may also access the text's companion Web site at www.pearsonhighered.com/leeds. Updated for the fifth edition, the Web site features chapter quizzes, current Web links, and additional sports data.

ACKNOWLEDGMENTS

In a project such as this, the list of people who contributed to its completion extends far beyond those whose names appear on the cover. We owe personal and professional debts of sincere gratitude to a great many people. First, we thank our team at Pearson including Noel Seibert, Emily Brodeur, Maggie Brobeck, and Carolyn Terbush. We also are grateful for the advice, encouragement, and suggestions from the ever-growing community of sports economists who use this book. Their input and support serve as a continuing source of motivation and assistance. We would particularly like to thank all of those who read and reviewed the manuscript as we prepared the fifth edition, including Andrew Zimbalist, Smith College; Bruce K. Johnson, Centre College; Mary N. Gade, Oklahoma State University; Nancy Jianakoplos, Colorado State University; Phil Miller, Minnesota State University–Mankato; Joshua Price, University of Texas–Arlington; and Wayne A. Grove, Le Moyne College. Their suggestions for improvements were excellent, and we tried our best to incorporate them wherever possible. A special thanks to Eva Marikova Leeds for her diligent review of the manuscript during the revision process. Finally, as always, we thank our families: Eva, Daniel, Melanie, Heather, Daniel, Thomas, and Eric, all of whom provided unwavering support.

Michael A. Leeds
Peter von Allmen

THE ECONOMICS OF SPORTS

PART ONE

Introduction and Review of Economic Concepts

CHAPTER 1

Economics and Sports

All I remember about my wedding day in 1967 is that the Cubs dropped a double-header.

—George Will[1]

INTRODUCTION

On December 10, 2011, in a game watched by over 60 percent of Spanish television viewers and millions more around the world, the two most successful teams in the top Spanish soccer league, La Liga, faced off in a game that has come to symbolize much more than a soccer contest.[2] Real Madrid, long allied with Spanish conservatism, jumped to an early 1–0 lead, only to lose 3–1 to its archrival, FC Barcelona. "Barça" is so much a symbol of Catalan pride that the team motto is "More than a club." As always, the win touched off an enormous celebration in the winning city. Just a few months later, more than a million New York Giants fans filled the streets of Manhattan for the ulti-mate celebration—a ticker tape parade—following the Giants Super Bowl victory, while at the same time the city of Boston was awash in the excitement brought on by the annual "Beanpot" hockey tournament between Northeastern, Harvard, Boston College, and Boston University.

Sports occupy a unique position in the human psyche. Athletic contests around the world have long been a way for individuals, institutions, cities, and nations to define themselves. Sports can bring out the best and the worst in people. As early as the 19th century, universities used football to give their students a sense of identity. Cities feel that they have achieved "big-time" status once

[1]George F. Will, *Bunts* (New York: Scribner, 1998), p. 22.

[2]"El Clasico TV ratings break record," December 13, 2011, at http://www.insidespanishfootball.com/el-clasico-tv-ratings-break-record/, viewed March 6, 2012.

3

they have attracted a major league franchise. At the national level, Japan's performance in the 2011 Women's World Cup provided a much-needed lift to a country devastated by the earthquake and tsunami and shaken by a near nuclear disaster. At the same time, police have had to quell riots on campuses in the wake of heartbreaking losses—or big victories. Reports of domestic violence rise in cities when "their" team is upset in the Super Bowl. In their pursuit of national pride, countries have sometimes sacrificed the physical well-being of their young athletes by giving them performance-enhancing drugs that have had dire side-effects.[3]

Sports can also serve as tools by which nations conduct foreign policy. They have brought people together, as was the case in 1971 when a team of American table tennis players and their "ping-pong diplomacy" marked the first step in the reopening of relations between the United States and China. They have also kept people apart, as demonstrated by the boycotts that disrupted the 1976, 1980, and 1984 Olympics.

The clamor over sports might lead one to think that the sports industry dominates the world economy. In fact, compared to many firms, let alone industries, it is a very small operation. According to *Forbes Magazine*, the total revenues generated by the four major North American sports leagues (basketball, baseball, football, and hockey) totaled about $21 billion in 2010, which would not rank among the top 100 revenue-generating companies. The sports' revenues are about one-twentieth of those of Walmart and roughly equal to the $21.6 billion generated by Northwestern Mutual, yet, unlike sports, Walmart does not have its own section in any newspaper, and the local insurance company does not merit a segment on the evening news.[4]

This book harnesses this enthusiasm for sports and uses it to introduce a variety of economic concepts. These concepts frequently have applications beyond the business of sports. For example, understanding how sports leagues exercise monopoly power provides deeper insight into the policies followed by the Organization of the Petroleum Exporting Countries (OPEC) or Google, and learning about the impact of free agency on team payrolls shows how free markets affect the distribution of incomes in an economy. Studying sports economics thus provides more than an appreciation for the sports industry. It also demonstrates how economic reasoning helps us understand the world around us.

1.1 THE ORGANIZATION OF THE TEXT

The text is divided into five parts. The remainder of this part provides an extensive review of basic economic theory, particularly supply and demand, the basics of production theory, and models of perfect competition and monopoly.

---

[3]See Katie Kindelain, "Kentucky Students Riot after NCAA Championship Win," *abcnews.com*, April 3, 2012, at http://abcnews.go.com/blogs/headlines/2012/04/kentucky-students-riot-after-ncaa-championship-win; David Card and Gordon B. Dahl, "Family Violence and Football: The Effect of Unexpected Emotional Cues on Violent Behavior," *Quarterly Journal of Economics*, vol. 126, no.1 (February 2011), pp. 103–143; Steven Ungerleider, *Faust's Gold: Inside the East German Doping Machine* (New York: Thomas Dunne Books, 2001).

[4]"Fortune 500," *Fortune*, May 12, 2012, at http://money.cnn.com/magazines/fortune/fortune500/2011/full_list/index.html, viewed March 8, 2012.

The tools introduced in Chapter 2 are used throughout the text to inform a wide variety of questions in the broader sports industry.

The next three parts of the text are devoted to showing how three particular areas of economics provide insight into how sports function. Part Two presents the industrial organization of sports. **Industrial organization** is the study of how firms maximize profit. In Chapter 3, we discuss the purpose and structure of a variety of professional leagues. We also review the competitive and monopoly market structures and discuss the implications for profit maximization in each case. In Chapter 4, we extend the discussion of monopoly and analyze the challenges that concentrated markets create for consumers. In Chapter 5, we investigate the desirability of competitive balance, how it can be measured, how it has changed over time, and how leagues have dealt with unbalanced competition.

Part Three contains two chapters on the public finance of sports. **Public finance** asks how and why governments provide goods and services and how they raise the funds to pay for them. In Chapter 6, we discuss the potential benefits of new arenas for both teams and the cities in which they play and describe how the size and shape of facilities have evolved. In Chapter 7, we turn to the cost of these facilities, including an analysis of why local governments might pay some or all of these costs as a form of investment and, if the investment is made, how to best fund it.

Part Four covers the labor economics of professional sports. **Labor economics** analyzes how markets determine the level of employment and compensation. In Chapter 8, we use labor markets to explain why professional athletes receive such high salaries. In doing so, we introduce basic labor market concepts, such as human capital, and analyze the potential impact of teams and leagues as powerful employers on wages. Chapter 9 explores labor market institutions, such as player associations, which also affect salaries and working conditions of players. In Chapter 10, we discuss the history and implications of discrimination in professional sports. From the informal yet strictly enforced "color lines" that marked the National Football League (NFL) and Major League Baseball (MLB) until 1946 and 1947, respectively, to the limits that such leagues as Nippon Professional Baseball still place on how many foreign players are permitted on team rosters, sports provide many examples of discriminatory behavior.

Finally, in Part Five (Chapter 11), we broaden our study of sports to include amateur athletics at the Olympic and major college levels. We present the history of amateurism and the consequences that misperceptions about this history have had for the National Collegiate Athletic Association (NCAA). This chapter also examines the effects of recent changes in admissions and eligibility standards on schools and athletes.

Special Features and Additional Resources

There are two types of feature boxes in the text. The first highlights specific legal decisions that have had a major impact on the structure of professional sports. Economics does not exist in a vacuum, and these cases are vitally important to understanding how certain groups have used or tried to use economic power to their advantage, sometimes in conflict with laws such as those that apply to discrimination, antitrust, and fair labor standards. The second contains biographical sketches. The world of sports is filled with colorful personalities that add to our enjoyment of the game. Some of these people are well known to even the casual sports fan. Others are less known, but all have played an important role in the evolution of the economics of sports. These biographical sketches, the first of which appears in this chapter, highlight both their accomplishments in the context of the chapter and their character as individuals.

As you progress through the course, we encourage you to make full use of the Internet as a powerful and easy-to-use source of further reading. First and foremost, the publisher of this text, Addison Wesley, maintains a Web site specifically designed to support the book. Log on to **www.aw-bc.com/leeds_vonallmen** and you will find a set of interesting links to other valuable sites as well as information that we provide directly to assist you. The site is updated regularly so that it contains links to sites and stories that are sure to be of interest.

In addition, virtually every major (and almost every minor) league team and individual sports league or association has its own Web site. These sites are continually updated with information about news (including economic events) from around the league. Finally, many sports magazines maintain Web sites that have current and archived information that can be very useful for term papers, projects, and general information. One caution: Beware of unreliable information that is rampant on noncommercial, individual blogs and private Web sites. The information they convey is often based on opinion rather than on fact and is of little or no value.

Let the games begin!

1.2 BABE RUTH AND COMPARATIVE ADVANTAGE

Economics can often help to resolve what at first glance seems to be puzzling behavior. We begin most chapters by posing a few puzzles that people have faced in the sports world. The material that we present in each chapter then helps us to solve the puzzles that we raise at the outset. This section provides a taste of what is to come. We use the theory of comparative advantage, a concept normally used by specialists in international trade, to explain why the Boston Red Sox stopped using the best left-handed pitcher in baseball in 1918.

Opportunity Costs

In 1915, a young left-hander for the Boston Red Sox emerged as one of the dominant pitchers in the game, helping the Red Sox to World Series championships in 1916 and 1918. In the 1918 World Series, he won two games and set a record for consecutive scoreless innings that stood until 1961. From 1915 through 1918, he won 78 games and lost only 40, and he allowed slightly over 2 runs per game. In 1919, he pitched in only 17 games and won only 16 more games in the rest of his career, yet no fans complained. The reason was that the young pitcher was none other than George Herman "Babe" Ruth, who went on to redefine baseball as a power-hitting rightfielder for the Red Sox and later for the New York Yankees.

Babe Ruth confronted the Red Sox with the classic economic problem of opportunity costs. An **opportunity cost** is the value of the best forgone alternative.

We all face opportunity costs in our everyday lives. Our limited time, income, and energy constantly force us to choose among alternative actions. When we go to the movies on Saturday night, we no longer have the time or the money to go to a concert that evening. When the Red Sox used Babe Ruth as a rightfielder, they gave up the chance to use him as a pitcher. (Because the main contribution of a rightfielder is as a hitter, we will use the term "hitter" rather than rightfielder from now on.) If the goal of a team is to win as many games as possible (an objective we will explore later in this text) then the opportunity cost of using a player at one position is the wins that the team sacrifices by not using him at another position. When the Red Sox used Babe Ruth as an outfielder, they sacrificed wins by not having a great pitcher in their rotation. If they had kept Ruth as a pitcher, they would have sacrificed wins by not having a great hitter in their lineup.

Absolute and Comparative Advantage

It is usually easy to decide where to use a player, as only a few players make good pitchers, and pitchers are typically bad hitters. Babe Ruth, however, was an exception. He was the best pitcher *and* the best hitter on the team. Being the best at everything meant that Babe Ruth had an absolute advantage at both pitching and hitting. A person or country has an **absolute advantage** in an activity when it is more efficient at that activity than another person or country. For example, if the United States can make cancer drugs using fewer resources than Japan can, it has an absolute advantage in making cancer drugs. Because Babe Ruth was a better pitcher and hitter than any other player on the Red Sox, he had an absolute advantage over all his teammates in both pitching and hitting.

The Red Sox decided to use Babe Ruth as a hitter because, although he had an absolute advantage as both a hitter and a pitcher, his absolute advantage as a hitter was much larger than his absolute advantage as a pitcher. This meant that Babe Ruth had a comparative advantage as a hitter. A person or country has a **comparative advantage** when the opportunity cost of an activity is lower than it is for another person or country. Because Babe Ruth was such a good hitter, the opportunity cost of using him as a pitcher (the number of wins the team would sacrifice) was extremely high, much higher than for other players on the team. This meant that, even though Babe Ruth had an *absolute* advantage over his teammates as a pitcher, he did not have a *comparative* advantage as a pitcher.[5]

To see the gains from moving Babe Ruth from the pitcher's mound to the outfield more clearly, we compare the opportunity cost of using Babe Ruth at each position in 1918. The opportunity cost of using Ruth as an outfielder was the additional runs given up by Red Sox pitchers, which would result in more losses. The opportunity cost of using Ruth as a pitcher was the reduction in runs scored by the Red Sox, which also might have led to more losses. Ruth's switch

---

[5]For a more complete explanation of Babe Ruth's comparative advantage during his career with the New York Yankees, see Edward Scahill, "Did Babe Ruth Have a Comparative Advantage as a Pitcher?" *Journal of Economic Education,* vol. 21, no. 4 (Fall 1990), pp. 402–410.

from pitcher to outfielder probably displaced Tilly Walker, arguably the worst of the Red Sox starting outfielders in 1917, and made room for Dutch Leonard, who had the highest earned run average (ERA) among the regular starting pitchers in 1918.[6] Ruth's last year as a full-time pitcher—1917—was an amazing one; he won 24 games, lost 13, and gave up about 2 runs per game. The first year that Ruth played mostly in the outfield was even more amazing. He led the league in slugging percentage (the average number of bases advanced per at bat), and his 11 home runs not only led the league but also were almost twice as many as the 6 hit by the entire Red Sox starting outfield in 1917.

Table 1.1 shows that replacing Ruth, who had a 2.01 ERA in 1917, with Leonard, who had a (still low) 2.72 ERA, meant that the Sox gave up 0.71 more runs per 9 innings than they would have if Ruth had had an identical year in 1918. Over the 14 games that Leonard pitched, that meant that the Red Sox' opportunity cost of using Babe Ruth in the field was about 10 runs over the course of the 1918 season.[7] Using the formula for runs produced (runs scored + runs batted in − home runs) shows that Ruth produced 29 more runs in 1918 than Walker had produced in 1917. Thus, the Red Sox came out 19 runs ahead from the switch.

At this point, one might ask why the Red Sox did not use Babe Ruth as a pitcher every four or five days and as a hitter every day in between. In baseball, the skills of pitching and hitting are so different that one cannot develop both at the same time. No player has ever managed to play every day and pitch every fourth or fifth day. Acquiring the skills needed to become an elite hitter or pitcher demands a great deal of intensive practice. This pre-commitment generally does not leave enough time or energy to develop alternative skills.

More generally, one of the most important conclusions of the theory of comparative advantage is that developing particular skills and specializing in activities that use these skills makes individuals, firms, and nations better off. Professors employ research assistants and working parents hire day care providers because

TABLE 1.1 The Gain and Loss from Moving Babe Ruth

Player	Runs Sacrificed	Runs Produced
Babe Ruth	2.01 per game	105 per season
Dutch Leonard	2.72 per game	—
Tilly Walker	—	76 per season
Net change	+9.94 per season[a]	+29 per season

[a]Uses 14 starts for the 1918 season.

Source: Baseball Almanac, at http://www.baseball-almanc.com.

---

[6]The earned run average is the average number of runs a pitcher gives up per nine innings, the normal length of a ballgame.

[7]The Boston Red Sox played only 126 games in 1918 because the season was terminated on September 1 due to the United States' entry into World War I.

trying to do everything would take them away from the activities that they perform best. It is cheaper (more efficient) for them to pay other people to provide the goods or services than to try to do everything themselves.

At the national level, if the United States has a comparative advantage in the production of cancer drugs, it is better off specializing in cancer drugs and importing TVs even if it has an absolute advantage over Japan in both products. The opportunity cost of sacrificing cancer drugs in order to make TVs ourselves is higher than the cost of sending cancer drugs to Japan in exchange for TVs. Like Babe Ruth, we are better off specializing in what we are relatively best at and leaving the rest to others.

BIOGRAPHICAL SKETCH

Babe Didrikson Zaharias   (1911–1956)

I knew exactly what I wanted to be when I grew up. My goal was to be the greatest athlete that ever lived.

—*Babe Didrikson Zaharias*[1]

The theory of comparative advantage tells us that athletes are better off when they specialize. A quick look at athletes from the professional ranks to middle schools seems to bear this hypothesis out. "Two-way" football players have become a rarity, and athletes who play more than one sport have all but disappeared. It is thus unlikely that the athletic world will ever see another Babe Didrikson Zaharias. Zaharias dominated the athletic world like no athlete before or since, achieving star status in the disparate worlds of basketball, track and field, and golf.

Mildred Ella Didriksen was born in 1911 to impoverished Norwegian immigrants in Port Arthur, Texas. The sixth of seven children and the youngest girl, Mildred got the nickname "Babe" while a young girl and still the "baby" of the family, though she later attributed the nickname to comparisons with baseball hero Babe Ruth. Her last name was changed to "Didrikson" as a result of a spelling error in her school records.

As a youth, Zaharias was drawn to sports at a time when sexual stereotypes still discouraged women from participating in "manly" sports, but Zaharias' working-class upbringing freed her from many of the restrictions that would have constrained her development as an athlete. She did not participate in organized sports, however, until she left high school in 1930 to play basketball for the Employers Casualty Insurance Company.

It may seem odd today for an athlete to advance her career by taking a job as a secretary for $75 a month with an insurance company, but at that time, many colleges did not offer athletic programs for women, and the fledgling National Collegiate Athletic Association (NCAA) was openly disdainful of women's athletics. Employers

(Continued)

(*Continued*)

Casualty played in the 45-member Women's National Basketball League, which played under the auspices of the Amateur Athletic Union (AAU). The AAU was then the dominant athletic body; it oversaw competitions by a few schools and by companies that sponsored teams.

The Employers Casualty "Golden Cyclones" were one of the best amateur teams in the nation. When the first All-American women's basketball team was announced in 1929, eight of its members were from Employers Casualty. Zaharias quickly established herself as a star among stars, being named an All-American for three straight years.

As good as she was on the basketball court, Zaharias found her greatest success in track and field. It was here that she recorded the greatest single performance in the history of track and field and perhaps of any athletic competition. The 1932 National Track and Field Competition served as the trials for the 1932 Los Angeles Olympic Games. Zaharias was the sole representative of the Employers Casualty team. In one afternoon, she ensured that Employers Casualty won the team championship by winning the shot put, the baseball throw, the javelin throw, the 80-meter hurdles, and the broad jump. She also tied for first in the high jump and finished fourth in the discus, an event in which she normally did not compete. In all, she won six gold medals and broke four world records in about three hours. Zaharias hardly skipped a beat in the Olympics, setting world records in the javelin throw and the 80-meter hurdles. She also tied for first in the high jump, though her then-unorthodox style (the so-called Western Roll that soon became the dominant style) caused a controversy among some of the judges, who thought it illegal. As a compromise, she was declared the second-place finisher and given the only half-gold-half-silver medal in the history of the modern Olympics.

As the dominant performer and personality of the 1932 "Hollywood Games," Zaharias quickly became a national celebrity. Her publicity, however, came at a considerable cost. The public did not know what to make of a woman who defied sexual stereotypes of the time. Zaharias seemed destined to fade from public view when the AAU stripped her of her amateur status for appearing in an automobile advertisement (even though, apparently, she had not given permission for the firm to use her likeness). After a year or so of stunts and exhibition tours, she returned to work for Employers Casualty.

Over the next several years, Zaharias reconstructed her personal and athletic lives. Stung by her treatment in the press, she strove to develop a more feminine image, playing up her role as a wife following her marriage to professional wrestler (and later sports promoter) George Zaharias in 1938, but she was anything but a typical housewife. Having picked up golf as a teenager, Zaharias threw herself into her new, more socially acceptable sport. In 1935, she won the Texas State Women's Golf Championship and was ready to enter full-time competition when the United States Golf Association banned her from amateur competition because of her appearance in the automobile advertisement. She responded by turning pro, but she quickly realized that professional golf provided neither adequate competition nor adequate remuneration. She succeeded in having her amateur status reinstated in 1943. Though she would have to wait until the end of World War II to enter the next stage of her athletic career, it was worth the wait.

Zaharias burst onto the women's golf tour in 1945, winning the Texas Women's Open and the Western Open, and being named "Woman Athlete of the Year" by the Associated Press (an award she had won 13 years earlier for her Olympic exploits). This proved merely a warm-up for 1946, when she won 14 straight tournaments. In 1947,

Zaharias became the first American woman to win the British Women's Amateur golf championship in the 55-year history of the event.

After her victory in the British Amateur event, Zaharias again turned pro and a year later became a charter member of the newly formed Ladies Professional Golf Association (LPGA—it chose the term "Ladies" to avoid conflict with the unsuccessful Women's PGA). Her talents led her to be a dominant figure in the LPGA—she won about two of every three events she entered in 1950 and 1951—and her showmanship, while not always appreciated by her competitors, helped market the new tour.

In 1953, Zaharias was diagnosed with cancer, and doctors told her family and friends (but not Zaharias herself) that she had less than a year to live. Within four months, however, she was back on the tour, finishing as the sixth-highest money winner for 1953. She did even better in 1954, winning five tournaments and having the lowest average on the tour. The cancer reappeared in 1955, and Babe Didrikson Zaharias, arguably the greatest athlete of the twentieth century, died in 1956.

[1]Susan Cayleff, *Babe: The Life and Legend of Babe Didrikson Zaharias* (Urbana, I.L.: University of Illinois Press, 1995), p. 46.

Source: Susan Cayleff, *Barbe: The Life and Legend of Babe Didrikson Zaharias* (Urbana, I.L.: University of Illinois Press, 1995).

Summary

Sports occupy a unique place in the public psyche. Although sports generate less revenue than many other industries, sports results are predicted, reported, and analyzed in newspapers, magazines, books, and TV and radio programs. This text presents economic models from industrial organization, public finance, and labor economics to provide insight into the economics of sports. One of the most important economic models is that of comparative advantage. Despite having an absolute advantage as both a pitcher and an outfielder, Babe Ruth specialized in playing the outfield because that was where he had a comparative advantage. He had a comparative advantage in playing every day as an outfielder because the opportunity cost of his playing outfield—the additional runs that other teams would score against a lesser Red Sox pitcher—was less than the opportunity cost of his playing every four to five days as a pitcher—the lower number of runs the Red Sox would score from playing a lesser outfielder. Following the law of comparative advantage made Babe Ruth and the Red Sox better off.

Discussion Questions

1. Why do sports generate so much more news coverage than other industries that are much larger in financial terms?
2. The theory of comparative advantage predicts that athletes perform better when they specialize. Studies show that young athletes are increasingly focusing on a single sport. Do you think this is a good idea?

Problems

1.1. Use an appropriate economic theory to explain why Kobe Bryant might employ someone to answer his fan mail even if he can read the letters and type the responses more
quickly than the person he employs?

1.2. Is the following statement true or false? Explain your reasoning. "I am attending
college on a full athletic scholarship, so the opportunity cost of attending college is
zero for me."

1.3. From 1946 through 1967, the placekicker for the Cleveland Browns, Lou Groza, was
successful on 54.9 percent of his field goal attempts. From 1999 through 2008, the
Browns' kicker was Phil Dawson, who was successful on 82.8 percent of his attempts.
Use the theory of comparative advantage to explain the massive improvement in the
Browns' kicking game.

1.4. The term "figure skating" refers to the shapes that skaters used to trace in the ice as
part of skating competitions. In the 1970s, this aspect of the sport was deemphasized
and eventually eliminated. Use the theory of comparative advantage to show why
eliminating this part of the competition has led skaters to perform much more difficult
and sophisticated jumps and spins.

CHAPTER 2

Review of the Economist's Arsenal

To be a sports fan these days is to be taking a course in economics.

—ALLEN BARRA[1]

INTRODUCTION

As noted in Chapter 1, many aspects of sports business are hard to explain from a casual fan's perspective. In this chapter, we review some of the basic economic models that allow us to formalize our analysis and, in turn, explain why these markets behave as they do.

LEARNING OBJECTIVES

After reading this chapter, you will be able to:

- Use the basic model of supply and demand to explain the relationship between prices and quantity, such as why collectors pay much more for Mickey Mantle baseball cards than for Hank Aaron baseball cards, even though Aaron had better career statistics.

- Describe how teams use their most fundamental input—player talent—to generate wins, and how the law of diminishing marginal returns impacts teams' decisions on how to allocate that talent.

---

[1]Allen Barra, "In Anti-Trust We Trust," *Salon Magazine,* May 19, 2000, at http://www.salon.com/news/feature/2000/05/19/antitrust/index.html.

- Distinguish the various market structures that are present in the sports industry and apply the appropriate model for analyzing questions such as why the Chicago White Sox do not lower their ticket prices when doing so would allow them to sell out like their neighbors, the Chicago Blackhawks.

- Explain why the era of professional sports began at the same time in two different countries with two different sports.

2.1 THE SUPPLY AND DEMAND MODEL

The supply and demand model is the first and simplest model that we encounter. Recall that a **model** is a simplification of reality that allows economists to isolate particular economic forces. A good model allows economists to make predictions and provide explanations about the world quickly and easily.

Unlike physicists and chemists, economists and other social scientists find it difficult to conduct experiments: It is far more difficult to control what people do than it is to control substances in a test tube. Even if economists were physically able to control what people do, ethical and legal considerations would make most experiments unfeasible. For example, it would be very hard—and certainly undesirable—for an economist studying bankruptcy to force a person or firm to go bankrupt. Instead, economists rely on theoretical and statistical models of market structure to make reliable predictions about behavior.

For all its simplicity, the supply and demand model has remarkable power to explain the world around us. At the same time, we must be careful to use the model under the appropriate circumstances. The supply and demand model is most suitable when there are many buyers and sellers of a homogeneous good (i.e., all suppliers are selling the same product), and consumers have good information about available prices across sellers.

Supply and demand show us how producers and consumers respond to price changes. Together, they determine how much of a good or service is produced and what value society places on it. In a different course, we might use these tools to analyze the financial meltdown of 2008 or the impact of a higher minimum wage on employment. In this section, we introduce the concepts of supply and demand and use them to show why Mickey Mantle cards cost so much more than Hank Aaron cards.

Demand, Supply, and Equilibrium

An individual consumer's **demand** for baseball cards (or for any good or service) is the relationship between the price of those cards and the number of cards that he or she is willing and able to buy. It is a sequence of answers to the question, "If baseball cards cost this much, how many of them would you buy?" Or, from the firm's perspective, "How many would we be able to sell?" We compute the **market demand**, which shows the quantity that all consumers combined purchase at each price by summing the individual demand curves, that is, by adding the quantity that each consumer purchases at each price. Figure 2.1 shows the **market demand curve** for a specific player's baseball card. Note that the curve

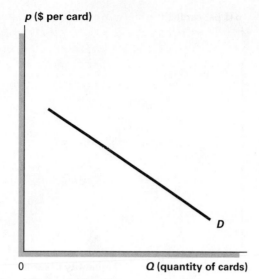

FIGURE 2.1 The Demand for Baseball Cards

As the price of baseball cards falls, the quantity demanded rises.

is downward sloping, as the relationship between price and quantity is invariably negative. As the price of cards falls, the number of cards that consumers buy rises. Economists call the negative relationship between price and quantity the **law of demand**. A change in a good's price causes a **change in quantity demanded**, moving quantity up along the demand curve when the price rises and down the demand curve when the price falls.

The **supply** of baseball cards relates price to the number of cards that sellers are willing and able to provide. Unlike consumers, who view the price of an item as the sacrifice they must make, producers view the price as a reward. As a result, higher prices encourage producers (sellers) to offer more cards. For existing cards, an increase in the price gives more card owners an incentive to offer their cards for sale. In addition, sellers have an incentive to produce more new cards as the price rises. At the same time, other producers have an incentive to stop what they are doing and start producing cards. Some economists call the positive relationship between price and quantity the **law of supply**.

Similar to market demand, the **market supply curve** is the sum of the individual supply curves. The market supply curve is typically upward sloping, as seen in Figure 2.2. Again, if the price of cards changes, the quantity moves along the supply curve, a movement that economists call a **change in quantity supplied**.

Taken alone, market demand says nothing about the amount consumers actually buy or the price they pay. Similarly, market supply alone does not say how much producers sell or the price they receive. To find out what happens in the marketplace, one must look at supply and demand together. Figures 2.3a and 2.3b show that the two curves cross at the point labeled e. Economists call e the **equilibrium point** because at that point, the actions of consumers and producers are in balance. Consumers are willing and able to buy Q_e cards at the price

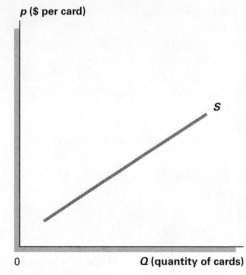

FIGURE 2.2   The Supply of Baseball Cards
As the price of baseball cards rises, the quantity supplied also rises.

p_e, which is exactly the quantity that producers are willing and able to sell at that price. As a result, neither consumers nor producers have any desire to alter their actions; thus, the price stays at p_e, and the quantity at Q_e.

Figure 2.3a shows that, at a price higher than p_e (such as p_h), **disequilibrium** occurs because producers want to sell Q_s while consumers want to buy only Q_d.

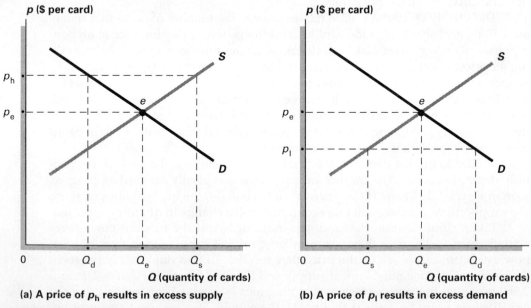

(a) A price of p_h results in excess supply   (b) A price of p_l results in excess demand

FIGURE 2.3   Equilibrium in the Baseall Card Market
Equilibrium occurs at price p_e, where the supply and demand curves meet.

Unable to sell all the cards they want, producers face a **surplus** or **excess supply**. Frustrated producers lower their prices in order to attract more customers. The lower price encourages consumers to buy more cards and discourages producers from selling them. As Q_d rises and Q_s falls, the excess supply falls until it equals zero, and equilibrium is restored at p_e.

Figure 2.3b shows that, at a price below the equilibrium (p_1), buyers want to purchase Q_d cards while sellers want to sell only Q_s. The **shortage** or **excess demand** for cards at p_1 drives the price upward until the shortage disappears at p_e.

We cannot actually see the supply and demand curves of the products we consume. We do, however, observe equilibrium prices. For example, baseball trading card prices are published regularly in price guides. In 1955, the Bowman Company produced a set of cards known as the "TV set," with pictures of players appearing on the face of the card bordered by what appears to be a television set. Included in that set are the cards of Mickey Mantle, perhaps the greatest switch-hitting power hitter ever, and Hank Aaron, who was Major League Baseball's all-time home run leader from 1974 to 2007.

According to the *Beckett Baseball* price guide, which tracks card values, the March 2012 prices of Mantle and Aaron cards from the 1955 Bowman set were $800 and $250, respectively.[2] Such a large difference in price is difficult to justify, given that Hank Aaron had more home runs (HR), hits (H), runs scored (R), runs batted in (RBI), and a higher batting average (Avg) than Mantle (see Table 2.1). We can use the simple supply and demand model as an analytical tool to investigate the difference in prices. Because the forces of supply and demand determine prices, the explanation must lie in differences in supply, in demand, or in both.

Changes in Supply and Demand

The supply and demand relationships are not permanently fixed. They can change for many different reasons. This section reviews why the supply or demand curve might shift and the effects that shifts have on the equilibrium price and quantity.

FACTORS THAT AFFECT THE LOCATION OF THE DEMAND CURVE   Economists call a shift of the demand curve a change in demand. A **change in demand** stems from a change in any of the five underlying factors: consumer income, the prices

TABLE 2.1   Career Statistics of Hank Aaron and Mickey Mantle

	AB	H	R	HR	RBI	Avg	Card Price
Hank Aaron	12,364	3,771	2,174	755	2,297	.305	$250
Mickey Mantle	8,102	2,415	1,677	536	1,509	.298	$800

Sources: Player statistics are from MLB.com; Card prices are from *Beckett Baseball*, March 2012, p. 34.

---

[2]*Beckett Baseball*, March 2012, p. 34.

of substitutes or complements, consumer tastes, the number of consumers in the market, and the expectations that consumers hold.

We have seen that consumers typically buy more of a good if their incomes increase, but frequent exceptions exist. If a hockey fan living in Providence, Rhode Island, gets a raise, he might buy more hockey cards of the Providence Bruins, the local minor league team. Alternatively, he might buy fewer cards of the Providence Bruins and more cards of the National Hockey League's (NHL's) Boston Bruins. If he buys more cards of the Providence Bruins as his income rises, then the cards are normal goods. **Normal goods** get their name because consumers normally buy more of a good or service when their incomes rise. If the fan buys fewer cards, then the cards are inferior goods. **Inferior goods** need not be undesirable or poorly made. One simply buys less of them as one's income rises.

If hockey fans buy fewer Providence Bruins cards when their incomes fall, it seems reasonable to conclude that they would go to fewer hockey games as well. We can also ask whether the recession of 2008–2009 had a negative impact on professional sports or are sports "recession-proof"? The evidence from the recent recession is mixed. Attendance at the four major sports in 2008 and early 2009 was not significantly below previous levels, but all else was not held equal, as incomes fell. Some NBA teams sold tickets at significant discounts to prop up attendance. According to ESPN.com, the Memphis Grizzlies drew about as many fans in 2008–2009 (about 12,600 per game) as they did in 2007–2008 (12,770), but they sold their tickets so cheaply that the team's gross revenue per game was only $300,000, an average of less than $24 per fan.[3] Similarly, some Major League Baseball teams discounted 2009 season tickets by up to 25 percent, and the New York Yankees were forced to cut the prices of some premium seats in the new ballpark by half.[4]

The major North American sports leagues do have a safety net in the form of long-term TV contracts. As long as recessions do not outlast these contracts, the guaranteed income of these contracts helps to sustain teams. Sports and athletes that rely heavily on year-to-year sponsorships, such as golf and tennis, are in a more vulnerable position. Formula-1 and the National Association for Stock Car Auto Racing (NASCAR) were particularly hard-hit by the downturn, as they rely heavily on sponsorships by car manufacturers that were devastated by the recession.[5] Similarly, the Ladies Professional Golf Association (LPGA) reduced its tournament schedule from 34 events in 2008 to 31 in 2009 and total prize money fell by about $5 million.[6]

---

[3]Bill Simmons, "Welcome to the No Benjamins Association," *ESPN.com*, February 27, 2009, at http://www.espn.go.com.

[4]Jon Birger, "Baseball Battles the Slump," *CNNMoney.com*, February 19, 2009, at http://money.cnn.com/2009/02/18/magazines/fortune/birger_baseball.fortune/index.htm; and Richard Sandomir, "Yankees Slash the Price of Top Tickets," *The New York Times*, April 28, 2009, at http://www.nytimes.com/2009/04/29/sports/baseball/29tickets.html?_r=1&scp=4&sq=+%20yankees%20+%20%22ticket%20prices%22&st=cse.

[5]Sean Gregory and Steve Goldberg, "Daytona Drag: NASCAR Tries to Outrace the Recession," *Time*, February 12, 2009, at http://www.time.com/time/business/article/0,8599,1879136,00.html.

[6]Ron Sirak, "LPGA Facing Economic Realities," *Golf Digest*, November 18, 2008, at http://www.golfdigest.com/golf-tours-news/2008-11/20081119sirak, viewed April 30, 2012.

When the price of a substitute good increases, the demand curve shifts to the right. If a card collector views Mickey Mantle cards and Yogi Berra cards as reasonable substitutes, an increase in the price of Yogi Berra cards causes the demand curve for Mickey Mantle cards to shift to the right.

The opposite effect occurs when the price of a complement increases. For example, older cards need protection from bending and other mishaps that reduce the value of the card. The best way to prevent such accidents is to keep the cards in protective sleeves. If the price of the sleeves rises, the demand for cards falls. This occurs because collectors use the two products together and think of them as a single commodity. When the price of sleeves rises, the price of a card with a sleeve also rises, reducing demand for cards. Figure 2.4a shows the impact of an increase in income and a reduction in the price of a substitute good on the demand curve.

In his book *The Blind Side*, Michael Lewis provides an interesting example of how tastes can affect the demand for a specific service.[7] Lewis notes that, until the 1980s, offensive linemen were regarded largely as interchangeable units and were among the lowest paid players on a football team. Today, left tackles are among the most highly paid players on the team. The premium paid to left tackles represents a change in tastes by football teams that have increasingly emphasized the forward pass.

The growing emphasis on the forward pass has made quarterbacks the stars of their teams and made protecting them a priority. It has become particularly

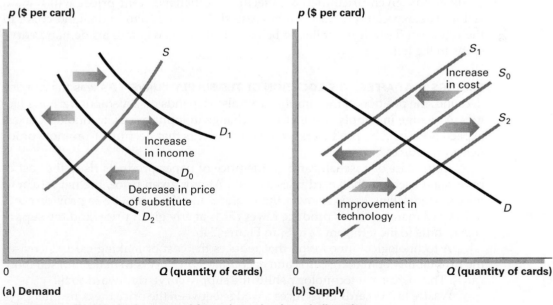

(a) Demand **(b) Supply**

FIGURE 2.4 **Changes in the Demand for and Supply of Baseball Cards**
Demand and supply curves can shift left or right.

[7]Michael Lewis, *The Blind Side: Evolution of a Game* (New York: W. W. Norton, 2006).

important to protect quarterbacks from behind, their "blind side," where they cannot see oncoming defenders. This required players big enough to stand up to defensive ends but fast enough to move over to block linebackers. Left tackle (which protects a right-handed quarterback's blind side) thus became a unique—and highly paid—position.

Another example of the impact of tastes on prices can be found in ticket prices charged by Major League Baseball teams. Traditionally, teams have charged a fixed price for a given seat location, regardless of the opponent. Recently, they have started to behave more like European soccer teams or Japanese baseball teams by charging higher prices when more popular teams, such as the New York Yankees or the Boston Red Sox, come to town in a strategy known as variable ticket pricing. Some teams, such as the San Francisco Giants, even change ticket prices based on pitching matchups. The practice of altering ticket prices after the season begins is known as dynamic pricing. We will return to this concept in Chapter 4, but even with our simple model of supply and demand, we can predict that, because the supply of seats is the same regardless of whom the visiting team is, differences in price must reflect changes in the demand curve. The demand curve for teams like the Red Sox and Yankees is farther to the right than for most other teams because of the greater taste of fans for seeing these teams play.[8]

Finally, expectations of future prices can affect demand. A collector who believes that the prices of cards will rise in the near future is willing to buy more cards at any given price than a collector who believes that prices will remain stable. The expectation of a price increase shifts the collector's demand curve to the right. Similarly, if the collector believes that prices will fall, his demand curve shifts to the left.

FACTORS THAT AFFECT THE LOCATION OF THE SUPPLY CURVE   As was the case for demand, the position of the supply curve also depends on several underlying factors. A **change in supply** results from a change in input prices, technology, taxes, expectations held by producers, and natural events that destroy or promote products or resources.

In the case of baseball cards, if the price of paper products rises, the cost of producing each baseball card rises as well. At any given price, the net return to making and selling cards is lower than before, and the incentive to provide cards falls. Card manufacturers produce fewer cards at any given price, and the supply curve shifts to the left from S_0 to S_1 in Figure 2.4b.

A technological innovation that reduces the cost of making cards increases the profitability of making cards and encourages producers to make and sell more cards. The increase in technology shifts the supply curve rightward to S_2.

A sales tax on cards introduces a wedge between the price the consumer pays and the price the producer receives. The difference between what the consumer

---

[8]Joshua Brustein, "Star Pitchers in a Duel? Tickets Will Cost More," *New York Times*, June 27, 2010, at http://www.nytimes.com/2010/06/28/technology/28tickets.html, viewed February 23, 2012.

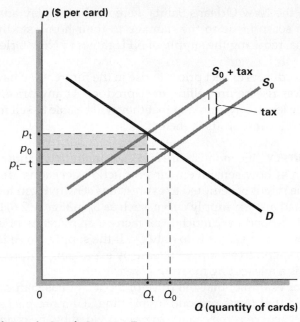

FIGURE 2.5   A Change in Supply Due to a Tax

A tax causes consumers to see the curve S_0 + tax while producers still act along S_0.

pays and what the producer receives means that the market has two supply curves, as seen in Figure 2.5. Figure 2.5 shows that the vertical difference between the two supply curves equals the amount of the per-unit tax. For example, a $0.10 per-card tax on producers results in a new supply curve that lies $0.10 above the original. The price that consumers must pay (p_t) is determined by the intersection of the demand curve with the supply curve that includes the tax. Quantity decreases to Q_t because consumers are willing to purchase fewer cards at the higher price. The price that sellers receive is the price for Q_t cards on the original supply curve and is equal to the price that consumers pay minus the tax ($p_t - t$). The difference between the price that consumers pay and the price that sellers receive is the per-unit tax, t. Multiplying the per-unit tax by the number of cards sold, Q_t, yields the tax revenue collected by the government. In Figure 2.5, this area is shaded gray.

Natural disasters can also affect the location of the supply curve. If a hurricane damaged the card factory, it would temporarily reduce the availability of new cards. The world saw stark evidence of this type of event when a major earthquake struck Japan in 2011. The quake and ensuing tsunami damaged many factories and a major nuclear energy facility, temporarily disrupting the production of products such as autos worldwide, as even non-Japanese automakers scrambled to find alternative suppliers of parts normally produced in Japan.[9]

---

[9]"Japan's Earthquake and Tsunami Hit Parts Supplies," *Motor Trend,* June 2011, at http://www.motortrend.com/features/auto_news/2011/1106_japan_earthquake_tsunami_hit_parts_supplies/viewall.html, viewed February 23, 2011.

Closer to home, the New Orleans Saints were unable to play any home games during the 2005 season due to the damage to their home stadium caused by hurricane Katrina, reducing the supply of NFL games in New Orleans to zero for the season.[10]

Finally, if producers expect prices to rise in the future, they have an incentive to wait until prices rise before selling their product. At any price, producers are willing to provide less today, thinking that they will be able to sell for more tomorrow, and the supply curve shifts to the left.

ELASTICITY OF SUPPLY   Economists are often less interested in how much producers produce than in how sensitive their production decisions are to changes in price. At first, one might be tempted to express this sensitivity in terms of slope. If card producers had a steep supply curve, such as S_0 in Figure 2.6, then it appears that firms do not respond very much to an increase in price. As price rises from p_0 to p_1, output grows from Q_0 cards to only Q_1. If the supply curve is relatively flat (S_1), producers respond to the price increase by expanding output from Q_0' to Q_1'. Slope, however, is a misleading measure of sensitivity.

Suppose, for example, that the price of a pack of baseball cards rises from $0.10 to $0.11 and that firms respond by printing 200 more packs of cards. The slope of the supply curve is the change in price divided by the change in quantity, or $0.01/200 packs.

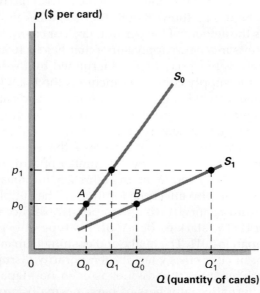

FIGURE 2.6   Relatively Elastic versus Inelastic Supply
Elasticity depends on more than just the slope of the curve.

[10]Associated Press, "Saints' home games: 4 at LSU, 3 in Alamodome," September 12, 2005, at http://sports.espn.go.com/nfl/news/story?id=2159595, viewed April 30, 2012.

The problem is that 200 packs can represent a big change in the number of packs produced or a very small change, depending on how many packs firms had been printing to begin with. Increasing production by 200 packs means much more to producers if they expand from 1,000 packs to 1,200 than if they expand from 10,000 packs to 10,200. As a result, slope cannot tell us how meaningful the increase of 200 packs really is. Thus, while the supply of cards appears to be more sensitive to price changes at point B on supply curve S_1 because of its relatively flat slope, supply might actually be more sensitive at point A on curve S_0 because the initial quantity of cards is lower.

Economists account for the producers' starting point by using percentage changes in price and output rather than absolute changes.[11] They use these percentage changes to measure the sensitivity of production to changes in price. We call this measure the elasticity of supply (which we denote as ε_s). The **elasticity of supply** is the percentage change in quantity that results from a given percentage change in price:

$$\varepsilon_s = \frac{\%\Delta Q^s}{\%\Delta p}$$

In the above example, the $0.01 increase in the price of a pack of cards corresponds to a percentage change of $0.01/$0.10 = 0.10, or 10 percent. If firms originally produced 1,000 packs of cards, then the percentage change in quantity is $(1,200 - 1,000)/1,000 = 0.2$, or 20 percent, and the elasticity of supply is $\varepsilon_s = 0.2/0.1 = 2.0$. When the price of a pack of cards rises by 10 percent, producers increase their output by 20 percent. The percentage increase in output is twice the percentage rise in price.

If firms originally produced 10,000 packs of cards, the percentage increase in output is $(10,200 - 10,000)/10,000 = 0.02$, or 2 percent, and the elasticity of supply becomes $\varepsilon_s = 0.02/0.10 = 0.20$. In this case, a 10 percent increase in the price of a pack of cards brings only a 2 percent increase in production, and firms are much less responsive to changes in price.

Although the supply curve's location and elasticity are important for many of the issues we deal with later in the book, they cannot resolve our question about the relative prices of Mantle and Aaron cards. To simplify the analysis, we will make two weak assumptions and one strong assumption. A **weak assumption** is likely to be true in real life, while a **strong assumption** is often not true. Strong assumptions can be valuable, however, as long as the conclusions we draw are valid even when the assumption is not strictly true. In this case, our weak assumptions are that the Bowman Company produced the same number of Mickey Mantle and Hank Aaron cards and that the same number of Mantle and Aaron cards have survived in perfect (mint) condition. Our strong assumption is that the owners of these cards are willing and able to sell a fixed number of cards regardless of the price they receive.

---

[11] We define the percentage change of the variable X (%ΔX) as $\Delta X/X = (X_1 - X_0)/X_0$. We use point elasticity rather than arc elasticity, which would replace the denominator with the mean of X_0 and X_1. If X_0 and X_1 are close together, the difference is negligible.

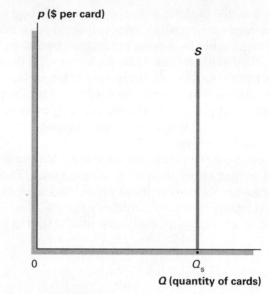

FIGURE 2.7   Perfectly Inelastic Supply
When the supply curve is vertical, quantity does not change, and the elasticity of supply is zero.

In this case, the supply curve is a vertical line. Because price changes do not affect the quantity supplied, the supply curve in Figure 2.7 is **perfectly inelastic**.

ELASTICITY OF DEMAND   As with supply, we are often interested in the sensitivity of demand to changes in price rather than absolute levels of price and quantity. The **elasticity of demand** (ε_d) is the percentage change in quantity demanded for a given percentage change in price. The only difference between the elasticity of demand and the elasticity of supply is that the elasticity of demand measures the price sensitivity of consumers rather than producers

$$\varepsilon_d = \frac{\%\Delta Q^d}{\%\Delta p}$$

For example, if the price of a card increases from \$0.10 to \$0.11 and the quantity demanded falls from 1,000 to 750 cards, the elasticity of demand is

$$\frac{(1,000 - 750)/1,000}{(0.10 - 0.11)/0.10} = -2.5$$

Elasticities of demand fall between zero (perfectly inelastic) and minus infinity (infinitely elastic).[12] When the elasticity lies between 0 and −1, we say that demand is **inelastic**, because the percentage change in quantity is less than the percentage change in price. When the elasticity is less than −1, we say that demand is **elastic**.

---

[12]Some microeconomics textbooks eliminate the negative sign by taking the absolute value of the elasticity formula. We use the negative number because it reinforces the notion that price and quantity move in opposite directions along the demand curve.

EXPLAINING THE DIFFERENCE IN CARD PRICES   We can now use the simple supply and demand model to show that the difference in value between Mickey Mantle and Hank Aaron cards stems from economic forces rather than accident or error. We previously noted that there is no reason to believe that the supply curves of Mantle and Aaron cards differ from each other. Because a fixed number of cards of each player were produced, we assume that supply is perfectly inelastic. As a result, differences in price must be the result of differences in demand. What factors might contribute to such a large difference in demand?

Mickey Mantle spent his entire career in New York, while Aaron spent his career in Milwaukee and Atlanta, which are much smaller cities. Even if Aaron and Mantle are equally popular with their hometown fans, the difference in population causes the demand curve for Mickey Mantle cards to lie far to the right of the demand curve for Hank Aaron cards. To see why, assume that a typical fan prefers players and memorabilia for his hometown team. We are not, however, interested in how many cards each individual Braves or Yankees fan buys at each price. We want to know how many cards all Braves fans combined buy at each price and how many cards all Yankees fans combined buy at each price. The total market demand curve is thus the horizontal sum of the individual demand curves. Figure 2.8 shows the individual demand curves for baseball cards by two baseball fans, Ray and Roy, and the market demand curve that would result if they were the only consumers. Because New York is a much larger city, adding all of the individual demand curves for Mickey Mantle cards results in a market demand curve for his cards that is farther to the right than the demand curve for Hank Aaron cards, increasing their price relative to Hank Aaron cards.

In addition to having more people, the New York metropolitan area has fans who are, on average, wealthier than Braves fans in either Milwaukee or Atlanta.

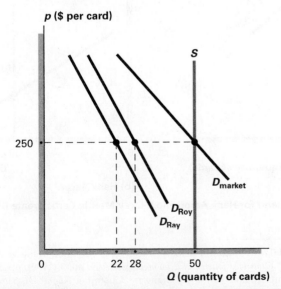

FIGURE 2.8   The Relationship between Individual Demand and Market Demand for Baseball Cards
Market demand is the horizontal sum of the individual demands.

If baseball cards are normal goods, the higher level of income causes the demand curve for Mickey Mantle cards to shift out still farther relative to the demand for Hank Aaron cards.

Finally, one must account for the unfortunate possibility that the tastes of baseball fans for baseball cards reflect the prejudices of the population at large. As we shall see in Chapter 10, most economists regard discrimination as a taste or distaste for members of a particular group. If some card collectors prefer Mickey Mantle, who was white, to Hank Aaron, who is black, simply because of their races, the demand for Mantle cards would be greater than the demand for Aaron cards.

Figure 2.9 shows that the combined effects of the differences in market size, income, and tastes and preferences of individuals with a taste for discrimination result in greater demand for Mantle cards than for Aaron cards. The differences in demand coupled with the identical, perfectly inelastic supply curves create the difference in equilibrium price. Several studies of trading card prices have established that race plays a significant role in determining the price of playing cards. Nardinelli and Simon (1990) were the first to establish such a link. Gabriel, Johnson, and Stanton (1999) found that discrimination was less likely to occur for rookie cards, when the future performance of a player was unknown, but reappeared as the player's ability was revealed over the course of his career.[13]

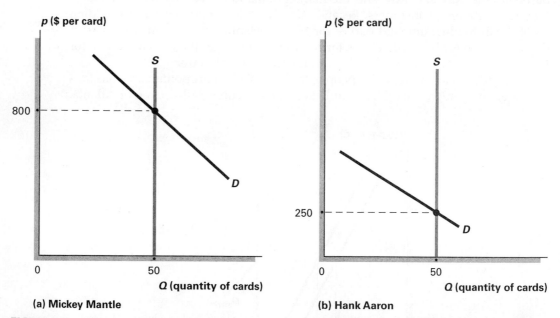

(a) Mickey Mantle   **(b) Hank Aaron**

FIGURE 2.9   Differences in Demand for Hank Aaron and Mickey Mantle Cards Create Differences in Price

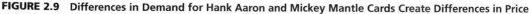

[13]Clark Nardinelli and Curtis Simon, "Customer Racial Discrimination in the Market for Memorabilia: The Case of Baseball," *Quarterly Journal of Economics*, vol. 105, no. 3 (1990), pp. 575–595; and Paul E. Gabriel, Curtis D. Johnson, and Timothy J. Stanton, "Customer Racial Discrimination for Baseball Memorabilia," *Applied Economics*, vol. 31, no. 11 (1999), pp. 1331–1335.

2.2 PRODUCING OUTPUT AND THE PRODUCTION FUNCTION

Producing a sporting contest, such as a football game, is much different from producing a pizza. Most obviously, a football game is service, like a play or movie, not a physical object. In addition, output must be produced in concert with another producer (team). Despite these differences, we can still apply the economic theory of production to sports. In this section, we review the basics of production theory, including why these concepts are so important to the study of team sports and the special nature of sports relative to other goods and services.

A Note on the Definition of Output

Before analyzing a market, economists must determine how to measure output. In some markets, such as the pizza market, defining output (Q) is easy. It is the number of pizzas produced in a given time period. In sports markets, defining and measuring output is more complicated. If we think of output as what a firm sells in order to obtain revenue, we could measure output as attendance or television appearances. If we focus on production, it may be more useful to measure output as games, because the team must combine inputs to produce games throughout the course of the season. Finally, if a team's popularity, and hence its revenue, depend on its performance, the appropriate output is wins or winning percentage rather than simply games played. Our problem resembles that facing those who study higher education. From the standpoint of revenue, a college or university may define output as the number of students enrolled. From the standpoint of input utilization, it may define output as the amount that its students learn, perhaps measured by their future incomes. Unfortunately, there is no simple resolution to this issue. To force a universal definition of output would cloud the issue as often as it would clarify it. In this text, we address this thorny issue by defining output according to the aspect of the market under consideration. For the remainder of this section, we consider output to be the number of wins produced per season.

The Production Function

Production transforms inputs into output. A **production function** shows the relationship between the quantity of inputs used and the quantity of output produced. This relationship is an expression of the technology of production and typically includes labor and capital as inputs because the firm can substitute between them. In sports, however, capital (the need for a field of play, for example) is fixed. In addition, the number of players is set by rule. Thus, as we consider a team's attempt to produce wins (Q), it makes more sense to speak in terms of units of talent. The more talent a team has on the roster, the more games it can expect to win. We can show a production function in which a football team can invest in either offensive talent (T_O) or defensive talent (T_D) as:

$$Q = f(T_O, T_D)$$

Another term for Q is the **total product of labor**. In order to evaluate the impact of increases in either input on the number of wins, we must hold the other input constant. Figure 2.10a shows the typical relationship between one variable input, offensive talent in this case, and output while holding the quantity of defensive talent constant. As T_O rises from 0 to T_{O1}, each successive unit of talent adds more to wins than the last. The intuition behind this is fairly simple. If a football team only has one or two talented players out of the starting 11, the team will benefit enormously from additional talent on the field. From T_{O1} to T_{O2}, wins continue to rise but at a decreasing rate. These players still improve the team but not as much as the first few talented players. Beyond T_{O2}, additional talent might actually cause the team to win less. Is this possible? Perhaps you are familiar with the saying, "there's only one ball" as a reference to the fact that having too many players want to carry the ball can damage team chemistry and reduce wins.

When coaches and general managers consider adding talent to a roster, they think like economists—by focusing on the margin. If they add one more talented player, how many more games might the team win? To focus on the change in output resulting from a small increase in one input, economists evaluate the player's marginal product. The **marginal product** of an input indicates the increase in output that results from a one-unit increase in that input, holding the other input constant. For both offense and defense we thus have:

$$MP_T = \Delta Q / \Delta T$$

Figure 2.10b shows the marginal product of offensive talent. From 0 to T_{O1}, as the slope of the total product curve increases, the marginal product increases. Again, the number of games the team wins increases quickly as the coach adds talent to the roster. From T_{O1} to T_{O2}, the slope of the total product curve decreases, and marginal product falls. The decline in marginal product, known

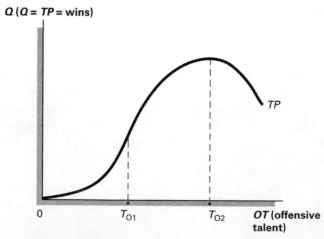

FIGURE 2.10a   The Total Product Curve

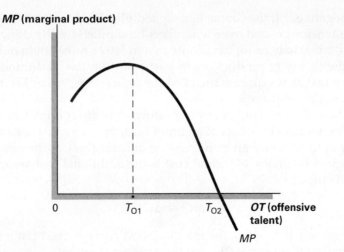

FIGURE 2.10b The Marginal Product Curve

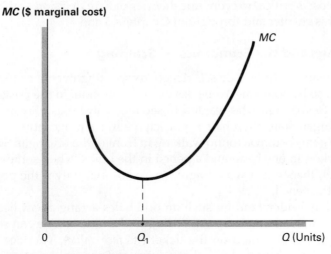

FIGURE 2.10c The Marginal Cost Curve

as the law of diminishing returns, is one of the most important concepts in all of economics. The **law of diminishing returns** states that as a firm (team) continually increases one input while holding the other fixed, the marginal product of that input must eventually fall. This concept explains why, for example, a baseball team with five good starting pitchers does sign yet another starter and why the Giants do not sign both Eli Manning and Tom Brady to play in the same year. Other than for a few trick plays, a team can use only one quarterback at a time, and, barring injury, additional quarterbacks rarely play. Finally, beyond T_{O2}, where the total product curve is downward sloping, the marginal product curve is negative.[14] If the Giants had signed Eli Manning, Tom Brady, and Drew Brees, the tension created over who plays how much (or the difficulty in trying to play all three) may cause the Giants to win fewer rather than more games. We will use the theory of production, in particular the law of diminishing returns, later in the text as we discuss the need for salary caps, roster limits, and teams' profit-maximizing strategies.

The law of diminishing marginal returns has direct implications for a firm's costs. As the marginal product of an input falls, the firm must use more and more of that input to achieve a given increase in output. Thus, as the marginal product falls, marginal cost rises. **Marginal cost** is the additional cost associated with an increase in output.

$$MC = \Delta C / \Delta Q$$

As Figure 2.10c shows, the marginal cost curve is essentially the inverse of the marginal product curve (though the axes are different). Marginal cost falls at first because additional units of talent are highly productive. Beyond Q_1, marginal costs begin to rise as the input is now subject to diminishing returns. The concept of marginal cost is critical to economic theories of firm decision making as we will see later in this chapter and throughout Chapters 3 and 4.

Price Ceilings and the Economics of Scalping

Today, fans wanting to buy or sell tickets to sporting events at the last minute can easily do so by accessing Web sites such as Stubhub. In the past, a University of Michigan football fan who wanted to see the Wolverines play archrivals Ohio State or Michigan State often had to participate in a strange ritual. Students with tickets to the game could be found walking in front of the Michigan Student Union with their tickets in one hand and a pencil in the other. When someone offered to buy the ticket, the student would agree to do so—but only if the potential buyer also bought the pencil.

The key to understanding such an odd sales arrangement lies in the state of Michigan's antiscalping laws. According to the law, no one can sell tickets for more than the value printed on the ticket (its *face value*). The face value of the ticket, however, was well below what a free market would dictate. In economic terms, the law placed a **price ceiling** on tickets, keeping their price far below equilibrium. If the face value of a ticket is $15, and no sales are permitted above this price, the price ceiling (p^c) is $15. Such a ceiling is shown in Figure 2.11.

A price ceiling creates two problems for buyers and sellers. First, the price ceiling ($p^c = \$15$ in Figure 2.10) creates excess demand for tickets, since the quantity of tickets demanded (Q_d) is much greater than the quantity of tickets supplied (Q_s). To make matters worse, there is no guarantee that the people who place the greatest value on tickets can get them. By limiting price to p^c, we know only that all buyers are willing and able to pay at least p^c to see a Michigan football game.

---

[14]The formula for marginal product is identical to the formula one would use to compute the slope of the total product ($\Delta Q / \Delta L$).

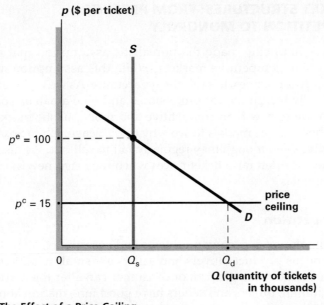

FIGURE 2.11   The Effect of a Price Ceiling
A price ceiling creates excess demand of $Q_d - Q_s$.

If price does not serve as an allocation mechanism, someone who is just willing to pay the face value for a ticket might get one while someone who values it far more highly might not. Many colleges and universities have a persistent excess demand for tickets. This frequently leads to scenes of students camped outside the ticket office for days at a time to be sure that they have a seat for the big game. Thus, when prices do not ration tickets, some other limited resource, in this case time, typically does.

Universities set low prices for one of several reasons. For example, they might do so out of a sense of fairness to students with limited incomes. Recognizing that athletics are a student activity, athletic departments might want to be sure that all (or at least most) students can afford to see "their" team play.

If those with tickets could sell freely to those without, a mutually beneficial trade could be arranged. Suppose, for example, that Daniel is a rabid Michigan fan who is willing to pay $100 for a ticket to see Michigan play Michigan State. Melanie—the lucky recipient of a ticket—thinks a ticket is worth only $15. If Daniel pays Melanie $70 for the ticket, he would pay $30 less than the ticket is worth to him while Melanie would receive $55 more than the ticket is worth to her. Daniel and Melanie would both benefit from such an exchange, yet the law prohibits it. That is why Melanie can be found on State Street in Ann Arbor, offering her ticket for the face value of $15, but only to those who are willing to pay $55 for her pencil and why Daniel is happy to pay so much for a pencil![15]

---

[15]A note of caution: It is doubtful that this practice is legal in most areas—and thus it is not one that we would advocate or condone.

2.3   MARKET STRUCTURES: FROM PERFECT COMPETITION TO MONOPOLY

So far, we have implicitly made the unrealistic assumption that all goods are bought and sold in competitive markets. While this assumption may work for some goods, such as potatoes, it is not always accurate. As we will see in Chapters 3 and 4, it is usually inaccurate for professional and elite amateur sports markets. In this section, we review both competitive and monopolistic market structures. We then use these simple models to see why the Chicago White Sox do not lower their ticket prices even though they regularly fail to sell out. We also use them to explain why teams often raise ticket prices when they sign new stars to lucrative guaranteed contracts.

Perfect Competition

Competitive markets have many producers and consumers, all buying and selling a homogeneous product. Buyers and sellers are small relative to the overall size of the market, so no single firm or consumer can alter the market price unilaterally. In addition, buyers and sellers have good information about prices. As a result, competitive firms have no market power. **Market power** is the ability to set or influence prices. If a firm in a competitive market tries to raise the price it charges, consumers will purchase an equivalent product elsewhere at the market price.

Although the *market* demand curve for a good sold in a competitive market is downward sloping, each *individual* competitive firm faces an L-shaped demand curve. The horizontal part of the curve shows the market price that is determined by market supply and demand. If a firm raises its price above that charged by its rivals in a perfectly competitive market, its sales fall to zero. The vertical part of the demand curve coincides with the vertical (price) axis and shows that the firm will not sell any output if it charges a price above the prevailing market price.

Figure 2.12 shows how a competitive market works for potatoes. Market demand and market supply yield an equilibrium price of \$4/bag in Figure 2.12a. Each farmer faces a demand curve that is horizontal at $p = \$4$ in Figure 2.12b. If a farmer charges more than \$4, his sales fall to zero. Since each farmer is so small relative to the size of the entire market, he can sell all the bags he wants at the market price without causing the market price to fall. Economists call firms in this position **price-takers**.

Because a farmer can sell each additional bag of potatoes for \$4, the extra revenue he receives from selling an additional bag—his **marginal revenue** (*MR*)—equals the price he charges for that last bag ($MR = p$). A farmer weighs the additional revenue received against the additional cost incurred to produce an additional bag of potatoes, his **marginal cost** (*MC*). He maximizes profits by producing and selling additional bags of potatoes until the extra revenue earned from selling the last bag equals the cost of producing that last bag (*MC*), as seen in Figure 2.13.

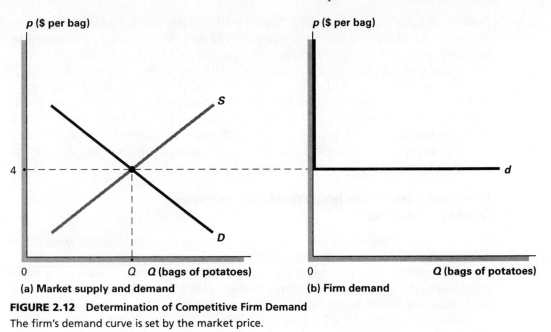

FIGURE 2.12 Determination of Competitive Firm Demand
The firm's demand curve is set by the market price.

Finally, economists assume that competitive firms can freely enter and exit the market. Thus, if potato farmers are making large profits, more farmers will plant potatoes. The increase in the number of farmers growing potatoes shifts the market supply curve to the right. The rightward shift of the supply curve causes

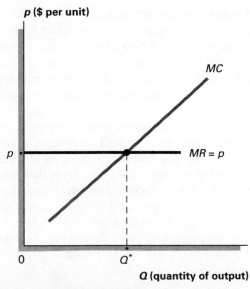

FIGURE 2.13 Marginal Revenue and Marginal Cost
The optimal quantity occurs where the $MR = MC$.

prices to fall, reducing individual firms' profits. This result is probably the single most important outcome of the competitive market. When firms in a competitive industry are profitable, other firms enter, causing price and profits to fall.

Free entry by producers benefits consumers in two important ways. It ensures that firms in the industry cannot restrict output in order to drive up prices and earn excessive profits. More importantly, competitive markets are **economically efficient**. An economically efficient outcome maximizes society's gains from exchange. In this context, profits attract new farmers and stimulate production by existing farmers so that society's desire for potatoes is satisfied. We discuss the concept of economic efficiency extensively in Chapter 4.

Monopoly and Other Imperfectly Competitive Market Structures

In reality, most goods have some characteristics that distinguish them from other commodities. Consumers may have no clear preferences over the type of potatoes they buy, but they may prefer buying tickets to see the Colorado Rockies play baseball to buying tickets to see the Denver Broncos play football. If we measure output as the number of fans in attendance, and if sports fans in Denver feel that there are no perfect substitutes for a Rockies game, the Rockies have market power, which enables them to raise prices without losing all of their customers. As a result, the demand curve for Rockies games is downward sloping rather than L-shaped. If the Rockies had no competitors at all and consumers had the choice of seeing a Rockies game or seeing nothing, they would be a monopoly. A **monopoly** exists when a single firm is the sole producer in the market. The demand curve faced by a monopoly is the market demand curve, because the firm does not share the market with any other firms.

All sports franchises exercise some degree of market power. This power stems from several sources. Baseball fans' preference for watching baseball games rather than other sporting events gives the Rockies a degree of market power. Moreover, potential competitors (i.e., teams seeking to enter the market) often face substantial barriers to entry, such as access to playing facilities or a television contract. These barriers prevent new entrants from providing a reasonable alternative.

Like a competitive firm, a monopoly maximizes profit when marginal revenue equals marginal cost. Unlike a competitive firm, a monopoly does not passively accept the price and quantity that are dictated by the intersection of supply and demand. The monopolist can set price at the level that maximizes its profits.

As a monopoly, the Rockies face a downward-sloping market demand curve and must lower their ticket prices if they want to sell more tickets than they did last year. Since the Rockies cannot easily identify all the fans who bought tickets at a higher price last year, they have to reduce the price of all the tickets they sell next year.[16] The extra revenue they receive from selling

---

[16]For now we ignore the complication raised by season tickets and by price discrimination. We also assume that there are no changes in anything but the price of Rockies tickets.

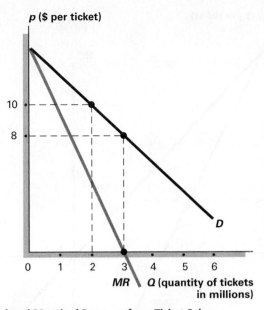

FIGURE 2.14   Demand and Marginal Revenue from Ticket Sales
Marginal revenue, the extra revenue from selling one more ticket, is less than the price of that ticket.

an additional ticket changes for two reasons. First, the team gains additional revenue from selling the extra tickets. Second, the team loses revenue because it must lower the price of all tickets in order to sell more of them. For example, suppose the Rockies sold 2 million tickets last year at $10 each and want to sell 3 million this year. If they attract the additional fans by charging $8 for all 3 million tickets, they gain $8 million in revenue from selling 1 million extra tickets at $8 apiece and lose $2 on each of the 2 million tickets they could have sold for $10 each. As a result, the additional revenue from increasing sales by 1 million tickets is $4 million (new revenue = $8 × 3 million = $24 million, less original revenue = $10 × 2 million = $20 million), not $8 million. As a result, the monopolist's marginal revenue curve lies below the demand curve, as seen in Figure 2.14.

As long as a team is not at capacity, the marginal cost of accommodating an extra spectator is close to zero. It costs the team relatively little to sell one more ticket and to admit and clean up after one more fan. As a result, economic analyses of ticket sales typically assume that the marginal cost of admitting an extra spectator equals zero. When ticket sales reach the capacity of the stadium, the marginal cost effectively becomes infinite since the team cannot sell any more seats at any price. Figure 2.15 illustrates the capacity constraint with a marginal cost curve that is effectively zero until 50,381 fans (the capacity of Coors Field) are admitted. At this point the marginal cost curve becomes vertical.

Figure 2.15 shows that market power allows the monopoly to charge a higher price than would a competitive industry. A perfectly competitive industry operates where the market demand curve cuts the MC curve. It sells Q^c and charges

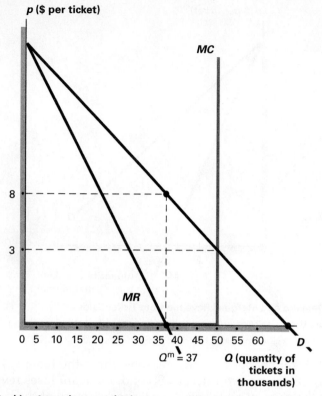

FIGURE 2.15   Rockies Attendance and Prices

The optimal quantity of tickets, Q^m occurs where $MR = MC$, and the optimal price lies on the demand curve, directly above Q^m

$p^c = \$3$. A monopolist produces $Q^m < Q^c$ because the MR curve cuts the horizontal axis at a much lower level of output.

To find the highest price the team can charge and still sell Q^m (37,000 tickets per game in this example), we look at the demand curve. In addition to telling us how much people are willing and able to buy at a given set of prices, the demand curve tells us the maximum amount consumers are willing and able to pay for a given quantity. The demand curve in Figure 2.15 tells us that the Rockies can sell 37,000 tickets per game if they charge no more than \$8 per ticket.

We can use this simple model of monopoly behavior to determine whether the Chicago White Sox or Chicago Blackhawks are irrational in their ticket policy. On the surface, it appears that someone is doing something wrong. After all, the Blackhawks regularly sold out the United Center during the 2010–2011 hockey season, while the White Sox rarely sold out U.S. Cellular Field during the 2011 baseball season.

In fact, both teams may be following optimal strategies. Having at least a degree of market power, both the White Sox and the Blackhawks face downward-sloping demand and marginal revenue curves. We continue to assume that marginal costs are zero, so their marginal cost curves lie along

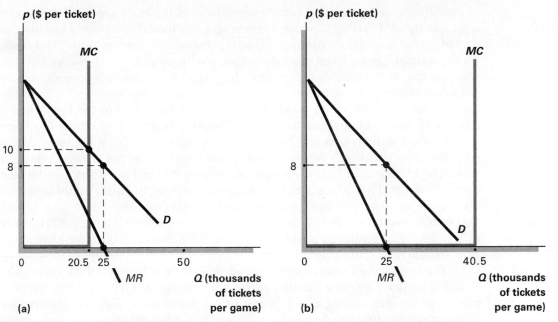

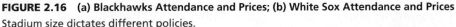

FIGURE 2.16 (a) Blackhawks Attendance and Prices; (b) White Sox Attendance and Prices
Stadium size dictates different policies.

the horizontal axis at all attendance levels below full capacity. However, the teams reach full capacity at very different points. The White Sox home games at U.S. Cellular Field can accommodate slightly over 40,500 fans. Blackhawk games at the United Center, however, can hold only 20,500 per game. Because the United Center is so much smaller, the marginal cost curve for Blackhawks games becomes vertical much earlier than the marginal cost curve for the White Sox, as seen in Figure 2.16.

The different *MC* curves mean that the White Sox and the Blackhawks follow different pricing policies even if they have identical demand curves. Because the *MC* curve for the White Sox is horizontal over such a large range of attendance, the marginal revenue curve probably crosses the marginal cost curve along the horizontal axis, as seen in Figure 2.16b. This means that the White Sox were maximizing their profits from attendance even though they played in a stadium that was 40 percent empty. By contrast, the Blackhawks' marginal revenue curve is far more likely to cross the marginal cost curve on its vertical segment. The Blackhawks maximize their profits from attendance by charging a relatively high price and selling out the United Center.

The Impact of an Increase in Costs

We have shown that teams determine how many tickets to sell—and how much to charge for their tickets—by equating the marginal revenue and marginal cost of selling an additional ticket. We have also shown that the marginal cost of providing an extra seat is generally very low until the team approaches the seat-ing capacity of its venue. Perhaps surprisingly, the model completely ignores the cost of guaranteed player contracts. That is because such contracts are fixed costs. As the term suggests, **fixed costs** do not vary with output, which we measure in this example as the number of fans attending a game. Because player contracts do not affect marginal costs, they have no bearing on ticket prices.

To see why Albert Pujols' salary represents a fixed cost to the Los Angeles Angels of Anaheim, just ask how much the Angels must pay him if the team draws only 1 million fans and how much they must pay him if the team draws 4 million fans. A player's salary—like any fixed cost—does not change as output rises. The $15.5 million that the Angels are paying Albert Pujols this year has the same impact that a $15.5 million legal judgment against the team might have. All else equal (or, as economists say, *ceteris paribus*), the price and quantity of tickets that maximized profits before the payment still do so after the payment. The only difference is that profits are lower than before. Why, then, might a team raise ticket prices after signing free agents?

The key can be found on the demand side of the ledger, not the supply side. Teams raise ticket prices when they sign a *new* free agent if they feel that the new player makes fans willing to pay higher prices than before. Teams charge higher ticket prices because the demand curve (and hence the marginal revenue curve) shifts outward, as seen in Figure 2.17. The higher demand and marginal revenue curves lead to a higher equilibrium price and (subject to capacity) quantity than before. In short, teams charge higher prices when they sign free agents because they *can* do so not because they *must*.

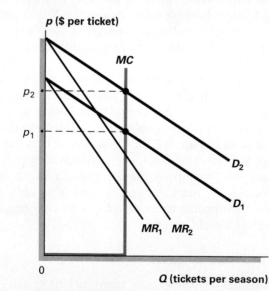

FIGURE 2.17   A Change in Demand Due to the Addition of a Marquee Player
Ticket prices rise because the demand for tickets rises, not because the team faces higher costs.

2.4   THE RISE OF PROFESSIONAL SPORTS

While "ball sports" date back to antiquity, baseball and soccer were the first sports to become widely popular, professional national pastimes.[17] Both sports developed and flourished when and where they did as the result of broad-based economic phenomena. Historians have drawn a link between the prosperity that accompanied the Industrial Revolution in the mid-19th century and the development of sport.[18] For a society to have a pastime, it first must have time to pass.

To see why, we use the same marginal analysis that we used earlier in the chapter. The same basic principle holds for consumers who want to maximize their well-being. In this section, we apply marginal analysis to the growth of leisure activity and then use this reasoning to show why spectator sports arose in the latter half of the 19th century in England and the United States.

Similar to a firm, a person spends an additional hour at an activity, whether it is work, studying, or leisure, until the benefit of an additional hour spent on that activity equals the cost of an additional hour. With a firm, benefits and costs are easy to understand and easy to measure. For an individual, the concepts can be more abstract. While the reward for work might be easily measured in terms of wages and salaries, the reward for many activities is the utility we gain from them, where **utility** is another word for pleasure. We call the extra happiness we get from a little more of a good or an activity the marginal utility we receive from it. The marginal cost of engaging in a little more of an activity might be monetary: the dollars we could have earned had we not studied economics or gone to a movie. It could also be the reduction in happiness we experience by making a different choice.

Figure 2.18 shows typical marginal utility and marginal cost curves. The marginal utility curve slopes down, indicating that the more we engage in an activity to begin with, the less a little more means to us. The marginal cost curve slopes up, showing that, as we engage more in an activity, we have to give up increasingly valuable alternatives.

To see how this applies to the rise of spectator sports, consider what life was like prior to the Industrial Revolution. Most people toiled in subsistence agricultural economies, meaning they spent all their waking hours growing enough food to survive. Anyone who did otherwise endangered his life and the lives of those around him. As Figure 2.18 shows, the marginal cost of leisure was extremely high for most people. That meant that most people devoted no time to leisure. While a few 18th-century French aristocrats enjoyed playing *jeu de pomme,* an early form of tennis, a poor peasant had no time for such a luxury.

Starting in the late 18th century, the Industrial Revolution significantly raised the living standards of large numbers of people in England. With higher incomes, people could spend time away from work without risking their lives. In terms of Figure 2.18, this meant that the marginal cost curve shifted down from MC_0 to MC_1.

---

[17]The ancient sports were typically associated with religious festivals, whereas movements such as the *Turnverein* in the early 19th-century German states were more expressions of nationalism than entertainment.

[18]For a good historical overview, see William Baker, *Sports in the Western World* (Totowa, N.J.: Rowman & Littlefield, 1982); and Robert Burk, *Never Just a Game: Players, Owners, and American Baseball to 1920* (Chapel Hill, N.C.: University of North Carolina Press, 1994).

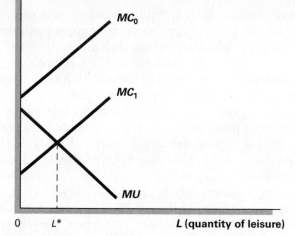

FIGURE 2.18 The Marginal Utility and Marginal Cost of Leisure Time
As the marginal cost of leisure fell, the time devoted to leisure rose.

As a result, people could spend time pursing non-labor activities, such as schooling or leisure—or both at once.

The modern version of soccer developed in the elite "public schools" of England (e.g., Eton, Charterhouse, Westminster, Harrow, and Rugby). Starting from a vaguely defined primitive sport, soccer evolved at each of the public schools in much the same way that different species of animals evolve from a common ancestor when they live on separate islands. Each school developed its own version of soccer based on the unique characteristics of the terrain on which it was played. At most schools, rough or muddy grounds made violent contact impractical. Schools that had large, open fields, such as the Rugby School, developed much rougher versions of the sport. Soccer's popularity soon spread to Cambridge University and Oxford University and to clubs formed by public school and university graduates. It is no coincidence that one of the most popular of the early clubs called itself "The Old Etonians."

In the United States, baseball also first appeared among the more prosperous elements of society. An early form of baseball was an adaptation of English games played by the Puritan upper-middle class in New England in the late 18th century. The first organized game did not appear until 1842, with the formation of the New York Knickerbocker Club.

Though they lacked the social imprimatur of the British public school, baseball clubs also strove to establish or maintain the social positions of their members. Games between baseball clubs in the pre–Civil War era were less a competition than an exercise in "manly upright fellowship, harmony, and decorum. For them, excellence in performance meant exhibiting character as well as skill...."[19]

---

[19]Robert Burk, *Never Just a Game* (1994), p. 6. For an excellent summary and comparison of the origins of baseball and soccer, see Stefan Szymanski and Andrew Zimbalist, *National Pastime* (Washington, D.C.: Brookings Institution Press, 2005).

In the second half of the 19th century, the benefits of the Industrial Revolution began to spread to all segments of society in England and in the United States. The higher standard of living of working-class families led to a broader pursuit of leisure activities. As a result, soccer spread northward from the public schools around London into the industrial heartland of England and Scotland, and baseball spread south and west from New York. In addition, playing baseball became a way for members of immigrant communities to assert their "Americanness." Thus, by the end of the 19th century, in England, soccer clubs of working-class people had largely displaced "Old Etonians," while in America, first-generation Americans of German and Irish descent had largely displaced "Yankee" baseball players.

The growing popularity of soccer and baseball among the working class led directly to the professionalization of the games. Working-class athletes lacked the independent means of earlier participants, so they could not afford to play regularly without being compensated for the opportunity cost of their time. The upper-class sportsmen on both sides of the Atlantic saw their roles change from amateur participants to financial backers of professional teams. While they remained firmly in charge of the management and financing of the clubs, the old guard roundly condemned the "moral declension" that accompanied both the increasing professionalism of sports and the participation of working-class athletes. Their concern did not keep them from recognizing that they could profit from marketing a superior, professional product to a public that now had the money and leisure time to attend sporting events regularly. We will return to the discussion of the spread of sports activities to the working class in Chapter 11 in the context of the history of amateurism.

BIOGRAPHICAL SKETCH

Silvio Berlusconi   (1936–)

We will make Italy like [AC] Milan.

—*Silvio Berlusconi*[1]

Take a little bit of Rupert Murdoch, add some Jerry Jones, sprinkle in a bit of George W. Bush, and you might just come up with Silvio Berlusconi. Like Murdoch, Berlusconi is a media magnate, controlling much of the information flow received by Italians each day. His road to the top, while not quite a rags-to-riches story, had many twists and turns.

Berlusconi showed an entrepreneurial flair at an early age, working his way through college and law school by booking bands on cruise ships. When an act fell through, he sometimes filled in as a singer. Berlusconi's first major success came in real estate, as the developer of a luxury complex outside Milan.

Berlusconi created the TV station TeleMilano to provide entertainment for the luxury community's residents. The TV station was a big hit, particularly his

(Continued)

(*Continued*)

pioneering of reality TV in Italy with an Italian version of the American show, *Big Brother*. TeleMilano's success led Berlusconi to transform it into the nationwide network Canale 5 in 1980. His media empire, which *Forbes* values at $5.9 billion, includes two other TV networks and the daily newspaper *Il Giornale.* Fininvest, the holding company that controls Berlusconi's media holdings, has made him one of the 200 richest people in the world.

Despite his power and wealth, Berlusconi remained relatively unknown until he purchased AC Milan in 1986. Like Jerry Jones, who purchased the Dallas Cowboys three years later, Berlusconi obtained a storied franchise that had fallen on hard times. AC Milan, founded by English expatriates in 1899, is one of the oldest soccer clubs in Italy and one of its most successful. By 1986, however, AC Milan's fortunes were in steep decline. It had won the Italian championship (the *Scudetto*) only once in the previous 18 years. In the early 1980s, it was implicated in a series of scandals and was briefly relegated from Serie A, Italy's top soccer league.

Like Jones, Berlusconi thrilled in the limelight of owning and transforming a popular sports team. He discarded the defensive style for which Italian teams were known and brought in many foreign players, including Ruud Gullit, a black player from Suriname. Integrating AC Milan was particularly controversial, as even today, Italian fans have a reputation for hostility to black players. Rather than simply call a press conference to introduce his new players, Berlusconi drew upon his media skills and flew his players into San Siro, the team's stadium, by helicopter to the strains of Wagner's *Ride of the Valkyries.*

Integrating the team and changing its style of play paid off, as AC Milan entered the most successful period in its history. It won the *Scudetto* in 1988, a feat it has repeated seven times. It has also been the most successful team in European soccer's (UEFA) Champions League, winning the title five times since 1989.

Like George W. Bush, Berlusconi used his celebrity as a team owner to begin a career in politics, when he founded the political party Forza Italia ("Go Italy"), named for the cheer that Italian fans chant for their national soccer team, in 1993. Bush, once the part owner of the Texas Rangers, was elected governor of Texas in 1994.

Berlusconi formed the party at an opportune time. The parties that had dominated Italian politics since the end of World War II, the Christian Democrats and the Communists, had both recently lost favor. Berlusconi exploited this vacuum, using sports metaphors to promote the message that he would bring a new energy and forcefulness to Italian politics. Berlusconi rode this message to three terms as prime minister. His first term lasted less than a year in 1994, but his second lasted from 2001 until a whisker-thin loss in 2006. This made his second administration the longest of any Italian government since World War II. In May 2008, Berlusconi was elected as prime minister a third time.

Berlusconi's political career has been stormy. He has been dogged by allegations of corruption since his time as a developer in Milan. Berlusconi's dominance of the press and TV is also cause for concern. In 2011, Freedom House estimated that, between Berlusconi's private holdings and his power over state-run networks, he controlled about 90 percent of the Italian media. Thus, during Berlusconi's second term, Freedom House rated Italy as the only nation in Western Europe not to have a free press, a rating that has improved since he left power.

In 2011, personal scandals and Italy's debt crisis caught up with Berlusconi, ultimately leading to his resignation from office. He remains, however, the owner and president of AC Milan, which may prove to be a springboard for yet another political comeback.

[1]Franklin Foer, *How Soccer Explains the World: An Unlikely Theory of Globalization* (New York: Harper Collins, 2004).

Sources: "Answers Please," *The Economist,* August 2, 2003, pp. 23–27; Silvio Berlusconi and Family, *The World's Billionaires,* March 2012, at http://www.forbes.com/profile/silvio-berlusconi/, viewed May 2, 2012; Geoff Andrews, *Not a Normal Country: Italy After Berlusconi* (London: Pluto Press, 2005); Rachel Donadio, "Berlusconi's Wife Says She Wants a Divorce," *The New York Times,* May 4, 2009, at http://www.nytimes.com/2009/05/04/world/europe/04iht-italy.html; Franklin Foer, *How Soccer Explains the World: An Unlikely Theory of Globalization* (New York: Harper Collins, 2004); Paul Ginsborg, *Silvio Berlusconi: Television, Power, and Patrimony* (London: Verso, 2004); Karin D. Karlekar and Jennifer Dunham, "Freedom of the Press 2012: Breakthroughs and Pushback in the Middle East," *Freedom House,* at http://www.freedomhouse.org/article/freedom-press-2012-breakthroughs-and-pushback-middle-east, viewed May 2, 2012.

Summary

Supply and demand are among the simplest but most powerful tools in the economist's arsenal. Understanding most economic relationships requires a solid grasp of this framework. If you have a clear understanding of which external forces affect demand and supply, then you can make accurate predictions regarding the direction of change in prices and output.

Firms produce output by combining inputs. All else equal, increases in any one input eventually are subject to the law of diminishing marginal returns. The marginal productivity of that input declines and, in turn, marginal costs rise.

When markets are competitive, prices are lower and output is higher than if a firm has market power such as in a monopoly; not all economic activity, though, occurs in competitive markets. Market power gives a firm the ability to set prices rather than simply accept the price as determined by the market. In most sports markets, teams have substantial market power. By setting ticket prices, teams have the ability to control attendance, subject to the capacity of their building.

Costs and the distinction between fixed and variable costs play a vital role in the determination of output and prices. For professional sports teams, players' salaries are often best treated as fixed costs, because they are unrelated to the number of games played.

Individuals also weigh marginal benefit and marginal cost when making decisions. People weigh the extra happiness, or marginal utility, that they get from leisure time and the marginal cost of an extra hour of leisure (the earnings forgone) when deciding how to allocate their time. The high marginal cost of leisure time prior to the Industrial Revolution explains why professional sports did not arise until the mid-19th century.

Discussion Questions

1. Does your college charge a higher price for football or basketball games against higher-profile opponents? If it does not charge different prices, do you think it should? Does it do anything else to differentiate games against more and less attractive opponents?

2. Who is made better off by sites such as stubhub.com? What reason do you have for your answer?

3. Explain why the marginal cost of winning increases even if players are available at a fixed salary (say, $500,000 each).

4. Given the law of diminishing marginal returns, how should a team with a fixed salary budget allocate its payroll between offensive and defensive players?

5. The National Collegiate Athletic Association (NCAA) does not allow its members to play against schools that the NCAA does not certify. Is this a good idea? Why or why not?

Problems

2.1. Some cities have several teams in England's Premier League (the country's top soccer league). Explain how this affects the monopoly power of those teams.

2.2. The marginal cost of admitting an additional fan to watch the Sacramento Kings play basketball is close to zero, but the average price of a ticket to a Kings game is about $60. What do these facts tell you about the market in which the Kings operate? Justify your answer.

2.3. The major North American sports leagues prohibit teams from locating within a specific distance of an existing team. Why do they have such a rule?

2.4. Use supply and demand to show why teams that win championships typically raise their ticket prices the next season.

2.5. Use a graph with attendance on the horizontal axis and the price of tickets on the vertical axis to show the effect of the following on the market for tickets to see the Vancouver Canucks play hockey.
   a. The quality of play falls, as European players are attracted to play in rival hockey leagues in their home countries.
   b. Vancouver places a C$1 tax on all tickets sold.
   c. A recession reduces the average income in Vancouver and the surrounding area.
   d. The NBA puts a new basketball franchise in Vancouver.

2.6. Use the law of diminishing returns to explain why pro golfer Rory McIlroy should not spend all of his practice time working on his putting.

2.7. Use a graph to show how the marginal product of offensive labor in the NFL might change if wide receivers in the NFL are no longer allowed to use gloves that make it easier to catch the ball on cold days.

2.8. The New York Jets football team raises ticket prices from $100 to $110 per seat and experience a 5 percent decline in tickets sold. What is the elasticity of demand for tickets?

2.9. Since the 1990s, many Major League Baseball teams have moved to new stadiums that are far smaller than the ones they have replaced. Use an appropriate graph to show what this has meant for ticket prices.

2.10. Suppose the Tampa Bay Rays baseball team charges $10 bleacher seats (poor seats in the outfield) and sells 250,000 of them over the course of the season. The next season, the Rays intends to increase the price to $12 and sell 200,000 tickets.

    a. What is the elasticity of demand for bleacher seats at Rays games?

    b. Assuming the marginal cost of admitting one more fan is zero, is the price increase a good idea?

APPENDIX 2A

Utility Functions, Indifference Curves, and Budget Constraints

This appendix reviews the basics of consumer theory. It contains an introduction to utility maximization, which involves the use of indifference curves and budget constraints. It then uses these tools to provide a more sophisticated account of the rise of spectator sports.

2A.1 CONSTRAINED MAXIMIZATION

Sandy is a graduate student who loves to go to baseball games and read economics textbooks. In fact, tickets and books are the only things she buys.[20] Economists evaluate Sandy's feelings toward baseball and economics books using her utility function. Sandy's **utility function** is a mathematical representation of the happiness she gets from her consumption decisions. In this example, Sandy's utility function contains only baseball tickets (T) and economics books (B), and so we can write her utility function as

$$U = u(B, T)$$

    Since Sandy wants both books and tickets (they are "goods," as opposed to "bads" that she does *not* want), whenever the number of either books or tickets increases, Sandy's **total utility** increases as well.

    Economists, like Freudian psychologists, believe that people are motivated by a desire for pleasure. Freudians call the pleasure impulse the "id." Economists call it "utility maximization." In this example, Sandy would maximize her utility by buying an infinite number of tickets and books.

    Also like psychologists, economists see forces that hold the pleasure impulse in check. Rather than the internal, psychological barrier of Freud's superego, economists see external constraints in the limited resources that people have at their

---

[20]Sandy surely buys more than just two items, but this simplification allows us to use two-dimensional pictures rather than multivariate calculus.

disposal. People have only so much money, time, and energy with which to satisfy their desires. As a result, they cannot have all things or engage in all activities that make them happy. Put simply, they have to make choices. They do not, however, choose randomly. Economists assume that people maximize their utility subject to constraint by making rational choices, the economic analog to Freud's ego. Sandy makes a **rational choice** when she uses all available information to make the decision that maximizes her happiness.

Many noneconomists use the idea of rational choice to claim that economists view people as walking calculators who carefully weigh all options and have no room for emotions of any kind. Such a characterization is unfair. In fact, rationality need not connote careful decision making—or even sanity. To an economist, actions that most people would regard as heinous or bizarre would still be rational as long as they maximized the decision maker's utility.

Indifference curves allow us to illustrate people's preferences in a world that contains two goods. Recall that Sandy likes to watch baseball games and buy economics texts. Sandy enjoys a certain amount of happiness from seeing 10 baseball games and buying four economics textbooks (a combination illustrated by point A in Figure 2A.1). If someone took away one of Sandy's books (moving her to point A'), she would not feel as happy as before. Sandy would not feel so bad, however, if the person who took away her book gave her a ticket to a ballgame in exchange. In fact, if the person gave her enough tickets (say three tickets, putting her at point B in Figure 2A.1), Sandy might feel just as happy as she did to begin with.

If Sandy feels exactly the same about the two combinations of ballgames and books, we say that she is **indifferent** between points A and B. There are typically many combinations of ballgames and books that make Sandy equally happy. Combining all these points yields an indifference curve, like the ones shown in Figure 2A.2.

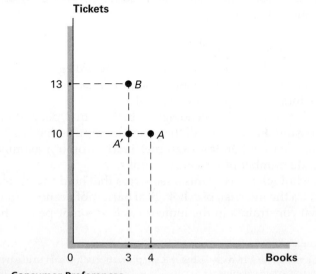

FIGURE 2A.1   Consumer Preferences

Sandy feels worse off at *A'* than at *A*, but she feels indifferent between *A* and *B*.

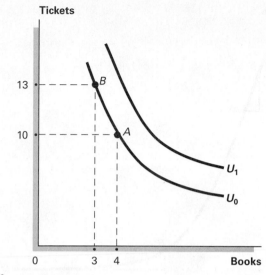

FIGURE 2A.2   Indifference Curves
Sandy feels the same everywhere along U_0, but she would be better off on U_1.

Because every combination of ballgames and textbooks yields some level of utility, every point in Figure 2A.1 is on *some* indifference curve. As a result, drawing all of Sandy's indifference curves would require filling in the entire area of the graph. We therefore draw only a sampling of her indifference curves. While indifference curves can come in many different shapes, most look like those in Figure 2A.2: They are downward sloping, convex, and cannot intersect.

Indifference curves slope downward any time we consider two products that the consumer likes. If we give Sandy more of a product that she likes, she is happier. To restore her initial utility level—and keep her on her original indifference curve—we have to take away some of something else that she values. More of one good means less of the other, and so the indifference curve slopes down. Having more of both goods makes Sandy happier, giving her a higher level of utility, shown by her being on a higher indifference curve in Figure 2A.2.

A convex indifference curve is typically very steep at first but becomes steadily flatter as one moves down and to the right. To see why, note that when Sandy sees many ballgames and reads few books, seeing one more or one less game means very little to her, but reading one more or one less book has a great impact on her happiness. As a result, she is willing to give up seeing a large number of ballgames in order to get only a few more books, as shown by the movement from point A to A' in Figure 2A.3. In this range, the indifference curve is steep. The same logic results in an almost flat indifference curve when Sandy has many books but sees only a few ballgames, as in the movement from B to B' in Figure 2A.3. Economists typically attribute Sandy's behavior to the principle of diminishing marginal rate of substitution. A **diminishing marginal rate of substitution** implies that, as consumers give up each successive unit of one good, they need increasing quantities of the other good in order to maintain the same level of utility. It is closely related

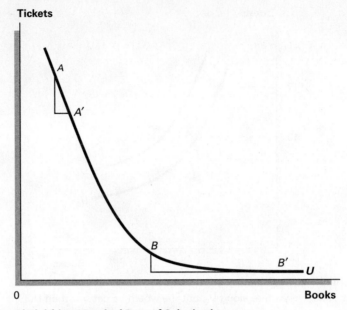

FIGURE 2A.3   Diminishing Marginal Rate of Substitution
Sandy values books relatively highly and tickets relatively little at *A*, but she feels just
the opposite at *B*.

to the law of diminishing marginal utility, which states that as a person consumes
increasing quantities of one good, holding the consumption of all other goods constant, the marginal utility of the additional units consumed will eventually fall.

If indifference curves intersected, we would have to make some rather
bizarre conclusions about how people behave. Figure 2A.4 shows what happens

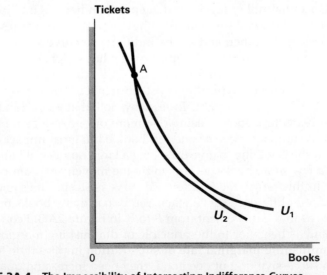

FIGURE 2A.4   The Impossibility of Intersecting Indifference Curves
If indifference curves cross, consumers' preferences become inconsistent.

if two of Sandy's indifference curves, U_1 and U_2, cross at point A. Above point A, indifference curve U_2 lies to the right of indifference curve U_1. That means that Sandy can have more books without giving up any ballgames, leaving her better off. As a result, Sandy prefers all points on U_2 to all points on U_1. However, below point A, the positions of the indifference curves are reversed, meaning Sandy prefers all points on U_1 to all points on U_2. To make matters still more confusing, since the two curves have point A in common, Sandy must get the same level of utility from both curves.

To maximize her utility, Sandy wants to be on the highest possible indifference curve. She is limited, however, by the amount of time, energy, and income at her disposal. For simplicity, assume that Sandy is constrained only by her income (I) of $800 and that tickets to a ballgame cost $10 while economics texts cost $20. Figure 2A.5 shows that she can buy 80 tickets if she buys only tickets and 40 textbooks if she buys only books. Since books cost twice as much as tickets, Sandy must give up two tickets in order to buy one more book. As a result, her budget constraint is a straight line with slope −2 that connects the points corresponding to 80 games and zero books, and zero games and 40 books.

We can write Sandy's constraint algebraically as

$$20B + 10T = 800$$

More generally, if p_b is the price of books and p_t is the price of tickets, then

$$p_b B + p_t T = I$$

To see how changes in income and prices affect the constraint, consider what happens when we change the two. If the price of a ballgame doubles to $20,

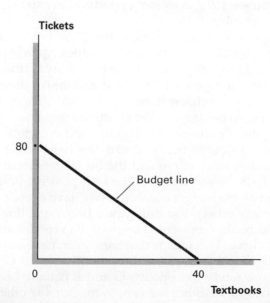

FIGURE 2A.5 Budget Constraint
Sandy's budget constraint shows the combinations of goods that she can afford.

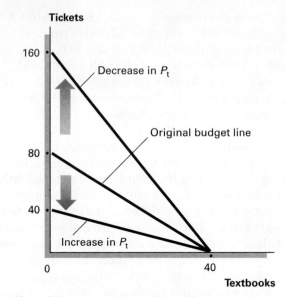

FIGURE 2A.6 The Effect of Changes in Price on the Budget Constraint
Sandy's constraint swivels out if the price of tickets falls and swivels in if the price of tickets rises.

Sandy's opportunities fall. She can now see only 40 games if she spends all her money on tickets. Figure 2A.6 shows that the vertical intercept slides down to 40 games, and the budget constraint becomes flatter. Since ballgames and textbooks now cost the same amount, Sandy can get one more book by sacrificing one ballgame, and the slope of the constraint becomes −1. If the price of a ballgame falls to $5, Sandy can see 160 games, her opportunities expand, and the slope of her constraint becomes −4.

If Sandy gets a raise so that she now has $1,000 at her disposal (and all prices stay at their original levels), her opportunities again expand. If she buys only tickets, she can go to 100 games. If she buys only textbooks, she can buy 50 books. Both intercepts in Figure 2A.7 increase, and the constraint shifts outward. Since the two prices have not changed, Sandy must still give up two ballgames to buy another book, and so the slope of her constraint remains −2.

Sandy's best possible choice of ballgames and economics texts comes on the highest indifference curve that still satisfies her budget constraint. This occurs where the indifference curve and the budget constraint are tangent, at point E in Figure 2A.8. To see that E is the best possible point, consider any other possible point on the budget constraint (we have chosen F in Figure 2A.8, but you can choose any other). You can draw a horizontal line from the combination of games and books represented by point F to combination G, which lies on the indifference curve. This means that Sandy can have more books without sacrificing any ballgames by moving from point F to point G, leaving her better off. We also know Sandy likes points G and E equally because they lie on the same indifference curve. Since we can do this for *any* other possible point,

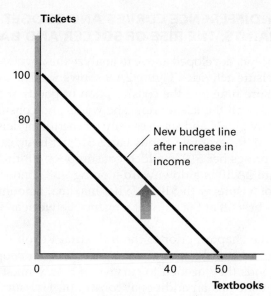

FIGURE 2A.7   The Effect of an Increase in Income

If Sandy's income rises, her constraint shifts out, but the slope does not change.

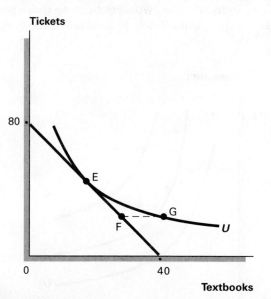

FIGURE 2A.8   The Utility-Maximizing Bundle

The best possible combination of tickets and textbooks occurs where an indifference curve is tangent to Sandy's constraint.

no other attainable combination of ballgames and textbooks provides as much utility as E. In addition, Sandy cannot afford a better combination of books and ballgames because any higher indifference curve lies outside her constraint.

2A.2 USING INDIFFERENCE CURVES AND BUDGET CONSTRAINTS: THE RISE OF SOCCER AND BASEBALL

We can use the concepts developed above to analyze the development of spectator sports and other leisure activities. Figure 2A.9 shows Sandy's indifference curves for two goods: leisure time and the consumption of goods and services. Sandy, however, cannot have all the leisure time she wants and consume all she wants. She can afford to buy goods and services only by sacrificing leisure time to work and earn income.[21] If, for example, Sandy earns $10 per hour, each hour of leisure that she sacrifices brings her $10 in added consumption. In this case, her budget constraint in Figure 2A.10 is a downward-sloping line connecting T hours, her maximal amount of leisure, with $10 \times T$, her maximal amount of consumption. As before, Sandy is best off at the point of tangency between an indifference curve and her constraint.

As noted in the chapter, prior to the Industrial Revolution, most societies could be characterized as subsistence economies in which people spent all their time generating goods they needed to survive. If Sandy must consume at least C_0 to survive, then she has an additional constraint. Her survival constraint is the horizontal line through C_0 in Figure 2A.11. Sandy cannot consume less and survive.

As an economy industrializes, workers become more productive, and their wages rise. A higher wage allows Sandy to generate more consumption for every

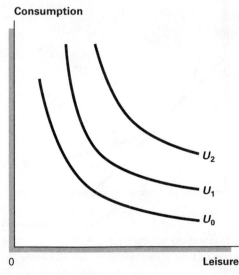

FIGURE 2A.9 **The Trade-Off between Goods and Leisure**
Sandy can also have a preference over goods and leisure time.

---

[21]Economists acknowledge that people can allocate their time in other ways. One example is "home production," the unpaid work that goes into cooking, cleaning, and similar household activities.

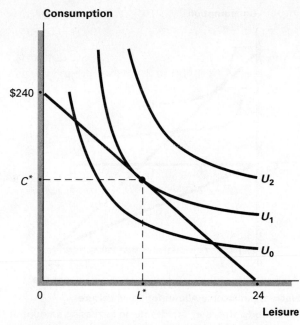

FIGURE 2A.10   The Utility-Maximizing Combination of Goods and Leisure
Sandy's optimal combination of goods and leisure time also comes at the tangency
of an indifference curve and her budget constraint.

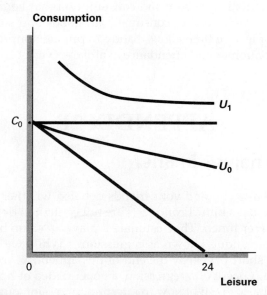

FIGURE 2A.11   Subsistence Level of Income Allows No Leisure
When people live at subsistence level, the optimal quantity of leisure is zero.

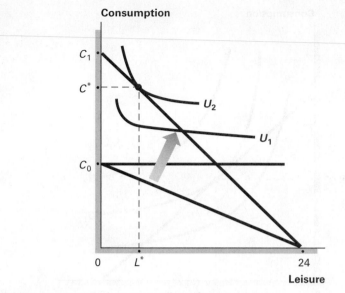

FIGURE 2A.12   An Increase in Income Allows for Some Leisure
As people become more productive, they can devote an increasing amount of time to leisure.

hour of leisure she sacrifices. Her budget constraint swivels outward, and her maximum possible consumption rises from C_0 to C_1 in Figure 2A.12. Sandy now has several combinations of leisure and consumption that lie above her survival constraint. She can now afford to consume both goods and services and leisure time. The advent of leisure time allows Sandy to pursue nonproductive activities such as the participation in and attendance at athletic events.

APPENDIX 2B

Regression Analysis in Brief

How many times have you and your friends debated whether a player is worth the money his team pays him? Economists are not content to debate the monetary value of a player over lunch. They estimate a player's value based on a sophisticated statistical technique known as regression.[22] While we cannot make you an expert in a few short pages, by the end of this appendix, you should have an appreciation of the concept of a regression, a general idea of how economists use regressions, and a basic grasp of how to interpret regression output.

---

[22]See G. S. Thomas, "Surhoff Proves to Be '99's Best Investment," *Street & Smith's SportsBusiness Journal*, October 25–31, 1999, p. 1, for an article that uses a technique such as this.

Suppose you want to figure out how much Alex Ovechkin, a star forward with the Washington Capitals, is worth to his team. Presumably, the Capitals pay him based on some measure of performance. (We discuss the precise measure in Chapter 8.) In a very simple world, teams may base the salaries of all players other than goalies on the number of goals they score:

$$\text{Salary} = f(\text{Goals})$$

In the equation above a player's salary is a **dependent variable**, because its value depends on (is determined by) the number of goals a player scores. Because the number of goals does not depend on another variable in the equation above, we call it an **independent variable**. If the relationship between goals scored and a player's salary (the "functional form" of $f(x)$ in the equation above) was a straight line like that in Figure 2B.1, you would be able to compute how much Alex Ovechkin was worth based on the number of goals he scored. Since you know that Ovechkin scored 32 goals in the 2010–2011 season, you could tell your friends how much he is worth to the team.

Unfortunately, life is not so simple. Salaries and goals scored do not line up perfectly along a straight line. Instead, the relationship is likely to be scattered around the line, as shown in Figure 2B.2. The points corresponding to players' goals and salaries may be scattered about the line for two reasons. First, there may be some error in measuring the variables involved. For example, Ovechkin's official salary may not include a bonus he received for making the NHL All-Star Team. If so, the official statistics understate his full compensation, and the point corresponding to his goals and salary lies below the line.

Second, a player's salary and goals scored may not lie on the line because of some factor for which we have failed to account. For example, Ovechkin also had 53 assists—plays that led to goals scored by his teammates. If teams reward both players for both goals and assists, then Ovechkin's goal–salary combination may lie above the line in Figure 2B.2 because his salary also reflects a factor that our goal–salary relationship ignores.

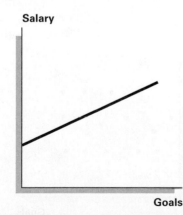

Salary

Goals

FIGURE 2B.1   The True Relationship between Goals and Salary
If we knew the true relationship between goals and salary, we would know what each hockey player's salary should be.

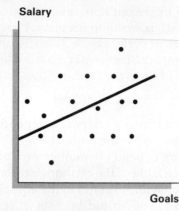

FIGURE 2B.2   Observations Scattered Around the True Relationship
A player's salary might be higher or lower than the true relationship predicts.

Making matters more difficult still, in real life, we do not observe the line in Figure 2B.2. All we see is the scatter of points. From this scatter of points, we must estimate the relationship between goals and salaries before making a statement about a given player.

Economists who want to know the relationship between goals scored and salary in the NHL must first estimate the true relationship from the scatter of points that appear in Figure 2B.3. They do so through a process known as ordinary least squares (OLS). The name **ordinary least squares** indicates that we choose the line that minimizes the sum of the *squared* distances between the points and the line. If e_i is the distance (measured as a vertical line) between each point $(i = 1, \ldots, n)$ scattered around the proposed line and the line itself, OLS minimizes the sum S, where

$$S = \sum_{i=1}^{n} e_i^2$$

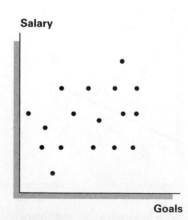

FIGURE 2B.3   OLS Fits a Line to the Scattering of Points
In reality, we see only the scattered points and must estimate the true relationship.

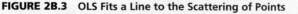

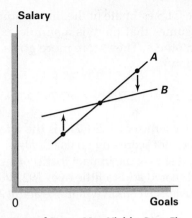

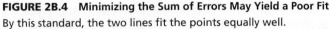

FIGURE 2B.4 **Minimizing the Sum of Errors May Yield a Poor Fit**
By this standard, the two lines fit the points equally well.

While we do not bother with all the theory behind OLS estimation, it helps to see why economists prefer it to two alternative estimation methods. One alternative is to minimize the total error (Σe_i), in effect adding the signed distances of the points from the proposed line. Figure 2B.4 shows this method fails to distinguish between lines A and B, even though line A clearly gives the better fit. The problem is that the error for line B is also zero because the negative error offsets the positive error.

We can solve the problem of offsetting positive and negative misses by either squaring the errors or taking their absolute value ($\Sigma |e_i|$). The two methods, however, are not identical. If we added the absolute value of the error terms, we would conclude that either line C or line D in Figure 2B.5 fits the data equally well. By squaring the errors, OLS places greater weight on the large miss made by line D. OLS thus fits our intuitive notion that a line with several small misses fits the data better than a line with a few very large ones.

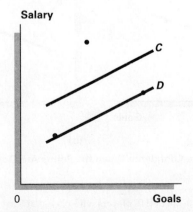

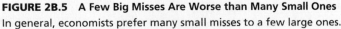

FIGURE 2B.5 **A Few Big Misses Are Worse than Many Small Ones**
In general, economists prefer many small misses to a few large ones.

Economists call the OLS estimate of the line relating salary to goals a *simple regression,* because it assumes that there is a simple explanation for why some players make more than others: They score more goals. Here is the output from one such simple regression[23]

$$\text{Salary} = 1{,}291{,}215 + 92{,}297 \times \text{Goals}$$

In this equation, the coefficient 1,291,215 is the *intercept term.* It is the salary a player receives if he does not score any goals (Goals = 0). The coefficient 92,297 represents the *slope term.* It shows the impact that scoring an extra goal has on salary. It says that each goal scored adds a little over $92,000 to a player's salary. This model thus predicts that Alex Ovechkin will make about 1,291,215 + 92,297 × 32 = $4,244,719.

We cannot, however, be certain that a player's salary will actually rise by about $92,297 per goal scored. Figure 2B.6 shows two different sets of points that both lead to the same slope term. While the estimate is the same for each, we are far more confident of our results in Figure 2B.6a. Statisticians measure their confidence in their estimates with a variable called the *standard error.* We shall not derive the formula for the standard error; we simply say that the closer the standard error of a coefficient is to zero, the more confident we are that our estimate accurately reflects the true value. A good rule of thumb is to look for a standard error that is no more than half the size of the coefficient. Computer programs generally compute the ratio of the coefficient to the standard error, a value called the *t-statistic.* Since we want the standard error to be no more than about half

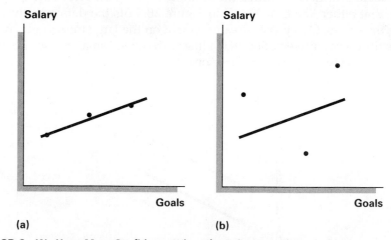

(a)   (b)

FIGURE 2B.6   We Have More Confidence When the Points Are Close to the Line

---

[23]The sample in this case is 2010–2011 NHL players who played at least 20 games and had averaged at least 5 minutes per game on the ice.

the value of the coefficient, we look for a *t*-statistic that is greater than 2.0. Most economics papers report the *t*-values in parentheses below the coefficients like this:

$$\text{Salary} = 1{,}291{,}215 + 92{,}297 \times \text{Goals}$$
$$(13.30) \quad (13.83)$$

In this case, both *t*-values are much greater than 2.0, so we can be confident that the true values of both the constant and the slope terms are not zero and that goals actually do have an impact on salary.

Multiple Regression and Dummy Variables

As noted earlier, we can probably make our measurement more accurate by including other variables that affect a player's salary. In fact, failing to include a key variable such as assists may cause our coefficient on goals to be off target, a problem statisticians call bias. We call a regression that has several explanatory variables a multiple regression, reflecting the fact that a dependent variable (in our case, salaries) may be affected by multiple factors. The results of a multiple regressions look very much like those of a simple regression. In this case, we find

$$\text{Salary} = 755{,}677 + 18{,}436 \times \text{Goals} + 74{,}820 \times \text{Assists}$$
$$(7.74) \quad (2.03) \quad\quad\quad (11.35)$$

The interpretation of the coefficients becomes a bit more complex in a multiple regression. Now the coefficient on goals, 18,436, reflects the impact of an additional goal on a player's salary *holding the number of assists constant*. It allows us to say that if two players have the same number of assists (and any other factor one might include) but one of the players has 10 more goals than the other, we expect the player with more goals to earn about $184,000 per year more than the other.

While standard errors and *t*-statistics give a good idea as to how well specific variables explain the data, they do not tell how good a job the regression as a whole does. Fortunately, most regression packages provide several overall measures of the quality of the regression. The most intuitive measure of a regression's "quality of fit" is its R^2. The value of the R^2 tells us how much of the variation in the dependent variable can be explained by the explanatory variables in the regression. In the above regressions, for example, the R^2 rises from 0.21 to 0.34 when we add assists as an explanatory variable. This tells us that goals alone explain about 21 percent of the variation in salary, while goals and assists combined explain about 34 percent. Using both goals and assists improves the regression because the R^2 of the second regression is closer to 1, meaning it comes closer to explaining 100 percent of the variation in salary.

One additional variable we might want to include in our multiple regression is the player's position. Neither goals nor assists are as important for defenseman, whose primary responsibility is to prevent scoring by the other team, as they are to an offensive player. We cannot add a player's position, however, in the same way that we would add the number of goals or assists he has. A player's position, like a worker's sex or race, is a qualitative variable; it does not have an obvious numerical value. To include position in our regression, we must first create a dummy variable. **Dummy variables** assign numerical values to qualitative variables. In this case, we let the dummy variable equal zero if the player was not a defenseman and one if the player was a defenseman. This changes the regression to

$$\text{Salary} = 418{,}312 + 45{,}715 \times \text{Goals} + 64{,}470 \times \text{Assists} + 694{,}374 \times \text{Defenseman}$$
$$\quad\quad\quad (3.55)\quad\quad (4.35)\quad\quad\quad\quad\quad (9.46)\quad\quad\quad\quad\quad\quad (4.92)$$

Since the variable *Defenseman* equals zero for all players who do not play defense, the coefficient has no impact for them. We can think of the coefficient as the impact of playing defense, *ceteris paribus*—the impact of playing defense for a player who scores a given number of goals and who has a given number of assists. These results suggest that defensemen are paid a premium of almost $700,000. This does not mean that defensemen are more valuable to hockey teams. Defensemen are less likely to score goals or have assists than wings or centers. An offensive player who scores about seven more goals and has six more assists than a defensive player more than makes up the difference of the dummy variable. As expected, adding a player's position improves the quality of the regression—the R^2 rises to 0.36.

PART TWO

The Industrial Organization of Sports

CHAPTER 3

Sports Franchises as Profit-Maximizing Firms

For almost twenty years I owned and ran a National Football League team, the San Diego Chargers. When I bought the Chargers I believed I could apply to professional football the same principles of good business management that had enabled me to succeed in the corporate world. There was also a time when I believed in Santa Claus, the Easter Bunny, and the Tooth Fairy.

—GENE KLEIN[1]

INTRODUCTION

If we judged Mark Cuban solely according to the bottom line, he would be one of the worst owners in professional sports. Figures from *Forbes magazine* show that in the 2010–2011 season his team, the NBA's Dallas Mavericks, ranked 24th in the league in operating income (a loss of $7.8 million), despite having the 9th highest revenue in the league ($146 million).[2] Any corporate executive who turned such high revenues into such low operating income would soon be scanning the classified

---

[1]Eugene Klein, *First Down and a Billion: The Funny Business of Pro Football* (New York: Morrow, 1987), p. 12.

[2]Operating income is closely related—but not identical—to profit. It is the difference between a team's revenue and the costs of its day-to-day functions. Unlike profit, it excludes costs not related to day-to-day operations, such as interest payments on loans or wear and tear on its facility. "NBA Team Values: The Business of Basketball," *Forbes*, at http://www.forbes.com/lists/2011/32/basketball-valuations-11_land.html.

ads for a new job. Instead, Cuban is celebrated as the ideal owner, and baseball fans in Cuban's hometown of Pittsburgh in the past have pleaded for him to take over the downtrodden Pirates.[3]

Sports fans clearly use a different yardstick for measuring success. They condemn team executives or owners whom they suspect of putting profit ahead of winning, and they have at times supported massive public subsidies unrelated to the profitability of the teams. While the Mavericks have lost more money than almost any other NBA team under Cuban's stewardship, the fans—and Cuban himself—would probably say that it was worth every penny. Not only has he built a winning franchise, he is, in the words of one observer, "a *bona fide* sports star, better known and more popular than most of his players."[4] Cuban clearly views the Mavericks as a consumption good, a chance to have fun and to rub elbows with athletes, celebrities, and fans, rather than as a source of income.

While Cuban's actions have endeared him to fans, they have not endeared him to the NBA league office. He has been fined repeatedly for offenses ranging from criticizing referees to commenting that he would love to sign LeBron James, when James was not yet a free agent. Like most sports teams, Cuban's Mavericks operate in the context of a league. As Cuban has discovered, leagues set and enforce many rules. In Section 3.4, we examine how and why leagues regulate what teams may do on the field and what owners may do off the field in their pursuit of wins and money.

While many owners have nonfinancial motives for owning a sports franchise—a factor we explore in Section 3.2—few of them show as much disregard for profit as Mark Cuban. From the beginning of organized sport, owners have dealt with the tension between being sportsmen, who want to win, and being owners, who seek profit. We begin this chapter by contrasting the implications of these two roles. We then explore how a variety of circumstances affect the ability of sports teams to earn a profit—or at least to break even.

LEARNING OBJECTIVES

After reading this chapter, you will be able to:

- Describe the various possible team goals and how those goals influence team behavior.
- Analyze team revenues and explain differences in revenues and operating income across sports.
- Describe how owners can manipulate their costs to make profits look like losses.

---

[3]See, for example, Ryne Gery, "Mark Cuban Deserves a Chance in Baseball, The Pirates Need Him," *Call to the Pen,* August 7, 2010, at http://calltothepen.com/2010/08/07/mark-cuban-deserves-a-chance-in-baseball-the-pirates-need-him/.

[4]Chris Suellentrop, "Mark Cuban: How to Meddle with Your Sports Team—The Right Way," *Slate Magazine,* December 4, 2002, at http://www.slate.com.

- Explain the role that leagues play in teams' pursuit of wins or profits.
- Explain and show how alternative league structures affect teams' behavior.

3.1 MAXIMIZING PROFITS OR MAXIMIZING WINS?

For most of the summer of 2011, the Philadelphia Phillies dominated the National League, while the New York Yankees led the American League. The Phillies had Major League Baseball's best regular season record and topped MLB in per-game attendance, while the Yankees were a close second in both categories. The Yankees took a back seat to no one when it came to revenues, earning over $439 million in 2011. The Phillies were also among the league leaders at $249 million. Table 3.1 contrasts these impressive figures with the performance of teams with much less enviable performances, the Cleveland Indians and the Kansas City Royals. Neither of these teams matched the Phillies or the Yankees in wins on the field, fans in the seats, or revenues on the books. In fact, the total attendance of the Indians and Royals combined did not equal that of either the Phillies or the Yankees, while their combined revenues fell short of the Yankees.

However, when it comes to operating income, the two weaklings looked more like bullies. In 2011, the Indians led MLB with $30.1 million in operating income, with the Royals close behind at $28.5 million. The Yankees were 22nd of 30 clubs with only $10 million in operating income, and the Phillies staggered home in 29th place, with $11.6 million in losses. While it is possible that the Indians and the Royals were simply more efficiently run organizations than the Phillies and the Yankees, it is more likely that the Phillies and the Yankees won more games because they spent a greater fraction of their revenues to secure the best possible players. In other words, they valued wins over profits.

Whether teams maximize wins or profits has been a hotly debated topic among sports economists because no one motivation can explain the behavior

TABLE 3.1   Performance Measures for the Phillies, Yankees, Indians, and Royals

Team	Winning Percentage	Attendance	Revenue[a]	Operating Income[a]
Phillies	0.630	3,680,718	439	−11.6
Yankees	0.599	3,653,680	249	10
Indians	0.494	1,840,835	178	30.1
Royals	0.438	1,724,450	161	28.5

[a] In millions of dollars

Sources: Forbes data on revenue and operating income are compiled by Kurt Badenhausen, Michael K. Ozanian, and Christina Settimi, "MLB Team Values," *Forbes*, at http://www.forbes.com/lists/2011/33/baseball-valuations-11_land.html; Winning percentages are from "MLB Standings—2011," *ESPN.com*, at http://espn.go.com/mlb/standings/_/year/2011/seasontype/2; Attendance data are from "MLB Attendance Report—2011," *ESPN.com*, at http://espn.go.com/mlb/attendance/_/year/2011.

of every team or even any one team.[5] Instead, teams trade off the two objectives, sometimes favoring one and sometimes favoring the other. As Table 3.1 suggests, though, some teams probably pursue one goal more than the other. In this section, we present a simple model of team behavior. This model will show the consequences of pursuing wins versus profits. The model also establishes a basic framework that will guide us through much of the rest of the book.

Maximizing Profit

Although not all teams maximize profits, they all have a limit as to how much they are willing and able to lose. Thus, a profit function, the difference between total revenues (R) and total costs (C), guides all teams' actions. As discussed in Chapter 2, we also assume that a team's total revenue and total cost are functions of its quality. In other words, better teams attract more fans but cost more to assemble. We can write the profit function of team i as

$$\pi_i = R(W_i) - C(W_i),$$

where W_i is the winning percentage of team i. For simplicity, we make two additional assumptions about the team's revenues and costs. First, we assume that revenues increase with winning percentage but at a decreasing rate. This assumption makes sense because, as we will see in Chapter 5, fans can be turned off by a team that wins too many games as well as by a team that wins too few. Second, we assume that teams can "buy wins" at a constant price, c_w. These assumptions yield the total revenue and total cost curves shown in Figure 3.1a.

The profit-maximizing team acquires wins until the difference between revenue and cost is maximized. In terms of Figure 3.1a, the team increases w until the total revenue curve is as far above total cost curve as possible. Because this

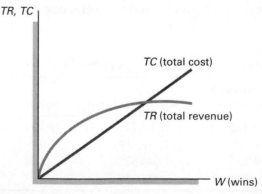

FIGURE 3.1a   Total Revenue and Total Cost Curves
The firm maximizes profit when TR is as far as possible above TC.

---

[5]For two recent entries in this debate see Stefan Késenne, "The Win Maximization Model Reconsidered: Flexible Talent Supply and Efficient Wages," *Journal of Sports Economics*, vol. 7, no. 4 (November 2006), pp. 416–427; and Rodney Fort, "Owner Objectives and Competitive Balance," *Journal of Sports Economics*, vol. 5, no. 1 (February 2004), pp. 20–32.

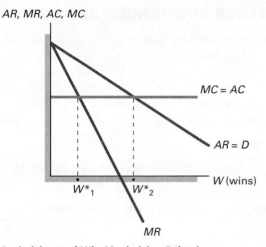

FIGURE 3.1b Profit-Maximizing and Win-Maximizing Behavior
The profit-maximizing team wins W_1^* games, and the win-maximizing team wins W_2^* games.

point is difficult to discern with the naked eye, it is easier to recall that the distance between total revenue and total cost is greatest when the slopes of the two curves—marginal revenue and marginal cost—are equal. Figure 3.1b shows this to be at the point W_1^*.

Maximizing Wins

To analyze the behavior of a win maximizer, we have to recognize that teams cannot simply maximize wins without regard to costs. The NHL's Ottawa Senators discovered this sad fact in 2002–2003, when they compiled the league's best record and then went bankrupt. Maximizing wins is sustainable as long as the team does not lose more money than the owner can tolerate. For simplicity, we assume that this means the firm's profits cannot be negative ($\pi \geq 0$).[6] To say that profits cannot be negative is equivalent to saying that total revenue is at least as great as total cost ($TR \geq TC$) or that average revenue is at least as great as average total cost ($AR \geq ATC$). Thus, the win-maximizing team acquires talent until the AR and ATC curves cross at W_2^*.

Comparing the optimal actions of the profit-maximizing and win-maximizing teams in Figure 3.1 yields the fairly obvious conclusion that, all else equal, win-maximizing teams win more often than profit-maximizing teams ($W_1^* > W_2^*$) while profit-maximizing teams earn higher profits. The value of this simple model comes from what we can add to it, that is, from seeing how other factors shift the curves in Figure 3.1 and alter the behavior of teams. In later chapters, we will use this model to analyze such issues as competitive balance and salary structures in professional sports. In the remainder of this chapter, we take a closer look at the revenue and cost functions that teams face.

---

[6]Short-run losses might be part of a strategy that maximizes long-run profits, but we ignore that possibility here.

3.2   A CLOSER LOOK AT REVENUES, AND COSTS

In the preceding section, we saw that, regardless of whether a team maximizes profits or wins, the relationship between its revenues and costs strongly influence its actions. In this section, we take a closer look at individual components of teams' revenues and costs. Table 3.2 shows *Forbes magazine's* estimates of the revenue, operating income, and market value of selected franchises from the four major North American sports leagues in 2011 (2010–2011 for the NBA and NHL).[7] It also

TABLE 3.2   Franchise Value, Total Revenue, Payroll, and Gate Revenue for 2011 (Millions $)

League/ Team	Market Value	Revenue[a]	Total Payroll	Gate Revenue	Operating Income
MLB					
Top 3	Dodgers: 2,150[b]	Yankees: 439	Yankees: 203	Yankees: 300	Indians: 30.1
	Yankees: 1,850	Red Sox: 310	Phillies: 173	Red Sox: 176	Royals: 28.5
	Red Sox: 912	Cubs: 266	Red Sox: 162	Cubs: 146	Cubs: 28.1
Middle 2	Mariners: 449	Braves: 203	Rockies: 88	Mariners: 63	Twins: 16.6
	Nationals: 419	Nationals: 200	Braves: 87	Nationals: 60	Pirates: 15.9
Bottom 3	Rays: 331	Rays: 161	Pirates: 45	Athletics: 29	Angels: −1.2
	Athletics: 307	Athletics: 160	Rays: 41	Pirates: 27	Phillies: −11.6
	Pirates: 304	Marlins:148	Royals: 36	Marlins: 25	Mets: −40.8
NBA					
Top 3	Knicks: 655	Knicks: 226	Lakers: 90	Lakers: 96	Knicks: 64
	Lakers: 643	Lakers: 214	Magic: 89	Knicks: 81	Bulls: 51.3
	Bulls: 511	Bulls: 169	Mavericks: 86	Celtics: 68	Rockets: 35.9
Middle 2	Cavaliers: 355	Warriors: 119	Bobcats: 66	Heat: 41	Bucks: −2
	Jazz: 343	Thunder: 118	Pistons: 66	Warriors: 41	Grizzlies: −2.6
Bottom 3	Grizzlies: 266	Grizzlies: 92	Cavaliers: 52	Pacers: 15	Pacers: −16.9
	Timberwolves: 264	Bucks: 92	Timberwolves: 46	Grizzlies: 15	Bobcats: −20
	Bucks: 258	Nets: 89	Kings: 44	Timberwolves: 14	Magic: −23.1
NHL					
Top 3	Maple Leafs: 521	Maple Leafs: 193	Flyers: 71	Maple Leafs: 93	Maple Leafs: 82
	Rangers: 507	Rangers: 169	Sabres: 70	Canadiens: 83	Canadiens: 47.7
	Canadiens: 445	Canadiens: 165	Blackhawks: 69	Canucks: 82	Rangers: 41.4
Middle 2	Oilers: 212	Wild: 97	Ducks: 58	Wild: 44	Stars: −1.1
	Sharks: 211	Oilers: 96	Canadiens: 55	Kings: 35	Kings: −2
Bottom 3	Blue Jackets: 152	Jets: 71	Jets: 45	Jets: 20	Lightning: −8.5
	Islanders: 149	Coyotes: 70	Avalanche: 41	Islanders: 20	Blue Jackets: −13.7
	Coyotes: 134	Islanders: 63	Islanders: 30	Coyotes: 18	Coyotes: −24.4

---

[7]The *Forbes* estimates are just that—estimates based on the best publicly available information. Nevertheless, they are widely used by economists as the best data available.

TABLE 3.2 Continued				

League/ Team	Market Value	Revenue[a]	Total Payroll	Gate Revenue	Operating Income
NFL					
Top 3	Cowboys: 1,850	Cowboys: 406	Giants: 138	Cowboys: 95	Cowboys: 119
	Redskins: 1,555	Redskins: 332	Dolphins: 126	Patriots: 93	Redskins: 65.6
	Patriots: 1,400	Patriots: 333	Texans: 122	Giants: 87	Cardinals: 56.4
Middle 2	Seahawks: 997	Colts: 252	Jaguars: 197	Cardinals: 49	Saints: 28.9
	49ers: 990	Chiefs: 252	Eagles: 106	Falcons: 48	Broncos: 28.5
Bottom 3	Rams: 775	Lions: 228	Seahawks: 89	Lions: 40	49ers: 1.5
	Raiders: 761	Vikings: 227	Bucs: 85	Rams: 39	Browns: −2.9
	Jaguars: 725	Raiders: 217	Chiefs: 82	Raiders: 35	Lions: −7.7

[a]Revenue figures reflect revenue sharing by teams.

[b]Reflects actual sale price of Dodgers as announced on March 28, 2012, and not the *Forbes* estimate.

Sources: Data on market value, revenue, and operating income are from Kurt Badenhausen, Michael K. Ozanian, and Christina Settimi, "NFL Team Values," *Forbes*, at http://www.forbes.com/lists/2011/30/nfl-valuations-11_land.html; "NBA Team Values," *Forbes*, at http://www.forbes.com/lists/2011/32/basketball-valuations-11_land.html; "MLB team Values," at http://www.forbes.com/mlb-valuations/list/; "NHL Team Values," *Forbes*, at http://www.forbes.com/nhl-valuations/, viewed March 21, 2012; Salary data are from "*USA Today* Salary Databases," *USA Today*, at http://content.usatoday.com/sportsdata/basketball/nba/salaries/team; http://content.usatoday.com/sportsdata/football/nfl/salaries/team; http://content.usatoday.com/sportsdata/hockey/nhl/salaries/team; http://content.usatoday.com/sportsdata/baseball/mlb/salaries/team, viewed March 21, 2012.

shows the *USA Today's* payroll estimates for that season. Specifically, the table shows the three teams with the largest and smallest values in each category as well as the two teams that bracket the league-wide median. (Because the leagues all have an even number of teams, there is no middle team.)

The revenue and cost figures require a bit of perspective. As we noted in Chapter 1, a professional sports team is a relatively small firm in the context of a large urban economy. An individual team typically generates less annual revenue than a large department store.[8]

Table 3.2 reveals four important features of sports leagues. First, the data generally support the view that profit-maximization is a reasonable first approximation of team behavior in these leagues. With a few notable exceptions, teams with high revenue also have high operating income, our measure of day-to-day profit. Thus, while profit-maximization clearly does not apply at all times to all teams, we shall use it as our rule of thumb for most of this book.

Second, the data in Table 3.2 suggest that it pays to be in a big city. New York, Los Angeles, and Dallas, the largest, second-largest, and fourth-largest metropolitan areas in the United States, dominate baseball, basketball, and football. Hockey is led by Toronto, by far the largest metropolitan area in Canada (with, not surprisingly, Montreal—the second-largest city in Canada—or New York second

---

[8]Roger Noll, "The Economics of Sports Leagues," in *Law of Professional and Amateur Sports*, ed. by Gary A. Uberstine, K. R. Stratos, and R. J. Grad (Deerfield, Ill.: The West Group, 1989), p. 17–2.

in most categories). Something about large cities appears to increase the revenue and profitability of sports franchises. We can show this relationship on a graph similar to Figure 3.1a. Figure 3.2 shows that small improvements in team quality add more to the revenue of a team from a large city (TR_L) than to the revenue of a team from a small city (TR_S). As a result, "big market" teams naturally tend to be more successful both on and off the field than "small market" teams, a point to which we return in Chapters 4 and 5. For now, we focus on how location affects an individual team's financial performance.

Third, the advantage of being from a large metropolitan area varies across the different sports. In general, the divide between "haves" and "have nots" appears greatest in baseball and hockey, with the Yankees' revenue being almost three times that of the Marlins and more than twice that of the median clubs. In hockey, the Maple Leafs also had about three times the Islanders' revenue and about twice the NHL's median. In contrast, basketball's Knicks made about 2.5 times that of the Nets and less than twice the NBA median. Football has an even more level playing field, with the Cowboys' revenue being less than twice that of the Oakland Raiders and only about 1.6 times the NFL's median. Clearly, something causes team revenues in some leagues to be more equal than revenues in other leagues.

Finally, some sports are much more profitable than others. The median football team had operating income of $29 million, and the median baseball team had about $16 million. Moreover, very few teams in either league lost money. Only the long-suffering Cleveland Browns and Detroit Lions had negative operating income in the NFL. In MLB, only three teams lost money, and of these, two teams—the Phillies and the New York Mets—were among the six highest-revenue teams in MLB. In contrast, the median operating income for both the NBA and the NHL was about negative $2 million. As might be expected, far more teams in these leagues (17 teams in each) had negative operating income. Much of the difference in profitability can be traced to differences in revenue. The median NFL

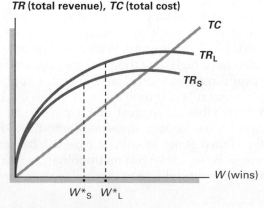

FIGURE 3.2 Revenue, Cost, and City Size
The total revenue curve is steeper for teams in large cities, so they tend to win more games.

franchise had revenues exceeding $252 million, with MLB just below $200 million. The NBA was far behind, with median revenues of about $120 million, while the median NHL franchise had revenues below $100 million.

A Detailed Look at Revenue

Professional teams generate revenue from five principal sources: ticket sales or gate receipts (R_G), local and national broadcasting rights (R_B), licensing income (R_L), other venue-related revenues, including luxury boxes, concessions, and stadium-naming rights (R_V), and transfers from other teams in the league (R_T):

$$TR = R_G + R_B + R_L + R_V + R_T$$

The size and variation of each of these revenue streams differs substantially from sport to sport, which helps to explain why some sports are more profitable and more equal than others.

GATE REVENUE   Gate revenue (revenue from ticket sales) is an important source of income for all professional teams. Figure 3.3 shows the gate revenue for all teams in the four major North American leagues in 2011 (or 2010–2011).

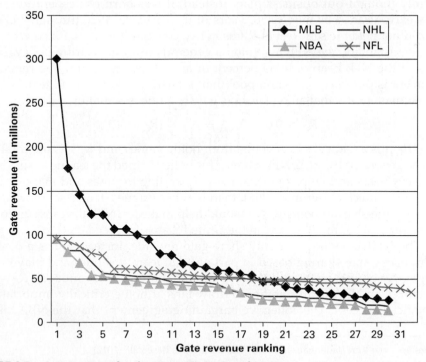

FIGURE 3.3   Gate Revenue for the NBA, NFL, NHL, and MLB

Gate revenue in MLB varies far more across teams than in the other sports.   *Source:* Team sites associated with Kurt Badenhausen et al., "NFL Team Values," *Forbes*, (2011), Kurt Badenhausen et al., "NHL Team Values," *Forbes*, (2011), Kurt Badenhausen et al., "NBA Team Values," *Forbes*, (2011), Kurt Badenhausen et al., "MLB Team Values," *Forbes*, (2012).

As expected, big-market baseball teams, with their 81 home games per season, generate the highest revenue. This revenue drops off fairly quickly, however, and the bottom half of MLB teams do not generate as much gate revenue as many NFL teams, which play only eight home games per season. In 2011, the Oakland Athletics, Pittsburgh Pirates, and Florida Marlins earned less than one-tenth the Yankees' $300 million in gate revenue. The rapid drop-off in baseball is partly because of lower attendance; the Athletics drew under 1.5 million fans, less than half what the Yankees drew. It resulted from lower ticket prices, as the average ticket price in Oakland was $33, about half that at Yankee Stadium.[9]

While baseball has the largest variation in gate revenue, the NFL has the smallest, with the Cowboys having only 2.7 times the ticket revenue of the Oakland Raiders. This is partly because football teams generally draw close to capacity crowds. On average, every stadium in the NFL was at least three-quarters full, a feat achieved by only 11 MLB teams. It is also partly because a ticket to see the Cowboys, Patriots, or Giants costs only a little over 50 percent more than a ticket to see the Cincinnati Bengals.[10]

One major reason why gate revenue in the NFL is so evenly distributed comes from the league's generous revenue-sharing policy, which reduces R_G for some teams and adds to R_T for others. Initially, this policy was not the result of a carefully thought-out business plan. Instead, it was born of desperation in the NFL's early years. For the first 16 years of its existence, 1920 through 1935, the NFL did not field the same set of teams in two consecutive years. Faced with such extreme instability, the NFL instituted a generous revenue-sharing policy. Home teams in the NFL keep only 60 percent of all net gate revenue. The remaining 40 percent is put into a common pool that is distributed among all teams.[11] This arrangement means that an NFL team's gate revenue is actually:

$$R_G = 0.6 \times R_{G,H} + 0.4 \times (R_{G,P}/32)$$

where $R_{G,H}$ is a team's gate revenue from home games and $R_{G,P}$ is the total gate revenue generated by all 32 NFL teams. This policy helped the league to survive its lean, early years and helps to explain why operating incomes and market values today are so much closer in the NFL than in other leagues. It also set the stage for other revenue-sharing policies that would help make the NFL the most uniformly profitable of all the major sports in the United States.

The NHL does not explicitly share gate revenue. Instead, it has a complex system of revenue sharing based in part on total team revenues and playoff gate receipts. As of 2011–2012, NBA teams do not share gate revenue, so $R_G = R_H$. This makes an NBA team's ability to draw fans at home critically important for its financial success. The collective bargaining agreement that the NBA and its

---

[9]Figures are from Kurt Badenhausen et al., "The Business of Baseball" (2012).

[10]Kurt Badenhausen et al., "The Business of Football" (2011).

[11]The NFL dates its founding from when the initial body, the "American Professional Football Association" took the name "National Football League" in 1922. See David Harris, *The League: The Rise and Decline of the NFL* (New York: Bantam Books, 1986), p. 12; and Eric M. Leifer, *Making the Majors: The Transformation of Team Sports in America* (Cambridge, Mass.: Harvard University Press, 1995), pp. 98–109.

players ratified in December 2011 calls for significant revenue sharing, but the plan has not yet been implemented.

MLB also shares a substantial portion of its net gate revenue. According to MLB's collective bargaining agreement, teams must place 31 percent of all "net local revenue" in a pool, from which all 30 teams then draw equally. Thus, teams with large gate revenue, such as the Yankees, effectively transfer some of that revenue to less well-off teams, such as the Athletics, so R_G falls for the Yankees and R_T rises for the Athletics.

BROADCAST REVENUE Few events have changed the finances of professional sports as much as the advent of television. All four major sports currently enjoy huge revenue streams from both local and league-wide national broadcast rights. Table 3.3 shows, however, that TV benefits some sports more than others. These differences have important implications for the overall prosperity of the leagues and the disparities of operating income within each league.

The prosperity of the NFL stems directly from its huge network contracts. To see the difference that TV can make, consider what would happen if the NFL and NHL had each other's TV contract. Table 3.3 shows that each NFL team gets almost $177 million more per year than each NHL team. If both leagues had equal TV contracts (adding $85 million to NHL teams' revenues and subtracting $85 million

TABLE 3.3 Revenue from League-Wide Broadcast Rights Agreements

Sport	Years	Stations	Total Fees[a] ($)	Annual Average Per Team[b] ($)
MLB	2006–2013[c]	ESPN; Fox; TBS	4.87	23.8
NBA	2009–2016	ABC/ESPN; TNT	7.44	31.0
NFL	2006–2013[d]	ESPN; CBS; Fox; NBC; DirecTV	46.2	184.4
NHL	2011–2021	NBC; Comcast; VERSUS; CBC[e]	2.2	7.8

[a]In billions.
[b]In millions.
[c]ESPN: 2006–2013; FOX: 2001–2006.
[d]ESPN: 2011–2019; CBS, Fox, NBC: 2012–2020; DirecTV: 2011–2015.
[e]This does not include some smaller revenue from French language broadcasts over RDS.

Sources: Andy Bernstein, "Flexibility a Key in New MLB-ESPN Deal," *SportsBusiness Journal,* at www.sportsbusinessjournal. com; Adam Fraser, "Rogers Acquires Canadian Rights to Major League Baseball," *SportsPro,* June 2, 2009 at http://www. sportspromedia.com/news/rogers_acquires_canadian_rights_to_major_league_baseball/; Dex McLuskey and Aaron Kuriloff, "NFL Signs Nine-Year Extensions of TV Contracts with CBS, Fox, NBC," *Bloomberg.com,* December 15, 2011, at http://www.bloomberg.com/news/2011-12-14/nfl-renews-television-contracts-with-cbs-fox-nbc-networks-through-2022. html; Rachel Cohen, "NBA extends TV deals with ESPN/ABC, TNT," June 27, 2007, at http://www.usatoday.com/sports/ basketball/2007-06-27-3096131424_x.htm; Maury Brown, "TSN and the NHL Reach Six-Year Broadcast and Digital Rights Deal," *bizofhockey.com,* June 4, 2008, at http://www.bizofhockey.com/?option=com_content&view=article&id=141&Itc mid=1; CBC Sports, "New Hockey Deal Keeps Hockey Night in Canada on CBC," *CBCSports.com,* March 26, 2007, at http:// www.cbc.ca/sports/hockey/story/2007/03/26/hockey-night-in-canada.html; Tony Keller and Neville McGuire, *The New Economics of the NHL* (Toronto: Mowatt Centre for Applied Public Policy Research, 2011), at http://www.mowatcentre.ca/ pdfs/mowatResearch/31.pdf; and Matt Egan, "Comcast Skates Away with 10-Year TV Deal for NHL," *FoxBusiness.com,* April 19, 2011, at http://www.foxbusiness.com/industries/2011/04/19/comcast-skates-away-10-year-tv-deal-nhl/.

from NFL teams' revenues), almost every NHL team would have *higher* annual revenue than the equivalently ranked NFL team. Only the Cowboys (for reasons we will explain later in this chapter) would earn more than the Maple Leafs.

Because almost all of its TV revenue is shared equally (one major exception being local preseason broadcasts), the NFL has no disparity between large-market and small-market teams. Green Bay is smaller than any city hosting an MLB team, but its TV revenue is not significantly lower than that of NFL teams playing in New York or Chicago. This is not the case in MLB, where local broadcast revenue exceeds national broadcast revenue. Thus, even with teams sharing 31 percent of all local revenue, MLB's Kansas City Royals are at a much greater disadvantage than the NFL's Kansas City Chiefs.

Major League Baseball's network contract for national broadcasts is far less lucrative than football's, but unlike the NFL, some baseball teams have another major source of TV revenue: TV contracts with local or regional broadcasters. The Yankees might receive only $23.8 million from the national contract, but their local broadcast rights bring in over $90 million per year. The Yankees are not the only team to benefit from local TV revenue. Two of the biggest free agent signings of 2012, Albert Pujols with the Los Angeles Angels and Japan's Yu Darvish with the Texas Rangers, were made possible by infusions of cash from huge broadcast rights deals, as both teams recently signed 20-year, $3 billion deals with Fox.[12]

One key to the explosion in local TV money for MLB is the rapid growth of cable television. Cable rights are more valuable than the rights to over-the-air broadcasts because, in addition to the advertising revenue that both forms of broadcasting bring, a cable company receives a subscription fee from each cable user. As a result, most local broadcasts are now seen on cable.

A second, related source of income is the growth of regional sports networks (RSNs). All MLB teams now belong to RSNs, which frequently feature teams from other professional and intercollegiate sports as well. For example, Rogers SportsNet in Canada carries both the Blue Jays and the Raptors, while Comcast SportsNet Chicago broadcasts the White Sox, Cubs, and Bulls. One can see the value of RSNs from the fact that the Los Angeles Dodgers, a team that had gone through bankruptcy proceedings the previous summer, were sold for $2.15 billion in the spring of 2012. A major reason for the Dodgers' huge price tag is that their media contract expires in 2013, at which time most experts expect the team's cash flow to increase by over $50 million per year.[13]

---

[12]The Rangers' deal begins in 2015; they currently receive "only" $80 million per year. Bill Shaikin and Kevin Baxter, "Angels Double-Play: Pujols and Wilson; Money from TV Allows Team to Acquire Stars," *Los Angeles Times*, December 8, 2011, p. C1; Howard Bryant, "Angels, Rangers Join the Big Boys," *ESPN.com*, March 29, 2012, at http://espn.go.com/mlb/preview12/story/_/id/7750708/los-angeles-angels-texas-rangers-now-baseball-superpowers.

[13]Maury Brown, "The Effect of Regional Sports Networks," *The Ledger Domain*, February 5, 2007, at http://www.baseballprospectus.com/article.php?articleid=5843; Michael Ozanian, "The Business of Baseball 2012," *Forbes*, March 21, 2012, at http://www.forbes.com/mlb-valuations/list; Chris Smith, "Baseball after Cable: Team Sales Prices Boosted by Cable Networks," *Forbes*, March 21, 2012, at http://www.forbes.com/sites/chrissmith/2012/03/21/baseball-after-cable-team-sale-prices-boosted-by-cable-networks.

Many franchises own a stake in the RSN to which they belong. In fact, the Cleveland Indians turned down a considerable sum from Fox to keep their sports broadcasts "in-house" with SportsTime Ohio. Baseball teams like to **vertically integrate** the successive functions of creating and then delivering their product—in this case, playing the game and then broadcasting it—because doing so helps them to avoid having to share revenue with the other teams. Team owners who also own the RSN can transfer revenue from one to the other by charging a low price for the broadcast rights. The low price hurts the team but helps the cable company, effectively taking money from one pocket and putting it in the other. However, money that appears in the team owner's pocket is subject to a 31 percent tax in the form of revenue sharing. Money that appears in the RSN owner's pocket is not shared with other teams.

The NBA's current agreement with ABC/ESPN and TNT provides the league with $930 million per year, but not every team receives $31 million per year. The disparity comes from what must be the oddest broadcast rights agreement in the history of sports. When the NBA and the old American Basketball Association (ABA) merged in 1976, only four teams (the Denver Nuggets, Indiana Pacers, New Jersey Nets, and San Antonio Spurs) joined the NBA. The other teams had to disband. The owners of the Nuggets, Pacers, Nets, and Spurs compensated most of their unfortunate brethren with lump-sum cash payments. Ozzie and Dan Silna, the owners of the Spirit of St. Louis, chose a different form of compensation. They agreed to take one-seventh of the TV revenue paid to the four former ABA teams in perpetuity. For several years, it appeared that the Silnas had gotten a poor deal, as the NBA's TV contracts generated little revenue. In the 1980s, things began to change, and the Silnas now claim tens of millions of dollars each year as a result of their 1976 buyout.[14]

While the NBA's network contract is less important to the NBA's revenue stream than the NFL's contract is to the NFL's revenue stream, it is still responsible for over one-fourth of the median team's total revenue and over one-third of the total revenue of the New Jersey Nets. If the NBA had the NHL's contract, only six teams would have had positive operating income in 2011. As in the case of baseball, however, local broadcast revenue plays an important role in team finances and accounts for much of the disparity in NBA team revenue and operating income. At one extreme, the Los Angeles Lakers benefit from a 20-year deal with Time Warner that pays them an estimated $150 million per year. At the other extreme, the Charlotte Bobcats receive only $9 million per year in local TV revenue. To make matters worse, until the recent collective bargaining agreement, the NBA did not share any local revenue, which meant that, unlike MLB, nothing mitigated the huge disparities in cable revenue.[15]

---

[14]Patricia Hurtado and Bob Van Voris, "Defunct Basketball Team Claims TV Revenue from Lawsuit Settlement in 1976," *Bloomberg.com*, November 22, 2011, at http://www.bloomberg.com/news/2011-11-22/decades-old-nba-antitrust-labor-case-filed-by-oscar-robertson-under-review.html.

[15]Joe Flint, "Time Warner Cable, Lakers Strike 20-year TV Deal," *Los Angeles Times*, February 14, 2011, at http://articles.latimes.com/2011/feb/14/sports/la-sp-0215-lakers-time-warner-20110215; Sam Amick, "Inside the NBA," *SI.com*, April 21, 2011, at http://sportsillustrated.cnn.com/2011/writers/sam_amick/04/20/sacramento.kings/index.html.

As with the NBA, much of the disparity in revenue among NHL teams stems from large differences in local TV revenue. These differences have even more serious consequences in hockey because the NHL receives far less than the other leagues in network revenue, with each team receiving only about one-fourth of what an NBA team receives, about $7.8 million per year. Teams in small media markets, such as the Winnipeg Jets, thus find it hard to compete financially with teams from larger markets, such as the Toronto Maple Leafs, whose local broadcast revenue ($34.5 million in 2010–2011) is more than double their network revenue.[16]

TELEVISION AND ATTENDANCE—EXPOSURE VERSUS SUBSTITUTION   Broadcasting games is a double-edged sword to teams. To the extent that fans prefer to watch games on television rather than at the stadium, televising home games reduces gate receipts. The impact of TV on attendance was first documented in 1948, when the Philadelphia Eagles saw attendance drop by 50 percent after they decided to televise all their home games. This decline led the NFL to "black out" (forbid networks from showing in the local market) games that were not sold out. Blacking out the home team's game may not stimulate ticket sales if a New England Patriots fan in Boston prefers watching a televised game between the Cowboys and Dolphins to shivering at Gillette Stadium on a cold December day. On the other hand, if television stimulates fans' interest in the game, more broadcasts may increase attendance. The NFL owes a good deal of its popularity to its focus on nationally broadcast games and the Sunday doubleheader, which allows fans to watch popular teams from other cities.

Networks televise games when they profit from doing so. The demand by networks or local stations to televise games is a **derived demand**. The demand for a good or service is *derived* from the demand for another when the quantity that people are willing and able to buy depends on the market for a different product. In the case of broadcasting rights, the demand by TV networks for sporting events is derived from the demand by sponsors for advertising time. A network's willingness to pay a league or team for the right to broadcast a game stems from its ability to sell advertising during the game.

The exposure that broadcasts give a network and its advertisers explains why the NFL can charge so much more than the other sports. However, a network might pursue broadcast rights even though it knows that it will lose money as a result. Networks may be willing to overpay if they view football as a "loss leader." The broadcast itself might lose money, but if it attracts viewers to other shows on the network, it may still be consistent with overall profit-maximization. Sports have also given new entrants, such as Fox or DirecTV, an air of credibility with sponsors and potential affiliates. Lucie Salhany, chairperson of Fox Broadcasting when Fox first began broadcasting NFL games, argued, "We had to have it and it didn't matter what we paid for it. It put us on the map. It got us more affiliates....Sales-wise,

---

[16]Rick Westhead, "Maple Leaf Sports Plans Broadcast Gamble," *TheStar.com*, November 27, 2011, at http://www.thestar.com/sports/article/1093199--maple-leaf-sports-plans-broadcast-gamble.

there were people we could never call on that we could call on once we got football."[17]

Television revenue has rivaled or surpassed gate revenue as the primary source of income for all major sports, and the sports have become so dependent on it that they have literally changed the way they play their games. Games are now interrupted by the infamous "TV time-out." Fans and players at the stadium wait while television viewers see advertisements, confident that play will not resume until the ads are over. Some sports, such as baseball, can easily accommodate such breaks. Other sports see stoppages in play extended for unnatural lengths. Football and basketball have gone so far as to introduce specific time-outs for no other purpose than to show commercials on TV. Fans at NHL games occasionally wait several minutes between face-offs to accommodate commercials. Football's two-minute warning came about as a concession to TV networks. The need to break for commercials represents a serious barrier to regular TV broadcasts of major league soccer in the United States, as play is continuous for long periods of time with no naturally occurring breaks.

LICENSING AGREEMENTS   All four major North American Leagues have created licensing arms—MLB Properties, NBA Properties, NFL Properties, and NHL Enterprises—to oversee the sale of "official" team paraphernalia to fans. This centralization has two consequences. First, as with league-wide TV contracts, league-wide licensing agreements prevent teams from competing with one another and give the teams greater market power when dealing with both manufacturers and retailers. Second, because the teams share licensing revenue (R_L), the agreements provide another way to level the financial playing field.

Perhaps owing to its longer season and greater attendance, MLB had the greatest licensing revenue in 2010 at $2.75 billion, with the NFL following closely at $2.70 billion. The NBA was well behind at $1.75 billion, and the NHL again trailed badly at $630 million.[18] How these figures translate to team revenue is not completely clear, as league offices claim a share, and a portion of licensing revenue is frequently set aside for official league charities.

Licensing is one area in which the NFL has moved away from equalizing revenue streams. Shortly after Jerry Jones bought the Dallas Cowboys in 1989, he signed licensing deals with Pepsi Cola and Nike. Because neither company had an agreement with NFL Properties at the time, the NFL tried unsuccessfully to block the deal. Thus, while the Cowboys remain part of NFL Properties, they have a number of lucrative side deals. In 2011, Silver Star Merchandising, the Cowboys merchandising arm, signed a 10-year apparel deal with the University of Southern California, a deal it hopes to extend to other universities.

Digital revenue is probably the most rapidly growing category of revenue in professional sports—one that soon may merit a separate category but which we

---

[17]Eric Schmuckler, "Is the NFL Still Worth It?" *Mediaweek* (September 28, 1998), pp. 26–32.

[18]Darren Rovell, "Publication: MLB Will Beat NFL in Licensing Revenue in '10," *Sports.biz with Darren Rovell*, June 14, 2010, at http://www.cnbc.com/id/37692194/Publication_MLB_Will_Beat_NFL_In_Licensing_Revenue_In_10.

now classify under licensing. Digital revenue actually refers to a wide variety of ventures, from licensing games, such as "Madden NFL," to broadened agreements with existing television partners, to arrangements with new media, such as Google, that bypass TV entirely. As with merchandising revenue, the NFL and MLB lead the pack in digital revenue, taking in roughly $500 million and $450 million in 2010. These revenues were enough to place the NFL and MLB among the top-25 U.S. companies in digital sales. The NBA generated about $225 million in digital revenue, while the NHL again trails the pack at $120 million.[19]

VENUE REVENUE   Until the blockbuster $2.15 billion sale of the Los Angeles Dodgers, the Dallas Cowboys were the most valuable professional franchise in the United States, a mantle they may assume again as the market for sports franchises adjusts to the Dodger sale. At first, it is hard to see why the Cowboys are so valuable. While the Cowboys have long been one of the most successful teams in the NFL, winning more Super Bowls than all teams except the Pittsburgh Steelers, the NFL did not give them much opportunity to capitalize financially on this success. While the Cowboys play in the NFL's third-largest stadium, the 60–40 split of gate revenues limits their allocated gate revenue. The Cowboys' media revenue is also limited by league policy, as all teams share the revenue from their national telecasts equally. The key to the Cowboys' financial success has been the team's extraordinarily profitable stadium agreements. Cowboys Stadium has 300 luxury boxes, more than twice as many as the average of the 31 other teams (143) and 15,000 club seats, almost twice as many as the remaining teams' average (8662).

Venue revenue, or nonticket revenue from the stadium (R_v), includes revenue from parking and concessions, but, more importantly, it includes revenue from luxury suites and other special seating, only a small portion of which counts as ticket revenue. Luxury seating has become particularly valuable in the NFL because teams share a substantial portion of ticket revenue with each other (and with their players as part of the salary cap, discussed in Chapter 8). For example, suppose a luxury suite in Texas Stadium rents for $500,000 per year and has 20 seats in it. If the Cowboys claim the value of the seats to be $50 each, they must share only $3,200 ($0.4 \times 20 \times 50 \times 8$ games), and they keep much of the remaining $496,800 for themselves. Much of this revenue enters as a lump sum per season because luxury boxes are typically leased on a per-season basis. Other attendance-related revenue, such as parking and concession, is directly connected to how many people come to the games, so it is more variable.

---

[19]Daisy Whitney, "Demand for Online Video Fuels Digital Revenue for Sports Programming," *ReelSEO.com*, at http://www.reelseo.com/digital-revenue-for-sports-programming, viewed April 15, 2012; Staci D. Kramer, "CES: NBA Digital Expands to More Connected TVs and Adds More Premium Live Games," *paidContent.org*, January 6, 2011, at http://paidContent.org/2011/01/06/419-ces-nba-digital-expanda-to-more-connected-tvs-and-adds-premium-live-gam; Dan Gallagher, "Electronic Arts' Riccitiello Aims High," *MediaWatch.com*, January 17, 2012, at http://articles.marketwatch.com/2012-01-17/industries/30800220_1_mobile-games-elevation-partners-john-riccitiello/3; Mike Tirone, "Top 25 Digital Media Companies, By Revenue," *Wealth Wire*, April 14, 2011, at http://www.wealthwire.com/news/economy/1005.

THE EFFECT OF STADIUM DEALS ON FRANCHISE LOCATION   Over the years, several NFL teams have moved away from their home cities to apparently illogical destinations. Both the Rams and Raiders left the Los Angeles market for far smaller markets in St. Louis and Oakland, respectively, leaving the nation's second-largest market without a team. The Houston Oilers abandoned what was then the nation's 10th-largest metropolitan area for the 40th-largest market in Nashville. Even the Cleveland Browns' move to Baltimore was from a larger city to a smaller one. On the surface, all these moves seem unprofitable, as they limit both the teams' fan base and media exposure. Why, then, do the teams move?

The answer can be found in the peculiar interaction of revenue sharing and stadium deals. Because the teams in the NFL split their national TV contract equally and their gate receipts almost equally, the impact of a team's moving to a smaller city is spread over all the teams in the league. In baseball, where teams depend so heavily on local media revenue, a team in a media market the size of Los Angeles would never leave for a much smaller city. The Yankees, for example, might threaten to move from the Bronx to Manhattan or northern New Jersey, but they would never threaten to leave the New York metropolitan area. The NFL's Raiders, who did not depend heavily on local media revenue, had no such qualms about leaving Los Angeles. The moves to smaller cities, however, may hurt the NFL's ratings in the nation's second-largest media market. This, in turn, could lead to worse TV contracts for the NFL—and less revenue for all teams, including the teams that moved—in the future.

The damage that an individual team's behavior can do to the NFL as a whole results in what economists call the **tragedy of the commons**. The "tragedy" gets its name from a problem that towns faced centuries ago when townspeople put their livestock out to graze on the town common. Because no one property owner had a claim on—or responsibility for—the town common, the cost imposed by a resident's livestock was shared equally by the entire town. Thus, the cost to residents was low and residents had no incentive to limit the amount of grazing that their livestock did on the common. If only one or two residents failed to limit their livestock, the cost to the town would have been negligible. The problem was that all residents had the same incentive. As a result, the commons were overgrazed and were eventually destroyed. Similarly, because NFL teams share TV revenue equally, a team in a large media market does not lose much revenue from abandoning it for a smaller media market that offers a better stadium deal. However, if all teams behave that way, the loss in revenue could be substantial.

For example, while the costs incurred because of the Rams's move from Los Angeles to St. Louis are spread over the entire NFL, the Rams get to keep almost all the benefits for themselves. The stadium arrangement for the TransWorld Dome (known as the Edward Jones Dome since 2002) granted the Rams all revenues from the 124 luxury suites. As noted earlier, most of this revenue is not shared with other teams. As long as municipalities continue to bid against one another for the right to host an NFL franchise, the league may continue to see teams move to smaller markets in pursuit of better stadium arrangements. Leagues have attempted to minimize the tragedy of the commons by trying to prevent teams from moving. These efforts have met with mixed success. The courts denied the NFL any right to regulate team moves as the result of an antitrust brought by the Oakland Raiders in 1980. However, the courts have not allowed this ruling to serve as a precedent for other leagues.[20] We discuss this problem in detail in later chapters.

NAMING RIGHTS   One of the newest sources of venue revenue comes from teams' selling the names of their facilities to the highest bidder. Stadium-naming rights are only one form of sponsorship. When watching a NASCAR race, a European soccer match, or even a golf tournament, fans can see the lengths to which companies go to associate their brands with a team, a player, or an event. Corporate names and logos adorn uniforms and equipment. All but two Women's National Basketball Association (WNBA) teams now bear the logo of the Boost Mobile phone company, with the Seattle Storm and the San Antonio Silver Stars receiving an exemption only because they had preceding deals with rival phone companies.[21] One enterprising boxer even had an advertisement temporarily tattooed on his body.

Even against this background, stadium naming rights stand apart. Rich Products, Inc. was the first company to purchase naming rights to a stadium when it put its name on the Buffalo Bills' new stadium in 1973 for $1.5 million over 25 years. For the next 20 years, professional sports in America largely ignored the revenue possibilities of naming rights. In 1990, only a handful of teams had sold such rights. Today, most stadiums and arenas bear corporate names. Naming rights have even filtered down to the college level. University of Maryland basketball fans can cheer on the Terrapins at the Comcast Center (rights sold for $20 million), while Rutgers University football fans root for the Scarlet Knights at High Point Solutions Stadium (rights sold for $6.5 million).

Corporate executives and sports marketers consider naming rights a great deal. In the words of Jeffrey Knapple, the president and CEO of Envision, "In a marketing landscape where corporations are continually striving to gain market share and 'share of mind' from their respective constituents, naming rights provides [sic] the ultimate opportunity to rise above the pack."[22]

Table 3.4 identifies the five most lucrative naming rights deals as of 2011. It shows that companies spend up to $20 million per year to put their names on sports facilities. Unfortunately, evidence suggests that, while naming rights add millions each year to many teams' coffers, the purchases add little to a firm's profitability. One recent study of 54 stadiums and arenas showed that only a handful

---

[20]See Michael Danielson, *Home Team: Professional Sport and the American Metropolis* (Princeton, N.J.: Princeton University Press, 1997), pp. 146–151.

[21]Ken Belson, "New Sponsor on WNBA Uniforms," *New York Times,* August 22, 2011, at http://www.nytimes.com/2011/08/22/sports/basketball/wnba-makes-sponsorship-deal-with-boost-mobile.html?_r=1.

[22]Jeffrey S. Knapple, "Naming Rights Industry," *Naming Rights Deals* (Chicago: Team Marketing Report, 2001).

Advertisements have begun to appear in the oddest places.

of purchases had any impact on the company's profitability and that the effect was as likely to be negative as it was positive.[23]

Companies pay impressive sums to put their names on an NFL or MLB stadium, but these amounts do not come close to what some companies pay to put their names on the jerseys of top soccer teams. The last major team not to bear a corporate logo, FC Barcelona of Spain's La Liga, has the most lucrative shirt sponsorship, having struck a five-year deal with the Qatar Foundation, a not-for-profit organization, which will pay about $40 million per year. Real Madrid and Manchester United follow, with shirt sponsorships that are worth over $30 million per year. Perhaps the most creative shirt deal was made by Tottenham Hotspur, which has two sponsors, one for when it plays in England's Premier League and one for when it plays in the pan-European Union of European Football Associations (UEFA) Champions League.[24]

---

[23]Eva Marikova Leeds, Michael A. Leeds, and Irina Pistolet, "A Stadium by Any Other Name," *Journal of Sports Economics*, vol. 8, no. 6 (December 2007), pp. 581–595.

[24]Richard Gillis, "Soccer's Biggest Signings," *Wall Street Journal*, November 1, 2010, at http://online.wsj.com/article/SB10001424052748703708404575586162309028930.html; Associated Press, "Barcelona Agree €150 Million Shirt Sponsor Deal with Qatar Foundation," *The Guardian*, December 10, 2010, at http://www.guardian.co.uk/football/2010/dec/10/barcelona-shirt-sponsor-qatar-foundation.

TABLE 3.4   The Ten Most Lucrative Naming Rights Deals (in millions)

Stadium	City	Sponsor	Annual Payment[a]	Number of Years
Citi Field	Queens, NY	Citigroup	$20	20
MetLife Stadium	East Rutherford, NJ	Metropolitan Life Insurance	$17–20	25
Reliant Stadium	Houston	Reliant Energy	$10	31
Gillette Stadium	Foxboro, MA	Gillette	$8	15
University of Phoenix Stadium	Glendale, AZ	Apollo Group	$7.7	20
FedEx Field	Landover, MD	FedEx	$7.6	27
Bank of America Stadium	Charlotte, NC	Bank of America	$7.0	20
Lincoln Financial Field	Philadelphia	Lincoln National	$6.7	20
Lucas Oil Stadium	Indianapolis	Lucas Oil Products	$6.1	20
Minute Maid Park	Houston	Coca-Cola Co.	$6.0	28

[a]In millions of dollars

Source: "Stadium Naming Rights," *ESPN Sports Business*, at http://espn.go.com/sportsbusiness/s/stadiumnames.html, viewed July 27, 2012; Evan Buxbaum, "Mets and the Citi: $400 Million for Stadium-Naming Rights Irks Some," *CNN.com*, at http://articles.cnn.com/2009-04-13/us/mets.ballpark_1_citi-field-mets-home-stadium-naming?_s=PM:US, April 13, 2009; Richard Sandomir, Jets-Giants Home Now Met-Life Stadium," *NYTimes.com*, at http://www.nytimes.com/2011/08/24/sports/football/metlife-signs-naming-rights-deal-with-jets-and-giants.html, August 23, 2011; Associated Press, "U. of Phoenix Buys Naming Rights to Cardinals Stadium," http://sports.espn.go.com/nfl/news/story?id=2603052, September 26, 2006; David Mielach, "A $122 Million Super Bowl Bet: Lucas Oil Stadium," *The Entrepreneurist*, at http://www.businessnewsdaily.com/1988-lucas-oil-success.html, February 4, 2012 "Naming Rights Deals," *Street and Smith's SportsBusiness Journal*, at http://www.sportsbusinessdaily.com/Journal/Issues/2011/09/19/In-Depth/Naming-rights-deals.aspx, September 19, 2011.

The Distributional Effects of Revenue Sharing

Leagues share revenue to promote financial parity in the front office and competitive balance on the field. If some teams have much greater revenue than others, the entire league's stability will be jeopardized as the "have not" teams struggle to survive financially and cannot afford to field competitive teams. Gross disparities in revenue undermined the North American Soccer League in 1984 and the United States Football League in 1987. More recently, the lockouts that destroyed the 2004–2005 season in the NHL and that threatened the 2011–2012 season in the NBA both stemmed as much from inequality among franchises as they did from traditional labor–management issues. In this chapter, we have focused on the financial ramifications of revenue sharing. From the standpoint of profits, shared revenues reduce some revenue streams for relatively wealthy teams, while other teams' profits are bolstered by revenue transfers (R_T). We discuss the impact of revenue sharing on competitive balance in Chapter 5 and its effect on payrolls in Chapter 9.

Table 3.2 and the ensuing discussion suggest that the NFL has the most extensive revenue sharing, followed by MLB, with the NBA and NHL trailing behind.

To check this, we compute the coefficient of variation of revenue in each league. The coefficient of variation is the ratio of the standard deviation of revenue to the mean level of revenue. The numerator of this fraction tells us how widely dispersed the revenue of each league is, while the denominator accounts for the fact that the standard deviation will naturally be larger if we are dealing with larger numbers in general. As expected, the coefficient of variation for the NFL (0.147) is far smaller than for any of the other leagues. This tells us that, after accounting for the overall level of revenue, the spread of revenue is far smaller for the NFL than for the other leagues. MLB is a fairly distant second (0.254), and the NBA (0.265) and NHL (0.294) follow.

The relatively narrow distribution of revenue for the NFL stems from two sources. First, as noted earlier, the NFL has long been the most generous of the four major North American leagues in terms of revenue sharing. Second, the most evenly shared source of revenue—the league's TV agreements—is also the league's greatest single source of revenue. Because the NFL's broadcast rights generate so much revenue, disparities in other sources of income are relatively small.

MLB has recently moved in a similar direction. Unlike the NFL, however, local revenue—particularly from regional sports networks—is a substantial source of income for MLB. Thus, disparities in local revenue have far more impact for MLB than for the NFL. Still, although MLB does not share as much revenue as the NFL and teams have developed ingenious ways to avoid sharing revenue, MLB has achieved a degree of revenue parity that seemed unthinkable a decade ago.

Instead of a simple gate revenue and broadcast revenue-sharing formula, the NHL has a complex revenue sharing system. Under the agreement, small-market, low-revenue teams receive transfer payments from large-market, high-revenue teams. The arrangement is so complex that "even some of the people who negotiated the deal confess that they don't understand it all."[25] Shared revenues come from playoff gate receipts, a portion of player salaries placed in escrow, and revenue from top-grossing clubs. Only teams with fewer than 2.5 million television households and payrolls below the midpoint of league salaries are eligible to receive funds.[26]

The NBA does not yet share gate and local broadcast revenue. As a result, it has large disparities in revenue despite its having the second-greatest level of revenue from equally shared, league-wide broadcast rights. Large—and growing—differences in local broadcast revenue have caused inequality among teams to increase in recent years. There are reports that the NBA has developed an ambitious revenue-sharing program, which it hopes to implement by the 2013–2014 season. The plan allegedly calls for all teams to contribute "roughly 50 percent, of their total annual revenue, minus certain expenses such as arena

---

[25]Andy Bernstein, "Inside the Complex NHL Deal," June 4, 2009, at http://www.sportsbusinessdaily.com/Journal/Issues/2005/08/20050801/Labor-Agents/Inside-The-Complex-NHL-Deal.aspx.

[26]Andy Bernstein, "Inside the Complex NHL Deal."

operating costs.... "[27] Each team will receive a payment equal to the NBA's average team payroll.

Revenue sharing is not universally praised. Yankees' president Randy Levine has likened revenue sharing to welfare.[28] Such critics claim that revenue sharing—like any tax—penalizes teams for producing a higher quality product, which in this case means spending more on salaries to field better teams. They argue that revenue sharing "simply creates a welfare class of teams that can turn significant profits by keeping payroll down, knowing that if revenues fall, they'll cash a big check from the Yankees, the Red Sox, the Cubs, the Dodgers."[29] The high operating incomes of mediocre baseball teams seem to support such cynicism. Nor is the problem confined to MLB. In the NFL, the five most profitable teams in 2010–2011 were the Dallas Cowboys, Washington Redskins, Arizona Cardinals, Tampa Bay Buccaneers, and Cincinnati Bengals. These five teams went a combined 31–49 that year with no playoff appearances among them. With a guaranteed source of income, some teams seem to maximize profits by constraining their expenditure on talent. We return to this issue in Chapters 5 and 9.

Cost

Like revenues, a firm's costs come in a variety of forms. Recall from Chapter 2 that variable costs change as a firm's output changes while fixed costs remain constant no matter how much or little the firm produces. Most models of firm behavior treat the cost of labor as a variable cost, since the firm must hire more labor in order to produce more output and can change the number of workers that it hires relatively easily. In professional sports, however, labor costs and most other costs are fixed (or variable over only a narrow range) in a given season. At the team level, the NBA, NFL, and NHL all designate a relatively narrow band within which a team's payroll must fall. Baseball is the only major North American sport that does not place direct limits on a team's payroll. At the individual level, once the season begins, a team is obliged to honor its contract with a player and may not reduce his salary if the team draws fewer fans than expected or if the player is injured. Thus, individual salaries and overall payrolls do not change significantly with output, as measured in the number of fans, over the course of a season.

The data in Table 3.2 show that, not surprisingly, players' salaries figure prominently in the total costs of professional franchises. Salaries, which include deferred payments, bonuses, workers' compensation expenses, and pension

[27]John Lombardo, "Inside NBA's Revenue Sharing: How Complex Plan Will Shift $140 Million to Needy Teams," *Street and Smith's Sports Business Journal*, January 23, 2012, at http://www.sportsbusinessdaily.com/Journal/Issues/2012/01/23/Leagues-and-Governing-Bodies/NBA-revenue.aspx, viewed April 26, 2012.

[28]Craig Calcaterra, "Yankees President Randy Levine Blasts Rangers Owner Chuck Greenberg," *Hardball Talk*, January 28, 2011, at http://hardballtalk.nbcsports.com/2011/01/28/yankees-president-randy-levine-blasts-rangers-owner-chuck-greenberg.

[29]Joe Sheehan, "Don't Blame the Pirates, Blame MLB's Revenue Sharing System," *SI.com*, August 25, 2010, at http://sportsillustrated.cnn.com/2010/writers/joe_sheehan/08/25/pirates.finances/index.html.

contributions, make up over half a team's costs in every major sport. With a few exceptions, player costs vary little over the course of a single year.[30]

The remaining expenses consist of travel, advertising, administration (both team and league), and venue expenses. For baseball, and, to a lesser extent, hockey, expenses also include player development. Travel expenses increase with the size of the team, the number of away games, and the distances traveled. Teams incur advertising and administrative costs at two levels. Each team does advertising specific to its own club and market, and each team has its own administrative costs, which include everything from office supplies to the salaries of the team executives. Advertising and administrative costs also occur at the league level. These costs include broad-based ad campaigns designed to increase demand for the sport, and administrative costs, such as the cost of paying a commissioner and maintaining league offices.

Total venue costs differ significantly across teams. Many teams pay rent to local governments that own the venues in which they play, but those rents might be close to or far below market value. Some teams that own their own venues receive millions in public subsidies, while others receive little or no public funds. We explore these issues in detail in Chapters 6 and 7.

In MLB and, to a lesser extent, the NHL, teams pay a portion of player development costs for players in their minor league systems. Each MLB team operates six minor league teams (in AAA, AA, and three single A leagues). Income statements for six major league teams that were leaked to the website Deadspin.com show player development costs in 2008 that ranged from $15.5 million for the Seattle Mariners to $23.2 million for the Pittsburgh Pirates.[31] Because each minor league system generates only a few major league players per year, developing a major league player costs millions of dollars.

Opportunity Cost and Team Movement

Opportunity cost never appears on a team's balance sheet, yet it figures vitally in the strategic decision making of all teams. When franchises move from one city to another, they are driven by the prospect of higher profits in the new city. The opportunity costs of staying in a given city are the profits forgone by not moving to the new city. When a team contemplates a move, its owner usually cites the need for more skyboxes, lower lease payments, and better practice facilities. The implied threat in such statements is that some other city is offering such facilities, as seen in two of the most infamous franchise moves, by baseball's Dodgers and football's Colts. In general, for a threat to be credible, the team must have a viable

---

[30]The exceptions include trades, waiving a player in midseason, very short-term contracts such as the 10-day contract in the NBA, and "two-way" contracts that allow the team to pay a player one salary if he is in the major leagues and a lower salary if he is sent to the minor leagues.

[31]The other teams were the Florida Marlins, the Tampa Bay Rays, the Los Angeles Angels of Anaheim, and the Texas Rangers. For the Pirates and Mariners figures, see "MLB Confidential: The Financial Documents MLB Doesn't Want You to See, Part 1," *Deadspin*, at http://deadspin.com/5615096, viewed April 2, 2012; and "MLB Confidential Part 2: Seattle Mariners," *Deadspin*, at http://deadspin.com/5619509, viewed April 2, 2012.

alternative location. If no city is willing and able to provide a media market or venue agreement that makes a move worthwhile, the current host city has no incentive to meet a team's demand for a new or improved facility. We explore the bargaining power of teams over cities further in Chapter 7.

While many teams move because they are suffering losses in their current city, not all teams that move are losing money. When the Dodgers moved to Los Angeles in 1957, they ended a remarkably successful run in Brooklyn. In the decade before they moved west, the Dodgers were the most profitable team in baseball, accounting for 47 percent of the profits of the entire National League. Similarly, in their last season before sneaking off to Indianapolis, the Baltimore Colts had operating income of $5.1 million, the third highest in the NFL.[32]

3.3 TAXES, PROFIT, AND OWNER BEHAVIOR

While most fans love Mark Cuban, they do not have similar affection for such owners as Michael Brown of the Cincinnati Bengals or Donald Sterling of the Los Angeles Clippers, who, in the fans' eyes, fail to measure up to the "sportsmen" of a bygone era. Fans of all sports look back fondly to owners who nurtured the game and viewed it as more than a profit center or ego boost. Unfortunately, that image is largely fiction. Over 100 years ago, Albert Spalding, the owner of the Chicago White Stockings, complained of his fellow owners, "[W]ith these men it was simply a mercenary question of dollars and cents. Everything must yield to the one consideration of inordinate greed."[33] Today's Toronto Blue Jays and the Colorado Rockies may owe their origins to their initial owners' desire to sell beer (Labatt's in Toronto and Coors in Colorado),[34] but these owners had a 19th-century role model in Chris von der Ahe, a brewer and the founder of the original St. Louis Browns, who used the ball club to boost his own beer sales. In this section, we explore ways in which team owners increase their profits. Some methods reflect poorly upon owners, as they involve using teams to maximize profits in other lines of business or manipulating the tax laws. We also show how one method, the vertical integration of teams and the TV stations that broadcast their games, could benefit the owner and the consumer alike.

Finding Profit in Losses

While teams worry about many different sources of revenues and costs, it still seems that one need only subtract total cost from the various forms of revenue to calculate profits. Unfortunately, nothing is simple in the finances of professional sports. Paul Beeston, once the Toronto Blue Jays' vice-president of business

---

[32]James Quirk and Rodney Fort, *Pay Dirt* (1992), p. 135; and Jon Morgan, *Glory for Sale: Fans, Dollars, and the New NFL* (Baltimore: Bancroft Press, 1997), p. 106.

[33]Albert G. Spalding, *America's National Game* (New York: American Sports Publishing Company, 1911), p. 302.

[34]Some claim that the very name of the Blue Jays stems from the desire to promote one particular brand of beer, Labatt's Blue. See John Helyar, *Lords of the Realm* (1994), p. 400.

operations, put it best: "[A]nyone who quotes profits of a baseball club is missing the point. Under generally accepted accounting principles, I can turn a $4 million profit into a $2 million loss and get every national accounting firm to agree with me."[35] In this section, we explore how teams use the rules of accounting to manipulate their measures of profit.

USING SPORTS TO MAXIMIZE PROFITS ELSEWHERE   Sometimes, team owners take advantage of the high visibility that professional sports offer in order to increase profits in another industry. Perhaps nowhere is this practice more prevalent than in Japan, where all but two NPB teams are named for the corporations that own them, as opposed to the cities in which they play. As a result, the teams play an important role in marketing products unrelated to baseball. For example, the Seibu Lions, who play in Saitama, are owned by the Seibu group. After a game, Lions fans can ride the Seibu-Ikebukuro train from the game to a Seibu department store which, not coincidentally, celebrated with a major sale when the Seibu Lions won the 2008 Japan Series.

An even more striking example is the Yomiuri Giants, who are owned by the Yomiuri Group, which also owns two newspapers and the NTV television network. In fact, professional baseball in Japan began as a way to increase newspaper sales. The *Yomiuri Shimbun*, Japan's largest newspaper, sponsored a trip by a U.S. All Star team to play a series of games in Japan in 1934. The centerpiece of the tour was Babe Ruth, who had just completed his last season as a Yankee and would play only part of one more season with the Boston Braves.[36] The tour was so successful that the owner of the paper, Matsutaro Shoriki, decided to keep the team together and go on a tour of U.S. cities. Interestingly, it was at that time that the uniforms of the Japanese teams were changed to English on the front and Arabic numbers on the back, a practice that continues today.[37]

Because of the ownership structure of Japanese baseball teams, profits are secondary to the teams' ability to publicize their sponsors. In fact, teams are regarded as advertising expenses by their parent companies, with front office positions often staffed from corporate headquarters rather than using baseball insiders. As a result, teams in Japan may be run by corporate managers from the company's home office who may neither know nor care about baseball.

While American teams are generally not as closely linked to a parent company, one striking example occurred in the NHL. The Anaheim Ducks of the NHL were originally named the Anaheim Mighty Ducks and were owned by the Walt Disney Corporation, the producer of the movie *The Mighty Ducks*. The team's logo and colors were announced in June 1993 following the 1992 release of the movie.

---

[35]Quoted in Andrew Zimbalist, *Baseball and Billions* (1992), p. 62.

[36]For an account of this tour, see Robert Fitts, *Banzai Babe Ruth* (Lincoln, Neb.: University of Nebraska Press, 2012).

[37]Joseph A. Reaves, *Taking in a Game: The History of Baseball in Asia* (Lincoln, Neb.: University of Nebraska Press, 2002), pp. 69–77.

Operating Income, Taxes, and Profit

To this point, we have been using operating income, the net revenue from day-to-day operations, when discussing the profitability of sports franchises. When teams, or firms of any kind, report profits, however, they use **accounting profit**, the difference between total revenue and total cost. Accounting profit differs from operating income in that it nets out interest expenses and depreciation as well as the day-to-day costs of production. Since corporate profit taxes are based on accounting profit, firms can deduct interest payments from their corporate profit taxes, while they must pay taxes on the profits that are paid out as dividends. Thus, profits are taxed twice, once as corporate profits and once as personal income. The asymmetric treatment of interest and dividends has led economists to conclude that firms generally prefer to raise funds by issuing debt (in the form of bonds and loans on which they pay interest) rather than stock, which results in dividend payments. Moreover, most borrowing in sports, and hence most interest payments, stem from the loans that owners take out to buy the team.

Tax laws treat depreciation as an expense. Thus, higher depreciation expenses result in lower tax burdens. Typically, firms apply depreciation to plant and equipment. In 1949, Bill Veeck, then owner of the Cleveland Indians, applied it to his players, claiming that their skills wore out over time. This allowed him to significantly reduce his tax burden despite the fact that, unlike bulldozers or ovens, professional teams do not become worthless after several years, and teams already deduct expenditures on minor league systems that re-stock their talent. A good example of this tax loophole came in 1964, when a syndicate bought the Milwaukee Braves (and moved to Atlanta a year later). The syndicate declared that only $50,000 of the $6.168 million it spent was for the team itself and that the remaining $6.118 million was embodied in the players. It also declared that the players were depreciable assets that wore out over a 10-year span, losing 10 percent of their original value each year. This allowed the Braves' owners to write off $611,800 as depreciation expenses on their income statement each year. At a 52 percent corporate tax rate, the team reduced its tax burden by over $300,000 per year for 10 years. The total tax savings meant that the new owners of the Braves were able to pass almost half the purchase price of the team on to the American taxpayer.

Vertical Integration

As noted earlier in this chapter, sports teams have become increasingly involved in the TV outlets that broadcast their games. We have seen that joint ownership enables teams to reduce the amount of revenue teams must share. However, it might also reflect efficiency gains from **vertical integration**, the combination of different stages of production.

Alone, both the team and the broadcaster have monopoly power. Bringing the two together seems to create a "super monopoly" with even greater power to exploit consumers. Economic theory shows, however, that the efficiency gains that accompany the vertical integration of a team and a media outlet may benefit both owners and consumers.

   To see why, consider two firms, each with monopoly power in its own market. Imagine that the two firms are located along a river. The **upstream firm** produces its output and floats it down the river to the **downstream firm**, which then sends the final output down the river to consumers. If the upstream firm has monopoly power, it can charge a monopoly price to the downstream firm. The downstream firm treats the price it pays as part of its marginal cost of production. It uses this high marginal cost to determine the (even higher) price it charges consumers.

   Figure 3.4 illustrates the impact of upstream and downstream monopolies. For simplicity, we assume that the upstream firm's marginal costs are constant, so that its *MC* curve is a horizontal line. We also assume that the downstream firm has no costs other than what it pays the upstream firm, so its *MC* curve is a horizontal line at the price it pays the upstream firm. Figure 3.5b shows that the consumer faces a double whammy of two monopolies. The higher price charged by the upstream monopolist raises the costs of the downstream monopolist, which then raises prices still higher in exercising its own monopoly power.

   If the downstream firm vertically integrates by buying the upstream firm, it has no reason to charge itself a high monopolistic price.[38] The cost of the upstream product to the downstream firm is now simply the marginal cost of production. The double whammy of Figure 3.4 now falls to a single blow in Figure 3.5.

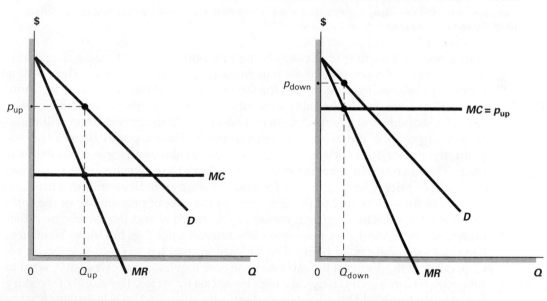

(a) Upstream firm   **(b) Downstream firm**

FIGURE 3.4   Monopoly Pricing by Upstream and Downstream Firms
When an upstream monopolist sells to a downstream monopolist, the downstream firm takes the price it pays the upstream firm (P_{up}) as marginal cost.

---

[38]In fact, we shall show in Chapter 4 that charging a high price would harm the firm by creating a deadweight loss.

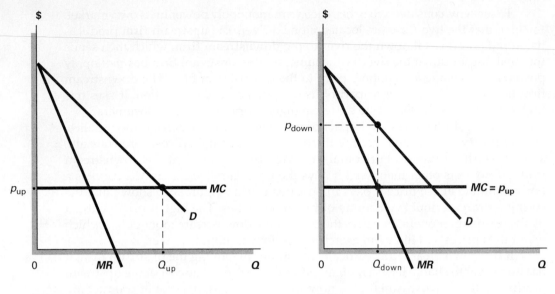

(a) Upstream firm   **(b) Downstream firm**

FIGURE 3.5   Vertical Integration with Competitive Pricing Upstream

When the upstream and downstream firms are vertically integrated, the downstream firm can purchase output at the competitive price ($MC = P_{up}$).

While two separate monopolies apply their monopoly power twice, a single, vertically integrated monopoly applies its monopoly power only once. The result is a lower price and higher quantity for the consumer. In this case, it means more games at a lower cost to the cable subscriber than would otherwise be the case.

An individual or group that owns two vertically integrated firms will maximize total profits of the two combined enterprises. From a purely financial standpoint, the owner does not worry whether one firm shows a larger profit than the other. The price at which the upstream firm sells to the downstream firm is called the **transfer price**. Changes in transfer prices change an individual firm's accounting profits (those reported to the IRS), but not the overall profitability of the combined enterprises. Thus, the joint owner of the franchise and the cable station that broadcasts the franchise's games sets a low transfer price (i.e., broadcast rights fee) if revenue-sharing, tax, or political considerations make it advantageous to do so. Conversely, if the profits of the cable company are regulated, the owner may want to minimize its earnings by charging a high broadcast rights fee. The moral of the story is that when teams and broadcasters are vertically integrated, as is increasingly common in the sports industry, one must view accounting profits with a skeptical eye.

3.4   THE IMPORTANCE OF LEAGUES

All major professional team and individual sports are organized into leagues. Leagues provide so many vital organizational and financial services to individual teams that forming a league appears to be a prerequisite for the financial stability of a sport, yet the arrival of leagues did not coincide with the advent of professional teams.[39] In this section, we assume that teams share the goal of profit-maximization and that leagues exist to help them meet this goal.[40] We focus on how leagues set rules, limit entry, promote competitive balance, share revenue, and market their product.

The Origin of Leagues in American Sports

Baseball's National League, the oldest existing professional league in the United States, did not appear until 1876, seven years after the Cincinnati Red Stockings, the first openly professional team, began to play in 1869. It took another 20 years for the National League to establish a stable set of teams. The NFL formed in 1920, two generations after William Heffelfinger became the first professional football player in 1876, and it did not field a stable set of teams until 1936.[41] The same pattern held in Europe, as a formal league structure for soccer arose in 1888, at least 12 years after the appearance of professional players, 25 years after the codification of the sport by the Football Association (FA), and decades after teams began playing the sport.[42] Despite these delays, professional team sports could not have survived without the formation of stable leagues.

Prior to the appearance of leagues, teams played each other on an informal, ad hoc basis. Until the latter part of the 19th century, most games involved teams from the same town. As transportation improved, matches were arranged between teams from increasingly distant towns.[43] Informal trips to play teams in other towns, a practice known as barnstorming, became popular, but there was no guarantee that the opposition would show up or that the game would draw a sizable crowd. The experiences of the old Cincinnati Red Stockings illustrate this problem. During their grand tour of 1869, the Red Stockings drew large crowds from coast to coast while compiling a 56–0–1 record. The next year, they lost only four games but disbanded when the season was over. The Red Stockings team resembled a strongman in a traveling carnival who offers to take on all comers. The sideshow may attract a crowd if it can bill the strongman as "undefeated." A strongman who has won two-thirds of his matches (an enviable record for most teams today), however, would not generate much interest.

---

[39]Eric M. Leifer, *Making the Majors* (1995), p. 15.

[40]See, for example, Gerald Scully, *The Market Structure of Sports* (Chicago: University of Chicago Press, 1995), pp. 3–40.

[41]James Quirk and Rodney Fort, *Pay Dirt* (1992), pp. 333–334.

[42]There are many wonderful histories of the origins of baseball and soccer. Two of the best are Harold Seymour, *Baseball: The Early Years* (New York: Oxford University Press, 1960) and David Goldblatt, *The Ball Is Round: A Global History of Soccer* (New York: Riverhead Books: 2006). For an excellent comparison of the two sports, see Stefan Szymanski and Andrews Zimbalist, *National Pastime* (Washington, D.C.: Brookings Institution Press, 2005).

[43]See Michael Danielson, *Home Team*, p. 20.

Setting the Rules

Formally speaking, a league is a voluntary association that promotes the common interests of its members. Hence, the League of Women Voters (LWV) was formed in 1920 to help women exercise their newly won right to vote and continues its efforts to register and inform voters. Just as the LWV was originally formed to promote the interests of women voters, the NFL, NBA, NHL, and MLB were formed to promote the interests of the teams that are their members.[44] In particular, leagues perform functions that no one team can do alone, such as establishing rules of play. However, the limits of these "core functions" has been the subject of much dispute, as owners often want to include more actions than players, other firms, and governments want them to.

As a result, leagues are by nature cooperative bodies. At one level, the teams are rivals that succeed at the expense of each other. At another level, each team's success depends on the success of the other teams in the league and on the success of the league as an institution. Leagues create a body of rules, set schedules, promote competitive balance, decide on revenue-sharing arrangements, stage championship tournaments, create a framework for the entry of new players and teams, and conduct advertising campaigns.[45]

Of the functions of leagues, the most important is establishing and enforcing rules of the game. Without a single, commonly accepted way to play, teams cannot play one another, and the sport cannot function, let alone grow. For example, the many different rules by which 19th-century English football clubs played created conflict between clubs and stymied the growth of the game. In 1863, many clubs joined to form the Football Association (FA) to establish a single set of rules.[46] In addition to standardizing rules, the FA gave football the nickname it now enjoys in England and the United States. The approved version of the game was dubbed "Association Football," later shortened to "Assoc. Football" or "soccer."

While the Football Association succeeded in establishing a common set of rules, its broad membership, from the most highly skilled teams to relatively informal clubs, prevented it from fulfilling other duties of a league. This undermined early attempts to play a fixed schedule, as games were often dull, one-sided affairs. Recognizing the need to provide stable competition between evenly matched teams, 12 of the strongest clubs formed an elite grouping in 1888 that called itself "the Football League" (FL). Despite the seeming conflict with the FA, the FL did not attempt to displace the FA entirely. The members of the FL recognized that they were motivated by the interests of their individual clubs and not the welfare of the FL or the sport as a whole, and they chose to share power with the FA, allowing it to serve as an outside arbiter.[47] Over the next century, the FL

---

[44]Interestingly, the leagues themselves are organized as not-for-profit associations.

[45]Groups such as the Professional Golfers' Association and the United States Tennis Association perform much the same function for these more individual-based sports.

[46]Unhappy that the new rules did not allow their rougher version of football, devotees of the style developed at Rugby formed their own association, the Rugby Football Union, in 1871.

[47]Wray Vamplew, *Pay Up and Play the Game: Professional Sport in Britain, 1875–1914* (Cambridge, U.K.: Cambridge University Press, 1988), p. 125.

grew to 92 teams, broken into four divisions. In 1992, the 20 teams in the strongest division broke away from the FL to form the Premier League (officially called the Npower Football League thanks to a 2010 sponsorship agreement with the British utility company Npower), with the FL supervising the 72 remaining teams.

Like soccer, baseball initially had different rules in different places. Two versions of the sport dominated, Massachusetts Rules and Knickerbocker Rules (also known as New York Rules). Knickerbocker Rules are the linear ancestor of modern baseball, while Massachusetts Rules may seem bizarre to the modern observer. Under Massachusetts Rules, a team got an opposing player "out" by hitting him with a thrown ball, the bases were arranged in a square rather than a diamond, and winning a game required 100 runs or getting every member of the other team out, as in cricket. By the middle of the 19th century, the Knickerbocker Rules had become the norm.[48]

Baseball went through several attempts to find a stable league structure. The earliest central authority, the National Association of Base Ball Players (NABBP), was formed in 1858. It did not arise out of a need to standardize rules, because the Knickerbocker Rules dominated the game played by the teams in the NABBP (largely in the New York area). Instead, it sought to combat professionalism and preserve the "gentlemanliness" of the game. The NABBP failed to achieve its goals, and it succumbed to the growing professionalism of the sport, being replaced by the National Association of Professional Base Ball Players (NAPBBP) in 1871. The NAPBBP also proved ineffectual, particularly in enforcing player contracts. In 1876, the financial backers of several teams effectively staged a coup d'état, casting aside the NAPBBP and forming the National League of Baseball Clubs. The National League remains the oldest functioning league in American sports (hence its nickname, "the senior circuit").

Sometimes leagues manipulate rules to create more excitement or to protect players. Both these motives have affected kickoffs in the NFL. For many years, the NFL made teams kick off from deeper and deeper in their own territory in an effort to generate longer and more exciting kickoff returns. Prior to the 2011 season, as part of its attempt to limit devastating head injuries, the NFL reversed itself and moved kickoffs from the kicking team's 30-yard line to its 35-yard line.

In an attempt to win back fans after the cancellation of the 2004–2005 season, the NHL instituted a number of changes designed to increase scoring. These included limiting the equipment and activities of goalies, allowing longer passes, and instituting "shootouts" to end tie games. After seeing how popular it had been in the rival American Basketball Association (ABA) and American Basketball League (ABL),[49] the NBA added the three-point basket to increase scoring and restore the value of outside shooting; more recently, they permitted teams to play "zone" defense.

---

[48]See Harold Seymour, *Baseball* (1960), pp. 23–30; and Robert Burk, *Never Just a Game: Players, Owners, and American Baseball to 1920* (Chapel Hill: University of North Carolina Press, 1994), p. 14.

[49]Terry Pluto, *Loose Balls: The Short, Wild Life of the American Basketball Association* (New York: Simon and Schuster, 1990), pp. 29–30.

Leagues establish and enforce rules governing behavior off the field as well. In its early years, baseball's National League expelled teams for failing to play out their schedules. Individual players were also banned from baseball for intentionally losing games, as was the case for eight of the Chicago "Black Sox" following the 1919 World Series, or for betting on baseball games, as Pete Rose was in 1989. The NFL suspended Alex Karras of the Detroit Lions and Paul Hornung of the Green Bay Packers for one year in 1963 for betting on league games. Players may also be suspended for engaging in activity that may reflect poorly on the league, as witnessed by Major League Baseball's suspension of Melky Cabrera in 2012 for using a banned substance.

Leagues have also played a role in purging the crowds of "undesirable elements" that discouraged attendance. For example, Sunday beer sales at baseball games have been allowed only fairly recently. In the 1890s, the National League tried to present a wholesome image by expelling the Cincinnati Red Stockings for serving beer at all. Prior to the 1930s, games were not even played on Sundays in many cities. Currently, in the NHL, teams can be penalized during a game if fans repeatedly throw objects onto the ice and delay the game. In the NFL, the home team can be penalized if its fans are so noisy that the opposing team cannot hear the snap count.

Limiting Entry

In recent years, one might be forgiven for thinking that American universities had lost the ability to count. How else can one explain the fact that, in 2011, the Big 10 athletic conference had 12 teams in it, while the Big Twelve Conference had only 10 teams? Their command of geography also seemed to be slipping. In 2011, the Pacific 12 Conference welcomed the University of Colorado, which is located about 1,000 miles from the Pacific Ocean. Not to be outdone, the Big East Conference was preparing to invite San Diego State University, which is only about 15 miles from the Pacific Ocean, but close to 3,000 miles from its new East Coast rival, the University of Connecticut. All across the country, major intercollegiate athletic conferences are reconfiguring in ways that destroy century-old rivalries and appear to make little sense.

To comprehend conference realignment, it is first important to understand why collegiate sports conferences or professional sports leagues place any limit on their size. In North America, MLB, the NBA, and the NHL have all restricted themselves to 30 teams, while the NFL has 32 teams. In Australia, by contrast, the Australian Football League has 16 teams. In Japan, the Nippon Professional Baseball League (NPB) has just 12 teams. For many years, NCAA conferences typically had 8–10 teams. Today, many observers think that the NCAA will eventually have 4 "super conferences," each with about 16 teams.

The forces that determine how large a league becomes can be found in the work of Nobel laureate James Buchanan.[50] In his theory of the economics of clubs,

---

[50]James M. Buchanan, "An Economic Theory of Clubs," *Economica*, vol. 32, no. 1 (February 1965), pp. 1–14; and John Vrooman, "Franchise Free Agency in Professional Sports Leagues," *Southern Journal of Economics*, vol. 64, no. 1 (July 1997), pp. 191–219.

Buchanan reasoned that admitting a new member to a club—in this case, a sports league—brings costs and benefits. Existing teams benefit from the admission fees that new teams pay to join the league and from the additional fan base and media outlets new teams bring.[51] Additional members also bring a cost. For example, admitting new teams to the league spreads any shared revenue over more members and reduces the ability of existing members to use the threat of moving to the new city as a bargaining chip when negotiating with their current home cities.

If the revenue from admitting one more team declines as the league grows— as one might expect if leagues admit cities from the most profitable cities first and then admit teams from less and less profitable cities—the marginal revenue curve slopes downward, as in Figure 3.6. Similarly, if the cost of admitting one more team rises, the marginal cost curve slopes upward. The equilibrium point occurs where the marginal revenue and marginal cost curves meet (e_0), which leads to optimal league size Q_0.

In recent years, several factors have changed the economic landscape of college sports, increasing the marginal value of new members to several conferences. Three of the most important reasons all come down to one thing: the growing importance of football as a source of revenue.

The growing importance of football created a problem for the Atlantic Coast Conference (ACC), which had a long history of success in basketball but little tradition in football, and the Big East Conference, which had been formed specifically as a basketball conference and had turned to football only as an afterthought. The ACC adjusted to the new reality by adding such football powers as Virginia Tech, the University of Miami, and Florida State University. The Big East failed to adjust, making such missteps as rejecting a bid by Penn State to join the conference in the early 1980s, and has seen a steady departure of teams, several of which (Boston College, Miami, Virginia Tech, West Virginia, and—in 2013—Pittsburgh and Syracuse) left for the ACC. To enhance the status of football, the Big East has invited such schools as Boise State and the University of Houston. Big *East*, indeed!

In addition, the growing popularity of—and revenue from—conference championship games in football vastly increased the desirability of such games. However, NCAA rules specify that conferences must have at least 12 members to hold a football championship game. This led the Pacific 10 to add Colorado and Utah, and the Big 10 (which already had 11 teams) to add Nebraska for the 2011 season. Both conferences held their first football championship game in 2011.

Figure 3.6 also shows the dangers that face professional leagues when they limit the number of teams. At the dawn of the 20th century, the National League, then the only major professional league in North America, restricted itself to only eight teams. It failed to recognize, however, that rising populations and incomes in urban centers had shifted the marginal revenue curve rightward from MR_0 to MR_1. The shift caused the equilibrium point to shift to e_1 and the optimal league size to grow from Q_0 to Q_1. The failure of the National League to expand led Ban Johnson to found the American League in 1901.

---

[51]More generally, Buchanan assumes that members of a club produce "club goods" that members of the club share with one another but outsiders cannot enjoy.

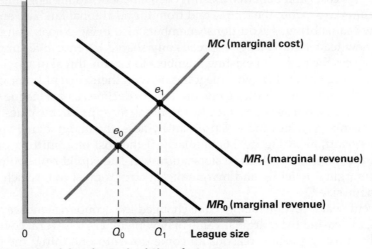

Marginal Revenue and Marginal Cost

MC (marginal cost)

e_1

e_0

MR_1 (marginal revenue)

MR_0 (marginal revenue)

0   Q_0 Q_1 League size

FIGURE 3.6   Determining the Optimal Size of a League
The optimal size of the league is set where the marginal revenue meets marginal cost.

Leagues also dictate *where* entry can occur. Table 3.5 shows that, in 2010, each of the 10 largest metropolitan areas had several professional franchises. As expected, New York, the largest market, had more franchises than any other area, with 11. Los Angeles and Chicago, the second and third most populous

TABLE 3.5   The Ten Most Populous Metropolitan Statistical Areas and Their Sports Teams in 2011

City (population)[a]	MLB	NBA	NFL	NHL	MLS	WNBA
New York (18.9)	2	2	2	3	1	1
Los Angeles (12.8)	2	2	0	1	2	1
Chicago (9.5)	2	1	1	1	1	1
Dallas (6.4)	1	1	1	1	1	0
Philadelphia (6.0)	1	1	1	1	1	0
Houston (6.0)	1	1	1	0	1	0
Washington, D.C. (5.6)	1	1	1	1	1	1
Miami (5.6)	1	1	1	1	0	0
Atlanta (5.3)	1	1	1	0	0	1
Boston (4.6)	1	1	1	1	1	0

[a]Population in millions.

Source: U.S. Census Bureau, "Population and Housing Occupancy Status: 2010—United States—Metropolitan Statistical Areas," *American FactFinder,* 2010, at http://factfinder2.census.gov/faces/tableservices/jsf/pages/productview.xhtml?pid=DEC_10_NSRD_GCTPL2.US24PR&prodType=table, viewed April 4, 2012.

metropolitan areas, had eight and seven. MLB and the NBA had franchises in all of the 10 largest metropolitan areas. It may seem odd that the business savvy NFL does not have a team in Los Angeles, but, as we see in Chapter 7, having a large city ready to bid away another city's team might be a good business strategy. The NHL was in every area except Houston. The WNBA had entered five of the ten largest metropolitan areas, while MLS was in eight.

Placing franchises in the largest cities has important implications for the individual teams, as it ensures that each team has a large fan base to which it can market. On the other hand, adding teams to a market dissipates the monopoly power of the existing teams. To have a monopoly, a firm must produce a good with no close substitutes. As the number of available substitutes increases, the demand curve facing the incumbent firm (team) becomes more elastic. In Figure 3.7, the addition of a new, nearby team shifts the demand curve from D_0 to D_1, reducing the profit-maximizing price from p_0 to p_1. The more teams that exist in any given area, the more vigorously they must compete with one another in all areas of revenue generation, from luxury box sales to regular ticket sales to advertising.

Placing teams in all the most desirable cities also helps to keep out competing leagues in much the same way that controlling access to a key input limits entry in other markets. The lack of profitable markets dogged the ABA, which competed with the NBA from 1967 to 1976. To avoid direct competition with the NBA, the ABA chose mostly midsized cities for its franchises. In part because of its weak locations, the ABA eventually folded, with only the Denver, New Jersey, San Antonio, and Indiana franchises surviving to join the NBA. The same fate awaited the World Hockey Association (WHA), which played from 1972 through 1979.

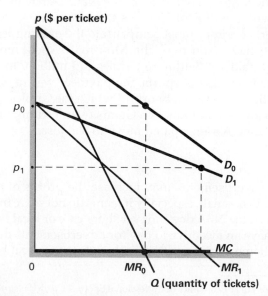

FIGURE 3.7   Effect of Entry on Demand
When a new team enters an existing market, the demand curve for the existing team shifts leftward and becomes more elastic.

Four of its teams joined the NHL, two were compensated for not joining the NHL, and the remaining teams disbanded. All teams that attempted to compete head-to-head with NHL teams in the same large-city market failed. The only teams to survive played in midsized markets where no other team already existed.

Limited Entry as Cooperative Behavior

Some analysts regard leagues as multiplant monopolies. According to this view, a season of games is a "peculiar mixture: it comes in divisible parts, each of which can be sold separately, but it is also a joint and multiple yet divisible product."[52] For example, part of the excitement of attending a single game comes from how the outcome relates to league standings, which involves all teams in the league and all games in the season.

Leagues carefully coordinate the output (here measured as games played) and prices charged to broadcasters or licensees by member teams for the betterment of the league, even if such restrictions reduce the profits of some member teams. Major network television contracts are negotiated at the league level rather than by individual teams. Such cooperative behavior allows the most popular games to be aired on national television, and it prevents teams from competing with each other for broadcast rights, thereby keeping prices high. Competition leads to lower revenues for the league because teams have an incentive to reduce prices to networks for broadcast rights. Restricting the number of teams (and the geographic locations they occupy) gives owners a guaranteed source of ticket and media revenue as well as a restricted market for apparel and other team-related enterprises. Leagues enforce territorial rights by setting a radius within which no other member of the league may locate. In the NFL, each team is given exclusive rights to an area with a radius of 75 miles from its home stadium. A team that moves into another's territory must compensate the existing team. For example, when MLB, which had taken over the Montreal Expos, moved the team to Washington, DC, it paid the Baltimore Orioles $75 million. In keeping with the changing economic landscape of sports, the payment was to get the Nationals a stake in the Mid-Atlantic Sports Network, of which the Orioles had owned 90 percent.[53] A dispute with the San Francisco Giants over territorial rights is currently holding up the Oakland A's anticipated move to San Jose.

Advertising

While one team's advertisements may increase the profits of other teams, such spillovers are likely to be small, especially if teams do not share much gate revenue. For example, because the NBA does not yet share gate or local media revenue, the Houston Rockets have an incentive to pay for advertisements that encourage fans to attend Rockets home games and to watch or listen to local broadcasts of their

---

[52]Walter C. Neale, "The Peculiar Economics of Professional Sports," *Quarterly Journal of Economics*, vol. 78, no. 1 (February 1964), p. 3.

[53]Graydon Ebert, "MLSE Buy" *Offside: A Sports Law Blog*, at http://offsidesportsblog.blogspot.com/p/mlse-buy.html, viewed April 5, 2012.

games. The revenue from attendance or local broadcasts in other cities accrues to other teams, and the revenue from national broadcasts is shared evenly, so the Rockets have little reason to pay for broadly focused ads. If all ads were aimed at increasing local revenues, analyzing their impact on demand and profit would be straightforward. Advertising expenditures would appear as a fixed cost, and, if effective, they would shift the demand curve for the team's games to the right. The optimal quantity of advertising (Q^*) occurs where the marginal benefit (MB) from the last dollar spent on advertising was equal to the marginal cost (MC) of the ad, as shown in Figure 3.8.

In contrast, leagues take a multilevel approach to marketing. As with traditional franchises, such as McDonald's, professional teams contribute to joint advertisements run at the league level. In turn, the leagues create a specific image designed to increase demand for the sport as a whole. For instance, the WNBA spent $15 million on marketing in its first year. The league developed a slogan ("We Got Next") and used it in a variety of ads designed to promote the league rather than any specific team.

Advertising at the league level promotes the welfare of all teams and thus is a **public good**. A public good is marked by **nonrival** consumption, which means that the benefit that one team receives from a league-wide marketing campaign does not reduce the benefit that any other team can receive from the same campaign. Public goods are also marked by **nonexclusion** in that one team cannot prevent another team from receiving the benefits of the ad campaign.

Financing public goods poses a serious problem. Asking teams to contribute voluntarily creates an incentive to free ride. Teams **free ride** when they attempt to pay less than their marginal benefit from a public good and to shift the financing burden

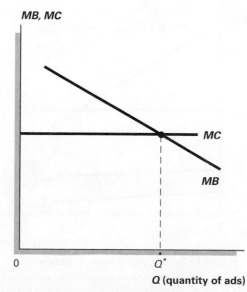

FIGURE 3.8   Determining the Optimal Quantity of Advertisements
Teams should advertise until the marginal cost of advertising equals its marginal benefit.

to other teams. Thus, there are two obstacles to providing the optimal amount of a public good. The first is to determine the marginal benefit of the good to society, and the second is to ensure that each consumer (team, in this case) pays its share.

As we saw in Chapter 2, the market demand for a private good, such as apples, is the horizontal sum of the individual demand curves. If Amy buys four apples and Pat buys six apples when the price is $1 per apple, their combined quantity demanded at $1 is 10 apples. With public goods, when we want to compute how much consumers are willing to pay for a given amount of the good, we add the individual demand curves *vertically* rather than horizontally. To see this, suppose that 60-second advertising slots for the NBA on network television are available at a constant marginal cost of $50,000. Figure 3.9 shows that no single team is willing to pay for such an advertisement. However, if the first 60-second preseason commercial is worth $10,000 to 15 small-market teams, such as the Sacramento Kings, and $20,000 to 15 larger-market teams, such as the Los Angeles Lakers, the first commercial is worth $450,000 to the 30 teams combined. Assuming marginal benefits decline as usual, so that the demand curves slope downward, the optimal number of commercials in Figure 3.7 is 30.

The second challenge, getting those who benefit from the good to contribute toward its production, can be very complex. Once built, public goods, such as parks and roads, can be used by anyone, so identifying the beneficiaries can be difficult. Because leagues provide marketing for a limited clientele, they have a much easier time identifying exactly who benefits. As a result, each team contributes to the league-wide marketing fund.[54]

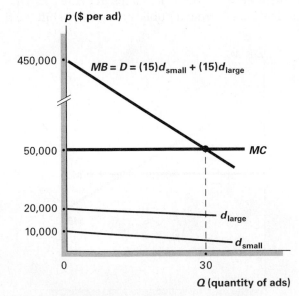

FIGURE 3.9 Total Marginal Benefit When Consumption Is Nonrival
The market demand for a public good is the vertical sum of the individual demand curves.

[54]Craig A. Depken, David R. Kamerschen, and Arthur Snow, "Generic Advertising of Intermediate Goods: Theory and Evidence," *The Review of Industrial Organization*, vol. 20, no. 3 (May 2002), pp. 205–220.

SPORTS AND THE LAW
The Limits of Leagues

In the often surprising world of sports law, few lawsuits had as many twists as *American Needle* v. *NFL*. In 2009, the NFL asked the Supreme Court to reconsider a decision that it had won, and, a year later, snatched defeat from the jaws of victory. As part of the brief it submitted to the U.S. Court of Appeals, the NFL claimed that it was taking a "nuanced economics-based approach," which brought a stinging response from several of the nation's top sports economists.[1] Finally, in losing the case, the NFL may have turned what some had derided as "American Needle management's sour grapes over being snubbed by the league" into the event that saved the 2011–2012 football season.[2]

Few could have foreseen the chain of events that would follow when, in 2000, NFL Properties terminated its licensing agreement with a variety of manufacturers to sign an exclusive deal with Reebok (now a part of Adidas).[3] Upset over the loss of a lucrative contract, American Needle sued, claiming that NFL teams had violated antitrust laws by acting as a single entity rather than as individual firms. American Needle lost its suit and multiple appeals, as the courts ruled that the NFL was entitled to negotiate apparel contracts as a single entity. Then, to everyone's surprise, the NFL joined American Needle in asking the U.S. Supreme Court to take up the issue.

While American Needle just wanted its contract back, the NFL saw an opportunity to expand the concept of a league. We have seen that leagues necessarily involve collusion by the teams they comprise and that, when the collusion involves core activities, such as rules of play or scheduling, this collusion is desirable, even necessary. The question is how far that collusion can go. Court rulings and acts of Congress had extended the NFL's core activities to negotiating broadcast rights and licensing agreements, but now the NFL wanted to push the boundary still further. In its appeal, the NFL claimed that the league was not 32 separate operations, but in effect one large firm.

If the Supreme Court had agreed with this argument, then *any* action the NFL took, from deciding where franchises located to setting limits on salaries, would be within the normal operation of one single entity. With the NFL embroiled in contentious negotiations with its players' union, a favorable ruling would have greatly strengthened its hand and encouraged it, in the words of one observer, to "really go for the jugular."[4] As it turns out, the Supreme Court agreed with the economists rather than the NFL and refused to extend the lower court ruling beyond the apparel agreement. Chastened by this ruling, the NFL finally reached an agreement with the players, and the 2011–2012 season was saved.

[1] Quoted in Craig Corbitt, Jan Yi, "*American Needle, Inc.* v. *National Football League, et al.*: Amicus Curiae Brief of Economists in Support of Petitioner," at http://www.scribd.com/bigtkirk/d/20345483-Sports-Economists-Amicus-Brief-in-American-Needle-Case, viewed May 1, 2012.

[2] Tom Van Riper, "The NFL Vs. American Needle," *Forbes*, January 7, 2010, at http://www.forbes.com/2010/01/06/american-needle-supreme-court-business-sports-nfl.html.

[3] For more background on the lawsuit, see Jennifer S. Forsyth, "American Needle Throws Downfield in NFL Licensing Dispute" *Law Blog: The Wall Street Journal*, September 18, 2009, at http://blogs.wsj.com/law/2009/09/18/american-needle-throws-downfield-in-nfl-licensing-dispute/.

(Continued)

[4] ESPN analyst John Clayton, quoted in Doug Farrar, "The NFL Loses American Needle: What It Means," *Shutdown Corner/Yahoo! Sports,* May 24, 2010, at http://sports.yahoo.com/nfl/blog/shutdown_corner/post/The-NFL-loses-American-Needle-What-it-means?urn=nfl,243282.

Sources: Doug Farrar, "The NFL Loses American Needle: What It Means," *Shutdown Corner/Yahoo! Sports,* May 24, 2010, at http://sports.yahoo.com/nfl/blog/shutdown_corner/post/The-NFL-loses-American-Needle-What-it-means?urn=nfl,243282; Jennifer S. Forsyth, "American Needle Throws Downfield in NFL Licensing Dispute" *Law Blog: The Wall Street Journal,* September 18, 2009, at http://blogs.wsj.com/law/2009/09/18/american-needle-throws-downfield-in-nfl-licensing-dispute/; Craig Corbitt, Jan Yi, "*American Needle, Inc. v. National Football League, et al.*: Amicus Curiae Brief of Economists in Support of Petitioner," at http://www.scribd.com/bigtkirk/d/20345483-Sports-Economists-Amicus-Brief-in-American-Needle-Case, viewed May 1, 2012; Tom Van Riper, "The NFL Vs. American Needle," *Forbes,* January 7, 2010, at http://www.forbes.com/2010/01/06/american-needle-supreme-court-business-sports-nfl.html.

3.5 SOCCER'S ALTERNATIVE BUSINESS MODEL

Every four years, the World Cup reminds us that most of the world pays little attention to baseball or American football and that hockey and basketball are distinctly secondary diversions. Soccer dominates the world stage. As Table 3.6 shows, professional teams, such as Manchester United and Real Madrid, have operating incomes and market values that rival those of the Los Angeles Dodgers and Dallas Cowboys. In Europe alone, merchandise sales for the top five European leagues (Spain's La Liga, England's Premier League, Germany's Bundesliga, Italy's Serie A, and France's Ligue 1) topped $800 million in 2009–2010.[55]

TABLE 3.6 Soccer Club Values and Revenues, 2011 ($ Millions)

Team	Country	Market Value	Revenue
Manchester United	England	1,864	428
Real Madrid	Spain	1,451	537
Arsenal	England	1,192	336
Bayern Munich	Germany	1,048	396
Barcelona	Spain	975	488
AC Milan	Italy	838	289
Chelsea	England	658	313
Juventus	Italy	628	251
Liverpool	England	552	276
Inter Milan	Italy	441	275

Source: Dan Bigman, "The World's Most Valuable Soccer Teams," *Forbes,* at http://www.forbes.com/2011/04/20/worlds-most-valuable-soccer-teams_slide.html, viewed April 5, 2012.

[55] Yahoo! Sport, "Ligue 1—France Fourth in Merchandise Sales," *EuroSport.com,* February 22, 2011, at http://uk.eurosport.yahoo.com/23022011/58/ligue-1-france-fourth-merchandise-sales.html.

Once one goes beyond the top few teams, however, the figures drop off dramatically. According to 2011 figures from *Forbes*, the 10th most valuable soccer team in the world, Inter Milan, was worth less than every NFL team. The 20th most valuable team, Borussia Dortmund, was worth less than every MLB and NBA team and was roughly equal to the Calgary Flames, the NHL's 13th most valuable franchise.[56] Despite Latin America's passion for the sport and the outstanding performance of several national teams, no Latin American country has a club in *Forbes'* top 20. European clubs employ almost all the top Latin American (and African and Asian) players.

The divide between rich and poor is not merely geographic. Even in the "major" soccer countries, teams outside the top division have difficulty making a profit. In Spain, 80 percent of all merchandise sold comes from either Real Madrid or FC Barcelona.[57] Twenty-two of the seventy-two Football League clubs that rank below England's Premier League effectively declared bankruptcy at some point between 2000 and 2006.[58] In contrast, teams in England's Premier League share in a four-year $2.85 billion contract with British Sky Broadcasting Group PLC that expires in 2013.[59] Until recently, teams in Italy's Serie A did not even share revenue with each other. As a result, Juventus and AC Milan had television revenues 20 times greater than smaller Serie A clubs. A new revenue sharing agreement does little to correct this imbalance. The five dominant teams (Juventus, AC Milan, Inter Milan, Roma, and Napoli) succeeded in basing much of the sharing formula on the number of fans a team has. Because these five teams have so many fans, they will continue to receive the lion's share of revenue.[60]

Profit-Maximization in Soccer

As we saw earlier in this chapter, profit-maximization is one of several possible motivations for a team owner in North America. The same can be said for European soccer teams. The Russian oligarch Roman Abramovich probably did not have profits on his mind when he bought a controlling interest in Chelsea of England's Premier League. His motivation was probably more in line with Mark Cuban's reasons for owning the Dallas Mavericks, as seen by Chelsea's Champion's League victory in 2012.

Broad social forces have also limited profit seeking by soccer team owners. In England, the limits were remnants of the social hierarchy that surrounded the origins of the sport. As recently as 1982, the Football League, which then oversaw the four top divisions of soccer in England, prohibited teams from paying salaries

---

[56]Dan Bigman, "The World's Most Valuable Soccer Teams," *Forbes,* at http://www.forbes.com/2011/04/20/worlds-most-valuable-soccer-teams_slide.html, viewed April 5, 2012.

[57]Yahoo! Sport, "Ligue 1—France Fourth in Merchandise Sales," (2011).

[58]Umberto Lago, Rob Simmons, and Stefan Szymanski, "The Financial Crisis in European Football," *Journal of Sports Economics,* vol. 7, no. 1 (February 2006), pp. 3–12.

[59]Aaron O. Patrick and Dana Cimilluca, "English Soccer's Morning After," *Wall Street Journal* June 5, 2009, at http://online.wsj.com/article/SB124346762522860417.html.

[60]SoccerEx, "Peace at Last as Serie A Clubs Agree Revenue Sharing Deal," *SoccerEx Business Daily,* copyright 2009–2012, at http://www.soccerex.com/industry-news/peace-at-last-as-serie-a-clubs-agree-revenue-sharing-deal/, viewed April 5, 2012

to club directors.[61] Thus, the business practices of English soccer teams have only recently begun to resemble those of North American teams. One example of the odd decisions that resulted from the lack of professional management came in 1967, when what is now the Premier League "rejected a BBC proposal of a million pounds for live broadcast of championship matches."[62] This is tantamount to the NFL's refusing to allow the networks to broadcast the Super Bowl.

In some countries, outside authorities limit the activities of teams. In France, the national soccer association strictly limits the teams' ability to borrow and spend. In Germany, the fact that loans must be personally guaranteed by team officials constrains the amount that teams borrow.[63] Both sets of limitations have restricted the ability of teams to obtain top-flight players, but they have also kept teams from overextending themselves financially.

The greater role of government in European economies further restricted team profits by limiting broadcast revenue. Unlike the United States, European countries have only recently opened the airwaves to private broadcasters. With leagues facing a monopsonistic buyer of broadcast rights, soccer broadcasts and broadcast revenues lagged badly behind those of the North American sports. For example, in the 1970s, when television had already become a dominant economic force for North American teams, teams in the top division of French soccer still derived over 80 percent of their revenue from ticket sales.[64]

With the growth of private TV stations, particularly via cable, television revenue has played an increasingly important role in the finances of European soccer teams. Today, French teams in Ligue 1 derive over 50 percent of their revenues from television. The same can be said for leagues in England, Italy, Germany, and Spain.[65] Aware of the value of integrating the game with the broadcast of the game, large cable companies have come to hold increasing stakes in teams themselves. Silvio Berlusconi's purchase of AC Milan through his broadcast company, Fininvest, is only one of many prominent cable broadcasters to invest in soccer teams.

The Impact of Promotion and Relegation

Unlike MLB, the NBA, the NFL, or the NHL, membership in a typical soccer league is not fixed. Each year, the three worst teams in most soccer leagues are relegated to a lower division, while the three best teams in the next division are promoted to a higher one. Imagine baseball's Colorado Rockies' being sent down to the International League and replaced in the National League by the Columbus Clippers, and you have an idea of what promotion and relegation can do.

---

[61]Stefan Szymanski and Andrew Zimbalist, *National Pastime* (2005), p. 132.

[62]Wladimir Andreff and Paul D. Staudohar, "European and US Sports Business Models," in *Transatlantic Sport*, edited by Carlos Pestana Barros, Muradali Ibrahimo, and Stefan Szymanski (Cheltenham, U.K.: Edward Elgar, 2002), p. 25.

[63]Umberto Lago et al. "The Financial Crisis in European Football," (2006), p. 8.

[64]Wladimir Andreff and Paul Staudoher, "European and US Sports Business Models," (2002), p. 25.

[65]Stefan Szymanski and Andrew Zimbalist, *National Pastime* (2005), p. 160.

The fact that a team could move from one league to another and back again greatly complicates the structure of and relationship between leagues. At minimum, one needs an overall authority to oversee the relationships between the various leagues. Table 3.6 shows the various affiliations that exist in English soccer (other nations have similar structures).

The best European teams have the chance to play in yet another league. Each year, the Union of European Football Associations (UEFA) invites the top teams in each country to play in the Champions League, an elite group of 32 teams to determine the European Champion.[66] The teams earn substantial rewards if they advance far in the Champions League playoffs. According to UEFA, the 32 clubs in the Champions League in 2010–2011 will share almost $1 billion, with FC Barcelona, the winning club, receiving almost $67 million.[67]

Finally, continental organizations such as UEFA answer to the Federation International de Football Association (FIFA). FIFA is best known for the World Cup championship it stages every four years. In the World Cup competition, players return from their club teams to their home countries to compete as a nation.

One last source of revenue for soccer teams stems from the open system of relegation and promotion, and explains how top Czech or Argentinean players wind up playing for Italian or Spanish teams. Many soccer teams keep themselves financially afloat by developing talented young players and then selling their rights to wealthier teams. A wealthy team such as Manchester United might purchase the rights to players from small "provincial" English teams, from teams from relatively poor countries such as Ukraine or Brazil, and from financially conservative teams such as Olympique Lyonnais in France's Ligue 1. This practice is more acceptable in an open system of promotion and relegation than in a fixed, closed system because teams face a natural limit to the sales they are willing to make. If a relatively small team, such as Stoke City, sells too many of its players, it will find itself relegated to a lesser league with a subsequent reduction in

TABLE 3.7   Organizational Structure of English Soccer

Organization	Jurisdiction
Premier League	20 Best teams
Football League	72 Teams in next 3 leagues
Football Association	500 + Teams in all leagues
UEFA	Football clubs throughout Europe
Champions League	32 best football clubs in UEFA
FIFA	Football clubs worldwide

---

[66]This happens on each continent. For example, in South America the Confederacion Sudamericana de Futbol (CONMEBOL) stages the Copa Toyota Libertadores.

[67]UEFA, "Champions League Financial Distribution," *Management*, August 16, 2011, at http://www.uefa.com/uefa/management/finance/news/newsid=1661038.html.

revenues. A team in a closed system faces no such disciplinary force. Thus MLB teams from the 1915 Philadelphia Athletics to the 1996 Florida Marlins have held periodic "fire sales" in which they auctioned off all their best players.

The Financial Dangers of an Open System

Promotion brings a huge reward to teams that advance to England's Premier League while relegation brings a huge penalty. This winner-take-all (or at least winner-take-most) structure provides a strong incentive for teams on the verge of promotion or relegation to invest heavily in players who will ensure promotion or stave off relegation. If this effort fails, a team can find itself with a bloated payroll and diminished revenues.

Elite teams also face pressure to invest heavily in players to ensure inclusion in the Champions League. The dangers of spending heavily can be seen in the sad case of Leeds United (a team particularly close to one coauthor's heart). In the late 1990s the team's management spent heavily in an effort to win the European Championship. However, Leeds lost in the 2001 semifinals, costing it about $18 million in lost revenue. Worse yet, Leeds failed to qualify for the Champions League the next season. With revenues far below expectations, the team had no choice but to sell off many of its high-price players. By 2005, the team had been relegated from the Premier League.[68] As of 2012, Leeds remains in the Championship League, just below the Premier League but with no immediate prospect of returning to its former glory.

The Single-Entity Ownership Model

All of the leagues we have discussed so far have one thing in common: They operate based on what is known as a franchise model. Each team is owned by a different individual, group, or corporation and is free to pursue its own goals, within limits imposed by the league. The teams also make all of their own player personnel decisions, such as whom to draft, whom to retain, and whom to dismiss. Although this model of ownership is popular, especially among long-established sports, some of the newer leagues in sports that do not have large followings have adopted a different ownership model: the single-entity league.

In a single-entity league, investors purchase a share of the league itself rather than an individual team or share of a team. All operations of the league, including the allocation of players to teams, are made by the central league offices.[69] This includes negotiation of player contracts, marketing and advertising decisions, and other expenditures. The advantage of this structure is the ability to manage costs across all teams—eliminating disparities between large markets and small markets.[70]

---

[68]See Stefan Szymanski and Andrew Zimbalist, *National Pastime* (2005), p. 139.

[69]Roger G. Noll, "The Organization of Sports Leagues," *Oxford Review of Economic Policy,* vol. 19, no. 4 (Winter 2003), p. 530.

[70]Tripp Mickle and Terry Lefton, "Several Leagues Later, Debate on Single Entity Model Still Lively," *Street and Smith's Sports Business Journal,* August 4, 2008, at http://www.sportsbusinessjournal.com/index.cfm?fuseaction=article.printArticle&articleId=59720, viewed June 8, 2009.

The challenge for single-entity leagues is to cater to demand differences across local markets. The advantage of the franchise system is that individual team owners can make decisions that they believe are best for their own team rather than have to bow to a single decision that may be good for some teams, but not for others.

Some leagues are transitioning from the single-entity model to a franchise model, such as MLS and the WNBA. Thus, while it seems clear that established leagues in well-known sports prefer the franchise model, it appears that there is no single answer as to which league structure is best for emerging sports.

BIOGRAPHICAL SKETCH

Bill Veeck

People need people (who else is there to take advantage of?)

—*Bill Veeck*[1]

 Many owners have won more games than Bill Veeck did with the Cleveland Indians (1946–1949), St. Louis Browns (1951–1953), and Chicago White Sox (which he owned twice, 1959–1961 and 1975–1980). It is safe to say, however, that no owner in the history of the game had nearly as much fun. Veeck was literally born into baseball—his father was president of the Chicago Cubs—and he never left. In the 1920s, young Bill helped plant the ivy that now covers the wall at Wrigley Field.

A self-described hustler, Veeck was a showman *nonpareil* who gave baseball such attractions as bat day and the exploding scoreboard, and such disasters as "disco demolition night," at which a sellout Chicago crowd ran amok after thousands of disco records were blown up. Veeck also proposed many innovations that baseball adopted only after he had passed from the scene. In his 1969 memoir, *The Hustler's Handbook*, for example, Veeck proposed using the scoreboard to do a variety of things—to review disputed plays or to inform the fans about the type and speed of pitch that had just been thrown—that teams took decades to implement.

Bill Veeck had an innate sense of how the market and social justice come together. Between 1947 and 1964, only two American League teams other than the New York Yankees—the Cleveland Indians and the Chicago White Sox—won pennants, and only one won a World Series. Veeck was the owner of the Cleveland Indians when they won the 1948 World Series, and he built the team that appeared in the 1954 World Series. He was later the owner of the Chicago White Sox when they made it to the 1959 World Series, their first appearance since the Black Sox scandal of 1919. It was no coincidence that these teams were among the leaders in integrating the American League. Veeck brought Larry Doby to the Indians in 1947, a few weeks after Jackie Robinson broke the color line with the Brooklyn Dodgers. Four years earlier, Veeck had tried

(Continued)

(Continued)

to integrate baseball when he sought to buy the sad sack Phillies, one of the worst and least popular teams in baseball, and stock the team with players from the Negro Leagues. Veeck had long opposed baseball's color line on moral grounds, but he also felt that integrating the game made good business sense. He thought that bringing in star players from the Negro Leagues would build a talented, exciting team that fans would want to see. According to Veeck, MLB Commissioner Kenesaw Mountain Landis stepped in at the last minute and found another buyer for the Phillies, preventing his purchase of the team.

Veeck also showed a sense of fairness as an outspoken critic of baseball's reserve clause, which effectively bound a player to a team for life. He was the only owner to testify against the reserve clause in Curt Flood's lawsuit against baseball in the 1970s.[2]

Veeck's unorthodox beliefs and promotions did little to endear him to the other owners. They went so far as to block his attempt to move the Browns, a poor relation of the more popular Cardinals, from St. Louis to Baltimore, allowing the move only after Veeck had sold the team. In an attempt to boost interest in his team, Veeck tried such stunts as sending 3'7" Eddie Gaedel to the plate as a pinch hitter (he walked) and holding "You Be the Manager Day," in which fans were given the opportunity to make substitutions and determine strategy. Predictably, some owners attempted to block Veeck's attempt to get back into baseball in the 1970s.

Veeck's last go-round as an owner—his second stint with the Chicago White Sox—was not as successful as his previous efforts. The advent of free agency and the growing importance of TV and venue revenue did not fit his limited means and hustler mentality. He was forced to sell the team after seven years. Fortunately, Bill's son Michael, the part-owner of several minor league teams, has kept the Veeck legacy alive. As owner of the St. Paul Saints, Michael Veeck staged such stunts as "Mime-O-Vision," in which mimes acted out the action on the field as a sort of living instant replay. The fans responded by pelting the mimes with hot dogs, a travesty trumpeted by headlines in all the local papers. Michael's father would have been proud.

[1]Bill Veeck, *The Hustler's Handbook* (Durham, N.C.: Baseball America Classic Books, 1996), p. 196.
[2] We discuss Flood's lawsuit in Chapter 4 and analyze the reserve clause in Chapter 8.

Sources: Bill Veeck, *The Hustler's Handbook* (Durham, N.C.: Baseball America Classic Books, 1996); and John Helyar, *Lords of the Realm* (New York: Ballantine Books, 1994).

Summary

Unlike most firms, sports teams do not necessarily maximize profit. Pursuing a different goal, such as maximizing wins, can lead to very different behavior by a team, but even if teams do not maximize their profits, they cannot afford to ignore them entirely. Teams derive their revenue from ticket sales, the sale of broadcast rights, licensing income, other venue-related income, and the transfer of funds from other teams. The degree to which revenues are shared among teams varies from league to league, with the greatest sharing occurring in the NFL.

In the sports industry, most sources of cost are fixed over the period of a single season. Primary sources of costs are player salaries, stadium leases, and administrative costs. In the NHL and MLB, subsidies to minor league affiliates for player development also add significantly to team total cost.

Leagues regulate the behavior of teams on the field and off it. Financially, leagues attempt to keep revenue imbalances in check and control costs. In some cases, it is more useful to view the league as the monopoly and teams as producers of a joint product.

European soccer teams face a very different business climate than do North American sports teams. While some teams are highly profitable, most struggle financially. This is partly due to the fact that soccer has only recently been regarded as a business and partly due to the relegation and promotion system. Some new leagues, such as MLS, have gone to a single-entity system in which the league directly controls the individual teams.

Discussion Questions

1. Are the New York Yankees correct when they claim that revenue sharing simply rewards teams that do not try to win?
2. Would professional leagues behave differently if teams had corporate affiliation (e.g., the IBM Lions) rather than city or state affiliation?
3. Has the NFL been foolish to allow Los Angeles to go so long without a team?
4. Should the NBA or NHL switch to a promotion and relegation system?
5. If you were CEO of a company, would you spend $10 million per year to put your company's name on a stadium?

Problems

3.1. Suppose that you are the owner of a professional baseball team in a major city, and MLB allows a second team to locate in your city. On what basis should you be compensated?
3.2. Draw a graph that shows the demand for seats at an NFL stadium. Show how demand for attendance at a given game would be affected if:
   a. The prices of parking and food at the games increase.
   b. Televised games switch from free TV to pay-per-view only.
   c. A new league forms with a team that plays nearby.
   d. The quality of the team decreases dramatically.
   e. The length of the season is increased.
3.3. True or false; explain your answer: "If all teams are of equal quality, it doesn't matter whether they share gate receipts or not—revenue will remain unchanged."
3.4. Some researchers argue that revenue sharing is like socialism in that it removes the incentive to outperform rivals. Do you agree with this statement? Why or why not?
3.5. Suppose that each team in a league has a demand curve for generic advertising (a league-wide, non-team–specific campaign) equal to $Q = 1,000 - 5p$. If there are 20 teams in the league, and ads cost $175 each, how many ads will the teams want to purchase as a group?

3.6. Use the marginal revenue and marginal cost curves from the economics of clubs to explain why the NFL has 32 teams, while Bundesliga-1, the top German soccer league, has only 20 teams.

3.7. Suppose that most of the teams in a given league are owned by individuals, while two are owned by corporations. If the profits of the individually owned teams rise, but that of the corporate-owned teams remains flat, is it fair to say that this is an inferior ownership structure? Why or why not?

3.8. Suppose an owner pays $500 million to purchase a hockey team that earns operating profits of $50 million per year. The new owner claims that $200 million of this price is for the players, which he can depreciate using straight-line depreciation in five years. If the team pays corporate profit taxes of 40 percent, how much does the depreciation of the players save the owner?

3.9. How can the San Diego Padres, one of the weakest teams in the National League from a wins-losses perspective, be one of the most profitable?

3.10. Why might a league favor a single-entity ownership model? Explain the differences in the risks and rewards of such a system compared to a franchise owner system.

CHAPTER 4

Monopoly and Antitrust

Gentlemen, we have the only legal monopoly in the country,
and we're [messing] it up.

—ATLANTA BRAVES OWNER, TED TURNER[1]

INTRODUCTION

Major League Baseball's National League is the oldest professional sports league in the United States.[2] Founded in 1876, it rested on two basic principles:

1. Member clubs had an exclusive right to their home territory.
2. A reserve system bound players to member clubs for as long as the team wanted them.

These principles proved so profitable that many succeeding North American sports leagues adopted them for themselves, often word for word. One need not look far to see why the leagues were so successful. The principle of "territorial rights" gave teams **monopoly power** in their host cities, as it precluded the entry of competing teams. The reserve system kept owners from bidding up salaries to lure away a rival team's players, giving each team **monopsony power** over its players. Baseball and all subsequent sports owe much of their early success to these two barriers. However, team success often came at the expense of the players whom the teams employed, the fans whom they entertained, and the cities where they played.

---

[1]John Helyar, *Lords of the Realm* (New York: Villard Books, 1994), p. 268.
[2]The fact that it predates the American League by about 25 years has led to its nickname, "the senior circuit."

LEARNING OBJECTIVES

After reading this chapter, you will be able to:

- Identify and illustrate the social costs of monopoly power.

- Analyze how teams apply pricing strategies that result in increased profits and reduced consumer well-being.

- Describe the circumstances under which society may be better off with a monopoly than a large number of competing firms.

- Recognize the importance of entry barriers for monopoly sports teams and leagues.

- Explain the importance of U.S. antitrust law and the significance of Major League Baseball's exemption to these laws.

- Learn how the NCAA became a cartel, and why it was sued by its own members.

- Use game theory and the concept of the prisoners' dilemma to show how seemingly rational actions by two competing firms can lead to outcomes that neither firm wants.

4.1 WHAT'S WRONG WITH MONOPOLY?

As we saw in Chapter 2, marginal revenue is less than price for a monopoly. To maximize profits, monopolies produce output where marginal revenue equals marginal cost, whereas perfectly competitive firms set price equal to marginal cost. Figure 4.1 illustrates the profit-maximizing attendance for a monopoly team with a marginal cost curve that coincides with the horizontal axis, and downward-sloping demand and marginal revenue curves. A competitive industry would sell Q_c tickets, where price equals marginal cost.[3] The NFL's market power allows it to restrict output to Q_m, charging a higher price ($20 in this case) and selling fewer tickets.

Monopolists and Deadweight Loss

Most noneconomists dislike monopolies because of the high prices they charge. High prices, however, are a two-edged sword. They may hurt the consumers who have to pay them, but they benefit the stockholders, employees, and other stakeholders in the firms that receive them. In Figure 4.1, consumers pay an amount equal to the area *EFBG* because they pay a price per unit equal to segment *EF* on *EG* units of output. While the price of $20 exceeds the competitive price (zero in this example), society—which consists of both consumers and producers—is not necessarily worse off, because producers receive *EFBG* more than if they charged

---

[3]Strictly speaking, the industry supply curve is the horizontal sum of all the individual marginal cost curves. For our purposes here, we ignore any complication raised by capacity constraints.

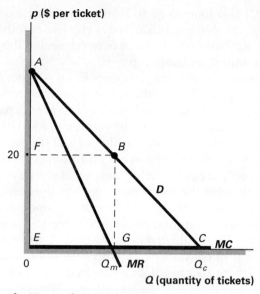

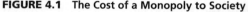

FIGURE 4.1 The Cost of a Monopoly to Society

When a firm charges the monopoly price of $20, it creates a deadweight loss equal to area *BCG*. Consumer surplus falls from *ACE* under competitive pricing to *ABF*.

the competitive price. Thus, higher prices reshuffle income without changing the total amount of income for society. The higher price simply transfers money from one pocket (the consumer's) to another (the monopolist's). Because one cannot say whether this transfer helps producers more than it hurts consumers, economists treat it as bringing no overall change in society's well-being.

Economists are much more concerned about the impact of the decline in output that accompanies monopoly. In particular, they worry about how monopoly affects the sum of consumer surplus and producer surplus. Consumer surplus stems from the fact that, despite our protestations to the contrary, we are never satisfied "getting exactly what we paid for." In fact, if all we got out of an item was what we paid for it, we would be just as happy without it.[4] **Consumer surplus** is the net value that flows to consumers because not all consumers are charged the maximum that they are willing to pay. **Producer surplus** is the net value that flows to producers because not all units are sold for the minimum that the producer would accept to sell them. Measuring consumer surplus is quite easy in theory. It is equal to the area that lies under the demand curve and above the price up to the last unit sold. In Figure 4.1, at a price of $20, consumer surplus is the area *ABF*.

To see how consumer surplus arises, consider the case of four football fans. Debbie loves the Carolina Panthers and is willing and able to pay $40 for a ticket

[4]Producer surplus is the extra revenue that a firm receives beyond what it requires to sell a given level of output. It is related to—but not identical to—profit. Economists calculate producer surplus as the area between the supply (or marginal cost) curve and the market price.

to see them play. Bill also likes to go to Panther games, though not as much as Debbie; he is willing and able to pay $20. Jeff is still less enthusiastic; he is willing and able to pay $10. Kathleen is indifferent between seeing the Panthers play and staying home; she is willing and able to pay $0.

If consumers must pay the competitive price of $0 from Figure 4.1, all four consumers buy tickets to see the Panthers, but none of them feels the same way about his or her purchase. Since Debbie is willing and able to pay $40 for the ticket but pays $0, she gets a bonus—or consumer surplus—of $40 (the vertical segment *YY* in Figure 4.2). Similarly, Bill has a surplus of $20 (the vertical segment *ZZ*), Jeff has a surplus of $10 (the segment *WW*), and Kathleen has no surplus whatever. Kathleen is the only consumer who "gets what she pays for." She is willing and able to pay exactly what the Panthers charge her. Purchasing the ticket leaves her no better off—and no worse off—than before. Economists refer to a person in Kathleen's position as a **marginal consumer**, since she is indifferent between buying and not buying. She could just as easily pass up the ticket as buy it.

In fact, thousands of consumers, all with their own desires and abilities to pay, want Panthers tickets. As a result, there are hundreds or thousands of vertical segments indicating consumer surplus for the fans who buy tickets. Eventually, these segments fill up the triangle formed by the demand curve and the horizontal line representing the market price (the horizontal axis in Figure 4.2).

Now let us consider the monopoly price of $20. If the Panthers charged $20, Kathleen would suffer a loss if she bought the ticket because she would pay $20

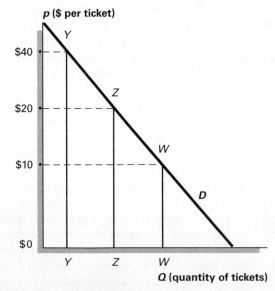

FIGURE 4.2 **Consumer Surplus for Individual Consumers**
Consumer surplus for each consumer is the difference between the price ($0 in this example) and the maximum that they would be willing to pay. Debbie is willing to pay $40 to see the game, and so receives a consumer surplus of $40. Kathleen, who values the game at $0, receives no surplus.

more than she was willing and able to pay. As a result, she no longer buys the ticket. Jeff, too, would suffer a loss and would not buy the ticket. Bill would now be the marginal consumer, because he pays exactly what the ticket is worth to him. Only Debbie would enjoy a consumer surplus, though her surplus is much smaller than it had been ($20 instead of $40). More generally, when a monopoly serves the market, consumers buy fewer tickets, and consumer surplus shrinks. In terms of Figure 4.1, consumer surplus would be *ACE* if the market for tickets were perfectly competitive. Because the equilibrium price in this example is zero, consumer surplus is the entire area under the demand curve. When the same market is a monopoly, consumers pay an amount equal to *EFBG*. As a result, consumer surplus shrinks to *ABF*. In addition to the rectangle *EFBG*, consumers also lose the area of the triangle *BCG* because they buy less than before. This loss is not offset by gains elsewhere. Economists call losses that do not have offsetting gains elsewhere in the economy **deadweight losses**. The deadweight loss *BCG* that accompanies monopoly reduces the well-being of society.

Some economists, in particular those who belong to a particular school of thought known as **public choice**, believe that the social costs of monopoly exceed the deadweight loss of triangle *BCG* in Figure 4.1. These economists regard the expenditure the monopolist makes to obtain and protect its market position—behavior they call **rent seeking**—as an unproductive expenditure that adds to society's deadweight loss. They would claim, for example, that the $1.6 million that the NFL spent lobbying Congress in 2011 represented an effort by football to protect its monopoly power.[5] As such, it imposed an additional cost on society, since that money could have been spent in more productive ways. In the limit, the monopolist would be willing to spend up to the total gains from its monopoly position, the area of the rectangle *EFBG*.[6] As a result, the total cost to society could be as large as the original deadweight loss plus the revenue of the monopolist (*BCG* + *EFBG*).

Do Monopolies Always Charge Monopoly Prices?

Figure 4.1 shows that a monopoly team maximizes profit by setting output where the *MR* curve crosses the horizontal axis (point *G*, where *MC* = 0). If *MC* > 0, then the monopolist operates to the left of *G*, where *MR* > 0. Because we never see *MC* < 0, monopolists should not set output higher than *G*. It is not hard to show that *MR* = 0 at the level of output where the price elasticity of demand equals −1.[7]

[5]"Center for Responsive Politics. Annual Lobbying by the National Football League," *OpenSecrets.org*, March 26, 2012, at http://www.opensecrets.org/lobby/clientsum.php?id=D000027847&year=2011.

[6]See, for example, Richard Posner, "The Social Costs of Monopoly and Regulation," *Journal of Political Economy*, vol. 83, no. 4 (August 1975), pp. 807–827; Robert Tollison, "Rent Seeking," in *Perspectives on Public Choice: A Handbook*, ed. by Dennis Mueller (Cambridge, U.K.: Cambridge University Press, 1997); Associated Press, "Commissioner Spent $1.2 Million on Lobbying in 2001," *ESPN.com*, at http://www.espn.com, viewed May 15, 2002.

[7]This is because $MR = P \times (1 + 1/\varepsilon_D)$, where ε_D is the price elasticity of demand.

Because the demand curve becomes less and less elastic as we move down and to the right, we can say that a monopolist should not operate where $0 > \varepsilon_D > -1$. That is, it should never operate on the inelastic part of the demand curve. Intriguingly, economists have found that sports teams often operate in that part of the demand curve. This seems to imply that monopolists set their price too low for them to maximize profit.[8] How could this be?

Research by David Berri and Anthony Krautmann, among others, has found that this seemingly irrational strategy may maximize profit if we recognize that stadium concessions (drinks, food, and souvenirs) are complements for tickets since consumers can purchase them only in the stadium.[9] In Figure 4.1, the optimal price for a team that earns no revenue from concessions is $20. If the firm does receive concession revenue, it should set a lower price so that more people enter the stadium and buy concessions. While the team sacrifices some revenue from attendance, the revenue it earns on concessions more than makes up for this loss.

Promotion, Relegation, and Monopoly Power

In Chapter 3, we saw that the promotion and relegation system can cause soccer teams to behave differently from teams in the North American leagues. Perhaps the most important difference lies in the consequences of an open league for monopoly power. A closed league can create local monopoly power because it is limited to a fixed set of teams. New teams can enter the league, and existing teams can enter a new market only with the permission of the existing teams.[10]

An open league has no such power. New teams can enter a low league and be promoted to better leagues until they compete at the highest level. Thus, while only the Giants and Jets are allowed to play the New York metropolitan area by the NFL, 14 members of the Football League play in the London metropolitan area. Of these, six teams (Arsenal, Chelsea, Fulham, Tottenham Hotspur, and Queens Park) played in the Premier League in 2011–2012. There is, moreover, no guarantee that this number could not rise even higher in the years ahead. Similarly, poor business or personnel decisions have caused some major metropolitan areas—such

[8]See, for example, Roger Noll, "Attendance and Price Setting," in *Government and the Sports Business*, ed. by Roger Noll (Washington, D.C.: Brookings Institution, 1974); Rodney Fort and Robert Rosenman, "Streak Management," in *Sports Economic: Current Research*, ed. by John Fizel, Elizabeth Gustafson, and Lawrence Hadley (Westport, Conn.: Praeger, 1999); and Jason Winfree, Jill McCluskey, Ron Mittelhammer, and Rodney Fort, "Location and Attendance in Major League Baseball," *Applied Economics*, vol. 36, no. 19 (October 2004), pp. 2117–2124.

[9]For a discussion of the previous literature on pricing decisions related to demand elasticity as well as the empirical results described here, see: Anthony C. Krautmann and David J. Berri, "Can We Find It in the Concessions: Understanding Price Elasticity in Professional Sports," *Journal of Sports Economics*, vol. 8, no. 2 (May 2007), pp. 183–191.

[10]For a good discussion of open vs. closed leagues, see Roger G. Noll, "The Organization of Sports Leagues," *Oxford Review of Economic Policy*, vol. 19, no. 4 (Winter 2003), pp. 530–551.

as Leeds or Bristol, England—to go without a franchise in the top professional league. With no way to regulate entry or exit of competitors, it is very difficult for teams in open leagues to exercise local monopoly power.

4.2 STRATEGIC PRICING AND PRICE DISCRIMINATION

We know from Chapter 2 that monopolies have market power (the ability to set or control price). Unlike teams in open leagues, teams in closed leagues have substantial market power, which stems from a lack of competition in their home markets. In this section, we describe ways in which a monopolist can increase its profits further by utilizing pricing strategies that are more sophisticated than a single price for all games.

Variable and Dynamic Ticket Pricing

For a Red Sox fan, there is nothing like going to a game when the Yankees come to town. In the NHL, Chicago Blackhawk fans circle the date on the calendar when the always good (and popular) Red Wings visit. These are just two examples of what we intuitively know to be true: Some games are much more attractive (at least expected to be more attractive) than others. Recall that the market demand curve is formed by adding the individual demand curves horizontally. When individual fans' desire to attend a game increases, the market demand curve shifts to the right.

The quality of the opponent and the existence of a long-standing rivalry are not the only reasons for differences in demand. Differences may arise from the presence of a star player on the opposing team, promotional events, such as give-aways and fireworks nights, the day of the week, and even the weather.[11] Rather than charge the same price for all games, teams can increase profits if they vary the price of tickets from game to game. **Variable ticket pricing (VTP)** sets ticket prices in accordance with expected demand for a future game. When a team believes that demand for a given game will be lower, it can reduce the price to compensate. Conversely, it can increase the price for a game it believes will be popular. For example, the Buffalo Sabres of the NHL rate their regular season games as platinum, gold, silver, bronze, or value. For the 2011–2012 season, a 200-level club seat for a particular game can range from $240 for a platinum game to $108 for a value game.[12] This increase in price of over 100 percent from the cheapest to most expensive games provides clear evidence that the demand curves for individual games vary substantially.

Some of the factors that affect consumer demand for a specific game, such as the day of the week, are known before the season even begins. Other factors, such as the home team's and opponent's records, may not be known until shortly before

---

[11]Dan Rascher et al., "Variable Ticket Pricing in Major League Baseball," *Journal of Sport Management*, vol. 21, no.3 (2007), pp. 407–437.

[12]Buffalo Sabres, "Tickets: 2011–2012 Individual Game Tickets," 2010, at http://sabres.nhl.com/club/page.htm?id=70166, viewed March 16, 2012.

the game. Many MLB teams, such as the San Francisco Giants, St. Louis Cardinals, and San Diego Padres, have taken the strategy of adjusting ticket prices a step further by adjusting the prices of unsold tickets during the course of the season. The Pittsburgh Pirates also adjust the ticket prices of 1,400 bleacher seats on a daily basis beginning 10 days before the day of the game.[13] This process, known as **Dynamic Ticket Pricing (DTP)**, allows the team to capture additional revenue based on individual game characteristics that are unknown at the start of the season, such as a matchup of All-Star pitchers, which might produce exceptionally high demand, or a game against a noncontender on a chilly weekday evening. For example, in 2009, the San Francisco Giants played a series against the New York Mets. For the first game, played on a cold Thursday night, upper deck prices were $1 off the usual $10 and bleacher seats were $2 off the usual $17. The next night, however, a weekend game with the Giants' best pitcher on the mound, those same seats went for $19 and $27. On Sunday, which featured a bobblehead doll give-away, the Giants raised the price of a bleacher seat to $23. Some of these price adjustments were made shortly before game day.[14] Variable and dynamic ticket pricing schemes appear to be gaining momentum across all professional sports. According to Patrick Rishe of *Forbes Magazine*, more than 30 teams in the NHL, MLS, MLB, and NBA utilize Dynamic Ticket Pricing and have increased revenue substantially because of it.[15]

The NFL does not make use of variable ticket pricing, perhaps because, with so few home games, relatively few empty seats exist for any given game, regardless of opponent. Stephen Jones, Chief Operating Officer of the Dallas Cowboys, cited league parity and timing as reasons why variable ticket pricing would be difficult in the NFL given that teams must finalize ticket prices long before they finalize roster moves that may alter team quality.[16]

From the team's perspective, differences in demand across games represent an opportunity to increase profits. When games are less popular, the team has an incentive to lower the price. With the marginal cost of attendance essentially zero, costs are about the same no matter how many fans attend. But, up to a point, revenues increase as more fans buy tickets at lower prices. We can see the impact of variable versus constant pricing in Figure 4.3. As usual, we assume that marginal cost is zero up to the point of stadium capacity (10,000). Demand for a less popular game is represented by D_0, and demand for a more popular game is shown as D_1. If the team uses a variable pricing strategy, it will set marginal revenue equal to marginal cost for each game ($MC = MR_0$ and $MC = MR_1$),

---

[13]Pirates Press release, *Pirates to Introduce Dynamic Ticket Pricing for 2012 Season*, at http://pittsburgh.pirates.mlb.com/news/article.jsp?ymd=20111216&content_id=26182894&vkey=pr_pit&c_id=pit, viewed May 8, 2012.

[14]Ken Belson, "Tickets Cost Too Much? Check Back Tomorrow," *The New York Times*, May 18, 2009. p. D2.

[15]Patrick Rishe, "Dynamic Pricing: The Future of Ticket Pricing in Sports." *Forbes.com*, January 6, 1012, viewed March 16, 2012.

[16]Darren Rovell, "Sports Fans Feel Pinch in Seat (Prices)," June 21, 2002, at http://espn.go.com/sports business/s/2002/0621/1397693.html, viewed June 10, 2009.

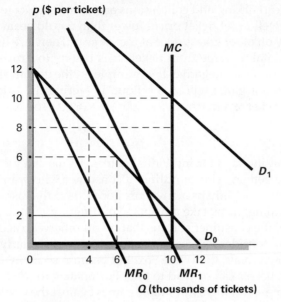

FIGURE 4.3   Variable Ticket Pricing

A team facing differential demand for its games (D_0 and D_1) maximizes profits by charging $10 per seat for the more popular game and $6 per seat for the less popular game, as opposed to a single price of $8 for both games.

resulting in prices of $6 and $10, respectively. The team will sell out the popular game and sell 6,000 tickets to the less popular game. Total revenue for the two games is $136,000. The graph indicates that if the team tried to sell tickets to the less popular game for $10, most of the seats would go unfilled. Similarly, if the team charged only $6 for the popular game, it would sell the same number of tickets as at the higher price, but make 40 percent less in revenue. Suppose that instead of charging two prices, the team charged a single intermediate price, such as $8, for both games. We can easily show that such a strategy results in a price that is too high for the unpopular game and too low for the popular game.[17] At a price of $8, the more popular game still sells out, but revenue falls from $100,000 to $80,000; for the less popular game, attendance falls to 4,000, resulting in revenue of just $32,000. Thus, overall revenue from charging a single price of $8 is $112,000, $24,000 less than the two-price scheme. This analysis is far from a theoretical abstraction. Barry Kahn, CEO of Qcue, a firm that provides computer software that allows teams to run dynamic pricing schemes, says that teams using this strategy have increased revenue by an average of 30 percent for high-demand games and 5–10 percent for low-demand games.[18]

With these advanced pricing strategies, teams maximize profit by maximizing ticket revenue. As Dan Rascher et al. note, however, there are other revenue

---

[17]The equation for D_0 is $Q = 12 - P$. The equation for D_1 is $Q = 20 - P$.
[18]Patrick Rishe, "Dynamic Pricing" (2012).

streams to consider. Parking and concessions are complements to tickets. As such, the team may do well to set ticket prices lower than would seem optimal because fans spend money on other goods once at the game.[19] There are limits to this strategy, however, as total revenue from ticket sales begins to drop off quickly once marginal revenue becomes negative. For example, in the graph, at a price of $2 per ticket the less popular game will be a sellout. Lowering the price from $6 to $2, however, reduces ticket revenue from $36,000 ($6 × 6,000) to $20,000 ($2 × 10,000).

Bundling

In addition to charging fans for individual games, teams can increase revenue by bundling games together. With **bundling**, a consumer who wants to buy good A must also buy good B (or perhaps many more goods, as in the case of season tickets). With product bundling, firms take advantage of differing demand across products to capture some of the consumer surplus that might otherwise accrue to buyers. To illustrate this point, consider Phil a huge Cubs fan who particularly likes to see them play their cross-town rivals, the White Sox. But because so many other Chicagoans feel the same way, tickets can be hard to find. Fortunately for Phil he can get tickets to a White Sox game—and highly desirable games against the Cardinals and Detroit Tigers as well—by purchasing a Cubs six-game pack. The six-game pack allows Phil to buy tickets to the White Sox game as long as he also purchases tickets to five other games, including a Wednesday afternoon game against the Pittsburgh Pirates for which demand is likely much lower than for the White Sox game.[20]

To see how this pricing scheme benefits both Phil and the Cubs, let's assume that a ticket for the White Sox game costs $30. Phil is willing to pay $100 to see a Cubs–White Sox game, but he would only pay $25 to see any other Cubs game. If the tickets were sold separately at the price of $30, he would go to the White Sox game and receive a surplus of $70, but would not buy a ticket to the other games. Suppose now that Phil can see the Cubs–White Sox game only if he buys a six-pack of tickets. Unlike variable ticket pricing, bundling does not rely on setting different prices for each game. Instead, it relies on the large surplus consumers would receive from seeing a specific game. If all tickets are sold at the regular price but must be purchased in a group of six, tickets to the hypothetical six-game set cost $180 [6 × $30]. Phil values the six tickets at $225 ($100 for the White Sox game and $25 for the other five games). At a price of $180, he is better off making the purchase because he still receives a surplus of $45. Even though he experiences a loss of $5 on the five less-popular games, the loss is more than offset by the surplus he receives from seeing the White Sox game. The Cubs are better off as well because they sell tickets to six games instead of only one. With the marginal cost of Phil's attendance at these extra games at or close to zero, the Cubs' profits also increase.

[19]Dan Rascher et al., "Variable Ticket Pricing in Major League Baseball," *Journal of Sport Management*, vol. 21, no. 3 (2007), pp. 407–437. They base this analysis on the work of Rodney Fort, "Owner Objectives and Competitive Balance," *Journal of Sports Economics,*" vol. 5, no. 1 (February 2004), pp. 20–32.

[20]Cubs.com, *Six Game Pack*, 2012, at http://chicago.cubs.mlb.com/chc/ticketing/sixpacks.jsp, viewed March 20, 2012.

Price Discrimination and Two-part Pricing

In our discussion of variable ticket pricing, dynamic pricing and bundling, teams used advanced pricing strategies based on differences in the perceived quality of the games by a given consumer. We now move on to a different strategy that relies on teams' identifying differences in willingness to pay *for the same game*.

Recall that in Figure 4.1, a single monopoly price led to a deadweight loss of area *BCG*, and left consumers with a surplus of area *ABF*. We know that consumer surplus is the extra benefit that consumers receive because the firm charges a single profit-maximizing price for all units it sells. Often, firms charge a single price to all consumers because they have no way to determine which consumers are willing to pay more, and consumers have no incentive to reveal their greater willingness to pay. If a monopolist could sort consumers by their willingness and ability to pay and set prices accordingly, it could capture some or even all of the consumer surplus. As we will see, such a pricing strategy also reduces or eliminates the deadweight loss associated with a single monopoly price. Economists call charging different prices to different consumers based on their willingness to pay **price discrimination**. Unlike the common use of the word *discrimination*, which refers to actions based on prejudice, price discrimination has nothing to do with dislike for a particular demographic group. Instead, a firm price discriminates when it charges more to customers who are willing and able to pay more. On the surface, charging a higher price to wealthy customers than to poor consumers sounds like the fair thing to do. We shall see, however, that firms that price discriminate seldom have such altruistic motives and that price discrimination does not leave consumers better off.

PERFECT PRICE DISCRIMINATION   If the Panthers know exactly how much Debbie, Bill, Jeff, and Kathleen are willing and able to pay, they can extract their consumer surplus by charging each person exactly what he or she thinks the ticket is worth. By charging Debbie $40, Bill $20, and Jeff $10, the Panthers turn all their consumers into marginal consumers.[21] All the consumers are now just willing to pay for the tickets because what was once their consumer surplus is now additional profit for the Panthers.

By treating each additional consumer like the marginal consumer, the Panthers no longer charge a lower price to everyone when they want to sell more tickets. The process of charging each consumer the maximum that he or she is willing to pay is known as **perfect price discrimination**. When the Panthers perfectly price discriminate, their marginal revenue is the price of the last, cheapest ticket that they sell. The marginal revenue of selling a ticket to Bill is thus $20, while the marginal revenue of selling a ticket to Jeff is $10. In terms of Figure 4.1, if the Panthers can perfectly price discriminate, their *MR* curve coincides with their demand curve. The Panthers now sell the same number of tickets as a perfectly competitive industry, and total surplus grows to *ACE*. Social

---

[21]Technically, the Panthers would have to charge $39.99, $19.99, and $9.99 to be sure that Debbie, Bill, and Jeff buy tickets. We round off for ease of exposition.

well-being is once again maximized, as the perfectly price-discriminating monopolist acts in an economically efficient manner. Consumers, however, do not receive any of the increase in social well-being. By charging all consumers exactly what the ticket is worth to them, the Panthers claim Debbie and Bill's consumer surplus for themselves. By charging all fans the maximum price they are willing and able to pay, the Panthers capture the entire area *ACE* in Figure 4.1 as revenue.

PERSONAL SEAT LICENSES   As a general rule, firms do not have enough information to extract all the consumer surplus. Few firms know exactly how much each consumer is willing and able to pay for an item. However, firms have other ways to extract at least part of the consumer surplus. One such method is two-part pricing. As its name indicates, **two-part pricing** involves two distinct segments—a fixed component and a variable component that changes with the amount of output the consumer purchases. Personal seat licenses (PSLs) are a form of two-part pricing that has become particularly popular in the NFL. They were first introduced by the Carolina Panthers to help finance the construction of Ericsson Stadium (now Bank of America Stadium) in 1993.[22]

The idea of a PSL is very simple. A person pays a fixed fee for the right to buy season tickets for a given period of time. This allows teams to capture a large portion of the consumer surplus and deadweight loss that ordinarily results from a monopoly. We can think of this strategy as a two-part process. First, the Panthers can eliminate the deadweight loss by charging the competitive price for season tickets and selling the competitive quantity. The lower price and higher quantity restore consumer and producer surplus to their competitive levels. The Panthers then exert their monopoly power by charging a fixed PSL fee that allows them to claim some of the consumer surplus that their fans enjoy. If the Panthers knew exactly how much consumer surplus the typical fan enjoyed, they could charge a PSL fee that extracted almost all of his or her surplus. This would leave the fan just willing to buy the season ticket. Figure 4.4 shows the demand curve for a typical fan (consumer). Instead of charging the monopoly price (p_m), the team can increase profits by utilizing a two-part price. The variable portion of the two-part price is zero, as the Panthers charge the competitive price for the ticket (which is 0 in our simple world where $MC = 0$). The fixed portion of the price is the cost of the PSL. If all fans have the same preferences, as described by the demand curve in Figure 4.4, the team sets the PSL fee equal to the shaded area and consumer surplus falls to nearly zero. The Panthers could thus keep all the benefits of a competitive market for themselves. If consumers do not all have the same preferences, the task of the team is more complicated. A low PSL fee leaves some surplus for high-demand consumers. A high PSL fee leads low-demand consumers to forgo the PSL.[23]

---

[22]The argument that follows is based on Roger Noll and Andrew Zimbalist, "Build the Stadium—Create the Jobs!" in *Sports, Jobs, and Taxes*, ed. by Roger Noll and Andrew Zimbalist (Washington, D.C.: Brookings Institution Press, 1997), pp. 20–25.

[23]For more on the role of PSLs in stadium funding, see for example, Robert Baade and Victor Matheson, "Have Public Finance Principles Been Shut Out of Financing New Stadiums for the NFL?" *Public Finance and Management*, vol. 6, no. 3 (2006), pp. 284–320.

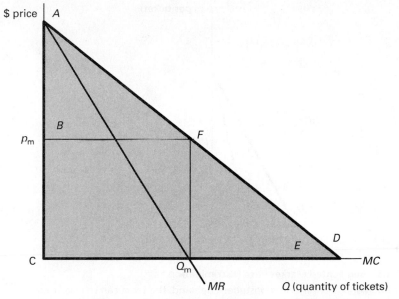

FIGURE 4.4   A Two-Part Price

A two-part price consists of a fixed fee and a per-unit price. In this case, the firm attempts to set the fixed fee equal to the shaded area *ACE*, and the per-unit price is zero. Deadweight loss is eliminated and consumer surplus falls from *BAF* to zero.

QUANTITY DISCOUNTS   Another way for firms to increase profit is to offer a menu of price–quantity combinations and to let consumers choose the combination they most prefer. As with perfect price discrimination, this allows producers to charge prices that reflect the intensity of the consumers' desire. Teams often offer an array of choices based on quantity.

   Quantity discounts take advantage of the team's knowledge that—assuming a given quality of games—fans' marginal utility from consuming a sporting event declines with the quantity of games they attend. While the team does not know exactly what the fan is willing and able to pay for each game, the team knows that the fifth hockey game is worth less than the first and the twenty-fifth is worth less still. Many teams, particularly those with longer seasons, offer a variety of partial- and full-season ticket plans in which the cost per ticket is lower than the cost of buying each ticket individually.

SEGMENTED MARKETS   Sometimes, the Panthers may know nothing about individuals, but they know that some groups are less willing or able to pay. For example, the Panthers may know that students on the whole have less disposable income and as a result are more sensitive to changes in price than are middle-aged adults.[24] If the Panthers can separate the student market from the nonstudent market (e.g., by requiring students to show their university ID cards), then they

---

[24]Senior citizens comprise another group that firms frequently feel is more sensitive to price.

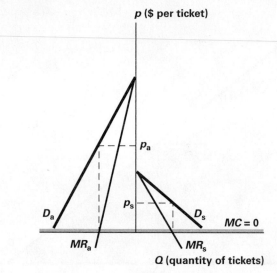

FIGURE 4.5 Segmented Market Price Discrimination

If student demand is lower than nonstudent demand, the team can charge students p_s and charge nonstudents p_a.

can practice third-degree price discrimination by charging a higher price to non-students than to students. **Segmented market (third-degree) price discrimination** occurs when a firm charges different prices for the same good in different segments of a market. Figure 4.5 shows what the Panthers can do if they can separate the demand by adults for Panthers tickets from the demand by students. Again ignoring capacity constraints, if the marginal cost of providing seats is approximately zero, the Panthers will maximize profit when the marginal revenue from selling to students (s) and the marginal revenue from selling to nonstudents (a) both equal zero. Figure 4.5 shows that the $MR_s = MR_a = MC$ rule results in a lower price for students than for adults. In effect, the Panthers maximize profits by charging a lower price to consumers whose demand is more elastic and a higher price to those with less elastic demand.

Monopoly Stood on Its Head: A Brief Introduction to Monopsony

Monopsony is essentially the mirror image of monopoly. Monopolists derive their power from being the only seller and use this power to drive up the price of what they sell. Monopsonists derive their power from being the sole consumer of a good or service and use their power to drive down the price of what they buy.

Until the 1970s, sports leagues held monopsony power through specific language in the standard player contract, called the **reserve clause**. The reserve clause effectively bound players to the team that held their contracts for as long as the teams desired their services. Thus, a player such as Otto Graham, who had a Hall of Fame career with the Cleveland Browns in the 1950s, could not sell his services to any NFL team except the Browns. For Graham, playing football in the NFL was indistinguishable from playing for the Browns. Facing no competition for

Graham's services, the Browns could pay him a far lower salary than they would have if the Giants, Bears, or Rams could have bid for his services. We discuss the history and economics of the reserve clause in greater detail in Chapter 8.

Sometimes, teams can also be the victims of monopsony power. As noted in Chapter 3, privately owned television stations are a relatively recent innovation in most countries. When only government-sponsored stations existed, sports leagues faced a single buyer for their broadcast rights. As a result, the revenues they received lagged badly behind those received by North American teams. In 1929, BBC radio went so far as to refuse to pay the Football Association for the right to broadcast the FA Cup Final.[25] The advent of private, pay TV broke the public stations' monopsony power and led to a dramatic rise in rights payment. In Italy, payments to Serie A and Serie B teams rose by almost 250 percent between 1993 and 1998.[26] While the payments to the NFL still dwarf those to soccer teams worldwide, television rights now bring teams in the major West European leagues tens of millions of dollars per year.

4.3 WHAT'S RIGHT WITH MONOPOLY?

While monopolies often impose deadweight losses on society, the case against them is not always as straightforward as it may appear. First, it is not always so easy to identify a monopoly. For example, since Detroit has only one football team, the Lions, one might logically conclude that the Lions are a monopoly. The Lions, however, could plausibly claim that they are not a monopoly and that they actually operate in a very competitive environment. The key lies in the definition of the market in which the Lions operate. If the market is defined as professional football teams in the Detroit area, then the Lions are clearly a monopoly. The Lions could respond that such a definition is far too narrow. In the sports industry alone, the Lions must compete for attention with professional baseball, basketball, and hockey teams in and around Detroit. They also must contend with Football Bowl Subdivision (formerly Division I-A) football teams, such as the University of Michigan and Michigan State University. If the market is expanded still further to include all possible leisure and cultural activities in the area, the market becomes very crowded, and the Lions begin to look like very small cats in a large jungle.

Even if the Lions fail to convince you that they are not a monopoly, they may be able to persuade you that their monopoly power arose from the natural functioning of the marketplace, not from any immoral or illegal actions on their part. In short, the Lions may claim that they are a **natural monopoly**. Natural monopolies result when large firms operate more efficiently than small firms. **Minimum efficient scale** is the point at which long-run average cost is minimized. If the firm's minimum efficient scale is sufficiently large compared with the

---

[25]Stefan Szymanski and Andrew Zimbalist, *National Pastime* (Washington, D.C.: Brookings Institution Press, 2005), p. 153.

[26]Alessandro Baroncelli and Umberto Lago, "Italian Football," *Journal of Sports Economics*, vol. 7, no. 1 (February 2006), p. 17.

number of customers, there may be no room for competing firms to enter. This generally results when firms face large start-up costs and low marginal costs.[27]

Figure 4.6a shows that a professional sports team may be a natural monopoly. As we illustrated in Chapter 2, a team's payroll is a fixed cost because the cost to the team is the same regardless of its "output" as measured in tickets sold. Except for that part of rent that is tied to attendance, the expense of renting or building a stadium also adds to fixed costs. Because the marginal cost of accommodating an additional fan is effectively zero, the Lions' costs do not rise very much beyond this fixed amount until they reach the capacity of their stadium. Using these assumptions, we can approximate the **average cost**, or per-unit cost, of the Lions as follows:

$$\text{Average cost} = \frac{\text{Total cost}}{\text{Quantity}} = \frac{\text{Fixed cost}}{\text{Number of tickets sold}}$$

As the number of tickets the Lions sell rises, their average cost gets closer and closer to MC_0. As a result, "bigger is better" to the Lions, since they can charge a lower price and still cover their costs as their output rises. Figure 4.6b again shows the cost curves for the monopolist and adds the demand and marginal

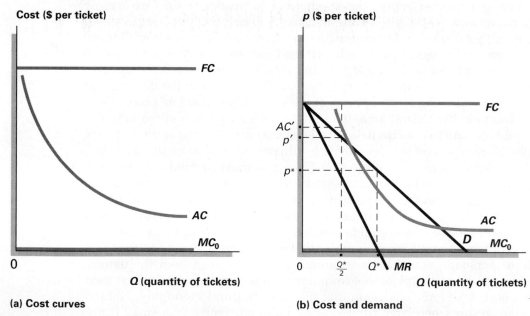

FIGURE 4.6

Part (a) shows the cost curves for a natural monopoly. Average cost declines continuously. In part (b), the firm maximizes profits by setting price p^* and selling Q^*. If the firm were broken into two equal-size smaller firms, each selling $\frac{Q^*}{2}$, both firms would suffer losses, as average cost (AC') exceeds price (p').

---

[27]For a good discussion of natural monopoly and the general issue of antitrust policy as it applies to the NFL see Robert Heintel, "The Need for an Alternative to Antitrust Regulation of the National Football League," *Case Western Reserve Law Review*, vol. 46, no. 4 (Summer 1996), pp. 1033–1069.

revenue curves. The monopolist produces Q^* and charges p^*. Note that if another firm entered the market, and output were divided equally, neither firm would be profitable, as price (p') is less than average cost (AC'). In such cases, as the term implies, the market structure naturally evolves to a single seller.

Leagues may also claim that, while perfectly competitive markets increase the amount of the product and reduce its price, a league's monopoly power delivers other benefits to fans. One of the major benefits that MLB's monopoly power has conferred on baseball fans has been the relative stability of franchises. Owners who want to move their teams have traditionally had to seek the approval of the other owners. The failure of MLB's Pittsburgh Pirates and Chicago White Sox to secure approval was instrumental in preventing their moves to St. Petersburg. Leagues use these aborted moves as evidence that the monopoly power of leagues protects the interests of the hometown fans.

4.4 BARRIERS TO ENTRY THAT LEAGUES CREATE

Not all monopolies stem from the natural working of the market or from explicit government policy. Some monopolies owe their existence to barriers created by the firms themselves. Sports leagues have become experts at erecting barriers to entry, and—when the barriers have failed to keep out competitors—at co-opting the opposition.

In the 1960s, the battle lines in professional football reflected network battle lines. Fans of the National Football League tuned in to CBS, while devotees of the American Football League watched their games on ABC and then NBC. Today, the NFL licenses its broadcasts to an alphabet soup of networks. In addition to providing a great source of revenue for the NFL, the variety of networks creates a crucial barrier to entry. Rival football leagues have long recognized that their livelihood depended on forming a lasting and profitable link with a television partner. The AFL owed its survival in the 1960s to the willingness of ABC and later NBC to pay for broadcast rights. The infusion of cash from network TV helped the AFL hang on through years of relatively low attendance. Much of the blame for the failure of the WFL in the 1970s and the USFL in the 1980s can be traced to their failure to get sufficient support from major television networks. The collapse of the XFL after only one season in 2002 stemmed largely from its steadily declining TV viewership and the imminent loss of its TV contract.

As noted in Chapter 3, leagues can create barriers and forestall entry by locating franchises in the appropriate cities. In baseball, the American League found sufficient markets to enter thanks to the dogged refusal of the National League to admit more than eight franchises. The AFL tried to exploit the NFL's refusal to expand in the late 1950s by planning flagship franchises for the rapidly growing cities of Dallas and Minneapolis. When the NFL got wind of these plans, it quickly convened an expansion meeting and awarded franchises to those same cities. This successfully prevented the AFL from entering Minneapolis and doomed the Dallas entry to failure. The AFL sued, claiming that the NFL had awarded these franchises solely to monopolize professional football. Despite the admission by Redskins' owner George Preston Marshall that the NFL had awarded the franchises just to prevent the AFL from penetrating the markets, the AFL lost a bench verdict.[28] In some cases, legal disputes have arisen within leagues when existing teams relocate without the permission of the league, effectively invading the protected market of another team. Such was the case when San Diego Clippers of the NBA moved to Los Angeles without league approval, as described in the box "Sports and the Law."

SPORTS AND THE LAW
Franchise Location

The NBA's Clippers have not always called Los Angeles home. In 1978, they moved from Buffalo, where they had played as the Braves, to San Diego (which had previously hosted the Rockets). The Clippers suffered from poor attendance in San Diego, so when the Donald Sterling purchased the team in 1984, he moved the franchise to Los Angeles without first obtaining league permission. Sterling likely assumed he would prevail in a legal battle because Al Davis had just successfully sued the NFL when it attempted to block his moving the Raiders from Oakland to Los Angeles. (See Chapter 7 for more information on the Raider's suit.) Most important in this context is that the courts found that the NFL had violated antitrust law by blocking the Raiders from relocating.

   Not surprisingly, the Lakers did sue the Clippers for invading their territory. Like the Raiders, the Clippers argued that any attempt by the league to block their move would violate antitrust law. While the case (*NBA* v. *San Diego Clippers Basketball Club*) was in process, the Clippers played in Los Angeles. With the Clippers already in Los Angeles (interestingly, with the permission of the Lakers) the league changed the rules on relocation to require any moving franchise to secure a majority vote of all other franchises. In the initial trial, the District Court granted a summary judgment in favor of the Clippers, which the league promptly appealed. In the Ninth Circuit Court of Appeals, the court rejected the Clippers' assertion that "a restriction on franchise movement in and of itself violates antitrust laws" and found that since the District Court had not employed the correct standard, the decision should be reversed and remanded the case for trial.[1] Though the Clippers were allowed to stay in Los Angeles, they were required to pay $6 million to the Lakers for invading their territory.

[1]Ronald J. Shingler, "Antitrust Law and the Sports League Relocation Rules." *Golden State University Law Review*, vol. 18, no. 1 (2010), article 5, at http://digitalcommons.law.ggu.edu/ggulrev/vol18/iss1/5, viewed April 4, 2012.

Sources: Rascher, Daniel A. 2008. "Franchise Relocation, Expansions, and Mergers in Professional Sports Leagues," in *The Business of Sports*, Vol. 2: *Economic Perspectives on Sport*, ed. by Brad H. Humphries and Dennis. R. Howard (Westport, Conn.: Praeger); Scully, Gerald W. 1995. *The Market Structure of Sports* (Chicago: University of Chicago Press); Shingler, Ronald J., "Antitrust Law and the Sports League Relocation Rules," *Golden State University Law Review*, vol. 18, no. 1 (1988) article 5, at http://digitalcommons.law.ggu.edu/ggulrev/vol18/iss1/5, viewed April 4, 2012.

---

[28]The AFL's Dallas Texans moved to Kansas City in 1963 to achieve great success as the Chiefs. See Gary Roberts, "Antitrust Issues in Professional Sports," in *Law of Professional and Amateur Sports*, ed. by Gary Uberstine (Deerfield, Ill.: Clark, Boardman, and Callaghan, 1992), pp. 19-8, 19-9; and James Quirk and Rodney Fort, *Pay Dirt* (Princeton, N.J.: Princeton University Press, 1992), pp. 346–347.

4.5   SOCIETY'S RESPONSE TO MONOPOLY AND MONOPSONY: ANTITRUST LAWS

In 1890, the United States made its first concerted effort to combat monopolies and monopsonies with the Sherman Antitrust Act. The Sherman Act was later supplemented by the Clayton Act, which allowed private lawsuits to recover three times the damages caused by subversion of the free market. The Sherman Act has two main clauses:

1. Every contract, combination in the form of a trust or otherwise, or conspiracy, in restraint of trade or commerce among the several states, or with foreign nations, is declared to be illegal.
2. Every person who shall monopolize, or attempt to monopolize, or combine or conspire with any other person or persons, to monopolize any part of the trade or commerce among the several States or with foreign nations, shall be deemed guilty of a felony.[29]

At first glance, the two clauses seem almost identical. The differences, while subtle, have been crucial in determining the course of antitrust suits against professional sports teams and leagues.

The first clause prohibits "independent entities that *ought* to be competing against one another from agreeing *not* to compete."[30] It prevents firms from joining together to form **cartels**, also known as *trusts* (hence the name of the act).

The second clause attacks monopolies themselves, regardless of how they are formed. It outlaws "conduct by a firm which creates, protects, or entrenches a dominant position in some relevant market."[31] Lawsuits brought under the second section, while well publicized, have generally had little impact on the sports industry.

The courts use two different standards when considering potential violations of the Sherman Act, which place very different demands on the litigants. The *per se* standard applies when there are what the courts have called "naked restraints" to competition, such as price fixing. Under this standard, the restraints on competition are inherently bad and no further information regarding damage to consumers or competitors need be demonstrated. One need only establish that prohibited activity took place for the *per se* standard to apply. The *rule of reason* standard takes a more nuanced view of monopolies and cooperative activities among firms. According to this standard, each case must be judged on its own merits. Some cooperative activities may be permitted or even encouraged and some monopolies may be best left intact. For example, a monopoly whose production is characterized by significant scale economies may be able to produce at lower average costs than if it were broken up into several small firms. Rather than break up such a firm, governments try to **regulate** natural monopolies, requiring

---

[29]Legal Information Institute. "15 USC Chapter 1—Monopolies and Combinations in Restraint of Trade," at http://www.law.cornell.edu/uscode/text/15/chapter-1.

[30]Gary Roberts, "Antitrust Issues" (1992), p. 19–10.

[31]Gary Roberts, "Antitrust Issues" (1992), p. 19-4.

that they receive the approval of an oversight board before raising price. Those who feel that professional sports leagues are natural monopolies openly advocate regulating the sports industry to prevent it from earning monopoly profits.[32]

The rule of reason is particularly important in professional sports because, on the surface, all leagues appear to violate antitrust legislation under the *per se* standard. By their very nature, leagues coordinate the actions of their member teams. The coordination can be relatively innocent, as in the establishment and enforcement of a common set of playing rules or the arranging of a commonly respected schedule. The coordination can also result in **collusion**, in which teams collude and act like one big monopoly.

An Important Anomaly: Baseball's Antitrust Exemption

Baseball occupies a unique place in the American economy. Unlike all other industries, it has long enjoyed an absolute exemption from all federal antitrust laws with no time limits, no governmental oversight, and no regulation of its pricing policies. Oddly, the courts recognize that baseball's exemption defies all legal and economic logic, yet have done nothing to terminate it for 90 years, and recent legislative changes have been merely cosmetic, with no real effect.

Baseball owes its exemption to the last serious challenge to its monopoly position, the attempt by the Federal League to form a third major league in 1914 and 1915. The outlook for a third league seemed promising at the time. The successful entry by the American League to major league status in 1901 showed that a rival league could succeed. In addition, the Federal League felt it could attract players from the American and National Leagues, as salaries had been steadily falling since the two leagues had ended their competition for players in 1903.[33]

As part of its assault on the two existing leagues, the Federal League filed an antitrust lawsuit against the 16 owners as well as the 3 members of the "National Commission" that oversaw the two major leagues. The lawsuit was based on both sections of the Sherman Act, charging the major leagues "with being a combination, conspiracy and monopoly."[34]

The Federal League filed its suit in the U.S. District Court of Northern Illinois before Judge Kenesaw Mountain Landis because Landis had acquired a reputation as a trustbuster. Unfortunately for the Federal League, he also proved to be a rabid baseball fan. Landis scolded the Federal League's lawyers, saying that

---

[32]See, for example, Gary Roberts, "Should Congress Stop the Bidding War for Sports Franchises?" Hearing Before the Subcommittee on Antitrust, Business Rights, and Compensation, Senate Committee on the Judiciary. "Academics," *Heartland Policy*, vol. 4 (November 29, 1995), pp. 4–5, at http://www.heartland.org/stadps4.html.

[33]Roger Abrams, *Legal Bases: Baseball and the Law* (Philadelphia: Temple University Press, 1998), pp. 53–60.

[34]The commission consisted of Ban Johnson, the president of the American League; John Tener, the president of the National League; and August Hermann, the owner of the Cincinnati (NL) team, who had been instrumental in brokering the peace between the National and American Leagues. See Harold Seymour, *Baseball: The Early Years* (New York: Oxford University Press, 1960), p. 212.

attacks on baseball "would be regarded by this court as a blow to a national institution."[35] After hearing the arguments, Landis refused to issue a ruling for over a year, by which time the Major Leagues had reached an agreement with all but one of the Federal League owners, driving the Federal League out of business.[36]

The one holdout was Ned Hanlon, the owner of the Federal League's Baltimore Terrapins. Hanlon was upset that his buyout offer of $50,000 was well below that offered to owners whose teams competed in cities with major league franchises.[37] He was also offended because Charles Comiskey, the owner of the Chicago White Sox, had called Baltimore a "minor league city, and not a hell of a good one at that," and that Charles Ebbets, owner of the Brooklyn Dodgers, had said that Baltimore was unfit to have a team because "you have too many colored population [sic]...." Hanlon filed his own antitrust suit—*Federal Baseball Club of Baltimore, Inc.* v. *National League of Professional Baseball Clubs* (hereafter *Federal Baseball*)—and won an $80,000 settlement (trebled under the provisions of the Clayton Act to $240,000) in a Washington, D.C., Federal District Court. The judgment was overturned on appeal, whereupon Hanlon took his suit to the Supreme Court.[38]

In 1922, the Supreme Court ruled unanimously that baseball was not subject to antitrust laws. In his opinion for the court, Justice Oliver Wendell Holmes Jr. wrote that baseball was a "public exhibition, not commerce and that the interstate travel," which would have made baseball subject to federal legislation, was purely incidental to staging these exhibitions.

The rationale for this ruling has never been clear. Some claim that the Court feared that ruling against MLB would do irreparable damage in the wake of the "Black Sox" scandal in which eight members of the Chicago White Sox had been accused of conspiring with gamblers to throw the 1919 World Series. Others point out that Chief Justice William Howard Taft had played third base for Yale University's baseball team and was related to William Wrigley, the owner of the Chicago Cubs.[39]

Subsequent court decisions made baseball's exemption increasingly difficult to justify. The Supreme Court consistently denied other industries, particularly other sports, the right to use the *Federal Baseball* ruling as a precedent. Somehow, the Court maintained that other sports were interstate commerce while baseball was not.

---

[35]Harold Seymour, *Baseball: The Golden Age* (New York: Oxford University Press, 1971), p. 212; and Roger Abrams, *Legal Bases* (1998), p. 55.

[36]Harold Seymour, *Baseball* (1971), pp. 212–213; and Andrew Zimbalist, *Baseball and Billions* (New York: Basic Books, 1992), p. 9.

[37]Some Federal League owners bought the Major League teams with which they competed. Wrigley Field was originally built for the Federal League's Chicago Whales. See Harold Seymour, *Baseball* (1971), pp. 215–243; and Andrew Zimbalist, *Baseball and Billions* (1992), p. 9.

[38]Roger Abrams, *Legal Bases* (1998), p. 56; Harold Seymour, *Baseball* (1971), p. 243; and John Johnson, "When a Professional Sport Is Not a Business: Baseball's Infamous Antitrust Exemption," in *Sports and the Law,* ed. by Charles Quirk (New York: Garland Publishers, 1996), p. 151.

[39]Roger Abrams, *Legal Bases* (1998), p. 57; and John Johnson, "Baseball's Infamous Antitrust Exemption" (1996), p. 151.

The Supreme Court's 1955 ruling in an antitrust lawsuit that the U.S. government had brought against the International Boxing Club is a prime example. The Supreme Court ruled that, while boxing matches occurred in a specific place and did not involve moving across state lines, deals for TV, radio, and motion picture rights did cross state boundaries. The Court acknowledged that this judgment contradicted previous rulings regarding baseball but declared that those rulings were "not authority for exempting other businesses merely because of the circumstance that they are also based on the performance of local exhibitions."[40]

The tortured logic required to justify baseball's exemption from the antitrust laws was never more evident than in the early 1950s, when George Toolson, a player in the New York Yankees' system, resisted being sent back to the minor leagues. He then sued the Yankees, claiming that the reserve clause violated antitrust laws. As Toolson's suit worked its way through the legal system, the House Subcommittee on the Study of Monopoly Power (chaired by Representative Emmanuel Cellar and hence called the "Cellar Committee") began to hold hearings on baseball's antitrust exemption. When it became obvious that the Toolson case was going to the Supreme Court, the Cellar Committee postponed further action under the assumption that the courts would settle the matter. The Supreme Court seized upon this inaction, saying that Congress had signaled its approval of baseball's antitrust exemption by refusing to take any action against baseball. The "approval" granted by the Cellar Committee formed the basis of the Supreme Court's ruling in favor of the Yankees.[41]

Perhaps the most misunderstood legal case surrounding the reserve clause is Curt Flood's antitrust suit of the early 1970s. Most people incorrectly think of Flood as the man who single-handedly overthrew the reserve clause in baseball. In fact, Flood lost his case as well as his career. After the ruling against him, baseball players had to wait another four years before their union was able to overturn the reserve clause.

In the late 1960s, Curt Flood was a star outfielder for the St. Louis Cardinals. In 1968, after a particularly good season, Flood asked the team for a $30,000 raise. Not one inclined to tolerate such demands, Cardinals owner Augustus Busch traded Flood to the Philadelphia Phillies after the 1969 season. Curt Flood had many reasons for objecting to this trade. It sent him from a team that had won a World Series in 1967 and had come within one game of another championship in 1968 to a team that was a perennial also-ran. It also sent him away from friends, family, and developing business interests in St. Louis to a town that had a history of bad relations with black ballplayers.[42] Because of the reserve clause and baseball's exemption from antitrust regulations, Flood had no say in his own destiny. As a black man who had endured severe discrimination early in his career, Flood

---

[40]Earl Warren writing for the majority. Cited in *United States* v. *International Boxing Club of NY, Inc.*, 348 US 236—Supreme Court 1955, at *FindLaw,* at http://caselaw.lp.findlaw.com/scripts/getcase.pl?court=us&vol=348&invol=236, viewed August 30, 2012.

[41]See Roger Abrams, *Legal Bases* (1998), p. 62; James Quirk and Rodney Fort, *Pay Dirt* (1992), pp. 188–189; Roberts, "Antitrust Issues" (1992), pp. 19-33–19-36; and Andrew Zimbalist, *Baseball and Billions* (1992), pp. 12–15.

[42]Personal communication with Andrew Zimbalist, 2012.

saw a parallel between his own position and that of enslaved blacks in America barely 100 years earlier. In asking Commissioner Bowie Kuhn to repeal the trade, Flood used words that Frederick Douglass might have chosen: "I do not feel I am a piece of property to be bought and sold irrespective of my wishes."[43]

In 1970, with the support of the Major League Baseball Players Association (MLBPA), Flood filed suit in U.S. Federal District Court against the commissioner's office, asking for $3 million (to be trebled) and for free agency. In language reminiscent of Kenesaw Landis's rhapsodies to baseball in the Federal League suit, the trial judge ruled in Kuhn's favor, arguing that baseball was on "higher ground" than mere commerce. An appeals court also ruled in Kuhn's favor, citing Congress's failure to act against the reserve clause, as the Supreme Court had argued almost 20 years earlier in its *Toolson* ruling.

The Supreme Court's decision, written by Harry Blackmun, was even more curious. Blackmun denied the basis for baseball's exemption by acknowledging that baseball was a business that engaged in interstate commerce. He called the exemption "an exception and an anomaly" and referred to the *Federal Baseball* and *Toolson* rulings as "aberration[s] confined to baseball." Despite these stinging condemnations of the reserve clause and of baseball's exemption from the antitrust laws, the Supreme Court ruled 6–2 (with one abstention) in Kuhn's favor in 1972. The Court based its decision on the principle of *stare decisis* ("let the old decision stand"), effectively saying that the original antitrust ruling was wrong but that too much now rested on the original decision for the Court to overturn it.[44]

In 1998, Congress finally placed limits on baseball's antitrust exemption by passing the "Curt Flood Act." The legislation, however, does little to change the status quo. It limits baseball's powers only in the area of labor relations, granting players the right to file antitrust suits to resolve labor disputes. For example, MLB can still limit the number of teams and restrict their ability to relocate. In addition, the legislation is likely to have no impact on labor markets, as the players' right to sue is highly limited. The Supreme Court's 1996 *Brown* v. *Pro Football, Inc.* ruling effectively states that the players association must decertify itself before a player can sue on antitrust grounds.[45] Given the baseball players' association history as the most effective of all sports unions, it is highly unlikely that it would ever be decertified.

---

[43]While playing for a minor league town in the Deep South early in his career, Flood was not allowed to mix his dirty laundry with that of his white teammates. White clubhouse attendants would not even handle his uniform. Flood's reference to slavery was not lost on Supreme Court Justice Thurgood Marshall, who also drew an analogy to slavery in his minority opinion.

[44]Blackmun's decision included the poems "He Never Heard of Casey," by Grantland Rice, and "Baseball's Sad Lexicon," by Franklin Pierre Adams. See Abrams, *Legal Bases* (1998), p. 62; Quirk and Fort, *Pay Dirt* (1992), pp. 188–189; Roberts, "Antitrust Issues" (1992), pp. 19-33–19-36; and Zimbalist, *Baseball and Billions* (1992), pp. 12–15.

[45]Gary Roberts, "Brown v. Pro Football, Inc.: The Supreme Court Gets It Right for the Wrong Reasons," *Antitrust Bulletin*, vol. 42, no. 3 (Fall 1997), pp. 595–639; and Sonya Ross, "Clinton Signs Bill Removing Baseball Antitrust Exemption for Labor Matters," *Associated Press*, October 28, 1998, at http://www.fl.milive.com/tigers/stories/19981028antitrust.html.

Leagues That Lack an Antitrust Exemption

Baseball's exemption from the antitrust laws has given it a greater ability to protect both its monopoly power and its monopsony power in the marketplace. It is no coincidence that the Federal League, whose antitrust suit was the basis for the antitrust exemption, was the last league to pose a serious challenge to Major League Baseball. Since then, baseball has faced only the feeble attempt to form a rival Mexican League in the 1940s and the stillborn attempts to form the Continental League in the late 1950s and the United Baseball League in the mid-1990s.

Unlike baseball, all the other major professional leagues have endured serious challenges to their monopoly power. In many cases, the existing league has had to absorb teams from a rival league and—in one case—to merge with a rival entrant. Forty of the 122 franchises in the 4 major North American leagues "began life as members of rival leagues, and 7 or 8 were created in direct response to the threats posed by rival leagues."[46] In 1976, the NBA ended a costly 10-year war with the American Basketball Association by allowing the Denver Nuggets, Indiana Pacers, New Jersey Nets, and San Antonio Spurs to join the NBA. Three years later, the NHL ended its own costly war with the World Hockey Association by absorbing the surviving WHA teams: the Edmonton Oilers, Hartford Whalers (now Carolina Hurricanes), Quebec Nordiques (now Colorado Avalanche), and Winnipeg Jets (now Phoenix Coyotes).[47]

Perhaps because it has been the most consistently profitable enterprise in last 65 years, the NFL faced the most frequent and the most successful challenges. In the midst of a war with the second of four challengers to call itself the "American Football League," the NFL persuaded the Cleveland Rams to join the NFL as a pseudo-expansion team in 1937. The AAFC, while it survived only from 1946 through 1949, had several lasting impacts on professional football. Of the four teams absorbed into the NFL in 1950—the Baltimore Colts, Cleveland Browns, New York Yankees, and San Francisco 49ers—two (the Browns and Colts) went on to become the dominant teams of the 1950s. More importantly, by allowing teams to employ black players, the AAFC helped force an end to the NFL's short-lived color line.

The most successful attack on the NFL's monopoly power came from the fourth and final iteration of the American Football League. After battling one another from 1960 through 1965, in 1966 the two leagues agreed to a full merger that was completed after the 1969 season.[48] In the 1980s, the USFL challenged the dominance of the NFL and precipitated perhaps the oddest antitrust decision of all. This suit alleged that the NFL had denied rival leagues access to television by

---

[46]James Quirk and Rodney Fort, *Pay Dirt* (1992), p. 297. The NFL's Yankees lasted for only a few years and played in Yankee Stadium.

[47]Interestingly, one man, a lawyer named Gary Davidson, was instrumental in the formation of both the ABA and the WHA.

[48]One sidelight to the agreement was the institution of an AFL–NFL Championship Game, later renamed the Super Bowl.

reaching agreements with all three major networks. A jury found the NFL guilty of violating the antitrust laws but assessed damages of only $1 (trebled to $3). Opinions regarding this ruling vary. Some say that the jury found the problems faced by the USFL to be largely self-inflicted, while others assert that the jury was confused and assessed the penalty under the—incorrect—assumption that the trial judge could later increase it.[49]

Limited Exemptions: The NFL and Television

When Alvin "Pete" Rozelle became commissioner of the NFL following the death of longtime commissioner Bert Bell in 1959, professional football still lagged badly behind baseball and college football in the nation's consciousness. The NFL now generates more broadcast revenue than any league in the history of professional sports, an agreement that pays each team over $180 million per year. While we all take "the NFL on Fox" or "the NBA on ABC" for granted, professional sports—and Rozelle in particular—had to overcome serious obstacles to obtain a league-wide contract.

The most significant obstacle was that such contracts were illegal. The NFL had been under an injunction since 1953 that expressly prohibited a league-wide contract.[50] Faced with a legal system that would not permit such "restraint of trade," Rozelle actively lobbied Congress to extend a limited exemption from antitrust laws to football, basketball, and hockey. The exemption would apply solely to these leagues' ability to negotiate league-wide broadcast rights. In 1961, Congress passed the Sports Broadcasting Act, granting the exemption.[51]

The exemption had an immediate impact on the market for broadcast rights. NFL teams no longer had to negotiate local contracts (often in markets that overlapped one another, further depressing prices). By 1969, a mere seven years after the exemption was granted, the revenue from broadcast rights had risen by a factor of 5 for the "big-market" New York Giants and by a factor of 13 for the "small-market" Green Bay Packers. The merger of the NFL with the rival AFL in the late 1960s further increased the monopoly power of professional football, giving yet another upward boost to broadcast revenues.

While professional sports in North America have generally succeeded in exercising monopoly power, European soccer leagues have had only mixed success. England's Premier League has been able to negotiate its own contract. In Italy, however, the courts ruled that the TV contract negotiated by Serie A and Serie B of the Italian soccer federation (Lega Calcio) violated antitrust laws. Teams must now negotiate their own contracts for broadcast rights. As a result,

---

[49]See Jim Byrne, *The $1 League* (1986), p. 346; Roberts, "Antitrust Issues" (1992); and Eric M. Leifer, *Making the Majors* (1995), p. 142.

[50]Due to its exemption from antitrust laws, baseball faced no such prohibition, though it did little in the 1950s to exploit this advantage.

[51]One of the concessions that the NFL had to grant Congress in order to get its limited exemption was a promise not to compete with college or high school football. As a result, the NFL does not play Saturday games until the high school and college seasons end in early December.

the TV revenue for teams like AC Milan is 10 times the revenue for the smaller clubs in Serie A, a gap that, as we saw in Chapter 3, revenue sharing has failed to close.[52]

4.6   THE NCAA: AN INCIDENTAL CARTEL

Supporters of the NCAA regard it as the guardian of integrity in intercollegiate athletics. Its foes see it as a money-grubbing cartel that ruthlessly exercises both monopoly and monopsony power. In fact, there may be elements of truth to both viewpoints. Former Executive Director Walter Byers described his job as "keeping intercollegiate sports clean while generating millions of dollars each year as income for the colleges."[53] Yet high-minded ideals, such as keeping professionalism out of collegiate sports and limiting the number of games schools can play, coincide with the goal of a monopsony to drive down labor costs and the monopoly goal of limiting output to drive up prices. However, the NCAA is neither a monopoly nor a monopsony in the classic sense. Instead, it is a collection of schools that have come together, for good or ill, to regulate intercollegiate athletics.

Economists call a group of firms that cooperate in order to exercise monopoly or monopsony power over a market a **cartel**. Members of cartels coordinate their activities so as to fix the market price, assign output levels to their members, divide profits, and erect barriers to entry by firms outside the cartel. The NCAA has—whatever its motives—done all these things, including erecting barriers to entry by driving out rival organizations. One example of the NCAA's predatory behavior came in the wake of federal legislation that vastly expanded funding for women's sports.[54] After first opposing the legislation because it might drain resources away from its traditional interests, the NCAA changed course and sought to extend its authority to cover women's sports. The only problem was that an oversight body already existed, the Association of Intercollegiate Athletics for Women (AIAW). In the early 1980s, the NCAA used its power over men's sports to cajole and coerce member schools to switch their affiliation from the AIAW to the NCAA. The NCAA also used its control over men's sports to guarantee superior media access for those schools that participated in NCAA-sanctioned events. By 1982, the AIAW had folded.

While the NCAA acts like a cartel, it differs from the classic image of a cartel in two important ways. First, it was not formed in order to monopolize (or monopsonize) a market. In fact, the colleges and universities formed the organization that evolved into the NCAA under duress. Their initial goal was to formulate rules of play on the football gridiron. From regulating behavior on the field, they

---

[52]Alessandro Baroncelli and Umberto Lago, "Italian Football," *Journal of Sports Economics*, vol. 7, no. 1 (February 2006), p. 17.

[53]Walter Byers with Charles Hammer, *Unsportsmanlike Conduct: Exploiting College Athletes* (Ann Arbor: University of Michigan Press, 1995), p. 5.

[54]This legislation, known as Title IX, will be discussed more thoroughly in Chapter 10.

quickly moved into regulating behavior off the field, eventually morphing into a multimillion dollar organization that carefully protects its financial interests. This gradual evolution into a collusive structure has led economists to call the NCAA an **incidental cartel**.

Second, unlike classic cartels, the NCAA does not seek to maximize the profits of its members. In fact, the members of the NCAA explicitly reject the profit motive. Eschewing profits does not mean, however, that academia is averse to money. As is the case for their explicitly professional brethren, colleges find ways to turn profits into expenses. Expensive, luxurious weight rooms, coaches whose salaries exceed those of college presidents, and subsidies to less profitable sports are all time-honored examples of ways to dissipate profits earned by a few select teams.[55]

The origins of the NCAA are inextricably bound up with the development of football in America. At the start, American football resembled the rougher versions of football played in England. Football teams (and all other athletic clubs) were student-run organizations, so colleges often developed their own set of rules. The lack of consistent rules forced schools playing each other into negotiations that were sometimes comical. A football game between Harvard and McGill in Montreal was played under Harvard's rules for one half and McGill's rules for the other.[56] The transaction costs of negotiating rules on a game-by-game basis discouraged the spread of football.[57] The lack of consistent rules also made it difficult to enforce any one set of rules. As a result, football became an alarmingly violent game.

Events came to a head after the 1905 season, during which 18 students were killed and 159 suffered relatively serious injuries. In the wake of this carnage, President Theodore Roosevelt summoned representatives of Harvard, Yale, and Princeton—three major football powers of the time—to the White House, where he warned them to regulate the game or see it outlawed. In response, representatives of 13 colleges met to adopt an explicit set of rules and to establish an enforcement mechanism. The resulting organization, the Intercollegiate Athletic Association of the United States (IAAUS)—renamed the National Collegiate Athletic Association in 1910—succeeded where prior organizations had failed. Within a year, it had established a common set of rules that a large number of schools could accept.

For the first several years, the NCAA was primarily concerned with standardizing rules in football and other intercollegiate sports. Soon, however, the NCAA turned its attention to rules for behavior off the field, passing numerous resolutions intended to discourage the professionalization of college sports.

---

[55]See James Koch, "Intercollegiate Athletics: An Economic Explanation," *Social Science Quarterly*, vol. 64, no. 2 (June 1983), pp. 360–374; and Arthur Fleisher et al., *The National Collegiate Athletic Association: A Study in Cartel Behavior* (Chicago: University of Chicago Press, 1992), pp. 73–94.

[56]See Eric M. Leifer, *Making the Majors* (1995), pp. 40–42.

[57]The most serious early attempt, the Intercollegiate Football Association, however, ended in failure in 1894 after 18 years.

One can argue whether the NCAA's adherence to amateurism represented a high-minded stand in defense of the academic integrity of its members or an attempt to guarantee its members a cheap labor force. One cannot deny, however, that the NCAA was trying to serve as a coordinating body for its membership, urging them to cooperate on actions far beyond its initial mandate.

The NCAA quickly learned, however, that a successful cartel must be able to monitor the actions of its members and punish cheaters. In 1948, the NCAA finally tried to put an enforcement mechanism in place with the so-called Sanity Code. In the **Sanity Code**, the NCAA specified a set of principles designed to govern the behavior of member schools and recommended expulsion for members who failed to abide by its principles. However, seven schools—which came to be known as the "seven sinners"—announced that they would not abide by the Sanity Code's restrictions on financial aid.[58] In the first and only test of the Sanity Code, the NCAA membership failed to muster the necessary two-thirds majority it needed to expel the seven sinners. With no way to enforce coordinated action, the NCAA appeared dead as a cartel.

Ironically, the NCAA cartel was saved in the early 1950s by one of the most serious scandals in the history of intercollegiate athletics. In the postwar era, college basketball enjoyed an unprecedented surge in popularity. At the height of the boom, the sport was rocked by a series of point-shaving scandals. Point shaving was a way for unscrupulous gamblers to ensure that they beat point spreads, the expected margin of victory that is set by bookmakers. Gamblers typically get players to shave points by paying them to win by a smaller margin than bookies predict. The gamblers then bet that the team will not cover the point spread.

The scandal destroyed the basketball programs of several schools in the New York area in 1952, including that of former national champion City College of New York.[59] It also implicated several members of the national champion University of Kentucky basketball squad. The ensuing investigation brought to light evidence that the Kentucky coach, Adolph Rupp, had associated with Ed Curd, a gambler with links to organized crime (and who may have abetted the point shaving), and that Rupp had flagrantly violated NCAA regulations regarding payments to athletes.

Unable to enforce its own guidelines, the NCAA was powerless to take action against Kentucky. The Southeastern Conference (SEC), the group of schools with which Kentucky was associated, however, was so embarrassed by Kentucky's actions that Bernie H. Moore, the SEC commissioner, suspended Kentucky from the SEC for the ensuing year. With no serious rival in the SEC, Kentucky retorted that it would simply play schools outside of the SEC. The NCAA then stepped in to back the SEC by writing to all its member schools and urging them to honor the

---

[58]The seven sinners were Boston College, the Citadel, the University of Maryland, the University of Virginia, Virginia Military Institute, Virginia Polytechnic Institute, and Villanova University.

[59]City College of New York is the only school ever to win the NCAA championship and the National Invitational Tournament (then the more prestigious event) in the same year. More recent point-shaving scandals have damaged programs from Boston College to Arizona State.

boycott. Rather than fight the boycott, Kentucky's faculty representatives accepted their punishment, an action that ex–NCAA Commissioner Byers claimed would be unthinkable in today's litigious climate.[60]

The "death penalty" levied on Kentucky was almost identical to the actions taken against the University of Pennsylvania over television rights. In 1951, The NCAA television committee determined that televising home games was detrimental to attendance at those games. Based on this conclusion, they limited television coverage to only one game per week in each market. When the University of Pennsylvania (Penn) announced it would broadcast its games anyway, the NCAA declared Penn to be a "member in bad standing," after which four opponents for the upcoming season declined to play them. The threat of severe consequences caused Penn to reverse its decision, and the games were not televised.[61] The realization that it had an effective threat mechanism gave the NCAA a new lease on life. By mobilizing its members into a boycott of Kentucky (not, as is popularly believed, closing the program), the NCAA again demonstrated that it had a weapon with which to penalize cheaters and had shown a willingness to use it. Schools now accept lesser punishments in part because of the fear that failure to do so will result in the death penalty.[62]

4.7   PRISONER'S DILEMMA: HOW RATIONAL ACTIONS LEAD TO IRRATIONAL OUTCOMES

As with many of the NCAA's anticompetitive actions, its restraint of trade in television began innocently. At a party in 1950, Dick Romney, the commissioner of the Mountain States Conference (now the Western Athletic Conference), approached University of Michigan coach Fritz Crisler and started discussing the TV package that the NCAA was then negotiating. He asked, half-seriously, if Crisler, who was on the NCAA's negotiating committee, would be willing to set aside some games for the other schools so that schools such as Michigan would not get all the publicity and glory. To Romney's surprise, Crisler agreed and helped push through a limit on the number of games that each school could have on the network broadcast.[63]

---

[60]See Murray Sperber, *Onward to Victory: The Crises That Shaped College Sports* (New York: Henry Holt and Co., 1998), pp. 330–343; Paul Lawrence, *Unsportsmanlike Conduct: The National Collegiate Athletic Association and the Business of College Football* (New York: Praeger, 1987), pp. 52–53; and Walter Byers, *Unsportsmanlike Conduct* (1995), pp. 55–61.

[61]U.S. Supreme Court, *NCAA v. Board of Regents of Univ. of Okla.*, 468 U.S. 85 (1984), at http://caselaw.lp.findlaw.com/scrips/getcase.pl?court=us&vol=468&invol=85, viewed March 20, 2012.

[62]The most prominent impositions of the death penalty came against the football program at Southern Methodist University, which suspended its football program for the 1987 and 1988 seasons and the basketball program at the University of Southwest Louisiana (now UL-Lafayette) in 1973–1974 and 1974–1975.

[63]Anecdote related in Walter Byers, *Unsportsmanlike Conduct* (1995), pp. 81–82. Schools were limited to three appearances over a two-year period. Each of 12 football conferences also had to be represented over this period.

As football became increasingly lucrative, the more powerful schools came to forget Crisler's spirit of fairness and wanted to increase their control over the flow of money. In 1976, 61 of the largest football powers in the NCAA formed the College Football Association (CFA), whose sole purpose was to lobby for greater control of television appearances and revenue. The NCAA responded in 1978 by recalculating its formula for dividing football programs. Previously, schools had been assigned to one of three divisions (Divisions I–III). These divisions were based on the size of their student populations in order to ensure competitive balance. In 1978, the NCAA split Division I, which consisted of the largest schools, into Divisions I-A and I-AA.

The two-tiered Division I arrangement increased the share of income flowing to the big-time programs, though not enough to satisfy the schools that had formed the CFA. In 1982, two members of the CFA, the University of Georgia and Oklahoma University, brought an antitrust suit against the NCAA. The suit alleged that the NCAA had conspired to prevent its own members from engaging in free commerce. Federal District Court Judge Juan Burciaga ruled against the NCAA in stinging terms. He called the NCAA "a classic cartel" and claimed that "[c]onsumer demand and the free market are sacrificed to the interests of the NCAA administration.... It is clear that [the] NCAA is in violation of Section 1 of the Sherman [Antitrust] Act."[64]

After a series of appeals, the case went before the Supreme Court in 1984. The majority of the court ruled that the television contract was not a *per se* violation of antitrust laws, since the "industry" of college football needed some restrictions in order to operate. The court ruled instead that the NCAA failed to meet the rule of reason and upheld Burciaga's initial ruling by a 7–2 vote. The dissenting opinion, written by Byron ("Whizzer") White, a former All-American at the University of Colorado, claimed that the majority had misapplied the rule of reason by ignoring the noncommercial goals of the NCAA, a sentiment reminiscent of the *Federal Baseball* ruling.[65]

As expected, the ruling led to the flood of college games that we now see on television every fall. The separate deal between Notre Dame and NBC in 1991 led some to say that the network's initials stood for "Notredame Broadcasting Corporation." Much to the surprise of the schools involved, their greater exposure did not bring about an immediate increase in revenue. In their haste to increase their TV exposure, the members of the CFA forgot that demand curves slope down. With more games on TV, the ratings for a typical broadcast fell by one-fourth. As a result, the fees schools could charge for broadcast rights plummeted. Four years after the decision, college football rights fees were only half of what they had been. In a crowning irony, Oklahoma, one of the plaintiffs in the case, saw its average revenue for a regional or national broadcast fall from

---

[64]Quoted in Murray Sperber, *College Sports Inc.* (New York: Henry Holt and Co., 1990), p. 51.

[65]See Eric Seiken, "The NCAA and the Courts: College Football on Television," in *Sports and the Law*, ed. by Charles Quirk (New York: Garland, 1996), pp. 56–62; and Sperber, *College Sports Inc.* (1990), pp. 51–52.

over $425,000 the year before the Supreme Court ruling to less than $190,000 the season after.[66]

The members of the NCAA seemed to defy one of the central tenets of economic theory by taking an action that made them all worse off. Outside of the sports world, there are many examples of seemingly self-destructive behavior, such as wasteful arms races or advertising campaigns that the participants would like to avoid but for some reason cannot. Economists call the broad set of seemingly optimal actions that lead to suboptimal outcomes a prisoner's dilemma. **Prisoner's dilemma** is a specific outcome of a tool of analysis called game theory.[67] While one can use game theory to analyze athletic situations, such as whether a pitcher should throw a curveball or whether a chess player should sacrifice a queen, it also has much wider applications. **Game theory** can shed light on any situation involving three elements: players (individuals, organizations, or nations), strategies, and outcomes.

With a few simplifications, one can use game theory to explain why Georgia and Oklahoma engaged in such seemingly self-destructive behavior. For simplicity, we shall consider only two "players," Florida State University (FSU) and the University of Miami, and assume that each faces two possible strategies: limiting its broadcasts in accordance with its agreement and breaking, the agreement and broadcasting many games. Two players, each with two strategies, results in four possible outcomes, or "payoffs," as illustrated in the **payoff matrix** in Table 4.1.

If both schools limit their appearances on TV, then both schools make high profits, as was the case under the NCAA-negotiated contract. The member schools that sued the NCAA thought that they could increase their profits by broadcasting unlimited games. In terms of Table 4.1, unlimited broadcasts are a **dominant strategy**, because each school finds it the best strategy regardless of what the other school does. If FSU limits its appearances, Miami will gain an advantage over FSU (moving from parity at $10 million to a $17 million advantage) by

TABLE 4.1   College Football Broadcasts as a Prisoner's Dilemma

	Miami Televises Many Games	Miami Limits Appearances
FSU Televises Many Games	Miami gets $5 million FSU gets $5 million	Miami gets $3 million FSU gets $20 million
FSU Limits Appearances	Miami gets $20 million FSU gets $3 million	Miami gets $10 million FSU gets $10 million

[66]Murray Sperber, *College Sports Inc.* (1990), p. 52; Francis Dealy, *Win at Any Cost: The Sell Out of College Athletics* (New York: Birch Lane Press, 1990), p. 150; and Roger Noll, "The Economics of Intercollegiate Sports," in *Rethinking College Athletics,* ed. by Judith Andre and David James (Philadelphia: Temple University Press, 1992), p. 202.

[67]Those desiring an overview of game theory basics and an additional example should refer to the appendix to this chapter.

televising many games. If FSU televises many games, Miami protects itself (moving from a $17 million disadvantage to parity at $5 million) by televising many games as well. The "dilemma" of the prisoners' dilemma stems from the fact that, while broadcasting many games is optimal for each individual school, it results in a suboptimal outcome if all schools decide on the same strategy. As a result, broadcasting many games leaves both Miami and FSU worse off than they were initially.

BIOGRAPHICAL SKETCH
Alvin "Pete" Rozelle   (1926–1996)

If he were in private business and accomplished what he had with the NFL, he'd be worth one hundred million dollars.

—Anonymous corporate executive[1]

Paul Tagliabue and Roger Goodell, the NFL's last two commissioners, may have brought the NFL's broadcast revenue to its current stratospheric heights, and David Stern of the NBA may be professional sports' resident wizard, but none of the magic they have worked would have been possible without the efforts of Alvin Ray "Pete" Rozelle. As the NFL's commissioner from 1960 to 1989, Rozelle transformed football from an afterthought on the American sports scene to the most popular of our major team sports. He also laid the groundwork on which the future success of other sports could be built.

Growing up just outside of Los Angeles, little about Rozelle's early life presaged a career in football. Rozelle entered the navy upon graduating from Compton High School in 1944 and entered Compton Junior College after being discharged in 1946. In one of the remarkable coincidences that seemed to guide his career, the Cleveland Rams moved to Los Angeles that same year and selected Compton Junior College as their training camp. Rozelle worked part-time work in the Rams' publicity department until he left to attend the University of San Francisco, which he chose after a chance meeting with USF's legendary basketball coach Pete Newell, who promised him a part-time job as athletic news director. When Rozelle graduated in 1950, he became USF's full-time news director. Thanks to the high profile of USF sports at that time (an undefeated football team and a basketball team that won the then-prestigious National Invitational Tournament), Rozelle had the opportunity to meet many prominent sports figures, including Tex Schramm, the general manager (GM) of the Los Angeles Rams. When the Rams' public relations director abruptly left for another team in 1952, Schramm offered Rozelle the chance to come back to Los Angeles. Rozelle worked with the Rams until 1955, when he moved back to San Francisco to become a partner in a public relations firm.

Rozelle might never have had any further contact with football had it not been for the turmoil that engulfed the Los Angeles Rams in the late 1950s. Ownership of the team was equally divided between longtime owner Dan Reeves and two partners who shared a hatred for Reeves. The result was a paralysis that drove Tex Schramm to seek a job with CBS Sports and caused NFL Commissioner Bert Bell to seek a GM who could mediate between the two factions. Bell was a friend of Rozelle's partner in the PR firm and recalled Rozelle's previous attachment to the Rams as well as the work the firm had done in marketing the 1956 Melbourne Olympic Games. In 1957, Rozelle once again headed south, to become GM of the Rams.

Two years later, fate again took a hand when Bell died suddenly of a heart attack, leaving no clear successor. At their annual meetings the next January, the owners spent 10 fruitless days trying to agree on a new commissioner. Finally, during a break, Dan Reeves proposed his 33-year-old GM to Wellington Mara, the son of New York Giants' owner Tim Mara, as a compromise candidate. When Mara suggested the owners consider Rozelle, the ensuing discussion was almost comical.

"What do you know about him?" [Steelers owner] Art Rooney asked.

"Reeves says he's good," Mara answered....

"Rozelle?" Frank McNamee of the Philadelphia Eagles blurted out, "Who's he?"[2]

Becoming "boy czar" of the NFL in 1960 was not the prize it would be today. The league had failed to capitalize on the popularity of its 1958 championship game between the Baltimore Colts and the New York Giants, and it remained a backwater. League offices were in the back room of a bank in Bell's hometown of Bala Cynwyd, Pennsylvania, and teams still struggled financially.

One of the main problems facing the NFL was the balkanized structure of its television dealings. With each team pursuing its own contracts, gross inequities in revenue resulted (the Baltimore Colts made $600,000 from television in 1959 while the Packers made only $80,000), though no team made very much. In the words of then-president of CBS Sports Bill McPhail, "Local stations made more money then by showing old movies than they did showing professional football games."[3]

Rozelle quickly responded to the challenge. To raise the profile and increase the marketability of the NFL, he immediately moved the league offices to Manhattan. He then set to work consolidating the league's television contracts. Rozelle faced two profound obstacles to his efforts. First, he had to instill a "league-think" mentality in owners who had previously had little ability or reason to look beyond their own survival. Using all the patience and marketing skills at his disposal, Rozelle convinced the owners of the big-city teams, such as the Giants and the Chicago Bears, to sacrifice their own short-term goals in favor of the long-term gains that would come from adopting a unified TV policy and sharing revenues equally.

Convincing the owners, however, was the easy part. Negotiating a league contract with the television networks was illegal for an entity that had lost any pretense of exemption from the antitrust laws with the *Radovich* decision of 1957. Rozelle spent the summer of 1961 lobbying Congress for a limited exemption that would allow the NFL to negotiate a single, leaguewide TV contract. His efforts were rewarded that September with the Sports Antitrust Broadcast Act, which allowed football, hockey, and basketball leagues to pool their revenues from television.

Even then, Rozelle's work was not over. Unlike the lords of baseball, who steadily put obstacles in the way of television coverage, Rozelle actively courted the networks and their affiliates. The results of Rozelle's league-think mentality became readily apparent. In 1962–1963, the NFL's first contract with CBS paid approximately $330,000 per franchise per year. By 1964–1965, the payments had risen to about $1 million per franchise per year.

(Continued)

(Continued)

While such figures are far below current contracts, they broke new ground at the time and induced a sense of unity among the owners. This unity allowed Rozelle to create NFL Properties, which pooled the revenues from league licensing agreements. It also allowed the owners to withstand conflict with a restive players' union far better than the fractious lords of baseball.

In later years, Rozelle would see much of this unity of purpose fracture. The first major setback came with Al Davis's successful antitrust suit over the NFL's attempt to prevent his Oakland Raiders from moving to Los Angeles in 1980. The second came with the entry of a new breed of owners, best exemplified by the Cowboys' Jerry Jones, who—having paid huge sums for their franchises—were determined to maximize their own revenues, even if that meant scrapping the old league-think mentality. Still, the continued prosperity of the NFL and of all professional sports is a testament to the work of the one-time gofer for the Los Angeles Rams.

[1]David Harris, *The League: The Rise and Decline of the NFL* (New York: Bantam Books, 1986), p. 13.
[2]Quoted in David Harris, *The League* (1986), p. 11.
[3]Quoted in David Harris, *The League* (1986), p. 13.

Sources: David Harris, *The League: The Rise and Decline of the NFL* (New York: Bantam Books, 1986); John Hilyar, *Lords of the Realm* (New York: Villard Books, 1994).

Summary

Monopolies maximize profit by raising prices and reducing output. Economists regard the higher prices as a transfer from consumers to producers that does not affect the overall well-being of society. The lower output, however, creates a deadweight loss that does reduce social well-being. Firms may be able to increase profits beyond the level they can earn with a single price by charging prices based on the quality of the game or by bundling games. In addition, monopolists may be able to capture some or all the consumer surplus by engaging in different forms of price discrimination. Group discounts, season ticket plans, and personal seat licenses are three forms of price discrimination practiced by sports franchises.

Unlike North American leagues, soccer leagues in Europe have limited ability to exert monopoly power. The promotion-relegation system can undermine a team's local monopoly power or even remove it from a specific market.

Since the late 19th century, the U.S. government has opposed monopoly. The basis of antitrust policy is the Sherman Antitrust Act, which has been applied against professional sports and the NCAA with varying degrees of success. Due to a series of bizarre court rulings early in the 20th century, baseball has enjoyed a blanket exemption from antitrust laws. It used the exemption to great effect, exerting monopsony power thanks to the reserve clause long after the clause was ruled illegal for other sports.

Some firms join together, forming cartels that exert monopoly power. The NCAA is one example of an "incidental cartel." It was originally formed to establish rules of play for colleges but soon learned to cooperate for financial matters as well.

Discussion Questions

1. Do you think that all professional sports should share baseball's exemption from antitrust laws or that baseball should lose its exemption?
2. Is it fair to fans when teams create a bundle of more popular games and less popular games that must be purchased together?
3. Do you feel that leagues are better described as cartels made up of independent firms or as a single, multiplant firm?
4. What strategy would you follow if you were trying to create a rival basketball league?
5. Why do you think that antitrust lawsuits brought under the second clause of the Sherman Antitrust Act have generally been so unsuccessful?
6. Should major college sports powers be allowed to operate as cartels?

Problems

4.1. An athletic director was once quoted as saying that he felt his school spent too much on athletics but that it could not afford to stop. Use game theory to model his dilemma.
4.2. You are the commissioner of the National Hockey League. You have been called to testify at an antitrust case against the NHL. Argue that
  a. The NHL is not a monopoly.
  b. Even if it is a monopoly, it is a natural monopoly.
4.3. Why can't Premier League teams like Arsenal exert as much monopoly power as the NFL's Chicago Bears?
4.4. Suppose that the demand curve for tickets to see a football team is given by $Q = 100{,}000 - 100p$ and marginal cost is zero.
  a. How many tickets would the team be able to sell (ignoring capacity constraints) if it behaved competitively and set $p = MC$?
  b. How many tickets would it sell—and what price would it charge—if it behaved like a monopoly? (*Hint:* In this case the marginal revenue curve is given by $MR = 1{,}000 - 0.02Q$.)
4.5. Why was the limited exemption from antitrust laws so crucial to the development of the NFL?
4.6. Suppose that all St. Louis Rams fans feel the same as Jane, who values every game at $28, regardless of the opponent. Can the Rams increase profits by bundling the Rams–Bears game with three others? Why or why not?
4.7. Suppose most fans prefer Sunday afternoon baseball games (regardless of opponent) to all other types of games. Describe two pricing strategies that a team could use to increase profits based on this difference in demand.
4.8. Suppose the typical Buffalo Bills fan has the demand curve for Bills football games: $p = 100 - 10G$, where G is the number games the fan attends.
  a. If the Bills operate in a perfectly competitive market and $MC = 0$, what are the equilibrium price and quantity of tickets?
  b. Suppose the Bills are a monopoly and that marginal cost is the same as in part (a). What are the equilibrium price and quantity (Hint: $MR = 100 - 20G$). What are the equilibrium price and quantity if the Bills can perfectly price discriminate?

4.9. Suppose the can segment their fans into young fans and senior citizens. Young fans have the demand curve $120 - 10G$ ($MR = 120 - 20G$). Senior citizens have the demand curve $p = 60 - 10G$ ($MR = 60 - 20G$). Assume again that $MC = 0$. What are the equilibrium price and quantity for young fans? What are the equilibrium price and quantity for senior citizens?

4.10. Suppose that, in order to protect Ronaldo from his adoring fans, soccer teams that host Real Madrid must hire extra security, and security costs go up as the number of fans at the game goes up. When a team such as Arsenal hosts Real Madrid, how do these extra costs affect the price of a ticket for that game compared with the price of a ticket when they host any other team? Is this price discrimination by Arsenal? Why or why not?

APPENDIX 4A

Overview of Basic Game Theory

In the body of the chapter, we describe a particular outcome from game theory known as the prisoner's dilemma. This appendix provides a basic introduction to game theory for those not familiar with it. Game theory is a tool used to evaluate strategic interactions among a limited number of players. The payoff matrix shows the outcome of the game (i.e., the payoff received by each player after the game ends). We typically assume that both players can see the entire matrix before choosing their strategy. Play can be either simultaneous or sequential, though here we consider only simultaneous play. Each player moves at the same time without knowledge of the other's choice.

Consider the game below in which two vendors (Joe and Jane) must decide whether to sell home team or visiting team jerseys outside the stadium. Joe's payoffs are shown in the upper right of each panel; Jane's payoffs are shown in the lower left.

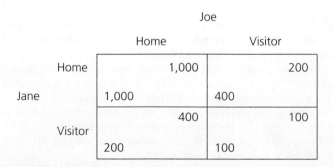

In this case, both players are better off if they choose home team jerseys. If Jane chooses to sell home team jerseys, Joe earns $1,000 if he chooses to sell home jerseys, but only $200 if he chooses visiting team jerseys. If Jane chooses visitor jerseys, Joe earns $400 if he chooses home and $100 if he chooses visitors' jerseys. The payoff matrix is symmetric, so Jane's options are the same. Because Joe and Jane are always better off choosing home jerseys, we say that each has a dominant strategy. A player follows a **dominant strategy** no matter what the other player chooses. Thus, the cell Home/Home is an equilibrium in dominant strategies. An equilibrium in dominant strategies is an equilibrium in which neither player has an incentive to change his or her strategy *regardless of the opponent's decision.*

Suppose instead that the game is played between the Bears and the Jets at a neutral site and each vendor can sell jerseys from only one team. The new payoff matrix is shown below:

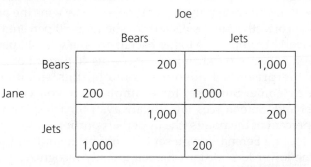

In this case, neither player has a dominant strategy. Both vendors fare poorly if they choose the same team. If they choose different teams, each does well, and neither has an incentive to change as long as the other player follows a given strategy. For example, if Jane chooses Bears and Joe chooses Jets, each earns $1,000. Thus, this game has two Nash equilibria. A **Nash equilibrium** is a solution in which both players keep their strategies constant *given the strategy of the other*. An equilibrium in dominant strategies is a special case of a Nash equilibrium, because in that case, neither player changes strategies no matter what the other player does.

An Alternative Application of Game Theory

The prisoner's dilemma is a particularly powerful and easily understood example of game theory and how it applies to economic settings. However, not all situations involving players, strategies, and payoffs result in a prisoner's dilemma, as the following example shows.[68]

You are playing at Centre Court at Wimbledon, down 6–5 in the third set of the Ladies' Finals. Serena Williams awaits your serve. You know from bitter experience that Serena has a devastating forehand. As a result, in this most important match of your life, you serve...directly to her forehand?

---

[68]For a more formal take on the game theoretic basis of tennis serves, see Mark Walker and John Wooders, "Minimax Play at Wimbledon," *American Economic Review*, vol. 91, no. 5 (December 2001), pp. 1521–1538.

Playing to an opponent's strength may seem like the height of folly, but athletes, generals, and CEOs do it all the time. They recognize that sometimes no single strategy dominates another and that their best hope lies in being unpredictable, following a **mixed strategy**.

Your match with Serena Williams is a perfect example of just such a strategy. It seems obvious to all that you should avoid Serena's forehand at such an important point in the game. Of course, one of those to whom this strategy seems obvious is Serena herself. As a result, she prepares herself mentally and physically for a serve to her backhand, leaving her vulnerable to a serve to her strength. The payoff matrix in Table 4A.1 clarifies the wisdom of this strategy. You have two choices when you serve: going to Serena's forehand or backhand. Serena, in turn, has two possible strategies: anticipating a serve to her forehand or backhand. If she correctly guesses that you are serving to her forehand, she wins the point 60 percent of the time. If she correctly guesses backhand, she wins 50 percent of the time. If she guesses forehand but you serve to her backhand, she wins 40 percent of the time. If she incorrectly guesses backhand, she also wins 40 percent of the time.

Unlike the prisoner's dilemma example, this situation has no single equilibrium outcome. Suppose, for example, that you consistently serve to Serena's forehand. Serena sees this. By always preparing for a forehand serve, she wins 60 percent of the points (the upper left portion). You realize that you can do better by fooling Serena, so you serve to her backhand and win 60 percent of the points (the lower left portion). Serena quickly recognizes your new strategy and begins to expect a serve to her backhand, winning 50 percent of the points (the lower right portion). You adjust again and now serve to Serena's strength. Because she still expects you to serve to her backhand, you manage to win 60 percent of the time (the upper right portion). Serena again catches on, however, and correctly anticipates the serve to her forehand, bringing us back to our starting point (the upper left portion), where you win 40 percent of the time.[69]

Since no strategy stays optimal for long, your greatest advantage comes from fooling Serena and hitting your serve where she least expects. This means that you

TABLE 4A.1   Mixed Strategies in Tennis

	Serena Guesses Forehand	Serena Guesses Backhand
You serve to Serena's forehand	You win 40% Serena wins 60%	You win 60% Serena wins 40%
You serve to Serena's backhand	You win 60% Serena wins 40%	You win 50% Serena wins 50%

[69]To see this problem carried out to comic extremes, see the confrontation between Vizzini and the Dread Pirate Roberts in *The Princess Bride*, by William Goldman (1974).

must follow a mixed strategy, serving sometimes to her forehand and sometimes to her backhand. When Serena guesses correctly, she may hit a devastating return. When she does not, you stand an excellent chance of winning the point. You must see to it that Serena does not guess correctly too often. Thus you must mix up your serves just often enough that Serena cannot gain any advantage by guessing that you will serve one way or the other.

Suppose your strategy is to serve to Serena's forehand with probability p (and hence to her backhand with probability $[1 - p]$). Suppose, further, that Serena's strategy is to anticipate a serve to her forehand with probability q (and a serve to her backhand with probability $[1 - q]$).[70] If Serena prepares for a serve to her forehand, then, from Table 4A.1, the probability that she wins the point is

$$\text{Prob}_{GF} = 0.6p + 0.4(1 - p)$$

because she wins 60 percent of the serves to her forehand and 40 percent of the serves to her backhand when she anticipates a serve to her forehand. By similar reasoning, the probability that she wins if she prepares for a serve to her backhand is

$$\text{Prob}_{GB} = 0.4p + 0.5(1 - p)$$

Your optimal strategy should be to serve to her forehand just often enough that Serena does not gain an advantage by guessing one way or the other. In other words, your best strategy is to choose p so that $\text{Prob}_{GF} = \text{Prob}_{GB}$. Setting these equations equal and solving for p, one finds that your optimal strategy would be to serve to Serena's forehand one-third of the time ($p = 1/3$) and to her backhand two-thirds of the time. Then, no matter how she guesses, you will win 53.3 percent of the points.[71]

---

[70]We assume that both decisions are random and that each player knows only the probabilities of her opponent's actions (e.g., from previous matches).

[71]Similar reasoning yields Serena's optimal guessing strategy—that is, what percentage of the time (q) she should prepare for a serve to her forehand. If either you or Serena deviates from your optimal strategy, the other will see this (i.e., you can tell how often Serena prepares for a forehand serve [q], and she can tell how often you serve to her forehand [p]). If Serena sees you are not following the best strategy of serving to her forehand one-third of the time, she can adjust her strategy to reduce your winning percentage below 53.3.

CHAPTER 5
Competitive Balance

*When you lose a couple of times, it makes you realize how difficult
it is to win.*

—Steffi Graf (German Tennis Player)[1]

INTRODUCTION

One of the oldest adages in professional football is that on any given Sunday, each team has a chance to beat the other. But what if, year after year, a few teams regularly win, while the rest almost always lose? No doubt, the games would be less interesting. As early as 1956, economists noted that successful leagues must be based on relatively even competition, but the degree of parity within a sports league can mean different things to different people.[2] To some, it means close competition every year, with the difference between the best and worst teams being relatively small. To others, it means regular turnover in the winner of the league's championship. Whatever the measure, we call the degree of parity within a league **competitive balance**. This chapter discusses competitive balance from the perspective of fans and owners. In addition, it explores how economists measure competitive balance, how leagues try to alter competitive balance in a league, and why such efforts might not be successful.

---

[1]"Sports Quotes—Another 'Top 10' List of Favorites...," at http://www.famous-quotes-and-quotations.com/sports_quotes.html.

[2]Simon Rottenberg, "The Baseball Players Labor Market," *Journal of Political Economy*, vol. 64, no. 3 (June 1956), pp. 242–258.

LEARNING OBJECTIVES

After reading this chapter, you will be able to:

- Understand why owners and fans care about competitive balance.
- Be able to use and interpret the different measures of competitive balance.
- Describe and compare the tools that leagues use to promote competitive balance and the limitations of those tools.

5.1   WHY FANS AND OWNERS WANT COMPETITIVE BALANCE

Fans and owners alike have a conflicted relationship with competitive balance. No Bears fan enjoys losing to the Packers, but they all recognize that an occasional loss makes the games more interesting. Similarly, the McCaskey family, which owns the Bears, gets a greater financial return—and greater satisfaction—if the team is successful but does not always win. In this section, we look a bit more deeply at the value of competitive balance to fans and owners.

The Fans' Perspective

Suppose you are an exchange student in the United States, and your host family takes you to see your first baseball game, one between the Houston Astros and the Texas Rangers. The game quickly gets boring because the talent on the two teams is very uneven. The Rangers score on the hapless Astros over and over again, and you notice that most fans leave by the seventh inning. The final score is 11–0. "That's OK," your host says, "the Astros lose most of the time, and the Rangers almost always win." If that were your only exposure to baseball, you would probably leave America thinking baseball was a waste of time. If instead you had seen the Cincinnati Reds beat the St. Louis Cardinals in a wild 5–4 game after a home run in the bottom of the ninth, and you learned that almost all games are like this, you might become a lifelong fan.

From the fan's perspective, an uncertain outcome is much more interesting than a foregone conclusion. Historically, fans have shown their displeasure with unbalanced competition, even when their own team did most of the winning. An often-cited example is the Cleveland Browns of the late 1940s; their dominance of the All-American Football Conference caused them to become less popular with their home fans.[3] In baseball, the Yankees may have had the same kind of negative effect on attendance at their own games and across the American League when they won eight pennants and six World Series between 1950 and 1958. Table 5.1 shows that between 1950 and 1958, a period generally marked by prosperity and economic growth, attendance at both Yankee games and those of the entire American League either stagnated or fell as the Yankees dominated the league.

---

[3]Over the four seasons of the AAFC's existence (1947–1949), the Browns won 47 games, lost 4, and tied 3.

TABLE 5.1 New York Yankees' Success and American League and National
League Attendance, 1950–1958

Year	AL Champion	World Series Champion	Yankees Attendance	AL Attendance	NL Attendance
1950	Yankees	Yankees	2,081,380	9,142,361	8,320,616
1951	Yankees	Yankees	1,950,107	8,888,614	7,244,002
1952	Yankees	Yankees	1,629,665	8,293,896	6,339,148
1953	Yankees	Yankees	1,531,811	6,964,076	7,419,721
1954	Cleveland	NY Giants	1,475,171	7,922,364	8,013,519
1955	Yankees	Brooklyn	1,490,138	8,942,971	7,674,412
1956	Yankees	Yankees	1,491,784	7,893,683	8,649,567
1957	Yankees	Milwaukee	1,497,134	8,169,218	8,819,601
1958	Yankees	Yankees	1,428,438	7,296,034	10,164,596

Source: Attendance data are from Rodney Fort and James Quirk, *Pay Dirt* (Princeton, N.J.: Princeton University Press, 1992). Performance data is from the official MLB Web site http://www.MLB.com.

By contrast, in the National League, which had four different champions (Phillies, Giants, Dodgers, and Braves), attendance grew substantially.

Fans enjoy a contest with an uncertain outcome even though they root for their team to win every game. Research shows that fans in most sports are interested in games in which the home team has a 60 to 70 percent chance of winning.[4] This does not mean that fans want their teams to lose 30 to 40 percent of the time. They just want them to have a chance of losing. If fans were certain that their team would win every week, a major source of excitement would disappear.

The Owners' Perspective

Perhaps the shortest explanation of why competitive balance matters to owners is that, as seen above, it matters to fans. As a result, competitive balance can have a strong influence on demand for the game, whether in person or on TV. In Chapter 3 we saw that owners may have a variety of objectives, such as maximizing profits or maximizing wins. No matter what the objective of individual team owners is, consistently unbalanced competition that alienates fans is not in the best interest of the league. Recall that one role of a league is to perform functions that individual teams either cannot do or have no incentive to do. Leagues adopt policies to promote competitive balance because they enhance fan demand for the league, and individual teams lack the means or the motivation to do so.

[4]See Glenn Knowles, Keith Sherony, and Mike Haupert, "The Demand for Major League Baseball: A Test of the Uncertainty of Outcome Hypothesis," *The American Economist,* vol. 36, no. 2 (Fall 1992), pp. 73–80; and Jeffrey Borland and Robert MacDonald, "Demand for Sport," *Oxford Review of Economic Policy,* vol. 19, no. 4 (2003), pp. 478–502. For a different view, see Babatunde Buraimo and Rob Simmons, "Do Sports Fans Really Value Uncertainty of Outcome? Evidence from the English Premier League," *International Journal of Sport Finance,* vol. 3, no. 3 (August 2008), pp. 146–155.

Leagues and professional associations would not need to take specific action if their members tended naturally toward equal strength. If, however, a few teams flourish while most teams languish, the league has an incentive to act. For example, in auto racing, NASCAR goes to great lengths to promote equal competition among cars. Each car in a NASCAR Sprint Cup race is measured using a device known as "the claw," which checks cars for uniformity. In addition, engines must meet an exacting set of criteria and are even restricted to reduce horsepower on larger tracks, where speeds are greatest. To further ensure even competition, some cars are retested at the conclusion of the race. By placing so many restrictions on the cars, racing leagues hope to ensure close competitions decided by the skills of the drivers and their teams.

There are two reasons why such intervention might be necessary in team sports: motivations of owners and the size of the market.[5] If some owners maximize wins rather than profits while other owners maximize profits, competitive balance can suffer, harming all teams financially. Even if all owners have the same motivation, the financial return to investing in talented players is likely greater for teams from large cities in the absence of revenue sharing. As the attendance data in Table 5.1 show, actions that maximize individual team profits or wins may be detrimental to competitive balance.

The Effect of Market Size

There is considerable disagreement among those who have studied the impact of market size on competitive balance. There appear to be three primary sources of contention: what to use as a measure of success, how to characterize market size, and how to measure the impact of such policies as revenue sharing that have, at some level, always been in place. Studies that use different measures of success or market size can therefore come to very different conclusions. For example, MLB's Blue Ribbon Panel reported in 2000 that low-payroll teams (their measure of market size) rarely succeeded in the playoffs (their measure of success) from 1995 to 1999. However, in *The Wages of Wins,* David J. Berri, Martin B. Schmidt, and Stacey Brook note that success in the playoffs is different from success in the regular season, and, using a longer data set, found that the correlation between payroll and wins is rather weak.[6] Other work by Schmidt and Berri tests several measures of market size and conclude that team quality is not strongly related to population or per capita income.[7]

The characterization of market size is particularly complex, in part because it continues to evolve. Before the television era, teams relied almost solely on gate revenue, so attendance was the most important source of revenue, and the

---

[5]For an excellent discussion of the possible motivations of owners, see Andrew Zimbalist, "Sport as Business," *Oxford Review of Economic Policy,* vol. 19, no. 4 (2003), pp. 503–511.

[6]David J. Berri, Martin B. Schmidt, and Stacey Brook, *The Wages of Wins* (Stanford, Calif.: Stanford University Press, 2006).

[7]Martin B. Schmidt and David J. Berri, "Competitive Balance and Market Size in Major League Baseball," *Review of Industrial Organization,* vol. 21, no. 1 (August 2002), pp. 41–54.

financial advantage of large cities was limited. The growth of Regional Sports Networks (and the revenue they provide) has created an income differential that is not limited by the size of a ballpark. It is therefore reasonable to conclude that teams in large markets can generate more revenue for each additional win than small ones can.[8] The impact of their greater revenue on competitive balance, however, remains a point of debate.

Even if fans desire some level of uncertainty, a profit-maximizing league prefers to have the teams in the largest markets win more often than teams elsewhere.[9] In a 30-team league, perfect parity means that the Yankees and Dodgers—teams in the two largest markets—would win the World Series only once every 30 years on average. If championships were allocated so that they were distributed equally on a per capita basis, rather than a per-team basis, the Yankees would win once every 9 years, the Dodgers once every 14 years, and the Milwaukee Brewers almost once a century. Over 108 World Series through 2011, the Yankees have won about twice as often as they would if wins were allocated evenly by population (27 vs. 12), the Dodgers come up a little short (6 vs. 8), and the Brewers' fans are still waiting, with 0 World Series wins in their 42 years of existence.

To see why big-market teams gain more from winning than small-market teams do, assume that each team gets its revenue only from tickets and local television revenue and that teams benefit from having a higher winning percentage, but the additional benefits of increasing the winning percentage become smaller as it approaches 1.000. Thus, the marginal revenue curve from additional wins is positive but downward sloping. Because teams in larger cities enjoy greater increases in fan support from an additional win than teams in small cities, an additional win generates more gate revenue, more media revenue, and more venue revenue for a team in Los Angeles than it does for a team in Indianapolis. Figure 5.1 illustrates the greater value of wins for a team in a large market. It shows the additional (marginal) revenue from one more win for a team in a small market (MR_S) and a team in a large market (MR_L).[10]

If all firms maximize profits then they will operate where the marginal revenue of wins equals the marginal cost of wins. To keep the focus on revenue, assume that the marginal cost of a win is constant and equal for all teams. For a small-market team, this occurs at W_S wins. A large-market team has an incentive to acquire more talent and wins $W_L > W_S$ games. Thus, even in a world without Mark Cubans or Jerry Joneses, where all teams maximize profit, the model predicts that, all else equal, teams from big cities win more frequently than teams from small cities.

---

[8]Players may also prefer to play in large markets for endorsement reasons, but we do not assume that in the foregoing analysis.

[9]Andrew Zimbalist, *May the Best Team Win: Baseball Economics and Public Policy* (Washington, D.C.: Brookings Institution Press, 2003), pp. 35–36.

[10]This model first appeared in Mohamed El-Hodiri and James Quirk, "An Economic Model of a Professional Sports League," *Journal of Political Economy*, vol. 79, no. 6 (November/December 1971), pp. 1302–1319.

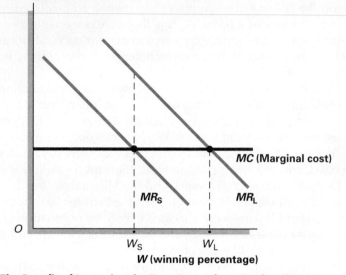

FIGURE 5.1   The Benefit of Improving the Team Depends on Market Size

Because winning is more valuable to a big-market team, it pursues winning more avidly than a small-market team does.

The Influence of Diminishing Returns

While teams from large cities may have a greater incentive to acquire talent and win games than teams from small cities, there is still a limit to how far they will go in pursuit of wins. Teams limit their pursuit of star players because of the law of diminishing marginal returns. Diminishing returns to labor are found in every industry. In the short run, as a firm adds units of labor, the marginal product (the additional output) of the last unit of labor must eventually fall, even if labor is homogeneous. The reason is straightforward: In the short run, capital is fixed, so the additional workers eventually have less capital to work with and are less productive.

In the context of sports, diminishing returns may set in very quickly, especially in basketball, where only five teammates play at a time, and, as the saying goes, "there is only one ball." The same logic applies across all team sports. With rare exceptions, professional football teams have only one quarterback on the field at a time. The New England Patriots would not dispute that Drew Brees is a great player, but his value to the Patriots is surely less than the salary that a team without a top quarterback would offer, given that the Patriots already have future Hall of Famer Tom Brady.

Diminishing returns act as a brake on team behavior because they reduce the incentive any one team has to stockpile talent. It does not make economic sense for a team to spend large sums of money acquiring all the best players at each position when some, perhaps many, of them will contribute very little. As we will learn later in the chapter, even with the influence of diminishing returns, variations in market size and owner motivations have led leagues to seek additional ways to equalize team quality.

A Brief History of Competitive Balance

In MLB, the New York Yankees have been a dominant franchise since the 1920s, when they won six American League championships between 1921 (the year after they acquired Babe Ruth) and 1928. It was even more pronounced when they won five straight World Series between 1949 and 1953. Two of the three other major sports have similar histories. The Boston Celtics won every NBA championship but one between 1959 and 1969. Between 1965 and 1979, the Montreal Canadiens won the NHL's Stanley Cup 10 times. The Canadiens' dynasty was followed by that of the New York Islanders, who won the Cup the next four years in a row. Only in the NFL has no team ever won the league championship—the Super Bowl—more than twice in a row, but three teams—the Steelers, Cowboys, and 49ers—have accounted for one-third of all Super Bowl victories, and two teams—the Browns and the Lions—have not appeared in a Super Bowl, despite being in the NFL for all 46 of them.

Internationally, unbalanced competition in the elite European soccer leagues is even more skewed toward a few dominant teams. Since the 2000–2001 season, FC Barcelona and Real Madrid have combined to win 10 of 12 La Liga championships in Spain, while Bayern Munich and Borussia Dortmund have won 9 of 12 Bundesliga championships, Manchester United, Chelsea, and Arsenal have won 11 of the last 12 English Premier League crowns, and AC Milan, Internazionale Milan, and Juventus have won 11 of 12 Serie A titles (and every title since AC Roma won in 2000–2001).

The San Antonio Spurs and Los Angeles Lakers won 9 of 13 NBA Championships between 1999 and 2011.

Competitive imbalance also appears at the amateur level. For example, since the formation of the college football's Big 10 Conference in 1896, the University of Michigan has won or shared 42 titles, more than one-third of the total. In contrast, Indiana University has won only two titles, five fewer than the University of Chicago, which gave up football in 1939.

Changes in the relative importance of the various revenue sources and the growth of the sports industry in general have increased the concerns that the financial consequences of unbalanced competition are becoming more severe. Accordingly, we must consider the owners' perspective on equalizing competition.

5.2   MEASURING COMPETITIVE BALANCE

There are two approaches to measuring competitive balance.[11] The first approach focuses on team performance over the course of a given season. To examine this, economists have developed measures of dispersion in single-season performance. A wide dispersion in winning percentages means that some teams are much better than others in that season. The second approach looks across several seasons. It measures the concentration of championships or turnover in the league's standings over a given period. Leagues with a high concentration of championships have a small set of teams winning year after year. No single approach is necessarily better than the other. To fully evaluate the competitive balance in a league, one should use both measures. Fans and owners are likely to desire both tightly contested seasonal competition and regular turnover in champions.

Within-Season Variation

In a way, sports fans resemble opera or classic rock buffs. Both are attracted by the absolute quality of the performers. Thus, the demand to see a big-time college football game between Texas and Oklahoma far outstrips the demand to see a game between Ivy League powers Harvard and Penn. However, absolute quality is not the only factor. While either Texas or Oklahoma would easily defeat an Ivy League opponent, most fans would prefer to see a tightly contested game between Harvard and Penn to a 49–0 shellacking of Oklahoma by Texas. Within-season variation in winning percentage focuses on the evenness of competition over the course of a season.

Most measures of within-season variation start with the standard deviation of winning percentage. The **standard deviation** is the distance of the typical

---

[11]For more sophisticated views of some of the techniques presented here, see Craig A. Depken II, "Free-agency and the Competitiveness of Major League Baseball," *Review of Industrial Organization*, vol. 14, no. 3 (May 1999), pp. 205–217; Brad Humphreys, "Alternative Measures of Competitive Balance," *Journal of Sports Economics*, vol. 3, no. 2 (May 2002), pp. 133–148; and P. Owen Dorian, Michael Ryan, and Clayton R. Weatherston, "Measuring Competitive Balance in Professional Team Sports Using the Herfindahl-Hirschman Index," *Journal of Industrial Organization*, vol. 31, no. 4 (December 2007), pp. 289–302.

observation from the sample mean. In the case of a professional sports league, there is a loser for every winner, so the mean winning percentage for a league must be 0.5.[12]

The formula for the standard deviation of winning percentages within a single season is

$$\sigma_{w,t} = \sqrt{\frac{\sum_{i=1}^{N} (WPCT_{i,t} - 0.500)^2}{N}}$$

where $WPCT_{i,t}$ is the winning percentage of the ith team in the league in year t, 0.500 is the average winning percentage of all teams for the year, and N is the number of teams in the league. The larger the standard deviation, the greater is the dispersion of the winning percentages. For example, consider the final standings for Major League Baseball's 1996 season. We use this season because it was before interleague play began in 1997, ensuring that the mean winning percentage in each league is exactly .500. Table 5.2 shows the final standings for both

TABLE 5.2   Winning Percentages for the National and American Leagues 1996

American League				National League			
Team	W	L	WPCT	Team	W	L	WPCT
Cleveland Indians	99	62	0.615	Atlanta Braves	96	66	0.593
New York Yankees	92	70	0.568	San Diego Padres	91	71	0.562
Texas Rangers	90	72	0.556	Los Angeles Dodgers	90	72	0.556
Baltimore Orioles	88	74	0.543	Montreal Expos	88	74	0.543
Seattle Mariners	85	76	0.528	St. Louis Cardinals	88	74	0.543
Boston Red Sox	85	77	0.525	Colorado Rockies	83	79	0.512
Chicago White Sox	85	77	0.525	Houston Astros	82	80	0.506
Milwaukee Brewers	80	82	0.494	Cincinnati Reds	81	81	0.500
Minnesota Twins	78	84	0.481	Florida Marlins	80	82	0.494
Oakland Athletics	78	84	0.481	Chicago Cubs	76	86	0.469
Kansas City Royals	75	86	0.466	Pittsburgh Pirates	73	89	0.451
Toronto Blue Jays	74	88	0.457	New York Mets	71	91	0.438
California Angels	70	91	0.435	San Francisco Giants	68	94	0.420
Detroit Tigers	53	109	0.327	Philadelphia Phillies	67	95	0.414
Mean			0.500				0.500
Standard deviation			0.067				0.054

Source: MLB.com Standings, at http://mlb.mlb.com/mlb/standings/index.jsp?tcid=mm_mlb_standings#19960929, viewed April 17, 2012.

---

[12]Note that when computing the standard deviation of winning percentages for a subset of teams in the league such as a conference or division (as opposed to the population of the whole league), the formula for the standard deviation of a sample should be used instead. To do so, we divide by $N–1$ instead of N teams. Because the average winning percentage may not be exactly 0.500, the average winning percentage should be used instead.

the American and National Leagues. One can get a first impression of how balanced the two leagues were by looking at the highest and lowest winning percentages. In the American League, the Cleveland Indians had the highest winning percentage in either league (0.615), while the 0.327 winning percentage of the Detroit Tigers was the worst in baseball. In the National League, the Braves led the league with a 0.593 winning percentage—with three fewer wins than the Indians. At the bottom of the standings, we see that, although the Phillies finished last, they won 14 more games than the Tigers. Computing the standard deviation of winning percentage confirms this impression. The standard deviation in the American League was 0.067, meaning that the typical observation varies by 0.067 from the mean winning percentage. In contrast, the standard deviation in the National League was just 0.054, which is about three-fourths that of the American League.

The standard deviation of winning percentages is a useful summary of competitive balance, but it has significant limitations. In particular, the standard deviation of winning percentages varies with the number of games in a season. To see why, try flipping a fair coin—one with an equal chance of coming up heads or tails—four times. This is the equivalent to two equally matched teams playing one another four times, with only random factors determining the outcome. More than 12 percent of the time (about once in eight tries), you will get an extreme outcome of all heads or all tails.[13] As you increase the number of flips to 40, 400, or 4,000, the chance of an extreme outcome becomes more and more remote. This experiment tells us that, even if a league were perfectly balanced, we might very well see some teams with many more wins than others in a short season. As the season gets longer, however, winning and losing streaks begin to offset one another, just like runs of heads and tails with coin flips.

Table 5.3 shows that the actual standard deviation of winning percentage in the NFL was about three times the standard deviation of winning percentage in MLB in 2011. This finding might reflect greater competitive balance in MLB, or it might result from the fact that the NFL has only a 16-game season while MLB

TABLE 5.3 Dispersion of Winning Percentages 2011			
League	**Actual**	**Ideal**	**Ratio**
MLB	0.069	0.039	1.77
NFL	0.201	0.125	1.61
NBA	0.158	0.056	2.82
NHL	0.080	0.056	1.43
English Premier League	0.109	0.081	1.34

Sources: MLB and NFL results are for the 2011 season. NHL, NBA, and English Premier League (EPL) results are from 2010 to 2011. All data are generated from the standings on the official league Web sites. Because teams receive one point for overtime losses and EPL teams receive one point for draws, winning percentages in the NHL and EPL are computed as the percentage of possible points and means are not equal to 0.50.

---

[13]This is a straightforward application of the binomial distribution.

has a 162-game season. To account for the fact that the standard deviation is larger for sports with shorter seasons, we do not directly compare standard deviations. Instead, we first compute what the standard deviation of winning percentage would be for a league that had completely equal teams. The ratio of the actual standard deviation to this "ideal" standard deviation tells us how far out of balance the league is. Because the ratios for MLB and the NFL account for the length of the season, we can use them to compare competitive balance in the two leagues.

The standard deviation that corresponds to a world in which each team has a 0.5 chance of winning each game is

$$\sigma_I = \frac{0.5}{\sqrt{G}}$$

where 0.5 indicates that each team has a 0.5 probability of winning, and G is the number of games each team plays.[14] Because each MLB team plays 162 games per season, the ideal is 0.039. Because NFL teams play only 16 games, a randomly occurring string of wins or losses has a greater impact on a team's final winning percentage, so the ideal standard deviation is much larger, 0.125. In the NHL and NBA, where teams play 82-game schedules, the standard deviations are 0.056.

To measure competitive balance within a single season, we use the ratio (R) of the actual standard deviation of winning percentages (σ_w) to the ideal standard deviation (σ_I).[15]

$$R = \frac{\sigma_w}{\sigma_I}$$

Thus, for the NBA in 2010–2011,

$$R = \frac{0.158}{0.056} = 2.82$$

Based on this result, we see that the standard deviation of winning percentages in the NBA is close to three times what it would be in a world with perfectly balanced teams. Again, this result is consistent with our casual observation that competition appears unbalanced in the NBA, as five teams had winning percentages of over 0.690, while six teams had winning percentages of less than 0.300.

Table 5.3 presents the actual and ideal standard deviations for five major sports leagues in 2011. It shows that the NHL was the most equally balanced North American league, with an R-value of 1.43. The NFL and MLB followed with R-values of 1.61 and 1.71. Competition in the English Premier League in soccer was only slightly less balanced than the NHL, with an R-value of 1.34. The NBA, with a ratio of 2.82, has a dispersion of winning percentages that is almost three times that of a perfectly balanced league, by far the highest of the five leagues.

---

[14]This results from the fact that the variance of the binomial distribution is $\sigma^2 = p \times (1 - p)/N$, where p is the number of successes and N is the number of trials.

[15]See Gerald Scully, *The Business of Major League Baseball*. Chicago: University of Chicago Press, (1989) for an early application of this method to professional baseball. We can use the same idea to evaluate competitive balance over many seasons by calculating the average value of the standard deviation over several years and using that value as σ_w when computing R.

The data in the table clearly show the NBA to be the least balanced league in North America. In *The Wages of Wins*, Dave Berri, Martin Schmidt, and Stacey Brook discuss why this might be so.[16] Their theory is based on the old adage "you can't teach height." In basketball, taller players have a distinct advantage over shorter ones. There are good players who are not tall, but if we compare two players of equal skill but substantially different heights, the taller player will be more effective. The number of very tall people who are also very gifted athletes—and whose athletic skills are well suited for basketball—is extremely small. Thus, a team lucky enough to get an unusually gifted player, such as Dwight Howard, has a competitive advantage.

Between-Season Variation

For baseball fans everywhere, spring is a special time of year that brings the promise of a new baseball season and the chance that "this could be the year" that their team wins it all. Across seasons, competitive balance implies that each team has the opportunity to move up in the standings each year and compete for playoff berths. This type of competitive balance is called turnover, or team-specific variation. It is different from within-season variation in that it considers the change in the relative positions of the teams in the standings each year rather than the distance between teams in a given season. Sports economists define team-specific variation as

$$\sigma_{i,T} = \sqrt{\frac{\sum_{i=1}^{T} \left(WPCT_i - \overline{WPCT}\right)^2}{T}}$$

where T is the number of seasons, and $\overline{WPCT}$ is the team's average winning percentage over the T seasons.[17] The larger σ_T becomes, the more a team's fortunes change from year to year. If every team always finished with the same record, σ_T would be zero. If fans support only teams that have a reasonable chance of winning their division or conference, variation across seasons is vital to maintaining fan interest over long stretches of time. If σ_T were zero for all teams, we would know how all teams would perform before the season even started. Such a situation would surely reduce demand for all teams.

One frustrating aspect of using the variation between seasons is that, unlike the within-season standard deviation, there is no obvious standard of comparison. It is not possible to say whether fans or owners care more about how much their team's winning percentage varies across the years or how their team's position changes relative to other teams. For example, would Philadelphia hockey fans be

---

[16]David J. Berri, Martin B. Schmidt, and Stacey Brook, *The Wages of Wins* (2006). The arguments presented here are based on a previous paper by David J. Berri et al., "The Short Supply of Tall People: Explaining Competitive Imbalance in the National Basketball Association," *Journal of Economic Issues*, vol. 39, no. 4 (December 2005), pp. 1029–1041.

[17]If you are interested in reading about the debate over which measures are most appropriate, or learn about additional measures of competitive balance, see the articles by Brad R. Humphreys and E. W. Eckard, in *Journal of Sports Economics*, vol. 4, no. 1 (February 2003), pp. 81–82.

happier if the Flyers had a very good record instead of a mediocre record but finished second to the New Jersey Devils every year or if they won the Stanley Cup once every few years but were a last-place finisher in every other year? Though turnover is certainly important, the absence of an absolute standard means that team-specific variation is useful only as a relative measure of dispersion (when comparing one time period with another or one sport with another).

FREQUENCY OF CHAMPIONSHIPS   One can also evaluate competitive balance by looking at the frequency with which teams win successive championships. At one extreme, if the Cardinals win the World Series every year, then the winning percentages of the teams in the league do not matter as much, since the league is clearly unbalanced. At the other extreme, if different teams win the American League and National League pennants every year, then one can argue that competition in each league is balanced, regardless of how bad the worst teams are relative to the best teams. This criterion is similar to the turnover criterion discussed above, but it relates to championships rather than regular season standings.

Table 5.4 shows that the NBA is also the least balanced North American league in terms of how often teams win championships. Just 2 of 30 teams won 6 of 10 championships between 2002 and 2011. No other North American sports league shows such imbalance. The English Premier League, however, is even more imbalanced, as Manchester United, Chelsea, and Arsenal were the only teams to win the championship over that time span. The NHL is the most balanced by this measure, with nine different winners of 10 Stanley Cups, while eight teams from MLB and seven teams from the NFL won championships between 2002 and 2011.[18]

TABLE 5.4   Distribution of Championships: 2001–2002 to 2010–2011

NBA	NHL[a]	NFL	MLB	Premier League
Spurs—3	Red Wings—2	Patriots—2	Red Sox—2	Manchester United—5
Lakers—3	Devils—1	Giants-2	Cardinals—2	
			Yankees—1	
Celtics—1	Avalanche—1	Steelers—2	Angels—1	Chelsea—3
		Bucs—1		
Heat—1	Ducks—1	Colts—1	Giants—1	Arsenal—2
Pistons—1	Hurricanes—1		White Sox—1	
Mavericks—1	Lightning—1	Saints—1	Marlins—1	
	Bruins—1	Packers—1	Phillies—1	
	Blackhawks—1			
	Penguins—1			
HHI = 0.22	*HHI* = 0.13	*HHI* = 0.16	*HHI* = 0.15	*HHI* = 0.38

[a] Hockey championships start with 1997–1998 because there was no champion in 2004–2005.

---

[18]The NFL championship (Super Bowl) is played in the calendar year following the regular season. Data here reflect the 2002–2011 regular seasons.

THE HERFINDAHL-HIRSCHMAN INDEX   Counting the number of teams that win a championship in a given period shows that the NBA and the Premier League are less balanced than the NFL, the NHL, or the MLB. Unfortunately, simply counting the number of teams that have won in a decade does not distinguish between a league in which five teams each win twice and a league in which one team wins six times and four teams win once. The Herfindahl-Hirschman Index (*HHI*) is a metric we can use to make such comparisons. The *HHI* was originally developed to measure the concentration of firms in an industry, but sports economists use it to measure the concentration of league championships.

We calculate the *HHI* by counting the number of championships team i won within a given period (c_i), dividing by the number of years in the period (T), squaring this fraction, and adding the fractions for all teams:

$$HHI = \sum_i \left(\frac{c_i}{T}\right)^2$$

If the number of years exceeds the number of teams in the league or conference, then the minimum value of the *HHI* is $1/N$, where N is the number of teams in the league. For shorter periods of time, the minimum value is $1/T$. Thus, the value of the *HHI* for the NHL (0.13) is very close to the minimum possible level (0.10) for a 10-year period. The NHL could not have been much more competitive by this standard. The maximum, 1, indicates perfect imbalance. To see this, consider two leagues, each with five teams. In one league each team has won two championships over the last 10 years. In the other league, one team has won all the championships. The *HHI* for each league is as follows:

$$HHI_1 = \left[\left(\frac{2}{10}\right)^2 + \left(\frac{2}{10}\right)^2 + \left(\frac{2}{10}\right)^2 + \left(\frac{2}{10}\right)^2 + \left(\frac{2}{10}\right)^2\right] = \frac{20}{100} = \frac{1}{5}$$

$$HHI_2 = \left[\left(\frac{10}{10}\right)^2 + \left(\frac{0}{10}\right)^2 + \left(\frac{0}{10}\right)^2 + \left(\frac{0}{10}\right)^2 + \left(\frac{0}{10}\right)^2\right] = \frac{100}{100} = 1$$

The *HHI* for the five leagues appears in the last line of Table 5.4. As expected, the *HHI* for the Premier League is far greater than for any other league, followed by the *HHI* for the NBA. The *HHI* for the NHL, NFL, and MLB are substantially smaller and are relatively close together, with the NHL having the smallest *HHI*. Thus, by this metric, the NHL was more balanced than any of the other four major North American leagues from 2001–2002 to 2010–2011.

Illustrating Competitive Imbalance

Thus far, we have measured competitive balance with sometimes complex statistics. In this section, we show how to express competitive balance graphically. To do so, we use an economic tool known as the Lorenz curve. Initially created to show wealth inequality, the **Lorenz curve**, illustrates how evenly distributed any resource or characteristic is in a population.

To see how the Lorenz curve works, consider the NBA's 2010–2011 regular season. Because the NBA has 30 teams that play an 82-game schedule, there are

1,230 games—and hence 1,230 possible wins—over the course of the season. The three weakest teams (the Minnesota Timberwolves, Cleveland Cavaliers, and Toronto Raptors) combined to win only 58 games. Thus, the bottom 10 percent of the NBA population accounted for about 4.7 percent of the NBA's total wins. The combination (10, 4.7) corresponds to point A in Figure 5.2. The next three teams combined for 71 wins, or almost 5.8 percent of the total. In terms of Figure 5.2, we move another 10 percent to the right and 5.8 percent up to point B. Point B shows that the bottom 20 percent of the NBA population accounted for slightly less than 10.5 percent of all wins. As we add better teams, we account for more and more wins, so the Lorenz curve becomes steeper as we move to the right. Finally, the three best teams (the Chicago Bulls, San Antonio Spurs, and Miami Heat) won 181 games, 14.7 percent of all wins. Moving the final 10 percent to the right and the final 14.7 percent up accounts for all teams and all possible wins, so we end up at the point (100, 100).

To evaluate the NBA's Lorenz curve, we compare it to the curve that would result if each team won 41 games and lost 41 games. In this case, it does not matter which three teams we choose first because any three teams combine for 123 wins, or 10 percent of the total. Thus, adding 10 percent of the population always adds 10 percent of the total wins. In this case, the Lorenz curve is a straight line from the origin to the point (100, 100).

NBA's Lorenz curve lies below the "ideal" Lorenz curve because the three weakest teams account for far less than 10 percent of the wins, causing the actual Lorenz curve to sag below the ideal. When all teams and all wins are counted, the actual curve rejoins the ideal curve at the point (100, 100). As competitive imbalance grows, the weak teams account for a lower percentage of wins, the strong

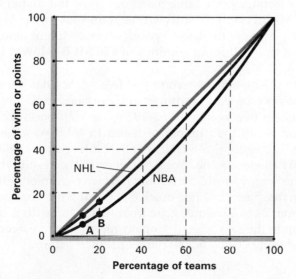

FIGURE 5.2 The Lorenz Curve

The lower Lorenz curve for the NBA shows that competitive balance was worse there than in the NHL in 2010–2011.

teams account for a greater percentage of wins, and the Lorenz curve sags farther below the ideal. Thus, performing the same exercise for the NHL yields a Lorenz curve that lies between the NBA's Lorenz curve and the ideal.[19] The gap between the two curves shows that the NHL is not perfectly balanced, but it is more evenly balanced than the NBA. Figure 5.2 thus reinforces the statistics in Table 5.3, which showed that the ratio of the actual to the ideal standard deviation of winning percentages was 1.25 for the NHL and 2.82 for the NBA.

In sum, there are many ways to measure competitive balance, and no single method should be regarded as most appropriate. To fully grasp the state of competitive balance in a league requires consideration of intraseason balance—the spread of winning percentages across teams—as well as interseason balance, the turnover of teams in the standings, and the frequency of championships. Leagues must be concerned about all these forms of competitive balance because fan interest—and correspondingly attendance, television ratings, and league profits—is likely to be affected by each.

COMPETITIVE BALANCE IN MAJOR LEAGUE BASEBALL   Many team owners in Major League Baseball have bemoaned what they see as a severe competitive imbalance between teams in big markets and teams in small markets. As noted above, the owners' Blue Ribbon Panel established in 2000 supported their claim that big-market clubs could afford more talent than the small-market clubs and win championship after championship. The owners were concerned that the imbalance had become particularly acute after 1976, when baseball players won the right to **free agency**, which allows a player to sell his services to the highest bidder.

The metrics described in this chapter suggest that competition in MLB is not particularly imbalanced. Table 5.3 shows that the dispersion of winning percentages in MLB is only slightly worse than that in the NFL. In addition, Table 5.4 shows that, over the last 10 years, seven different teams have won the World Series and the *HHI* for championships in MLB is lower than in the NBA and the NFL.

Contrary to the owners' assertion that free agency has harmed competitive balance, there has been greater turnover in champions in the free agency era. In the 15 years prior to free agency (1962–1976), the *HHI* was 0.12. In the 15 years after free agency, when the number of teams in MLB was the same as in the 15 years before free agency, the *HHI* was 0.09. Over the next 20 World Series, from 1991 to 2011 (there was no World Series in 1994), despite the dominance of the Yankees, who won 5 World Series, the *HHI* was again only 0.12, the same as 15 years prior to free agency. While much else in MLB has changed since 1976—it has expanded from 24 to 30 teams, gone from two to three divisions, and added a "wild card" team to the playoffs—championships in the free agency period are, if anything, spread more evenly across the league than before.

---

[19]Because the NHL distinguishes wins from "overtime wins," we use the total number of points (two points for a win, one for an overtime loss) rather than wins for the NHL.

5.3 ATTEMPTS TO ALTER COMPETITIVE BALANCE

All the major North American sports leagues have developed policies designed to promote competitive balance. These policies—revenue sharing, salary caps and luxury taxes, and the reverse-order draft—are designed to limit the advantages of big-market teams by reducing the benefits or increasing the costs that big-market teams face when pursuing talent. Whatever impact these policies have on competitive balance, many players believe that the true goal is to depress salaries. We analyze the impact of these policies on salaries in Chapter 9. In this section, we focus on their impact on competitive balance.[20]

The Invariance Principle

Many of the tools we consider in this section are designed to limit or prevent **free agency**, which is the right of a player to sell his services to the highest bidder. Team owners have consistently asserted that free agency and competitive balance cannot coexist. Economic theory, however, says that free agency should have no impact on competitive balance. A basic principle of economics is that freely functioning markets distribute resources to where they are most highly valued. Changing **property rights**—the ownership or control of resources—affects who gets paid but not where the resources are employed. The fact that the allocation of resources does not vary when property rights change is known as the **invariance principle** and was first applied to sport over 50 years ago by Simon Rottenberg.[21]

To see how the invariance principle works, consider how FIFA, the international body governing soccer, might allocate tickets for the 2014 World Cup in Brazil. Brazil is such a soccer-mad country, and its citizens are so confident about their national team, that Brazilian fans would buy far more than the 92,000 tickets available for Estádio do Maracanã, the site of the 2014 championship in anticipation of Brazil's reaching the final game. As seen in Figure 5.3, the final game would sell out if tickets cost $150. (For simplicity, we assume that all seats are equally valuable.) Suppose that FIFA decides that $150 is too much to charge and declares that tickets will cost only $10. At a price of $10, however, 500,000 people are willing and able to buy tickets. At that price, FIFA must ration the tickets. FIFA could, for example, institute a lottery in which 92,000 people are chosen at random. Those lucky winners can buy tickets for $10.

The invariance principle says that, as long as people are free to transact with one another, the final allocation of tickets will be the same under both the free market and the lottery. Assume, for example, that Barry is willing to pay $300 for

---

[20]For a more detailed account of how leagues use these tools to promote competitive balance see Michael A. Leeds, "Salary Caps and Luxury Taxes in Professional Sports Leagues," in *The Business of Sports*, ed. by Brad R. Humphreys and Dennis R. Howard, vol. 2 (Westport, Conn.: Praeger, 2008), pp. 181–206.

[21]The invariance principle is sometimes attributed to 1991 Nobel Laureate Ronald Coase. However, Coase's contribution was to apply the invariance principle in the context of externalities, a concept we cover in Chapter 7. See Ronald Coase, "The Problem of Social Cost," *Journal of Law and Economics*, vol. 3 (October 1960), pp. 1–44. See also Rottenberg, "The Baseball Players' Labor Market" (1956).

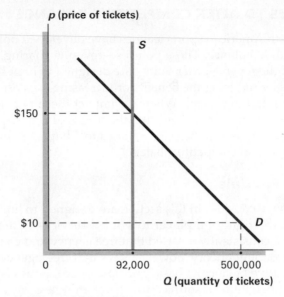

FIGURE 5.3 **The Market for World Cup Tickets in Brazil**

At the equilibrium price of $150, FIFA can sell exactly 92,000 seats. At a price of $10, there is an excess demand of 408,000.

a ticket, while Ann won a ticket, which she values at $20. As we saw in Chapter 2, Barry and Ann can become better off if Barry buys the ticket at a price between $20 and $300. For example, if Barry pays Ann $150, he enjoys a consumer surplus of $150. In addition, Ann enjoys a producer surplus of $130.

More generally, if people are free to transact with one another, there are two results. First, the market price of a ticket rises from the official price of $10 to the equilibrium price of $150. Second, because the market price is now $150, all ticket holders place a value of at least $150 on their tickets. By transferring the property rights to the ticket holders, FIFA has not altered the ultimate distribution of tickets. It has simply changed who gets paid for them.

In the context of professional sports, consider the case of Albert Pujols, the star first baseman who moved from the St. Louis Cardinals to the Los Angeles Angels of Anaheim after the 2011 season. As one of the best hitters in baseball, Pujols is a popular draw and adds greatly to the gate and media revenue of any team for which he plays. In a midsize city like St. Louis, he might generate $15 million per year in additional revenue. However, in a much larger, wealthier metropolitan area, such as greater Los Angeles (which has roughly 4.5 times the population of the St. Louis consolidated metropolitan area), Pujols adds considerably more. As a free agent, Pujols was able to sell his services to the highest bidder, and the Cardinals lost out to the Angels because the Angels were willing to pay Pujols $24 million per year.

Consider now what would happen in a world in which players are not free to move but profit-maximizing owners were free to sell the rights to players' services for cash or payment in kind. The Angels would still get Pujols because they would be willing to pay the Cardinals more than he was worth to St. Louis but less than he was worth to Los Angeles. As a result, both teams profit. Such a transaction sent Babe Ruth from the Boston Red Sox to the New York Yankees in 1920. An avid fan of musical theater, Red Sox owner Harry Frazee sold the rights to Babe Ruth to the Yankees for $100,000 so that he could finance his Broadway productions.

This example shows that property rights do not affect where top players like Albert Pujols play. They do, however, determine whom the Angels pay to obtain his services. Under free agency, the player owns the rights to his services. In such a world, the Angels lure Pujols from St. Louis to Los Angeles by offering him a higher salary. If Pujols were unable to move freely, the Angels would not have to worry about enticing Pujols to Los Angeles. Instead, they would have to pay the Cardinals.

In some situations, the invariance principle fails to hold. For our purposes, the most important situation occurs when there are substantial transactions costs. As the term suggests, a **transaction cost** is the expense of dealing with a buyer or seller in a market *in addition to* the price one pays for the good or service. Returning to our World Cup ticket example, suppose Barry had to take out a $200 advertisement in the newspaper to find Ann. He would face a market price of $150 plus a transaction cost of $200. Because the ticket is worth only $150 to Barry, the transaction cost would discourage Barry from buying the ticket. More generally, when there are substantial transaction costs, resources might not flow to their most valued use. In this section, we analyze several ways in which leagues have imposed transaction costs that prevent the free flow of players to their most valued positions.

Revenue Sharing

As we showed in Chapter 3, revenue sharing equalizes teams' profits. Some team owners also claim that revenue sharing is necessary to equalize the demand for talent. As the magnitude of revenue and the variety of revenue sources continues to increase, leagues have initiated an increasingly sophisticated array of revenue sharing mechanisms that typically treat revenue generated at the league-wide level differently from revenue generated locally.

Revenue sharing in the NFL is extensive. Teams share equally in the large national television revenue. With very little local media revenue, this has been a strong equalizer. While less important than it used to be, the 60–40 split of gate revenues described in Chapter 3 has also had a big impact.

The most recent NBA contract is expected to substantially increase the amount of revenue sharing.[22] In addition to sharing national television and sponsorship revenue, all teams will submit up to 50 percent of their revenues, less

---

[22]The collective bargaining agreements for all leagues are discussed in detail in Chapter 9. In this section we limit the discussion to the portions of the agreements that relate to competitive balance.

certain expenses, to a common pool, from which they will receive an amount equal to the average payroll. Teams that contribute less than the average payroll are net receivers of income while high-revenue teams that contribute more than the average payroll are "net payors."[23]

Since the early 2000s, Major League Baseball has significantly increased the percentage of revenue shared across clubs. Beginning with the 2002 labor agreement, teams have paid 31 percent of their net local revenue (which includes gate and local broadcasting revenue) into a pool that is divided equally among the 30 teams. They also redistribute a portion of the Central Fund, which includes all nonlocal revenue (including national television revenue), which helps to even out revenue disparities. Teams with the largest local revenues receive smaller shares, while teams with the smallest local revenues receive larger shares.[24] Beginning with the 2012 agreement, additional restrictions are being phased in on these distributions. Teams in the 15 largest markets will be ineligible for larger shares by 2016 even if they have low local revenues.[25] Further, teams will not be allowed to use these revenues to pay down team debt (and so increase profits) and will have to report how the funds increased team quality.[26] To the extent that these new restrictions induce net recipients to increase player quality, competitive balance will increase.

Following the 2004–2005 lockout, the NHL adopted a complex formula that transfers money from high-revenue teams to low-revenue teams to equalize payrolls. In order to qualify for these revenues, a team must be among the bottom 15 in revenue and play in a city with a media base of less than approximately 2 million people.[27]

Interestingly, the model shown in Figure 5.1 predicts that if teams are profit maximizers, revenue sharing will not increase competitive balance, as shared revenue represents a tax on wins for all teams, shifting both MR_L and MR_S downward equally, leaving the distribution of wins unchanged. A recent paper by John Solow and Anthony Krautmann supports this prediction.[28] Revenue sharing can

---

[23]John Lombardo, "Inside NBA's Revenue Sharing: How Complex Plan Will Shift $140 Million to Needy Teams," *Street and Smith's Sports Business Journal*, January 23, 2012, at http://www.sportsbusinessdaily.com/Journal/Issues/2012/01/23/Leagues-and-Governing-Bodies/NBA-revenue.aspx.

[24]According to the collective bargaining agreement that established this process (2007–2011 *Basic Agreement*) the net result is that all teams that pay more than they receive have a "Net Transfer Value" equivalent to that which would result from a 48 percent straight pool plan (not including the Commissioner's discretionary Fund) mlb.mlb.com/pa/pdf/cba_english.pdf, viewed April 25, 2012.

[25]"Summary of Major League Baseball Players Association: Major League Baseball Labor Agreement," *MLB.com*, at http://mlb.mlb.com/mlb/downloads/2011_CBA.pdf, viewed April 25, 2012.

[26]Jason Stark, "How the New BCA Changes Baseball," *ESPN.com: Baseball*, November 22, 2011, at http://espn.go.com/espn/print?id=7270203&type=story, viewed April 24, 2012.

[27]Tim Campbell, "Jets Will Not Need NHL's Revenue-Sharing," *Winnipeg Free Press*, April 25, 2012, at http://www.winnipegfreepress.com/breakingnews/Jets-will-not-need-NHLs-revenue-sharing—146445605.html, viewed April 25, 2012.

[28]John L. Solow and Anthony C. Krautmann, "Leveling the Playing Field or Just Lowering Salaries? The Effects of Redistribution in Baseball," *Southern Economic Journal*, vol. 73, no. 4 (2007), pp. 947–958.

increase competitive balance if the league requires the teams that receive revenue to use it to improve the quality of the team (i.e., maximize wins).[29]

From a league-wide profitability standpoint, revenue sharing is problematic because the league as a whole benefits when large-market teams win more often. To see why, think of revenue sharing as charging a tax on big-market teams and paying a subsidy to small-market teams. At its most extreme, the tax/transfer system equates all incomes, effectively directing all revenue to a central pool from which each team takes out an equal share. Even if post-tax revenues are all equal, large pretax differences mean that the central pool will be larger if big-market teams win more often. If the central pool is larger, then the post-tax payment to all teams—small-market as well as big-market—is larger if big-market teams win more often. Thus, all teams have a financial interest in the success of big-market teams.

Salary Caps and Luxury Taxes

Of the major North American sports leagues, only MLB does not have a salary cap. A **salary cap** is a direct restriction on the amount a team is allowed to pay its players. In Chapter 9, we will see how caps operate and affect payrolls. Here, we focus on their impact on competitive balance. The term "salary cap" is a misnomer for two reasons. First, while caps have become increasingly complex, their basic target is *payrolls*, not individual salaries. Second, salary caps are bands, setting both a ceiling and a floor on what teams can spend on players. Most of the attention has focused on the ceilings, which were $120 million in the NFL, $64 million in the NHL, and $58 million in the NBA for the 2012 (2011–2012) season.

Salary caps are effectively a form of revenue sharing, not among teams but between teams and players. They are set by identifying two factors: a revenue base, which specifies the amount of revenue to be split between the players and teams, and a player share, which specifies the percentage of the revenue base that goes to the players. The revenue base typically does not include all league revenues. For example, in the NBA, the revenue base, called basketball-related income (BRI), includes ticket sales, television fees, and most other operating income, but only a portion of revenues from luxury suites, fixed signage, and stadium-naming rights.[30] The NFL's 2011 labor agreement specifies different player shares for different sources of income and does not allow the owners to deduct any expenses before the split. Under this plan, the players receive the following:

- 55 percent of national media revenue
- 45 percent of NFL Ventures revenue
- 40 percent of local club revenue

---

[29]For an advanced treatment of the differential outcomes resulting from profit maximization versus win maximization, see John Vrooman, "Theory of the Perfect Game: Competitive Balance in Monopoly Sports," *Review of Industrial Organization*, vol. 34, no. 5 (2009), pp. 5–44.

[30]For complete details on the definition of BRI and the sharing arrangement with the players, see article VII of the collective bargaining agreement, available through the NBPA at http://www.nbpa.org/sites/default/files/ARTICLE%20VII.pdf, viewed April 26, 2012.

In addition to the maximum salary set by the cap, the agreement sets minimum expenditure levels. For example, in 2013 and beyond, NFL teams as a group must spend at least 95 percent of the cap and each club must spend 89 percent of its cap.[31] Although the specific forms of revenue that teams share and percentage that they share are different for the NBA and the NHL, the impact on competitive balance is similar in both leagues. Lower bounds on team payrolls can also improve competitive balance if they compel teams to pursue a minimum level of talent. The lower bounds of the salary cap thus limit the ability of teams to maximize profits by minimizing their labor costs. This is particularly important for closed leagues (without relegation) in which teams share extensive revenue.

The big difference between the salary restrictions in the NFL and the NBA is that NFL payrolls have a hard cap, while NBA payrolls have a soft cap. A **hard cap** is an absolute limit. NFL teams must stay within the limits of the cap. A **soft cap** has exceptions to the limits that the cap imposes. The NBA's soft cap has numerous exceptions, the three most important of which are the midlevel exception, the rookie exception, and the Larry Bird exception. The midlevel exception allows each team to sign one player to the average NBA salary even if the team is already over the salary limit or if signing a player to such a contract would put the team over the limit. Under the rookie exception, a team can sign a rookie to his first contract even if doing so puts the team over its cap limit. The Larry Bird exception permits teams to re-sign players who are already on their roster even if doing so would exceed the cap limit. This rule got its name because its first use permitted the Boston Celtics to re-sign their star player in 1983. In 1983, the Celtics were loaded with stars, and a hard cap would have forced the Celtics to break up this very popular team to re-sign Larry Bird. To avoid this, the NBA softened the cap, permitting the Celtics to keep their team intact. The soft cap may explain why competitive balance in the NBA is so low. A soft cap makes it easier for teams to stock up on and retain talented players.

Because all of the exceptions have undermined the soft cap, the NBA developed a number of supplemental measures to reinforce it. These include caps on salaries that teams can pay individual players and a luxury tax. The cap on individual salaries classifies players according to their years of experience and specifies maximum and minimum salaries that a team can pay players with a given amount of experience.

A **luxury tax** has nothing to do with luxury boxes; it is a surcharge the league imposes on teams whose payroll exceeds a specified level. The 2011 collective bargaining agreement significantly tightens the NBA's luxury tax. Prior to 2012–2013, teams that exceeded the cap had to pay a $1 tax for every $1 by which they exceed the cap. Now, teams must pay a tax rate that increases for every $5 million by which they exceed the cap. For example, a team that is $15 million over the cap used to pay a $15 million tax but now must pay a $37.5 million (2.5 × $15 million)

---

[31]"NFL Clubs Approve Comprehensive Agreement," July 21, 2011. *NFL.com*, at http://www.nfl.com/news/story/09000d5d820e6311/article/nfl-clubs-approve-comprehensive-agreement, viewed April 26, 2012.

tax. Penalties are greater still for teams that exceed the cap in any four years of a five-year period.[32]

Baseball's luxury tax (now known as a "competitive balance tax") also charges teams for paying more than a prespecified threshold ($178 million in 2011–2013 and $189 million for 2014–2016). Like the NBA, MLB charges a higher tax rate to repeat offenders. Teams that violate the threshold for the first time pay a 17.5 percent tax rate. Subsequent violations increase the tax rate to 30 percent, then to 40 percent, and finally to 50 percent for four-time violators.[33] Between 2003 and 2011, the Yankees have paid the luxury tax every year, with a total payment in excess of $200 million, more than 10 times as much as the Boston Red Sox, who have paid the second most.[34] The Yankees' continued willingness to exceed the threshold indicates that the luxury tax has had a limited impact on their behavior.

The Reverse-Order Entry Draft

The reverse-order entry draft allows teams to select players according to their order of finish in the previous season. The team with the worst record chooses first, the second-worst team chooses second, and so on, until the team that won the previous season's championship chooses last. The same procedure continues through subsequent rounds. All players not chosen in the draft are free to sign contracts with any team.

The origin of the draft can be traced to 1934, when two NFL teams—the old Brooklyn Dodgers and the Philadelphia Eagles—bid against each other for the services of Stan Kostka, an All-American player at the University of Minnesota. The resulting bidding war drove salary offers to the then-unbelievable level of $5,000 (what Bronko Nagurski—the greatest player of the era—made). At the next annual league meeting, Bert Bell, the Philadelphia Eagles owner, proposed a unique way to avoid future bidding wars. Teams would select the rights to unsigned players, with the order of selection determined by each team's performance in the previous season.

All the major North American leagues now have a reverse-order draft. Partly because NBA rosters are so small—each team has only 12 players on its active roster—the NBA draft lasts only two rounds. Because other leagues have larger squads and because success at the professional level has traditionally been harder to predict, they have longer drafts: the NHL draft lasts five rounds, the NFL draft lasts seven rounds, and the MLB draft continues until all teams decide to stop drafting players.

---

[32]Larry Coon, "Breaking Down Changes in the New CBA," *ESPN.com*, December 3, 2011, at http://espn.go.com/espn/print?id=7289447&type=story, viewed April 26, 2012.

[33]Maury Brown, "Inside MLB/s New 5-year Labor Agreement," *The Biz of Baseball*, November 22, 2011, at http://bizofbaseball.com/index.php?option=com_content&view=article&id=5521:ins ide-mlbs-new-5-year-labor-agreement&catid=30:mlb-news&Itemid=42.

[34]Maury Brown, "Yankees Surpass $200 Million in Total Luxury Tax Payments," *The Biz of Baseball*, December 22, 2011, at http://bizofbaseball.com/index.php?option=com_content&view=article&id= 5560:yankees-surpass-200-million-in-total-luxury-tax-payments&catid=26:editorials&Itemid=39, viewed April 26, 2012.

EVALUATING THE REVERSE-ORDER DRAFT   In theory, reverse-order drafts can promote competitive balance by allocating the best new players to the weakest teams. However, its success in equalizing talent depends on the teams' motivations—the draft will be most effective if all teams are win-maximizers—and on the ability of teams to identify and develop talented players. Some teams (such as the NFL's Green Bay Packers) seem to be consistently able to find talented players despite having poor draft picks, while other teams (such as the NFL's Cincinnati Bengals) regularly fail to find good players despite having excellent draft positions.[35]

Because the reverse-order draft rewards failure with high draft picks, it can worsen competitive balance. As teams fall out of competition, they could begin to lose deliberately in order to improve their position in a future draft.[36] In response to teams' intentionally losing, the NBA and NHL have instituted lottery systems in which teams with the worst records have the best chance of securing the top draft pick but are not sure to get it. While a lottery reduces the incentive to lose games intentionally, it also reduces the possibility that the weakest teams will benefit most from the draft. For example, the NBA's Orlando Magic won the 1993 draft lottery despite having just missed the playoffs the previous season and having the best record of any teams eligible for the lottery.

The reverse-order draft could also serve rather selfish interests. It certainly benefited Bert Bell's Eagles, which were a last-place team when he proposed the draft. More importantly, the dubious impact of the reverse draft on competitive balance and the clear limitations drafts place on the market power of drafted players have led critics to claim that the reverse-order draft is nothing more than a tool to keep players' salaries low. Still, some teams gave up a considerable advantage by agreeing to the draft. The New York Giants and the Chicago Bears, two teams from the biggest markets at the time, dominated the NFL's early years. Giving up the right to bid against other teams was not in their immediate self-interest, as the Giants and Bears could have outbid all other teams for any player they desired. However, the owners of the Giants and Bears recognized that a larger issue was at stake. In the words of Tim Mara, the owner of the Giants at the time, "People come to see a competition. We could give them a competition only if the teams had some sort of equality."[37]

EVALUATING TALENT: THE OAKLAND ATHLETICS AND *Moneyball*   In the early 2000s, the management of the Oakland Athletics baseball team seemed to find a new way to evaluate talent. Despite being a quintessential small-market team that

---

[35]Patrick Rishe, "The Best and Worst NFL Teams Regarding Drafting Proficiency," *Forbes,* April 25, 2012, at http://www.forbes.com/sites/prishe/2012/04/25/the-best-and-worst-nfl-teams-in-drafting-collegiate-talent/, viewed May 11, 2012. Perhaps the best selection by the Patriots came in 2000, when they chose future Hall of Fame quarterback Tom Brady in the sixth round of the draft, meaning that all other NFL teams had five or more chances to select Brady before the Patriots chose him.

[36]See Beck A. Taylor and Justin G. Trogdon, "Losing to Win: Tournament Incentives in the National Basketball Association," *Journal of Labor Economics,* vol. 20, no. 1 (January 2002), pp. 23–41; and Joseph Price, Brian Soebbing, David Berri, and Brad Humphreys, "Tournament Incentives, League Policy, and NBA Team Performance Revisited," *Journal of Sports Economics,* vol. 11, no. 2 (April 2010), pp. 117–135.

[37]Michael MacCambridge, *America's Game* (New York: Random House, 2004), p. 44.

regularly had among the lowest revenues and payroll in MLB, the Athletics became a consistent winner. They finished first in their division four times between 2000 and 2006 and finished second the other three years.[38]

Michael Lewis analyzed the Athletics' astonishing run in the best-selling book and hit movie *Moneyball*.[39] Lewis attributes much of the Athletics' success to their General Manager, Billy Beane. Lewis claims that Beane stood much of the conventional wisdom regarding player evaluation on its head.[40] Teams traditionally looked for players with good physical tools, players who could run fast, throw far, and hit the ball hard. The standard yardstick for batting performance was slugging percentage, which relates a player's total bases per at bat. A player who hits a lot of home runs will, all else equal, have a much higher slugging percentage than a player who hits a lot of singles. Beane, a follower of baseball statistician Bill James, claimed that the key to success lay in a team's getting on base as often as possible, which is best measured by a player's on-base percentage.[41] Lewis asserts that, while traditional scouts look for physically gifted athletes, Beane looked for players who were disciplined and received a lot of bases on balls (walks), even if they were not much to look at in a uniform.

In their economic analysis of *Moneyball*, Jahn Hakes and Raymond Sauer find evidence to support Lewis's claim that Beane discovered an unexploited imperfection in the market.[42] Applying multiple regression analysis, they show that increasing a team's on base percentage contributes more to wins than increasing its slugging percentage. Using salaries to measure the value that teams place on a player's characteristics, they also show that teams generally valued slugging percentage more highly than on-base percentage. Emphasizing on-base percentage allowed Beane to acquire players whose contribution to success had been undervalued by other teams. This gave the Athletics a competitive advantage and allowed them to win consistently with far lower payrolls than other teams.

Unfortunately, the Athletics were not able to translate their success in the regular season to a World Series appearance. As Beane himself admits, his strategy was better suited to a 162-game season than to a 7-game series.[43] More importantly, as in any competitive market, the first mover enjoys a relatively brief

---

[38]They finished second in 2001 despite winning 102 games because the Seattle Mariners won an American League record 116 games.

[39]Michael Lewis, *Moneyball* (New York: Norton, 2003).

[40]The credit for the approach made famous by Beane belongs at least in part to his predecessor, Sandy Alderson, who preceded Billy Beane as the A's General Manager.

[41]Slugging percentage is computed as $(1B + 2 \times 2B + 3 \times 3B + 4 \times HR)/AB$, where $1B$ is the number of singles a player hits, $2B$ is the number of doubles, $3B$ is the number of triples, HR is the number of home runs, and AB is the number of at bats. On-base percentage equals $(H + BB + HBP)/(AB + BB + HBP + SF)$, where H is the number of hits, BB is the number of bases on balls ("walks"), HBP is the number of times the player was hit by a pitch, and SF is the number of sacrifice flies. Appearances that result in BB, HBP, or SF are not counted as an AB.

[42]Jahn Hakes and Raymond Sauer, "An Economic Evaluation of the *Moneyball* Hypothesis," *Journal of Economic Perspectives*, vol. 20, no. 3 (Summer 2006), pp. 173–185.

[43]David J. Berri, Martin B. Schmidt, and Stacey Brook, *The Wages of Wins* (2006).

advantage. Hakes and Sauer demonstrate that the relative valuation of slugging percentage and on-base percentage had begun to shift by 2004. With other teams now applying Bill James's principles, the Athletics were relegated to also-ran status by 2007.

Schedule Adjustments in the NFL

The NFL has introduced an additional element of parity across seasons, which is unrelated to the movement or acquisition of players. Each team's schedule is determined in part by the team's performance in the previous season. Each team plays 16 games. The first 14 are independent of the success of the team: Each team plays the other three teams in its own division twice, plus all four teams in one other division within the conference, plus all four teams from one division in the other conference, for a total of 14 games. The relevant portion of the schedule for this discussion is that for each team, the remaining two games are played against opponents determined by their performance in the previous season. The first-place team in each division plays the two first-place teams in its conference that it would not otherwise have played; the second-place team plays the other two second-place teams, and so on. As a result, stronger teams play stronger schedules the following year, and weaker teams play weaker schedules the following year, creating a natural tendency toward parity.

Promotion and Relegation

The promotion and relegation system provides an additional incentive mechanism that may increase competitive balance. We saw that top European leagues, such as the English Premier League and the Bundesliga, have actual-to-ideal competitive balance ratios that are second only to the NHL, North America's most balanced league. Yet, if we consider frequency of championships as the measure of balance, Table 5.3 provides strong evidence that these same leagues are among the least competitive. The promotion and relegation system provides an explanation to this puzzle.

When a team in a North American league is having a bad season and stands to finish near the bottom of the standings, it may not have much incentive to win. Once eliminated from the playoffs, the team may instead use the remaining games to try out new players in its minor league system, or raise capital by selling off some of its top players to playoff-bound teams that are in search of that "missing piece" needed to make them a championship contender. Thus, the winning percentage of the poor team may erode further, increasing the standard deviation of winning percentage.

In a promotion and relegation league, teams near the bottom of the standings have no such luxury. If they let their performance slide further, they may be relegated to a lower league. Teams that are near the bottom of the standings have an incentive to continue to play to win right to the end. Thus, promotion and relegation may not create turnover of the league champion, but it may decrease the standard deviation of wins within the league.

BIOGRAPHICAL SKETCH
Bud Selig   (1934–)

Selig listened and questioned and murmured empathetically, all of the things he did best.

—John Helyar[1]

Perhaps no person symbolizes the struggle over competitive balance more than baseball Commissioner Alan H. ("Bud") Selig. Selig's Wisconsin roots run deep. Born in Milwaukee, he graduated from the University of Wisconsin at Madison in 1956 and, after serving in the military for two years, joined his father's automobile business. Business proved so good that, when major league baseball came to Milwaukee, Selig was able to act on his love of baseball by becoming a part-owner in the Milwaukee Braves. Selig's ties, however, were to the *Milwaukee* Braves. When the team moved to Atlanta in 1965, Selig promptly sold his share of the team and formed a group dedicated to bringing a new team to Milwaukee. His efforts bore fruit when the Seattle Pilots, a badly financed expansion team, went bankrupt after the 1970 season. Selig immediately bought the team for $10.8 million and moved it to Milwaukee.

With Selig as their president, the Brewers gained a reputation as an exemplary organization, and the team came within a game of winning the 1982 World Series. The Brewers' performance on and off the field led Selig to play a growing role in the governance of Major League Baseball's affairs. When the owners forced Fay Vincent to resign as commissioner in 1992, Selig, as chairman of the owners' executive council, effectively took over the duties of commissioner. For the next six years, Selig walked a tightrope, serving the interests of all of baseball while working to advance the interests of his own Milwaukee Brewers. Finally, in July 1998, Selig's fellow owners elected him as commissioner. Selig then put his holdings in the Brewers into a blind trust and turned operations of the Brewers to his daughter Wendy Selig-Preib.

Selig's popularity with his fellow owners and his insistence on consensus has brought the owners unprecedented cohesion. That has enabled him to introduce a variety of innovations designed to bring greater excitement to the game. Under his tenure, baseball raised the number of divisions per league from two to three, increasing the number of teams in the postseason. The number was further increased by the introduction of "wildcard" playoff teams (which won the 2002, 2003, and 2011 World Series). He also oversaw a greater consolidation of the American and National Leagues, whose war of the early 1900s did not fully end until Selig brought both leagues under the authority of the commissioner's office in 2000.

Most importantly, by bringing the often-fractious owners together, Selig reversed a trend of over 20 years. All labor stoppages prior to Selig's becoming commissioner had effectively ended with the owners' capitulating. The 1994–1995 strike ended in a draw, with neither side achieving its aims. In the near-strike of 2002, the ownership succeeded in forcing the players association to blink and to approve a revenue-sharing

(Continued)

(*Continued*)

plan and luxury tax that it had bitterly opposed. This marked ownership's first outright victory in negotiations since the first dispute in 1972. Sadly, the 1994–1995 strike caused the cancellation of the 1994 World Series, something two world wars had failed to do. The willingness of owners to forgo the rest of the season severely tarnished the game's reputation. The resurgence of baseball's popularity in the late 1990s has since been marred by allegations that many of the period's greatest stars used performance-enhancing drugs. The allegations of drug use and of the weak antidrug stance by MLB led to a series of congressional hearings at which Selig, union representatives, and star players were subjected to embarrassing questions on national television.

Because of his controversial record, some see Bud Selig as a man who saved the game. Others feel that he was ill-suited to be anything other than the owner of a small-market team. Whatever one's opinion of him, few can deny that he has had a major impact on the game.

[1]John Helyar, *Lords of the Realm* (New York: Ballantine Books, 1994), p. 505.

Sources: Associated Press, "MLB Official Says 'Nothing Improper' About 1995 Loan," *ESPN Baseball*, January 9, 2002, at http://espn.go.com/mlb/news/2002/0108/1307601.html; Anonymous, "Bud Selig," *BaseballLibrary.com*, at http://www.baseballlibrary.com/baseballlibrary/ballplayers/S/Selig_Bud.stm; Anonymous, "Alan H. 'Bud' Selig," *Commissioners*; John Helyar, *Lords of the Realm*, New York: Ballantine Books, 1994, at http://mlb.mlb.com/mlb/history/mlb_history_people.jsp?story=com_bio_9.

Summary

For a league to be financially successful in the long run, there must be a semblance of even competition among teams. Given that the value of a win is much greater in large cities, it is unlikely that leagues would maximize revenue from perfect parity across teams, and would likely do better to have better teams in cities where demand for the sport is greatest.

Fans and owners both have an interest in competitive balance. Fans enjoy contests that have uncertain outcomes. If the home team wins too much or too little, attendance will decline. The fact that fans are less likely to follow a team that wins or loses too often gives owners a financial stake in maintaining competitive balance. Because teams typically try to win as often as possible, moves to assure competitive balance typically originate from the central league office.

There are several ways to measure competitive balance, no one of which is necessarily better than the others. A popular way to measure within-season balance is to take the ratio of the standard deviation of winning percentages to the "ideal" standard deviation that would prevail if all teams were equally talented. A popular way to measure across-season balance is to use the Herfindahl-Hirschman Index, which shows how narrowly concentrated the champions have been over a given time period. By both measures, MLB is relatively competitive compared to other sports. This contradicts the claims that MLB owners have made that baseball has had a competitive balance crisis since the advent of free agency.

Economic theory predicts that free agency will not affect the distribution of talent in a sport as long as the team owners maximize profit, players maximize income, and transaction costs are low. Sports leagues have implemented a number of policies—such as revenue sharing, salary caps, luxury taxes, and the reverse-order draft—to increase transaction costs and limit the movement of players from small-market to big-market teams. These measures have met with uneven success.

Discussion Questions

1. How far should leagues go to ensure parity among teams?
2. What do you believe means more to fans, winning the championship once in a while or being competitive every year?
3. Should Major League Baseball adopt a system of promotion and relegation?

Problems

5.1. Suppose, as an owner, you could leave the highly competitive league (in terms of closeness of contests) that you currently play in and enter a league that assured that your team would never lose again. Would you want to do so? Why or why not?
5.2. Explain how the law of diminishing returns provides a natural tendency toward competitive balance.
5.3. Suppose the winning percentages in a six-team league were as follows at the end of the season— Team A: 0.750, Team B: 0.600, Team C: 0.500, Team D: 0.500, Team E: 0.400, Team F: 0.250. Compute the standard deviation of winning percentages.
5.4. In question 5.3, suppose each team plays a 50-game schedule. Compute the "ideal" standard deviation based on equal playing strength, and the ratio of the actual to the ideal.
5.5. If the NFL increased its schedule from 16 games to 36, what would the new benchmark ideal standard deviation be (assuming equal playing strength)?
5.6. Why do many economists believe that free agency has not affected competitive balance?
5.7. Draw the Lorenz curves from Figure 5.2. Based on what you know from this chapter, add a Lorenz curve for the NFL and a Lorenz curve for the English Premier League. Why did you place them where you did?
5.8. Suppose that over five seasons, the order of finish for five teams in the West League and the East League are as follows. Use the *HHI* to determine which league has better competitive balance across seasons.

West League Season					East League Season				
1	2	3	4	5	1	2	3	4	5
A	A	A	E	E	A	B	C	D	E
B	B	D	D	D	C	A	A	A	A
C	C	C	C	C	C	B	D	E	D
D	D	B	B	B	B	D	B	B	B
E	E	E	A	A	D	E	E	C	C

5.9. If you were a fan of Team A, which set of distributions shown in the previous question (West or East) would you prefer? Why?

5.10. Go to the NFL regular season standings for 2009 (http://sports.espn.go.com/nfl/standings) and compute the standard deviation of winning percentage and the ratio of actual to ideal standard deviation. Was competitive balance in 2009 better or worse than it was in 2008?

PART THREE

Public Finance and Sports

CHAPTER 6

The Public Finance of Sports: Who Benefits and How?

The pride and the presence of a professional football team is far more important than 30 libraries.

—ART MODELL, FORMER OWNER OF THE BALTIMORE RAVENS[1]

INTRODUCTION

"Build it, and they will come." The vision that worked such wonders for Kevin Costner in *Field of Dreams* has long been a mantra for sports teams at all levels.[2] To the team that occupies it, a new venue means more fans, additional luxury boxes or premium seating, and enhanced gate and venue revenue. However, teams are quick to point out that they are not the only ones to gain. Building a new stadium or attracting a new team seems to have something for everyone.

---

[1]Quoted in Joanna Cagan and Neil deMause, *Field of Schemes* (Monroe, Maine: Common Cause Press, 1998), p. 137.

[2]Students of film or the book on which it is based, *Shoeless Joe*, by W. P. Kinsella, will know that the correct quotation is "Build it and *he* will come." (Emphasis added)

Many state and local officials see sports facilities as the anchors around which their cities can revive decaying downtown areas.[3] They have visions of tourists drawn to their towns to attend sporting events, of residents staying in center city areas for entertainment and shopping rather than heading for the sub-urbs, and of local merchants relocating to prosperous downtown sites.

At the same time, sports fans in cities without franchises long for the status of a "big-league" city in which they can at last root for "their" team. Fans who live in cities that already have a franchise hope that a new home will enable their team to attract free agents that will make them a winner. Even if they are not sports fans, local construction workers look forward to the jobs cre-ated by the extensive building project and members of the hospitality industry eagerly await the fans that will visit—and spend money in—their city.

In the next two chapters of this text we examine the economic impact of new sports venues, sports franchises, or of major athletic events, such as the Olympics, Super Bowl, or World Cup. In this chapter, we focus on the benefits that they con-fer on teams, fans, and cities. In Chapter 7 we turn to who pays for the facilities that the teams or events use and the different ways in which they pay for them.

LEARNING OBJECTIVES

After reading this chapter, you will be able to:

- Show how a new facility can increase a team's revenue stream.

- Recognize how new facilities might make fans better off even if they never attend a game.

- Appreciate how new facilities, new teams, or new events might contribute to a local economy—and why they generally add little.

6.1 HOW TEAMS BENEFIT FROM NEW FACILITIES

Ray Kinsella may have been moved to build a baseball diamond in the middle of his corn field in the movie *Field of Dreams*, but today's sports teams want a bit more. Construction costs for football and baseball stadiums now approach or exceed $1 billion. Even basketball arenas now cost over $600 million.[4] It was not always so. Ebbets Field, a structure so extravagant that Brooklyn Dodgers' owner Charles Ebbets had to sell half his share of the team to finance it, cost $750,000 when it was built in 1913. Even accounting for inflation, that would come to only a little over $17 million in 2011. With the costs of new facilities skyrocketing, the cities and teams that pay for them must expect the benefits to skyrocket as well.

---

[3]Mark Rosentraub, "Stadiums and Urban Space," in *Sports, Jobs, and Taxes,* ed. by Roger Noll and Andrew Zimbalist (Washington, D.C.: Brookings Institution Press, 1997), pp. 178–180.

[4]According to Paul Munsey and Corey Suppes, *Ballparks,* 2012, at http://Ballparks.com, Cowboys Stadium cost about $1.15 billion to construct, Yankee Stadium cost $1.3 billon, and the Barclays Centre, which will host the NBA's Brooklyn Nets starting in 2012, is expected to cost $637 million.

Facilities, Attendance, and Profits

New stadiums and arenas almost invariably lead to increases in attendance in the years following their construction. The Baltimore Orioles and the Cleveland Indians, the two teams whose new stadiums in 1992 and 1994 touched off the boom in "retro" stadiums in the early 1990s, saw their average attendance rise by 40 percent and 31 percent in their first year in Oriole Park and Jacobs (now Progressive) Field.

Over time, however, the novelty of a new ballpark fades. Attendance at Oriole Park and Progressive Field steadily declined, as the Orioles and Indians, which fielded powerful teams in the 1990s, fell back to also-ran status in the 2000s. In 2011, attendance at Oriole Park was only 21,672 per game, less than half their 1992 figure. The Indians did a little better, drawing 22,726 fans, less than two-thirds what they drew in 1994.[5] More significantly, Orioles and Indians drew more fans in their last year in their old ballparks than they did in 2011.

The "honeymoon effect" of a new facility on attendance has received a great deal of attention with the construction boom of the 1990s and early 2000s.[6] Studies have shown that a new facility has a greater impact on baseball teams than on teams in the other major sports, increasing attendance by about one-third. The greater impact on baseball probably stems from the fact that baseball games do not sell out as much as basketball, football, or hockey games. The lack of sellouts comes from baseball's long season—about twice as long as basketball and hockey seasons and over 10 times as long as football's—and from the large size of its facilities compared to basketball and hockey. Thus, there is typically more room for a baseball team's attendance to increase than for the three other sports. As the experience of the Orioles and Indians suggests, the increase does not last forever. All else equal, attendance falls back to its original level after about 10 years.

Over time, a new facility cannot disguise the quality of the team that plays there, as the experience of the Milwaukee Brewers has shown. When Miller Park first opened in 2001, attendance rose by 80 percent, going from 19,427 to 34,704 per game. Attendance fell quickly, however, as fans were turned off by poor performance on the field. Just two years later, attendance had fallen to 20,992, nearly pre–Miller Park levels. Since then, an improving team has attracted more and more fans. In 2011, the Brewers won their division for the first time since 1982 and drew a record 37,918 fans per game.

---

[5]Attendance figures are based on "Baltimore Orioles Attendance Data" and "Cleveland Indians Attendance Data," *Baseball Almanac,* copyright on 2000–2012, at http://www.baseball-almanac.com, viewed April 21, 2011.

[6]The following discussion is taken from Christopher M. Clapp and Jahn K. Hakes, "How Long a Honeymoon? The Effect of New Stadiums on Attendance in Major League Baseball," *Journal of Sports Economics,* vol. 6, no. 3 (August 2005), pp. 237–263; John C. Leadley and Zenon X. Zygmont, "When Is the Honeymoon Over? National Basketball Association Attendance 1971–2000," *Journal of Sports Economics,* vol. 6, no. 2 (May 2005), pp. 203–221; John C. Leadley and Zenon X. Zygmont, "When Is the Honeymoon Over? Major League Baseball Attendance 1970–2000," *Journal of Sport Management,* vol. 19, no. 3 (July 2005), pp. 278–299; and John C. Leadley and Zenon X. Zygmont, "When Is the Honeymoon Over? National Hockey League Attendance 1970–2003," *Canadian Public Policy,* vol. 32, no. 2 (June 2006), pp. 213–232.

New hockey and basketball arenas have a smaller, shorter-lived effect on attendance. Perhaps due to the smaller capacity of such arenas, attendance rises by only 15 to 20 percent in the facility's first year. In addition, the honeymoon effect quickly diminishes. Hockey attendance falls back to previous levels within five to eight years, while basketball attendance returns to previous levels by year nine.

In a few cases, new ballparks have failed to draw additional fans. In part because of the financial meltdown of 2008–2009, the New York Yankees drew almost a half-million fewer fans in 2009—their first year in the new Yankee Stadium—than they did in 2008. However, despite this decline in attendance, *Forbes* magazine states that the team's gate revenue rose by over $100 million. The reason lies in the fact that, in addition to drawing more fans, teams in new facilities put fans into different, more expensive seats. According to *Forbes*, the average ticket price in the new Yankee stadium cost $26 more than in the old stadium.[7] The increase in revenue indicates that, at least in the case of the New York Yankees, the income elasticity of demand and the price elasticity of demand were low.

While new stadiums affect all ticket prices, the biggest impact is typically on the number, size, and cost of luxury boxes and other special seating. Surprisingly, until the Astrodome opened in 1965, no modern stadium had luxury boxes. Roy Hofheinz, part-owner of the Houston Astros and the moving force behind the building of the Astrodome, was inspired to create his "Skyboxes" by the "high perch for noblemen in Ancient Rome's Colosseum."[8] Indeed, the whole idea for a domed stadium came from the Colosseum's use of a retractable roof.[9] Since the Astrodome was constructed, luxury boxes and other premium seating have become an indispensable part of the contemporary sports facility.

While much of an NFL team's revenue is shared with other teams in the league, most of the revenue from luxury boxes is retained. It therefore provides an important source of profits for owners. As a result, the average NFL team has 140 luxury boxes, over 50 percent more than in the NHL, which has the second most boxes. It also has 8,675 club seats, which is over twice as many as the average

---

[7]The Yankees attendance was 4,298,655 in 2008 and 3,719,358 in 2009. Their gate revenue was $217 million in 2008 and $319 in 2009. Average ticket prices were $41 in 2008 and $67 in 2009. See "New York Yankees Attendance Data," *Baseball Almanac,* 2000–2012 at http://www.baseball-almanac.com/teams/yankatte.shtml, viewed May 21, 2012; Kurt Badenhausen and Michael Ozanian, "The Business of Baseball," *Forbes,* April 22, 2009, at http://www.forbes.com/lists/2009/33/baseball-values-09_New-York-Yankees_334613.html; and Kurt Badenhausen, Michael Ozanian, and Christina Settimi, "The Business of Baseball," *Forbes,* April 7, 2010, at http://www.forbes.com/lists/2010/33/baseball-valuations-10_New-York-Yankees_334613.html.

[8]Peter S. Canellos, "In City with Short Memory, Astrodome May Become History," *Milwaukee Journal-Sentinel,* July 27, 1997, p. 26A, at http://news.google.com/newspapers?nid=1683&dat=19970727&id=q0MqAAAAIBAJ&sjid=Ky4EAAAAIBAJ&pg=6675,7160037. The Colosseum, which held 80,000 people, also had drinking fountains and elevators that allowed animals to appear in the arena as if by magic. Unlike most stadiums today, it was privately funded (by slaves and booty taken during the conquest of Jerusalem) and remained in use for 500 years. See Joe Meyer, *The Roman Colosseum,* March 10, 2009, at http://www.synthreal.com/Colosseum.htm; and Elissa Michelle Zacher, *The Colosseum in Rome: Part One,* September 1, 2011, at http://socyberty.com/history/the-colosseum-in-rome-part-one.

[9]Edgar W. Ray, *The Grand Huckster: Houston's Judge Roy Hofheinz, Genius of the Astrodome* (Memphis: Memphis State University Press, 1980), pp. 230–231.

Team	Market Value[a]	Revenue	Year Stadium Opened	Number of Luxury Boxes (Rank)
Dallas Cowboys	$1,850	$406	2009	300 (1)
Washington Redskins	$1,555	$352	1997	280 (2)
New England Patriots	$1,400	$333	2002	88 (29)
New York Giants	$1,300	$293	2010	200 (4t)
New York Jets	$1,223	$285	2010	200 (4t)

TABLE 6.1   Stadium Revenue, Age, and Luxury Seating for the Five Most Valuable NFL Franchises

[a]All dollar figures in millions.

Sources: Kurt Badenhausen et al., "NFL Team Values," 2011, at http://www.forbes.com/lists/2011/30/nfl-valuations-11_land.html; Paul Munsey and Corey Suppes, *Ballparks*, 2012, at http://*Ballparks.com*; "Gillette Stadium," *ESPN.com* at http://espn.go.com/travel/stadium/_/s/nfl/id/17/gillette-stadium, viewed April 23, 2012.

MLB team has, which is second-most in this category.[10] Recent history suggests that the NFL's reliance on luxury seating is still growing. NFL stadiums built since 2001 have an average of 157 luxury boxes, about 29 more than are in the 11 stadiums built prior to 1990. That difference is probably a significant understatement of the trend in luxury boxes, as six of the older facilities have undergone extensive renovations since then.[11]

The impact of luxury seating on a team's profit can be seen in the *Forbes* data. Table 6.1 shows financial and seating information for the five most valuable NFL teams in 2010, which—not coincidentally—also have the five highest revenue streams.

Of these five teams, four have stadiums that were built since 2000, and three occupy the two newest facilities in the NFL. (The Giants and Jets share MetLife Stadium.) While the Redskins have a comparatively old facility, they are the only team that comes close to the Cowboys in the number of luxury boxes, with 280 to the Cowboys' 300. The Giants and Jets tie for fourth in the NFL, with 200 luxury boxes. Only the Patriots break the trend with a relatively low total of 88 luxury boxes, though this figure might be partly offset by the fact that the Patriots' suites are among the largest in the NFL and include two "Super Suites" that seat up to 36 people.[12]

6.2   HOW FANS BENEFIT FROM A NEW FACILITY

In the next two sections, we examine how fans and host cities gain from having a new facility. It might seem odd to distinguish between how a city benefits from hosting a sports franchise and how a team's fans benefit. After all, the population

---

[10]*Revenues from Sports Venues*, at http://www.sportsvenues.com/info.htm#Suites, viewed May 14, 2012.

[11]Figures are from Paul Munsey and Corey Suppes, *Ballparks*, at http://*Ballparks.com*, viewed April 23, 2012.

[12]Paul Munsey and Corey Suppes, *Ballparks*, at http://*Ballparks.com*, viewed May 15, 2012.

of the host city typically forms a great part of the team's fan base, and the fan base is often a large segment of the city's population. Our distinction, however, is not based on differing constituencies. Rather, it refers to the type of benefits each receives. In this section, we examine the generally intangible benefits that come from attending a game in a new stadium and from rooting for the "home team" regardless of whether one actually attends a game. In the section that follows, we evaluate the impact of teams and facilities on measures of economic activity, such as jobs, incomes, and tax revenues.

The Size and Shape of Baseball and Football Stadiums

In 1999, their last year in the Astrodome, the Houston Astros filled their home park to 61.0 percent of capacity. In 2008, the Astros filled 82.7 percent of the seats of Minute Maid Park. One might conclude from these figures that fans flocked to watch a much more attractive team or revel in a more attractive stadium in 2008. However, the Astros' average attendance in 2008 (34,741) was only marginally larger than a decade earlier (33,408). The percentage rose largely because Minute Maid Park has only 42,000 seats, while the Astrodome had almost 55,000. This jump in the percentage of capacity was not unique to the Astros, as most baseball stadiums have shrunk over the last two decades. In this section, we show how the size and shape of baseball and football stadiums—but not basketball and hockey arenas—have changed over the last 30 years. As football and baseball teams have moved from shared to separate facilities, they have been able to offer their fans seating arrangements that are adapted specifically to their sports.

Tables 6.2a and 6.2b contrast the two most recent eras of stadium construction. In the 1960s, 1970s, and 1980s, cities constructed large, circular, multipurpose

TABLE 6.2a   **The Capacity of Shared Baseball and Football Stadiums Built Between 1961 and 1982**

City	Stadium	Year Opened	MLB Team	MLB Capacity	NFL Team	NFL Capacity
Washington	RFK Stadium	1961	Senators	45,016	Redskins	56,692
New York	Shea Stadium	1964	Mets	55,601	Jets	57,333
Houston	Astrodome	1965	Astros	48,297[a]	Oilers	62,439
St. Louis	Busch Stadium	1966	Cardinals	49,676	Cardinals	60,000
San Diego	Jack Murphy Stadium	1967	Padres	53,539[a]	Chargers	56,586[a]
Cincinnati	Riverfront Stadium	1970	Reds	52,952	Bengals	60,389
Pittsburgh	Three Rivers Stadium	1970	Pirates	47,971	Steelers	59,594
Philadelphia	Veterans Stadium	1971	Phillies	62,382	Eagles	65,352
Seattle	Kingdome	1976	Mariners	59,166	Seahawks	66,403
Minneapolis	Metrodome	1982	Twins	55,883	Vikings	63,000

[a]Figures changed over time. This is a weighted average.

TABLE 6.2b The Capacity of Separate Baseball and Football Stadiums				
City	**MLB Stadium**	**MLB Capacity**	**NFL Stadium**	**NFL Capacity**
Washington	Nationals Stadium	41,888	FedEx Field	91,704
New York	Citi Field	45,000	MetLife Field	82,500
Houston	Minute Maid Field	40,963	LP Field[a]	68,798
St. Louis	Busch Stadium II	46,861	Edward Jones Dome[b]	65,321
San Diego	Petco Field	46,000	Qualcomm Stadium	71,294
Cincinnati	Great American Ball Park	42,059	Paul Brown Stadium	65,535
Pittsburgh	PNC Park	38,365	Heinz Field	65,050
Philadelphia	Citizens Bank Park	43,000	Lincoln Financial Field	68,532
Seattle	Safeco Field	46,621	CenturyLink Field	67,000
Minneapolis	Target Field	40,000	Metrodome	64,035

[a]The Houston Oilers moved to Nashville and became the Tennessee Titans.
[b]The NFL's St. Louis Cardinals moved to Phoenix and were replaced by the St. Louis Rams.
Source: Paul Munsey and Corey Suppes, *Ballparks,* at http://Ballparks.com, viewed April 24, 2012.

stadiums. The stadiums' distinctive, round shape and their close resemblance to one another led critics to call them "cookie-cutter stadiums." The average capacity of these facilities for baseball was 53,048 fans. The capacity expanded slightly for football games, growing to an average of 60,779.

Starting in the 1990s, a new era began in which baseball and football teams occupied separate facilities. Table 6.2a shows the seating capacities of the "cookie cutter stadiums" that were built to house both football teams and baseball teams. Table 6.2b shows the capacities of the single-purpose stadiums that replaced them in the 1990s and 2000s. No longer limited by having to share with a very different sport, new baseball stadiums shrank about 10,000 from 53,048 to 43,074. In contrast, football stadiums grew by about 10,000 from 60,779 to 71,247.

The reason for the changes in size can be found in the histories of the sports. Until the 1960s, most football teams were tenants in stadiums built by baseball team owners specifically to house the teams they owned.[13] By the 1960s, football had become increasingly popular, and municipalities were paying much or all of the construction costs. As a result, cities opted to build large,

---

[13]NFL teams even adopted variants of the names of MLB teams whose facilities they used (e.g., the Chicago Bears, who rented Wrigley Field from the Cubs) or took on the names of the teams themselves (e.g., the New York Giants of the NFL, who rented the Polo Grounds from MLB's Giants).

multipurpose stadiums. The size of the multipurpose stadiums was thus a compromise, too large for baseball and too small for football. The move back to single-use stadiums that began in the 1990s allowed each sport to find its optimal size.

Baseball and football stadiums also began to change shape in the 1960s. Circular stadiums were an attempt to meet the desires of both baseball and football fans. Unfortunately for the fans of both sports, the ideal seating arrangements for football and baseball look nothing alike. Football teams play on a standardized, rectangular field. Teams score by going to one end of the field or the other, but the bulk of the action takes place in the middle of the field. Seats at either end of the field give little perspective on the action and provide a poor view of what is happening for most plays. Figure 6.1 shows a diagram of Reliant Stadium, which was built for the NFL's Houston Texans. It was built specifically for football and thus has the ideal configuration for that sport.

By contrast, most of the action on a baseball field takes place within the diamond that forms the infield. Baseball stadiums built in the 19th and early 20th centuries thus consisted of grandstands that extended outward from home plate along the foul lines and did not encompass the outfield. Interestingly, stadiums built since 1990 closely resemble the ballparks from 100 years earlier. Figure 6.2 shows

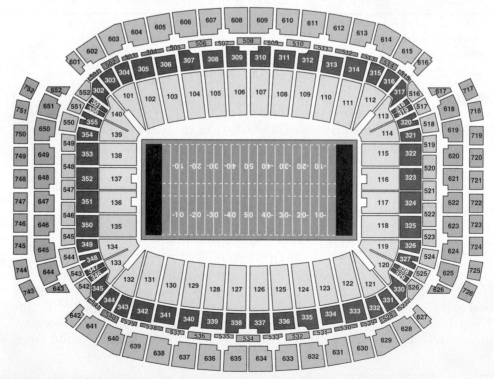

FIGURE 6.1   Reliant Stadium—Home of the NFL's Houston Texans
Source: Based on seating chart at Reliant Stadium found at http://reliantpart.com/reliant-stadium.

Minute Maid Park
Houston, Texas

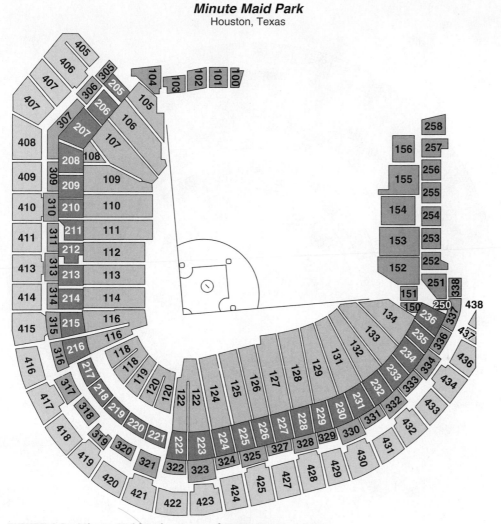

FIGURE 6.2 **Minute Maid Park—Home of MLB's Houston Astros**

Source: Minute Maid Park (Baseball Only), at http://www.Gotickets.Com/Venues/Tx/Minute_
Maid_Park.Php.

a diagram of Minute Maid Park, Houston's baseball-only facility. Notice that most of their seats near home plate and the infield, and relatively few seats far from the action in the outfield.

While the new, single-purpose facilities allow baseball and football teams to place seats in the optimal positions, the multipurpose facilities built in the 1960s and 1970s presented an unavoidable conflict between what worked for one sport and what worked for the other. The resulting compromise was the circular, cookie-cutter stadium, which provided poor sight lines for both sports.

The Astrodome
Houston, Texas

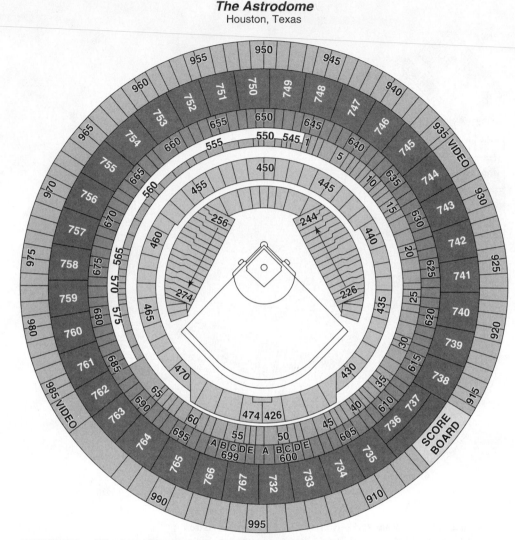

FIGURE 6.3a **The Astrodome—Configured for Baseball**

Source: The Astrodome, at http://www.gotickets.com/seating_charts/baseball/astrodome.php.

Figures 6.3a and 6.3b show the previous home of Houston football and baseball, the Astrodome, built in 1965 configured for baseball (Figure 6.3a) and football (Figure 6.3b). Because of its "cookie cutter" design, the stadium had many seats in the least desirable locations. When arranged for football, there were too many seats in the end zone and too many of the seats near midfield were far from the action. When arranged for baseball, there were too many seats deep in the outfield. As a result, fans of both sports had poor views of the action, and teams had trouble selling large blocks of tickets.

The Astrodome
Houston, Texas

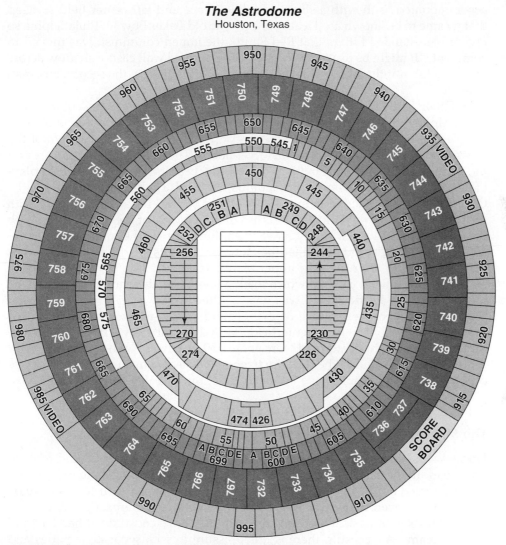

FIGURE 6.3b   The Astrodome—Configured for Football

Source: Based on figure "Astrodome configured for football" found at http://football.ballparks.com/NFL/HoustonOilers/seats.htm.

The cookie-cutter shape also imposed uniformity on baseball, which had previously been characterized by idiosyncratically shaped ballparks. While the size and shape of a football field and a baseball infield are carefully specified, the shape of a baseball outfield has few restrictions. As a result, stadiums built early in the 20th century came in a dizzying array of sizes and shapes. Some were designed around the particular strengths or weaknesses of the home team. Yankee Stadium may have been the "house that Ruth built," but it was also built to order for Babe Ruth, a left-handed batter who hit prodigious home runs. Yankee Stadium accommodated Ruth with a short right field fence and left-center field so deep that it came to be known as "Death Valley." The old Baker Bowl in Philadelphia so favored left-handed hitters that Red Smith, the famed columnist, was moved to comment, "It might be exaggerating to say the outfield wall casts a shadow across the infield. But if the right fielder had eaten onions at lunch, the second baseman knew it."[14]

Other fields were shaped to fit into a preexisting city plan. Centerfield in Philadelphia's Shibe Park came to a distinctive point 515 feet from home plate so that the stadium could fit in the square grid formed by city streets. Two of the most dramatic plays in baseball history—Bobby Thomson's "shot heard round the world," a dramatic 9th-inning home run that beat the Dodgers in a 1951 play-off game, and Willie Mays's miraculous catch of a mammoth drive by the Cleveland Indians' Vic Wertz in the 1954 World Series—had as much to do with the configuration of the Polo Grounds as with the talents of the two players. With one of the oddest shapes of any baseball stadium, the Polo Grounds, named for an area north of Central Park that the New York Giants shared with polo teams before moving to their home in upper Manhattan, could be a very easy place or an incredibly difficult place in which to hit a home run, depending on where one hit the ball. The leftfield wall was only 258 feet away, with an overhang that reduced the effective distance of the leftfield seats—where Thomson hit his home run—to only 250 feet. Centerfield was a different story. The stands in left-centerfield and right-centerfield were about 450 feet away, with a cutout in dead centerfield that extended the distance to about 480 feet.[15] In almost any other stadium, Willie Mays would have been staring at the ball Vic Wertz hit as it sailed out of the park.

The Size and Shape of Basketball and Hockey Arenas

Hockey and basketball franchises have a similar history to baseball and football franchises. In the early years of professional basketball, hockey team owners frequently rented out their buildings to basketball teams when their teams were on the road. However, the similarity ends there. Multipurpose arenas have not constrained hockey or basketball teams the way they have constrained baseball and football teams. As a result, there is less pressure to seek separate facilities and relatively small changes in capacity when hockey and basketball teams move to separate facilities. Table 6.3a shows that, as of the 2011–2012 season, 11 basketball teams still shared arenas with 10 hockey teams. (The Lakers and Clippers both share the Staples Center with the Kings in Los Angeles.) As seen in Table 6.3b, only four teams shared a city (or were located close to one another) and did not share a facility. The tables also indicate that the capacity of basketball and hockey arenas do not change as dramatically when teams go from shared to separate facilities. Hockey-only arenas hold only about 1,000 fewer fans than shared arenas, while

---

[14]Quoted in Rich Westcott, *Philadelphia's Old Ballparks* (Philadelphia: Temple University Press, 1996), p. 32.
[15]Stew Thornley, *Land of the Giants: New York's Polo Grounds* (Philadelphia: Temple University Press, 2000), p. 3.

TABLE 6.3a	Capacity of Shared Basketball and Hockey Arenas in 2011			
Arena	**NBA Team**	**NBA Capacity**	**NHL Team**	**NHL Capacity**
TD Garden	Boston Celtics	18,624	Boston Bruins	17,565
United Center	Chicago Bulls	21,711	Chicago Blackhawks	20,500
American Airlines Center	Dallas Mavericks	21,041	Dallas Stars	18,532
Pepsi Center	Denver Nuggets	19,155	Colorado Avalanche	18,007
Staples Center	Los Angeles Lakers/Clippers	19,028[a]	Los Angeles Kings	18,118
Madison Square Garden	New York Knicks	19,763	New York Rangers	18,200
Wells Fargo Center	Philadelphia 76ers	20,328	Philadelphia Flyers	19,537
Air Canada Centre	Toronto Raptors	19,800	Toronto Maple Leafs	18,819
Verizon Center	Washington Wizards	20,282	Washington Capitals	18,506
Prudential Center	New Jersey Nets[b]	18,103	New Jersey Devils	17,655

[a]Average of capacity for Lakers and Clippers.
[b]The Nets moved to the Barclays Center in Brooklyn in 2012.

TABLE 6.3b	Capacity of Separate Basketball and Hockey Arenas in 2011				
NBA Team	**NBA Arena**	**NBA Capacity**	**NHL Team**	**NHL Arena**	**NHL Capacity**
Detroit Pistons	The Palace of Auburn Hills	22,076	Detroit Red Wings	Joe Louis Arena	20,066
Miami Heat	American Airlines Arena	19,600	Florida Panthers	BankAtlantic Center	19,250
Minnesota Timberwolves	Target Center	19,356	Minnesota Wild	Xcel Energy Center	18,064
Phoenix Suns	US Airways Center	19,864	Phoenix Coyotes	Jobing.com Arena	17,125

Source: Paul Munsey and Corey Suppes, *Ballparks*, at http://Ballparks.com, viewed April 24, 2012.

basketball-only arenas are indistinguishable from shared arenas. With identical 82-game seasons and similar fan bases (at least for live attendance), hockey and basketball arenas tend to have similar sizes. Like football teams, both basketball and hockey teams move up and down rectangular surfaces, and scoring occurs at opposite ends of the rectangle. As a result, hockey and basketball use surfaces that have roughly the same size and shape, and there is little tension over the shape of the shared arenas.

The main conflict between basketball and hockey teams has been financial. In recent years, NBA teams have typically been the primary tenants of the arenas that they share with NHL teams and hence have benefited much more from their facilities. A hockey team that is a secondary tenant generally faces worse financial arrangements than the basketball team with which it shares the arena.[16] It is no surprise that the four most profitable teams in the NHL—the Toronto Maple Leafs, New York Rangers, Montreal Canadiens, and Detroit Red Wings—are all primary tenants in their facilities. The Maple Leafs and Rangers have arrangements with the Air Canada Centre and Madison Square Garden that are equal or superior to those of their cotenants, the NBA's Raptors and Knicks, while the Canadiens and Red Wings have their own arenas.

Do New Facilities Create Better Teams?

Team owners do not just promise that a new stadium will bring better seats, they invariably claim that the increased attendance and revenue will allow them to field better teams. However, research by Jahn Hakes and Christopher Clapp and by Kevin Quinn et al. suggests that the link between new stadiums and better teams is tenuous at best.[17] Both papers assume that teams maximize profits and that both winning and playing in a new facility increase revenues. In terms of the basic profit function first presented in Chapter 3,

$$\pi = R(w, A) - C_0 - C(w)$$

Revenue (R) increases with wins, w, and decreases with the age of the team's facility, A, as fans prefer to watch games in new facilities. We assume that cost has two components, one independent of wins, C_0, and one that increases with additional wins, $C(w)$. We assume that a new stadium increases costs only through a fixed cost that is associated with building the stadium. For example, the team might take out a loan to pay its share of construction costs, and pay its creditors C_0 every year. Because C_0 does not change with the number of number of games a team wins or the number of fans it attracts, it does not influence the teams desire to win. In this simple model, a new stadium increases profit if the added revenue

---

[16]See Robert La Franco, "Profits on Ice," *Forbes*, May 5, 1997, pp. 86–89.

[17]Jahn Hakes and Christopher Clapp, "The Edifice Complex: The Economics of Public Subsidization of Major League Baseball Facilities," *The International Journal of Sport Finance*, vol. 1, no. 2 (2006), pp. 77–95; and Kevin Quinn, Paul Bursick, Christopher Borick, and Lisa Raethz, "Do New Digs Mean More Wins? The Relationship between a New Venue and a Professional Sports Team's Competitive Success," *Journal of Sports Economics*, vol. 4, no. 3 (August 2003), pp. 167–182.

MR, MC (marginal revenue and marginal cost)

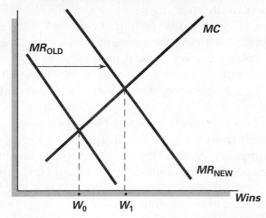
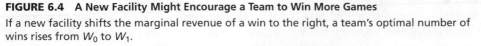

FIGURE 6.4   A New Facility Might Encourage a Team to Win More Games

If a new facility shifts the marginal revenue of a win to the right, a team's optimal number of wins rises from W_0 to W_1.

exceeds the fixed cost C_0, but does it also increase the number of games the team wins? The answer is yes if new facilities increase the impact of an additional win on revenue—that is, if fans are more attracted to a winning team when it plays in a nice new facility. As Figure 6.4 shows, if having a new facility increases the marginal revenue of a win, then teams with new facilities have a greater incentive to acquire talented players and win games.

Kevin Quinn et al. test the relationship between a facility's age and winning directly by analyzing how a new stadium affects the winning percentage of teams in the four major North American sports. They find that stadium age has no impact on winning percentage in any sport except baseball, where it has only a small effect. Jahn Hakes and Christopher Clapp test whether the impact of a win on revenue and attendance for baseball teams is greater in new stadiums than in old ones. They find that winning teams bring more fans and revenue and newer stadiums bring more fans and revenue but that winning teams do no better in new stadiums than they do in old ones. They conclude that baseball teams in new stadiums have no financial incentive to re-invest their revenue into hiring better players.[18]

Teams as Public Goods

One does not have to attend a game to benefit from the presence of a sports franchise. Just as a nation takes pride in the accomplishments of its Olympic athletes or national teams, states, cities, and neighborhoods can feel a sense of identity

---

[18]See Kevin Quinn et al., "Do New Digs Mean More Wins?" (2003); and Jahn Hakes and Christopher Clapp "The Edifice Complex" (2006).

from having a professional franchise in their midst.[19] A successful team, in particular, may contribute to a city's self-image. As Bill Veeck said of his 1948 Cleveland Indians, "[T]here is that feeling of reflected glory in a successful baseball team. Cleveland is winning the pennant. The eyes of the whole country are upon Cleveland, upon us, upon me and you. *We're looking pretty good, aren't we, Mac?*"[20] All the residents of a community can share in the goodwill and sense of community that their hometown team generates without attending a game or watching it on TV.

When teams become closely integrated into their communities, they become public goods. Recall from Chapter 3 that a public good is nonexcludable and nonrival in consumption. Nonrivalry in consumption means that one person's consumption does not prevent another person from consuming the good, while nonexcludability means that once the good is available to anyone, it is available to everyone. In the context of professional sports, attending the game is not a public good because fans can be excluded from Fenway Park unless they buy a ticket. However, a citizen of Red Sox Nation can consume the good feeling that comes from the Red Sox winning the World Series without ever having attended a game. Generally, teams are local public goods in the sense that the feelings they generate apply to a particular geographic area. At times, the feelings could extend beyond a city's borders, particularly if the feelings of community or pride apply to a different aspect of personal identity, such as ethnicity or religion, as has long been the case with Notre Dame's so-called "subway alumni," a term first applied to the large number of Catholics in New York who devotedly followed Notre Dame football.

Residents of small to midsized cities feel they are part of a "big-time" city when their hometown has a major league franchise. Indianapolis may not be able to compete with New York in terms of economic or cultural clout, but its residents derive a sense of superiority to New York whenever *our* Indiana Pacers defeat *their* New York Knicks. It may therefore come as no surprise that a survey of residents of Indianapolis in the 1990s found that the Indiana Pacers were a close second to the city's museums as a source of civic pride, with the Indianapolis Colts placing third.[21]

The links between sport and society can run far deeper than good feelings about one's hometown and can have far more serious consequences than just

---

[19]Michael Danielson, *Home Team: Professional Sport and the American Metropolis* (Princeton, N.J.: Princeton University Press, 1997); Rosentraub, *Major League Losers: The Real Cost of Sports and Who's Paying for it* (New York: Basic Books/Princeton University Press, 1997), pp. 30–73; and David Swindell and Mark Rosentraub, "Who Benefits from the Presence of Professional Sports Teams? The Implications for Public Funding of Stadiums and Arenas," *Public Administration Review*, vol. 58, no. 1 (January/February 1998), pp. 11–20.

[20]Bill Veeck and Ed Linn, *Veeck as in Wreck* (Chicago: University of Chicago Press, 1962), p. 121.

[21]Mark Rosentraub, "Stadiums and Urban Space," in *Sports, Jobs, and Taxes*, ed. by Roger Noll and Andrew Zimbalist (Washington, D.C.: Brookings Institution Press, 1997), pp. 189–190; and David Swindell and Mark Rosentraub, "Who Benefits from the Presence of Professional Sports Teams?" (1998), pp. 11–20.

a pride in being part of "Red Sox Nation."[22] Local sports teams sometimes reflect the aspirations of rival ethnic groups. For example, the Glasgow Rangers and Glasgow Celtic soccer teams play out the rivalry between Protestants and Catholics in Glasgow in the Scottish Football League. The Montreal Canadiens and FC Barcelona have been symbols of something even larger: the nationalist yearnings by ethnic minorities.

French Canada has long identified with the Canadiens. In fact, some historians trace the separatist movement in Quebec to "Richard riot" of 1955. The riot ostensibly began in response to the suspension of hockey great Maurice Richard for several games at the end of the 1954–1955 NHL season and the ensuing playoffs. In fact, Richard's suspension might have simply been the last straw for Montreal's French-Canadian residents, who had long felt shut out from opportunities by the English-speaking élite.

While some French-Canadian fans speak of separation, FC Barcelona fans actually fought for it during the Spanish Civil War. "Barça," as the football team is called, has long been a symbol of Catalan separatist aspirations and, from 1938 to 1975, of opposition to Fascist rule of Francisco Franco. With the Catalan language banned and the Franco régime openly supporting archrival Réal Madrid, "[o]nly the Camp Nou [FC Barcelona's home field] provided Catalans a place to yell and scream against the regime in their own, banned vernacular."[23]

6.3 HOW CITIES BENEFIT FROM TEAMS, FACILITIES, AND EVENTS

Candidates for public office often claim that government should be run like a business. If that were the case, then many stadiums would not be built, and cities would not compete so vigorously for events such as the Olympics. The central question facing any private business is whether a project is profitable. By this standard, most studies find that sports facilities fall short. Without public support, most contemporary facilities fail to cover their costs of construction and operation.[24] Building a stadium (or subsidizing its construction) thus seems to be a losing proposition that cities should avoid. While cities might spend too much on stadiums and arenas, people who insist that the facilities be profitable misunderstand the role of government. Economists agree that the private sector's pursuit of profit generally does a good job of allocating resources. However, they also agree that unfettered markets sometimes fail to provide the socially desired amount of a good or service. When markets fail, government intervention can lead to improved outcomes.

---

[22]This term is often used to denote the collective fans of the Boston Red Sox, particularly those living in New England. The term has been traced to an article about the split loyalties of Connecticut residents during the 1986 New York Mets–Boston Red Sox World Series. Nathan Cobb, "Baseball Border War: In Milford, Conn. Geography Brings Sox and Mets Fans Cheek to Jowl," *Boston Globe*, October 20, 1986, p. 8.

[23]Franklin Foer, *How Soccer Explains the World: An Unlikely Theory of Globalization* (New York: Harper Collins, 2004), p. 195.

[24]See, for example, Jahn Hakes and Christopher Clapp "The Edifice Complex" (2006), p. 78.

Market failure can occur for several reasons. For example, market outcomes may provide too little of a public good and consumers may attempt to free ride. Alternatively, market outcomes may lead to overconsumption of a common resource, as the case in the tragedy of the commons. Monopolies maximize profit by producing less than the socially optimal amount of output. In this chapter, we focus on the market failure caused by externalities. An **externality** is an unintended and uncompensated cost or benefit that a firm imposes on a third party who has no part in the firm's provision of a good or service.

Governments exist in part to bring a broader perspective to the allocation of goods and services by ensuring that firms pay the full costs and receive the full benefits of their actions. When the presence of a team, a new facility, or a mega-event such as the Olympics or Super Bowl brings large benefits that are not captured by the private sector, local governments can prevent market failure and improve economic well-being by providing subsidies to teams and event-organizing committees. In this section, we examine some of the benefits of teams and mega-events that the private sector does not take into consideration but that governments can and should. The focus in this section broadens from just facilities to the presence of the team or event itself. This is because cities typically confront the decision to build a new facility in the context of the broader decision to attract a team or event or to prevent a team from leaving.

Positive and Negative Externalities

Governments subsidize facilities and mega-events because of the externalities they cause. A **positive externality** occurs when a party not directly involved in a transaction receives unintended benefits from a transaction, and a **negative externality** occurs when a party bears unintended costs from a transaction for which they do not receive compensation. The rationale for public funding of a stadium or arena rests largely on the belief that the positive externalities of sports franchises outweigh the negative externalities for their communities.[25]

Positive and negative externalities interfere with the market's ability to allocate resources. Consider, for example, a typical Chicago Cubs game. In addition to whatever direct costs and benefits the Cubs convey to the residents of Chicago, they also create negative externalities each time they play a game. In deciding how much to produce, the Cubs and MLB as a whole are typically concerned only with the private cost of operation—how much they must spend on salaries, travel, and a host of other inputs. They do not usually consider—and may not even be aware of—the external costs of the health problems and inconvenience they create for people affected by the traffic congestion caused by people who attend the game and the resulting noise, overcrowding, and pollution. The private costs that underlie the Cubs' and MLB's profit maximization decisions understate

---

[25]Externalities can result from either production or consumption. Here, we consider only negative production externalities and positive consumption externalities.

the full social costs, which include both the private costs and the costs imposed on third parties.[26] If the Cubs or any firm considered all these costs, the net rewards associated with any given price—and the incentive to produce—would be lower. As a result the "private" supply curve (S_p) in Figure 6.4, which includes only private costs experienced directly by the firm, lies to the right of the "social" supply curve (S_s), which includes all private and social costs.

The market equilibrium that results from the private decisions of producers and consumers in Figure 6.5 is Q_p, while the socially optimal quantity is only Q_s. The difference ($Q_p - Q_s$) shows that the negative production externality causes the Cubs to schedule too many games when left to their own devices. Similarly, the difference between the price that the Cubs charge and the price that society would like them to charge ($p_p - p_s$) shows that a negative externality causes the Cubs to charge their fans too little.

Because the Cubs do not pay for the congestion and pollution they cause, the negative externality makes them better off. The lower cost of production allows the Cubs to charge a lower price, which benefits fans who attend Cubs games. Chicago residents, most of whom do not attend games, suffer, however, from the costs that the Cubs impose on them.

Surprisingly, Chicago generally does not want to entirely eliminate the negative externalities that the Cubs impose on it. The only way to ensure that the Cubs

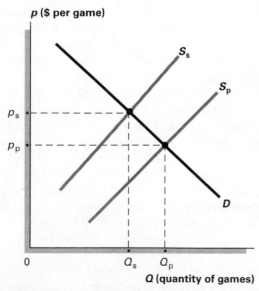

FIGURE 6.5 Negative Production Externalities Shift the Supply Curve Leftward
The socially optimal quantity of games (Q_s) is less than the privately optimal quantity (Q_p).

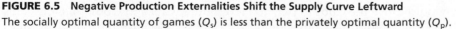

[26]Some teams, including the Cubs, have tried to reduce or eliminate negative externalities. The Cubs provide shuttle buses to reduce traffic and cleanup crews to reduce litter in the surrounding community. See Christopher Hepp, "Near Fabled Park, Ambience a Lure," *Philadelphia Inquirer* (September 29, 1999), pp. A1, A6.

impose no negative externalities would be for them to play no games. Ending Cubs games to get rid of the negative externality would probably leave Chicago worse off because negative externalities are undesirable by-products of a desirable action. In general, people would be worse off without the output even if it meant a cleaner, safer environment. In this example, Chicagoans want to see the number of games reduced to Q_s, where the benefits and social costs of one more ballgame are equal, but they do not want to eliminate the games entirely.

The negative production externalities associated with sports facilities tend to decline over time. Residents of neighborhoods where a proposed structure will be built often complain bitterly about the problems it will bring. However, residents are almost rhapsodic about long-existing structures. In the words of baseball historian Harold Seymour, a ballpark is "a landmark, an asset to city life—especially to the lives of those who live in the neighborhood."[27]

The change in attitudes does not come because the stadium or the fans change. It comes because the residents change. None of the homeowners who lived in what is now called "Wrigleyville" when the stadium was built in 1914 are still alive. Almost all the residences and businesses have been sold several times over since then. The turnover has two effects. First, Wrigleyville might attract people and businesses that enjoy having a team in the neighborhood. These gains could outweigh the losses of the negative externalities and leave residents and local merchants better off. Second, even if the negatives dominate, the turnover has internalized the externality because people who have bought homes or businesses in Wrigleyville have been compensated for any inconvenience. The compensation comes in the form of lower real estate prices. The only ones to be hurt were the original homeowners and businesses. They paid full price for their locations and were not compensated for the costs imposed on them. The negative externalities generated by newer facilities, such as Nationals Park in Washington, DC, which was built in 2009, have yet to be fully internalized. People who own nearby housing may see the value of their property decline. Unlike the residents of Wrigleyville, few of them paid a discounted price for their property.

Sports facilities also bring benefits to the neighborhoods, cities, and metropolitan areas in which they are located. Many firms and households that have no direct connection to the facility see their incomes rise as a result of its construction. Because they do not compensate the team for locating in the city, these firms and households benefit from a positive externality.

Just as the costs imposed by a negative externality cause the private supply curve to be too far to the right in Figure 6.5, the benefits brought by a positive consumption externality cause the private demand curve to be too far to the left. Figure 6.6 shows that, in the absence of government intervention, a positive externality would cause the Cubs to play too few games. Chicago would like the Cubs to play Q_s games, but the Cubs would play only Q_p. Because the Cubs' revenues understate the total benefit to the residents of Chicago, the city must provide an

---

[27]See the Foreword to Michael Betzold and Ethan Casey, *Queen of Diamonds: The Tiger Stadium Story* (West Bloomfield, Mich.: Northfield Publishing, 1992).

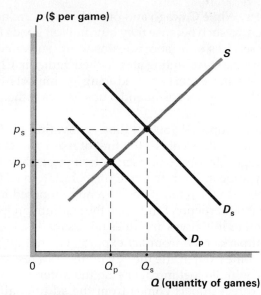

p ($ per game)

FIGURE 6.6 **Positive Consumption Externalities Shift the Demand Curve Outward**
The socially optimal quantity (Q_s) is greater than the privately optimal quantity (Q_p).

additional incentive for the Cubs to play in Chicago rather than elsewhere. In the case of professional sports franchises, these incentives often take the form of public funding of sports facilities.

Facilities, Spending, and Tax Revenue

New facilities generate many different forms of spending. Constructing even the simplest of major league facilities produces hundreds of millions of dollars in spending and income. Once the facility is built, fans will spend tens of millions of dollars to attend and enjoy a game. From the standpoint of a team, the story ends there. Cities, however, have a broader perspective. Businesses and households that have nothing to do with the facility or the team that occupies it benefit if people who come for a game stay in the city for dinner or spend the night at a local hotel. Nor do the benefits stop there. The stadium employees and restaurant workers who earn higher incomes because of the new facility now have more money to spend, which increases the incomes of still other people in the local economy. We next examine the impact of these direct and indirect benefits to cities.

DIRECT BENEFITS   The direct benefit of the Cubs to Chicago is the new spending that is attributable to the team. New spending takes one of two forms. First, a franchise might cause Chicagoans to spend more—and save less—than they otherwise would. Second, and more importantly, the Cubs stimulate net exports by Chicago. International trade economists define **net exports** as the difference between the value of goods and services that a nation exports and the value of goods and services it imports. While Chicago and other US cities are not separate countries, we can treat them as such because they buy and sell goods from one another. Chicago exports the services of its sports teams to the surrounding region if the teams attract fans from the surrounding area to their games in Chicago. The teams also increase Chicago's net exports by reducing its imports from other cities. Chicago's imports fall if Chicagoans attend Cubs games rather than spend their money outside Chicago.

Advocates of the proposed $500 million renovation of Wrigley Field cite the construction jobs it would create as the first of many direct benefits the project would bring Chicago. However, a closer look suggests that the benefits might be smaller than they appear. First, the benefits come from *additional* spending. If Chicago's contribution to the renovation (currently proposed to be $250 million) comes out of a general construction fund, then the stadium project simply **crowds out**—or displaces—other initiatives and does not increase spending. Second, the benefits from the ballpark come from *net* exports, but not all the inputs to the construction project come from inside the city limits. As a result, it increases both exports and imports, with the net impact being the difference between the two.

A longer-term direct impact comes from the additional money that Cub fans will spend at the newly renovated ballpark and its surroundings. The Fan Cost Index reports that a family of four would spend a little over $300 on a trip to Wrigley Field in 2012.[28] Using these spending figures, if the renovations to Wrigley Field attract 250,000 additional fans and the index remains unchanged, the renovations will generate over $18 million in additional spending per year— or will it?

The true annual impact is likely to be far less than $18 million. The main reason is that much of the additional expenditure in Wrigleyville would not be additional expenditure in Chicago. Cubs fans would have spent much of that money elsewhere in Chicago if there had been no renovation to Wrigley Field or even if Wrigley Field did not exist. To a great extent, the renovation merely induces **substitution spending**, as Chicagoans shift their spending from one local leisure activity to another. Even the money spent by out-of-towners in Wrigleyville might not be new spending if residents of other cities decide to visit Wrigley Field rather than other attractions, such as the Chicago Art Institute, while they are visiting Chicago.

Finally, despite their high profile, sports franchises are really rather small businesses. In the words of one expert, "the sales revenue of Fruit of the Loom exceeds that for all of Major League Baseball."[29] Applying the Fan Cost Index to

---

[28]The Fan Cost Index computes the average cost of four nonpremium tickets, two beers, four sodas, four hot dogs, two programs, two hats, and parking for one car at each ballpark. We divided this figure by four and multiplied it by total attendance. See "Team Marketing Research," *Team Marketing Report*, April 2011, at http://www.teammarketing.com/public/files/2011_mlb_fci.pdf.

[29]Robert Baade, "Should Congress Stop the Bidding War for Sports Franchises?" Hearing Before the Subcommittee on Antitrust, Business Rights, and Compensation, Senate Committee on the Judiciary, November 29, 1995, vol. 4, "Academics," *Heartland Policy*, at http://www.heartland.org/stadps4.html, p. 19.

overall attendance in 2011 indicates that fans spent about $230 million at Cubs games in 2011. While that looks like a lot of money, it comes to less than one-tenth of one percent of the total income generated by the Chicago economy. The total revenue of all five Chicago franchises comes to less than one-half of one percent of all local incomes.[30] The impact of sports franchises on local economies is thus very small.

MULTIPLIER EFFECTS   The money spent at Cubs games also has an indirect effect on Chicago's economy, which benefits people who have nothing to do with the Cubs. This indirect benefit stems from the higher incomes of people who work at or near Cubs games. Their higher incomes lead to added spending elsewhere in Chicago. This spillover of added income and spending into the broader economy is known as the **multiplier effect**.

To envision the multiplier effect, think of Chicago's economy as a still pond. Spending additional money at a Cubs game is like throwing a pebble into the pond. The direct impact of the spending is the splash caused by the pebble's hitting the water. A series of ripples quickly spreads out from the initial point of impact. As they spread out, the ripples become fainter and fainter, until they are indistinguishable from the flat pond. The multiplier effect is like those ripples, spreading the direct impact of the spending throughout the city. To illustrate this, suppose that Rachel, a Chicago resident who runs a restaurant in Wrigleyville, earns an additional $30,000 thanks to the increased patronage that is generated by the renovations at Wrigley Field. That added income is part of the direct impact of the renovation and is part of the initial splash the pebble makes in the pond. Rachel saves some of her income and spends, say $27,000, on a new kitchen installed by a local company. Her expenditure on the kitchen becomes part of the first ripple. Her purchase, in turn, increases the income of the contractor who works on her kitchen. The contractor saves some of his additional $27,000 and spends, say $24,300, on a new car from a local dealer, forming yet another ripple, and so on.

The ripples get smaller because people do not spend all their additional income. Economists call the fraction of an additional dollar of income that consumers spend the **marginal propensity to consume** (MPC). They call the fraction of an additional dollar that they save the **marginal propensity to save** (MPS). Consumers must spend or save that entire additional dollar, so

$$MPC + MPS = 1$$

Studies indicate that Americans spend more than nine-tenths of each additional dollar that they earn. In the preceding example, Rachel's $MPC = 0.9$, so she spends

$$(0.9)(\$30,000) = \$27,000$$

---

[30]The total revenue data come from the *Forbes* team valuations for 2010–2011. Personal income data for Cook County, Illinois comes from U.S. Department of Commerce, "Table CA1-3: Personal Income Summary," *Regional Data: GDP & Personal Income,* at http://www.bea.gov/iTable/iTable.cfm?reqid= 70&step=1&isuri=1&acrdn=5, viewed April 27, 2012.

The $27,000 that Rachel spends is additional income to the contractor, who then spend nine-tenths of that income, or

$$(0.9)[(0.9)(\$30,000)] = \$24,300$$

The process continues in steadily decreasing ripples until the additional expenditure becomes indistinguishable from zero, and the ripples effectively disappear.

The total impact of Rachel's $30,000 increase in income on Chicago's economy is

$$T = \$30,000 + \$27,000 + \$24,300 + \$21,870 + \dots$$

While the numbers in this sum decline steadily to zero, it is not clear what the total impact is. We can, however, find the limit of this infinite sum. Using what we know about the numbers in the sum, we can rewrite T as

$$T = \$30,000 \times M$$

where

$$M = 1 + 0.9 + 0.9^2 + 0.9^3 + 0.9^4 + \dots$$

It is not hard to solve for M, which in this case equals $\dfrac{1}{1 - 0.9}$ or 10. The total impact of Rachel's additional earnings is thus $30,000 \times 10$, or $300,000. Because we multiply the initial expenditure by M, we call M the **multiplier**. Of course, the MPC need not equal 0.9. More generally, we compute the multiplier as follows:

$$M = \frac{1}{1 - MPC} = \frac{1}{MPS}$$

The multiplier effect means that a relatively small direct increase in incomes can have a huge impact on the well-being of a city. For example, a multiplier of 10 means that the impact of the $18 million in added spending in Wrigleyville has a total impact of $180 million.

The simple multiplier, however, vastly overstates the impact of professional sports teams.[31] The most important reason for this inaccuracy is that the simple multiplier applies to a **closed economy**, one that does not engage in trade. Cities, however, are **open economies** that trade extensively with other cities as well as with foreign countries. In open economies, much of the added consumption that results from higher incomes consists of imports from other economies. In our example, that would happen if Rachel spent some of her $30,000 on a Japanese-made camera or a laptop made in California. Any leakage from the local economy reduces the ripple effect in two ways. First, it causes local incomes to rise by less,

---

[31]The following argument is based on John Siegfried and Andrew Zimbalist, "A Note on the Local Economic Impact of Sports Expenditures," *Journal of Sports Economics*, vol. 3, no. 4 (November 2002), pp. 361–366.

as Rachel might spend only $20,000 on her new kitchen. Second, the contractor, who now receives less income, spends less of *his* additional income locally, causing the next ripple to be smaller still.

We can account for the impact of leakages from the system by adding the **marginal propensity to import**, the amount of an extra dollar of income that is spent on imported goods, to the multiplier. A more accurate multiplier would therefore be

$$M = \frac{1}{(1 - MPC + MPI)}$$

If we assume that 50 cents of every additional dollar of income leaves Chicago, the multiplier shrinks from 10 to 2.5 $(1/(1 - .9 + .5)) = 1/.4 = 2.5$). As a general rule, local multipliers are much smaller than national multipliers.

Much of the leakage from cities reflects the fact that most players do not live in the city where they work. Most of the full-time jobs and most of the income generated by the Cubs go to the team's athletes, coaches, front-office staff, executives, and owners, relatively few of whom live year-round in Chicago. To see this in another setting, while 93 percent of average employees live near where they work, only 29 percent of NBA players do. In all, while over 58 percent of an average employee's income is injected into a local economy, only about 10 percent of an NBA player's income is.[32] Sports teams thus serve as a conduit, transferring money from one set of out-of-town residents to another set of out-of-town residents.

Leakages are also inversely related to the size and diversity of the local economy. Large cities, which provide more opportunities to buy locally-made items, generally have larger multipliers than do small cities. However, the larger multiplier is at least partly offset by greater substitution spending. A larger local economy provides residents with more alternative outlets for their leisure time, reducing the likelihood that a sports franchise generates new spending that would not otherwise take place.[33]

Two additional factors further reduce the multiplier effect of professional sports franchises. First, because professional athletes' salaries are much higher than for most workers, they are taxed at a higher rate, leaving less of their income available for consumption. Second, as income increases, workers have a greater tendency to save, so the *MPC* falls. Because professional athletes' careers tend to be relatively short, they have an additional incentive to save, so their *MPC* is even smaller. In sum, the local multiplier is unlikely to be much bigger than 1.0, meaning that spending on a professional sports franchise has no multiplier effect on the local economy.

---

[32]John Siegfried and Andrew Zimbalist, "The Economics of Sports Facilities and Their Construction," *Journal of Economic Perspectives*, vol. 14, no. 3 (Summer 2000), pp. 95–114.

[33]See Roger Noll and Andrew Zimbalist, "The Economic Impact of Sports Teams and Facilities," in *Sports, Jobs, and Taxes*, ed. by Roger Noll and Andrew Zimbalist (Washington, D.C.: Brookings Institution Press, 1997), pp. 79–80; and Peter von Allmen, "Multiplier Effects and Local Economic Impact," in *The Oxford Handbook of Sports Economics*, vol. 2, ed. by Stephen Shmanske and Leo Kahane (Oxford: Oxford University Press, 2012).

STUDIES OF ECONOMIC IMPACT   Many economists have studied the impact of sports facilities, franchises, and mega-events on cities.[34] Most studies analyze potential increases in economic well-being (such as median income or employment) due to the presence of an athletic team or a new facility after controlling for other factors that are unrelated to sports. From the pathbreaking work of Robert Baade and Richard Dye to recent research by Dennis Coates and Brad Humphreys, economists have consistently found little or no evidence that facilities and teams affect the level of employment, incomes, or wages in a city.[35]

A more recent strand of the literature studies the impact of teams and facilities on property values. It asks whether the presence of a team makes a city more attractive even if it does not directly increase incomes or employment. If so then the increased demand for home and office space drives up property values. The results of this literature are mixed. Studies by Gerald Carlino and Edward Coulson and by Charles Tu find a positive impact on property values. These findings, however, might be specific to the data they use.[36] Papers by Coates and Humphreys and, more recently, by Xia Feng and Humphreys find small effects that drop off rapidly with greater distance from the facility.[37] Both papers conclude that, all else equal, a professional sports franchise makes the immediate neighborhood more attractive to potential homebuyers but that it has little effect on the city as a whole.

INTEREST GROUPS AND PUBLIC CHOICE   Even if new facilities are losing propositions, cities might still pursue them. One explanation for this seemingly irrational behavior is that specific interest groups, particularly in the construction and hospitality industries, might gain a lot. If these interest groups have disproportionate influence over the city's politicians, then the project might go forward even if a majority of the city's population opposes it. This helps to explain how cities like Phoenix and Pittsburgh got new ballparks after the proposal had been rejected in a referendum.[38] In this section, we use an area of economic theory known as public choice to develop an economic framework for such behavior.

---

[34]For a good survey of this literature, see Dennis Coates, "Stadiums and Arenas: Economic Development or Economic Redistribution?" *Contemporary Economic Policy,* vol. 25, no. 4 (October 2007), pp. 565–577.

[35]Robert Baade and Richard Dye, "Sports Stadiums and Area Development: A Critical Review," *Economic Development Quarterly,* vol. 2, no. 3 (August 1988), pp. 265–275; Dennis Coates and Brad Humphreys, "The Effect of Professional Sports on Earnings and Employment in U.S. Cities," *Regional Science and Urban Economics,* vol. 33, no. 2 (March 2003), pp. 175–198.

[36]Tu's case study of FedEx Field in Landover, MD does not account for the fact that another venue— U.S. Airways Arena—closed at about the same time that FedEx Field opened, while Carlino and Coulson exclude a large number of low-value properties. See Gerald Carlino and N. Edward Coulson, "Compensating Differentials and the Social Benefit of the NFL," *Journal of Urban Economics,* vol. 56, no. 1 (July 2004), pp. 25–50; and Charles Tu, "How Does a New Stadium Affect Housing Values? The Case of FedEx Field," *Land Economics,* vol. 81, no. 3 (August 2005), pp. 379–395.

[37]Dennis Coates and Brad R. Humphreys, "Professional Sports Facilities, Franchises and Urban Economic Development," *Public Finance and Management,* vol. 3, no. 3 (2003), pp. 335–357; and Brad Humphreys and Xia Feng, "Assessing the Economic Impact of Sports Facilities on Housing Values: A Spatial Hedonic Approach," *IASE/NAASE Working Paper 08-12,* August 2008.

[38]See Kevin Delaney, *Public Dollars, Private Stadiums* (New Brunswick: Rutgers University Press, 2003); and Robert Trumpbour, *The New Cathedrals* (Syracuse, N.Y.: Syracuse University Press, 2007).

Public choice theory stems from the work of Nobel laureate James Buchanan, Gordon Tullock, William Niskanen, and others in the 1960s. Its premise rests on the notion that decision makers in the public sector do not automatically act to resolve the market failures of public goods and externalities. Instead, public officials behave like consumers and producers in the private sector. They maximize their own well-being subject to constraints.

According to public choice theory, the interests of politicians and the owners of sports franchises dovetail neatly. Politicians want to attain, maintain, and improve their political standing. They therefore take actions designed to ensure their re-election or election to higher office. Since it is costly to determine the specific interests of large numbers of disparate voters, politicians are most responsive to organized group interests; the more highly organized the group, the more influence it wields over officeholders.[39]

Team owners, often in alliance with business and labor interests, have sought to use their organized influence over the political process. By expressing the intensity of their desires, interest groups may—through a process known as **logrolling**—induce politicians to pass legislation that majority rule would deny. To see this, suppose a legislature consists of three equal groups, each representing one-third of the state (i.e., East, Central, and West). The state is considering building two stadiums, one each in the East and West of the state. Suppose each new stadium would greatly benefit the region in which it is located but mildly hurt—through higher taxes that everyone in the state must pay to fund the stadiums—the other two portions of the state, as seen in Table 6.4. If the politicians voted according to the impact of the stadium on their constituents, they would defeat both stadium proposals, because each proposal hurts two-thirds of the state. However, according to the payoffs in Table 6.4, each proposal benefits the host constituency so much that majority rule leaves the state worse off.

Logrolling allows each group to express the intensity of its desires, thereby improving the efficiency of the political process. While residents of the East are harmed by the facility in the West and vice versa, if each agrees to support the other's proposal, the gain from their own stadium outweighs the cost of the other's

TABLE 6.4 How Logrolling Can Improve Social Well-Being

Region	Payoff to Proposal #1	Payoff to Proposal #2
East	+$10 million	−$2 million
Central	−$2 million	−$2 million
West	−$2 million	+$10 million
Overall impact	+$6 million	+$6 million

---

[39]See, for example, Arthur Seldon, "Public Choice and the Choices of the Public," in *Democracy and Public Choice*, ed. by Charles Rowley (London: Basil Blackwell, 1987), pp. 122–134.

stadium, leaving both better off. Each proposal passes by a 2–1 margin, and the overall well-being of the state improves, despite the fact that each facility benefits only one region.[40]

Group interests do not always have a positive impact on social well-being. Sometimes they are simply an attempt to claim economic rent. **Economic rent** is the extra return received by a producer or by an input above and beyond the opportunity cost of providing the output or input. Monopoly and monopsony power and public subsidies are common sources of economic rents. With tens or hundreds of millions of dollars in public funding for a new stadium or arena at stake, teams, leagues, and other stakeholders are willing to spend heavily to influence the political process in their pursuit of economic rents.

Pro-stadium forces regularly outspend their opponents in public referenda on stadium funding. In Seattle, Paul Allen used some of the fortune he made from Microsoft to cover the $4.2 million cost of the state referendum on financing a new football stadium for his Seattle Seahawks. He went on to spend $5 million to convince voters to support the proposal. His return, $300 million in state funding for Seahawk Stadium (now CenturyLink Field), made the $9.2 million investment one of Allen's most profitable moves since joining with Bill Gates to form Microsoft.[41]

Even when the vote does not go their way, lobbyists often find ways to get what they want. Frequently, that involves getting state legislators to provide what their constituents will not. For example, supporters of new stadiums for the Steelers and Pirates in Pittsburgh successfully turned to a "Plan B" in the state house—one that, in a neat application of logrolling, involved building two new stadiums in Philadelphia—after voters in Pittsburgh had rejected public funding. In 2012, voters in Minnesota saw their rejection of public funding overturned by the state house, which approved $498 million in funding for a new $975 million home for the Minnesota Vikings.[42]

While economists generally take a dim view of rent seeking, interest groups can sometimes have a positive impact by backing sports initiatives. New facilities and particularly mega-events can lead to investments in local infrastructure that will benefit the city for years but which never would have been approved without a specific event to focus the energy of interest groups. The 2008 Olympics transformed much of Beijing, leading in particular to a massive expansion of the city's subway system and the construction of the world's largest terminal at Beijing Airport.

---

[40]See, for example, Thomas Stratmann, "Logrolling," in *Perspectives on Public Choice: A Handbook*, ed. by Dennis Mueller (Cambridge, U.K.: Cambridge University Press, 1997), pp. 322–341.

[41]Joanna Cagan and Neil deMause, *Field of Schemes* (1998), pp. 16, 44, 166–168.

[42]See Kevin Delaney, *Public Dollars, Private Stadiums* (2003); and Robert Trumpbour, *The New Cathedrals* (2007); and Baird Helgeson and Jennifer Brooks, "After Years of Dealing and Debate, Viking Get their Biggest Win," *Minnesota Star-Tribune*, May 11, 2012, at http://www.startribune.com/politics/statelocal/150960525.html, viewed May 12, 2012.

Location, Location, Location

The impact of a team or facility on the local economy also depends on its precise location. A city maximizes the positive externalities associated with a sports franchise if it integrates the facilities into the urban fabric.[43] To do so, a city must develop an urban plan that exploits the attractions of a ballpark. Baltimore attempted to do just that when it placed Camden Yards and then M&T Bank Stadium in the Inner Harbor. Tourists could come to the Inner Harbor, spend time at other attractions, such as the Baltimore Aquarium, see a ballgame, and have nearby hotels to stay overnight. Cleveland followed a similar strategy. Jacobs (now Progressive) Field, which kept the Indians in town, and Gund (now Quicken Loans) Arena, which brought the Cavaliers back to Cleveland from suburban Richfield, were all part of a broader Gateway Project designed to revitalize downtown Cleveland.

The results of these projects have been mixed. While Cleveland experienced job growth following the construction of its sports facilities, the growth was actually lower downtown than elsewhere in the region and was slower than in the years immediately preceding the project.[44] Studies of Baltimore show that Orioles Park created fewer than 600 jobs and left the typical household roughly $12 poorer through the taxes paid to support the construction. Estimates suggest that, if anything, Baltimore's M&T Bank Stadium did even less.[45]

Baltimore's Oriole Park at Camden Yards also touched off a nostalgia craze among fans and stadium designers. Most baseball stadiums built since the early 1990s have a distinct "retro" feel. Not only are they built to look like the old ballparks (both Miller Field in Milwaukee and Citi Field in New York deliberately evoke memories of the Brooklyn Dodgers' old Ebbets Field), but they are also frequently in downtown areas, reminiscent of the old parks' locations.

The warm feeling associated with the downtown location of many of the newest stadiums is proof that nostalgia is not what it used to be. When they were first built, the old ballparks were built at the edge of town. When Shibe Park (later Connie Mack Stadium) was built at 21st Street and Lehigh Avenue in North Philadelphia in 1909, it stood near the site of a recently demolished hospital for communicable diseases. Given the state of medical knowledge at the turn of the 20th century, society tended to deal with communicable diseases by locating the patients as far from the center of town as possible. For several years after Shibe Park was built, Philadelphians complained about the distance they had to travel

---

[43]Thomas Chema, "When Professional Sports Justify the Subsidy," *Journal of Urban Affairs*, vol. 18, no. 1 (1996), p. 20; and Robert Baade and Allen R. Sanderson, "The Employment Effect of Teams and Sports Facilities" in *Sports, Jobs, and Taxes*, ed. By Roger Noll and Andrew Zimbalist. Washington, D.C.: Brookings Institution Press, (1997), pp. 94–95.

[44]Ziona Austrian and Mark Rosentraub, "Cleveland's Gateway to the Future," in *Sports, Jobs, and Taxes*, ed. by Roger Noll and Andrew Zimbalist (Washington, D.C.: Brookings Institution Press, 1997), pp. 355–384.

[45]Bruce Hamilton and Peter Kahn, "Baltimore's Camden Yards Ballparks," in *Sports, Jobs, and Taxes*, ed. by Roger Noll and Andrew Zimbalist (Washington, D.C.: Brookings Institution Press, 1997), pp. 245–281.

to reach it.[46] Similarly, the South Bronx, home of the New York Yankees was not always associated with urban congestion. The original Yankee Stadium was built on an empty 10-acre lot, bordered by unpaved roads, in a part of town known as "Goatville," hardly a metropolitan setting.[47] Brooklyn's Ebbets Field was not much different. By the mid-1950s, it may have come to epitomize the urban ball-park, but in 1913, the neighborhood in which it was built bore the nickname "Pigtown...where poor Italian immigrants lived in miserable shanties amidst goats and dandelions."[48]

As time went on, urban areas first developed and then decayed around many of the old ballparks. As the old parks themselves began to decay, team owners and cities considered relocating to the outskirts of town and the suburbs for sociologi-cal, technological, and economic reasons. An increasingly suburbanized fan base was more and more reluctant to attend games in the crumbling inner city.

Suburbanization also brought a need to accommodate fans who drove to the game. Any new ballpark would have to come packaged with acres of parking lots, and this vastly increased the space required for a stadium. Since fans found it inconvenient to go into town to enjoy restaurants, taverns, and other forms of entertainment, the stadium took on many of those functions itself, further isolat-ing the stadium and its income flows from the city. In the words of Robert Baade, "[I]n many cases the modern sports facility resembles a small walled city."[49] In moving stadiums back to the center of town, cities are expressing a willingness to spend more in order to generate greater spillovers for the community. With both greater benefits (in the form of consumer spending at local businesses) and higher construction costs, there is little reason to believe that the new trend in building stadiums downtown will result in substantial benefits for the cities that fund the stadiums.

The Impact of Special Events

Even if cities do not gain much from hosting a sports franchise, they might profit from hosting a special event, such as the Super Bowl, the Olympics, or the World Cup finals. Special events like these differ from a game played by local franchises in that they do not appeal specifically to local fans. While much of the money spent by local fans on a baseball game or a regular season football game may just replace money they would have spent on something else, special events attract people from all over the country (as in the Super Bowl) or all over the world (for the World Cup or Olympics) who would not have come to the host city had the event not taken place. Because fans coming from outside the local economy increase net

---

[46]See Bruce Kuklick, *To Everything a Season: Shibe Park and Urban Philadelphia, 1909–1976* (Princeton, N.J.: Princeton University Press, 1991), pp. 21–25; and Rich Westcott, *Philadelphia's Old Ballparks* (Philadelphia: Temple University Press, 1996), pp. 104–105.

[47]William Nack, "This Old House," *Sports Illustrated*, June 7, 1999, pp. 100–116.

[48]Harold Seymour, *Baseball: The Golden Years* (New York: Oxford University Press, 1971), p. 52.

[49]Robert Baade, "Should Congress Stop the Bidding War for Sports Franchises?" *The Heartland Insitute*, August 1, 1996, at http://heartland.org/policy-documents/should-congress-stop-bidding-war-sports-franchises-baade.

exports, the impact of special events might therefore be significantly larger than those of a franchise over a similar period of time.

Economists who have studied the impact of a variety of mega-events, from Olympics to Super Bowls, find mixed evidence regarding the impact of these events. Most of the studies are retrospective, as they look back at the impact of past mega-events on the local economy. In one of the earliest such studies, Philip Porter examines the effect of the Super Bowl on Miami, Tampa, and Phoenix by using a methodology similar to that used to measure the impact of a sports facility. His study focuses on the dollar value of county-wide sales revenue and on the economic impact of the 1979, 1984, 1989, 1991, 1995, and 1996 Super Bowls. With one exception, Porter finds that no Super Bowl had a statistically significant impact on the home county. Only the 1984 Super Bowl in Tampa had a significant effect, and that shows an increase of only $1.3 million in local sales during the month of the Super Bowl.

Porter finds far less impact than studies by the cities' host committees and the NFL, which consistently found a $120 to $160 million impact.[50] Much of the difference in the findings stems from the fact the NFL and host committees seem to have assumed that all spending on the Super Bowl was new expenditure by additional tourists. Super Bowls draw thousands of fans to the host city, but this causes little or no increase in local spending if the football fans displace other business people who cannot find room in hotels or who choose to hold their convention elsewhere. Like cities that spend money on renovating a stadium instead of a museum or local sports fans who spend their money on a hockey game rather than going to a show in town, mega-events like the Super Bowl crowd out one form of spending in the local economy with another.

Estimates of the impact of the Olympics have more varied results. In their study of several recent Olympic Games, Baade and Matheson estimate the impact of several Olympics on employment levels and find that, despite being hailed as an economic success, the 1984 Summer Olympics had no lasting impact on the Los Angeles economy. They conclude that, as with the Super Bowl, the Olympics draw tourists to the host city, but they also drive tourists away. For example, the Utah Tourism Office expected the 2002 Olympics to reduce the number of "non-resident skiers" by as much as 50 percent.[51] Additional spending by spectators crowded out spending by skiers.

Julie Hotchkiss, Robert Moore, and Stephanie Zobay focus on the 1996 Summer Olympics and find that it had a strong, lasting impact on employment and wages in Atlanta economy. Robert Baade and Victor Matheson agree that the Atlanta Games had a positive effect on the local economy but find that the impact of the Atlanta Olympics was transitory and might have harmed job creation in the

---

[50]Philip Porter, "Mega-Sporting Events as Municipal Investments: A Critique of Impact Analysis," in *Sports Economics: Current Research,* ed. by John Fizel, Elizabeth Gustafson, and Larry Hadley (Westport, Conn.: Praeger Publishers, 1999).

[51]See Michael Leeds, "Do Good Olympics Make Good Neighbors?" *Contemporary Economic Policy,* vol. 26, no. 3 (July 2008), pp. 460–467.

years following the Games. A more recent study of the Atlanta Games by Arne Fedderson and Wolfgang Maenning confirms Baade and Matheson's claims that the Atlanta Games had little to no effect.[52]

Several recent studies have taken a prospective look at the economic impact of mega-events by using a financial technique called "event analysis." Most event analyses examine the impact of an action or incident on the profitability of a firm by evaluating the influence of the event on the company's stock price.[53] If investors make rational use of all available information—a common assumption in finance—the company's stock price should respond rapidly to an event and its impact on the future profits of the firm. Several studies have used this technique to test whether overall stock market indices change in response to the announcement that the country will host the Olympics. A rise in the indices predicts that the country will prosper as a result of its hosting the Olympics. Again, the findings are mixed. Gabrielle Berman et al. find that the announcement that Sydney would host the 2000 Summer Olympics had no impact on the Australian exchange. Nikolaos Veraros et al. find a positive overall impact on the Athens exchange in response to the announcement of the 2004 Summer Olympics. They also found a positive impact on indices for the industrial and construction sectors. Leeds et al. find only a short-lived impact on the Shanghai exchange following the announcement that Beijing would host the 2008 Olympics. They attribute this to momentary euphoria that was quickly swept away. They also find mixed effects for sectoral indices, with some rising while others fell.[54] Thus, whether one looks retrospectively or prospectively, at Super Bowls or Olympics, there is no clear evidence that such mega-events bring large, lasting benefits to the host cities.

---

[52]Julie Hotchkiss et al. used a differences in differences estimation procedure, while Arne Feddersen and Wolfgang Maenning accounted for possible serial correlation and run a modified differences in differences equation. Robert Baade and Victor Matheson, "Bidding for Fool's Gold?" in *Transatlantic Sport*, ed. by Carlos Barros, Muradali Ibrahimo, and Stefan. Szymanski (Cheltenham, U.K.: Edward Elgar, 2002), pp. 127–151; Julie Hotchkiss, Robert Moore, and Stephanie Zobay, "Impact of the 1996 Summer Olympic Games on Employment and Wages in Georgia," *Southern Economic Journal*, vol. 69, no. 3 (2003), pp. 691–704; and Arne Feddersen and Wolfgang Maenning, "Wages and Employment Effects of the Olympic Games in Atlanta 1996 Reconsidered," *IAASE/NAASE Working Paper 09-16*, November 2009.

[53]More precisely, it looks at the holding period return, the value owning the stock over a given period of time. For more on event analysis and its application to sports, see Eva Marikova Leeds and Michael A. Leeds, "Event Analysis" in *The Oxford Handbook of Sports Econmics*, vol. 2, ed. by Stephen Shmanske and Leo Kahane (Oxford: Oxford University Press, 2012).

[54]Gabrielle Berman, Robert Brooks, and Sinclair Davidson, "The Sydney Olympic Games Announcement and Australian Stock Market Reaction," *Applied Economics Letters*, vol. 7, no. 12 (December 2000), pp. 781–784; Nikolaos Veraros, Evangelia Kasimati, and Peter Dawson, "The 2004 Olympic Games Announcement and Its Effect on the Athens and Milan Stock Exchanges," *Applied Economics Letters*, vol. 11, no. 12 (October 2004), pp. 749–753; and Michael Leeds, John Mirikitani, and Danna Tang, "Rational Exuberance? An Event Analysis of the 2008 Olympic Announcement," *International Journal of Sport Finance*, vol. 4, no. 1 (February 2009), pp. 5–15.

BIOGRAPHICAL SKETCH

Al Davis   (1929–2011)

To me, professional football is a business and an avocation. I never wanted to hurt anybody. To Davis, it is a war.

—Gene Klein[1]

For most of the 2000s, the Oakland Raiders were known as a dysfunctional, losing team. In the 1980s and 1990s, they were a successful but peripatetic franchise, moving from Oakland to Los Angeles and back again. From the late 1960s through the 1970s, all they did was win. All three of these eras reflected the personality of their longtime owner, Al Davis. Until his death in 2011, Al Davis *was* the Raiders. He had been their head coach, general manager, team owner, even—briefly—the commissioner of the league in which they played. In so doing, he infuriated his fellow team owners, as well as the residents of Northern and Southern California as his team moved from Oakland to Los Angeles and back again.

As an undergraduate at Syracuse University in the early 1950s, Davis became enchanted by the innovative offensive schemes of the team's football coach, Ben Schwartzwalder. Although he had no official position with the team, Davis became a fixture at team practices. Never one to let the lack of credentials get in his way, Davis talked his way into a job as an assistant coach at Adelphi University after graduating from Syracuse. Later stops at the Citadel and the University of Southern California confirmed Davis as a first-rate offensive mind and a brilliant recruiter. These qualities also had a downside, as Davis constantly battled with fellow assistant coaches and never hid his desire to be head coach. To make matters worse, his aggressive recruiting practices often ran afoul of NCAA rules.

Tainted by scandal and unable to find a head coaching position, Davis found himself adrift in 1960 when the fledgling AFL opened up a realm of new opportunities. He soon found a position on the staff of the Los Angeles (later San Diego) Chargers' head coach Sid Gillman, a widely acclaimed offensive genius. With the Chargers, Davis refined the concept of an attacking, pass-oriented offense and applied his marketing skills to stealing players from the NFL and rival AFL clubs. In 1963, Davis's success with the Chargers brought him the chance of a lifetime—though it hardly seemed so then.

When Davis became head coach in Oakland, the Raiders were the laughingstock of the AFL. They were, in fact, something of an accidental franchise. The AFL had originally hoped to locate a flagship franchise in Minneapolis. Caught unprepared when the NFL hastily expanded to Minneapolis, the AFL awarded the Minnesota franchise to Oakland even though no one had expressed an interest in owning a franchise there. A group led by developer Wayne Valley eventually stepped forward, but the Raiders reflected their slapdash origins, compiling an appalling record in front of minuscule crowds. In 1963, desperate for a respectable team, the Raiders hired Davis as head coach.

(Continued)

(Continued)

Within a year, Davis made the Raiders competitive, and within five years, they were playing in the Super Bowl. By that time, however, Davis had already moved beyond the coaching ranks.

In 1966, the AFL's owners narrowly approved Davis as the league's second commissioner. Six months later, they negotiated a merger with the NFL behind his back. This experience confirmed Davis's low opinion of football's owners and instilled a deep dislike of NFL Commissioner Pete Rozelle, whom Davis—Rozelle's opposite in upbringing and temperament—felt had undermined him during the merger talks. Some even believe that Davis felt that he should have been named commissioner of the expanded league.

His term as commissioner quickly over, Davis again was a man without a team until Wayne Valley brought him back in 1966 as a "managing general partner" with a one-tenth interest in the team. Valley soon regretted bringing Davis back to Oakland. In 1972, Davis masterminded a coup that reduced Valley to a figurehead position and—after four years of bitter legal battles—gave Davis control of the team.

As effective owner of the Raiders, Davis quickly became a pariah among the other owners, who were deeply committed to the "league-think" approach of Commissioner Rozelle. Whether out of principle or personal animosity, Davis repeatedly challenged the rest of the league. Unlike his peers, he welcomed free agency, declaring, "Just cut all the players and make everybody a free agent." He testified on behalf of the USFL in its antitrust suit against the NFL. (In return, the USFL pointedly sued only 27 of the 28 NFL teams.) He even refused to sign over the Raiders' share of profits from NFL Properties to the NFL Charities Foundation, claiming that the Raiders did their charity work locally.

Davis's biggest challenge to Rozelle and the NFL came in March 1980, when he sought to move the Raiders to Los Angeles. Davis had long coveted a larger stage than Oakland afforded, and he was among the first owners to see that favorable stadium deals would affect the balance of power in the NFL. The other owners, however, forbade him from moving the team, citing the league's constitution, which barred a team from moving into another's home territory without the league's unanimous consent. Davis responded by filing an antitrust suit against the NFL. After a series of trials that were finally settled in 1989, the NFL dropped its objections to the move and agreed to pay the Raiders $18 million. Davis quickly became disenchanted with Los Angeles. The rush to an agreement had left much of the language open to multiple interpretations, and Davis soon saw that his move would not bring the financial benefits that he had anticipated.

The return to Oakland in 1995 was not a joyous homecoming. Perhaps because of their many moves, the Raiders were not the dominant team that they were in the 1970s and 1980s. Almost constant litigation since the mid-1970s absorbed much of Davis's time and energy. In addition, the rest of the league finally caught on to Davis's tactics, both on the field and off. In the end, the man who had for so long been one step ahead of his colleagues found himself behind the times.

[1]Eugene Klein, *First Down and a Billion: The Funny Business of Professional Football* (New York: Morrow, 1987).

Sources: Glenn Dickey, *Just Win, Baby: Al Davis and His Raiders* (New York: Harcourt, Brace and Jovanovich, 1991); David Harris, *The League: The Rise and Decline of the NFL* (New York: Bantam Books, 1986); and Mark Ribowsky, *Slick: The Silver and Black Life of Al Davis* (New York: Macmillan, 1991).

Summary

Teams, fans, and cities all benefit from the presence of new facilities, though not in the same way or to the same degree. New facilities typically mean more fans for the teams that play in them, as a "honeymoon effect" can last for up to a decade. In addition, new facilities typically bring additional premium seating, which adds further to teams' revenues.

Baseball and football fans have benefited from the new configuration of stadiums. As teams moved from shared, multipurpose stadiums to their own facilities, they have been able to change their size and shape to conform to their specific needs. Because basketball and hockey draw similar crowds and have similar playing areas, there has not been a similar move to separate, uniquely shaped facilities for these two sports.

A new facility can increase a city's net exports, increasing the amount that outsiders spend in the city and reducing what city residents spend elsewhere. This added spending could have a multiplied effect, as people with higher incomes spend more, increasing the incomes of others, and so on. Unfortunately, studies have shown that the impact on net exports is relatively small, as spending on sports displaces other spending. The multiplier effect is also small.

Mega-events, such as the World Cup or Olympics, could have a larger effect on a city, as many fans travel long distances to attend them. Again, however, there is little evidence that local well-being is significantly affected.

Discussion Questions

1. Describe the externalities associated with a football stadium compared with an amusement park. Which would have greater positive externalities? Which would have greater negative externalities?
2. Suppose your city (or the nearest city housing an NBA franchise) is trying to decide where to build a new arena. Think of two or three possible sites and describe the pros and cons of each. Which site do you think is best?
3. Who will benefit most from the new stadium in Minneapolis, the Vikings, their fans, or the city as a whole?
4. If you had a choice between your city's (or the nearest large city's) hosting either a sports franchise or a World Cup, which would be more beneficial to your city? Why?

Problems

6.1. Why is the multiplier effect for the Los Angeles Lakers likely to be greater than the multiplier effect for the Sacramento Kings even though they are both teams in the NBA?
6.2. Why are the negative externalities associated the newly opened Barclays Centre in Brooklyn likely to be greater than the negative externalities associated with the Staples Center in Los Angeles, which opened in 1999?

6.3. If a majority of people do not want a stadium built in their town, how can building it lead to an improvement in social well-being?

6.4. While football and baseball teams have gone from multipurpose to football- and baseball-only facilities, basketball and hockey teams continue to share arenas. Why?

6.5. If the marginal propensity to consume in a municipality is 0.8, what is the value of the simple multiplier? If a new stadium that adds $30 million in new consumption expenditures is built, what is the impact on the economy based on this multiplier? Suppose the marginal propensity to import is 0.3, what happens to the multiplier and to the impact on the economy?

6.6. How does your answer to 6.5 change if city residents spend 60 cents of every additional dollar on goods made in other cities or countries?

6.7. Why does the fact that the NFL does not have a franchise in Los Angeles give its teams greater leverage with their host cities than teams in the other sports have?

6.8. If a new baseball stadium has only a very short-term impact on a team's attendance, why do MLB teams still pursue them?

6.9. Why would a Super Bowl played in Detroit probably have more of an impact than a Super Bowl played in Miami, even if both were to draw the same amount of fans? Why would a Super Bowl at Ford Field in Detroit have more of an impact on Detroit than a regular season Detroit Lions game that draws the same number of fans?

CHAPTER 7

The Public Finance of Sports: Who Pays and Why?

*[T]hey ain't going nowhere 'cause they're the **Brooklyn** Dodgers.*

—Usher at Ebbets Field[1]

In sports today the Phoenix Cardinals, who used to be the St. Louis Cardinals, took a seemingly insurmountable three-touchdown lead into the fourth quarter of their game against the Indianapolis Colts, who used to be the Baltimore Colts—not to be confused with the Baltimore Ravens, who used to be the Cleveland Browns—only to see the game slip from their grasp when, with three seconds left in the game, the Colts announced that they were moving to Albuquerque to become a professional hockey team.

—Dave Barry[2]

---

[1]Quoted in Michael Danielson, *Home Team: Professional Sport and the American Metropolis* (Princeton, N.J.: Princeton University Press, 1997), p. xvii.

[2]Dave Barry, *Dave Barry Turns 50* (New York: Random House, 1999), p. 62.

INTRODUCTION

One day in the late 1950s, Jack Newfield and Pete Hamill, both reporters for New York newspapers, discussed writing an article called "The Ten Worst Human Beings Who Ever Lived." On a whim, each wrote the names of the three people he regarded as "the all-time worst" on a napkin. To their amazement, they had listed the same three names: Adolf Hitler, Joseph Stalin, and Walter O'Malley.[3]

Since Newfield and Hamill lived in a nation with fresh memories of World War II and new worries over the Cold War, their inclusion of Hitler and Stalin was no surprise, but their both naming O'Malley, then-owner of the Los Angeles Dodgers, was. Unlike his companions on the list, O'Malley committed neither war crimes nor genocide. Instead, he forever changed the landscape of professional sports by moving the Dodgers from Brooklyn to Los Angeles. From that point on, sports franchises recognized that they had tremendous leverage in their dealings with the cities that hosted them. They were quick to exercise that market power, insisting that cities bear a much greater share of the burden of constructing and maintaining sports venues than they had in the past. In this chapter, we explain the source of the teams' market power and show how teams exercise it in their dealings with cities. We extend this reasoning to see how the sponsors of mega-events, such as the International Olympic Committee, exert similar market power in choosing a host city. Finally, we consider costs from the viewpoint of cities. We show that the cost of construction helps dictate where cities place stadiums, and we evaluate the ways cities fund the construction of facilities that now typically cost about $1 billion.

LEARNING OBJECTIVES

After reading this chapter, you will be able to:

- Appreciate the connection between the mobility of sports franchises and the increase in public funding of stadiums and arenas.

- Understand the ways that sports teams, leagues, and institutions exercise monopoly power in their dealings with municipalities.

- Grasp the impact that exchange rates and stadium location have on the ability of cities to retain franchises and subsidize facilities.

- Appreciate the advantages and disadvantages of different methods of financing public support of sports facilities.

7.1 HOW CITIES CAME TO FUND STADIUMS

Today it seems normal for teams to threaten to find a new home unless their current host city builds a new facility or restructures the rental agreement on the current one. It was not always this way. Until the 1950s, teams seldom moved, and few

---

[3]Geoffrey Ward and Kenneth Burns, *Baseball: An Illustrated History* (New York: Alfred A. Knopf, 1994), pp. 351–352.

noticed or cared if one did. This section provides a historical context for the growing mobility of sports franchises and their consequent increase in market power.

Teams on the Move

While the Dodgers' move to Los Angeles was the most notorious relocation, the Dodgers were not the first team to change cities. Nor was baseball the only sport to experience such moves. In the 19th century, teams entered, exited, and moved so frequently that they were reluctant to erect permanent facilities. As a general rule, they moved from small towns to large cities. The NFL likes to reminisce about its small-town, Midwestern origins, but professional football did not become financially stable until teams like the Decatur Staleys and Portsmouth Spartans had moved to large cities to become the Chicago Bears and Detroit Lions.[4] Unfavorable locations proved the undoing of entire leagues, as seen by the demise of baseball's American Association in the 1890s, the National Basketball League in the 1940s, and the women's American Basketball League in the 1990s.

The "Golden Age" of baseball marked the longest period of franchise stability. Between 1903, when the Baltimore Orioles left for New York to become the Highlanders (and later the Yankees), and 1953, when the Braves left Boston for Milwaukee, no Major League Baseball team entered, left, or changed cities. Baseball's growing prosperity led to the construction of its historic ballparks, starting with Shibe Park in Philadelphia and Forbes Field in Pittsburgh in 1909 and by Comiskey Park in Chicago a year later. The construction boom effectively ended with Yankee Stadium in 1923. Over the next 30 years, only one new baseball stadium was built, Cleveland's Municipal Stadium.

The Braves' move to Milwaukee did not necessarily signal the end of MLB's Golden Age. The Boston Braves; the Philadelphia Athletics, who moved to Kansas City in 1954 (and then to Oakland in 1968); and the St. Louis Browns, who moved to Baltimore and were rechristened the Orioles in 1953, were all neglected stepsisters in cities whose hearts belonged to the Red Sox, Phillies, and Cardinals, respectively. When the Braves left Boston, few fans noticed and fewer still mourned their loss. In the Braves' first nine games in Milwaukee, they drew as many fans as they had attracted in the entire preceding year.[5]

Unlike the franchises that had moved in the early 1950s, the Brooklyn Dodgers were second to none. In the 11 years prior to their move, from 1947 to 1957, the Dodgers were the most successful and most profitable team in the National League. Their value, moreover, went beyond dollars and cents. The Dodgers were "a cultural totem" for the residents of Brooklyn, a rallying point for those who felt scorned by the wealthier, more sophisticated Manhattanites.[6] It was this sense

---

[4]See Michael Danielson, *Home Team* (1997), pp. 20–24; and Charles Euchner, *Playing the Field* (Baltimore: Johns Hopkins University Press, 1993), p. 4. The NFL Hall of Fame Is in Canton, Ohio, home of the long defunct Canton Bulldogs.

[5]Neil J. Sullivan, *The Dodgers Move West* (New York: Oxford University Press, 1987), p. 42.

[6]See Neil J.Sullivan, *The Dodgers Move West* (1987), p. 15; and Michael Danielson, *Home Team* (1997), p. 9. Manhattan was the home of the Dodgers' archrivals, the New York Giants, who, ironically, moved to San Francisco when the Dodgers left for Los Angeles.

of loss—and the feeling of powerlessness that accompanied it—that prompted the sportswriters to elevate O'Malley to the elite company of Stalin and Hitler.

To O'Malley, the issue was a simple matter of economic profit. While the Dodgers did well in Brooklyn, he realized that the Dodgers would do even better if they had Los Angeles and, at the time, all of Southern California to themselves. O'Malley recognized the difference between accounting and economic profit. **Accounting profit** is what we typically think of as profit, the revenue a firm makes minus its explicit cost of production. **Economic profit** equals revenue minus all opportunity costs of the firm's production decision. Opportunity costs include the explicit costs of the resources used in the production process *plus* the profit that could have been earned in the firm's best alternative activity. In this case, a major opportunity cost of the O'Malleys' keeping the Dodgers in Brooklyn was the revenue they could have earned had they moved to Los Angeles. Because economic profit subtracts all costs, a firm could have negative economic profit even when its accounting profit is very high. The Dodgers thus had very high accounting profits, but the profit they sacrificed by playing in front of about 1 million fans each year in Brooklyn rather than over 2 million fans in Los Angeles was too great to ignore.

The Three Eras of Stadium Construction

Judith Grant Long identifies three phases of stadium funding.[7] The first phase, which she calls the "entrepreneurial period," lasted from 1890 to 1930. During this period, the owners of baseball teams built and operated their own ballparks. The owners of several hockey teams did the same thing, though we shall focus here on baseball, as it was the dominant organized professional sport in the United States at that time. In contrast, football teams lacked both the money and the fans to construct their own stadiums, and basketball did not even have a stable league yet.[8]

Almost all of the facilities built during this period had two common features. First, only one facility had the word *stadium* in its title. The rest had names like Wrigley Field or Shibe Park.[9] The use of the words *park* and *field* reflects the pastoral origins of baseball. Prior to the enclosure of games in private structures, baseball teams played in open fields or parks. They typically built ballparks to prevent bystanders from seeing ballgames for free.[10] The term *stadium* was not used until Jacob Ruppert applied the name to his new "Yankee Stadium" in 1923 in a deliberate attempt to recall the grandeur of classical architecture. (*Stadium* comes from the Greek word *stadion*, which originally meant a specific distance,

---

[7]Judith Grant Long, "Public Funding for Major League Sports Facilities Data Series: A History of Public Funding, 1890–2005," *Center for Urban Policy Research Working Paper Series* (2004). Edward J. Bloustein School of Planning and Public Policy, Rutgers University.

[8]Charles Clotfelter, *Big-Time Sports in American Universities* (Cambridge: Cambridge University Press, 2011), p. 47, notes that many of today's major college football stadiums were built in the 1920s.

[9]Wrigley Field was originally named Weeghman Field for the owner of the Chicago Whales of the Federal League, which first occupied the stadium. When William Wrigley bought the team and the stadium, he renamed it for himself.

[10]In 1936 Connie Mack went so far as to erect a "spite fence" behind right field of Shibe Park to prevent fans from viewing the game from the roofs of nearby apartment buildings.

later referred to a race of that distance, and eventually came to mean the seats for spectators who watched the race.) Second, most of the ballparks, with exceptions like Fenway Park, bear the name of the owner of the baseball team for which the stadium was built.

The unparalleled stability that baseball enjoyed during its "Golden Age" kept teams in the facilities they built in the early 20th century. Prior to 1950, Cleveland's Municipal Stadium and the Los Angeles Coliseum were the only major publicly built facilities, and the Coliseum was built for Olympics, not baseball or football. The aging of the facilities, the changing face of American cities, and the growing market power of franchises have led to the gradual disappearance of facilities built in the first period. Only Wrigley Field and Fenway Park still exist.

Long refers to the second period as the era of "civic infrastructure," in which cities viewed teams and stadiums as centerpieces of urban development. With franchises becoming mobile, cities frequently bid against one another to attract or retain them. As a result, the public sector often bore the full cost of stadium funding. The second period began in 1953, with the construction of Milwaukee's County Stadium and Baltimore's Memorial Stadium, and lasted until about 1980. Many of the stadiums built during this period were named for the cities or counties that funded them, such as Atlanta-Fulton County Stadium or Seattle's (King County) Kingdome. Others, such as Cincinnati's Riverfront Stadium or Pittsburgh's Three Rivers Stadium, were identified with distinctive local geographical features. Still others, such as Veterans Stadium in Philadelphia, took on patriotic names.

Long's third period, which she calls the "public-private partnership," began after 1980 and is still ongoing. During this period, local and state governments have funded about half the construction costs, with teams and leagues paying the rest. With the decline in public subsidies, teams have sought out new sources of income. One such source is found in the names of the facilities, which take the name of private sponsors that had purchased naming rights. The sale of naming rights even extends to totally publicly financed facilities, such as the Toyota Center in Houston or the FedEx Forum in Memphis.

SPORTS AND THE LAW

Who Can Move?

While it did not rival baseball's "Golden Age," the NFL had its own period of stability in the 1960s and 1970s. For 15 years after the Chicago Cardinals moved to St. Louis, no NFL team changed cities. The first crack in the system—the New York Giants' move from Yankee Stadium in the Bronx to Giants Stadium New Jersey in 1976—was so short that it might have gone unnoticed were it not for the flap caused by the Giants' crossing state lines but not changing their name. The move actually put the Giants closer to midtown Manhattan. Similarly, the Los Angeles Rams did not bother to change their name when they moved down the freeway to Anaheim in 1980. In addition, both team

(Continued)

(Continued)

owners—Wellington Mara of the Giants and Carroll Rosenbloom of the Rams—were liked and respected by their peers. This last point was crucial, as the NFL Board of Governors had to give unanimous approval to any move.

The next move proved harder to swallow. No sooner had the Rams left town, than Al Davis moved his Oakland Raiders into the now-empty Los Angeles Memorial Coliseum. To use a baseball metaphor, this move had three strikes against it. First, the move was so far—close to 400 miles—that Davis could not argue—as Mara and Rosenbloom did—that his team was still serving its long-time fans. Second, in relocating to Los Angeles, Davis was moving within 75 miles of the Rams' new home in Anaheim. Third, Davis was as unpopular with his fellow owners as Mara and Rosenbloom were popular. The result was another unanimous vote by the NFL Board, 22-0 against the move.

Al Davis and the LA Memorial Coliseum Commission responded with the groundbreaking lawsuit *LA Memorial Coliseum Commission* v. *NFL*, in which they claimed that the NFL had violated section 1 of the Sherman Antitrust Act when it had tried to prevent the Raiders from moving. The Los Angeles District Court found, using the rule of reason standard, "that the restriction on franchise movement was anti-competitive because it perpetuated local monopolies,"[1] a ruling that was upheld in 1984 by the Ninth Circuit Court. Rather than appeal the awarding of $4.6 million to the Coliseum, and $11.5 million to the Raiders—both of which would be trebled—the NFL settled out of court, agreeing to pay $18 million and to grant formal approval to the Raiders' move. (They had moved anyway in 1982.)

The ruling opened the floodgates to moves by other NFL franchises. The Baltimore Colts moved to Indianapolis in 1984, the Rams moved again, this time to St. Louis in 1995, the Cleveland Browns departed for Baltimore (and became the Ravens) in 1996, and the Houston Oilers decamped for Tennessee (and became the Titans) in 1997. In a crowning irony, the Raiders returned to Oakland in 1995, leaving the Los Angeles area without a franchise.

Similar moves occurred in basketball and hockey, though the courts did allow the leagues to block some moves, such as the Phoenix Coyotes' attempt to move to Winnipeg, if the league had a reasonable relocation policy in place. Only baseball, thanks to its antitrust exemption, managed to avoid wholesale moves. The Montreal Expos, which moved to Washington DC and which were a ward of the league at the time, were the only baseball team to move since the court ruling.

[1]Glenn Wong, *Essentials of Sports Law,* 4th ed. (Santa Barbara: Praeger, 2010), p. 468.

Sources: David Harris, *The League: The Rise and Decline of the NFL* (New York: Bantam Books, 1986); and Glenn Wong, *Essentials of Sport Law* 4th ed. (Santa Barbara: Praeger, 2010).

7.2   HOW TEAMS EXPLOIT MONOPOLY POWER

The Dodgers' move fundamentally altered the relationship between teams and the cities that host them. If the highly profitable Dodgers could be uprooted, so could any team. Teams began to exploit the monopoly power they exerted by encouraging bidding wars between cities hoping to attract a team and cities that were just as determined to keep "their" team. The bids have generally taken the form of new facilities that are either subsidized or entirely funded by the host city.

Leagues, Cities, and Market Power

For over 100 years, North American sports leagues have limited the number of teams to increase both competitive balance and profits. They have feared that admitting too many teams would lead to competitive imbalance, which can cause fans to lose interest and harm all teams. The fear of instability made all sports leagues reluctant to expand until the 1960s. Financial instability is not the only reason to restrict the number of teams. Leagues limit the number of teams and raise the "price" cities pay to attract or retain teams to maximize the profits of the members of the cartel.

As early as the 1930s, demographic changes and falling transportation costs began to put pressure on Major League Baseball to expand, but the Great Depression and World War II delayed any moves. By the mid-1940s the distribution of teams made little financial sense. At that time, for example, Los Angeles had no major league teams, while Boston had two baseball teams and a hockey team.[11]

After the war, both MLB and the NFL placed teams on the West Coast, but neither sport increased the number of teams. The NFL's Rams left Cleveland for Los Angeles in 1946, a move prompted by the creation of the Cleveland Browns of the new All-American Football Conference.[12] Baseball had an explicit offer to expand westward when the Pacific Coast League (PCL), a high minor league that had sent such stars as Joe DiMaggio and Ted Williams to MLB, broached the idea of becoming a third major league. The negotiations collapsed when MLB, which regarded its own reserve clause as sacrosanct, refused to honor the PCL's contracts with its own players. Instead, MLB allowed the Giants and Dodgers to move to the West Coast, reducing the PCL to truly minor-league status.[13]

MLB seemed content to respond to demographic pressures by rearranging franchises until it undertook the first systematic expansion by a professional sports league in 1961. The new policy, however, did not reflect a new business plan. Instead, it was a direct response to pressure from Congress. Seeing the controversial moves of the Dodgers and Giants and aghast at the impending loss of the Washington Senators to Minneapolis–St. Paul (where they became the Twins), Congress once again began to investigate baseball's antitrust exemption. In addition, Branch Rickey, the man who built the great Cardinal teams of the 1930s and Dodger teams of the late 1940s and 1950s, was looking into forming a new league, with two of the flagship teams planned for Houston and New York. Not surprisingly, three of MLB's first four expansion teams were located in Houston, New York, and Washington, DC.[14] Creating these three teams placated Congress and

---

[11]See Michael Danielson, *Home Team* (1997), p. 25.

[12]The Rams feared the popularity of a new team headed by the legendary Ohio State coach Paul Brown, who gave his name to the new team. See Jon Morgan, *Glory for Sale: Fans, Dollars, and the New NFL* (Baltimore: Bancroft Press, 1997), p. 59.

[13]See Neil J. Sullivan, *The Dodgers Move West* (1987), pp. 90–94.

[14]See Andrew Zimbalist, *Baseball and Billions* (New York: Basic Books, 1992), pp. 16–17; and James Miller, *The Baseball Business: Pursuing Pennants and Profits in Baltimore* (Chapel Hill: University of North Carolina Press, 1990), pp. 78–84.

prevented the rival league from forming. The fourth team, the Los Angeles Angels, gave the American League the West Coast presence that it had long coveted.

The NFL's first several expansions also came under duress. As noted in Chapter 4, the NFL had no intention of expanding in the early 1960s until it learned that the fledgling AFL planned to put teams in Dallas and Minneapolis. The AFL also spurred the NFL's second expansion in 1967. This time, however, the motive was peace, not war. The NFL and AFL recognized that their impending merger would violate antitrust laws and requested special legislation that would allow them to merge. In their path stood two powerful legislators from Louisiana, Representative Hale Boggs and Senator Russell Long, who could have delayed or derailed the legislation. Fortunately for the NFL, both men were keen to have an NFL franchise in New Orleans. Not surprisingly, less than two weeks after Congress passed the legislation granting the NFL and AFL the right to merge, the NFL approved the creation of the New Orleans Saints.[15]

Cities sometimes contribute to the monopoly power of teams by committing themselves to projects despite having no corresponding guarantee from the franchise. For example, in May 1990, the residents of Cuyahoga County, which includes Cleveland, voted to approve the construction of a new baseball stadium for the Indians and a new basketball arena for the Cavaliers, who were playing in the Richfield Coliseum in a nearby suburb. Unfortunately for Cuyahoga County, neither the Indians nor the Cavaliers had agreed to lease terms or to architectural plans for the facilities before the referendum. Having committed themselves to new facilities, the civic leaders forfeited any bargaining power with the franchises. The teams then insisted on such added features as stadium suites, office complexes, and restaurants, all at no extra charge to them. These add-ons increased the cost of Jacobs Field from $127 million to $175 million and Gund (now Quicken Loans) Arena from $79 million to $152 million.

In recent years, some leagues may have undermined their monopoly power by creating too many teams. The difficulty that MLB had in stimulating serious competition for the Montreal Expos (now the Washington Nationals) suggests that baseball might have overexpanded. Monopoly power may also be limited if leagues locate their franchises in an unbalanced manner. Of the 18 teams in the Australian Football League, 9 are located in Melbourne, with a 10th located in nearby Geelong. While the fans of the Western Bulldogs might be upset if the team threatens to move to Canberra, Melbourne itself is not likely to suffer. As with baseball, bidding wars for Australian Football franchises is unlikely.

Similarly, as we saw in Chapter 3, the promotion and relegation system of many soccer leagues reduces a team's ability to threaten to move. Every potential location is already likely to have a franchise either in the team's league or with the potential to be in its league. In addition, unlike the case in North America, local governments have gained some managerial control over franchises in exchange for their investment in the franchise, further reducing the chance of a move.[16]

---

[15]Jon Morgan, *Glory for Sale* (1997), p. 89; and David Harris, *The League: The Rise and Decline of the NFL* (New York: Bantam Books, 1986), p. 17.

[16]See Stefan Szymanski and Andrew Zimbalist, *National Pastime* (Washington, D.C.: Brookings Institution Press, 2005), p. 130.

THE ALL-OR-NOTHING DEMAND CURVE   When NASCAR sought a host city for its Hall of Fame, it did not offer cities a choice of how much material they wished to house. Cities had to host the entire NASCAR collection or none at all. The **all-or-nothing** choice gave NASCAR an advantage that very few monopolists ever get to exercise. While a monopoly has the power to set the price it charges or the quantity it sells, it typically cannot do both at once. If a monopolist sets the price of its product, consumers respond by buying as much of the good or service as they want. If it decides how much to produce, then by trial and error consumers will determine the price they will pay. The monopoly's power is thus limited by the demand curve that it faces. Even the most powerful monopolist cannot tell consumers how much to pay *and* how much to buy.

Under certain circumstances, however, a monopolist can dictate both price and quantity. Foot-long hot dogs at the ballpark or one-pound boxes of Milk Duds at the movie theater may have become something of a tradition, but they are also far bigger than most consumers want. This enables producers to extract consumer surplus by getting consumers to buy more than they wish to buy. Similarly, sports teams, sports leagues, or institutions such as the International Olympic Committee or NASCAR exploit their monopoly power by auctioning off teams or events to an array of eager cities. They also confront cities with an all-or-nothing choice. Since the city cannot choose to host part of a franchise or event at a lower overall cost, it must pay the full price or host nothing at all.

If NASCAR had acted like a typical monopolist, it would have charged cities the monopoly price of p_1 per unit (where, to make matters concrete, we let one unit be a room in the Hall of Fame) and let them "buy" as much of the Hall of Fame as they wanted. As seen in Figure 7.1, a city would choose to buy Q_1 rooms, and its residents would enjoy consumer surplus AEC. Figure 7.1 shows that NASCAR

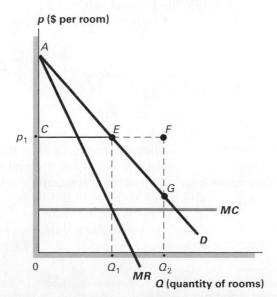

FIGURE 7.1   **A Monopolist Can Extract Consumer Surplus by Setting Price *and* Quantity**
Monopolists can force consumers to pay p_1 for Q_2 units of output, confronting them with an all-or-nothing choice.

could take some of this surplus by telling the city that if it wanted to host any of the Hall at all, it had to build all Q_2 rooms. Buying more rooms than it wants at the price p_1 results in a loss equal to EFG because residents of the city must pay more than the additional quantity is worth to them. The city will accept this loss as long as the surplus that residents enjoy on the first Q_1 rooms is greater than the loss residents suffer on the next $Q_2 - Q_1$. As long as consuming "too many" rooms is preferable to consuming none, the city chooses to consume too many. The franchise can push the city to build more rooms until the size of the loss (EFG) catches up with the size of the surplus (AEC).

How does a city decide how much a team, stadium, or event is worth? Objectively, it could calculate the item's present value. The **present value** (or present discounted value) of a good or service is what a stream of future benefits is worth today. To see how cities, firms, or consumers compute present value of, say, the Olympics, we make three simplifying assumptions. First, all costs to host the Olympics (C) are paid the moment the city wins the bid. Second, the revenue the city receives from the Olympic Games (e.g., revenue from the Games themselves and future use of the facilities built for the Games) comes in annual lump sums. Third, cities know exactly how much revenue they will receive, so expected revenue always equals actual revenue.

Under these assumptions, if the city receives benefits of B_t for each of T years after it wins the bid, then it is willing to pay up to V, where V is the value of the future stream of returns. One might expect V to equal the sum of payments the city receives ($B_1 + B_2 + B_3 + \ldots$), but the reality is a bit more complicated. Because one can save the dollar that one receives today and earn the market rate of interest, r, a dollar today actually equals $1 + r$ dollars a year from today, $(1 + r)^2$ dollars two years from today, and so on. The **future value** that \$1 today will have in t years is thus \$$(1 + r)^t$, while the **present value** of \$1 that one will receive t years from today equals \$$1/(1 + r)^t$. The present value of the stream of benefits to the city equals

$$V = \frac{B_1}{(1 + r)} + \frac{B_2}{(1 + r)^2} + \frac{B_3}{(1 + r)^3} + \ldots + \frac{B_T}{(1 + r)^T}$$

The city then compares its costs with its future stream of benefits. The project is profitable if $V > C$ and is not profitable if $C > V$.

Unfortunately, objective calculations might not reflect the subjective feelings of the city's residents. The contingent valuation method (CVM) says that one good way to determine how much a city's residents are willing to pay is to ask them.[17] **Contingent valuation** confronts individuals with a hypothetical event and asks them how much they would be willing to pay to ensure that the event occurs (or does not occur). It was originally devised by environmental

---

[17]For a good introduction to CVM, see Bruce K. Johnson and John C. Whitehead, "Contingent Valuation of Sports" in *The Oxford Handbook of Sports Economics*, ed. by Stephen Shmanske and Leo Kahane (Oxford: Oxford University Press, 2012).

economists as a way to simulate a market for goods that have no natural market, such as clean air.

In the context of sports, a CV survey presents a scenario, such as the chance to attract the NASCAR Hall of Fame or the possibility of losing the Minnesota Vikings to a different city, and it asks the respondent to state how much he or she is willing to pay to ensure that the event does or does not occur. The "willingness to pay" question comes in one of three forms. It can be open ended, asking the respondent the maximum he or she is willing to pay. It can be bracketed, asking the respondent to choose from among several options. Finally, it can be closed-ended, giving the respondent one possible payment (randomly selected from several possibilities) and asking whether the respondent would be willing to pay that amount.

CV surveys have several potential drawbacks. The most obvious is that they are not binding. Unless respondents believe that they will be held to their responses and that the gain or loss of the team depends on their answer, there is no strong incentive for them to answer truthfully. Because people are generally more willing to spend hypothetical dollars than real dollars, CV responses are typically taken as the upper bound on what residents are willing to pay. In addition, some economists believe that respondents have difficulty understanding payments made over a period of time and typically understate the burden of a series of payments relative to a single upfront payment. Thus CV surveys can come up with different answers depending on how they structure the payments. Still, a CV survey designed to determine the value of a new facility for the NHL's Pittsburgh Penguins closely paralleled the results of a referendum. Both found that about 40 percent of the population of Pittsburgh supported the construction of a new facility.[18]

The Winner's Curse

Even the pressures created by the all-or-nothing demand curve understate the power of sports leagues or teams to extract consumer surplus. They often solicit bids that exceed the value of the franchise to the winning city. In an auction in which the bidders do not know the value of the prize with certainty, the winner may well overpay for what has been won, falling victim to the **winner's curse**. The winner's curse was first applied to oil leases, when researchers sought to explain why investments by oil companies in the oil-rich Gulf of Mexico "paid off at something less than the local credit union." Since then, it has been applied to settings as diverse as advances paid to authors and the salaries paid to baseball players.[19]

---

[18]Peter Groothuis, Bruce Johnson, and John Whitehead, "Public Funding of Professional Sports Stadiums: Public Choice or Civic Pride?" *Eastern Economic Journal*, vol. 30, no. 4 (Fall 2004), pp. 515–526. Pittsburgh built the Consol Energy Center anyway.

[19]Richard Thaler, "The Winner's Curse," *Journal of Economic Perspectives*, vol. 2, no. 1 (Winter 1988), pp. 191–202. For an application to sports, see James Cassing and Richard Douglas, "Implications of the Auction Mechanism in Baseball's Free Agent Draft," *Southern Economic Journal*, vol. 47, no. 1 (July 1980), pp. 110–121.

To see how the winner's curse works, consider the fact that Charlotte had to outbid several other cities (e.g., Daytona Beach and Atlanta) to host the NASCAR Hall of Fame. Suppose all competing cities based their bids on how much they expected the Hall of Fame to be worth and hired experts to evaluate the benefits of the Hall. Based on these estimates, each city submitted bids to NASCAR.[20] Charlotte won the auction by bidding more than any other city. It might have won the bidding for any of three reasons.

First, it might be able to make more profitable use of the Hall than any other city. For example, the Hall of Fame might create synergies with other attractions in Charlotte that do not exist elsewhere. In this case, Charlotte's winning the auction is an efficient outcome.

Second, Charlotte might overestimate the benefits that the Hall would bring. In addition to any objective advantages it may have over other cities, Charlotte's winning bid reflects its optimism about the uncertain value of the Hall. If Charlotte overstates the value of the Hall, it might submit a winning bid that exceeds the true value of the NASCAR Hall of Fame. In this case, Charlotte falls prey to the winner's curse because it is the most optimistic bidder.

Finally, the auction process itself might lead Charlotte to bid more than the Hall of Fame is worth by making winning the auction more important than the value of the prize. Charlotte might get caught up in trying to win the right to host the Hall of Fame, independent of the expected benefits. Empirical studies and clinical experiments of bidding behavior have shown that, on average, bidders accurately assess the value of uncertain prizes. The winning bid, however, consistently overstates the value of the prize. Moreover, the amount by which a winner overbids, and hence the degree of loss, generally rises with the number of bidders. This has led some economists to conclude that participants get caught up in the action and begin to set winning the auction as a goal in itself. As a result, bids by cities and individuals alike may reflect both the value of the prize and the desire to win the prize regardless of its inherent worth.

7.3   STADIUM LOCATION AND COSTS

As noted in Chapter 6, the Minnesota Vikings' new home will cost approximately $975 million. That is an increase of over $900 million from their old home.[21] What could have caused such an increase? The cost of sports facilities has risen for many reasons. All facilities are far more elaborate than even the fanciest stadium in the early 20th century, with sophisticated scoreboards, fine restaurants, even wireless Internet connections. Much of the added luxury has also expanded the "footprint" of contemporary facilities. New stadiums take up more space to accommodate all the extra amenities they offer. In addition, the per-unit cost of urban space has

---

[20]Since cities have much greater access to capital than individuals do, we ignore the question of the city's ability to pay.

[21]According to Paul Munsey and Corey Suppes, *Ballparks.com* (2012), the Hubert H. Humphrey Metrodome cost $68 million to build in 1982.

risen. Because stadiums are so "space-intensive," teams and cities must account for the cost of space when they choose the precise location of the facility.

Location decisions also take place on a larger scale when leagues cross national boundaries. From the mid-1990s to the mid-2000s, there was a steady flow of Canadian hockey franchises to the United States. Even the Montreal Expos baseball team moved south to Washington, DC. In 2011, the flow reversed itself, and a U.S. hockey franchise moved north. In this section, we explore how location affects the cost of building a facility and operating a franchise, whether one is considering a move across town or across national boundaries.

How Exchange Rates Affect Costs

When the Winnipeg Jets left Canada in 1996 to become the Phoenix Coyotes, they were just one in what seemed like a steady progression of teams leaving Canada. The Quebec Nordiques had decamped for Colorado (to become the Avalanche) the year before and there was concern that Vancouver or Edmonton franchises might soon follow. Observers had begun to speculate that Canada might soon be left with only the Toronto Maple Leafs and Montreal Canadiens.[22] That sense of doom has long since disappeared, and in 2011 something that was once unthinkable occurred: a U.S.-based franchise (the Atlanta Thrashers) moved to Canada, and the Winnipeg Jets were reborn.

Many changes took place between 1996 and 2011 that made such a move possible. For example, greater revenue sharing and a vastly improved U.S. television deal made small-market Canadian cities more viable homes for franchises. However, what may have been the greatest factor in Canada's hockey renaissance had nothing to do with the NHL or local governments—it was the growing strength of the Canadian dollar.

With 7 of 30 NHL teams located in Canada, players and teams frequently move back and forth between U.S. and Canadian currencies. The Canadian franchises must pay particular attention to the two currencies, as much of their revenue (ticket sales, venue revenue, etc.) is denominated in Canadian dollars, while the fact that they must compete for players on a cross-national market means that their payroll—their largest single cost—is effectively in U.S. dollars. Fluctuations in the relative value of the two currencies—their exchange rate—thus affect the ability of Canadian franchise to compete both on and off the ice.

To show the impact of exchange rates on Canadian franchises, we make the simplifying assumption that a Canadian team pays its team in U.S. dollars. Since its revenues are all in Canadian dollars, the team must buy U.S. dollars on a currency market before it can pay its players. **Currency markets** allow people to trade dollars, yen, or euros for any other currency. Figure 7.2 shows the market for U.S. dollars. The "price" of U.S. dollars is the number of Canadian dollars it takes to buy US$1. This price is called the **exchange rate**, because it determines how many Canadian dollars must be exchanged to get US$1. In January 2003, the Canadian dollar fell to its lowest point, requiring C$1.55 to buy US$1.

---

[22]Michael Farber, "Giant Sucking Sound," *Sports Illustrated*, March 20, 1995.

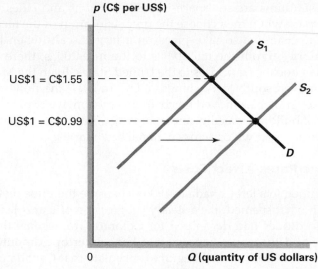

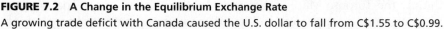

FIGURE 7.2   A Change in the Equilibrium Exchange Rate
A growing trade deficit with Canada caused the U.S. dollar to fall from C$1.55 to C$0.99.

At this exchange rate, Canadian hockey teams' expenses were magnified 55 percent by the exchange rate with the U.S. dollar. This created an "exchange rate deficit" of up to C$8 million for some teams, despite tax breaks of up to C$4 million given by some Canadian provinces. Team owners could escape this burden—and lessen their tax burden as well—by moving south of the border.

Since January 2003, the increasing U.S. trade deficit has steadily weakened the U.S. dollar.[23] The United States supplies dollars to currency markets when it buys more from abroad than it sells abroad. This shifts the supply curve of U.S. dollars rightward, as in Figure 7.2. The exchange rate has fallen as a result, reaching C$0.99 per US$1 in May 2012. The financial pressure on Canadian hockey teams that was such a burden in the 1990s has now disappeared.

Why Most Stadiums Are Not in the Center of Town

In Chapter 6, we saw that a sports facility typically provides the greatest benefits to a city if it is integrated into the fabric of the city and not banished to the edge of town. Yet that is precisely where most facilities are located. The reason is neither incompetence nor corruption—it is economic reality.

Arenas and stadiums take up a lot of space. Even disregarding the "sea of asphalt" that accommodates the thousands of cars in which fans arrive, one can shrink a football field or basketball court only so much. As we will see, this space costs money and becomes increasingly costly as one moves toward the center of town.

---

[23]In 2011, the U.S. trade deficit with Canada was $35.6 billion.

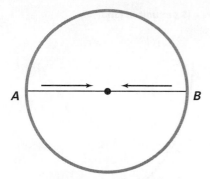

FIGURE 7.3   Competing Firms Move to the Center of Town
If the population is spread evenly in a circular city, rival firms locate in the central business district.

Consider, for example, the case of two jewelry shops that are trying to decide where to locate in the circular city shown in Figure 7.3. If the population is evenly spread over the city, then the best place for the stores to locate is in the very center of the circle. To see why, assume that store *A* and store *B* initially consider locating at the edge of town, along the diameter *AB* in Figure 7.3. Since the stores are identical in every way but convenience, customers base their purchases on how close they are to each store. In this case, half the city's population is closer to store *A*, and half is closer to store *B*. As a result, each store gets an equal share of the city's business. The managers of store *A* understand how customers decide to shop and recognize that they can capture some of *B*'s business by moving to a more convenient location. They do so by moving along the diameter toward the center of the circular town. The managers at store *B* also see this and try to do store *A* one better by moving still closer to the center of the circle. The process continues until both stores compete for space in the center of town. The tendency of businesses to locate in the center of a city has given rise to the term **central business district**.

The competition for space also explains why property values are so much higher near the center of town. Urban economists call the rise in property values as one moves toward the center of town the **rent gradient**. Figure 7.4 shows a typical rent gradient. As the price of land rises, people seek out ways to economize on their use of it. If the cost of land rises high enough, developers find it cheaper to build vertically—high-rise offices and apartment buildings—than to build horizontally. Buildings therefore tend to become taller as one moves toward the city center, and Figure 7.4 could illustrate the heights of buildings as well as the cost of land. A stadium surrounded by parking facilities requires so much space that the cost of land can make locating in the center of town prohibitively expensive. As a result, when cities replaced the old, urban ballparks in the 1960s and 1970s, they frequently moved them to the outskirts of town. Of course, that was where team owners put the original stadiums a half century earlier.

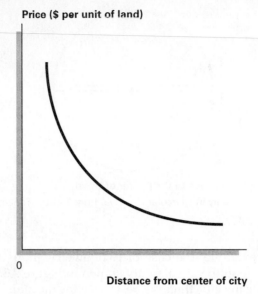

FIGURE 7.4   The Rent Gradient

Because firms want to locate in the center of town, land prices rise as one moves closer to the center.

7.4   STADIUM COSTS AND FINANCING

Recent estimates indicate that from 1995 to 2009—which roughly spans Long's third period of stadium construction—teams, leagues, and cities spent almost $18 billion on sports facilities. Of this total, teams spent a little over $7 billion, while the public sector spent over $10 billion, almost 60 percent of the total.[24] This section examines how cities underwrite the construction of new facilities and shows that the actual subsidy might be far greater than what the official figures indicate.

Bidding wars for sports franchises differ from normal auction markets in two important respects. First, a city's successful bid for a team does not bring ownership rights. In fact, professional leagues have gone to considerable lengths to prevent cities from owning franchises. For example, MLB owners blocked Joan Kroc's attempt to give the Padres to San Diego after she inherited the team from her late husband. The NFL's bylaws specifically require that teams have an individual majority owner. The Green Bay Packers are frequently cited as an exception to the rule against public ownership, but, contrary to popular belief, the Packers are not owned by Green Bay; they are a publicly held corporation. Thus, in 2000, this supposedly city-owned team threatened to leave Green Bay if the city did not accede to its demands for stadium improvements.[25]

---

[24]Mayya Komisarchik and Aju Fenn, "Trends in Stadium and Arena Construction, 1995–2015," *Colorado College Working Paper 2010-03*, April, 2010.

[25]The Packers are, however, the only NFL team that does not have a single managing partner. See Joanna Cagan and Neil de Mause, *Field of Schemes* (Monroe, Maine: Common Courage Press, 1998), pp. 93–94 and 191–192; Richard Jones and Don Walker, "Packer Boss Warns of Move If Stadium Doesn't Get Upgrade," *Milwaukee Sentinel Journal*, March 1, 2000, at http://www.jsonline.com/packer/news/feb00/lambeau01022900.asp; and Barry Lorge, "Kroc Wanted to Give Padres to City," *San Diego Union-Tribune*, July 29, 1990, p. H1.

Leagues oppose municipal ownership for two reasons. Because a municipally owned team is by definition an immobile team, the city could provide facilities on its own terms, thereby undercutting much of the market power that teams hold over cities. In addition, city ownership would make the finances of the team a matter of public record.

The second unique characteristic of the market for teams is the way in which cities pay for "their" teams. Unlike auctions, which result in monetary payments, cities do not pay directly for the teams they have "won." Their payment is a form of barter, in which cities provide teams with facilities.

Table 7.1 shows the total cost and public share of facilities built for major league sports teams since 2000. Adding up the figures in Table 7.1 shows that $11.34 billion has been spent since 2000 to construct new facilities for the major North American sports leagues. More than half this amount, about $6.1 billion, has come from state and local governments. Sometimes, the spending on sports facilities comes when the city has other pressing needs. Over the course of the 1990s, Cleveland, a city whose school system had gone into receivership, committed over a billion dollars to new facilities for its baseball, football, and basketball teams. Like individuals and firms, governments face opportunity costs. They must consider the alternative uses to which public funds can be put when evaluating public policy.

The data in Table 7.1, however, tell only part of the story. These data alone can lead analysts to misstate the full burden of a facility on a city. Construction costs are not the only expenditure that a city makes on a sports facility. It also pays for infrastructure, such as roads and utilities, and for support services, such as police and sanitation. Some costs do not involve any expenditure by the government. For example, cities frequently donate the land on which the facility is built, thereby sacrificing revenues that could have been made from using, renting, or selling the property. As with alternative expenditures, alternative uses of public resources, such as land and police, are an opportunity cost of building and operating a sports facility. If the stadium is owned by the state or local authority or by a public–private partnership, the city could also lose tax revenue, as a local government cannot tax itself.

As Table 7.1 shows, the public share of the expenditure on individual facilities has ranged from 0 to 100 percent. This variation is reflected in the facilities' ownership structure. Of the five facilities built since 2010, two—Amway Center

TABLE 7.1 Facilities Built between 2000 and 2012

Year	League	City	Facility	Construction Cost[a]	Percent Public
2000	MLB	Houston	Minute Maid Park[b]	$ 269	80.7
2000	MLB	San Francisco	AT&T Park[b]	$ 343	4.4
2000	MLB	Detroit	Comerica Park	$ 365	31.8
2000	NFL	Cincinnati	Paul Brown Stadium	$ 475	79.4
2000	NHL	St. Paul	Xcel Energy Center	$ 131	73.3

(Continued)

TABLE 7.1   Continued

Year	League	City	Facility	Construction Cost[a]	Percent Public
2000	NHL	Columbus, OH	Nationwide Arena	$ 152	0.0
2001	MLB	Pittsburgh	PNC Park	$ 262	91.2
2001	MLB	Milwaukee	Miller Park	$ 357	58.0
2001	NBA/NHL	Dallas	American Airlines Arena	$ 380	32.9
2001	NFL	Pittsburgh	Heinz Field	$ 233	84.1
2001	NFL	Denver	Sports Authority Field	$ 510	60.8
2002	NFL	Detroit	Ford Field	$ 300	86.7
2002	NBA	San Antonio	SBC Center	$ 186	100.0
2003	MLB	Cincinnati	Great American Ballpark	$ 325	86.2
2003	NBA	Houston	Toyota Center	$ 175	100.0
2003	NFL	Philadelphia	Lincoln Financial Field	$ 512	41.4
2004	MLB	Philadelphia	Citizens Bank Park	$ 346	50.3
2003	NHL	Phoenix	Jobing.com Arena	$ 180	100.0
2004	MLB	San Diego	PETCO Park	$ 457	66.5
2004	NBA	Memphis	FedEx Forum	$ 250	100.0
2006	MLB	St. Louis	Bush Stadium III	$ 365	12.3
2006	NBA	Charlotte	Time Warner Cable Arena[b]	$ 265	100.0
2006	NFL	Phoenix	University of Phoenix Stadium	$ 455	100.0
2007	NHL	Newark	Prudential Center	$ 375	56.0
2008	NFL	Indianapolis	Lucas Oil Stadium	$ 720	87.0
2008	MLB	Washington, DC	Nationals Park	$ 611	100.0
2009	MLB	New York	Citi Field	$ 600	27.0
2009	MLB	New York	Yankee Stadium II	$1,300	17.0
2009	NFL	Arlington, Tex.	Cowboys Stadium	$1,000	35.0
2010	MLB	Minneapolis, MN	Target Field	$544.4	72.0
2010	NBA	Orlando, FL	Amway Center	$ 480	87.5
2010	NFL	East Rutherford, NJ	MetLife Stadium	$1,600	0
2010	NHL	Pittsburgh, PA	Consol Energy Center	$ 321	0[c]
2012	MLB	Miami, FL	Marlins Park	$ 525	70.5

[a]In millions of current dollars.

[b]Originally named Enron Field, Pacific Bell Park, and Charlotte Arena respectively.

[c]Isle of Capri Casinos agreed to fully fund the arena if they were awarded a state gambling license and allowed to build a new $500M casino in the city.

Sources: Data for facilities built from 2000–2002 come from Judith Grant Long, "Full Count: The Real Cost of Public Funding for Major League Sports Facilities," *Journal of Sports Economics*, vol. 6, no. 2 (May 2005), pp. 119–143. Data from 2003–2011 come from National Sports Law Institute, "Sports Facilities Reports," *Marquette University Law School*, at http://law.marquette.edu/national-sports-law-institute/sports-facility-reports, viewed April 13, 2012; Data for Marlins Park come from Paul Munsey and Corey Suppes, *Ballparks.com* (2012).

and Marlins Park—are owned and operated outright by the cities in which they are located. Two others—Target Field and Consol Energy Arena—are run by public authorities created by the state of Minnesota and Allegheny County for the express purpose of operating stadiums and arenas. Finally, MetLife Stadium, which is home to the New York Giants and the New York Jets and received no state funding, is jointly operated by Giants Stadium LLC and Jets Development LLC. While these two companies are technically separate from the two football teams, they are effectively run by the teams.[26]

Because many stadium costs are indirect or unobservable, they are hard to measure. As a result, estimates of the public share of stadium costs can vary widely. For example, the Steinbrenner family might regard Long's estimate that New York paid 17 percent of the cost of the new Yankee Stadium as an overstatement, as the Yankees paid all the actual construction costs. Having spent $1.1 billion, the late George Steinbrenner felt justified in saying to New Yorkers, "It's a pleasure to give this to you people."[27] But was Yankee Stadium really a gift? The city donated the land on which the stadium was constructed, built parking facilities, and made a variety of improvements to transportation and other infrastructure. Mayya Komisarchik and Aju Fenn estimate the city's contribution to be about $220 million, or about 13.8 percent of total expenditure on the stadium, close to Long's estimate of 17 percent.[28] Paul Munsey and Corey Suppes go much higher on their *Ballparks.com* website; they put the figure at $430 million, about 28 percent, on their Ballparks.com website. The *Sports Facility Report* of the National Sports Law Institute goes higher still. It says that public expenditure came to $480 million or 32 percent of the total.

7.5 PAYING FOR STADIUMS

We have seen that there are two basic motivations for publicly funding sports facilities. First, if the team is a public good, people can enjoy the team without paying for it by watching it on TV, following it in the newspaper, or simply discussing it around the water cooler. These consumers can free ride by letting someone else spend money on the team. Second, if teams provide positive externalities, people benefit from the presence of the team even if they pay no attention to it and have no say in how often or how well it plays. In both cases, the free market will not provide as much of the good as the economy desires.

Governments can fill this void by providing public goods and subsidizing firms whose production gives off positive externalities. The public goods aspect of sports teams is particularly difficult for governments to fund because consuming

---

[26]Giants Stadium LLC is co-owned by John Mara, who is president, CEO, and co-owner of the New York Giants. "Company Overview of Giants Stadium LLC," *BusinessWeek*, August 31, 2012, at http://investing.businessweek.com/research/stocks/private/snapshot.asp?privcapId=36320464, viewed May 19, 2012.

[27]Karen Mathews, "Yankees Break Ground on New $1 Billion Stadium," *USA Today*, August 16, 2006, at http://www.usatoday.com/sports/baseball/al/yankees/2006-08-16-stadium-groundbreaking_x.htm.

[28]Mayya Komisarchik and Aju Fenn, "Trends in Stadium and Arena Construction, 1995–2015," (2010).

a sports team can be so intangible. All we can really say is far more people enjoy the team than just the fans in the arena or the residents of the city. People who gain from spillovers are a bit easier to identify, as one can trace at least the first round of beneficiaries from a team's presence, such as the construction and hospitality industries. For these reasons—and because the major North American sports leagues prohibit public ownership of franchises—we focus on subsidies rather than outright government provision.

Deciding to subsidize a new sports facility raises a crucial question: How does the government raise the revenue to provide the subsidy? Economic theory suggests that governments maximize the well-being of their residents if they finance the subsidy by imposing taxes or fees according to the benefits each resident or business receives. Unfortunately, one of the reasons positive externalities are external to the market mechanism is the difficulty in identifying exactly who benefits. Fortunately, it is possible to establish some general principles for determining who should pay how much for a sports franchise.

One such principle—known as the **Ramsey rule**—dictates that sales taxes should be levied in inverse proportion to the price elasticity of demand for the good or service on which the government places the tax. Such a tax is more efficient than alternative tax schemes in the sense that it minimizes the deadweight loss. For example, suppose Charlotte, North Carolina, considered two ways to raise revenue for the NASCAR Hall of Fame: a tax on hotel stays and a tax on kidney dialysis.[29] Assume, for simplicity, that the local government thinks it can raise all the revenue it needs by imposing a $4 tax on either. Figure 7.5 shows the impact of a tax on

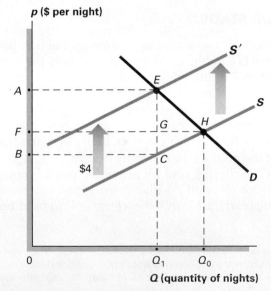

FIGURE 7.5   The Impact of a $4/Night Tax on Hotel Stays
The tax shifts the supply curve upward to S'. A deadweight loss of *ECH* results.

---

[29]In fact, it has imposed a 2 percent hotel tax.

the number of hotel stays. As shown in Chapter 2, a $4 sales tax causes consumers to see a supply curve that is $4 higher than the supply curve without the tax.

Since the equilibrium number of nights spent at local hotels falls from Q_0 to Q_1, the deadweight loss imposed by the tax equals the area of the triangle *ECH*. This burden consists of lost consumer surplus for hotel guests (*EGH*) and lost producer surplus for hotel operators (*CGH*). We explore the implications of this shared burden later in the chapter.

Contrast the deadweight loss from a hotel tax with the deadweight loss from a tax on kidney dialysis, as seen in Figure 7.6. A $4 tax on dialysis shifts the supply curve (which, for simplicity, we assume to be identical to the supply curve in Figure 7.5) up by $4, just like before. Unlike hotel stays, kidney dialysis has no good substitutes. The quantity of dialysis demanded is therefore much less sensitive to changes in price than the quantity of hotel stays demanded. Since the demand curve is so inelastic, the quantity of dialysis hardly changes, and the price rises by almost the full amount of the tax. Because the tax on dialysis causes little loss of output, there is very little deadweight loss (the area of the triangle *ECH*). If the city wants to impose a tax that minimizes deadweight loss, then a tax on dialysis may be just the thing. Most people, however, would not choose to impose a greater burden on people who are unfortunate enough to require dialysis.

Society must often choose between policies that are efficient and policies that satisfy some notion of fairness or equity. Tax analysis applies two forms of equity: horizontal and vertical. A policy satisfies **vertical equity** if it falls most heavily on those with the greatest ability to pay and places a smaller burden on those with low incomes. Since hotel stays are generally either part of a vacation by relatively well-to-do households or underwritten by businesses, while dialysis is an undesired

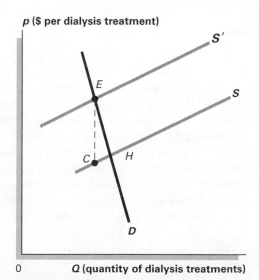

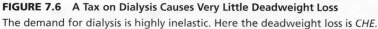

FIGURE 7.6   A Tax on Dialysis Causes Very Little Deadweight Loss
The demand for dialysis is highly inelastic. Here the deadweight loss is *CHE*.

burden borne by people from a variety of income groups, a hotel tax is more verti-cally equitable than a dialysis tax.

While vertical equity applies across income levels, horizontal equity refers to fairness at a given income level. A tax is **horizontally equitable** if it treats equals equally. Since public expenditure often confers unequal benefits on the popula-tion, the pursuit of horizontal equity leads governments to levy taxes in propor-tion to the benefits received from the expenditure. In this example, the tax on hotel stays seems more horizontally equitable, as staying at a local hotel is more likely to be connected to enjoying the home team than a visit to the dialysis unit.

Some economists think that governments should rely on **user fees** rather than public taxation to fund facilities. They claim that the public good aspects of a professional franchise are dwarfed by the private consumption that takes place. The emphasis that teams now place on luxury boxes and prime seating has made it difficult for middle- or low-income fans to attend the major professional sports games on a regular basis.[30] If this is the case, then consumption by the wealthy few has reduced consumption by the broader population.

In addition to spanning the income distribution, benefits can cut across geo-graphic boundaries. Many of the consumption benefits of a major league fran-chise flow out of the city to the residents of the relatively wealthy suburban ring. The suburbs disproportionately house the people who can most afford tickets to sporting events. They also disproportionately house corporate executives who use the luxury boxes and other premium seating that now account for so much of the cost of a facility. In addition, as explained earlier, most cities get only a small fraction of the revenue from luxury boxes. Taxes that fall on residents of the city that houses the team therefore allow suburbanites to escape the taxes that fund the facility, while local residents, who bear the heaviest tax burden, seldom if ever attend a game.

Who Pays a Sales Tax?

In addition to creating a deadweight loss, sales taxes often place a burden on groups that the government does not wish to target. Depending on the products subject to tax, the burden may fall upon people who do not benefit from the new facil-ity, thereby violating horizontal equity. The merits of sales taxes on items directly related to sports facilities are considered later in the chapter. This section explores the problem posed when the burden of a sales tax does not fall solely on the people who ostensibly pay the tax. The tax burden shifts because people respond to the world around them. Governments that impose a tax expecting people to behave the same way they did before the tax was levied are in for a rude awakening.

The Dallas Cowboys stirred up a major controversy when they proposed raising a portion of the $1.15 billion for their new stadium with a three percentage

---

[30]For interesting examples, see John Pastier, "Diamonds in the Rough: Two Cheers for the New Baseball Palaces," *Slate Magazine,* July 31, 1996, at http://slate.msn.com/feature2/96-07-31/feature2.asp; and John Siegfried and Andrew Zimbalist, "The Economics of Sports Facilities and Their Construction," *Journal of Economic Perspectives,* vol. 14, no. 3 (Summer 2000), pp. 95–114.

point increase (up to 18 percent total, among the highest in the nation) in the tax on hotel stays in the Dallas–Fort Worth area. Such a tax would seem to be a very popular way to raise funds. After all, the tax was designed to fall on out-of-town visitors, thereby exporting the burden of paying for a new stadium to taxpayers from other states. The proposed tax, however, drew a firestorm of protest from the local Visitors Bureau and—of all groups—Mary Kay Cosmetics.[31] Mary Kay's opposition was understandable. The company holds its annual convention in the area and did not want to see its expenses rise. Why, however, did the Visitors Bureau, which represents the local hospitality industry, object to having out-of-towners pay?

To see why local hotel owners might object, we simplify the problem and assume that the city passes a hotel tax of $4 for each person spending an evening in a local hotel. We further assume that before the tax is imposed 1 million people spend an average of 5 nights each in hotels in the Dallas–Fort Worth area in a typical year. One might initially conclude that the tax would raise $20 million ($4 per night ×1 million people ×5 nights per person) per year. This naïve calculation, however, assumes that visitors do not respond to the higher cost of staying in a local hotel.

Recall from Figure 7.5 that the tax causes the price of a night in a hotel room to rise—though by less than $4—and the number of nights spent at hotels to fall. The higher price that people pay per night spent at a hotel (segment *AF* in Figure 7.5) is the portion of the $4 tax that they bear. Since the government has imposed a $4 tax but the price of a night at a hotel has risen by less than $4, hotel operators receive a lower price per night than they did before the tax was imposed. The drop in payment that hotel operators receive (segment *FB* in Figure 7.5) is the portion of the $4 tax passed on to the local hotel industry.

The total tax burden equals the $4 tax (segment *AB* in Figure 7.5) times the number of rooms rented (segment *AE*). This product, the total tax revenue, equals the area of the rectangle *ABCE* in Figure 7.5. The portion of this rectangle that lies above the original price of the room (the rectangle *AFGE* in Figure 7.5) is the burden borne by people who stay at hotels. The rectangle below the original price (*FGCB* in Figure 7.5) is the burden borne by local hotel operators. When tourists or business travelers respond to the higher price of hotel stays by making fewer or shorter visits, local businesses are hurt—hence the opposition by the Dallas–Fort Worth Visitors Bureau—and the revenue generated by the tax falls short of its target.

Cleveland applied a different kind of sales tax to help fund the facilities it built. It imposed a 15-year sin tax on residents of Cuyahoga County (which consists of Cleveland and its immediate suburbs). Like most sin taxes, these taxes consisted of sales taxes on tobacco products and alcohol. **Sin taxes** are popular with many citizens because they impose a burden on people who engage in or cater to "sinful" behavior. Most of the public thus view sin taxes as a way to raise revenue by taxing other people and as a way to discourage undesirable activity.

---

[31]See Hugh Aynsworth, "Owner of Dallas Cowboys Seeks $1 Billion in Tax Funds," *Washington Times,* February 2, 2004, at http://www.washingtontimes.com/national/20040202-120350-8901r.htm.

Unfortunately, sin taxes cannot achieve both of these ends. As shown in Figure 7.5, if a tax discourages behavior, it creates a large deadweight loss and fails to raise the anticipated amount of revenue. In contrast, if drinking and smoking are addictive behaviors, the demand for them is highly price inelastic. Figure 7.6 shows that taxes on goods for which demand is inelastic create very little deadweight loss and come much closer to raising the desired revenue. However, because the change in quantity due to the tax is so small, the tax fails to discourage the sinful behavior.

Public choice theory helps to explain why Cleveland's sin taxes stirred less organized opposition than the Dallas area's proposed hotel tax. The deadweight loss of a tax adds to the burden on the group that pays the tax and hence subsidizes the publicly funded facility. A larger burden makes that group more likely to organize opposition to the tax. Since the demand curves for cigarettes and alcohol are far less price elastic than the demand curve for hotel stays, a smaller deadweight loss and less opposition arose to the sin tax.[32]

Incremental Financing

San Francisco and San Diego have attempted to finance their new facilities (AT&T—originally Pacific Bell—Park and PETCO Park) through a new technique that tries to avoid raising taxes. **Tax increment financing** (TIF) does not impose a new tax. Instead, it earmarks increased tax revenue to pay the city's debt to its bondholders. The idea behind this is that the new facility will stimulate tourism. The additional tourists will increase hotel occupancy rates, increase patronage at local restaurants, and generally increase expenditure in the community. This added expenditure will lead to higher revenues from existing sales taxes and hotel taxes without the city's having to increase tax rates at all. The city just commits to using this additional tax revenue to pay its bondholders. San Francisco has committed to raising $15 million through TIF, while San Diego hopes to raise $29 million.[33]

If incremental financing succeeds, it minimizes the burden on both tourists and local merchants. To succeed, however, the new facility must cause tourist expenditure to rise for a sustained period. Unfortunately, the honeymoon period for a new stadium might not be long enough. TIF appears particularly risky in San Diego. After spiking to 3 million in PETCO Park's first season (2004), attendance fell dramatically. In 2011, it was only 2.1 million, well below both the National League average and the Padres' average attendance in their last five years at Qualcomm Stadium. The Giants might not have such worries. They have drawn 3 million fans in 10 of the last 12 years, and—thanks to their 2010 World Series victory—they drew a record 3.4 million fans in 2011.

---

[32]See Gary Becker, "A Theory of Competition among Pressure Groups for Political Influence," *Quarterly Journal of Economics,* vol. 98, no. 3 (August 1983), pp. 371–400.

[33]San Jose Redevelopment Agency, *Economic Impact Analysis: Proposed Major League Ballpark in San Jose, CA,* September 22, 2009, at http://www.sjredevelopment.org/ballpark/meetings/092409/SanJosePresentation092109.pdf.

Taxes That Spread the Burden

In general, taxes aimed at out-of-towners or those behaving "sinfully" do not meet the criteria set out at the beginning of this section. Some are inefficient; others fail on equity grounds. We now turn to two funding mechanisms that, while flawed, do a better job of meeting the criteria. Each tries to allocate burdens more equitably, though they do so differently.

The first mechanism thinks big, as exemplified by how the Milwaukee metropolitan area has funded Miller Park. It instituted a general sales tax on Milwaukee and the surrounding five-county region. The broad geographic reach of this tax accounts for the regional impact of a stadium, reducing the vertical and horizontal inequities that result when inner-city taxpayers finance a facility that benefits wealthy suburbanites. However, while the sales tax does a better job of targeting the beneficiaries of the stadium, it remains a rather broad brush, as it is based on people's purchases of goods and services and not on their benefits from having the Brewers in town.[34]

The second mechanism thinks small, as demonstrated by the way that Seattle and the state of Washington have funded Safeco Field. This package of taxes is targeted at those who benefit most from the presence of the facility. It imposes a special sales tax of 0.5 percent on restaurants, bars, and taverns in King County and a tax of up to 5 percent on admissions to Safeco Field. They have also sought to export some of the burden with a 2 percent tax on rental cars. The sales tax tries to match burdens to benefits by placing the greatest tax burden on those who benefit from having the Mariners in town, though it does not get things quite right. By charging a five-star French restaurant at the opposite end of the county the same tax as a bar across the street from the stadium, the government does not match costs to benefits particularly well. The tax on admissions does a far better job of matching costs and benefits. The tax on car rentals has the same imperfect impact as the hotel room tax example discussed earlier.[35]

The Benefits of Debt

If a city does not raise taxes to pay for a new stadium, it must borrow. According to economic theory, borrowing to finance a new stadium does not lessen the tax burden on a community. It simply delays the inevitable, as it substitutes taxes now for taxes later, when it repays the debt. Since David Ricardo first stated the famous "equivalence theorem," economists have known that borrowing and taxation could have the same impact on residents, at least in theory.[36] State and local governments, however, face several institutional factors that lead them to prefer debt funding to direct taxation.

---

[34]See Dennis Zimmerman, "Subsidizing Stadiums: Who Benefits, Who Pays?" in *Sports, Jobs, and Taxes*, ed. by Roger G. Noll and Andrew Zimbalist (Washington, D.C.: Brookings Institution Press, 1997), p. 137.

[35]MSC Sports, *New Park Financing: How the Deals Got Done*, (1999), at http://www.wcco.com/sports/stadiums.html.

[36]In fact, Ricardo rejected the notion that the two were equivalent.

Individuals and small firms typically borrow money from a financial intermediary, such as a bank. Large corporations and governments typically borrow directly from financial markets by issuing bonds. A **bond** is a promise to pay its holder a fixed amount, the **face value** of the bond. This occurs at a future point in time, called the **maturity**. Both the face value and maturity are stated on the bond, as is the interest rate of the bond, also known as its coupon rate. The interest payment on a bond is given by the bond's coupon rate times the face value, which is usually $1000. Thus, a 5 percent coupon bond pays its holder $50 each year, usually in the form of two $25 semi-annual payments.

Bonds issued by state or local governments have an advantage over otherwise identical bonds offered by corporations. Tax laws allow bondholders to deduct the interest they earn from state and local bonds from their federal taxes. If a $1000 municipal bond pays 5 percent, the holder keeps $50 ($1000×0.05) after taxes. If a corporate bond pays $50, the holder keeps less after taxes. For example, the after-tax interest payment to a person in the 28 percent tax bracket is only $36 ($50 × [1 − 0.28]). The higher after-tax interest payment on municipal government bonds drives up the demand for them and causes their price to rise from p_0 to p_1, as shown in Figure 7.7. Because of their lower after-tax return, the demand for corporate bonds is also lower. This, in turn, lowers their price. In equilibrium, the after-tax interest rate on otherwise identical corporate and municipal kinds of bonds of the same risk must be the same, otherwise no one would buy the bond with the lower return. At tax rates of 28 percent a corporate bond must pay a pre-tax rate of 6.94 percent to have a post-tax return of 5 percent (6.94 × [1 − 0.28] = 5.0). This is why the interest rate on municipal bonds is lower than the rate on otherwise identical corporate bonds.

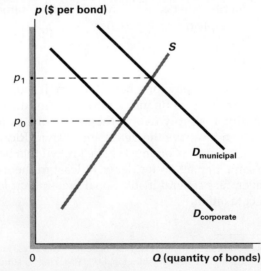

FIGURE 7.7   Tax Breaks Favor Municipal Bonds
Because they are tax exempt, all else equal, the demand for municipal bonds is greater than for corporate bonds.

Because they pay a lower rate, municipal bonds reduce the cost of building a stadium, by reducing the cost of borrowing. According to the National Sports Law Institute, "The use of tax-exempt bonds will save the Yankees an estimated $786 million over 40 years."[37] The lower federal tax revenues mean that taxpayers in other states and municipalities will have to pay higher taxes, that federal programs will have to be cut, or that the federal government will have to borrow more and drive up interest rates in general. No matter what, the tax deductibility of interest on municipal bonds imposes costs on the rest of the nation. The Internal Revenue Service has tried to limit the use of municipal bonds to purposes that serve public, rather than private, interests.[38] States and cities must now convince the IRS that private interests receive no more than 10 percent of the proceeds of the bond issue and that no more than 10 percent of the repayment of the debt comes from private sources. This restriction did not prevent New York from issuing $240 million in bonds to pay for the new Yankee Stadium's parking garages.[39]

While the Miami Marlins did not run afoul of the IRS, they may be in trouble with the Securities and Exchange Commission (SEC). In December 2011, the SEC opened an investigation into whether the Marlins committed fraud in convincing Miami and Dade County to provide over 70 percent of the funding for Marlins Park. At issue is whether the team—and Major League Baseball—misled government officials by claiming that the team could not afford to build a new stadium without substantial assistance from local government.[40] If the SEC finds that the Marlins and MLB knowingly misled local officials, they could be subject to substantial fines or even criminal prosecution.

Even if debt does not export the burden geographically, it can export the burden intertemporally. If future generations enjoy the benefits of the new facility, then economic theory says that society is better off if they pay some of the burden. Debt financing allows a city to impose some of the burden of a new facility on future generations. Unfortunately, stadiums do not last as long as they once did, and future generations might be stuck with the bill for a facility that their teams have already abandoned. Taxpayers in New Jersey, for example, still owed over $100 million in bond debt on Meadowlands Stadium when it was torn down to make way for MetLife Stadium in 2010.[41]

---

[37]National Sports Law Institute, "Sports Facility Reports: Major League Baseball," (2012), p. 18.

[38]Kevin McManimon, "The House That Debt Built," *McManimon and Scotland, LLC,* May 29, 2006, at http://www.mandslaw.com/articles/the-house-that-debt-built-will-the-irs-allow-cities-to-finance-construction-of-stadiums-on-a-tax-exempt-basis/.

[39]Money and Company, "Yankee Stadiums Troubled Tax-Free Financing," *Los Angeles Times,* June 17, 2011, at http://latimesblogs.latimes.com/money_co/2011/06/yankee-stadiums-troubled-tax-free-financing-.html.

[40]Charles Rabin, Martha Brannigan, and Patricia Mazzei, "Feds Open SEC Probe into Miami Marlins Stadium Deal," *Miami Herald,* December 3, 2011, at http://www.miamiherald.com/2011/12/02/2529191/feds-open-sec-probe-into-miami.html.

[41]Jonathan Berr, "New Stadiums Strike Out for Investors and Taxpayers," *DailyFinance,* September 20, 2010, at http://www.dailyfinance.com/2010/09/20/defaulting-new-stadiums/.

BIOGRAPHICAL SKETCH

Willard "Mitt" Romney   (1947–)

It was like stepping into an elevator shaft.

—Mitt Romney describing his feelings on taking over the Salt Lake Organizing Committee in 1999.[1]

Seldom have politics and sports been more intertwined than in the recent career of Willard ("Mitt") Romney. Mitt Romney was born and raised in Michigan; his father, the late George Romney, had served as the state's governor and had once been a presidential candidate. Romney graduated with highest honors from Brigham Young University in 1971, and in 1974, he received both a JD and an MBA from Harvard.

After spending two years on a Mormon mission to France, Romney went to work at Bain and Co., a Boston management consulting firm. In 1984, he founded Bain Capital, a venture capital firm that invested in hundreds of companies, including Staples, Domino's Pizza, and The Sports Authority.

In 1994, Romney entered the political arena by challenging Senator Edward Kennedy's reelection bid. The election's outcome was a foregone conclusion, as Kennedy garnered 60 percent of the vote. This might have been the end of Romney's political career were it not for a surprising move he made five years later.

In late 1998, the Salt Lake Organizing Committee (SLOC), the body charged with organizing and financing the 2002 Winter Olympics, was facing a severe crisis. With the Olympics just three years off, the SLOC was almost $400 million in debt, having badly underestimated the cost of staging the Olympic Games. To make matters worse, fundraising was at a standstill, with no new sponsors secured in over a year. Voluntarism was also lagging, and the leadership of SLOC was under investigation by the U.S. Justice Department for allegedly giving bribes exceeding $1 million to International Olympic Committee officials in order to secure the Games. The SLOC was in desperate need of a person who could combine business connections and savvy with unquestioned integrity and would not mind moving to Utah for the next three years. The job requirements seemed to fit Romney perfectly, and he soon showed why.

In February 1999, Romney took over as CEO and president of the SLOC and quickly put his personal stamp on the process. Recognizing that the allegations of corruption had demoralized workers and frightened off donors, Romney insisted on strict ethical standards in all SLOC's activities. He opened all meetings and records to the public. He also demanded that all employees and board members report any possible conflicts of interest and complete annual surveys of ethical conduct.

Knowing that morality alone would not balance the budget. Romney cut the Olympic Games' budget by about $200 million and vigorously pursued his political and business connections. The results were impressive. Romney's governmental contacts helped secure an estimated $1.5 billion from the federal government, almost 10 times more than the amount of federal support per athlete provided to the 1996 Summer Olympics in Atlanta. Between the government support and private sponsorships, the SLOC pulled out of its financial hole and wound up slightly in the black. The citizens of Utah were also energized, as 67,000 people volunteered for 23,000 volunteer positions.

Although the Olympics did little to revive the flagging business community in Salt Lake City, they were a public relations triumph. As head of the SLOC, Romney had become a celebrity. Less than six weeks after the Olympic flame had been extinguished, Romney had become the Republican candidate for governor of Massachusetts. This time he won and served as governor from 2002 to 2006. In 2012, he became the Republican nominee for president. The path that almost led to the White House thus began in the afterglow of the 2002 Winter Olympics.

[1]Michael De Groote, "Games Not Over: Financial Principles That Saved the 2002 Olympic Games," *Deseret News,* February 5, 2012, at http://www.deseretnews.com/article/700222487/Games-not-over-Financial-principles-that-saved-the-2002-Olympic-Winter-Games.html?pg=all.

Sources: Donald Bartlett and James Steele, "Snow Job," *Sports Illustrated,* December 10, 2001, pp. 79–97; Paul Foy, "Romney Just Glad Olympics Worked," *2002 Winter Olympic Games,* at http://olympics.hiasys.com/olympics_main/news/ap_olynewsscene 02252002.htm; "Governor MittRomney," *MassachusettsOfficeoftheGovernor,* athttp://www.mass.gov/portal/index.jsp?pageID= agccagid=govagca=biographiesagcc =mittromneybio; Paula Parrish, "Leap of Faith: Mitt Romney Embraces Challenges, and This Might Be His Biggest One," *Rocky Mountain News,* February 4, 2002, p. 8S; Lewis Rice, "Games Saver," *Harvard Law Bulletin,* Spring 2002, at http://www.law.harvard.edu/alumni/bulletin/2002/spring/feature_1-1.html.

Summary

Cities began to underwrite sports facilities in the 1950s and 1960s, after teams showed that they would move to new cities in response to economic incentives. Over the next several decades, cities came to see stadiums as part of their infrastructure and paid most or all of the expenses of new stadiums. Since the 1980s, there has been a more equal partnership, with cities paying about 60 percent of the costs of new construction, though the precise degree of public support is often hard to measure, as many of the costs are implicit or difficult to quantify.

Teams have exploited their monopoly power in several ways. Like any monopoly, they have limited output, in this case by limiting the expansion of teams. They have also extracted the cities' consumer surplus by confronting cities with an all-or-nothing choice through which the teams are able to get cities to "buy" a greater quantity than they wish. Finally, by effectively creating an auction for teams, leagues are able to exploit the winner's curse and get cities to bid more than the team is worth to them. The cost of attracting and retaining a team is affected by its location. When leagues cross national borders, exchange rate movements can create problems for franchises located in a country whose currency is weakening. Within a city, the cost of constructing a facility depends on how close it is to the center of town.

To subsidize a facility, cities must raise funds. Economists have established standards by which they evaluate a tax's efficiency as well as its vertical and horizontal equity. Most cities' tax schemes are neither particularly efficient nor equitable. In addition, the taxes often fall on people whom the city did not intend to burden. Still, by targeting individuals and firms that benefit from the facilities for taxes, some cities and regions have designed taxes that are more efficient and more horizontally and vertically equitable than others.

Discussion Questions

1. Are the stadiums or arenas of your local sports franchises located downtown or on the edge of town? Do you think that is the best place for them? Why or why not?
2. Standard economic theory is based on the assumption that people behave rationally. The winner's curse implies that people behave irrationally by paying more for an asset than it is worth. Can we reconcile the winner's curse with rational behavior?
3. What do you believe is more important in taxing the public to provide funds for stadiums—horizontal equity or vertical equity? Why?
4. How has your city raised funds to subsidize its sports facilities? Would you use a different method? Why?

Problems

7.1. Evaluate the following taxes from the standpoint of vertical and horizontal equity:
   a. A 25-cent per-gallon tax on milk
   b. A tax on stock market transactions
   c. A sales tax on men's clothing
   d. A tax on cigarettes

7.2. Suppose the demand for toothbrushes is perfectly inelastic, at $Q_d = 3,000$. The market supply curve is perfectly elastic and is equal to $p = 2.00$. What would be the deadweight loss associated with a $0.20 tax on toothbrushes? Based on the Ramsey rule, would this be a good product to tax?

7.3. Suppose a city is laid out along a major highway, so the city is shaped like a straight-line segment rather than a circle. If the city wants to build a sports arena, where along the segment should the city build the arena? Why?

7.4. True or false; explain your answer: "The new stadium was entirely privately funded because the city contributed only a 50-acre lot on which to build it."

7.5. Suppose the International Olympic Committee announced that it would hold all of its Summer Games in Athens, Greece and all of its Winter Games in Sapporo, Japan. What is the likely impact on the monopoly power of the IOC, the IOC's ability to exploit an all-or-nothing demand curve, and the winner's curse?

7.6. Use the rent gradient to show why New York did not build a new stadium for the Yankees in midtown Manhattan.

7.7. Your city is committed to raising $100 million for a new arena. The mayor suggests putting a tax on taxicab rides since out-of-towners disproportionately use taxicabs. Evaluate the wisdom of this policy decision.

7.8. Use the all-or-nothing demand curve to explain why the IOC is unlikely to accept a bid by Los Angeles to host only the track and field events in its bid for the 2020 Summer Olympics.

7.9. Why might a city want to go into debt as a way to fund a new stadium?

7.10. Suppose New York wants to build a new facility to replace Madison Square Garden. Assume that the cost of building a new arena in midtown Manhattan is $2 billion and that all the costs occur right away. Also assume that New York will receive annual benefits of $100 million for the next 30 years, after which the new arena becomes worthless. Does it make financial sense to build the new facility if interest rates are 5 percent?

PART FOUR

The Labor Economics of Sports

CHAPTER 8

An Introduction to Labor Markets in Professional Sports

After my fourth season I asked for $43,000 and General Manager Ed Barrow told me, "Young man, do you realize Lou Gehrig, a 16-year-man, is playing for only $44,000?" I said, Mr. Barrow, there is only one answer to that—Mr. Gehrig is terribly underpaid.

—YANKEES OUTFIELDER JOE DIMAGGIO[1]

INTRODUCTION

Joe Louis and Oscar de la Hoya were among the best—perhaps *the* best—fighters in the history of boxing. Joe Louis was heavyweight champion for 12 years (1937–1949) and successfully defended his title 25 times (still a record for the heavyweight division). Louis was so dominant that people took to calling his opponents "The Bum of the Month Club." De la Hoya won a gold medal in the 1992 Barcelona Olympics and went on to win 10 titles in six different weight classes.[2]

---

[1]Jeff Euston, "Cots Baseball Contracts," *Baseball Prospectus*, February 4, 2005, at http://www.baseballprospectus.com/compensation/cots/?author=2.

[2]De la Hoya won the super flyweight, lightweight, light welterweight, welterweight, junior middleweight, and middleweight titles.

In addition to sharing glorious careers, both staged less than glorious comebacks. Louis re-entered the ring almost two years after retiring but lost a title fight to Ezzard Charles in 1950. In 1951, Louis's career finally ended when he was knocked out by future champion Rocky Marciano. De la Hoya's comeback, also after almost two years away from fighting, met with initial success, when he won the middleweight title in 2006. However, de la Hoya then lost two of his next three fights before retiring in 2009.

While Louis and de la Hoya both attempted comebacks, their motivations for doing so could not have been more different. Louis started fighting again out of poverty. In his 12 years as heavyweight champion, Louis was paid $800,000 (roughly $10.4 million in 2011 dollars), a large sum to most people at the time, but small change by today's standards for heavyweight champions.[3] Moreover, mismanagement of Louis's funds and tax problems with the Internal Revenue Service (IRS) left him with almost nothing to live on after retirement. With no skills other than his fading boxing talents, Louis had no choice but to fight again.[4]

De la Hoya had no such money worries. His nickname, "Golden Boy," might have referred to his prodigious skills, but it could just as easily have applied to his extraordinary earnings.[5] De la Hoya earned over $600 million in his career and earned more than twice the value of Joe Louis's lifetime earnings for just one fight (about $23 million for a 2007 loss to Floyd Mayweather). He has also parlayed his success in the ring into a variety of business ventures, most notably Golden Boy Enterprises, whose activities have ranged from promoting boxers to real estate development to a 25 percent stake in the Houston Dynamo soccer team.[6]

Oscar de la Hoya did not have Joe Louis's monetary worries, but he also could not afford to turn down the offer to return to ring as the monetary rewards for fighting were too high for him to turn down.

The salaries paid to professional athletes in all sports have risen greatly in recent decades. In 2011, the average *weekly* earnings in the NBA were more than twice the average *annual* earnings of nonathletes in the United States. In this chapter, we analyze the forces that have caused the incomes of professional athletes to reach such levels.

---

[3]"Joe Louis (Barrow)," *Arlington National Cemetery Web site*, April 13, 1981, at http://www.arlingtoncemetery.net/joelouis.htm, viewed July 27, 2009.

[4]See, for example, Chris Mead, "Triumphs and Trials," *SIVault*, September 23, 1985, at http://vault.sportsillustrated.cnn.com/vault/article/magazine/MAG1119926/4/index.htm.

[5]It is probably no coincidence that *Golden Boy* is also the title of a play (later made into a musical) about a prizefighter.

[6]Tom van Riper, "Boxing's Last Golden Boy?" *Forbes*, January 15, 2009, at http://www.forbes.com/2009/01/14/boxing-oscar-de-la-hoya-biz-sports_cx_tvr_0115delahoya.html?partner=whiteglove_google; and Simone Walker, "De la Hoya—Boxing's Future Is Golden," *SportsPro*, October 13, 2009, at http://www.sportspromedia.com/notes_and_insights/de_la_hoya_-_boxings_future_is_golden/.

LEARNING OBJECTIVES

After reading this chapter, you will be able to:

- Understand the basic model of wage determination in labor markets
- Be able to describe why the salaries of superstars are much higher than the salaries of average players.
- Analyze the markets for individual sports, such as golf and tennis, and explain why players use performance-enhancing drugs despite knowing their harmful effects.

8.1   AN OVERVIEW OF LABOR SUPPLY AND LABOR DEMAND

As noted in the introduction, Oscar de la Hoya earned more for one fight than Joe Louis earned during his entire career. Similarly, the salaries paid to professional athletes in the four major North American sports were not always as high as they are now. Figure 8.1 shows that in the last 20 years alone, the average salary of a Major League Baseball player has almost quadrupled (from about $850,000 to over $3.3 million). To put this in perspective, the average salary was approximately 36 times per capita GDP in 1991. By 2011, it was over 65 times per capita GDP. The other major team sports in the North America show similar salary growth. In just the 10-year period from 2002 to 2011, average NHL salaries grew by over $700,000, average NFL salaries more than doubled to about $1.8 million, while average salaries in the NBA increased by over $1 million.[7]

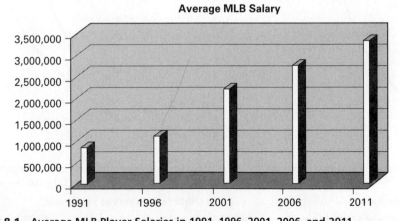

Average MLB Salary

FIGURE 8.1   **Average MLB Player Salaries in 1991, 1996, 2001, 2006, and 2011.**
The average salary of Major League Baseball players has risen significantly since 1991.

Source: "USATODAY Salaries Databases," *USAToday.com*. At http://content.usatoday.com/sportsdata/baseball/mlb/salaries/team/2011. Viewed May 22, 2012.

---

[7]NBA data, "USAToday Salary Databases," *USAToday.com*. 2012, at http://content.usatoday.com/sportsdata/basketball/nba/salaries/team/2001. Data from other sports can be reached from that site, viewed May 22, 2012. NFL data are for the ten-year period ending 2009–2010.

Such extraordinarily high salaries are not limited to North America. Argentinian soccer player Lionel Messi earned $39 million in 2011, while the GDP per capita in his country was just under $10,000 per year, and Spanish race car driver Fernando Alonso earned $40 million, over 1,300 times the per capita GDP in Spain.[8] In this section, we discuss both sides of the labor market. On the supply side, individual players offer their services to professional sports teams in order to maximize their utility. Teams demand labor in order to maximize profits. Although we know from Chapter 3 that some owners may benefit from fielding a low-quality team, in this chapter we assume that team quality and profits are directly related. Better teams earn higher profits, and the interaction of labor supply and labor demand determines the labor market for professional athletes.

Labor Supply

In many ways, a worker's labor supply decision resembles a firm's output supply decision. As Figure 8.2a shows, the labor supply curve looks like the supply curve for a product.[9] There are, however, several important differences. One important difference occurs in the units of measurement. The horizontal axis of a product supply curve refers to the amount of output the firm provides and is typically

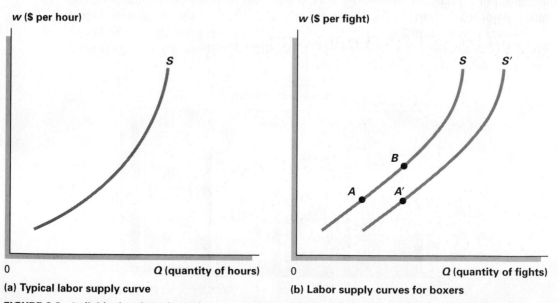

FIGURE 8.2   Individual and Market Labor Supply Curves for Workers and Boxers
The labor supply curve slopes upward, just like the supply curve for a good or service.

---

[8]"Best Paid Athletes from 200 Countries," *ESPN the Magazine,* April 26, 2012, at http://espn.go.com/espn/story/_/id/7858737/floyd-mayweather-united-states-best-paid-athlete-espn-magazine, viewed May 14, 2012; "10 Highest Earning Players," *Forbes.com,* at http://www.forbes.com/pictures/mlh45eel/no-3-lionel-messi/#gallerycontent, viewed May 23, 2012.

[9]For a more complete treatment of the labor supply curve and the labor–leisure choice model, see Appendix 8A.

measured in physical units (e.g., the number of shoes or automobiles), and the vertical axis denotes the price per unit of the firm's output. Labor markets do not involve the exchange of physical units. Instead, firms buy the services that people offer, typically measured in units of time. Thus, the quantity axis in Figure 8.2a refers to the hours of work that a person is willing to provide. Similarly, the vertical axis is now the price per unit of time. In most cases, economists use the worker's hourly pay, the **wage**, as the unit price of a worker's time.[10] The upward-sloping labor supply curve thus indicates that a worker responds to higher wages by offering more work time to employers.

In professional sports, we cannot use hours as the unit of labor because almost all athletes contract for a fixed amount of time, be it a football season, a tennis tournament, or a boxing match. Figure 8.2b modifies the standard labor supply curve to reflect this fact. The horizontal axis now measures the quantity of fights a boxer has over the course of his career, and the vertical axis measures the boxer's earnings per fight (which, for simplicity, we assume to be uniform). In team sports, the quantity of labor provided by a player is again typically set for a given season.[11] The price variable is thus the amount paid per season, or **salary**. The quantity variable depends on what we want to evaluate. If we analyze the labor market in a given season, the quantity variable refers to the number of players employed in that season. Alternatively, if we look at a typical player's career, the quantity variable refers to the number of seasons that player plays.

Returning to our boxing example, moving from point A to point B in Figure 8.2b shows that a boxer is induced to take on more fights as his pay increases, as was the case for Oscar de la Hoya. By this reasoning, the lower pay that Joe Louis received should have led him to fight less. As noted earlier, lower pay was not the only problem facing Louis. After retiring, Louis discovered that his manager had mishandled his funds and that he owed the IRS hundreds of thousands of dollars in back taxes. The lower savings—and hence the lower income that Louis would have received in retirement—meant that Louis had to fight more to maintain his standard of living. His labor supply curve shifted right to S', moving his number of fights from point A to point A'.

To see why the labor supply curve looks and shifts the way it does in Figure 8.2b, we must recognize that people choose how much to work based on the wage and the value they place on the alternative to work—leisure. At first, such a model seems ill-suited to professional sports, an industry in which the personnel are referred to as *players* rather than workers. This distinction suggests that professional athletics is a leisure activity rather than a way to make a living, but such a conclusion would be a mistake. While most, if not all, professional players might still play "for fun" if they could not play professionally, playing professionally requires a level of dedication that goes well beyond what the players would choose for pure recreation.

---

[10]Using the wage can significantly understate the unit price of labor, as it ignores many other factors, such as taxes and fringe benefits. Still, it is a useful first approximation.

[11]While the actual number of minutes or innings played may vary, the players make themselves available for the full season.

To understand the shape of the individual labor supply curve, think of leisure as a good that a worker can "purchase" by choosing to not work. The opportunity cost of one more hour of leisure is one less hour's worth of earnings. Thus, the cost of leisure is equal to the wage rate. When wages are low, the opportunity cost of not working is low. As wages increase, workers are subject to two separate effects: an income effect and a substitution effect. The substitution effect captures the increased cost of not working as wages rise, because workers must sacrifice higher earnings when they choose to "purchase" leisure. Thus, the substitution effect leads workers to work more as wages rise. The income effect reflects the increased purchasing power that comes from the increased wages. If leisure is a normal good, then workers buy more leisure—and work less—as their income rises. In this case, the income effect counteracts, rather than reinforces, the substitution effect.

In general, the substitution effect is stronger than the income effect, so higher wages lead workers to supply more labor, and the labor supply curve slopes upward.[12] As nonlabor income falls or when the value of one's assets declines—as has happened to many people's home values in 2008–2009—the demand for all goods and services falls. One such good is the quantity of leisure. A decline in the demand for leisure is equivalent to an increase in the supply of labor. Thus, Joe Louis's tax troubles led him to fight more frequently than he otherwise would have.

Labor Demand

Much of the debate among sports fans regarding athletes' salaries stems from a failure to understand the demand for labor. Many armchair quarterbacks spend Sunday afternoons yelling at their televisions, complaining about overpaid athletes. If these same fans understood the factors underlying the demand for labor and combined labor demand with labor supply, they would discover that many highly paid professional athletes are actually underpaid, a topic we explore extensively in the next chapter.

MARGINAL REVENUE PRODUCT We begin our analysis by assuming that firms produce a single output using two inputs, capital (K) and labor (L). We also assume that the firm is operating in the short run (so capital is fixed) and that the firm can alter output (Q) only by changing the labor input. Finally, we assume that all markets are perfectly competitive, so firms cannot affect the market price of their output. In such a setting, firms maximize profit by choosing L to maximize the difference between revenue and cost. This occurs where the marginal revenue from employing one more worker equals the marginal cost of employing that worker.

Ignoring all employment costs except for a worker's pay, the marginal cost of one more hour of labor is the worker's wage, w. The benefit of adding a worker is the extra revenue that worker generates. Economists call the extra revenue

---

[12]At high wage rates, it is possible that the income effect becomes stronger than the substitution effect. This would cause higher wages to reduce the number of hours worked, leading to a "backward-bending" labor supply curve.

created by an additional worker the **marginal revenue product**. Since marginal revenue equals price in a competitive market, marginal revenue product is simply the price per unit of output times the additional output produced:

$$MRP_L = MR \times MP_L = p\left(\frac{\Delta Q}{\Delta L}\right)$$

For example, if increasing the workforce from nine workers to 10 results in an additional 20 units that can be sold for $5 each, the value of the 10th worker to the firm is $100 = \$5 \times 20$.

The profit-maximizing firm balances marginal benefits and marginal costs. This means that it hires just enough workers so that the marginal cost, w, equals the marginal benefit, MRP_L:

$$MRP_L = w$$

Figure 8.3 shows a firm's marginal revenue product curve. Because the MRP_L curve shows the quantity of labor that the firm hires at each wage, it is also the firm's demand curve for labor. The reason for this downward slope is the decline in the marginal product of labor as more workers are added in the short run. Because of the law of diminishing marginal returns, the more workers the firm hires, the less each successive worker adds to output, and the less the firm is willing to pay them. Suppose the wage w_1 equals the MRP_L at the employment level L_1. If the wage falls to w_2, the revenue generated by the last worker exceeds his cost to the firm, and the firm responds by hiring more workers until $w = MRP_L$ is restored. If we relabel the vertical axis with the wage, the curve shows that

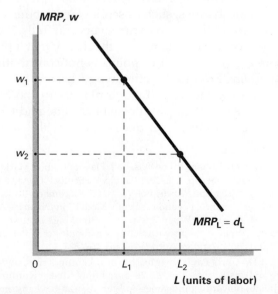

FIGURE 8.3   The Labor Demand Curve
The demand for labor slopes downward, just like the demand curve for a good or service.

the unit price of labor and the quantity of labor demanded by the firm are negatively related, just like the demand curve for a good or service.

MEASURING A PLAYER'S MRP   While the theory behind a player's value is quite simple, determining what a particular player is worth can be very complex. One major reason for the complexity is the fact that players are not homogeneous inputs that can be increased or reduced at will. Another is the difficulty in measuring output. Players do not directly produce a saleable good. Instead, players are an important input in the production of wins. If teams maximize profits, we must then establish the relationship between wins and profits. Economists have produced numerous estimates of the value of professional athletes' output since Simon Rottenberg's pioneering work in 1956.[13] We present one relatively intuitive measure developed by David Berri, Martin Schmidt, and Stacey Brook, who calculated the marginal revenue product for several players in the NBA.[14] They started by assuming that teams produce wins using players as inputs. The value of a player is thus

$$MRP_{ij} = MR_{win} \times \Delta wins_{ij}$$

where MRP_{ij} is the marginal revenue product of player i when he plays for team j, MR_{win} is the value of an additional win to a team, and $\Delta wins_{ij}$ is the additional number of wins that team j can attribute to player i. Berri et al. estimated that the monetary value of a win to a team is about \$1.67 million. They measure each player's contribution to teams wins using the following formula:

$$\Delta wins = \text{points} + \text{total rebounds} + \text{steals} + \tfrac{1}{2} \times (\text{blocked shots} + \text{assists})$$
$$- \text{field goal attempts} - \text{turnovers} - \tfrac{1}{2} \times (\text{free throws} + \text{personal fouls})$$

This equation (from which we have deleted subscripts for simplicity) rewards players for positive contributions, such as scoring and rebounding, and penalizes them for negative contributions, such as turnovers and fouls. It subtracts the number of field goal and free throw attempts on the theory that a player who requires more shots to score a given number of points is not contributing as much to his team. Based on the Wins Produced methodology, Lebron James, Chris Paul, and Tyson Chandler were the most productive players in the NBA in 2011–2012. James produced 17.3 wins, Paul produced 14.2 wins, and Chandler produced 13.3 wins.[15] The value of a star player does not end with his contributions to his

---

[13]See, for example, Simon Rottenberg, "The Baseball Players' Labor Market," *Journal of Political Economy,* vol. 64, no. 3 (June 1956), pp. 242–258; Gerald W. Scully, "Pay and Performance in Major League Baseball," *American Economic Review,* vol. 64, no. 5 (December 1974), pp. 915–930; Andrew Zimbalist, "Salaries and Performance: Beyond the Scully Model," in *Diamonds Are Forever: The Business of Baseball,* ed. by Paul M. Sommers (Washington, D.C.: Brookings Institution, 1992), pp. 109–133; Anthony C. Krautmann, "What's Wrong with Scully's Estimates of a Player's Marginal Revenue Product?" *Economic Inquiry,* vol. 37, no. 2 (April 1999), pp. 269–381.

[14]David J. Berri, "What Do Chris Paul, Dwight Howard, LeBron James, and Tim Duncan Have in Common?" *The Wages of Wins Journal,* May 22, 2008, at http://dberri.wordpress.com/2008/05/22/what-do-chris-paul-dwight-howard-lebron-james-and-tim-duncan-have-in-common/.

[15]"Geekstats for NBA Players," *The NBA Geek,* at http://www.thenbageek.com/players, viewed May 15, 2012.

own team. Because star players attract many fans to other teams' home arenas and NBA teams do not yet share gate revenue, star players in the NBA generate substantial positive externalities for other teams.

There are many other methods by which one might estimate the marginal product of a player, though the method used depends heavily on both the sport and the position. For example, in football, one might measure the marginal product of a running back by rushing yards, receiving yards, or some combination of the two. For quarterbacks, statisticians have developed composite indexes of productivity, such as the quarterback rating system, which distills a variety of statistical measures into a single index. Particularly in football, there is no universal agreement on which metrics best capture player productivity, in part because it is so hard to separate a player's performance from that of his teammates. A long reception by a receiver depends upon the quarterback who threw the ball, the linemen who gave the quarterback time to throw, and perhaps even the running back, whose presence on the field kept the defense from expecting a long pass.

As technology has improved and teams increasingly rely on number-crunchers to find a competitive advantage, analysts have developed an array of new performance measures, from WAR (wins above replacement) to WHIP (wins plus hits per innings pitched) to DICE (defense-independent component ERA). Analysts have also questioned the value of many commonly used performance measures. In *Stumbling on Wins*, for example, David Berri and Martin Schmidt are critical of goals against average—the number of goals per game—as a measure of a goalie's performance in hockey. Their objection is simple: the measure of performance is far too random to be a reliable indicator of talent. Presumably, the best goalies should have the best performance from year to year. However, the variability in goals against average is extremely high. For example, only three of the goalies with the top 10 goals against average in 2010–2011 (with a minimum of 25 games played) were also among the top 10 in 2011–2012. Berri and Schmidt claim that too many outside factors affect the number of goals a goalie allows, such as the play of the defensemen in front of him.[16]

Variability in defense has also led analysts to turn away from earned run average (runs allowed per nine innings pitched) as a measure of pitching performance. In an attempt to separate pitching performance from the quality of the other eight players on the field, analysts have developed defense-independent pitching statistics, or DIPS. DIPS look only at pitching outcomes that have nothing to do with fielding. They focus solely on outcomes like walks (*BB*—for bases on balls), home runs (*HR*), and strikeouts (*K*). Among the most popular DIPS is the fielding independent pitching (*FIP*), which is calculated in a way that makes it comparable to a pitchers ERA:

$$FIP = 3.10 + \frac{13 + HR + 3 \times BB - 2 \times K}{IP}$$

where *IP* is innings pitched. By this measure, Roy Halladay was by far the best pitcher in MLB in 2011. Despite having an ERA (2.35) that was slightly worse

---

[16]David J. Berri and Martin B. Schmidt, *Stumbling on Wins* (Upper Saddle River, N.J.: FT Press, 2010).

than Clayton Kershaw's (2.28) and roughly the same as Justin Verlander's (2.40), Halladay's FIP (2.22) was far lower than either Kershaw's (2.50) or Verlander's (3.03).[17]

IMPERFECT COMPETITION AND LABOR DEMAND   While the competitive model forms a useful baseline, the labor markets in professional sports frequently violate its underlying assumptions. We examine many labor market imperfections in Chapter 9. One imperfection, however, comes not from the labor market but from the product market. Recall that a monopoly sets a price that exceeds marginal revenue because the marginal revenue curve lies below the demand curve. In this case, the labor demand curve slopes downward because of both diminishing returns and declining marginal revenue. As a result, the MRP_L curve for the profit-maximizing monopolist lies to the left of the MRP_L curve of the competitive industry. If the labor supply curve has its typical upward slope, the monopolist hires fewer workers and pays lower wages than it would if the industry were competitive. This is consistent with the fact that monopolists restrict output as part of their strategy to maximize profits. Figure 8.4 shows that if demand were based on competitive markets, teams would pay higher salaries and hire more players. However, because demand is based on a monopoly in the output (games)

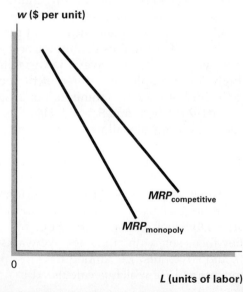

FIGURE 8.4   **The Monopolist's Marginal Revenue Product Curve**
A monopoly's labor demand curve will lie below the labor demand curve of an otherwise identical competitive industry.

---

[17]FIP figures were calculated using data from *Baseball-Reference.com* http://www.baseball-reference. com. For more on advanced pitching statistics, see Dan Basco and Michael Davies, "The Many Flavors of DIPS: A History and an Overview," *Society for American Baseball Research*, Fall 2010, at http://sabr. org/research/many-flavors-dips-history-and-overview, viewed May 23, 2012.

market, *MRP* is below and to the left of the competitive market labor demand curve, and the firm reduces both wages and employment.

Labor Market Equilibrium

Recall from Chapter 2 that market demand (supply) is the horizontal sum of all individual demand (supply) curves. The same principle applies to labor markets as well. Figure 8.5 shows the market supply (S_L) and market demand (D_L) of players in a sports league. As was true for the product markets described in Chapters 2 and 3, the equilibrium quantity of labor (L^e) and the equilibrium level of compensation (w^e) are given by the intersection of the supply and demand curves.

Figure 8.6 shows what happens to pay when market conditions change. When basketball became much more popular in the 1980s, thanks to the arrival of charismatic stars such as Magic Johnson, Larry Bird, and Michael Jordan, the demand to see professional basketball both in person and on TV rose. This, in turn, increased the value of each player's contribution to the product provided by the NBA. As a result, the marginal revenue product of all NBA players rose. The increase was not due to higher productivity. Instead, it was due to the rise in the marginal revenue that resulted from greater fan interest. A higher MR_{win} led to a higher *MRP*, which, in turn, caused the demand for labor to shift to the right and led to higher pay. Declining economic conditions in 2008 reduced the demand for tickets to NBA games.[18] This, in turn, caused the *MRP* of players in the NBA to

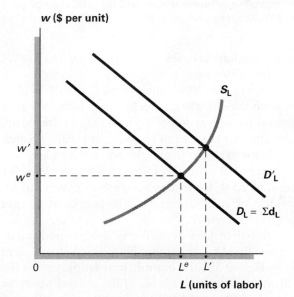

FIGURE 8.5   The Equilibrium Wage and Quantity in the Labor Market
The equilibrium wage, w^e, and employment, L^e, in a labor market are set by the intersection of the labor supply curve, S_L, and labor demand curve, D_L. If demand increases to D'_L, both the equilibrium wage and employment increase.

---

[18]Because the NBA contract was still in force, TV revenues had not declined.

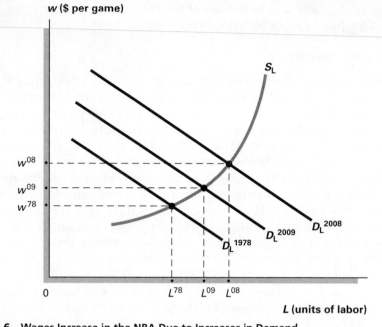

FIGURE 8.6 Wages Increase in the NBA Due to Increases in Demand

As basketball became more popular, the MRP of basketball players rose, shifting the labor demand curve to the right. This increased the pay and the level of employment. When the economy slowed in 2008–2009, team revenues fell, and the MRP curve shifted left.

decline. As a result, median salaries in the NBA for the 2009–2010 season fell slightly from their 2008–2009 level.

The number of teams also affects the overall demand for players. The number of teams can vary with the entry of rival leagues (a factor we revisit in Chapter 9) or with the expansion or contraction of a given league. Increasing the number of teams shifts the demand for labor from D_L to D_L' in Figure 8.5 and causes the equilibrium quantity of labor to rise to L' and the equilibrium level of pay to rise to w'. The impact of the number of teams explains why players associations oppose any form of contraction. In 2004, for example, baseball players in Japan staged their only strike, a two-day job action to protest the proposed merger of the Kintetsu Buffaloes and the Orix Blue Wave.[19]

Finally, the number of jobs available is determined partly by roster size. Roster limits are determined by agreement between the team owners and the players' associations. In Figure 8.7, the equilibrium employment level is L^e. We can show the roster limit, as a vertical line set at the agreed upon number of players (L^r). In this case, total employment falls and wages rise. Whether the players are made better off by this limit depends on the criteria used. Players who retain their jobs are paid more, but fewer players are employed. In addition, we can evaluate

---

[19]The two teams did merge to form the Orix Buffaloes, but the owners agreed to keep the number of teams at 12 by admitting the Rakuten Golden Eagles as an expansion team.

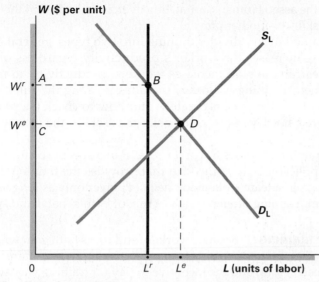

FIGURE 8.7 The effect of roster limits
With no roster limit, the teams employ L^e *players*. With a roster limit set at L^r employment falls and wages rise. Whether the total payments to players increases or decreases depends on the relative sizes of rectangle $0ABL^r$ (total payments with the roster limit) and rectangle $0CDL^e$ (total payments without the roster limit).

the total payments made to all players by comparing rectangles $0ABL^r$ to rectangle $0CDL^e$. If the former is larger, total payments to players increase. If it is smaller, total payments to players fall.

HUMAN CAPITAL AND PLAYER COMPENSATION   If workers are more productive, the MP_L, MRP_L, and wages all rise. **Human capital** is the set of skills that contribute to a person's productivity. The term implies that each person has a stock of skills that can be increased by investing in additional skills.

According to Nobel laureate Gary Becker, who developed the theory of human capital in the 1960s, a person investing in human capital resembles a business investing in physical capital.[20] When a firm purchases a drill press, it makes a one-time expenditure in return for an expected stream of benefits over the life span of the equipment. Similarly, a student who spends four years studying economics in college, or a hockey player who spends four years developing his skills in the minor leagues, endures an up-front cost to acquire skills that he can use for his entire career.

Unlike physical capital, human capital depreciates with age or disuse rather than with use. Many of the skills an athlete acquires, such as learning the basic rules of play, will not depreciate until long after retirement. Although physical abilities eventually depreciate with age, an athlete's knowledge of the game may increase throughout his or her career. An important difference between human and physical capital is that a firm can generally transfer physical capital to another

---

[20]Gary Becker, *Human Capital, 3rd ed.*, (Chicago: University of Chicago Press, 1993).

firm by selling the asset. Human capital, however, is embodied in the worker, who cannot sell his skills to another player.

Human capital theory divides training into two types: **general** and **specific**. General training increases the worker's productivity regardless of the setting. For example, learning to read increases workers' productivity no matter where they work. General training in hockey includes learning the rules of the game, how to pass or shoot the puck accurately, and how to check (stop) an opposing player. The more a hockey player can master these skills, the more valuable he is to all teams.

Specific training increases a worker's *MRP* in a specific context. At the most extreme, it is applicable only at the firm that provides the training. For example, learning the plays in a team's playbook helps a player only as long as he or she is part of that team. Training often provides a mix of both general and specific skills.

WHO PAYS FOR TRAINING?   Because workers and firms both gain when the workers are more skilled, both groups have an incentive to provide training. However, the benefits to each group and the incentive to pay for training vary with the skills that are imparted.

Becker concluded that the type of training a worker receives determines who pays for it. When a player receives specific training, he is more valuable to his current team than to other teams. The team can therefore capture much of the return to the training it provides because it must pay the player only enough to prevent him from moving to another team.

When a player receives general training, his productivity rises at all teams. If the team has no way to restrict player mobility, such as with the reserve clause, it is unwilling to pay for the training. Suppose, for example, the Toronto Maple Leafs of the NHL pay for a player's training costs by hiring coaches and providing training facilities while the player plays for the Maple Leafs' minor league team. With no restrictions in place, the player could leave the Leafs for another team when his contract expires, taking his human capital with him. The Maple Leafs would have paid for the training without receiving the benefit of the player's increased productivity. Because all teams recognize this potential loss of their investment, they force players to pay for general training in the form of low minor league salaries. We can formalize the model a bit to see why this is so.

For simplicity, assume that a player's career lasts only two seasons. In the first season, he costlessly receives skills, which he can then apply in the second season. Using the concept of present value that we introduced in Chapter 7, we can show that the player's value over the two seasons is his value in the first season (MRP_1) plus the present value of his *MRP* in the second season (MRP_2). If the interest rate is r, the player generates benefits (B):

$$B = MRP_1 + \frac{MRP_2}{1 + r}$$

In the first period, the team pays him $w_1 = MRP_1$ and in the second period, it pays him $w_2 = MRP_2$. If helping the player to acquire skills is not costless because the team must pay training costs, T, it faces the problem shown in the inequality below, as the player's costs exceed his contribution to the team

$$w_1 + \frac{w_2}{1 + r} + T > MRP_1 + \frac{MRP_2}{1 + r}$$

To restore equality, the team must reduce the player's pay. If training provides team-specific skills, the team can capture a return on its investment by paying the player less than he is worth to them but more than he is worth to other teams. If training increases the player's general skills, the player can apply his new skills equally well for any other team. Any attempt to reduce w_2 will induce the player to leave for another team. The team provides training only if the player pays for the training costs (usually in the form of lower pay) in the first period.[21]

For example, minor league hockey and baseball salaries are very low compared to salaries in the NHL and MLB. By accepting relatively low salaries while in the minor leagues and during their first several years in the major leagues players are helping to pay for the training they need.

8.2   THE ECONOMICS OF TOURNAMENTS AND SUPERSTARS

The theory of labor market equilibrium implies that players who are slightly more productive than other players should receive slightly higher rewards. Sometimes, however, small differences in performance translate into huge differences in compensation. For example, Roger Federer won the 2009 "Gentlemen's Singles" Championship at Wimbledon in a grueling five-set match with Andy Roddick that lasted more than four hours and took 77 games to complete (the equivalent of playing more than two 6–4, 6–4, 6–4 straight-set victories). It is hard to imagine a closer match. For winning the tournament, Federer received £850,000 (almost $1.41 million), while Roddick received only half that amount. The huge difference in payoffs seems even more drastic considering that a player who was eliminated in the second round earned just £7,000 more than a player who was eliminated in the first round.[22] The return to winning a match increases dramatically as a player advances through the tournament. Similar conclusions hold for golf, bowling, and most other individual sports.

In such cases, *relative* productivity rather than *absolute* productivity matters. Roger Federer would have received the same prize for winning Wimbledon regardless of his margin of victory. Winning is all that matters. The only objective is to beat the other player.[23] Because the order of finish is the only performance criterion, such contests are known as **rank-order tournaments**.

---

[21]In a world of uncertainty, where neither the player nor the team is sure that the training will result in higher skills and higher pay, there is an incentive for the two to share the costs of training.

[22]"Wimbledon 2009 Prize Money," *The Tennis Times,* June 2009, at http://thetennistimes.com/here-are-prizemoney-breakdowns-for-wimbledon-2009/.

[23]Two men were being chased by a grizzly bear when one of them stopped and began to put on track shoes. The other stopped and said, "You don't think track shoes are going to help you outrun a grizzly, do you?" The first man looked up and replied, "It's not the grizzly I'm trying to outrun."

Why would the organizers of a tournament set prizes based on rank order rather than absolute quality of performance? In all individual sports, the quality of any single performance depends on a long list of factors that have nothing to do with individual ability, such as the quality of the playing surface, the weather conditions, or the ability of the opponent.[24] To determine the absolute level of a player's marginal product, judges would have to account for all these factors, a difficult and expensive task. If tournament organizers cannot measure marginal product, they cannot provide a reward based on the players' *MRP*. They must devise a new way to distribute prize money and provide appropriate incentives for participants. Fortunately, relative performance is more readily measured. By setting a highly nonlinear prize structure, in which the increase in winnings grows as a player moves up the leaderboard, organizers give athletes a powerful incentive to do their best. This highly uneven distribution of the purses appeals to the most basic of economic tenets: self-interest.[25]

We start by assuming that participants maximize utility and that their utility increases with income and leisure and, hence, decreases with effort. Organizers of the tournament want players to give their best effort, thereby providing fans with the most exciting contest, maximizing their own profits. Figure 8.8 shows how a player determines her optimal level of effort in a tournament. Casual observation is enough to show that the marginal cost of effort is positive, which means that there are costs associated with trying harder to win (more hours of practice, learning to handle pressure situations, and extra effort in the contest itself). Thus, the marginal cost curve slopes upward in Figure 8.8. In this model we assume that the marginal cost curve not only slopes upward; it also becomes steeper as the amount of effort rises. The increasing slope means that changes in effort level become costlier as effort level rises. For example, moving from E_0 to E_1 adds little to the player's cost. In contrast, increasing effort from an already high level, such as from E_2, to an even higher level, E_3, comes at a great cost.

Because the tournament's organizers (reflecting the desires of the fans who buy tickets and the advertisers who sponsor broadcasts) want to see the players try their hardest, they must make sure that the differences between the prizes increase for players who reach the top of the rankings. Figure 8.9 shows why. In a contest with one winner and one loser, such as the finals of a tennis match, and with contestants who are roughly equal in ability, the difference between winning and losing may come down to random factors, such as playing conditions.[26] The increasing marginal cost of effort is MC^I. A player will set her level of effort (E_1) where *MR*, her additional revenue from moving up one position, equals the marginal cost of advancing on position. By creating a large difference between

---

[24]In one famous example, the course of the 1960 World Series was changed when a ground ball to the Yankee shortstop hit a pebble, took an unexpected bounce, and sustained a key Pirate rally in the seventh and deciding game.

[25]This theory was first put forth in Edward Lazear and Sherwin Rosen, "Rank Order Tournaments as Optimum Labor Contracts," *Journal of Political Economy*, vol. 89, no. 5 (October 1981), pp. 841–864.

[26]If the contestants are not equal in ability, the resulting tournament may be poor entertainment. If the weaker opponent knows he or she has no chance to win, there is no incentive to try.

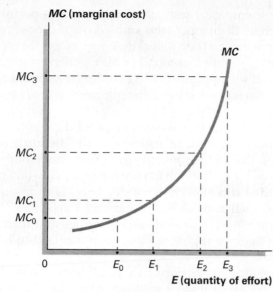

MC (marginal cost)

FIGURE 8.8 The Increasing Marginal Cost of Effort

Because providing greater effort means working harder, the marginal cost of effort slopes upward.

first and second prize, MR_1, the players have an incentive to expend more effort than if the difference were small (MR_2). If the marginal cost of effort is linear, as shown by the line MC^C, the organizers can elicit the same level of effort with a much smaller difference between prizes (MR_1').

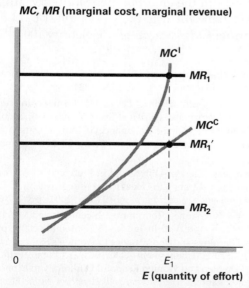

MC, MR (marginal cost, marginal revenue)

FIGURE 8.9 Creating the Incentive for a High Level of Effort in a Tournament

Increasing the reward for additional effort increases the optimal level of effort by a player in a tournament.

One of the first empirical tests of this theory was performed by Ronald Ehrenberg and Michael Bognanno, who studied the response of PGA golfers to differences in prize money.[27] They found that, just as the theory predicts, incentives matter. Particularly in the last round of play, golfers shot significantly lower scores when they had the opportunity to earn larger prizes. Later research has tested for incentive effects in variety of different sports, including distance running and tennis.[28]

There is some evidence that women respond differently from men to the pressure of an economic contest. In a survey of the literature on gender differences in preferences, Rachel Croson and Uri Gneezy note that women are more reluctant to engage in competition than men are and that women do not perform as well in competitive situations as men do. This claim is supported by controlled experiments, such as those by Gneezy and Rustichini.[29] They had Israeli fourth-graders run in timed, noncompetitive settings and then in head-to-head competitions. They found that girls ran slower in the head-to-head competition, while boys ran faster.

Studies that analyze the performance of athletes in actual competition, as opposed to analyzing experimental settings, generally provide mixed results. Keith Gilsdorf and Vasant Sukhatme find that women and men respond similarly to elimination tournaments, as in tennis. XiaoGang Che and Brad Humphreys find that women skiers do not respond at all to the incentives present in ski competition, though there are no studies of men's performance to provide a comparison. Finally, Eva Leeds and Michael Leeds show that women respond more to incentives than men in elite figure skating competition.[30]

Extraordinary rewards for top performers are not limited to sports. Compared to top earners in the entertainment industry, athletes' salaries seem much less impressive. Table 8.1 lists the five highest-paid celebrities and five highest-paid athletes from *Forbes Magazine's* "Celebrity 100."[31] While most people

---

[27]Ronald G. Ehrenberg and Michael L. Bognanno, "Do Tournaments Have Incentive Effects?" *Journal of Political Economy*, vol. 98, no. 6 (December 1990), pp. 1307–1324.

[28]See for example, Bernd Frick and Joachim Prinz, "Pay and Performance in Professional Road Running: The Case of City Marathons," *International Journal of Sport Finance*, vol. 2, no. 1 (February 2007), pp. 25–35; and Uwe Sunde, "Heterogeneity and Performance in Tournaments: A Test for Incentive Effects Using Professional Tennis Data," *Applied Economics*, vol. 41, no. 25–27 (November–December 2009), pp. 3199–3208.

[29]Rachel Croson and Uri Gneezy, "Gender Differences in Preferences," *Journal of Economic Literature*, vol. 47, no. 2 (Summer 2009), pp. 1–27; and Uri Gneezy and Aldo Rustichini, "Gender and Competition at a Young Age," *American Economic Review*, vol. 94, no. 2 (May 2004), pp. 377–381.

[30]Keith Gilsdorf and Vasant A. Sukhatme, "Tournament Incentives and Match Outcomes in Women's Professional Tennis," *Applied Economics*, vol. 40, no. 16–18 (September 2008), pp. 2405–2412; XiaoGang Che and Brad Humphreys, "Earnings and Performance in Women's Skiing," *The International Handbook on the Economics of Women's Sports* (Cheltenham, U.K.: Edward Elgar, forthcoming); Eva Marikova Leeds and Michael Leeds, "Do Men and Women Respond Differently to Economic Contests? The Case of Men's and Ladies' Figure Skating," *The International Handbook on the Economics of Women's Sports* (Cheltenham, U.K.: Edward Elgar, forthcoming).

[31]This list is technically of the most "powerful" celebrities, but income is an important factor in *Forbes's* rating system.

TABLE 8.1 The Five Highest-Paid Celebrities and Athletes in the *Forbes* 2011 "Celebrity 100"

Rank/Name	Occupation	Earnings (in millions)
Celebrities		
1. Oprah Winfrey	Multimedia Personality	$290
2. U2	Musicians	$195
3. Tyler Perry	Entertainer	$130
4. Bon Jovi	Musician	$125
5. Jerry Bruckheimer	Movies/Television	$113
Athletes		
1. Tiger Woods	Golf	$ 75
2. Kobe Bryant	Basketball	$ 53
3. LeBron James	Basketball	$ 48
4. (T) Phil Mickelson	Golf	$ 47
Roger Federer	Tennis	$ 47

Source: Dorothy Pomerantz, "The World's Most Powerful Celebrities," *Forbes.* May 16, 2011, at http://www.forbes.com/wealth/celebrities#p_2_s_dsalary, viewed May 14, 2012.

in the entertainment industry struggle to make ends meet, the table shows that becoming a star brings a huge reward. Without exception, these rewards dwarf the compensation of professional athletes. Tiger Woods, the highest paid athlete on the list, ranks 14th in overall income, and Kobe Bryant, the second-highest paid athlete on the list, is tied for 24th. (The highest-paid female athlete on the list, Maria Sharapova, is 72nd.)

Economic contests also apply in the corporate world. The salary of a top executive in a large corporation is likely to be at least twice that of his or her nearest rival. This does not mean that the *MRP* of the top-ranked executive is twice that of his or her nearest rival. In fact, the value of their marginal product is very difficult to determine because they do not produce output that can be readily measured. To ensure that second-tier executives give their best effort, tournament-style wages create disproportionately large rewards for increases in rank.

8.3 TOURNAMENTS, CHEATING, AND THE DISTRIBUTION OF INCOME

While tournaments might provide athletes with an incentive to do their best, a large spread in rewards can negatively affect athletes' behavior in both individual and team sports. When teammates feel they are competing for individual rewards, the result can sometimes be selfish play, which undermines the cooperation that teams need to succeed. The inability of Kobe Bryant and Shaquille O'Neal to cooperate was widely blamed for the breakup of the great Los Angeles Lakers teams of the late 1990s and early 2000s, while the later success of the Lakers was frequently attributed to the maturation of Kobe Bryant into a team player.

In extreme cases, a tournament can lead to outright sabotage. The most famous such case might be that of Tonya Harding, a former national champion figure skater who admitted to "hindering prosecution" in the plot to injure fellow skater Nancy Kerrigan prior to the 1994 Winter Olympics. Kerrigan was attacked during the National Championships, at which the Olympic team was to be chosen. Harding's ex-husband and an accomplice confessed to carrying out the attack and claimed that Harding herself was involved in planning it.[32] The primary motivation behind the attack was to remove Kerrigan as the preeminent U.S. woman figure skater so that Harding could assume that role, thus providing her with a "ticket to fame and fortune."[33]

More Potential Pitfalls of High Rewards: The Case of NASCAR

The reward scheme used in NASCAR racing is an interesting exception to both the standard model of wage determination and the highly nonlinear rewards used in golf and tennis. Although stock car racing satisfies the basic conditions for a rank-order tournament, the per-race reward structure is nearly horizontal. Figure 8.10 shows the prize money for a single NASCAR race and, for comparison, for a single PGA tournament. The reward increases much more dramatically in the golf tournament. The winner of the golf tournament receives about $1.7 million, while the

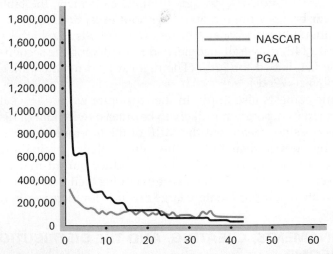

FIGURE 8.10   Comparison of the Rewards in the 2012 Players Championship versus the 2012 Bojangles Southern 500

The reward structure in NASCAR is far flatter than for the PGA.

Sources: Results: 2012 Official Race Results: Bojangles' Southern 500. At http://www.nascar.com/races/cup/2012/11/data/results_official.html; and *ESPN GOLF: The Players* Championship. At http://espn.go.com/golf/leaderboard?tournamentId=1004. Viewed May 21, 2012

[32]Sonja Steptoe and E. M. Swift, "A Done Deal," *Sports Illustrated,* March 28, 1994, pp. 32–36.

[33]E. M. Swift, "Anatomy of a Plot: The Kerrigan Assault," *Sports Illustrated,* February 14, 1994, pp. 28–38.

winner of the race receives just $320,000. The 15th-place finisher in either event receives roughly the same prize (around $130,000). Moving down to 43rd place, golfer receives $37,050, but the racer earns as much as $72,139. So while the rewards in racing are nonlinear, the changes in prize money are not as extreme as in golf. This raises a couple of questions about the payouts. First, why are NASCAR's payouts so different from other sports? Second, are NASCAR's incentives large enough to influence driver effort? To address the latter question, several economists have used econometric models to estimate the effect of changes in the prize structure. Brad Humphries and Bernd Frick have recently found that drivers respond to the incentives in the payout scheme. Using a sample of over 1,000 races, they show that the larger the spread between the prizes, the faster the average speed in the race.[34] Thus, while the increases in payouts are relatively modest, they do appear to generate an incentive to drive faster.

Returning to the first question of why NASCAR organizers set payouts so differently than other rank-order sports, we must consider several unique features of racing that work against steep increases in payouts for higher finishers. As noted earlier, in most individual sports, competitors cannot prevent their opponents from succeeding. In racing, drivers all compete on the same track at the

NASCAR drivers battle for position.

[34]Bernd Frick and Brad Humphries, "Prize Structure and Performance: Evidence from NASCAR," *Working Paper* 2011–12, at http://www.economics.ualberta.ca/~/media/economics/FacultyAndStaff/WPs/WP2011-12-Humphreys.pdf.

same time, so tournament-style wages may lead to reckless driving—with catastrophic results.[35] A win-at-all-cost strategy in auto racing could lead to a severe accident and high social costs, while an analogous strategy in figure skating would lead to an embarrassing fall on the ice and to costs only to one's ego. In addition, NASCAR teams that sponsor cars have relatively complex revenue and profit functions that include payments from sponsors, year-end prize money, and a wide variety of bonuses that drivers can win during races. Because stock cars are covered with advertisements for their sponsors, being on the track—and on camera—for a long period of time becomes very important to racers. Season championship points also give drivers a powerful incentive to remain on the track for the entire race rather than risk crashing in an attempt to earn points that may lead to a large end-of-season prize. Thus, highly nonlinear reward schemes for individual races may do more harm than good. Given that the spread of payouts is much less extreme than those of golf or tennis, yet are large enough to influence drivers' behavior, NASCAR officials seem to have set these payouts at levels that create exciting racing while being mindful of potential risks.

Too Much of a Good Thing

The disproportionate rewards that accompany even small differences in performance sometimes induce coaches, trainers, and athletes to push themselves and others too hard.

Possibly the most disturbing example of the undesirable outcomes in tournaments comes from a surprising yet familiar source. Imagine a country in which selected children are put to work full-time. School, friends, a normal childhood are all denied them as they perform hours of backbreaking work. When they try to get away, they are subjected to physical and emotional abuse, sometimes at the hands of their own parents. By the time they reach adulthood, many of them are physically broken—some even killed—by the arduous demands of their supervisors. Still others bear permanent emotional scars. Unable to form normal relationships with their peers, some take solace in drugs and others in self-abusive behavior. The country is the United States, and the abused children are the same ones we cheer on at events such as the Olympics, Wimbledon, and the NCAA championships. Severe abuses have also been well-documented in other countries, such as China.[36]

These youths are victims of a reward system in which first place counts for everything and second place for next to nothing. Adolescent girls take to the ice for the Olympic figure skating championship with greater individual rewards at stake than for any single event except, perhaps, a heavyweight boxing

---

[35]This argument is based on Peter von Allmen, "Is the Reward System in NASCAR Efficient?" *Journal of Sports Economics*, vol. 2, no. 1 (February 2000), pp. 62–79.

[36]Joan Ryan, in *Little Girls in Pretty Boxes* (New York: Doubleday, 1995), catalogs the horrors confronting many young female gymnasts and figure skaters. The dark side of the Chinese athletic system is described in Andrew Jacobs, "Heavy Burden on Athletes Takes Joy Away from China's Olympic Success," *New York Times*, August 7, 2012, at http://www.nytimes.com/2012/08/08/sports/olympics/chinas-quest-for-olympic-gold-takes-toll-on-athletes.html?pagewanted=all.

championship.[37] A gold medalist may get TV specials and starring roles in skating exhibitions. Her name will be entered in record books, and fans will remember her performance fondly for years to come. In contrast, all but a few relatives and friends will soon forget the performance of the fourth-place finisher.

As a result of the highly skewed reward structure, young girls are willing to work extremely long hours, some in excess of 45 hours per week. Their coaches and gyms, which stand to benefit mightily from the publicity these girls bring them, would be violating child labor laws if they paid the girls for their efforts. The long hours of training can cause permanent physical and psychological damage. Hoping to please their parents and coaches and yearning for a chance to stand on the Olympic podium, young gymnasts suffer through severe injuries that they do not allow to heal for fear of missing a championship or an Olympics before they become too old. One elite coach discouraged girls from having casts put on fractured limbs because "he feared it would hurt their muscle tone."[38] Some take an array of "laxatives, thyroid pills, and diuretics to lose the weight brought on by puberty."[39] The obsession with weight can become so serious that eating disorders can develop. Surveys show that almost a third of female college athletes—and up to two-thirds of female gymnasts surveyed—admit to some sort of eating disorder. One young gymnast, Christy Henrich, literally starved herself to death. The eating disorders can have long-term effects, leading to menstrual dysfunction and osteoporosis.[40]

Performance-Enhancing Drugs

In recent years, professional sports seem to have been plagued by the widespread use of performance-enhancing drugs (PEDs). PEDs present athletes with a dilemma. Sports celebrate athletes who push themselves to their absolute limits. The swimmer who shaves his head and body, the high-jumper who finds a new way to clear the bar, and the running back who has experimental knee surgery rather than retire are all seeking an edge that will propel them to (or keep them at) the top of their fields. While some changes, such as Babe Didrikson's use of the "Western Roll" high jump in the 1932 caused controversy at first (and cost her an Olympic gold medal), the advantage that such innovations bring quickly dissipates as they become widely adopted.

As fans, we perceive PEDs as somehow different from shaving one's body, finding a new way to jump, or having career-extending surgery. One reason for this difference is that many of the drugs that athletes take are controlled substances, which are used illegally when taken without a prescription. Another reason is

---

[37]Joan Ryan, *Little Girls in Pretty Boxes* (1995), p. 193.

[38]Merrell Noden, "Dying to Win," *Sports Illustrated,* August 8, 1994, pp. 52–59.

[39]Robert Frank and Phillip Cook, *The Winner-Take-All Society* (New York: The Free Press, 1995), p. 132.

[40]See Susan Gilbert, "The Smallest Olympians Pay the Biggest Price," *New York Times* (July 28, 1996), p. E4; Merrell Noden, "Dying to Win" (1994), pp. 52–59; Ryan, *Little Girls in Pretty Boxes* (1995), pp. 17–54; Ian Tofler, Barri Katz Stryer, Lyle Micheli, and Lisa Herman, "Physical and Emotional Problems of Elite Female Gymnasts," *New England Journal of Medicine,* vol. 335, no 4 (July 25, 1996), pp. 281–283.

that, unlike different jumping techniques, one cannot be sure that athletes are doping just by looking at them. Perhaps most important, though, is the danger that PEDs present. The risk associated with PEDs is not new; the first documented doping-related fatality came during a bicycle race in 1879. More recently, the fall of the Berlin Wall in 1989 and the resulting publication of state secrets showed the high cost of East German Olympic success. Physical disabilities, birth defects, even a change in sexual identity were all attributed to the "vitamins" that unsuspecting East German girls were given as part of their training regimen. In the United States, some estimates show that as many as 1 million high school students have used anabolic steroids, a popular PED. Researchers claim that the use of steroids causes heart and liver damage, violent mood swings ("roid rage"), and psychological dependency.[41]

Brad Humphreys and Jane Ruseski use data collected by the Youth Risk Behavior Surveillance System, a nationwide survey of high school-age students, to study steroid use among U.S. youths from 1991 to 2005. They find that boys are much more likely than girls to use steroids (an average over the sample period of about 5.4 percent versus an average of about 2.8 percent). Steroid usage was greater among multisport athletes, particularly among those in the higher grades, and was negatively related to parental education and income. Finally, they found that steroid use was positively related to risky behavior in general, such as the use of other, "recreational" drugs.[42]

The dangers of PEDs have not deterred athletes from using them. Some insight into the mind-set of elite athletes can be found in a survey of almost 200 sprinters, swimmers, powerlifters, and other athletes. The survey confronted the athletes with a hypothetical situation:

You are offered a banned performance-enhancing substance that comes with two guarantees:

1. You will not be caught.
2. You will win every competition you enter for the next five years, and then you will die from the side-effects of the substances.

Would you take it?

More than half the athletes surveyed said they would accept such an offer.[43]

Such attitudes among athletes have led economists to model PED use as a prisoner's dilemma.[44] Figure 8.11 provides a simple model of PED use. It begins

[41]See Aleksander Berentsen, "The Economics of Doping," *European Journal of Political Economy,* vol. 18, no. 1 (2002), pp. 109–127; Steven Ungerleider, *Faust's Gold: Inside the East German Doping Machine* (New York: Thomas Dunne Books, 2001); and Jane Weaver, "Steroid Addiction a Risk for Young Athletes," *MSNBC,* April 5, 2005, at http://www.msnbc.msn.com/id/7348758.

[42]Brad Humphreys and Jane Ruseski, "Socio-Economic Determinants of Adolescent Use of Performance Enhancing Drugs: Evidence from the YRBSS," *The Journal of Socio-Economics,* vol. 40, no. 2 (April 2011), pp. 208–216.

[43]Michael Bamberger and Don Yaeger, "Over the Edge," *Sports Illustrated,* April 14, 1997, pp. 61–70.

[44]For more detailed treatments of doping as a prisoner's dilemma, see Aleksander Berentsen, "The Economics of Doping." and Kjetil K. Haugen, "The Performance Enhancing Drug Game," *Journal of Sports Economics,* vol. 5, no. 1 (February 2004), pp. 67–86.

	Mark	
	Doesn't use PEDs	Uses PEDs
Sam Doesn't use PEDs	(2,2) No advantage/No harm	(5,0) Mark wins/Sam loses
Uses PEDs	(0,5) Mark loses/Sam wins	(1,1) No advantage/harm

FIGURE 8.11 **PED Use as a Prisoner's Dilemma**

with the simplifying assumption that we have only two athletes, Mark and Sam, each of whom has the choice of using PEDs or not using them. Using PEDs positively impacts performance and gives each player an advantage if the other does not use them.

The payoffs (expressed as units of happiness experienced by Mark and Sam) in the upper-left diagonal square occur when neither athlete takes PEDs, while the payoffs in the lower-right occur when both do. In both situations, neither Sam nor Mark has an advantage over the other. The only difference is that both athletes are risking their health if they both take PEDs. As a result, the payoffs in the upper-left square are superior to the outcomes in the lower-right square. The off-diagonal payoffs reflect the fact that, as the survey suggests, an athlete's happiness heavily depends on his winning. If one athlete takes PEDs and the other does not, then the athlete taking PEDs wins (by setting a world record, winning the home run title, or becoming world champion) and the other loses. The payoff structure in Figure 8.11 reflects the results of the survey cited earlier, that athletes place greater emphasis on success in their chosen fields than on a long and healthy life. Such preferences can, as shown in Figure 8.11, cause taking PEDs to be a dominant strategy. The result of the game is a prisoner's dilemma because both players take PEDs despite the fact that they would be better off if neither did.

Although PED usage is not new, many major sports have recently experienced embarrassing scandals involving PEDs. Perhaps the best-known scandal involves the Bay Area Laboratory Co-Operative (BALCO), whose founder, Victor Conte, served a short prison sentence after pleading guilty to steroid distribution and money laundering in June 2005. When the government seized BALCO's records, it found evidence that many well-known athletes had used steroids, human growth hormones, and other PEDs.

The track star Marion Jones was probably the most prominent athlete caught up in the BALCO scandal. She was stripped of the five medals that she had won at the 2000 Sydney Olympics (gold in the 100- and 200-meter sprints and the 1,600-meter relay, and bronze in the long jump and the 400-meter relay). Jones was also sentenced to six months in prison for lying to federal prosecutors about her steroid use.

The BALCO scandal has also implicated MLB's all-time home-run champion Barry Bonds. Although it may never be clear whether Bonds knowingly used

PEDs, the allegations made Bonds's pursuit of Hank Aaron's home-run title an embarrassing episode.[45] Roger Clemens, generally regarded as one of the best pitchers of his generation, has also been caught up in a perjury trial for his denial of steroid usage. Although he was acquitted in court, Clemens' once sure entry to baseball's Hall of Fame is now in jeopardy. The legacies of Mark McGwire, Raphael Palmiero, Manny Ramirez, Alex Rodriguez, and Sammy Sosa have also been tainted by PED usage. MLB now has safeguards in place against PED usage. However, Melky Cabrera's 50-game suspension for abnormal testosterone levels while leading the National League in batting average and after being named the MVP of the 2012 All Star Game shows that the controversy has not yet gone away.[46]

No other sport has been as severely damaged by PEDs than bicycling. Though allegations and suspensions are not new to cycling, the credibility of the entire sport was in doubt following the embarrassment surrounding the 2006 Tour de France. Just days before the race was to begin, nine riders, including pre-race favorites Jan Ullrich and Ivan Basso, were barred from the race for suspicion of doping. The race itself proved to be one of the most dramatic ever. Floyd Landis, who was in 11th place after the 16th stage of the race, came back to win the 17th stage by almost six minutes, an unheard-of margin, and went on to win the race. A few days later, however, all the good will generated by Landis's comeback was dashed. A drug test administered after the 17th stage had found abnormal levels of testosterone. Landis was subsequently stripped of his title and banned from competitive cycling for two years. With Lance Armstrong's decision to end his fight against allegations of PED usage, 80 percent of the Tour de France winners and almost 37 percent of all top-10 finishers since 1998 have either admitted that they took PEDs or have been officially tied to PED use.[47]

How often, under what circumstances, and for which substances athletes will be tested are matters of collective bargaining in most professional sports, including the four major North American team sports. While it may seem a simple matter to invoke rules that any player can be tested at any time for any substance, the player associations that represent all players in collective bargaining worry about invasions of privacy, inconvenience, and perhaps most frightening—the negative consequences of a false positive test. Nevertheless, with each successive agreement, owners and the players have agreed to test for an increasing number of substances, often with increased penalties for violations. In Major League Baseball for example, the *Baseball Almanac* reports that as of May 2012, there have

---

[45]Aaron declined the offer to attend games at which Bonds might break his record. See also Mark Fainaru-Wade and Lance Williams, *Game of Shadows: Barry Bonds, BALCO, and the Steroids Scandal That Rocked Professional Sports* (New York: Gotham Books, 2006).

[46]Jack Dickey, "Melky Cabrera Tests Positive for Testosterone, Is Suspended 50 Games, Can Still Win The Batting Title," *Deadspin*, August 15, 2012, at http://deadspin.com/5935082/melky-cabrera-tests-positive-for-testosterone-suspended-50-games-can-still-win-the-batting-title.

[47]Alan McLean, Archie Tse, and Lisa Waananen, "Top Finishers of the Tour de France Tainted by Doping," *New York Times*, at http://www.nytimes.com/interactive/2012/08/24/sports/top-finishers-of-the-tour-de-france-tainted-by-doping.html?smid=tw-nytimes, August 24, 2012.

been 30 suspensions (issued to fewer than 30 players as due to repeat violations) since the performance-enhancing drug policy was put into place in 2005.[48]

The ongoing scandals reveal how widespread the incentive to cheat has become, and how difficult it is for sports leagues and international antidoping agencies to keep up with the development of new and increasingly sophisticated PEDs. Perhaps nothing reflects the times as well as the fact that FIDE, the World Chess Federation, now requires that participants in international chess tournaments undergo drug testing after their matches.[49]

The Distribution of Income

Because financial rewards for individual victories are so heavily weighted in favor of top performers, the distribution of income in individual sports is highly skewed. For example, through July, the top 10 prize winners on 2011 WTA tennis tour accounted for over 42 percent of the total winnings of the top 100 players.[50] As in Chapter 5, we can illustrate the inequality on the women's tennis tour with a Lorenz curve. The horizontal axis in Figure 8.12 shows the cumulative percentage of the population (trivial here because each player accounts for 1 percent of the

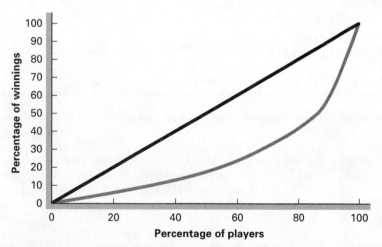

FIGURE 8.12 The Lorenz Curve for the WTA's Top 100 Money Winners in 2011

Source: "WTA Prize Money Leaders," at http://www.wtatennis.com/SEWTATour-Archive/ Rankings_Stats/prize_money_2011.pdf, viewed May 21, 2012.

---

[48]"Steroid Suspensions," *Baseball Almanac* at http://www.baseball-almanac.com/legendary/ steroids_baseball.shtml, viewed May 14, 2012. Although the article title refers to steroids, the list refers to players suspended for all banned substances.

[49]Vassiliy Ivanchuk, the third-ranking chess player in the world, was in danger of receiving a two-year suspension from international competition after he refused to submit to a drug test after the 2008 Dresden Chess Olympiad. A FIDE panel ruled that he had misunderstood the request because of language difficulties and the fact that he was distraught after a loss.

[50]A similar situation holds for team sports as well.

population). The vertical axis shows the cumulative percentage of earnings. The Lorenz curve sags below the straight line, as the bottom 10 percent of the money winners on the tour account for less than 3 percent of total winnings (point *A*), and the bottom 90 percent of the players account for less than 60 percent of the earnings on the tour.

The salary structure in most professional sports is highly uneven due to the earnings of superstars. Even at the highest levels of competition, a few players often have abilities and charisma that set them apart from the rest.[51] In 2011, the average salary for the New York Yankees was over $6.7 million, while the median salary was just over $2 million. The salaries of their top three players (Alex Rodriguez, CC Sabathia, and Mark Teixeira) were over 39 percent of the total team payroll. The same skewed distribution exists on almost all teams. Players such as Roberto Luongo, Kobe Bryant, Peyton Manning, and Alex Rodriguez stand at the extreme right-end of the talent distribution. The extraordinary performances of which these athletes are capable vastly increase the demand to see the games in which they play. Most fans would rather see a matchup of two of a sport's top stars than to see five games played by teams stocked with mediocre players. Fans' desire to see the very best players causes the demand for their services, and hence their earnings, to be much greater than those of players of only slightly lesser ability.

BIOGRAPHICAL SKETCH

Scott Boras   (1952–)

Talking to Boras about baseball executives is like talking to a lion about red meat.

—*Matt Taibbi*[1]

While players like Alex Rodriguez, Mark Teixeira, and Barry Zito would be millionaires no matter who represented them, there can be little question that they, and dozens of other baseball players, have benefited significantly from their association with Scott Boras. In securing high earnings for his clients, Boras has earned the universal scorn of owners. In the words of one reporter, they regard Boras as "Shiva god of destruction, sent to Earth to wreck all that is holy." Boras has proven so successful, and so popular with players, however, that few teams can afford not to deal with him.

Unlike many other agents, Boras did not set out to become an agent. When he was a young man, it looked like he might be a baseball player instead. Boras grew up on a farm in northern California and played baseball at the University of the Pacific, eventually becoming team captain. He was not, however, the stereotypical "jock," majoring in chemistry and taking Ph.D.-level classes in

---

[51]For a detailed description of the nonlinear returns to ability, see Sherwin Rosen, "The Economics of Superstars," *American Economic Review,* vol. 71, no. 5 (December 1981), pp. 845–858.

industrial pharmacology. This sometimes forced Boras to schedule private labs, some of which lasted until midnight, after baseball practice.

Boras was good enough at baseball to sign a contract with the St. Louis Cardinals in 1974, but he did not let his professional career derail his graduate studies. He would offer his coaches beer to proctor exams for him while he was with the team. A series of knee injuries ended Boras's hopes of making the major leagues, and he left baseball in 1978. At the same time, he began studying for a law degree at Pacific's McGeorge School of Law. After graduating from law school, Boras continued to use his background in chemistry, defending drug companies against class-action suits for a large law firm in Chicago, hardly the type of work one would expect of a man who would soon take on the moguls of baseball.

In 1985, Boras helped Bill Caudill, a former minor league teammate, negotiate a contract with the Toronto Blue Jays. The result, a five-year, $7 million contract that made Caudill the second-highest paid relief pitcher in baseball, caught the baseball world's attention and led to Boras's switch full-time to representing players. (Boras insists that he acts as players' legal representative and is not their agent.)

Today, Boras is the head of the Scott Boras Corporation. The company has about 45 employees, including a large research staff, and represents more than 60 players. He has negotiated some of the most lucrative contracts in baseball history, including Alex Rodriguez's 10-year, $252 million contract with the Texas Rangers, Barry Zito's 7-year $126 million deal with the San Francisco Giants, and Stephen Strasburg's record-setting 4-year $15.1 million deal as the first-round pick of the Washington Nationals. At the time, these contracts were records for a position-player and pitcher.

Boras has achieved these results by adopting tactics that neutralize or reverse the traditional monopsony power of MLB owners. He has, for example, effectively used the fact that he can speak with multiple teams while the teams are legally forbidden from speaking to each other about player negotiations. Boras used this asymmetric information to convince Texas Rangers majority owner Tom Hicks that other teams were interested in Rodriguez. Hicks responded by increasing his offer despite the fact that no other team was willing to surpass his previous offer. The result was a contract whose monetary value was greater than the sum Hicks's partnership, which included George W. Bush, had paid for the entire team.

Boras has also used the draft to obtain leverage for his clients. Traditionally the draft has been a source of monopsony power for teams, as they have exclusive rights to negotiate with the players they draft. Boras, however, convinced Tim Belcher, a top draft choice of the Minnesota Twins, to return to college rather than sign with the Twins (Belcher could do so because his college—Mount Vernon Nazarene—belonged to the National Association of Intercollegiate Athletics (NAIA) and not the NCAA). He later convinced J. D. Drew, the first overall choice of the 1997 draft, to play with the St. Paul Saints, an independent minor league team, rather than sign with the Philadelphia Phillies. Both Belcher and Drew signed much more lucrative contracts with different teams a year later.

At times, Boras's techniques have backfired. Boras's hardball tactics in negotiating a new contract for Alex Rodriguez were so aggressive—he announced that Rodriguez would opt out of the remaining three years of his contract during game 4 of the 2007 World Series—that Rodriguez eventually dropped him as an agent. It has also become

(Continued)

(Continued)

clear that many of the contracts Boras has negotiated have resulted in compensation far greater than the players' value. For example, Bill Caudill had only one good season for the Toronto Blue Jays, and Barry Zito's career with the San Francisco Giants (a 43–61 record and a 4.83 earned run average from 2007–2011) has hardly been that of a player Boras described as "one of the best left-handed pitchers of all time."[2]

[1]Matt Taibbi, "The Devil's Doorstep: A Visit with Scott Boras," *Men's Journal,* February 23, 2009, at http://www.mensjournal.com/the-devil%E2%80%99s-doorstep.

[2]Quoted in Bob Nightengale, "Boras Is Baseball's Bigger Deal Man, *USA Today,* November 14, 2006, at http://www.usatoday.com/sports/baseball/2006-11-14-boras-cover_x.htm.

Sources: Ben McGrath, "The Extortionist," *The New Yorker,* October 29, 2009, at http://www.newyorker.com/reporting/2007/10/29/071029fa_fact_mcgrath; Bob Nightengale, "Boras Is Baseball's Bigger Deal Man, *USA Today,* November 14, 2006, at http://www.usatoday.com/sports/baseball/2006-11-14-boras-cover_x.htm; and Matt Taibbi, "The Devil's Doorstep: A Visit with Scott Boras," *Men's Journal,* February 23, 2009, at http://www.mensjournal.com/the-devil%E2%80%99s-doorstep.

Summary

In this chapter, we examined how labor markets work in professional sports. The forces of labor supply and labor demand do a good job of explaining why the salaries of professional athletes have grown so much over the last several decades. Increasing demand by fans for the sport translates into higher demand for labor by teams. Athletes can increase their own earnings by investing in human capital. To the degree that the skills they acquire are general skills, the athletes will have to pay for the training by accepting lower salaries.

The distribution of income in professional sports is highly skewed toward those with the most talent. Tournament organizers and teams provide disproportionate rewards to get players to provide more effort. This reward system has some dangers, as it can lead to poor teamwork, sabotaging one's opponents, and carrying effort to unhealthy extremes. The unhealthy extremes include levels of practice that lead to permanent disability later in life or to the abuse of performance-enhancing drugs.

Discussion Questions

1. Has the recent focus on measuring individual performance harmed professional sports?
2. Should baseball and football follow the example of the IOC and disregard records set by players who have used PEDs?
3. If PEDs do not cause irreparable harm to an athlete's health, should they be permitted?
4. Are disproportionately high rewards to star athletes a bad thing for team sports?

Problems

8.1. Suppose that the market demand for baseball players is perfectly inelastic (vertical) at 750 players. If the market supply increases due to an increase in the number of available international players, use a graph to show how wages will change as a result.

8.2. Suppose that there are two types of players, good and medium. The team demand curve for top-quality players is $Q = 27 - 5w$, and the market supply of top players is $Q = 4w$, where w is the wage in millions of dollars. How many top-quality players will the team hire? What will they be paid?

8.3. Use a graph similar to Figure 8.5 to show the effect on league salaries of
  a. An increase in the number of players available
  b. A decrease in television revenues due to fan preferences for drama shows
  c. A minimum salary set above the equilibrium wage

8.4. Based on the following player statistics, compute the Win Score values. Assuming the players have equal star power to attract fans and players are rewarded only based on Win Score values, which player deserves to be paid the most? Who should be paid the least? How would your answer change if players were only rewarded for scoring?

Statistic	Players			
	Joe	Bob	Fred	Jim
Points	17	25	10	20
Total rebounds	7	5	10	6
Steals	3	0	4	2
Blocks	2	2	0	0
Assists	3	4	6	8
Field goal attempts	18	28	8	13
Free throw attempts	10	9	4	5
Turnovers	2	3	2	4
Personal fouls	4	5	3	3

8.5. Go to the Web site http://www.basketball-reference.com and find the statistics and salary of your favorite NBA player. Use the equation on p. 258 for additional wins and the value of a win to determine what he is worth and compare it with his actual salary. Is he overpaid, underpaid, or accurately paid?

8.6. Use a labor supply and labor demand graph to show the impact on salaries in the NBA of a strong economic recovery. Explain why the curves moved the way they did.

8.7. Explain and show using a graph why, at any given wage, a monopoly firm will hire less labor than the total employment if the industry were competitive.

8.8. Using a graph, show what happens to player effort in a tournament if the marginal cost-of-effort curve shifts upward.

8.9. Show what would have happened to the Lorenz curve in Figure 8.12 if the three top-ranked players on the women's tennis tour had all lost in the first round of the U.S. Open in September 2011.

8.10. Use the supply and demand model to explain why top athletes are paid less than top celebrities.

APPENDIX 8A

The Labor–Leisure Choice Model of Indifference Curves

Like all decisions in economics, the decision to work is one of choosing among alternatives. In the simple labor–leisure choice model, a person chooses between working for pay and not working (consuming leisure). Each person possesses a **utility function** as defined in Appendix 2A. Labor economists typically assume that utility results from consuming goods (X) and leisure (Z), both of which are normal goods, as shown in the following equation:

$$U = u(X, Z)$$

We can illustrate the utility function using indifference curves, as shown in Figure 8A.1. Each curve represents a specific level of utility, and utility increases as we move northeast, away from the origin (i.e., $U_2 > U_1$). The slope of an indifference curve, also called the **marginal rate of substitution**, represents the rate at which the person is willing to exchange one good for the other, holding utility constant. Recall that the negative slope of an indifference curve implies a trade-off: The person must receive more of one good if he or she receives less of the other in order to hold utility constant. The convex shape of the indifference curves reflects the diminishing marginal utility associated with consuming more and more of any single commodity.

Consumption is limited by an **income constraint** and a **time constraint**. A person's income consists of his or her earnings from working h hours at wage

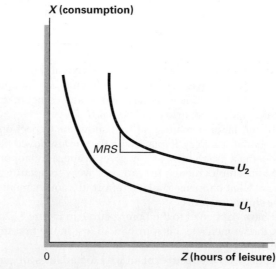

FIGURE 8A.1   Indifference Curves

w, and exogenous income V, which consists of all nonlabor income such as dividends, inheritances, and so on:

$$X = wh + V$$

The time constraint reflects the fact that there are only so many hours in a day (T) that must be allocated to either work or leisure.

$$T = h + Z$$

The time constraint implies that the opportunity cost of consuming one additional hour of leisure equals the hourly wage. In Figure 8A.2, the time constraint mandates that a person cannot spend less than zero hours working and more than T hours at leisure (and vice versa). Because many people receive some exogenous income even if they do not work, the budget constraint begins from a point $\$V$ directly above T. The constraint has a slope equal to $-w$ since the person must give up $\$w$ for every hour of leisure he or she consumes.

We can combine the person's utility function with his or her budget constraint to determine the person's utility-maximizing choice. Suppose a local golf pro, Bill, can earn income by giving golf lessons for $20 per hour. In addition, he receives $100 per day in dividend income.[52] His constraints are

$$X = 20h + 100$$
$$24 = h + Z$$

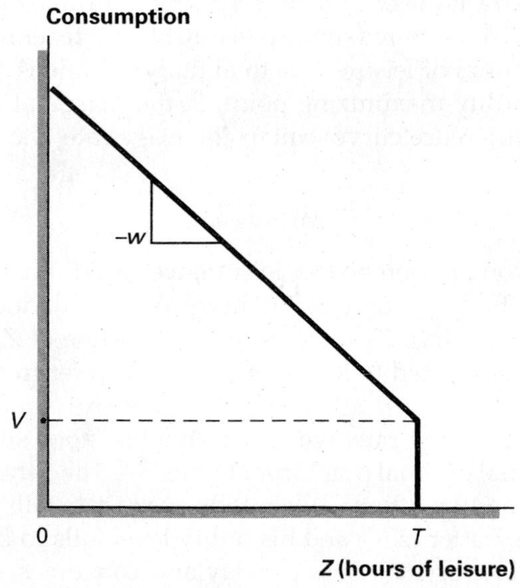

Consumption

FIGURE 8A.2   The Income and Time Constraints

---

[52]We could alter the model by assuming that Bill needs to devote a certain portion of each day to personal needs such as sleeping and eating, but the framework would be the same. With such an allowance, T would simply shift to the left by the amount of personal time, p, per period $(T - p = h + Z)$.

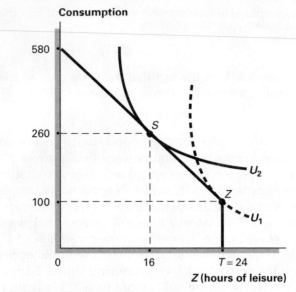

FIGURE 8A.3   **Individual Utility-Maximizing Curves**

Bill can teach all the lessons he wants, but each hour that he spends teaching requires that he give up one hour of leisure. Conversely, the opportunity cost of consuming an extra hour of leisure is $20. Bill's utility-maximizing solution is shown in Figure 8A.3. He maximizes his utility by teaching 8 hours per day and consuming 16 hours of leisure. His total daily income is $260, and his utility level is U_2. At the utility-maximizing point, S, the marginal rate of substitution (the slope of the indifference curve) equals the wage rate, the slope of the budget constraint:

$$MRS = w$$

If Bill had a strong preference for leisure, we could illustrate his preferences with the dashed indifference curve U_1. In this example, Bill does not want to work at all. The indifference curve U_1 touches the budget line at Z, which means that $h = 0$, and all time is devoted to leisure. Economists refer to such an outcome as a **corner** solution.

By varying Bill's wage rate, we can derive his labor supply curve. Figure 8A.4 shows Bill's initial optimal point from Figure 8A.3 and the effect of a decrease in his hourly wage to $10 per hour. When Bill's wage rate falls to $10 per hour, his budget line becomes flatter (ZB') and his utility level falls to U_1 at point R. At the new, lower wage, Bill works 6 hours per day and consumes 18 hours per day of leisure. His total income is now $160 per day. Finally, Bill responds to an increase in his wage to $30 per hour (which shifts the budget line to ZB'') by choosing the consumption–leisure combination, labeled T on the indifference curve U_3. Again Bill decides to work 6 hours per day, giving him an income of $280, and he consumes 18 hours per day of leisure.

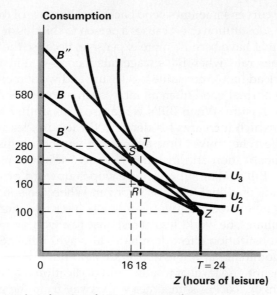

FIGURE 8A.4 Changes in Labor Supply Due to Wage Changes

From Figure 8A.4 we can easily derive Bill's labor supply curve. Like any supply curve, a labor supply curve shows the quantity (of hours in this case) that Bill supplies at various prices. In Figure 8A.5, points R', S', and T' correspond to the tangencies R, S, and T in Figure 8A.4. The line ll that connects these points is Bill's labor supply curve. The difference between this supply curve and a typical product supply curve is that it bends backward at wages above \$20. To see why, we must look further into the labor–leisure decision.

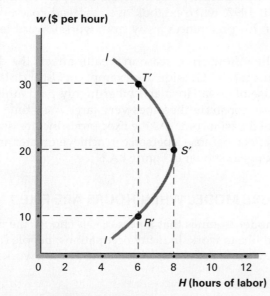

FIGURE 8A.5 The Individual Labor Supply Curve

Labor supply curves sometimes bend backward because of the *income* and *substitution effects*. The substitution effect causes a person to shift his or her consumption away from goods that have become more expensive. Because the opportunity cost of leisure is the wage rate, when Bill's wage rate increases, it increases the cost of leisure, which will lead him to consume less leisure and work more.

If leisure is a normal good, then an increase in income results in an increase in the demand for leisure. When Bill's wage rises, his ability to obtain income increases as well, which increases his demand for leisure, leading him to work fewer hours. In effect, he "buys" time away from work with his increased earning power. The substitution and income effects work in opposite directions in this case. Whether Bill's labor supply curve slopes upward or backward at any given point depends on which effect is stronger. When the substitution effect is larger than the income effect, Bill works more as his wage increases. When the income effect dominates, he works less in response to a wage increase. Figure 8A.5 shows that Bill's substitution effect dominates at wages below $20 per hour, but his income effect dominates at wages above $20 per hour.

Because of the intense level of training and dedication required at the professional level, players or coaches sometimes walk away from the game despite still being able to compete at the highest level in order to pursue other activities, such as spending more time with their families. Dick Vermeil, coach of the 2000 Super Bowl champion St. Louis Rams, had become a classic case of burnout almost two decades earlier. While coaching the Philadelphia Eagles from 1976 to 1983, Vermeil worked so many hours that he noticed a growth spurt of his second oldest son only while watching game film with his assistant coaches and seeing his son standing on the sidelines.[53] He left coaching at the end of the 1982–1983 season after working himself to the point of complete physical exhaustion. Although he worked after that as a broadcaster and motivational speaker, he did not return to coaching again until 1997, when he took over as head coach of the Rams. For Vermeil, a change in his preferences away from work toward leisure led him to leave the game.

We can also show how an increase in wealth affects the decision to work using the labor–leisure model. Consider the example of Oscar de la Hoya described in the text. In the case of de la Hoya and other highly paid athletes, the vertical portion of the income constraint becomes very large over time due to endorsement and accumulated past income. As the exogenous income segment increases, so does the income effect, because a person can achieve greater and greater utility levels without working, as shown in Figure 8A.6.

THE LABOR–LEISURE MODEL WHEN HOURS ARE FIXED

The labor supply model assumes that a person can choose the number of hours that he or she would like to work. In many occupations, people cannot choose the number of hours they work. For example, some production workers may prefer to

---

[53]Gary Smith, "A New Life," *Sports Illustrated* (March 28, 1983), pp. 60–67.

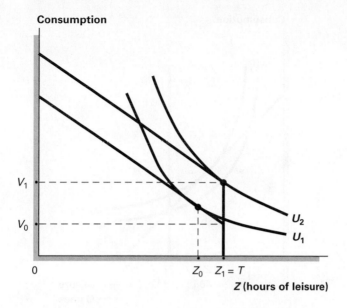

FIGURE 8A.6   **Increases in Wealth That Result in No Labor Supplied**

work part-time but must work a full 40-hour week in order to keep their jobs. The same is true in sports. Athletes face two possible constraints when they play in a professional league: The season may be either shorter or longer than they prefer. For example, Nikki McCray originally chose to play in the American Basketball League (ABL) because she preferred to play a longer season.[54] At the time, the ABL played a 40-game season, while the WNBA played only a 28-game season. When the ABL folded and her only option was the WNBA, her hours were set at a level below the level she would have chosen. We illustrate the effects of the shorter season on her utility maximization problem in Figure 8A.7 by imposing another constraint, fixing hours (or games in this case) along the vertical line set at Z_0. In the absence of this constraint, McCray maximizes her utility on U_1 by playing 40 games. In the presence of the games constraint, however, she cannot play more than 28 games (WNBA players are contractually forbidden to play in other leagues or for other teams). Thus, she maximizes her utility by playing only 28 games and consuming more leisure than she would like. While some leisure is a good thing, when a person consumes very large quantities of any good, leisure included, the marginal utility received from the last hour becomes very small.

Athletes who play individual sports typically do not face such stringent quantity constraints. For example, a professional golfer with a newborn child may elect to take several weeks away from the tour.[55] For athletes involved in team

---

[54]Steve Lopez, "They Got Next," *Sports Illustrated* (June 30, 1997), pp. 44–47.

[55]The LPGA now maintains a day-care center that travels with the tour, allowing golfers to keep their small children with them rather than be forced to choose between playing and staying home.

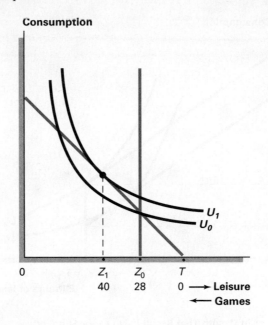

FIGURE 8A.7   The Effect of an Additional Constraint on Work Hours

sports, part-time play is generally not an option. For them, when family needs dictate time away from the game, retirement may be the only option. Such was the case with Mark Rypien, who retired from the Atlanta Falcons in order to care for his terminally ill son. In other cases, players leave the labor force temporarily. For example, Buffalo Bills linebacker Chris Spielman left the team for a full season to care for his critically ill wife.

CHAPTER 9

Labor Market Imperfections

There isn't a day where I don't hope for peace. At the same time, there isn't a day we don't prepare for war.

—NFLPA Executive Director DeMaurice Smith[1]

INTRODUCTION

As we saw in Chapter 8, the salaries paid to professional athletes grew significantly in the last quarter of the 20th century. While salaries grew rapidly in all the major North American team sports, as did the prize money in most individual sports, they grew more rapidly in some sports than in others. For example, in 1980 the average salary in MLB was about $68,000 more than the average salary in the NFL.[2] By 2010, average salaries in MLB were more than $1 million higher than

---

[1]Quoted in Monte Burke, "Is DeMaurice Smith the Most Important Man in Football?" *Forbes*, October 28, 2010, at http://www.forbes.com/sites/monteburke/2010/10/28/is-demaurice-smith-the-most-important-man-in-football/, viewed June 4, 2012.

[2]Michael J. Haupert, "The Economic History of Major League Baseball," in *EH.Net Encyclopedia*, ed. by Robert Whaples, December 3, 2007, at http://eh.net/encyclopedia/article/haupert.mlb; and, UPI International, "Average N.F.L. Salary Is $90,102, Survey Says," *New York Times*, January 29, 1982, at http://www.nytimes.com/1982/01/29/sports/average-nfl-salary-is-90102-survey-says.html, viewed May 25, 2012.

in the NFL.[3] The faster growth of salaries in baseball is surprising for two reasons. First, revenues in football have grown more rapidly than in baseball. Rising revenues should increase the *MRP* of players and their salaries. In addition, thanks largely to baseball's exemption from the antitrust laws, baseball players were not able to challenge the owners' monopsony power in court. The answer lies in part in the relative power of the sports' players associations. Baseball owners have been less successful in suppressing players' salaries because the Major League Baseball Players Association (MLBPA) has been more adept at overcoming the monopsony power of the owners than the National Football League Players Association (NFLPA). For example, MLB is the only league in which there is no salary cap on either teams or individual players that limits team payroll.

In this chapter, we examine how professional sports leagues have exerted monopsony power. We then show how the different sports unions have exerted countervailing monopoly power by controlling the labor input.

LEARNING OBJECTIVES

After reading this chapter, you will be able to:

- Understand how leagues exert monopsony power over players and the impact of monopsony on salaries.
- Describe how unions act as a countervailing force on teams' monopsony power and how the player associations have increased players' incomes.
- Describe how the most recently negotiated agreements in the NFL and NBA have changed the economic relationship between players and owners.

9.1   THE MONOPSONY POWER OF SPORTS LEAGUES

The labor markets in all the major North American sports are marked by deviations from the assumptions of the competitive model. As we saw in Chapter 4, the reserve clause gave teams considerable monopsony power over their players. In this section, we take a closer look at the reserve clause, the advent of free agency in professional sports, and how monopsony power continues to suppress the salaries of players who are not yet eligible for free agency. We also describe how leagues have used other mechanisms (such as salary caps) to slow the salary growth of players who have earned free agent status.

The Economics of Monopsony

A monopsony is the sole buyer of a good or service. Firms that sell goods or services in a monopsonistic market can sell them to no one except the monopsony.

---

[3]Maury Brown, "Average Salary for MLB in 2009," *The Biz of Baseball,* at http://bizofbaseball. com/index.php?option=com_content&view=article&id=3777:inside-the-numbers-average-salary-2009&catid=26:editorials&Itemid=39; and Jarret Bell, "NFL Salaries: Top NFL QBs Could Be in Line for Contract Hikes," *USA Today,* March 9, 2010, at http://www.usatoday.com/sports/football/nfl/2010-03-09-nfl-salaries-story_N.htm, viewed May 25, 2012.

In a monopsony labor market, workers can sell their services only to the monopsony employer. A monopsony exerts its market power like a monopoly, though its impact is the mirror image of a monopoly. While a monopolist uses its power to drive up the price it can charge consumers, a monopsonist uses its market power to drive down the prices it pays producers or workers. A monopsonist and a monopolist are similar in one respect. Both maximize profits by restricting the quantity of transactions relative to a perfectly competitive industry. The lower output and consumption impose a deadweight loss on society.

Figure 9.1 shows that, since the monopsonist is the only buyer in a market, its supply curve is the market supply curve (just as the monopolist's demand curve is the market demand curve). Because the supply curve is upward-sloping, the monopsonist can buy more only if it is willing and able to pay a higher price. Since a monopsonist usually cannot tell exactly how much each seller is willing to charge, it generally must pay a higher price for all the items it buys—not just for the additional items. The cost of buying a little more, the **marginal expenditure**, is thus greater than the cost of the additional purchases because the monopsonist must spend more on both the marginal unit and all preceding units. As a result, the monopsonist's **marginal expenditure curve** lies above the supply curve (just as the monopolist's marginal revenue curve lies below the demand curve). The monopsonist maximizes its profits when it buys just enough that its marginal benefit (here given by marginal revenue product) equals its marginal expenditure.

In Figure 9.1, the demand curve shows the monopsonist's marginal benefit (recall that the demand curve for labor is derived from the additional revenue one more worker generates for the firm). The monopsonist hires workers until marginal

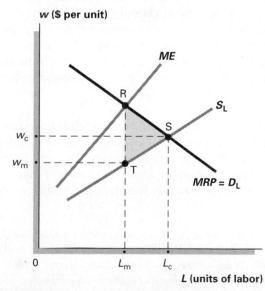

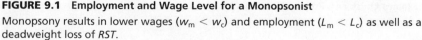

FIGURE 9.1 **Employment and Wage Level for a Monopsonist**

Monopsony results in lower wages ($w_m < w_c$) and employment ($L_m < L_c$) as well as a deadweight loss of *RST*.

revenue product equals marginal expenditure. Just as the monopolist determines the price it charges by looking up to the demand curve, the monopsonist sets the price it pays by looking down to the supply curve. Thus, the monopsony price in Figure 9.1 is w_m, not the competitive wage w_c. In the graph, the marginal expenditure curve cuts the marginal benefit curve at point R, and the monopsony level of employment is L_m. If the labor market were competitive, firms would hire L_c workers, which is where the marginal benefit of hiring the last worker equals the competitive wage (w_c). Thus, monopsony results in lower wages and lower employment than in a competitive market. It also results in a deadweight loss (the area RST). Monopsony power was once a cornerstone of professional sports. As noted in Chapter 4, the formation of the National League in baseball can be traced directly to its exerting monopsony power over players through the creation of the reserve clause.

The Reserve Clause

Prior to the reserve clause, professional baseball players moved freely from team to team, sometimes jumping contracts in the middle of the season.[4] This changed in 1876. Envious of the success of the Boston Red Stockings, William Hulbert, the financial backer of the Chicago White Stockings, lured away four of Boston's star players (and one from Philadelphia) late in the 1875 season. In a remarkable display of chutzpah, Hulbert then appealed to the other backers to create a new system that would—among other things—stop the bidding war for players. This coup d'état overthrew baseball's existing structure, the National Association of Professional Base Ball Players. The name of the new organization—the National League of Professional Baseball Clubs—was highly significant. Prior to Hulbert's coup, players' associations had run baseball. Now the clubs—and their owners—reigned supreme, and the players occupied a secondary position.[5]

Just how secondary became apparent in 1887, when the owners unveiled what had been an implicit "gentlemen's agreement" for the previous decade. With the formation of the National League, each owner had reserved the rights to five players' services for as long as he wanted them.[6] By 1889 the system of reserving players had expanded to the entire roster and had been installed as a clause in the standard player's contract:

> [I]f, prior to March 1,... the player and the club have not agreed upon the terms of such contract [for the next playing season], then on or before ten days after said March 1, the club shall have the right to renew this contract for the period of one year on the same terms except that the amount payable to the player shall be such as the club shall fix in said notice.[7]

[4]One of the institutional weaknesses of the Negro Leagues was the teams' inability to maintain stable rosters. See Robert Peterson, *Only the Ball Was White* (New York: Gramercy Books, 1970), pp. 95–98.

[5]Harold Seymour, *Baseball: The Early Years* (New York: Oxford University Press, 1960), p. 80.

[6]Not surprisingly, this was exactly the number that Hulbert had signed away in 1875.

[7]Quoted from James Quirk and Rodney Fort, *Pay Dirt* (Princeton, N.J.: Princeton University Press, 1992), p. 185.

On the surface, the clause seemed fairly innocuous. It restricted a player to a team for the length of the contract plus, if the team renewed the existing contract, one additional year of service. The catch lies in the fact that the owners interpreted the right to "renew this contract...on the same terms" as renewing all the terms of the contract, including the reserve clause, thus binding the player to the team for yet another year. Using this recursive system, a team could restrict a player from selling his services for as long as it wanted to keep him. Leagues in other sports saw the value of the reserve clause in keeping down costs and copied this clause almost word for word in their standard contracts.

With no competing employer able to bid away the services of their players, teams drove down their players' salaries to levels that just kept them in the sport. While players today can afford to support small entourages, even stars of an earlier time had to hold second jobs. Imagine walking into an appliance store and buying a washing machine from Albert Pujols. In 1951, you could have done just that from Jackie Robinson.[8]

The monopsony power conferred on owners by the reserve clause left Major League Baseball players in an extremely weak position. In an effort to improve their bargaining power, players formed the Major League Baseball Players Association (MLBPA) in 1953. In 1968, the MLPBA negotiated its first collective bargaining agreement with the league. Players in the other major leagues have formed similar associations—the National Basketball Players Association (NBPA), the National Hockey League Players Association (NHLPA), and the National Football League Players Association (NFLPA)—all of which are unique forms of unions. A **union** is an organization of workers who agree to act collectively to improve their, wages and working conditions. In the next section, we show how unions can counteract the monopsony power of team owners.

9.2 UNIONS IN PROFESSIONAL SPORTS

Unions have played a steadily decreasing role in the private sector of the U.S. economy. In 2011, only 11.8 percent of all employed wage and salary workers were union members, less than half their representation in the early 1980s.[9] American unions have been in steady decline since the early 1950s, when they represented about one-third of the U.S. labor force. Globalization, technological advances, and demographic changes of the workforce (particularly the growing participation of women) have all contributed to the decline. By contrast, unions in professional sports have continued to thrive. Union representation of the major sports leagues remains at or near 100 percent. In this section, we examine the impact that unions have had on the labor market for professional athletes.

---

[8]John Helyar, *Lords of the Realm* (New York: Villard Books, 1994), p. 12.
[9]Bureau of Labor Statistics, *Economic News Release: Union Members Summary*, January 28, 2012, at http://www.bls.gov/news.release/union2.nr0.htm, viewed June 2, 2012.

A Brief Introduction to the Economics of Unions

Unions typically fall into one of two categories: craft unions and industrial unions. **Craft unions** are by far the older of the two. Their origins can be traced back to the medieval guilds, groups of skilled artisans who joined together to prevent others from entering the city to undercut their prices. Modern craft unions consist of workers who share a common skill. For example, it is easy to guess what the members of the International Brotherhood of Electrical Workers do or what task the members of the Screen Actors Guild perform.

Industrial unions are much younger than craft unions. Workers first formed these unions in response to the harsh conditions they confronted as a result of the rise of large employers in the 19th century. Partly because they opposed the entrenched interests of their employers, organizers of industrial unions faced greater hostility than did organizers of craft unions. Industrial unions take their names from the types of output they produce, such as the United Auto Workers or the United Steel Workers.

The different organizational structures of the two types of unions cause them to use different tactics on behalf of their members.[10] Craft unions increase wages by limiting access to the union and to skills. Firms do not hire workers in a craft union. Instead, the union assigns workers to employers through a (literal or figurative) hiring hall. In effect, they shift the labor supply curve left, as seen in Figure 9.2a. The result is a union wage (w^u) that exceeds the competitive wage (w^{nu}).

Industrial unions represent workers with many different skills. As a result, they leave hiring and firing to the employer. Like craft unions, industrial unions push up wages, but they do so through collective bargaining. In **collective bargaining**, unions meet with employers to produce an agreement that specifies pay and other working conditions. Industrial unions induce employers to accept their demands by engaging in or threatening to engage in strikes. A **strike** occurs when workers act together to remove the labor input from the production process. A **lockout** occurs when the management of the firm does not permit the labor input to operate. The need to stage or threaten a damaging strike means that industrial unions derive their strength from being inclusive. A union cannot succeed unless the firms' employees remain loyal to it during a strike. This loyalty allows the union to function as a monopolist in the labor market, as seen in Figure 9.2b. In contrast, craft unions' power comes from being exclusive and keeping out competing workers.[11]

Opponents of unions assert that unions create inefficiency in the economy. They say that unions limit employment and production, thereby harming the economy. Higher wages mean higher costs of production, which puts domestic producers at a competitive disadvantage and encourages producers to relocate abroad.

---

[10]While workers and unions negotiate over many different aspects of the job, we simplify the analysis by focusing solely on wages.

[11]The NFLPA had difficulty maintaining unity during a strike due to racial divisions among players. See Cynthia Gramm and John Schnell, "Difficult Choices, Crossing the Picket Line During the 1987 National Football League Strike," *Journal of Labor Economics,* vol. 12, no. 1 (January 1994), pp. 41–71.

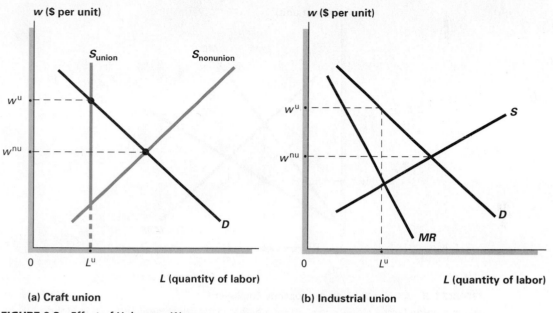

FIGURE 9.2   Effect of Unions on Wages
Craft and industrial unions both cause wages to rise, but they do so in different ways.

Union supporters feel that the opponents of unions paint an unnecessarily harsh picture. They claim that unions provide an important outlet for workers, which improves efficiency. They point out that unions formalize grievance procedures by workers, giving them a way to express their concerns to employers and allowing employers to respond to the needs of their workforce, thereby reducing conflict in the workplace. By making workers more productive, unions increase their MRP and cause the demand for labor to shift to the right. The higher MRP thus increases the equilibrium level of employment and justifies the higher wage that union workers receive. To the extent that the union increases employment by increasing MRP, efficiency in the market is improved relative to the monopsony outcome.

Union supporters also point out that there is no clear evidence that unions either reduce productivity or slow productivity growth. Finally, some economists suggest that unions serve as a countervailing force against the monopsony power of employers, forcing employers to pay workers their marginal revenue product and—perhaps—making the labor market more closely resemble a competitive market.[12]

Figure 9.3 shows that a monopsony drives down the wage from the competitive level, w^c, to the monopsony level, w^m. It also drives down employment from L^c to L^m, creating a deadweight loss. By setting a wage above w^m, a union may actually increase employment and reduce or eliminate the deadweight loss.

---

[12]See Richard Freeman and James Medoff, *What Do Unions Do?* (New York: Basic Books, 1984) for a good example of this more positive view of unions.

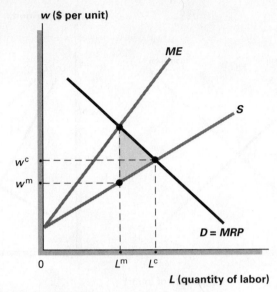

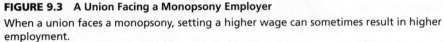

FIGURE 9.3   A Union Facing a Monopsony Employer
When a union faces a monopsony, setting a higher wage can sometimes result in higher employment.

For example, setting the wage at w^c makes the marginal expenditure curve a horizontal line at that level and forces the monopsony to act like a competitive industry.

When a monopoly union confronts a monopsony employer—a situation that economists call **bilateral monopoly**—the wage falls into an indeterminate range between the union wage and the monopsony wage. In Figure 9.4, the union would like to set its wage where the marginal revenue of union members (MR) equals the supply of labor (S). The monopoly wage w^u is determined by looking up from this intersection to the demand curve for labor. The monopsonist would like to set the quantity of labor where the marginal expense of the last worker (ME) equals the marginal revenue product ($MRP = D$) of the last worker. The monopsony wage w^m comes from looking down to the supply curve of labor. The precise settlement lies somewhere between w^u and w^m in Figure 9.4 and depends on the bargaining strength of the two sides.

In 1950, Nobel laureate John Nash developed a model to solve these types of bargaining problems that still serves as the basis for much of the work on bargaining. One of the Nash model's central findings was that a group's bargaining power stems from its ability to walk away from the bargaining table. Nash calls the value of each side's alternative activity its **threat point**. The more valuable the threat point for either side, the greater its bargaining power and the more favorable a solution it can achieve.

If, for example, the employer has a readily available source of labor (perhaps due to high unemployment rates), the benefits of permanently dissolving its relationship with the union may be very high. All else being equal, this allows the

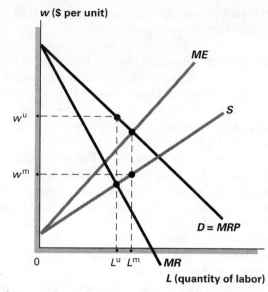

FIGURE 9.4 **Bilateral Monopoly**

In a bilateral monopoly, the wage lies somewhere between the monopsony wage and the union wage. The outcome depends on the two sides' bargaining power.

firm to drive a harder bargain and reach a lower wage settlement. Alternatively, if union workers have high-paying jobs awaiting them elsewhere, their threat point and the resulting wage both rise.

Unions in professional sports do not readily fit into any of the categories outlined above. On one hand, they represent workers with similar and distinct skills, like a craft union. On the other hand, they engage in collective bargaining with employers who do the hiring and firing, like an industrial union.

More important, unlike other unions, sports unions do not engage in wage negotiations. Instead, they bargain over the general framework within which individual players and their agents negotiate with teams.[13] Finally, the major sports unions and the leagues with which they negotiate sometimes advocate positions that are unlike those of other unions or firms. For example, during the 1998–1999 lockout, the NBA advocated a fixed salary scale for players while the union championed the free market. These stances are diametrically opposed to the stances taken by most firms and unions. Typically, unions push for salary scales, and firms want salaries to be set by the market.

For decades, all four players associations strove for some form of free agency so their players could receive competitive wages. In the section that follows,

---

[13]The NFLPA has reserved the right to conduct salary negotiations in its collective bargaining agreement, but it has never exercised this right. See Paul Staudohar, *Playing for Dollars: Labor Relations in the Sports Business* (Ithaca, N.Y.: ILR Press, 1996), p. 67.

we describe how the player associations accomplished that goal and how the leagues tried to maintain their economic power.

THE ADVENT OF FREE AGENCY   Baseball players initially felt that being subject to the reserve clause was an honor. Because, at first, teams could reserve only five players, being subject to the reserve clause meant that a player was regarded as one of the team's stars. Once the impact of the reserve clause on salaries became clear, players in all leagues became implacably opposed to it. Rather than face a monopsony employer as depicted in Figure 9.3, through collective action, they sought to gain a more favorable outcome, as in Figure 9.4. Eventually, the unions in all four sports overturned the reserve clause. Three unions did so through the court system, and, as we will see, one union did so by outmaneuvering the owners.

Football players were the first to achieve free agency, though they were not the first to take advantage of it. The Supreme Court's 1957 *Radovich* v. *National Football League* concluded that football—unlike baseball—was interstate commerce and therefore subject to the antitrust laws. In particular, the decision formally rejected NFL teams' right to reserve players.

Despite this resounding court victory, players had to wait another 35 years for true free agency. At first, NFL team owners responded by entering into an informal "gentlemen's agreement" not to pursue each other's players. When this broke down in the early 1960s, NFL commissioner Pete Rozelle unilaterally imposed the "Rozelle rule":

> Whenever a player, becoming a free agent in such manner thereafter signed a contract with a different club in the league, then unless mutually satisfactory arrangements have been concluded between the two League clubs, the Commissioner may name and then award to the former club one or more players from the Active, Reserve, or Selection List (including future selection choices of the acquiring club as the Commissioner in his sole discretion deems fair and equitable); any such decisions by the Commissioner shall be final and conclusive.[14]

The Rozelle rule thus recognized the players' right to free agency in theory but effectively killed it in practice. The rule turned signing a free agent into a trade in which the team had no control over the players it would lose. A form of the Rozelle rule survived until 1992, when a U.S. District Court ruled in *McNeil et al.* v. *National Football League* that it violated antitrust laws (see Sports and the Law, below).

The reserve clause in professional hockey and basketball were both overturned as the result of competition from rival leagues. In 1972, the World Hockey Association (WHA) sued the NHL for violating antitrust laws when the NHL tried to block players from jumping to the WHA. The resulting ruling (*Philadelphia World Hockey Club* v. *Philadelphia Hockey Club*) struck down the NHL's reserve clause.

---

[14]Quoted from the standard player contract in Dworkin, *Owners versus Players: Baseball and Collective Bargaining* (Boston: Auburn House, 1981), p. 250.

SPORTS AND THE LAW:

McNeil v. The National Football League

NFL players officially were the first to obtain free agency in 1957 but the last to enjoy its benefits. The delay was the result of clever maneuvering by the owners, missteps by the NFLPA, and a crucial legal principle known as the *non-statutory labor exemption.* The dispute over this principle continues to this day and played a key role in settling the 2011 lockout.

As noted in this chapter, the Rozelle rule stifled all attempts by players to exploit the gains of the *Radovich* decision by effectively turning a free agent signing into a trade with arbitrarily imposed, and potentially steep, costs. In 1976, an antitrust lawsuit brought by John Mackey, the great tight end and NFLPA President, struck down the Rozelle rule. The court found in *Mackey* v. *NFL* that the rule had been imposed unilaterally by the league and violated the principles of collective bargaining. This win was almost immediately neutralized when the NFLPA, which was near bankruptcy due to the cost of Mackey's lawsuit, agreed to a modified form of the Rozelle rule (which replaced the commissioner's whim with a fixed compensation formula) in exchange for the automatic payment of union dues. Free agency was again neutralized, as only one player changed teams as a free agent from 1977 to 1987. Even the great Walter Payton found no team interested in his services in 1981.

Realizing its error, the NFLPA again brought suit, but the *Powell* v. *NFL* lawsuit led to a far different result, thanks to the **non-statutory labor exemption**. A non-statutory law is one that results from court decisions rather than from Congressional action. The non-statutory labor exemption refers to the court's ruling that unions did not violate antitrust laws when they bargained on behalf of their members. In other words, the NFLPA could not sue the NFL over a rule that it had accepted in collective bargaining. The court effectively said, "You are right that this rule restrains trade, but you bargained this limitation into the contract. You will have to bargain it out." Unfortunately, the union could not get the owners to budge, despite strikes in 1982 and 1987. The continued impasse following the collapse of the 1987 strike did have one important result. The owners implemented "Plan B" free agency, which granted unrestricted free agency to a limited number of players. Ironically, only marginal players could become free agents, as teams were allowed to reserve 37 players. As a result, free agent reserves were sometimes paid more than starters.

In 1990, the NFLPA took the unusual step of decertifying, saying that it no longer represented the interests of the players. With no union, there was no collective bargaining agreement and no conflict with the non-statutory labor exemption. The NFL protested that the decertification was "in name only" and was just a charade. The court disallowed this protest and permitted the lawsuit brought by star New York Jets running back Freeman McNeil and seven other players to go forward. Allowed to rule on the merits of the case, the U.S. District Court ruled that the NFL's restrictions on free agency were a violation of antitrust laws. The 1992 *McNeil* v. *NFL* decision finally brought free agency to the NFL. While Freeman McNeil, then near the end of his career, did not benefit from the ruling, other players have. Despite the imposition of a salary cap, average salaries in the NFL have more than quadrupled since the *McNeil* ruling.

With the recent negotiations at an impasse, the NFLPA—which had reconstituted itself soon after the *McNeil* decision—again voted to decertify. Again, the NFL claimed

(Continued)

(Continued)

that the decertification was a ruse. The lockout was resolved before the courts ruled on the merits of the most recent decertification (which lasted only as long as the lockout), but it is clear that the non-statutory labor exemption is still an open issue in NFLPA–NFL negotiations.

Sources: Carol Rieger and Charles Lloyd, "The Effect of *McNeil* v. *NFL* on Contract Negotiation in the NFL—That Was Then and This Is Now," *Marquette Sports Law Review,* vol. 3, no. 1 (Fall 1992), pp. 45–58; David Harris, *The League: The Rise and Decline of the NFL* (New York: Bantam Books, 1986); Paul Staudohar, *Playing for Dollars: Labor Relations and the Spots Business* (Ithaca, N.Y.: ILR Press, 1996), pp. 82–83; Andrew Harline, "The NFL Lockout: The Current NFLPA Antitrust Strategy Lacks Staying Power," *Vanderbilt Journal of Entertainment and Technology Law,* March 19, 2011, at http://www.jetlaw.org/?p=5938; and Jarrett Bell, "Freeman McNeil Sees History Repeating in NFL Labor Dispute," *USAToday,* April 3, 2011, at http://www.usatoday.com/sports/football/nfl/2011-03-31-freeman-mcneil-nfl-labor_N.htm.

In the NBA, the antitrust lawsuit was brought by players rather than by the rival league. Oscar Robertson, a star player and president of the National Basketball Players Association (NBPA), sued the league (*Robertson* v. *NBA*) in response to the NBA's attempt to end a costly war with the rival American Basketball Association through a partial merger. Faced with an unfavorable court ruling and the prospect of continued rivalry with the ABA, the NBA dropped its appeal of the *Robertson* case in 1976 and agreed to phase in free agency.

Unlike the players in other sports, baseball players could not resolve their problem through the courts. The 1922 Supreme Court decision in the *Federal Baseball Club* v. *National League* gave MLB a blanket exemption from antitrust laws. Even though subsequent rulings recognized the absurdity of the *Federal Baseball Club* decision, they repeatedly upheld the monopsony power of baseball teams (e.g., *Toolson* v. *New York Yankees* in 1953 and *Flood* v. *Kuhn* in 1971).

The MLBPA was able to overthrow the reserve clause by outsmarting the owners rather than by suing them. Prior to 1970, all grievances by players were filed with the Commissioner, who typically sided with the owners. In the 1970 contract negotiations, Marvin Miller, the MLBPA's Executive Director, got the owners to agree to replace the commissioner with a three-person panel, with one member appointed by the owners, one member appointed by the union, and one member drawn from a mutually agreed upon list. The owners agreed to the commission after Miller assured them that the panel would deal only with trifling monetary matters. Then-Commissioner Bowie Kuhn would have the final say in all overarching matters that affected the integrity of the game. By couching its challenge to the reserve clause as a financial matter, the MLBPA was able to force the issue into the hands of an outside arbitrator, who ruled in favor of the players (and who was promptly dismissed by the owners).[15]

---

[15]For a complete account, see John Helyar, *Lords of the Realm* (1994).

FORMS OF FREE AGENCY   While the idea of **free agency**—the right of a player to sign with any team that offers him a contract—is universal, different sports leagues have placed different restrictions on when and how a player becomes a free agent. There is a seemingly endless list of qualifications and exceptions contained in the collective bargaining agreements that establish the rules for free agency.[16] Before focusing on the economic implications of restrictions on free agency, below, we summarize the various forms of free agency.

To begin with, some sports have two different levels of free agency. Most fans who discuss free agents are actually thinking of unrestricted free agents. An **unrestricted free agent** is a player with no strings attached; he is free to sign with any team that makes him an offer.

In MLB, a player can become an unrestricted free agent after six years of service at the major league level. In the NHL, most players become unrestricted free agents based on what is known as the 27 or 7 rule. Once the player has reached age 27 or has seven years of service and his contract has expired, he is declared an unrestricted free agent. In the NBA, players can become unrestricted free agents after four years if they are either not first-round draft picks or they are first-round picks and their team does not exercise its right of first refusal. NFL players become unrestricted free agents following their fourth year of service if their contract has expired.

Restricted free agents are free to solicit offers from other teams but not to sign with them. If the player does sign an offer sheet with another team, his original team has the **right of first refusal**, meaning it can retain the player by matching the other team's offer. While restricted free agency affords the player the opportunity to "test the market" to see how much his services are worth to other teams, it does not allow a player to decide where he will play. In addition, the expectation that the original team will match any offers may reduce the size or number of offers a restricted free agent receives. We discuss some of the empirical findings on this topic later in the chapter. In the NFL, a player with three years of experience can become a restricted free agent after his contract has expired. In the NBA, a first-round draft pick can become a restricted free agent after his fourth year. The National Hockey League has a dizzying array of categories related to a player's age and level of experience. For example, a player whose contract has expired, who first signed a contract when he was 18–21 years old, and who has three years of experience can become a restricted free agent. The experience requirement is shorter for players who signed their initial contracts when they were older. The MLB player agreement does not include restricted free agent status, though MLB and the NHL do include an important intermediate step between reserved status and unrestricted free agency known as salary arbitration.

---

[16]Interested readers can see the actual collective bargaining at the player association Web sites for each league. These agreements contain complete details on the rules for both unrestricted and restricted free agency.

Salary Arbitration

Before players become free agents, teams can exert monopsony power, confronting them with the kind of "take it or leave it" contract offers depicted in Figure 9.3. Athletes in MLB and the NHL, however, have an intermediate stage that gives them some recourse. Players in these two sports can submit disputes to salary arbitration. **Arbitration** occurs when parties to a dispute submit proposals to an **arbitrator**, a neutral third party who then suggests or imposes a resolution. Both baseball and hockey have **binding arbitration**, in which both sides commit to accepting the ruling of the arbitrator. Outside the sports world, binding arbitration is particularly popular in the public sector. Fearful of the consequences of a strike by police or firefighters, municipal officials often offer binding arbitration in exchange for the unions' accepting laws that prohibit them from striking. However, the NHL and MLB have different forms of arbitration.

ARBITRATION IN THE NHL Salary arbitration is open to NHL players who are eligible for restricted free agency (typically those with at least four years of experience). The players who file for arbitration and the teams for which they play both submit proposals based on factors related to the player's productivity. These factors include the performance of the player, his contribution to the overall performance of the team, and the performance and pay of comparable players in the NHL. The arbitrator then has 48 hours to choose one of the proposals or to impose a decision of his own. A recent study has shown that arbitration rulings are roughly equivalent to what statistical analysis predicts the players are worth to their teams.[17] Thus, arbitration appears to aid efficiency by bringing players and teams to a resolution that they would otherwise have trouble achieving.

ARBITRATION IN MLB MLB uses a different process, known as final offer arbitration. In **final offer arbitration (FOA)**, arbitrators cannot impose their own solutions; they must choose one of the two proposals submitted to them. The goal of FOA is to prevent the two parties from becoming addicted to arbitration. Arbitration addiction often results from the incentives that the parties to binding arbitration face. Arbitrators, who are generally well compensated, do not wish to jeopardize their employment by appearing prejudiced toward one side or the other. As a result, they have an incentive to "split the difference" of any two offers put in front of them. If the two parties to the negotiation recognize this tendency, they have little reason to compromise, as any moderation of their stance would lead the arbitrator to impose a less favorable ruling.[18] FOA reverses this incentive. The goal of each party is to convince the arbitrator that its proposal is the more reasonable one. This forces the two sides to adopt moderate positions. Ideally, the two positions will move so close together that the two sides reach an agreement

---

[17]See James Lambrinos and Thomas D. Ashman, "Salary Determination in the National Hockey League: Is Arbitration Efficient?" *Journal of Sports Economics*, vol. 8, no. 2 (April 2007), pp. 192–201.

[18]For more on the addictive nature of binding arbitration, see Ronald Ehrenberg and Robert Smith, *Modern Labor Economics* (Boston: Prentice Hall, 2011).

without recourse to arbitration. FOA is open to all players with at least three years of major league experience. The criteria on which a judgment is based are very similar to those used in hockey.

The results of the 2009–2011 arbitration proceedings support this view of FOA.[19] Of the 111 players who filed for arbitration in 2009, 65 settled with their teams before the time came to file briefs with the arbitrator. Of the remaining 46, only three actually went forward with arbitration. In two of the three cases, the arbitrator ruled in favor of the player, making 2009 the first year since 1996 that players won a majority of the hearings. In 2010, arbitrators ruled on eight cases, and the owners won five. In 2011, 34 players exchanged offers with teams. Of these, 31 settled before formal arbitration. Of the three cases that went through the full process, the players won twice and a team won once. Overall, the owners have won about 57 percent of the arbitration cases.

Despite the players' overall losing record in arbitration hearings, FOA has had a significant impact on player salaries. Former MLBPA Executive Director Marvin Miller has gone so far as to say that FOA has done more for player salaries than free agency. The evidence from recent history suggests that Miller might be correct in his assessment of FOA. Based on Maury Brown's figures from the *Biz of Baseball*, the 78 players who exchanged figures with their clubs in 2010 and 2011 earned average raises of well over 100 percent.[20]

Measuring Monopsony Power

Despite the advent of free agency and salary arbitration, teams can still exert a degree of monopsony power, particularly over players who have few years of experience. Economists measure the degree to which teams exploit their monopsony power by comparing the estimated value of a player (as measured by his MRP) with his wage. As we saw in Chapter 8, computing a player's MRP can be a complicated task. Today, most studies use a methodology first proposed by Anthony Krautmann.[21] Krautmann assumes that the salary received by a free agent reflects his marginal product. This changes the equation

$$MRP_i = \beta_0 + \beta_1 Perf_i + \beta_2 Z_i + \varepsilon_i$$

into

$$w_i = \beta_0 + \beta_1 Perf_i + \beta_2 Z_i + \varepsilon_i$$

where $Perf_i$ is a vector of performance measures for player i, Z_i is a vector of control variables, w_i is player i's salary, and ε_i is a random error term. This change transforms an equation in which the key variable is unobservable (MRP) into one

---

[19]See Maury Brown, "2009 MLB Salary Arbitration Vital Stats," *The Biz of Baseball*, February 20, 2009; and, Maury Brown, "Arbitration Figures," *The Biz of Baseball*, February 19, 2011, at http://bizofbaseball. com/index.php?option=com_content&view=article&id=599&Itemid=72, viewed May 25, 2012.

[20]Maury Brown, "Arbitration Figures," 2011, viewed May 26, 2012.

[21]See Anthony Krautmann, "What's Wrong with Scully Estimates of a Player's Marginal Revenue Product?" *Economic Inquiry*, vol. 37, no. 2 (April 1999), pp. 369–381.

in which the key variable is readily observable (w_i). One can then estimate the coefficients of the equation using regression analysis. Applying the resulting estimated coefficients to data for players who are not free agents allows us to see whether the "restricted" players also receive salaries that equal their marginal revenue products. Recently, Anthony Krautmann, Peter von Allmen, and David J. Berri have used this methodology to measure the degree of monopsony power exercised by teams in baseball, basketball, and football. They find that considerable monopsony power remains, particularly for players with the least amount of experience. These players, whom they call "apprentices," are not eligible for arbitration or restricted free agency. They find that, on average, such players receive 66 percent of their *MRP* in the NBA, 50 percent of their *MRP* in the NFL, and only 19 percent of their *MRP* in MLB. "Journeyman" players, who are eligible for arbitration in baseball or restricted free agency in football, did much better.[22] In the NFL, such players received 77 percent of their *MRP*. The impact of arbitration, or at least the threat of arbitration, was strongly felt in MLB, as journeyman players received 86 percent of their *MRP*.

Salary Caps

No matter how unified the players may be, they rarely get all that they ask for. The collective bargaining process is typically a matter of compromise. This has been true in the case of salary negotiations, where the four major North American sports leagues have sought countermeasures to free agency. Three of the four major sports leagues—the NHL, NBA, and NFL—now have salary caps. MLB owners have tried but failed to impose a cap for three decades. In Chapter 5, we described the impact of salary caps on competitive balance. Here we examine their impact on team payrolls.

THE SALARY CAP IN THE NBA   The NBA was the first league to create a salary cap. Unlike the reserve clause, the salary cap arose out of weakness rather than strength. During the 1970s, the salary war with the ABA and free agency had pushed payrolls in the NBA to 70 percent of the league's gross revenues.[23] Prior to the 1984–1985 season, desperate team owners convinced the players to accept a salary cap as part of a revenue-sharing agreement that gave players a percentage of league revenues. NBA owners credit the cap with saving the league in the 1980s.

Team owners were so convinced of the value of the cap that they locked out players in 1998–1999 and again in 2011 to tighten it. In 1999, the owners supplemented the cap on team payrolls with a cap on individual salaries and imposed an escrow tax on salaries. The individual cap sets a salary scale for players based on their years of experience in the league. In 2011, the owners reduced the players'

---

[22]The authors find that almost no players were restricted free agents in the NBA. See Anthony C. Krautmann, Peter von Allmen, and David Berri, "The Underpayment of Restricted Players in North American Sports Leagues," *International Journal of Sport Finance*, vol. 4, no. 3 (August 2009), pp. 75–93.

[23]For a historical discussion of salary caps in the NFL and the NBA, see Paul Staudohar, *Playing for Dollars* (1996).

share of revenues from 57 percent of basketball-related income (BRI) to between 49 and 51 percent. In sum, the limits on the players' share of revenue, and team and individual maximum salaries create a highly constrained environment for salary negotiations. For example, in 2013–2014, an NBA rookie must be paid between $490,000 and $4.4 million. A player with five years of experience must receive between $1.03 and $12.9 million.[24]

The NBA's escrow tax further tightens the salary cap. Under this system, the league sets aside 10 percent of each player's salary. If total player salaries and benefits—regardless of the exceptions mentioned in Chapter 5—exceed the agreed upon percentage of BRI, then the funds in escrow are remitted to the league until the total is equal to the players' negotiated level. Otherwise, players receive the funds held in escrow at the end of the season.

As we discussed in the context of competitive balance, the NBA salary cap is a "soft cap," containing many exceptions that allow teams to exceed the official cap. To dissuade high revenue teams from doing so, the league has instituted yet another mechanism to control salaries—the luxury tax, which we discuss below.

THE SALARY CAP IN THE NHL   NHL owners felt so strongly about a salary cap that they locked out their players for the entire 2004–2005 season to get one. Like the NBA and NFL, the NHL's cap guarantees the players a share of league revenue. Unlike the other two leagues, the NHL players' share is set by a sliding scale. Players receive 54 percent of defined revenues when "hockey-related" revenue is below $2.2 billion, and up to 57 percent when revenue exceeds $2.7 billion. With revenues exceeding $3 billion, owners paid the higher percentage to players in 2011–2012. The standoff that threatens the 2012–2013 season stems from the owners' desire to reduce the players' share of league revenue.[25]

The NHL agreement that ran through September 2012 had a hard cap, which included all salaries, signing bonuses, and performance bonuses.[26] The NHL cap also adopted limits similar to those that had been imposed by the NBA in 1999. It limited individual player salaries to be no more than 20 percent of the team's allowable payroll, and it used an escrow system to ensure that payments stayed within the salary cap limits. In the 2008–2009, players put 13.5 percent of their salaries (increased to 25 percent in midseason) into escrow.

THE SALARY CAP IN THE NFL   The NFL negotiated a salary cap in 1994 with the National Football League Players Association (NFLPA) in response to the 1992 court ruling that had granted players free agency. Like the NHL, the NFL has a

---

[24]Rookies drafted in the first round were paid according to a prespecified rookie salary scale. The maximum salaries were set according to prespecified formulae. Under a limited set of performance and seniority criteria, players can earn slightly higher than the specified maximum. See Larry Coon, "Larry Coon's NBA Salary Cap FAQ," Copyright 1999–2012, at http://www.cbafaq.com/salarycap.htm#Q13, viewed May 28, 2012.

[25]See, for example, Pierre LeBrun, "The State of CBA Negotiations," *ESPN: NHL*, September 6, 2012, at http://espn.go.com/nhl/story/_/id/8344702/state-discussions.

[26]At the time of this writing, the NHLPA and the league had not yet reached a new agreement.

hard cap, in which almost all payments to players count against the cap. Beginning with the 2011 CBA, the NFL's salary cap grants players varying shares of revenue depending on the source: 55 percent of national media revenue, 45 percent of NFL Ventures revenue, and 40 percent of aggregated local club revenue. Collectively, the clubs must spend 95 percent of the total cap value and the player's share must average at least 47 percent of revenues over the life of the agreement.[27]

Two factors complicate the NFL's salary cap computations. First, although NFL teams have 53 players on their active rosters, the salary cap applies only to the 51 highest-paid players. Second, the bonuses a team pays might or might not count toward its salary cap.

Bonuses have become an important part of player contracts in the NFL because football players generally do not have guaranteed contracts. A player who has signed a multiyear contract that is not guaranteed will not be paid if he does not make the team. This has led some teams to cut players with multiyear contracts and then sign them to much lower salaries a few days later. A large signing bonus (which is effectively guaranteed if paid at the start of the contract) or easily obtained incentive bonus can protect a player with a long-term contract by providing a source of guaranteed income. Signing bonuses, roster bonuses (paid if a player makes the team roster), workout bonuses (paid if the player attends off-season team workouts), and any bonus paid for meeting conditions that the player had also satisfied the previous year are all considered *likely to be earned* (LTBE) bonuses and count against the salary cap. However, the NFL allows teams to prorate them over the length of the contract rather than count them at the time they are paid. Thus, for cap purposes, a contract that pays a player $35 million in equal $7 million increments over five years is indistinguishable from one that pays the player a $15 million signing bonus and $4 million over five years.[28] Bonuses for meeting previously unmet goals (e.g., a running back's running for more yards than he has before) count as *not likely to be earned* (NLTBE) and do not count against the cap.

THE IMPACT OF SALARY CAPS   For all the emphasis placed on salary caps, they do not always limit what teams actually pay in a given year. The payroll data from *USA Today* show that the caps appear to work much better in some leagues

[27]*NFL Clubs Approve Comprehensive Agreement*, at http://www.nfl.com/news/story/09000d5d820e6311/article/nfl-clubs-approve-comprehensive-agreement, viewed May 28, 2012. The full agreement can be viewed at "NFL Collective Bargaining Agreement," at http://images.nflplayers.com/mediaResources/files/PDFs/General/2011_Final_CBA_Searchable_Bookmarked.pdf, viewed May 28, 2012. Despite the phrase, there are some revenues that are not included in "all revenue." For example, owners get credit for a portion of stadium construction costs. For more details on the revenue exceptions, see Daniel Kaplan, "NFL Labor Deal Paying Off," *Street and Smith's Sports Business Journal,* January 30, 2012, at http://m.sportsbusinessdaily.com/Journal/Issues/2012/01/30/Super-Bowl/Lead.aspx, viewed June 4, 2012.

[28]If a player is released or traded, bonus payments that have not yet been counted are counted in the year in which the player was released. Because such payments go for players who are no longer with the team, they have come to be called "dead money."

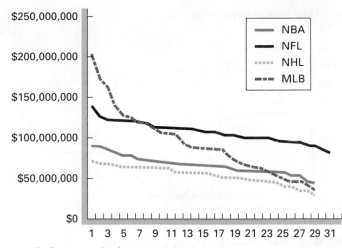

FIGURE 9.5 Payrolls for Teams in the Four Major Leagues

Payrolls in baseball, which does not have a salary cap, vary far more than payrolls in the three other major sports.

Source: Data are from "USA Today Salaries Databases" *USA Today,* at http://content.usatoday.com/sportsdata/baseball/mlb/salaries/team/2011 (baseball). Other data can be reached from that site, viewed May 28, 2012. Seasons shown: NFL: 2009, NBA, NHL: 2010–2011. MLB: 2011.

than in others.[29] In 2009–2010, only one of the 32 NFL teams exceeded the cap of $128 million, but 11 of 30 NHL teams exceeded the $59.4 million cap, and all but 6 of 30 NBA teams exceeded the $58 million salary cap. The challenges brought about by the soft cap in the NBA were most notable, as 10 teams spent more than $70 million and the Lakers, Magic, and Mavericks all had payrolls in excess of $86 million.

Although many teams exceed the salary cap in any given year, the cap seems to have had an effect. Figure 9.5 illustrates the payrolls of the teams in the four major North American sports. The graph shows that the payrolls of teams in the three leagues that have salary caps are far more equal than the payrolls in MLB.

Even discounting the New York Yankees, whose payroll is exceptional even by MLB standards, the variation in MLB payrolls is far greater than in than any other league. The highest NFL payroll would only rank fifth on the list of MLB payrolls despite the fact that MLB rosters are less than half as large as NFL rosters, while the lowest MLB payroll would rank last in every sport but the NHL, where it would rank 27th. Thus, particularly for the NHL and NFL, which have hard salary caps, setting bands within which teams are supposed to operate seems to have greatly equalized payrolls.

---

[29]Data are from the 2009–2010 NFL season and the 2010–2011 NBA and NHL seasons. Data for the NBA can be found online at *USA Today,* "USA Today Salaries Databases," *USA Today,* at http://content.usatoday.com/sportsdata/basketball/nba/salaries/team, viewed May 28, 2012. Data for the other sports are available at analogous sites and can be accessed from this site.

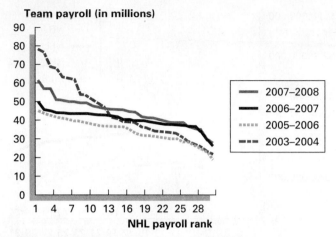

Team payroll (in millions)

Legend:
- 2007–2008
- 2006–2007
- 2005–2006
- 2003–2004

NHL payroll rank

FIGURE 9.6 NHL Team Payrolls from 2003–2004 to 2007–2008

The salary cap lowered and compressed salaries in the NHL.

Source: Data for the 2007–2008 season can be found at "USA Today Salary Databases," *USA Today*, at http://content.usatoday.com/sports/hockey/nhl/salaries/totalpayroll.aspx?year=2007–08, viewed August 8, 2009. Other data can be reached from that site.

Figure 9.6 shows payrolls for the 30 NHL teams from 2003–2004 through 2007–2008 (recall that the 2004–2005 season was lost to a lockout).

This figure looks remarkably like Figure 9.5. In this case, the outlier is the NHL's 2003–2004 season. The figure shows that team payrolls varied far more in 2003–2004, the year before the cap than in the following years. Although several teams exceeded it, the cap significantly reduced and equalized salaries. One cause for concern, however, is that the payroll curve became significantly steeper in 2007–2008, as the high-payroll teams began to separate themselves from the rest of the league. In the ensuing years, payrolls have become increasingly unequal, as the lowest payroll has remained nearly constant at just under $30 million while the top payroll has grown substantially—from about $61.8 million to just over $71 million through 2011–2012.[30] This skewing of payrolls might lie behind the owners' insistence on reducing the players' share of revenue in the new CBA.

Luxury or Competitive Balance Taxes

In Chapter 5, we discussed the impact of luxury taxes (also known as competitive balance taxes) on competitive balance. We recall them here because they were implemented through collective bargaining and have the potential to reduce overall payrolls. Under the current MLB agreement, the threshold

---

[30]"USA Today Salary Databases: NHL," *USA Today*, at http://content.usatoday.com/sportsdata/hockey/nhl/salaries/team, viewed June 3, 2012.

levels are $178 million for 2012 and 2013, and $189 million for 2014–2016. Teams that exceed this threshold must pay a tax of 17.5 percent if they are first-time violators. The penalty increases to 30 percent, 40 percent, and finally 50 percent for teams that exceed the threshold for the second, third, and fourth (or more) times.[31] Tax revenue is not redistributed to non-taxpayers. Instead, 50 percent of the revenue is devoted to player benefits, 25 percent goes to the industry growth fund, and 25 percent goes toward funding baseball development internationally.[32] The Yankees have paid the tax every year since its inception, with over $200 million in payments through 2011 (a sum that exceeds the 2011 payroll of all 29 other teams). Of the $227 million paid by all teams in taxes, the Yankees have paid $206 million. The Red Sox, Tigers, and Angels are the only other teams ever to have paid the tax. Between 2006 and 2012, however, the Yankees' payroll stabilized, varying in a relatively narrow range (between about $190 and $210 million). With the Yankees' payroll leveling off and most teams staying consistently under the tax threshold, the tax does appear to influence team behavior.[33]

The NBA also has a luxury tax, though it differs from the MLB tax in that tax revenues from payer teams are redistributed to the remaining clubs. In the most recent NBA agreement, the luxury tax penalty was increased substantially. Beginning in 2013–2014, teams must pay $1.50 for every dollar over the cap for the first $5 million and up to $3.25 for every dollar over the cap for all salaries in excess of $15 million above the cap.[34] While it remains to be seen how much this dissuades teams from spending more than the threshold, it serves as a potentially severe penalty to teams willing to exceed the soft cap.

The Impact of Rival Leagues

The periodic entry of competing leagues has also caused player salaries to rise. As we saw earlier, the appearance of rival leagues was an important factor in undermining the reserve clause in professional basketball and hockey. Rival leagues can also directly undermine a sports league's monopsony power. Figure 9.7 shows how a rival league affects salaries and employment. Initially, the monopsony hires L_m workers and pays the monopsony wage w_m. When the rival league enters,

---

[31]"MLB, MLBPA Reach New Five-Year Labor Agreement," *mlb.com* at http://mlb.mlb.com/news/article.jsp?ymd=20111122&content_id=26025138&vkey=pr_mlb&c_id=mlb, viewed May 28, 2012.

[32]Kristi Dosh, "MLB's Luxury and Tax and Revenue Sharing Are Not One and the Same," *The Biz of Baseball*, at http://bizofbaseball.com/index.php?option=com_content&view=article&id=4298:dosh-mlbs-revenue-sharing-and-the-luxury-tax-are-not-one-in-the-same&catid=29:articles-a-opinion&Itemid=41, viewed June 3, 2012.

[33]Associated Press, *Yanks, Red Sox Hit with Luxury Tax*, December 22, 2011, at http://espn.go.com/mlb/story/_/id/7381414/new-york yankees-boston-red-sox-only-teams-hit-luxury-tax, viewed May 28, 2012. Salary data are from the "USA Today Salaries Databases: MLB," *USA Today*, at http://content.usatoday.com/sportsdata/baseball/mlb/salaries/team, viewed June 4, 2012.

[34]Sam Amick, "Inside the NBA: Summary of the Tentative NBA Deal," *SI.com* at http://sportsillustrated.cnn.com/2011/writers/sam_amick/11/26/tentative.deal/index.html, viewed May 28, 2012.

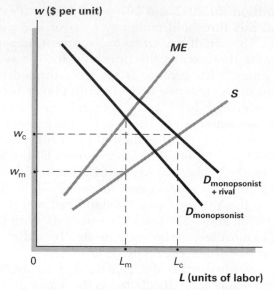

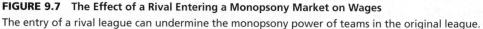

FIGURE 9.7   The Effect of a Rival Entering a Monopsony Market on Wages
The entry of a rival league can undermine the monopsony power of teams in the original league.

the teams must compete for players. Even if the increase in demand is relatively small, total employment increases to L_c, and the competition for players could force the wage up to w_c.

Salary increases caused by the entry of rival leagues have occurred in all major U.S. sports leagues. The appearance of the American League as a rival to the National League in 1901 caused the salaries of baseball players to rise sharply. The fear of higher salaries attending the entry of the Federal League led Connie Mack to sell off the star players from a powerful Philadelphia Athletics baseball club in 1915, an act from which it took the team over a decade to recover.

Since its merger with the American Football League in 1969, the NFL has faced down several rival leagues. The most serious challenges were posed by the World Football League, which operated in 1974 and 1975, and the United States Football League (USFL), which operated from 1983 through 1985. Between 1982 and 1986, the average salary in the NFL almost doubled as a direct result of the USFL's attempt to lure away players.

Similar "wars" drove up salaries when the ABA challenged the NBA in the 1960s and 1970s and when the WHA opposed the NHL in the 1970s. Between 1970 and 1976, when the WHA actively competed against the NHL for players, salaries in the NHL more than tripled. One study found that the pay in the NHL rose so much that players received more than their marginal revenue product.[35]

---

[35]J. C. H. Jones and William D. Walsh, "The World Hockey Association and Player Exploitation in the National Hockey League," *Quarterly Review of Economics and Business*, vol. 27, no. 2 (Summer 1987), pp. 87–101.

9.3 LABOR CONFLICT AND COMPROMISE IN COLLECTIVE BARGAINING

Compared to the rest of the economy, labor relations in professional sports have been particularly contentious.[36] From 1972 through 1994, every renewal of the collective bargaining agreement in MLB was accompanied by a strike or lockout. As Table 9.1 shows, each of the four major North American sports has experienced a work stoppage since 1980. Recently, the NFL and NBA both suffered protracted work stoppages in 2011. The NFL lost no regular season games, but the NBA's lockout shortened the regular season from 82 to 66 games. Had the lockout gone any longer, it is likely that the entire season would have been cancelled. The 2012–2013 NHL season is currently endangered by yet another lockout.

At first glance, labor conflict seems inconsistent with the economic assumption that workers and firms behave rationally. Like wars and lawsuits, strikes and lockouts seem willfully to waste resources. For example, the NHL's 301-day lockout in 2004–2005 is widely credited with the imposition of a salary cap. The settlement came, however, only after the cancellation of the entire season and the attendant loss of team revenue and player salaries. Both team owners and players would have been better off if they had agreed to implement a salary cap at the beginning of the season and avoided the loss of income.

In 2004, owners entered negotiations determined to install a salary cap, while the players were equally determined to avoid one. Thus, in the words of Paul Staudohar, "[T]he dispute was more about each side's philosophical approach than numbers."[37] As we describe below, when the parties disagree over such broad issues, they are less flexible in their positions and more uncertain about the

TABLE 9.1 Labor Unrest in Professional Sports since 1980

Year	MLB	NBA	NFL	NHL
1981	50-day strike			
1982			57-day strike	
1985	2-day strike			
1987			24-day strike	
1989	32-day lockout			
1992				10-day strike
1994–1995	232-day strike			103-day lockout
1998–1999		191-day lockout		
2004–2005				301-day lockout
2011		149-day lockout	132-day lockout	
2012				Ongoing lockout

[36]For a direct comparison, see James Quirk and Rodney Fort, *Hardball* (Princeton, N.J.: Princeton University Press, 1999), p. 68.

[37]Paul Staudohar, "The Hockey Lockout of 2004–2005," *Monthly Labor Report*, December 2005, p. 26.

implications of their positions. Seeking to avoid a strike during the postseason, when the players' leverage would be greatest, the owners locked out the players at the start of the 2004–2005 season. With neither side willing to budge, the stand-off resulted in the cancellation of the season.

ECONOMIC THEORY AND LABOR CONFLICT Economists reconcile strikes with rational behavior by acknowledging the role played by uncertainty. Uncertainty affects negotiations in one of two ways. If one side is overly pessimistic—either because it underestimates its own bargaining power or because it overstates the power of its opposition—it may settle for a less favorable agreement than it could have reached. If the participant errs on the side of optimism—overestimating its own bargaining power or understating the power of its opposition—conflict may result. Unduly optimistic perceptions of reality can prevent one or both parties from making the necessary concessions in time to prevent conflict. Uncertainty might be aggravated by a mistrust of the other side. If one party has reason to mistrust its counterpart, then it runs the risk of disregarding a truthful position.

If both labor and management know exactly how far they can push the other side, they can typically reach a settlement without resorting to conflict. Figure 9.8 illustrates how this might come about. In the figure, the union wants to push wages higher while the employer wants to drive wages lower. Unless labor and the employer are better off separating permanently, each side will be willing to accept a range of wages or salaries that is also acceptable to the other side. We have labeled this range of wages the **contract zone**.

The precise position of the contract zone depends on the two sides' threat points. If the union has strong alternative opportunities, then its threat point corresponds to a higher wage and the lower end of the contract zone moves to a higher wage, as shown in Figure 9.9a. If the firm has better alternatives, the upper end of the contract zone moves to a lower wage, as shown in Figure 9.9b.

The precise settlement depends on the bargaining strength of the two parties. A problem arises when workers, firms, or both do not know how far they can push the other side—or even how far they are willing to go themselves. When

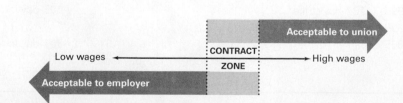

FIGURE 9.8 The Contract Zone
Unions try to find the highest wage that is acceptable to the firm. The firm tries to find the lowest wage that is acceptable to the union. The overlap of acceptable wages is the contract zone.

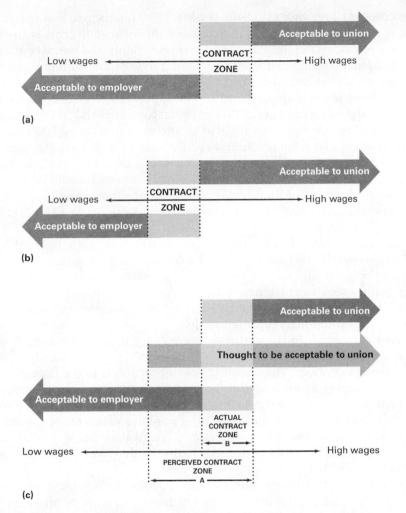

FIGURE 9.9 (a) Contract Zone with Powerful Union; (b) Contract Zone with Powerful Employer; (c) Mistaken Perceptions about the Contract Zone

The contract zone will shift left or right depending on the bargaining strengths of the union and the firm. If the firm mistakenly believes the union will accept a wage below the contract zone (or when the union believes the firm will accept a higher wage proposal), conflict might result.

they are overly pessimistic, they are likely to concede too much and reach an unfavorable settlement.[38] When they are overly optimistic during negotiations, neither side proposes a settlement in the contract zone, and conflict results, as illustrated in Figure 9.9c.

[38]See, for example, Beth Hayes, "Unions and Strikes with Asymmetric Information," *Journal of Labor Economics,* vol. 2, no. 1 (January 1984), pp. 57–84; and Michael A. Leeds, "Bargaining as Search Behavior under Mutual Uncertainty," *Southern Economic Journal,* vol. 53, no. 3 (January 1987), pp. 677–684, for two different perspectives on the role uncertainty may play.

LABOR CONFLICT AND PROFESSIONAL SPORTS   The unique role that sports unions play in negotiating broad frameworks rather than dollars and cents issues such as wages and salaries naturally leads to greater uncertainty and hence conflict. Most unions are legally prohibited from negotiating over "basic entrepreneurial decisions," which are the responsibility of management. Entrepreneurial decisions on aspects such as revenue sharing and league expansion or contraction, however, are often at the heart of negotiations in professional sports.[39] For example, the NFLPA staged two strikes in the 1980s in an attempt to get the NFL to agree to free agency, which would have revolutionized the way in which salaries were determined. The high stakes involved led both sides to take more extreme positions than they otherwise would have. They also caused both sides to be less certain about the implications of their bargaining positions than would have been the case if they had been haggling over whether starting quarterbacks should be paid $5 or $6 million per year.

The MLBPA often faced a unique source of uncertainty. Because baseball teams rely so heavily on local revenue, the owners often disagreed among themselves on the goals and strategies in their negotiations with the MLBPA. Big-market teams, such as the Yankees and Dodgers, were reluctant to implement changes designed to level the financial playing field. Because they played in such large markets, the big-market teams also lost much more gate and media revenue from labor stoppages. As a result, they were eager to avoid prolonged conflict. Small-market teams, such as the Kansas City Royals or Milwaukee Brewers, had very different incentives. They pushed heavily for limits to the financial advantages of big-market teams and were willing to endure long work stoppages to implement such limits. The conflicting goals of the teams made it hard for MLB ownership to present a coherent bargaining position, which made it hard for the union to know where the other side stood.[40] The relative peace in MLB since the strike of 1995–1995 is due in part to the harmony that MLB Commissioner Bud Selig has been able to instill among the owners.

Strikes are particularly likely if the parties do not trust one another. Unfortunately, mistrust has been a frequent feature of labor relations in professional sports. Jerry McMorris, the former owner of the Colorado Rockies, once said of baseball's negotiations, "I never would have believed the level of mistrust and lack of confidence in each other........ It made it very difficult for people to compromise or experiment."[41]

The mistrust can sometimes be well founded. For example, the NHL's 103-day work stoppage in 1994–1995 was due in part to the ill will created by one man: Alan Eagleson. As Executive Director of the NHLPA from its inception in 1967 until 1992, Eagleson was responsible for representing the interests of the

---

[39]Robert N. Covington, "(How Much) Is the Law to Blame for Baseball's Turbulent Labor Relations?" *Journal of Sports Economics*, vol. 4, no. 4 (November 2003), pp. 357–361.

[40]See Paul Staudohar, "Why No Baseball Work Stoppage?" *Journal of Sports Economics*, vol. 4, no.4 (November 2003), pp. 362–366; Andrew Zimbalist, "Labor Relations in Major League Baseball," *Journal of Sports Economics*, vol. 4, no. 4 (November 2003), pp. 332–355; and John Helyar, *Lords of the Realm* (1994).

[41]John Helyar, *Lords of the Realm* (1994), p. 602.

players. However, he frequently pursued other interests at the expense of the players he supposedly represented. While director of the NHLPA, Eagleson was also an agent for many players and often favored his clients over players who had other agents. Even players who had him as an agent were often not well represented. Eagleson saw to it that Bobby Orr, the great Boston Bruins player, was delivered to the Chicago Blackhawks by failing to convey the Bruins' final offer (which included part-ownership of the team) to Orr. Most serious was Eagleson's role as director of a foundation that oversaw international hockey exhibitions, such as the Canada Cup series. Eagleson convinced NHL players to participate in these exhibitions without pay by assuring them that a percentage of revenue had been earmarked for the NHLPA pension fund. However, a 1989 investigation showed that the owners had used the Canada Cup funds to replace their own contributions, all with Eagleson's knowledge and approval. The NHLPA successfully sued the NHL for $50 million, and Eagleson, who resigned under fire from the NHLPA in 1992, was imprisoned on fraud and mail fraud charges.[42]

Negotiations between NHL players and owners in the mid-1990s were doomed from the beginning. First, the two sides were negotiating large, defining issues, such as the creation of a salary cap. Second, both sides faced increased uncertainty due to the recent naming of Gary Bettman as new NHL Commissioner and Bob Goodenow as new executive director of the NHLPA. Finally, the players entered the negotiations still bitter over their betrayal by Eagleson and mistrustful of owners who had misallocated their pension funds. The two sides were unable to reach an agreement, and the 1994–1995 season began without a contract in place. Fearful that the players would strike on the eve of the playoffs, when their leverage would be greatest (and when they had held a 10-day strike in 1992), the owners staged a preemptive lockout.

Comparing the 2011 NBA and NFL Negotiations

When the NFL lockout began on March 12, 2011, it marked the first work stoppage between the most profitable of the four North American sports leagues and its players since 1987. Just four months later, the NBA owners also locked out their players creating professional basketball's first work stoppage since 1998–1999. With two of the four major sports leagues at a simultaneous standstill, one might conclude that the two leagues had a common problem. In reality, their circumstances were very different. As noted, the NFL was very profitable. With annual revenues exceeding $9 billion and significant revenue sharing, owners could not credibly claim that the league was in distress. The NBA was a much different story. In 2010–2011, 22 of 30 NBA teams lost money.

THE 2011 NFL AGREEMENT The NFL's lockout seems particularly illogical. With huge salaries and profits at stake, players and owners had strong incentives to reach an agreement. Yet we know from Figure 9.9c that if either side mistakes the

---

[42]Jane O'Hara, "In the Name of Greed," *Maclean's*, January 19, 1998, pp. 22–24; Paul Staudohar, *Playing for Dollars* (1996), pp. 140–141; and Russ Conway, *Game Misconduct: Alan Eagleson and the Corruption of Hockey* (Buffalo, N.Y.: MacFarlane, Walter, and Ross, 1997).

other's true position, standoffs can occur. In this case, two factors undermined an atmosphere of trust. First, both sides had new leadership since the previous CBA. Roger Goodell had succeeded Paul Tagliabue as commissioner in 2006, and Gene Upshaw, long time head of the NFLPA, had died in August of 2008. He was succeeded by DeMaurice Smith in early 2009, leaving both sides with inexperienced leadership.[43] Second, the owners, anticipating labor troubles, had negotiated a television contract that would pay them $4 billion even if no games were played. The players took this as a sign of bad faith and sued, arguing that the league had violated its mandate to maximize all profits that are shared with players. Although Judge David Doty sided with the players, the owners' move was a source of significant tension and likely eroded whatever trust may have existed. As a result of this mistrust, the NFLPA insisted that the NFL teams provide complete access to the owners' certified financial statements. The level of mistrust rose still further when the owners refused to comply.

In a surprising display of brinksmanship, the NFLPA decertified one day before the lockout began, declaring it no longer represented the players and was merely a trade association. In announcing the decertification, DeMaurice Smith claimed that "the lack of trust was too much to overcome following two years of negotiation."[44] At the same time, nine players, including stars Drew Brees, Tom Brady, and Payton Manning, and one a top college prospect, Von Miller, filed an antitrust suit against the owners (also in David Doty's court). Involving the courts complicates and slows matters because it introduces another party into the negotiations. Bargaining did not resume until mid-May and then it did so only under court order. By mid-summer, with the season rapidly approaching and the loss of revenue and salaries a real possibility, the two sides finally reached a new, ten-year agreement in late July, which preserved both revenues and salaries through the 2020 season.

The final agreement was, as expected, a compromise. Most notably, the owners achieved a significant reduction in the overall salary cap (a 7 percent reduction from 2009), a rookie pay scale, and credit for stadium investment up to 1.5 percent of revenues each year. Owners can deduct this credit for stadium investment before computing the players' share. The players received a commitment that the owners would spend at or close to the maximum allowed under the salary cap, significant funding for retirees and health and safety research, restrictions on preseason practices, and no expansion of the season to 18 games.[45]

---

[43]Mike Sando, "10 Things to Know about NFL Labor Situation," *ESPN NFL,* January 31, 2011, at http://espn.go.com/blog/nfcwest/post/_/id/32363/10-things-to-know-about-nfl-labor-situation.

[44]Alex Marvez, *NFL Owners Lock Out Players,* March 12, 2011, at http://msn.foxsports.com/nfl/story/NFL-Players-Association-union-decertifies-labor-talks-owners-031111, viewed May 29, 2012.

[45]"History of the NFL Salary Cap," *Business Insider,* at http://articles.businessinsider.com/2011-07-20/sports/30074982_1_nfl-salary-cap-nfl-lockout-history; Nate Davis, "NFL, Players Announce New 10-Year Labor Agreement," *USA Today,* July 25, 2011, at http://content.usatoday.com/communities/thehuddle/post/2011/07/reports-nfl-players-agree-to-new-collective-bargaining-agreement/1. "Summary of the New NFL Collective Bargaining Agreement," *SI.com,* July 25, 2011, at http://sportsillustrated.cnn.com/2011/football/nfl/07/25/cba-settlement-summary/index.html. "Terms of the Owners' Proposed CBA," *Fox Sports,* July 21, 2011, at http://msn.foxsports.com/nfl/story/Terms-of-NFL-owners-proposed-collective-bargaining-agreement-072111, viewed May 29, 2012.

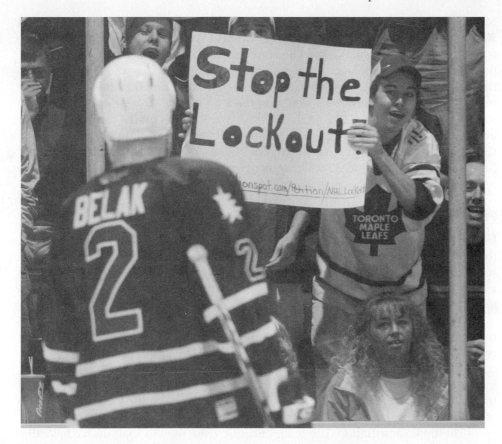

THE 2011 NBA AGREEMENT   In contrast to the NFL, the NBA talks, led by Billy Hunter, Executive Director of the NBPA, and NBA Commissioner David Stern, occurred in an environment of economic distress. As early as 2009, a dozen teams had expressed interest in obtaining loans totaling $200 million from the league due to financial hardship.[46] From the outset, the league let it be known that it intended to cut players' share of revenue from 57 to 50 percent, trimming $750 million per year from player costs. In addition, the owners wanted a hard salary cap. The two sides exchanged offers throughout 2010 and early 2011 without significant progress, as owners rejected a proposal from players to cut their revenue share to 54.3 percent, and the players rejected the owners' proposal of a "flex-cap" as a hard cap on salaries. The lockout officially began on July 1, 2011.

Several star players, such as Kobe Bryant, raised the stakes by publicly discussing the possibility of leaving the NBA to play overseas. Similar to the impact of rival leagues discussed earlier in the chapter, losing star players to leagues in other countries could have seriously undermined the bargaining power of the

---

[46]"NBA Lockout Timeline," *NBA.com*, December 9, 2011, at http://www.nba.com/2011/news/09/09/labor-timeline/index.html, viewed May 29, 2012.

NBA.[47] Throughout the negotiations, the players steadfastly refused to accept a 50–50 split of revenues. Unlike the NFL, no deal was complete at the start of the season and the league was forced to cancel games. With the season melting away, the NBPA followed the lead of the NFLPA and decertified in mid-November. As the lockout approached its 150th day and the cancellation of the season was imminent, the players and owners finally agreed on a new 10-year contract with a 66-game season in 2011–2012. In the end, the owners won on the most substantive issue—the division of revenue. For the length of the agreement, the players will receive between 49 and 51 percent of BRI. Players do benefit from a commitment that all teams will spend 85 to 90 percent of the salary cap but are likely made worse off by the dramatic increase in the luxury tax discussed earlier.[48]

Professional Tennis Associations

Individual sports, such as tennis or golf, also have associations that represent the interests of the players. These unions, however, differ from those in the team sports in several important ways. This section examines the unique aspects of the unions representing men and women tennis players. It also points out some differences in the goals of the men's and women's unions.

In 1968, the first year of "open" tennis, in which professionals and amateurs could both compete, the prize for winning the men's singles at Wimbledon was only £2,000. By 2012, the prize had risen to £1,150,000, an increase of 57,400 percent. The prizes in women's tennis had finally become as large as for men, so their increase was even more spectacular, growing from £750 to £1,150,000.[49] Much of the increase can be attributed to the presence of two organizations, the Association of Tennis Professionals (ATP) and the Women's Tennis Association (WTA).

These two associations differ significantly from the associations we have discussed thus far. First, they are relatively young. Until the late 1960s the Grand Slam events—the Australian, French, and U.S. Open and Wimbledon—were known as Championships (Wimbledon's official name is the "All England Lawn Tennis Championship") and were restricted to amateurs. The participants were largely well-to-do men and women who played tennis for a few years before going on to what they regarded as their adult lives.[50] When these tournaments welcomed professional players, a wider array of people sought to make a living

---

[47]A number of players did sign to play overseas but with one or two exceptions, they were not star players. For a few, the strategy backfired, as they had failed to negotiate opt-out clauses with the foreign teams and could not return to the NBA when the lockout ended. "NBA Players in China Might Be Stuck," *Fox Sports*, December 1, 2011, at http://msn.foxsports.com/nba/story/NBA-players-who-went-to-China-in-lockout-might-be-stuck-once-it-ends-113011, viewed May 29, 2012.

[48]Larry Coon, "Breaking Down Changes in the New CBA," *ESPN NBA*, November 28, 2011, at http://espn.go.com/nba/story/_/page/CBA-111128/how-new-nba-deal-compares-last-one, viewed May 29, 2012.

[49]Figures from "Prize Money," *Wimbledon: The Official Site*, at http://aeltc.wimbledon.org/en_GB/about/history/prizemoney_history.html.

[50]See E. Digby Baltzell, *Sporting Gentlemen: Men's Tennis form the Age of Honor to the Cult of the Superstar* (New York: The Free Press, 1995), for a highly entertaining, if very opinionated, history of men's tennis.

by playing tennis.[51] While recognition by the Grand Slam tournaments conveyed prestige on professional tennis, even today only a few tennis players would be able to make a living on their winnings from that handful of major events. The players needed a body that would represent their interests to venues and sponsors who sought to hold professional tournaments. Unfortunately, the tournament committees at the time had been created by and for amateur players and were either inexperienced at dealing with professionals or openly hostile toward them. To fill this void, the men formed the ATP in 1972, while the women formed the WTA a year later.

Unlike the unions we have encountered so far, the ATP and WTA resemble craft unions fairly closely. Like craft unions, the ATP and WTA define who is and who is not a qualified employee. As we saw in Figure 9.2, craft unions increase the pay of their members by restricting the supply curve of labor. Like firms that come to a hiring hall to obtain labor, venues that wish to establish tournaments obtain different classes of labor by applying to the unions for a tournament of a given status. Higher-status tournaments with higher payments and better benefits then receive higher-quality players. Because they sanction the events in which players take part, the ATP and WTA have become synonymous with the men's and women's professional tennis tours.

Like other unions in team sports, the ATP and WTA do not specify how much tournaments pay specific players. They do, however, establish the reward structure of the tournaments, so all players know what they will earn from a particular outcome They also negotiate all aspects of the "working conditions" of each tournament, from the types of hotel rooms the players occupy, to the uniforms of the "ballpersons," to the nature of the bathroom facilities in the locker rooms. The ATP and WTA rulebooks, which specify these regulations, are themselves significant. Unlike the major North American team sports, tennis players have a rulebook rather than a collective bargaining agreement. The source of this difference lies in the fact that the ATP and WTA do not engage in negotiations with a single management group. Instead, they set rules for employers who wish to hire tennis players for a tournament, much like construction unions (a typical craft union) set rules for developers who wish to construct offices or apartment buildings.

Also unlike most other unions, the ATP and WTA are strictly segregated by gender. In part, this is because men and women do not play against one another (except in mixed doubles). In fact, except for the Grand Slam and a few other similar events, men and women do not even compete in the same venues. Moreover, the needs of women who play tennis professionally differ significantly from the needs of men. The WTA, for example, specifies how long a woman may retain her status on the tour after having a child, while the ATP rulebook makes no mention of paternity leave.[52]

---

[51]By the 1960s, many of the tournaments were offering so many benefits and side payments to players that detractors called the participants "shamateurs." See E. Digby Baltzell, *Sporting Gentlemen* (1995), pp. 335–336.

[52]ATP Tour, Inc. *The 2012 ATP Official Rulebook*, 2012, at http://www.atpworldtour.com/Corporate/Rulebook.aspx; WTA Tour Incorporated, *WTA Women's Tennis Association 2012 Official Rulebook*, 2012, at http://www.wtatennis.com/SEWTATour-Archive/Archive/AboutTheTour/rules.pdf.

BIOGRAPHICAL SKETCH
Marvin Miller

*Man, don't the owners know that there's going to be a whole generation
of ballplayers' sons who grow up with the middle name Marvin?*

—*New York Yankees pitcher Rudy May*[1]

When reporters first asked Marvin Miller why he had gone
from being chief economist of the United Steelworkers (USW),
one of the nation's foremost unions, to heading a ragtag
players association that did not even have a permanent office,
he had a simple response for them: "'I grew up in Brooklyn,'
I said, 'not far from Ebbets Field.' . . . Heads nodded. No further
explanation was required."[2] Further explanation *is* required,
however, of a man who almost single-handedly overthrew the
powers of one of the most powerful monopsonies in America
and transformed the face of professional sports. In so doing,
Marvin Miller evolved from a man who might be the subject
of an occasional dissertation on the history of unions to one of
the towering figures in professional sports.

Miller did grow up in the shadow of Ebbets Field, the son of a storekeeper and
a teacher in the New York public school system. He got his first taste of labor relations
during World War II when he worked at the National War Labor Board, which adjudi-
cated union–management disputes as part of labor's pledge not to impede the war effort
by going on strike.

After the war, Miller worked at a variety of jobs with little clear direction when,
in 1950, Otis Brubaker, the research director at the United Steelworkers and an acquain-
tance from the National War Labor Board, asked Miller to join his staff at the USW.
Miller found a home at the USW and worked his way up to becoming the USW's chief
economist and assistant to the union's president, David J. McDonald. Ironically, Miller's
most notable accomplishment at USW was the creation of a "productivity sharing plan"
at Kaiser Steel that became a model for promoting good union–management relations
and preventing conflict.

In 1965, however, I. W. Abel defeated McDonald in a hotly contested union election that centered on McDonald's reliance on "technicians," such as Miller, rather than
elected officials. With his future at USW uncertain, Miller was intrigued when several
player representatives approached him about becoming the first full-time executive
director of the Major League Baseball Players Association.

The road to becoming director, however, was not smooth. In a full vote, the player
representatives chose their part-time director, Robert W. Cannon, instead. When Cannon
attached additional conditions to becoming full-time director, refusing, for example, to
move from his office in Milwaukee to New York, the players turned to Miller as their
second choice. Even then, Miller's selection was far from certain, as he had to secure the
approval of the full membership. Egged on by owners who viewed Miller as a rabble-
rousing union boss, the players were skeptical. The Cleveland Indians' manager, Birdie
Tebbetts, openly asked Miller, "How can the players be sure you're not a Communist?"

(*Continued*)

(Continued)

After a rocky start—Miller was voted down by the players at the Arizona spring training facilities 102–17 before being approved overwhelmingly by the players at the Florida camps—Miller quickly earned the players' approval and then their fierce devotion.

Miller viewed the MLBPA as a chance to practice principles of democratic unionism that would have been so hard to implement in a huge union such as the USW. He won the players' confidence not by using the sophisticated arguments that Ed Garvey used with the football players or by intimidating the players like Alan Eagleson did in hockey, but by listening. He made a point of meeting every player during spring training and meeting every team's player representative at least four times a year. These meetings, moreover, were not intended to rubber-stamp prearranged positions. The meetings were often lengthy, untidy affairs with players arguing with Miller and each other at great length. The one rule that Miller imposed was that the players had to leave the meeting unified. "'Anything less than 100 percent is unacceptable,' was his unshakable motto."[3] The result was a union that managed to do what many thought impossible, overturn the reserve clause when it lacked any legal standing to do so.

[1] Quoted in Helyar, *Lords of the Realm* (New York: Villard Books, 1994), p. 239.

[2] Quoted in Marvin Miller, *A Whole Different Ballgame* (New York: Carol Publishing Group, 1991), pp. 11–12.

[3] John Helyar, Lords of the Realm (1994), p. 84.

Sources: James Dworkin, *Owners versus Players: Baseball and Collective Bargaining* (Boston: Auburn House, 1981); Charles Korr, "Marvin Miller and the New Unionism in Baseball," in *The Business of Professional Sports,* ed. by Paul Staudohar and James Mangan (Urbana: University of Illinois Press, 1991); Marvin Miller, *A Whole Different Ballgame* (New York: Carol Publishing Group, 1991); and John Helyar, *Lords of the Realm* (New York: Villard Books, 1994).

Summary

Labor markets in the four major North American sports leagues were marked by significant monopsony power for most of the 20th century. As the sole buyer, a monopsony can drive down the price it pays. The reserve clause, the main source of monopsony power, bound players to the team that held their contract for as long as the team wanted them. By 1976, however, all four sports had discarded the reserve clause and had adopted some form of free agency. Leagues have tried to limit the impact of free agency in a number of ways. Salary caps have proven effective at both limiting player salaries and reducing the differences in team payrolls.

Unlike unions elsewhere in the economy, unions in professional sports have proven remarkably successful at organizing their workforce. The sports industry has also experienced far more labor conflict than have other labor markets. Economists have difficulty explaining conflict, as it seems to defy rational behavior. When one accounts for uncertainty, however, one can explain strikes as a mistake by one or both of the negotiating parties.

Some unions have proven more successful than others at promoting the interests of their players. The NFLPA has had trouble keeping pace with other unions, notably the MLBPA. Some of these problems have been unavoidable, while others have been the result of mistaken policies by the union.

Professional tennis players and golfers have established their own associations. These unions resemble craft unions in that they set out rules for players that limit the supply of labor and rules for employers (tournaments) that seek to hire players. Unlike most craft unions, the tennis and golf player associations are strictly segregated by sex.

Discussion Questions

1. Are salary caps good for professional sports? Would you want to have a salary cap in your job? If your answers differ, how do you justify the different answers?
2. Are unions good or bad for professional sports?
3. Should the government step in when there is a strike or lockout in professional sports?

Problems

9.1. Explain in everyday language the meaning of the deadweight loss in Figure 9.1.
9.2. Draw and compare figures similar to Figure 9.9 for both the NBA and NFL showing the contract zone at the start of their 2011 lockouts.
9.3. Would a craft union or an industrial union be more inclined to argue against the designated hitter? Why?
9.4. Suppose that Congress repeals MLB's exemption from the antitrust laws. How might this affect the contract zone between MLB and the MLBPA?
9.5. MLB has adopted final offer arbitration because it fears that regular binding arbitration is addictive. In what way can binding arbitration be addictive? Why isn't FOA addictive?
9.6. Explain how each of the following would affect the NHLPA's bargaining position.
    a. Russia's Kontinental Hockey League signs a large number of NHL stars.
    b. A change in the tax laws increases the profitability of owning stock and decreases the profitability of owning a sports franchise.
9.7. In what way are sports unions like craft unions? In what way are they like industrial unions? In what way do they differ from both?
9.8. Use what you have learned in this chapter to explain why "journeymen" in MLB earn 86 percent of their *MRP* while "apprentices" earn only 19 percent.
9.9. Use supply and demand curves to show how the ATP and the WTA increased the prize money offered on the men's and women's professional tennis tours.

CHAPTER 10

Discrimination

The biggest thing I don't like about New York are the foreigners.
I'm not a very big fan of foreigners. How the hell did they get in this country?
I'm not a racist or prejudiced person, but certain people bother me.

—JOHN ROCKER, FORMER MAJOR LEAGUE PITCHER[1]

I was raised on the beliefs of my father, my uncle, and Dr. Martin Luther King which,
in essence, are "Don't do me any favors. Let's agree on what the rules are,
and then judge me fairly."

—ARTHUR ASHE[2]

INTRODUCTION

On April 18, 1946, in a minor league game between the Montreal Royals and the Jersey City Little Giants, Jackie Robinson crossed the color line and became the first African American baseball player since the 1880s to be employed by a major league-affiliated team. His first at bat, a ground ball to the Jersey City shortstop, ended more than 50 years of segregated professional baseball in the United States.[3] Almost

---

[1]Jeff Pearlman, "At Full Blast," *Sports Illustrated* (December 27, 1999–January 3, 2000), pp. 62–64.

[2]Francis Dealey, *Win at Any Cost: The Sell Out of College Athletics* (New York: Birch Lane Press, 1990), p. 101.

[3]He did, however, hit a home run later in the same game. From Robert Peterson, *Only the Ball Was White: A History of Legendary Black Players and All-Black Professional Teams* (New York: Gramercy Books, 1970), p. 194.

exactly one year later, on April 15, 1947, he took the field as a Brooklyn Dodger. Over the objections of many fans, players, and owners, Dodgers' president Branch Rickey had reintegrated baseball. Three months after Robinson broke the color barrier in the National League, Larry Doby became the first black to play in the American League when Bill Veeck signed him to a contract with the Cleveland Indians. Doby suffered much of the same treatment as Robinson, including endless streams of insults from fans and players, death threats, and segregated hotels and restaurants that often prevented him from staying and eating with his teammates. It is remarkable that Robinson and Doby flourished despite the tense atmosphere in which they played. While baseball's history of discrimination against black players is surely the most widely known case of discrimination in sports, it is by no means the only one. Just as discrimination has long been a source of concern in almost every walk of life, it has been an issue in virtually every sport. The purpose of this chapter is to show how economists study and measure discrimination and to discuss some of the instances when those methods have uncovered significant evidence that discrimination exists in the sports industry.

LEARNING OBJECTIVES

After reading this chapter, you will be able to:

• Understand the Becker model of discrimination.

• Describe how various forms of discrimination can occur in professional sports.

• Evaluate gender discrimination in college sports.

While the overall evidence is mixed, a good deal of current research finds that players' opportunities today are free from discrimination.[4] For example, *The Racial and Gender Report Card*, which is published annually by The Institute for Diversity and Ethics in Sport at the University of Central Florida, gives the NFL, NBA, MLS (Major League Soccer), WNBA, and MLB straight A+'s for their performance in racial equity among players for 2011 (the report did not include the NHL).[5] The reports generally graded the leagues lower in areas such as coaching and management opportunities.

In contrast, a number of recent studies by economists find evidence that discrimination is still a concern. For example, Chih Hai Yang and Hsuan Yu found that foreign players in the NBA are systematically underpaid by 17.4 percent

---

[4]A good overview of early studies of discrimination in sports can be found in Lawrence M. Kahn, "The Sports Business as a Labor Market Laboratory," *Journal of Economic Perspectives,* vol. 14, no. 3 (Summer 2000), pp. 75–94.

[5]Richard E. Lapchick, et al., *The 2011 Racial and Gender Report Card: Major League Soccer; The 2011 Racial and Gender Report Card: The National Football League; The 2011 Racial and Gender Report Card: Major League Baseball; The 2011 Racial and Gender Report Card: National Basketball Association;* and *The 2011 Racial and Gender Report Card: The Women's National Basketball Association,* The Institute for Diversity and Ethics in Sport (TIDES), all reports can be accessed through the TIDES home page, at http://www.tidesport.org/, viewed May 30, 2012.

relative to U.S. natives, though the difference becomes smaller as the population of the player's home country increases.[6] The NBA is not the only place in which foreign players may suffer discrimination. Later in the chapter, we discuss discrimination against non-native players in European soccer. Michael Conlin and Patrick Emerson study hiring discrimination in the NFL by comparing the draft position of white and black players to how much they played and found significant evidence of hiring discrimination against blacks. An interesting element of this study is that, while blacks were discriminated against in the hiring (i.e., draft) process, there is no evidence of discriminatory behavior by coaches.[7] Finally, Joseph Price and Justin Wolfers find that the racial makeup of the referee crew has a significant impact on the number of fouls called on black and white players. They find that black players receive approximately 4 to 4.5 percent more fouls per 48 minutes than white players when the number of white referees increased from zero to three, and that, given the average difference in the racial composition of the teams in a typical game, the probability of victory for the team with more white players rose by about three percentage points as the referee crew changes from all black to all white.[8]

As we explore discrimination in professional and college sports, we need to distinguish between prejudice, which is a feeling or emotion, and discrimination, which is an action. A simple economic definition of discrimination is the "unequal treatment of equals." This chapter focuses solely on the economic effects of discrimination in the labor market. Thus, we use human capital theory and productivity data to discuss the existence, measurement, and changes in discrimination over time. The underlying question for all studies in this area is whether people of different demographic groups are evaluated and rewarded solely on the basis of their productivity.

Economists who study discrimination usually focus on two areas of concern. The first is whether equally qualified people have equal access to labor markets. This issue can be summarized as *equal access to work.* For example, if, as Conlin and Emerson have found, black NFL players are systematically drafted in lower positions than whites, they would have unequal access to work. The second criterion, *equal pay for equal work,* asks whether equally productive workers in identical positions are paid equally. For example, if foreign basketball players are paid less than otherwise identical U.S.-born players, our second criterion is violated.

Nobel Prize–winning economist Gary Becker, whose work on human capital is discussed in Chapter 8, also made major contributions to the way economists

---

[6]Chih-Hai Yang and Hsuan-Y Lin, "Is There Salary Discrimination by Nationality in the NBA?: Foreign Talent or Foreign Market," *Journal of Sports Economics*, vol. 13, no. 1 (February 2012), pp. 53–75. The authors also found evidence of discrimination against white players, though they note that the observed wage difference may be a function of playing time rather than discrimination.

[7]Michael Conlin and Patrick M. Emerson, "Discrimination in Hiring versus Retention and Promotion: An Empirical Analysis of Within-Firm Treatment of Players in the NFL," *Journal of Law, Economics & Organization*, vol. 22, no. 1 (April 2006), pp. 115–136.

[8]Joseph Price and Justin Wolfers, "Racial Discrimination among NBA Referees," *Quarterly Journal of Economics,* vol. 125, no. 4 (November 2010), pp. 1859–1887.

view discrimination. In this chapter, we focus much of our attention on his model. The next section describes how Becker's model approaches and measures discrimination.

10.1 BECKER'S THEORY OF LABOR DISCRIMINATION

Before focusing on the economics of discrimination, we should acknowledge that economics is not the only lens through which one can view discrimination. The economic approach to discrimination is relatively new. In fact, before Gary Becker introduced the neoclassical theory of discrimination in his groundbreaking *The Economics of Discrimination* in 1957, economists had generally left the field to other disciplines.[9] For example, psychologists and sociologists have spent a great deal of time studying discrimination and its roots. A distinguishing aspect of the economic approach to discrimination is that economists tend to focus much more on the outcome of discrimination than on its origin.

Becker's theory differs from the social–psychological approach in that it rests the concept of a **taste for discrimination**. Tastes are one of the basic building blocks of consumer theory in economics. As such, they are generally taken as given. To see the futility of challenging tastes, ask a friend what her favorite flavor of ice cream is. When she responds, ask her why she chose that flavor (say, peach). She will probably say something like, "Because peach tastes good." Now try asking her why peach tastes better than chocolate chip. Odds are she will shrug her shoulders and say she does not know why, or she will offer a variant on "Because it tastes good." As we describe below, it is possible to alter people's decisions, regardless of their tastes.[10]

Your friend's inability to explain the reasons behind her tastes does not mean that you cannot alter her actions. If you offer your friend a large enough cash payment along with the chocolate chip ice cream or charge a high enough price for the peach ice cream, you might convince her to eat the flavor that she does not most prefer. Becker's central insight was that people could have a taste for discrimination just like they can have a taste for a specific flavor of ice cream. People have a taste for discrimination if they act as if they are willing to pay to associate with one group rather than another.

Rather than wrestle with the complexity of the roots and mechanics of prejudice, Becker's theory allows economists to focus directly on behavior. It uses money to measure a person's taste for discrimination, avoiding the challenge of uncovering why someone discriminates. With this approach testing for the presence of and measuring the results of discrimination are fairly straightforward. In addition, Becker's theory enables analysts to predict how discrimination affects the people who practice it and who are victimized by it.

---

[9]Gary S. Becker, *The Economics of Discrimination*, 2nd ed. (Chicago: University of Chicago Press, 1971).

[10]A classic treatment of tastes and how economists regard them can be found in George Stigler and Gary Becker, "De Gustibus Non Est Disputandum," *American Economic Review,* vol. 67, no. 1 (March 1977), pp. 76–90.

In labor markets, the payment a discriminator makes to avoid associating with another group can take many forms, such as lower profits, higher prices, or lower wages. We distinguish among these payments because the source of discrimination and the nature of the payment depends on which party (if any) gains and which party loses.

10.2   DIFFERENT FORMS OF DISCRIMINATION IN PROFESSIONAL SPORTS

This section describes how Becker's model analyzes discrimination by employers, employees, and consumers. Although in each case the model uses money to measure the intensity of the discrimination, the model is based on utility maximization. As people with a taste for discrimination maximize their utility, their willingness to pay in order to indulge their tastes has a variety of effects on the market. In addition, the structure of the market has important implications for both the discriminator and the groups that are discriminated against.[11]

Employer Discrimination

Because it is based on utility maximization, Becker's model takes a broader view of the firm than simple profit-maximization. For example, an employer may be willing to sacrifice profits to avoid associating with a group of people that reduces his or her utility. Because a firm may be willing to sacrifice profits to satisfy the owner's taste for discrimination, we can make specific predictions regarding firms that discriminate in competitive, monopoly, or monopsony markets. We discuss these outcomes below in greater detail, as they have significant bearing on the persistence of discrimination in the sports marketplace.

In Becker's model, employers have preferences regarding employees with whom they do and do not want to associate. For example, a number of economists have studied discrimination against French-speaking hockey players (Francophones).[12] Some have found that whether a team discriminates depends in part on the players' positions—whether they are forwards or defensemen—and where the team is located. One study finds evidence of employer discrimination against French-speaking defensemen but not forwards.[13] Though some researchers have argued that the discrimination is rooted in differences in the style of play, other research focuses on evidence of

---

[11]Material in this section is based on Gary S. Becker, *The Economics of Discrimination* (1971).

[12]See, for example, Neil Longley, "The Underrepresentation of French Canadians on English Canadian Teams," *Journal of Sports Economics*, vol. 1, no. 3 (August 2000), pp. 236–256 Marc Lavoie, Gilles Grenier, and Serge Columbe, "Discrimination and Performance Differentials in the National Hockey League," *Canadian Public Policy*, vol. 13, no. 4 (December 1987), pp. 407–422; and Marc Lavoie, Gilles Grenier, and Serge Columbe, "Comment: Performance Differentials in the National Hockey League: Discrimination versus Style of Play Thesis," *Canadian Public Policy*, vol. 15, no. 1 (December 1989), pp. 461–469.

[13]J. C. H. Jones and W. D. Walsh, "Salary Determination in the National Hockey League: The Effects of Skills, Franchise Characteristics, and Discrimination," *Industrial and Labor Relations Review*, vol. 44, no. 4 (July 1988), pp. 592–604.

French Canadian Mathieu Darche plays for the Montreal Canadiens.

discrimination only by teams based in the English-speaking provinces of Canada. A more recent study finds strong evidence of a bias toward lower wages for French-speaking players born in Quebec by English-speaking Canadian teams but does not definitively attribute this difference to discrimination.[14]

To simplify matters, assume that there are only two groups of players, English-speaking (E) and French-speaking (F). To keep the focus on discrimination, assume for the moment that, although the players' styles may differ, they are equally productive. This way, in the absence of discrimination, demand for the two types of players would be equal. Becker measures the distaste that owners

---

[14]Neil Longley, "Salary Discrimination in the National Hockey League: The Effects of Location," *Canadian Public Policy*, vol. 21, no. 4 (December 1995), pp. 413–422. Others dispute these claims, criticizing the statistical analysis. See William D. Walsh, "The Entry Problem of Francophones in the National Hockey League: A Systematic Interpretation," *Canadian Public Policy*, vol. 18, no. 4 (December 1992), pp. 443–460, for a critique of Lavoie, Grenier, and Columbe. See Michael Krashinsky and Harry D. Krashinsky, "Do English Canadian Hockey Teams Discriminate Against French Canadian Players?" *Canadian Public Policy*, vol. 23, no. 2 (June 1997), pp. 212–216, and Longley's reply that immediately follows in the same issue (217–220). by Michael A. Curme and Greg M. Dougherty, "Competition and Pay for National Hockey League Players Born in Quebec," *Journal of Sports Economics*, vol. 5, no. 2 (May 2004), pp. 186–205.

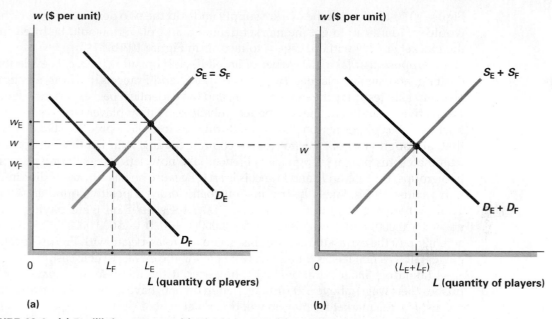

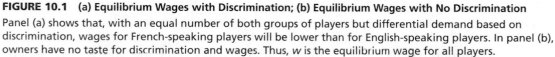

FIGURE 10.1 **(a) Equilibrium Wages with Discrimination; (b) Equilibrium Wages with No Discrimination**
Panel (a) shows that, with an equal number of both groups of players but differential demand based on discrimination, wages for French-speaking players will be lower than for English-speaking players. In panel (b), owners have no taste for discrimination and wages. Thus, w is the equilibrium wage for all players.

have for French-speaking players with the **discrimination coefficient** d_i (following Becker's notation, we use the subscripts i to denote employers, j to denote employees, and k to denote consumers). The discrimination coefficient is greater than zero if an owner feels that he pays an emotional (or *psychic*) cost in addition to the wage he pays a French-speaking player. He acts as if the wage were w for all E players and $w(1 + d_i)$ for all F's. If NHL owners have a taste for discrimination and prefer hiring English-speaking Canadians to hiring French-speaking Canadians, the demand for English-speaking Canadians (D_E) will be greater than that for French-speaking Canadians (D_F). In Figure 10.1a, we assume that there is an equal supply of each type of player ($S_E = S_F$). The difference in demand based on employer preferences leads to a difference in wages as well as a difference in the number of players hired.

As Michael Curme and Greg Dougherty point out, if the supply of English-speaking Canadians is greater than that of French-speaking Canadians, or the taste for discrimination (that creates the differences in demand) is great enough, teams may hire no French-speaking Canadians.[15] That is, there would be unequal access to work. To use an example from another sport, the National and American Leagues in baseball hired no blacks at all between 1890 and 1947. Alternatively, if there were no discrimination at all, we could simply add the two supply curves in

---

[15]Michael A. Curme and Greg M. Dougherty, "Competition and Pay for National Hockey League Players Born in Quebec," (2004).

Figure 10.1a to arrive at the market supply and add the two demand curves (which would be identical) to get the market demand, and players would be hired from the market supply without regard to race, as in Figure 10.1b.

Suppose that Jake, the owner of an NHL club outside Quebec, is evaluating, drafting, and signing players. Two players, Eddie and François, perform identically on every skill test, play the same position, and have identical past experience. From a productivity standpoint, they are perfect substitutes. Either player would sign a contract for $500,000 per season. However, during the interview process, Jake discovers that, although François has no trouble communicating with his English-speaking teammates, his primary language is French. Jake now separates the prospects into two groups: Eddie is an E, and François is an F. Because he has a taste for discrimination against all F's, Jake's discrimination coefficient is a positive number, say 0.2. Thus, when making his final decision, Jake feels as if he were paying Eddie $w_E = \$500,000$, and François $w_F = \$500,000(1 + 0.2) = \$600,000$. Jake does not actually pay the extra $100,000, but his desire not to associate with French-speaking players makes him feel as though he were paying the extra, psychic cost.[16]

Jake does incur additional cost, however, if the increase in demand for E's pushes their wages above $500,000. If enough owners have a taste for discrimination against F's, the market for players will be similar to that shown in Figure 10.1a, and owners with a taste for discrimination will pay higher wages than those without.

Discriminating clearly makes the team owner worse off financially. If Jake's taste for discrimination against F players makes the psychic and monetary wage of group F players greater than what he actually pays English-speaking players, w_E, he will not hire any players from group F. Jake is happier paying w_E to fill his roster with English speakers than he is paying a mixed team the competitive wage w. The economic cost of employing only English speakers depends on the elasticities of supply and demand. For example, if the supply of English-speaking players is perfectly elastic (a horizontal line), then owners do not have to increase w_E at all to hire more of them.

However, even prejudiced owners may employ F players if the players are willing to work for wages that are low enough. In the previous example, Jake's discrimination coefficient makes him feel that he is paying a wage premium of 20 percent. If the F's are willing to work for 20 percent less than E's, Jake would be willing to hire them. In this case, there would be unequal pay for equal work.

If the market for players is not competitive because players are heterogeneous, Jake may also end up with a mixed team. For simplicity, suppose E's and F's consist of good players (E_g and F_g) and bad players (E_b and F_b). If the E_g's are relatively scarce, Jake may exhaust the supply of E_g's, and he must choose between the less productive E_b's and the more productive F_g's. In such a case, Jake may maximize his utility by hiring some F_g's.

Discrimination clearly makes players in group F worse off. F's receive no offers as long as employers feel they pay F's more than the wage of equivalent

---

[16]As noted above, the neoclassical model does not explain *why* the owner feels this way. We discuss later the question of why people develop tastes for discrimination.

players in group *E*. Even if *F*'s are hired, they receive lower offers than equally productive *E*'s. *E* players are better off as a group because their chances of making the team, and their pay if they do, both increase. Although owners avoid associating with group *F* players, they pay for the privilege in the form of reduced profits. We stress that owners are worse off *financially* and not that they are worse off overall. Owners who discriminate do so willingly in order to maximize utility. In this case, utility maximization comes at the cost of reduced income.

STATISTICAL DISCRIMINATION   It is also necessary to consider the possibility that differences in average performance across groups exist. For example, on *average*, French-speaking Canadian players might have better offensive statistics and worse defensive statistics in college or junior hockey (the stepping-stone to the NHL for most Canadian players) than their English-speaking Canadian counterparts. The problem is that group averages are just that. They mask the individual variation *within* groups. Each player should be judged on his own merits, rather than those of the group to which he belongs. The use of group averages to judge individual productivity levels is called **statistical discrimination**.[17] Statistical discrimination differs from ordinary discrimination because it is based on incomplete information (group averages as opposed to individual-level data) rather than on the utility-maximizing choices of people with accurate information.

While it does not result from prejudice, statistical discrimination can have a very strong impact on a team's hiring practices. Consider, for example, a team that believes that a young French Canadian player has a 49 percent chance of being a successful player in the NHL, while a young English-speaking Canadian has a 51 percent chance of success. That team would not seek to have an almost equal split of French-speaking and English-speaking players. Because the team believes that any one English-speaking player is more likely to succeed than any one French-speaking player, it will hire only English speakers, at least until the pay differential becomes so great that the team is willing to take on players who are, on average, of lower quality.

Statistical discrimination is troublesome for two reasons. First, it may be profit-maximizing behavior on the part of firms. Even though assuming that all French-speaking Canadian players are weaker defensively than all English-speaking Canadian is inaccurate, teams may be correct on average if they always make this assumption when choosing individual players. Thus, they may feel justified in acting as discriminators. Second, statistical discrimination can become a self-fulfilling prophecy. If offensive-minded French-speaking Canadian forwards are drafted and defensive-minded ones are not, over time, league statistics will reflect that French-speaking Canadians are offensive-minded. Unfortunately, this means

---

[17]In the case of ethnicity, players are not able to switch groups. In some cases, however, employees may be able to switch from a less preferred group to a more preferred group in an attempt to signal to potential employers that they are highly productive. For example, a college degree may signal to employers that a person is highly productive. Employers would want potential employees to send this signal if it is costly to find out the truth about whether they are highly productive. For a detailed explanation of signaling, see Michael A. Spence, "Job Market Signaling," *Quarterly Journal of Economics,* vol. 87, no. 3 (August 1973), pp. 355–374.

that statistical discrimination and its consequences can occur even if the initial difference in offensive versus defensive ability stemmed from inaccurate perceptions.

Does Anyone Win with Employer Discrimination?

The impact of discrimination is clear for some groups. For example, discrimination harms employees who are the victims of discrimination. Employers lose profits but do so willingly in order to maximize utility. To see if any groups benefit economically from the employers' taste for discrimination, consider the case of racial discrimination in Major League Baseball. Blacks were effectively barred from organized baseball from 1888 to 1947 by a "gentlemen's agreement." Many black players who were good enough to play in the major leagues—some of them good enough to be admitted to baseball's Hall of Fame—were confined to the Negro Leagues, which lasted until the late 1950s.[18] Such players were certainly worse off.

One group that benefited from discrimination was white players of that era. Because blacks were excluded, more white players played in the major leagues than would have been possible otherwise. For purposes of illustration, we begin by assuming that all players are equally productive (homogeneous) and subsequently consider the more realistic case of variation in player quality. If all labor was equally productive, and 30 percent of the available labor force was black, in the absence of discrimination, roughly 30 percent of the players would be black. If there was a very large pool of available labor, the market supply curve (S) of players would have been a horizontal line, as shown in Figure 10.2. Players' wages would

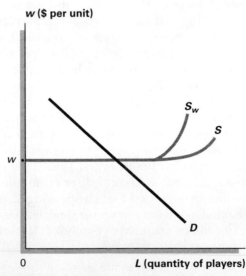

FIGURE 10.2   Discrimination with a Large Pool of Players
If the supply of players is large enough, discrimination by owners does not reduce wages.
Instead, owners hire only white players, and blacks are excluded from the market.

---

[18]For an excellent history of the Negro Leagues, see Robert Peterson, *Only the Ball Was White* (1970).

be set at the market level (w). In this case, the labor force is so large relative to demand that the labor supply curve for white players (S_w) results in the same wage. Because employers have a taste for discrimination, no blacks are hired, and far more whites are employed than if there were no discrimination.

In practice, players vary greatly in ability. If a team owner has a taste for discrimination against black players, and the quality of players of both races varies, that owner will choose marginal white players over blacks of greater ability to fill out the team's roster. In this case, white players of marginal ability would be the beneficiaries of the owners' taste for discrimination. Even with no formal or informal color line, as long as the increased utility from hiring a white player more than offsets the loss of utility from lower revenue, a discriminatory owner would hire the white player.

While white players would benefit and black players would be hurt by the color line, one set of beneficiaries may come as a surprise. The color line allowed owners of Negro League baseball teams—themselves largely African American— to draw on a large pool of players with few alternatives.[19] In addition, demand for Negro League baseball was much greater than it would have been with integrated major leagues. Figures 10.3 and 10.4 show that black fans' desire to see black players reduced their demand for Major League Baseball and increased their demand for Negro League baseball. In each case, D_S represents the level of demand for tickets when the leagues were segregated, and D_I represents the demand

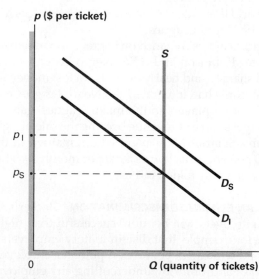

FIGURE 10.3   The Market for Attendance at the Negro League baseball games
When the National and American Leagues were integrated, demand for attendance at Negro League baseball games fell, as top players moved to the previously segregated leagues.

---

[19]While the word *Negro* is no longer used to describe African Americans, historians and economists still use the term *Negro Leagues* to describe the collection of all-black teams that competed in the era when baseball was segregated.

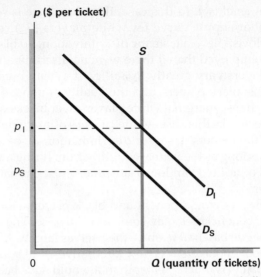

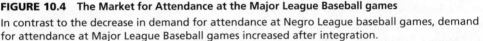

FIGURE 10.4   The Market for Attendance at the Major League Baseball games

In contrast to the decrease in demand for attendance at Negro League baseball games, demand for attendance at Major League Baseball games increased after integration.

for tickets when leagues were integrated. If each league plays a set schedule, the supply curve is a vertical line. Integration brings higher prices in the major leagues and lower prices in the Negro Leagues.

To see the Negro Leagues' reliance on segregation, one need look no further than their demise after Robinson and other Negro League stars jumped leagues. Attendance dropped sharply, and nearly every team lost money in 1947. By 1950, all but five major league teams had integrated. As Negro League teams lost increasing numbers of talented young players to the major leagues, gate receipts dwindled, teams folded, and a chief source of revenue became the sale of rights to their players to major league teams. Salaries for players who remained in the Negro Leagues dropped by about 50 percent, to as low as $200 per month. Despite valiant efforts to keep the league going, it finally folded in 1960.[20]

HOW COMPETITION CAN ELIMINATE DISCRIMINATION   Becker's theory implies that less discriminatory employers will be more successful than highly discriminatory employers. Suppose, for example, that discriminatory employers are willing to pay blacks $10 per hour and whites $15 per hour. A potential employer who is not prejudiced ($d_i = 0$) can enter and profit by undercutting any employer who uses white labor. He does so by hiring only blacks and paying them $11 per hour. Continued entry by unprejudiced employers increases the wage paid to black workers, driving down profits, which discourages further entry. If there are enough employers who do not discriminate, profits will eventually be driven to zero. At that point, any

[20]Robert Peterson, *Only the Ball Was White* (1970), pp. 203–204.

discriminatory employers who continue to pay higher wages to white workers are driven from the market because of their higher costs. They can remain only if they pay white workers the same wage that black workers receive. In professional sports, although the markets are not perfectly competitive, the competition to win games and championships is a powerful motivating force for owners to overcome their prejudices in order to maximize team quality. Allen Barra relates an example of how the pressure to win can overcome prejudice in his biography of legendary Alabama football coach Paul "Bear" Bryant. After reading a news account of Bryant's claim that African Americans would eventually play for Alabama, a fan remarked, "Well, I hope there're some Negro linebackers available. We need linebackers."[21]

A quick review of baseball's history supports the hypothesis that discriminators pay a price measured in wins for indulging their tastes. Historically, employers who integrated their teams more quickly generally won more games than those who were slower to integrate. For example, the Dodgers, who led the way to racial integration of the National League, won NL pennants in 1947 and 1949, and five pennants in the 1950s after winning only three in the previous 56 years. The Giants, who were the second fastest to integrate, won pennants in 1951 and 1954. Five of the six most successful teams (in terms of winning percentages) in the 1950s were the five teams that integrated most quickly.[22] Only the Yankees stood among the top teams in the 1950s with a relatively low percentage of black players.

While most owners were aware of the large pool of talent in the Negro Leagues before the color line was broken, only a few were willing to act on this knowledge. Bill Veeck attempted to purchase the Philadelphia Phillies in 1943 and planned to stock the team with stars from the Negro Leagues (for more information on Veeck, see his biographical sketch in Chapter 3 on pages 107–108). Major league owners blocked him by selling the team to someone else for much less than Veeck was willing to pay.[23]

More formally, Stefan Szymanski has demonstrated the impact of discrimination in a sample of teams from England's Football League over the period 1978 to 1993. Using a multiple regression model that holds team payroll constant, he has shown that teams with more black players during this period also won more frequently. Thus, a nondiscriminatory team could "buy" wins more cheaply than a team that wished to hire only white players.[24]

WHEN MARKETS ARE NOT COMPETITIVE Becker's theory also applies when workers are not homogeneous—and hence not perfect substitutes for one another—and when markets are not competitive, as is the case in professional sports. As in competitive markets, monopsonistic employers with a taste for discrimination

---

[21]Allen Barra, *The Last Coach: A Life of Paul "Bear" Bryant* (New York: W. W. Norton, 2005), p. 330.

[22]These teams were the Brooklyn (Los Angeles) Dodgers (0.592), Cleveland Indians (0.588), Boston (Milwaukee) Braves (0.554), Chicago White Sox (0.550), and New York (San Francisco) Giants (0.532).

[23]James A. Gwartney and Charles Haworth, "Employer Costs and Discrimination: The Case of Baseball," *Journal of Political Economy*, vol. 82, no. 4 (July–August 1974), pp. 873–881.

[24]Stefan Szymanski, "A Market Test for Discrimination in the English Professional Soccer Leagues," *Journal of Political Economy*, vol. 108, no. 3 (June 2000), pp. 590–603.

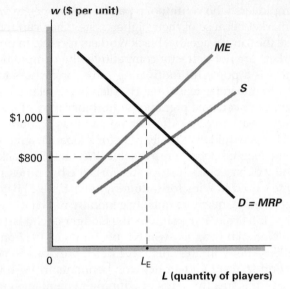

FIGURE 10.5   Monopsony Market for *E* Players
In a monopsony market, a single employer hires workers up to the point where the marginal expense for labor (*ME*) is equal to the *MRP*. At this employment level (*L*$_E$), the value of the last player is $1,000, but his wage is set at $800.

treat the wage of the less preferred group as though it were the $w \times (1 + d_i)$. Unlike competitive markets, which have many employers, a monopsonistic discriminatory employer is not driven from the market because workers have nowhere else to sell their services. Also, if a monopsony employer discriminates, players with lesser ability might earn more than players with greater ability. For example, suppose that *E*'s value to the team is $1,000 per game, and *F*'s value to the team is $1,500. If the employer has no taste for discrimination against *E*, it sets the monopsony wage at $w = $800 in Figure 10.5. Note that the demand curve in Figure 10.5, is also labeled as the marginal revenue product (*MRP*). Recall from Chapter 8 that the *MRP* is the value of an additional unit of labor to the firm. By setting the *ME* equal to *MRP*, the firm equates the marginal benefit and cost of additional labor.

Figure 10.6 shows the wages paid to *F* players by both a nondiscriminatory employer and one with a taste for discrimination. For the nondiscriminatory employer, the relevant demand curve is *D*, which, again, is also *MRP*. As in Figure 10.5, the nondiscriminatory monopsonist sets *ME* equal to the *MRP* and then takes the wage of $1,200 from the supply curve for the more productive *F* players. The discriminatory employer has a taste for discrimination coefficient equal to 0.2. This reduces the employer's demand curve from *D* to *D'* in Figure 10.6. Because the employer is a monopsonist, *F* players must accept $w/(1 + d_i) = $960 per game or be excluded from the market. As *F*'s cannot earn more than $960 in any other labor market, they accept the offer. Thus, despite earning 20 percent more than *E* players, who earn $800, *F* players are victims of discrimination.

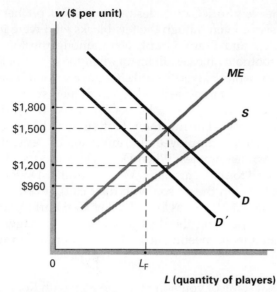

FIGURE 10.6 Monopsony Market for *F* Players

When a monopsonist also has a taste for discrimination, the wage of the group that is discriminated against may still receive higher wages than the preferred group. In this case, *F* players are more productive than *E* players, but the monopsonist employer has a taste for discrimination against *F*'s. They receive a wage of $960, but would have received $1,200 with no discrimination.

The actual *MRP* of *F*'s is $1,800, and they receive only $960 because of the combined forces of monopsonistic exploitation and discrimination. As such, they are paid $840 less than their contribution to the team, whereas *E*'s are paid only $200 less than their contribution to the team. Thus, *F*'s are paid more but are exploited to a much greater extent than *E*'s.

Employee Discrimination

Discrimination is not limited to employers. Prejudiced employees can also discriminate against their coworkers. Employees with a taste for discrimination regard the market wage, w, as $w(1 - d_j)$ if they must work with members of a group they do not like. Here, d_j represents the coefficient of discrimination for employees.

In the 1880s, a small number of black baseball players played in the American Association, then a "major" league. The first was Moses Fleetwood Walker, who played for Toledo in 1884. Fleetwood's brother Weldy also played part of one season with Toledo. A somewhat larger number of blacks played in the International League, which was a minor league. Some white players refused to play for teams that also hired blacks. Others played only grudgingly. In 1887, Douglas Crothers was suspended from the Syracuse Stars of the International League for refusing to appear in a team photo with Bob Higgins, a black pitcher on the team. Cap Anson, a star white player of the same era with a well-known dislike for black players, gained much notoriety from his refusal to play against blacks (though he did play when he learned he would not be paid otherwise) and his opposition to the New York Giants' desire to sign black pitcher George Stovey.[25] Such behavior persisted even though the few blacks who were in the game, such as Fleetwood Walker and Frank Grant, were among the top players in their leagues. It is a sad footnote on baseball history that the origin of the feet-first slide was from attempts of white players to spike Grant, a second baseman; he eventually invented the shinguard to protect himself from their spikes.

Discriminatory behavior toward blacks continued when the major leagues were reintegrated in 1947. During their first season, Larry Doby and Jackie Robinson were subjected to employee discrimination by several opposing teams and even by their own teammates. When Doby was introduced to his new team, several players refused to shake his hand. When the other Dodger players learned that Robinson was to begin the season with their club, several of his teammates, including such prominent players as Dixie Walker, Carl Furillo, and Eddie Stankey, circulated a petition opposing the decision. Dodger manager Leo Durocher's response was to call a team meeting at 1:00 in the morning in which he told his players, in part:

> Boys, I hear that some of you don't want to play with Robinson. Some of you have drawn up a petition. Well you know what you can use that petition for. . . . I'm the manager and I'm paid to win and I'd play an elephant if he could win for me and this fellow Robinson is no elephant. You can't throw him out on the bases and you can't get him out at the plate. This fellow is a great player. He's gonna win pennants. He's gonna put money in your pockets and mine. . . . Unless you wake up, these colored ball players are gonna run you right outa the park. I don't want to see your petition. . . . . The meeting is over. Go back to bed.[26]

Ironically, Pee Wee Reese, a Kentucky native and shortstop who ran the risk of losing his position to Robinson, refused to sign.[27] Early in the 1947 season, both the Philadelphia Phillies and St. Louis Cardinals threatened to strike rather than play against Robinson when he came to town. They relented only when faced with forfeiture and suspensions for not playing. In Robinson's first game in Philadelphia, however, the Phillies, led by their manager, Ben Chapman, hurled such savage abuse and obscenities at Robinson throughout the game that even those Dodgers who had opposed Robinson rallied around him.[28]

The extent of the economic harm prejudiced workers do to others and themselves depends on the nature of the labor market. If players are perfect substitutes for one another and the labor market is competitive, the Becker model predicts that prejudiced employees would never accept employment on a team that

---

[25]Robert Peterson, *Only the Ball Was White* (1970), p. 28.

[26]From Roger Kahn, *The Era: 1947–1957* (New York: Ticknor and Fields, 1993), p. 36.

[27]Ken Burns, "Bottom of the Sixth" episode, *Baseball* miniseries (Alexandria, Va: PBS video, 1994).

[28]Robert Peterson, *Only the Ball Was White* (1970), p. 199. Neither strike occurred after the league threatened suspensions.

is integrated because they perceive the market wage, w (that is offered to all employees), to be $w \times (1 - d_j)$. Thus, they require a wage of $w/(1 - d_j)$ in order to feel as though they have received the market wage. However, no such offers exist in a market with a perfectly elastic supply of players (horizontal supply curve). Crothers and others who refused to play alongside black players were simply replaced by those who would. If a prejudiced player with a taste for discrimination was traded to an all-white team, he would no longer require a wage premium. Thus, one possible outcome of employee discrimination is segregation. Although segregation is usually considered to be employer-driven, in this case, the taste for discrimination by employees creates the segregated market.[29]

As with employer discrimination, the results of the model are different when markets are not competitive. If players have different abilities, more than one market wage exists, and prejudiced employees may end up as teammates of players they dislike. For example, an owner may be willing to pay the wage differential demanded by a top player with a taste for discrimination because there are no viable substitutes of equal quality. Sometimes, workers are so necessary that employers cannot substitute for them. For instance, a title boxing match must, by definition, include the reigning champion. No black boxer fought for the world heavyweight championship between Jack Johnson's loss of the title in 1915 and Joe Louis's winning the title in 1937. The reason was not a lack of good black boxers. Instead, one could not substitute away from the white champions, and the white champions had such a strong distaste for fighting blacks (such a large d) that no match was possible.[30]

If markets cannot be segregated, and players of different groups are perfect substitutes for one another, those with a taste for discrimination will be driven from the market. The players who discriminate, not the players discriminated against, end up suffering the most. Becker argued that this eliminates employee discrimination from the market in the long run. Although employer and employee discrimination may have significantly depressed salaries of minorities as recently as the mid-1980s, many recent studies find that in the NFL, NBA, and MLB, wage differentials based on race have been eliminated.[31] If Becker's theory

---

[29]Gary Becker, *The Economics of Discrimination* (1971), p. 56.

[30]See David Margolick, *Beyond Glory: Joe Louis vs. Max Schmeling, and a World on the Brink* (New York: Alfred A. Knopf, 2005), p. 11.

[31]Orn B. Bovarsson, "A Test of Employer Discrimination in the NBA," *Contemporary Economic Policy*, vol. 17, no. 2 (April 1999), pp. 243–256, cites several recent studies that find no statistical evidence of employer discrimination. In addition, Jeffrey A. Jenkins, "A Reexamination of Salary Determination in Professional Basketball," *Social Science Quarterly*, vol. 77, no. 3 (September 1996), pp. 594–608, and Matthew S. Dey, "Racial Differences in National Basketball Association Salaries: A New Look," *American Economist*, vol. 41, no. 2 (Fall 1997), pp. 84–90, find no significant differences in NBA salaries by race. Lawrence M. Kahn, "The Effects of Race on Professional Football Players' Compensation," *Industrial Labor Relations Review*, vol. 45, no. 2 (January 1992), pp. 295–310, finds that as early as 1989 racial differences between blacks and whites were no more than 4 percent. In a survey article, Kahn also claims that there is no significant discrimination against blacks or Latinos in Major League Baseball. See Lawrence M. Kahn, "Discrimination in Professional Sports: A Survey of the Literature," *Industrial and Labor Relations Review*, vol. 44, no. 3 (April 1991), pp. 395–418.

is correct, there are two explanations for why this has happened. The competition between teams could have driven discriminatory owners or players from the market. Alternatively, the utility derived from the financial gains could be so much greater than the utility derived from discriminating that those with a taste for discrimination choose to stay in the market and bear the disutility of playing with groups they do not like.

Consumer Discrimination

Most research on salary differentials among black, white, and Latino baseball players indicates that neither race nor ethnic background affects salaries.[32] However, as we discuss below, evidence from both baseball and basketball indicates that discrimination still exists among consumers in the sports industry.

Consumers have a taste for discrimination if they prefer not to purchase goods or services from members of a specific group. For example, if a basketball fan has a taste for discrimination against black players, she perceives the price of admission to a game involving only white players to be p and the price of admission to a game in which blacks also play to be $p(1 + d_k)$, where d_k is the discrimination coefficient for consumers.

Consumer discrimination can be difficult to isolate in a typical product market because product characteristics, particularly product quality, can cause variations in demand that are not the result of discrimination. This is probably why evidence from empirical studies from studies of consumer discrimination is decidedly mixed. One study finds that Nielson television ratings of basketball games are higher when white players play more, but another finds that *Monday Night Football* ratings are higher when the game features a black quarterback.[33] Some also suggest that the recent influx of players from Europe and Latin America, such as Pau Gasol and Manu Ginobili, to the NBA reflects the desire of fans to see more white players.[34] By contrast, Ian Preston and Stefan Szymanski find no evidence that consumers have driven discrimination by professional soccer teams in England.[35]

To conclude that consumers discriminate, one must isolate the effect of players' race or ethnicity from other factors that affect consumer demand, such as the quality of the team or the facility in which it plays. To do this, some researchers have turned to the market for trading cards.[36] The results of these studies are also

---

[32]For more study results and discussion on this point, see Kahn, "Discrimination in Professional Sports" (1991).

[33]Mark T. Kanazawa and Jonas P. Funk, "Racial Discrimination in Professional Basketball: Evidence from Nielson Ratings," *Economic Inquiry*, vol. 39, no. 4 (October 2001), pp. 599–608. Eric M. Aldrich, Peter S. Arcidiacono, and Joseph L. Vigdor "Do People Value Racial Diversity? Evidence from Nielsen Ratings," *The B.E. Journal Of Economic Analysis and Policy*, vol. 5, no. 1 (2005), Article 4.

[34]Dan McGraw, "The Foreign Invasion of the American Game," *The Village Voice Online*, May 28–June 3, 2003, at http://www.villagevoice.com/news/0322,mcgraw,44409,1.html.

[35]Ian Preston and Stefan Szymanski, "Racial Discrimination in English Football," *Scottish Journal of Political Economy*, vol. 47, no. 4 (September 2000), pp. 342–363.

[36]For a different approach to consumer discrimination, see Daraius Irani, "Estimating Consumer Discrimination Using Panel Data: 1972–1991," in *Baseball Economics: Current Research*, ed. by John Fizel, Elizabeth Gustafson, and Lawrence Hadley (Westport, Conn.: Praeger, 1996).

mixed. A study by Curtis Nardinelli and Clark Simon finds that cards for white pitchers were 13 percent more expensive than the players' performances would justify and that nonwhite hitters' (i.e., non-pitchers') cards a about 10 percent too expensive. They found that the difference i particularly great for Latino players. A study by Torbin Anderson and Sumner J. La Croix, however, finds little evidence of discrimination against Latino players but indicates that black players are the victims of discrimination.[37]

Rodney Fort and Andrew Gill posit that some of the disagreement stems from consumers' confusion regarding race. They developed a continuous measure of race by showing people pictures and names of players and asking them "how black" and "how Hispanic" the players appeared to be.[38] Fort and Gill use these ratings to evaluate the impact of race and ethnicity on the price of the cards. They find that consumers discriminate more against players who, in the eyes of the respondents, appear to be "more black" or "more Hispanic."

Consumer discrimination can affect attendance in several ways. First, consumers could show their taste for discrimination by supporting teams that have fewer players from the group that they dislike. Second, consumers could follow teams that are integrated but do so with less intensity—going to fewer games, buying fewer jerseys, watching the team less on television. Perhaps most extreme, they could stop following the sport altogether if too many players come from the group they dislike.

Consumer discrimination is also reflected in advertising firms' choices of athletes as sponsors. Demand for athletes as endorsers is driven by consumers' desire to emulate people they admire. If audiences are predominantly white, and consumers have a taste for discrimination, firms seeking sponsorship opportunities may in turn discriminate against black athletes.

Evidence suggests that consumer discrimination continued in the NBA until the early 1990s. Salary differentials between blacks and whites persisted, and discriminatory consumers seemed to be the source of the differential in pay.[39] Lawrence Kahn and Peter Sherer find that blacks in the NBA earned about 20 percent less than equally productive white players in the mid-1980s.[40] A follow-up study by Barton H. Hamilton finds that the average salaries of black and white players had become virtually identical by the 1994–1995 season.

---

[37]See Curtis Nardinelli and Clark Simon, "Customer Discrimination in the Market for Memorabilia: The Case of Baseball," *Quarterly Journal of Economics,* vol. 105, no. 3 (August 1990), pp. 575–595; and Torben Anderson and Sumner J. La Croix, "Customer Discrimination in Major League Baseball," *Economic Inquiry,* vol. 29, no. 4 (October 1991), pp. 665–677.

[38]Rodney Fort and Andrew Gill, "Race and Ethnicity Assessment in Baseball Card Markets," *Journal of Sports Economics,* vol. 1, no. 1 (February 2000), pp. 21–38.

[39]Lawrence M. Kahn and Peter Sherer, "Racial Differences in Professional Basketball Players' Compensation," *Journal of Labor Economics,* vol. 6, no. 1 (January 1988), pp. 40–61; and Barton H. Hamilton, "Racial Discrimination and Professional Basketball Salaries in the 1990s," *Applied Economics,* vol. 29, no. 3 (March 1997), pp. 287–296.

[40]Lawrence M. Kahn and Peter Sherer, "Racial Differences in Professional Basketball Players' Compensation" (1988), p. 51.

However, Hamilton also finds, all else equal, that white players were more likely to be at the bottom end of the pay scale, near what was then the league minimum of $150,000 but that, at the upper end of NBA salaries, whites earned 19 percent more than equally productive blacks. He concludes that highly paid, highly visible stars are more likely to be subject to discrimination, while less visible bench players are not.[41]

Evidence of consumer discrimination also exists in men's Division I college basketball. Statistical techniques similar to those described above show that fans spend an additional $121,000 (as measured by home-gate revenues) if a white player is added to the team.[42] It is encouraging to note that research on consumer discrimination using the results of fan voting for all-stars in baseball shows that this type of discrimination has declined sharply since the 1970s and that a study on salaries of NBA players using data from the 1995–1996 season finds no evidence of discrimination, contradicting Hamilton's findings from just one year earlier. The lack of clear evidence of the presence of discrimination is itself a good indication that it is less prevalent than in the past.[43]

Unfortunately, consumer discrimination differs from other types of discrimination in one important regard: Market forces do not eliminate it over time. In fact, if consumers have a taste for discrimination against a particular group, and employers maximize profit, employers will not hire any members of that group. In the Becker model, it is the only form of discrimination that harms the group that is discriminated against without in turn damaging those with the taste for discrimination.

Discrimination by National Origin in European Soccer

Civil rights legislation the world over outlaws discrimination on the basis of "race, color, religion, sex, or national origin." Discrimination on the basis of national origin, however, has been a matter of dispute among the Union of Economic Football Associations (UEFA), the governing body of European Football; FIFA, the international governing body; and the European Union (EU) for more than 20 years. The problem lies in the conflicting motivations facing European club teams. Collectively, teams in each country worry that the influx of foreign players may reduce interest in their product. Individually, however, each team wants to put the best possible team on the field, regardless of where the players come from. This is particularly true of the Premier League teams in England, Germany, Italy, and Spain, who are constantly under pressure to advance to the Champions League. As a result, each individual club has a strong incentive to use foreign players. As a

---

[41]Barton H. Hamilton, "Racial Discrimination and Professional Basketball Salaries in the 1990s" (1997).

[42]Robert W. Brown and R. Todd Jewell, "Is There Customer Discrimination in College Basketball? The Premium Fans Pay for White Players," *Social Science Quarterly*, vol. 75, no. 2 (June 1994), pp. 401–412.

[43]Andrew F. Hanssen and Torben Anderson, "Has Discrimination Lessened over Time? A Test Using Baseball's All-Star Vote," *Economic Inquiry*, vol. 37, no. 2 (April 1999), pp. 326–352; and Mark Gius and Donn Johnson, "An Empirical Investigation of Wage Discrimination in Professional Basketball," *Applied Economics Letters*, vol. 5, no. 11 (November 1998), pp 703–705.

reflection of just how important foreign players are to European teams, only once in the 14 years from 1999 to 2012 has the winner of the "Golden Ball" (officially known as the "Ballon d'Or"), which is awarded to the European player of the year, played for a club in his native country.[44] While star players have long crossed national—and continental—boundaries, until 1991 UEFA rules strictly limited the number of foreign players, allowing only two per team. Such a policy, however, ran contrary to the letter and spirit of the Treaty of Rome, the agreement that has formed the groundwork of the European Union since 1957. In 1991, UEFA and the EU reached a compromise known as the "3 + 2 rule."[45] This rule limited each team to three starting players from other countries. Two more starters could be foreign citizens if they had lived in the club's country long enough.

Ironically, the incident that brought down both the 3 + 2 rule as well as the transfer system in Europe was not momentous. Jean-Marc Bosman tried to move from Liege (a team in the Belgian League) to Dunkerque (a French team) after his contract had expired. Liege blocked the move because it felt that Dunkerque did not offer a sufficient transfer fee. A **transfer fee** is a payment from one team to another to compensate for signing away a player. Bosman sued the Belgian League, claiming that the transfer system blocked the free flow of resources across European boundaries, a key element of the Treaty of Rome. In December 1995, the European Court of Justice ruled in Bosman's favor. It declared that the transfer system applied only when a player was under contract with a team and could not be applied at the end of the contract. It went on to declare that the 3 + 2 rule also blocked the free movement of resources and was illegal.[46]

Because the Court of Justice ruled that soccer was not exempt from the Treaty of Rome, UEFA changed its tack. It instead proposed several alternatives to the strict numerical quotas that had existed. However, none of these proposals were acceptable to the EU.[47]

UEFA's current regulation requires "eight players from every 25-man squad to have been developed in the fielding club's national association."[48] Research by

---

[44]Agence France Presse, "*Previous* FIFA Ballon d'Or Winners," *The Times of India,* January 10, 2012, at http://timesofindia.indiatimes.com/sports/football/top-stories/Previous-FIFA-Ballon-dOr-winners/articleshow/11430535.cms. Michael Owen was the only player who won the award playing in his native country, playing for Liverpool in 2001.

[45]Lindsey Valaine Briggs, "UEFA v. The European Community: Attempts of the Governing Body of European Soccer to Circumvent EU Freedom of Movement and Antidiscrimination Labor Law," *Chicago Journal of International Law,* vol. 6, no. 1 (Summer 2005), pp. 440–441.

[46]Wladimir Andreff and Paul Staudohar, "European and US Sports Business Models" (2002), p. 41.

[47]For more on the alternatives, see Lindsey Valaine Briggs, "UEFA v. The European Community" (2005), pp. 441, 448; "FIFA thumbs-up for 'six-plus-five' player rule," May 30, 2008. http://soccernet.espn.go.com/news/story?id=540901&cc=5901; and Andrew Hodgson, "Blatter bid to put limit on foreign players wins FIFA backing," May 30, 2008. *London Evening Standard* (Standard.co.uk), at http://www.thisislondon.co.uk/standard-sport/article-23488572-details/Blatter+bid+to+put+limit+on+foreign+players+wins+FIFA+backing/article.do, viewed August 4, 2009.

[48]Matt Scott, "Phil Jones's deal shows FIFA new rule drives up the price of English talent," *The Guardian,* June 9, 2011, at http://www.guardian.co.uk/football/2011/jun/10/phil-jones-fifa-rules-price/print, viewed May 31, 2012.

Roberto Pedace supports the idea that individual teams prefer to hire foreign players but not because it helps them win more games. Ironically, he finds that foreign players in the English Premier League (EPL) tend to be overpaid (i.e., are favored rather than discriminated against), and that the apparent source is customer discrimination. Pedace finds that having more players from South America significantly increases attendance.[49]

Positional Discrimination or Hiring Discrimination

Earlier in the chapter, we noted that the evidence on equality of access to North American professional leagues is mixed. A different but related question is whether minorities have equal access to all positions.[50] For example, since about two-thirds of the players in the NFL are black, one would expect about two-thirds of the players at each position to be black. One would also expect the racial balance of the coaches in the league to be similar to that of the players. As it turns out, these expectations are not realized.

Historically, positional discrimination, also known as **stacking**, has been an issue in both the NFL and MLB. Even today, whites dominate at some positions while blacks dominate at others. As recently as 2010, 83 percent of the quarterbacks in the NFL were white, as were 87 percent of the centers and 54 percent of the tight ends. At the opposite end of the spectrum, 86 percent of the running backs and 84 percent of wide receivers were black, as were 98 percent of the cornerbacks and 84 percent of safeties. In general, white players are more likely to be found on offense than on defense.[51]

Economists call the systematic steering of minorities to specific positions on the field and within the coaching ranks **role discrimination**. For example, if coaches erroneously assume that black players lack the strong arm and quick reactions needed to be a quarterback, then they discourage young black players from investing in the skills required to play quarterback.[52] If blacks are continually underrepresented at quarterback in youth, high school and collegiate football, an imbalance at the professional level naturally results.

Table 10.1 shows the racial and ethnic breakdown of Major League Baseball players for 2004. It shows that, although Latinos made up 26 percent of the league overall, 64 percent of shortstops and 32 percent of second basemen were Latino. In contrast, blacks were much more likely to be outfielders than their overall percentage would suggest, and whites were much more likely to be pitchers.

---

[49]Roberto Pedace, "Earnings Performance, and Nationality Discrimination in a Highly Competitive Labor Market as an Analysis of the English Professional Soccer League," *Journal of Sports Economics*, vol. 9, no. 2 (April 2008), pp. 115–140.

[50]Data in this section, unless otherwise noted, are from Richard E. Lapchick, et al., *The 2011 Racial and Gender Report Cards.*

[51]Despite these highly lopsided percentages, Richard E. Lapchick et al., state in *The 2011 Racial and Gender Report Card: National Football League* that stacking is much less of a concern than it has been historically because blacks now appear to have broken down the barrier at the quarterback position.

[52]The same argument is frequently used to explain why women are overrepresented in certain occupations and underrepresented in others.

TABLE 10.1 Racial and Ethnic Breakdown of MLB Players in 2004 at Selected Positions (%)

	Total	Pitchers	Catchers	First Base	Second Base	Third Base	Shortstop	Outfield
White	63	72	65	64	53	75	28	46
African American	9	3	2	15	15	5	7	26
Latino	26	22	33	20	32	19	64	25
Asian	3	3	0	2	0	0	1	3

Source: Richard E. Lapchick, et al., *The 2011 Racial and Gender Report Card: Major League Baseball,* The Institute for Ethics and Diversity in Sport, at http://www.tidesport.org/RGRC/2011/2011_MLB_RGRC_FINAL.pdf, viewed May 31, 2012.

The Racial and Gender Report Card does not separate players into specific infield positions after 2004, but in 2010, there were no African American catchers and only 5 percent of pitchers and 11 percent of infielders were African American, compared to 29 percent of outfielders. Thus, while opportunities for all races exist in the major leagues, positional segregation appears to be an ongoing concern.

There is simply not enough evidence to discuss race and positional segregation in hockey, as there have only recently been more than a handful of players of color. The most significant change in the makeup of hockey personnel in recent years is the large influx of European—particularly Eastern European—players since the fall of the Berlin Wall in 1989. The large influx of star players such as Peter Forsberg, Jaromir Jagr, and others improved the quality of play in the NHL. Although not all European players have enjoyed immediate success in the NHL due to the differences in the size of the ice surface and style of play, some teams have thrived after successfully signing top players from former Eastern Bloc countries such as Russia and the Czech Republic.

Role discrimination is a form of statistical discrimination. For example, if on average women do not know as much as men about sports, they could be systematically discouraged from pursuing roles as officials or broadcasters. The problem is that uncertainty causes employers to attribute the characteristics of the average person in the group to each member of the group. There is no way to determine without testing whether a specific woman has the knowledge to officiate a game. Unfortunately for women, if discrimination occurs early in the application process, they may never get the opportunity to reveal their skills. The same is true in positional discrimination. If, for example, black quarterback prospects are never given the opportunity to try out, they cannot demonstrate their skills to coaches and prove they are capable of playing the position.

Recent research by David Berri and Rob Simmons finds evidence of both role discrimination and employer discrimination against black quarterbacks in the NFL.[53] They note that, while about two-thirds of the players in the league are black, 73 percent of the quarterbacks who attempted 100 or more passes between 2000 and 2006 were white. In addition, they find that wage differences across race exist in some portions of the salary range. They construct a performance measure

---

[53]David J. Berri and Rob Simmons, "Race and the Evaluation of Signal Callers in the National Football League," *Journal of Sports Economics,* vol. 10, no. 1 (February 2009), pp. 23–43.

of quarterbacks that includes both running and passing productivity and show that, controlling for this measure, black quarterbacks at the upper half of the salary scale are compensated less than white quarterbacks of equal productivity. Thus, while salaries and playing opportunities have increased, Berri and Simmons' results indicate that more must be done to completely close the racial divide at the quarterback position.

DISCRIMINATION IN COACHING AND ADMINISTRATIVE RANKS   Concerns over equal access to work in the professional sports industry is not limited to players. A discrimination-free work environment should extend to the coaching ranks as well. If blacks had only recently entered professional sports in significant numbers, one might not expect to find many black head coaches. However, the racial composition of NFL players has been relatively constant for the last 10 years (as mentioned above, it is roughly one-third white and two-thirds black). Since many coaches are former players, one might expect two-thirds of the coaches to be black as well. However, from 2007 to 2010, 81 percent of head coaches in the NFL were white and only 19 percent were black. In 2011, the percentage of white head coaches dipped to 75 percent (26 white, 7 black, and 1 Latino).[54] While still far below the percentage of players, this represents an all-time high for coaching diversity in the NFL and is more than double the percentage of black coaches in 2003.

Latino and black baseball players are also less likely than whites to become coaches. The data in Table 10.2 show that, while the percentage of MLB managers who are black has remained roughly constant over the last decade, there has been a substantial increase in the number of Latino managers. It is also encouraging to see the upward trend in minority head coaches in the NBA, especially given that it has the highest percentage of black players of all the major professional sports leagues.

While women have had little more than a token role in the NBA and NHL and have not appeared at all as players in MLB or the NFL, they do work in administrative positions in all sports. The obstacles facing women in such positions vary with the nature of the jobs they hold. The value of having previously played the game is different for different jobs. General Managers, for example,

TABLE 10.2   Percentage of Black and Latino Head Coaches and Managers in the NBA, NFL, and MLB in 1991, 2000, and 2010

	1991	2000	2010
NBA	7	34	67
NFL	7	10	19
MLB			
Black	7	13	13.8
Latino	<4	3	13.8

Source: Richard E. Lapchick, et al., *The 2011 Racial and Gender Report Cards for the NFL, MLB and NBA,* The Institute for Ethics and Diversity in Sport, at http://tidesport.org, viewed June 1, 2012.

[54]Richard E. Lapchick, et al., *The 2011 Racial and Gender Report Card: The National Football League* (2011).

often evaluate talent and work closely with the coach on roster decisions, so people who have played the game have a significant advantage in obtaining these positions.[55] Thus, it is no surprise that none of the major sports teams has a woman in charge of personnel decisions.

Hiring records at the collegiate level are very similar to those at the professional level. In both coaching and administrative positions, Division I athletic programs are dominated by white males, but colleges' hiring records vary widely by sport. *The 2010 Racial and Gender Report Card: College Sport* gives Division I basketball programs an "A–" for providing opportunities to black basketball coaches, as 21 percent of all Division I coaches are black, and a "B" for FBS Football teams. Unfortunately, the number of female head coaches continues to decline, as about 60 percent of women's teams are coached by men. Also disappointing is that in Divisions II and III, the percentages of coaches who are minorities and women are typically worse than for Division I. As Richard Lapchick and his coauthors note, there are so few black head coaches in Division II and III that the number of women coaching men's teams is about equal to the number of blacks. Given these figures, it should not come as a surprise that white men hold the vast majority of positions at the highest administrative level. In 2009–2010, 100 percent of Division I conference commissioners were white and all but five were men, and almost 82 percent of Division I Athletic Directors were white males.[56]

We will return to the question of discrimination in collegiate athletics in Section 10.3. For now, we simply note that the imbalance at the collegiate level is likely to slow changes at the professional level, because top-level collegiate programs often serve as training grounds for future professional coaches. Thus, the argument that the absence of minority professional coaches is simply a "pipeline" problem (i.e., that the data will improve over time as more top-level candidates become available) seems misguided. If increases in the number of black NFL head coaches must be preceded by increases in Division I minority representation, the status quo will continue for some time. To date, the results of economic research on the topic are mixed. Research by Janice Madden shows that between 1990 and 2001, minority head coaches in the NFL have been significantly more successful than their white counterparts, raising the question of whether a double standard is in force in which blacks must have higher qualifications to reach the level of head coach than whites. In contrast, a study by Lawrence Kahn finds that race does not play a role in the dismissal of NBA coaches.[57]

---

[55]It may also be the case, however, that having prior playing experience does not yield any significant advantage. For example, it seems likely that a top-caliber women's basketball player would also be an effective evaluator of male basketball talent. If this is the case, then the absence of women as general managers in basketball would also represent role discrimination.

[56]Richard Lapchick, et al., *The 2010 Racial and Gender Report Card: College Sports,* The Institute for Diversity in Sport, at http://www.tidesport.org/RGRC/2010/2010_College RGRC_FINAL.pdf, viewed June 1, 2012.

[57]Janice Fanning Madden, "Differences in the Success of NFL Coaches by Race, 1990–2002: Evidence of Last Hire, First Fire," *Journal of Sports Economics,* vol. 5, no. 1 (February 2004), pp. 6–19; and Lawrence Kahn, "Race, Performance, Pay, and Retention among National Basketball Association Head Coaches," *Journal of Sports Economics,* vol. 7, no. 2 (May 2006), pp. 119–149.

Gender Equity—A Special Case?

Women rarely attempt to enter traditionally male professional or college sports, such as football. Gender differences in size, weight, and strength make such occurrences unlikely in the future as well. The only sports where men and women routinely compete against one another at the professional level are mixed doubles in tennis, auto racing, and as jockeys in horse racing. Mixed doubles (with one man and one woman per team) is a somewhat contrived event at major professional tournaments. Only in auto racing and thoroughbred horse racing do men and women regularly compete against one another under a common set of rules. Thus, those sports provide a unique opportunity to test for the existence of gender discrimination. A 1993 study of thoroughbred racing showed that, holding performance and experience constant, female jockeys receive significantly fewer racing opportunities. As a result, they have significantly fewer winnings than similarly qualified male jockeys.[58]

No systematic research has investigated the economics of gender discrimination in auto racing, most likely because there simply are too few women in racing for systematic study. Drag racing may be the exception. According to the *USA Today*, as of 2008, 39 women have competed in the four pro classes of drag racing, winning a combined total of over 80 races.[59] The relatively small number of successful female race drivers outside of drag racing (such as Danica Patrick) raises the question of whether so few women are found in the sport because of low demand or low supply. If no evidence exists that women are inferior race drivers or that they lack the human capital needed to become professional drivers, a lack of demand for women drivers represents employer discrimination. If the small number of drivers is the result of low supply (not many women pursue this career), it could be caused by role discrimination or not be discrimination at all.

FAN DEMAND FOR WOMEN'S SPORTS   Recall from Chapter 3 that television rights are a derived demand, driven by the demand of advertisers that are in turn determined by ratings. If the demand for women's sports is as high as that for men's sports, and no other cost differences exist, then in the absence of discrimination, there should be equal prize money.[60] Sponsors should have the same willingness to pay for advertising time regardless of gender.

Unfortunately for the players, owners, and fans of women's sports, there appear to be significant differences in the public demand for professional teams across gender. The demise of the U.S. women's professional soccer league (the WUSA) serves as a case in point. Although the league was unquestionably

---

[58]Margaret A. Ray and Paul W. Grimes, "Jockeying for Position: Winnings and Gender Discrimination on the Thoroughbred Track," *Social Science Quarterly*, vol. 74, no. 1 (March 1993), pp. 46–61.

[59]Gary Graves, "Women Are No Strangers to Drag Racing Success," *USA Today*, June 4, 2008, at http://www.usatoday.com/sports/motor/nhra/2008-06-04-women-drag-racing_N.htm, viewed June 1, 2012.

[60]It should be noted that men and women do not produce equivalent output in tennis matches, because men's matches are typically best of five sets and women's are best of three.

the preeminent women's league in the world, employed top stars from the Women's World Cup team such as Mia Hamm, and had benefited from over $100 million in initial investments, there simply was not enough demand from fans and sponsors to keep the league from folding in 2003. A retooled Women's Professional Soccer league began play in 2009 but lasted only until 2012.

Historically, women have fared better when it comes to individual sports. A striking example of how players can raise both awareness and earnings comes from the world of tennis. Open tennis tournaments began in the late 1960s. Today, both amateurs and professionals can qualify to play in an open tournament through a series of local and regional competitions. Initially, men's prize money was approximately 10 times that of women. In November 1972, the Women's U.S. Open champion, Billie Jean King, threatened to lead a boycott of the 1973 Open unless the prize money was equalized. Her protest succeeded, and prize money was eventually equalized. Gender-based differences in prize money persisted, however, in other major tournaments, such as Wimbledon and the French Open. As noted, prize differences in and of themselves are not sufficient for most economists to conclude that discrimination exists. However, in 1998, the ratings of HBO's coverage of Wimbledon went up by over 18 percent after it increased its coverage of women's play, which suggests that consumer demand for women's tennis was strong. However, women still received less than men for winning the singles title until 2007.[61] More recently, problems have arisen in women's professional golf and its organization, the LPGA. In 2009, Commissioner Carolyn Bivens was forced to resign amid concerns by top players over the loss of seven tournaments between 2007 and 2009 and a failed attempt to force the players to adopt an English-only policy.[62]

10.3 TITLE IX AND DISCRIMINATION IN COLLEGE SPORTS

Title IX is the most important measure ever undertaken to promote gender equity in sports in the United States. It has completely changed the face of scholastic and collegiate opportunities for women. Some even ascribe the success of the WNBA and the U.S. Women's World Cup soccer team directly to Title IX. It has not, however, been universally praised. Many claim that Title IX has denied opportunities to as many people as it has helped.

Though Title IX is a lightning rod for both proponents and detractors of women's athletics, it began as a seemingly innocuous section of the 1972 Educational Amendments to the 1964 Civil Rights Act. For such an important

---

[61]"Not about Money: HBO Declines to Renew Wimbledon Contract after 25 Years," *CNN/SI*, June 28, 1999, at http://www.cnnsi.com/tennis/1999/wimbledon/news/1999/06/28/hbo_wimbledon/index.html. Another frequently cited example of women's sports eclipsing men's in popularity is that ratings from television broadcasts of the Olympics show that women's figure skating and gymnastics are consistently among the most watched events.

[62]Associated Press, "Evans Takes Over as Acting Commish," *ESPN Golf*, July 13, 2009, at http://m.espn.go.com/golf/story?storyId=4323583, viewed September 11, 2012.

piece of legislation, Title IX itself is remarkably unimposing, measuring only one sentence in length. It reads:

> No person in the United States shall, on the basis of sex, be excluded from participation in, be denied the benefits of, or be subjected to discrimination under any educational program or activity receiving federal financial assistance.[63]

Three years later, the Department of Health, Education, and Welfare established three areas of regulatory jurisdiction:

1. Financial aid
2. Other benefits and opportunities
3. Participation in athletics

The third of these areas is directed at providing equal access to interscholastic and intercollegiate athletics. Congress established compliance guidelines for athletics in a 1979 amendment to the original legislation. Compliance can be achieved in one of three ways: proportionality, program expansion, or accommodation of the interests and abilities of the student body.

Proportionality means that the percentage of women who participate in sports at a university should approximate the percentage of female undergraduates enrolled at the school. For example, if women make up 55 percent of a school's undergraduate enrollment, approximately 55 percent of the athletes participating on the school's teams would have to be women. The Office of Civil Rights of the Department of Education oversees the enforcement of Title IX and uses a ± 5 percentage point rule in its interpretation of this test (e.g., if a school's enrollment is 55 percent female and 50 percent of the school's athletes are women, the school would be in compliance).

To show program expansion, the college must demonstrate that it has increased and continues to increase opportunities for the underrepresented gender. This criterion is open to interpretation. Depending on how one interprets the word *expansion*, women's sports could achieve proportionality with men in very short order, or it could take an extremely long time to reach equal or proportional programming levels for men and women.

Finally, colleges may show that they have fully accommodated the interests and abilities of the underrepresented sex. It is also difficult to use this criterion to challenge a school, because the school itself can be the judge of a student's ability to participate.

Each of these criteria leaves room for interpretation. Perhaps because it is a numerical measure and thus most easily checked, challenges to schools' compliance with Title IX have generally been based on the proportionality standard.[64]

---

[63]U.S. Dept. of Justice, Civil Rights Division, *Title IX Legal Manual,* January 11, 2001, at http://www.usdoj.gov/crt/cor/coord/ixlegal.htm.

[64]Andrew Zimbalist, *Unpaid Professionals* (Princeton, N.J.: Princeton University Press, 1999), p. 63.

Like most legislation, Title IX has had both intended and unintended effects. The balanced-budget approach to changes in athletic funding, in which one program's budget must be cut to increase another's has greatly contributed to the controversy over the implementation of Title IX guidelines, as men's sports have at times paid the ultimate price—cancellation of their program—in order to accommodate new women's programs. According to the Independent Women's Forum, which documents the effect of Title IX quotas, over 350 men's programs were discontinued between 1992 and 1997.[65] Among Division I schools, in 54 percent of cases, schools that dropped men's teams cited gender equity as a "great or very great" influence on their decisions.[66] These schools claimed that, by forcing them to cut opportunities for men in order to open opportunities for women, Title IX imposed a zero-sum game on them.

Whatever its impact on men's sports, Title IX has clearly increased the number of women taking part in athletics. The participation in sports by high school girls (also covered by Title IX) increased from 294,000 in 1971 to over 3 million in 2011.[67] Unfortunately, as noted above, as the number of women and girls participating at the high school and collegiate level has increased, the number of women working as head coaches has steadily fallen since the passage of Title IX. There are several potential explanations for this decline, ranging from the extraordinary time demands required to work as a head coach, which may disproportionately burden women who are also primary care givers at home to discrimination by employers (Athletic Directors), who are mostly male, to the increased attractiveness of women's team head coaching positions as salaries increased after Title IX. Recent research on coaching quality in Division I women's softball has shown that the difference is not attributable to differences in ability.[68]

Although Title IX is almost certain to continue as a source of ongoing debate, it seems clear that it will remain. After much contention, the Secretary of Education's Commission on Opportunity in Athletics concluded that Title IX had resulted in 30 years of great progress for women and girls and that it should remain, with the dual goals of continuing this progress and retaining opportunities for boys and men. In the words of then- U.S. Secretary of Education Rod Paige, "Without a doubt, Title IX has opened the doors of opportunity for generations of women and girls to compete, to achieve and pursue their American Dreams. This Administration is committed to building on those successes."[69]

---

[65]Jessica Gavora, *Tilting the Playing Field* (San Francisco: Encounter Books, 2002), p. 53.

[66]" 'Open to All' Title IX at Thirty," *Report of the Secretary of Education's Commission on Opportunity in Athletics*, p. 19, at http://www.nacua.org/documents/TitleIX_Report_022703.pdf.

[67]" 'Open to All' Title IX at Thirty," p. 13; and Kelli Anderson, "Nine for IX," *Sports Illustrated*, May 7, 2012, p. 49.

[68]Peter von Allmen, "Coaching Women and Women Coaching: Pay Differentials in the Title IX Era," in *The International Handbook on the Economics of Women's Sports*, ed. by Eva Marikova Leeds and Michael A. Leeds (Cheltenham, U.K.: Edward Elgar, forthcoming).

[69]" 'Open to All' Title IX at Thirty," p. 2.

BIOGRAPHICAL SKETCH

Branch Rickey

The greatest proof of Rickey's genius was that you always knew what he was doing—except when he was doing it to you.

—*Bill Veeck*[1]

Even if Branch Rickey had never broken baseball's color line, he would still be remembered as one of baseball's greatest innovators. In fact, by the time Rickey first joined the Dodgers at the age of 62, he had already experienced a full career in baseball.

Born in 1881, Wesley Branch Rickey was raised in a staunch Methodist family. A budding baseball career pretty much ended one day in 1903 when he refused to play on a Sunday. For the rest of his life—with the exception of a special war bonds drive during World War II—Rickey never attended a ballgame on a Sunday, though—some were quick to point out—that did not stop him from calling the ballpark to check on the day's gate receipts.

Rickey's preoccupation with money probably stemmed from an impoverished upbringing. Rickey was so poor that he had to delay going to college for several years after he graduated from high school. He later recalled that when he finally went to Ohio Wesleyan University, "[d]uring my first term . . . I had only one pair of pants, and nobody saw me wear anything else."[2]

Rickey's frugality was to follow him when he assumed a front office job with the St. Louis Cardinals, which had hired him away from their crosstown rivals, the Browns, in 1916. Frustrated that his scouts would frequently identify talented minor league players only to lose them to wealthier teams such as the New York Giants, Rickey began to buy minor league teams so as to keep players within the fold. This was the beginning of baseball's "farm system." The Cardinals' system became so extensive and so laden with talent (the products of that system included Hall of Famers Dizzy Dean, Joe Medwick, and Stan Musial) that the Cardinals displaced the Giants as the National League's dominant team in the 1930s. Rickey's spending on the team, however, eventually ran afoul of the team's ownership, and in 1943, at the age of 62, he headed east to Brooklyn to become president and 25 percent owner of the Dodgers.

While rebuilding the Dodgers' farm system in the early and mid-1940s, Rickey introduced a number of other innovations that are now taken for granted. He was the first to use a pitching machine and to have players practice their slides in sliding pits. Inspired by Dwight Eisenhower's account of preparations for D-Day, Rickey borrowed the philosophy to create "Dodgertown," in Vero Beach, Florida. Dodgertown was a vast complex where the entire Dodger system, minor leaguers and major leaguers alike, could receive instruction at one time.

Rickey became a well-known figure to New York sportswriters, who dubbed him "The Mahatma" because they saw Rickey's image in John Gunther's description of Mohandas "Mahatma" Gandhi as "a combination of God, your father, and Tammany Hall."[3] His double-talk was so renowned that his office in Brooklyn became known as "The House of Winds." One thing about which Rickey was absolutely silent was his plan to break baseball's color line.

Rickey took great care in finding the right player to integrate the major leagues. With a stealth that befitted a Cold War spy novel, Dodger scouts fanned the nation, ostensibly looking to recruit players for a new Negro League team to be called the "Brooklyn Brown Dodgers." Ruling out established stars, such as Satchel Paige or Buck O'Neill, as being too old to be able to establish careers in a new league and young stars, such as Roy Campanella or Don Newcombe, as being too inexperienced to withstand the pressures of being the first player to cross the color line, Rickey settled on Jackie Robinson, a rising star with the Kansas City Monarchs.

On October 23, 1945, the Brooklyn Dodgers revealed that they had signed Robinson to a contract with their top farm club, the Montreal Royals. Rickey had carefully chosen both the signing date and the ball club to which he assigned Robinson. The date was early enough that other players would know that they were likely to play with a black ballplayer and could arrange for a trade if they objected to doing so. The Montreal club was far enough out of the limelight and from America's overheated racial environment to allow Robinson some chance at a normal environment. (Even so, he recalled being close to a nervous breakdown by the end of the season.)

Soon after signing Robinson, Rickey had to withstand pressure from other owners—among them the legendary Connie Mack—who called to complain that he was ruining the game; they arranged a vote on the Dodgers' move in which Rickey cast the only approving vote. Far from being discouraged at the attitudes of the other owners, Rickey quickly soon signed the second, third, fourth, and fifth black baseball players to contracts.

Rickey also had to deal with on-the-field problems. At first he had to reassure the manager in Montreal, a Mississippian named Clay Hopper, who asked, "Mister Rickey, tell me—do you really think a nigra's a human being?"[4] Rickey was so reassuring and Robinson's play and demeanor so exemplary that Hopper eventually became one of Robinson's biggest backers. After Robinson's outstanding year in Montreal, Rickey then had to convince the Dodgers' manager, Leo Durocher, and the team's Mississippi-born broadcaster, Red Barber, to support his move.

Though he is fondly remembered by many as the first owner to sign a black player and promote him to the major leagues, some have questioned both his motivation and methods. For example, Rod Fort and Joel Maxcy note that while most MLB teams compensated the Negro League teams for signing away their players, Rickey did not compensate the Monarchs for signing Robinson. They go on to argue that the Negro Leagues were a viable competitor to MLB and that the strategy of signing top Negro League players was consistent with that of a monopoly defending its markets, dooming the rival league to failure. Whatever his motivation, Branch Rickey's efforts against considerable resistance from other owners paved the way for integrated baseball by the latter 1940s.

In 1950, Walter O'Malley, who also owned 25 percent of the Dodgers and was Rickey's rival for control of the club, gained control of another 25 percent of the Dodgers and forced Rickey out as president. Rickey quickly landed a position as vice-president and general manager of the Pittsburgh Pirates, where he built the foundation of a team that won the 1960 World Series (including stealing a young prospect named Roberto Clemente from the Dodger organization).

Rickey continued to affect baseball well in the 1960s. His attempt to create a rival Continental League forced the National League into its first expansion of the century and led the National League to replace the departed Dodgers and Giants with the

(Continued)

(*Continued*)

New York Mets. In 1963, Rickey returned to the Cardinals as a consultant. He helped oversee the 1964 Cardinals as they appeared in and won the World Series, their first win since the 1946 team, which Rickey also built. Branch Rickey died in 1965, after spending almost 70 years in baseball and living long enough to share the podium at the Baseball Hall of Fame induction of his good friend, Jackie Robinson.

[1]Bill Veeck, *The Hustler's Handbook* (Durham, N.C.: Baseball America Classic Books, 1996), p. 100.

[2]Harvey Frommer, *Rickey and Robinson* (New York: Macmillan, 1982), p. 38.

[3]Harvey Frommer, *Rickey and Robinson* (1982), p. 87. Tammany Hall was where New York City's notorious political machine had been headquartered, so that any political boss in New York was dubbed "a Tammany Hall politician."

[4]Harvey Frommer, *Rickey and Robinson* (1982), p. 120.

Sources: John Helyar, *Lords of the Realm* (New York: Ballantine Books, 1994); Harvey Frommer, *Rickey and Robinson* (New York: Macmillan, 1982); and Bill Veeck, *The Hustler's Handbook* (Durham, N.C.: Baseball America Classic Books, 1996). Rodney Fort and Joel Maxcy, "The Demise of the African American Baseball Leagues: A Rival League Explanation," *The Journal of Sports Economics*, vol. 2, no. 1 (February, 2001), pp. 35–49.

Summary

This chapter introduces economic theories of discrimination and uses them to describe how the tastes and preferences of employers, employees, and consumers can affect wages of athletes. Evidence shows that, although discrimination was overt in the 1940s, it has diminished over time. Examples from baseball in the 1950s support the hypothesis that discriminators will suffer lower profits or at least lower success rates, as measured in wins. There is evidence that some discrimination on the part of consumers still creates wage differentials in sports such as basketball. There is also substantial evidence that positional discrimination still exists in the NFL and in other sports on the playing field as well as in the coaching ranks. The implementation of Title IX in the 1970s stands as a watershed event in the effort to achieve gender equity in college sports.

Discussion Questions

1. Think of recent events from the sports industry that show a taste for discrimination. Do they represent consumer, employer, or employee discrimination?
2. Discuss the role of the media in shaping perceptions about racial and ethnic diversity in professional and amateur sports.
3. How might the development of the NFL and MLB have been different if blacks had not been excluded from these leagues during the years that spanned World War II?
4. Identify specific economic concepts and theories about discrimination in Leo Durocher's statement about Jackie Robinson on page 338.

5. If implementing Title IX means that men's sports must experience a reduction in funding, should it be eliminated?

6. Discuss the implications of a government policy that any network that intends to cover the Olympics must devote equal air time to men's and women's events.

Problems

10.1. Suppose the competitive salary in independent league baseball is $20,000 per season. One team owner has a taste for discrimination against all nonwhite players. Her coefficient of discrimination against Latinos is 0.20, and her coefficient of discrimination against blacks is 0.18. What would she consider the salaries of people who are members of these two groups to be? If the supply of players were perfectly elastic, how many of each group would be hired?

10.2. How can you determine if a running back in the NFL is suffering from wage discrimination? Would the process be the same for a lineman?

10.3. Under what circumstances would an owner be able to practice employer discrimination over a long period of time?

10.4. Suppose that the supply of both Hispanic and white pitchers (of equal quality) were perfectly elastic. Using supply and demand graphs, show the number of each player type hired by an owner with a taste for discrimination against Hispanics and those hired by a nondiscriminating owner.

10.5. Use Becker's model to explain why sponsors who discriminate will likely experience lower profits for doing so.

10.6. Is discrimination by referees best characterized as employer discrimination, employee discrimination, customer discrimination, or none of these? Explain your reasoning.

10.7. Using supply and demand graphs, show how positional segregation can occur even if only the players (including potential future players) believe that such discrimination exists.

10.8. True, false, or uncertain: Title IX compliance requires equal expenditures on men's and women's sports. Explain your answer.

10.9. Use what you know about the prisoner's dilemma to explain why the English Premier League teams such as Arsenal have so many foreign players even when, as a group, the Premier League teams agree that they want to limit the number of foreign-born players.

10.10. Draw a set of indifference curves (as described in Appendix 2A) depicting an owner with a taste for discrimination against Francophones. Put Anglophones on the horizontal axis.

PART FIVE

Sports in the Not-for-Profit Sector

CHAPTER 11

The Economics of Amateurism and College Sports

*I hope **he** doesn't fire **me**.*

—Gordon Gee, President of Ohio State University,

when asked if he would fire the school's football coach[1]

INTRODUCTION

At first glance, a chapter on intercollegiate athletics might seem like a departure for a book that has thus far focused on professional sports. After all, colleges and the NCAA spend considerable time, money, and energy reminding the public that intercollegiate athletics is an *amateur* undertaking. In fact, though, an analysis of intercollegiate athletics echoes themes and uses techniques from all the preceding chapters.

How and whether to maximize profits are just as relevant questions for an athletic director as for a team owner. Similarly, the exercise of monopoly and monopsony power plays a significant role in college athletics. While intercollegiate teams do not play one college off against another in an attempt to get a better stadium deal, colleges are very concerned about the public-good aspects and

---

[1] Pat Forde, "Tressel's End Fits with Saga's Pattern," *ESPN College Football,* at http://sports.espn.go.com/ncf/columns/story?columnist=forde_pat&id=6607408, viewed May 26, 2012.

spillovers of their athletic teams. Finally, many of the factors that determine how labor markets in professional sports function—and fail to function—are again relevant at the college level.

LEARNING OBJECTIVES

After reading this chapter, you will be able to:

- Appreciate how the "Olympic ideal" of amateurism developed and was integrated into intercollegiate sports.

- Identify the benefits and costs of intercollegiate sports to a university, and explain why colleges might want to support athletics even if they are not profitable.

- See how the NCAA can be viewed as a regulatory agency, a club, and a cartel and how each framework affects the interpretation of the NCAA's actions.

- Recognize how student-athletes benefit—and fail to benefit—from their college experience.

11.1 THE TROUBLESOME CONCEPT OF AMATEURISM

Much of the controversy surrounding college sports and the NCAA centers on the role of amateurism in college sports. The Knight Commission, an independent organization, founded in 1989 in response to the "commercialization of college sports," nicely summarized the case for amateurism in 2001.[2] In its otherwise critical report on the state of college sports, it claimed, "At one time…[a]mateurism was a cherished ideal. In such a context, it made sense to regard athletics as an educational undertaking. Young people were taught values ranging from fitness, cooperation, teamwork, and perseverance to sportsmanship as moral endeavor."[3] Many of the restrictions that colleges routinely place upon themselves—and violate—stem from the tension created by trying to uphold the notion that student-athletes are students first and athletes second. The idealized image of the past, however, is an illusion.

A Brief History of Amateurism and the Olympic Ideal

Long after the Olympics abandoned amateurism as a condition for competing, American colleges and universities remain wedded to the idea that their athletic teams should consist of students who engage in sports as a pastime rather than as a profession. Those who call for the "deprofessionalization" of college athletics

---

[2]Knight Foundation Commission on Intercollegiate Athletics, 2001. A Call to Action: Reconnecting College Sports and Higher Education (Miami: John S. and James L. Knight Foundation), p. 13, at http://www.knightcommission.org/images/pdfs/2001_knight_report.pdf.

[3]Mark Alesia, "Tourney Money Fuels Pay-to-Play Debate," *Indianapolis Star*, April 1, 2006, at http://www.indystar.com/apps/pbcs.dll/article?AID=/20060401/SPORTS/604010509.

often evoke the image of Olympic purity and sometimes explicitly urge colleges to "return to the Greek notion of amateur competition."[4] However, the historical record shows that the modern view of amateurism is shaped less by the Greek Olympic ideal than 19th-century British class divisions.

THE ORIGINAL OLYMPIC GAMES   The Olympic Games were one of four sets of Greek athletic contests, the other three being the Pythian, Nemean, and Isthmian Games. The Olympics were first held in 776 B.C. (the earliest recorded date in history) and continued every four years for over a millennium to honor the Greek god Zeus. These athletic competitions had a deeper, more spiritual role in the lives of the ancient Greeks than sporting events have in the lives of people today. Athletic contests were an integral part of religious festivals, not a sideshow like the modern Thanksgiving Day football games. The ancient Olympic Games arose "because Olympia was already an established sacred site, not the other way round."[5]

In the worldview of the ancient Greeks, people could rise above the limits of their mortality by defying death and performing heroic deeds in war. When there was no war to fight, the Greeks replaced the battlefield with the athletic field. The word *athlete* comes from the Greek word *athlos,* which means "conflict," or "struggle." In struggling against one another and against adversity, the participants came to resemble the gods they worshipped. Initially, the rewards for success at the Games were crowns of olive sprigs, which became the reward when the modern Olympic Games were revived. This practice was supposed to symbolize the pure motives of the competitors, who sought only the joy and glory of competition.

The practice of awarding an olive crown stems from the legend that surrounds the origins of the Games. It states that in order to win the hand of the daughter of King Oenomaus and hence inherit the kingdom, Pelops, a young Greek hero, first had to beat Oenomaus in a chariot race. Having won the race—and in the process killing Oenomaus—by sabotaging the king's chariot, Pelops tried to dispel the impression that he sought personal gain. He turned down the gold that was part of his prize for winning the race and asked instead to mark his victory with a crown made of a branch from a wild olive tree.

---

[4]Gordon Gee, then-president of the University of Colorado, quoted in Shannon Brownlee and Nancy Linnon, "The Myth of the Student-Athlete," *U.S. News and World Report,* January 8, 1990, p. 50. See also Welch Suggs, "The Demise of the 'Amateur Ideal,' " *Chronicle of Higher Education,* October 29, 1999, pp. A75–A76. The earliest known reference to an athletic contest was the funeral games that Achilles staged for his friend Patroclus in *The Iliad.*

[5]Quotation taken from Moses Finley and H. W. Pleket, *The Olympic Games: The First Thousand Years* (New York: Viking Press, 1976), p. 15. The other games honored Apollo, Zeus, and Poseidon. See Finley and Pleket, *The Olympic Games* (1976), pp. 23–25; Lynn Poole and Gray Poole, *History of Ancient Greek Olympic Games* (New York: Ivan Obolensky, Inc, 1963); B. Kidd, "The Myth of the Ancient Games," in *Five Ring Circus: Money, Power and Politics at the Olympic Games,* ed. by Alan Tomlinson and Garry Whannel (London: Pluto Press, 1984), p. 73; Francis Dealy, *Win at Any Cost: The Sell Out of College Athletics* (New York: Birch Lane Press, 1990), pp. 31–32 and 60; and Lawrence Hatab, "The Greeks and the Meaning of Athletics," in *Rethinking College Athletics,* ed. by Judith Andre and David James (Philadelphia: Temple University Press, 1991), pp. 32–35.

Even in ancient Greece, amateurism had little to do with reality. The olive crown given to the winners of the Olympic Games masked an array of greater rewards. Those selected to compete in the Games were regarded as heroes in their home cities. Honors, favorable marriages, and cash awaited them, especially if they returned victorious. According to Plutarch, Athenian winners at the Olympic Games were awarded 500 drachmai by their grateful city as early as 600 B.C. An Athenian inscription from the fifth century B.C. notes that Athens rewarded citizens who won an Olympic event with a free meal every day for the rest of their lives.[6] As a result of the ever-increasing prizes for victors at the Olympic Games, athletes earned enough to train full-time. "[A] rising young sports star [could] support himself entirely by athletics.... Awards in Athens, for example, totaled an estimated $600,000 in today's terms."[7] They also began to specialize in certain events, further detaching the Games from their original connection to warfare.[8] After the Romans conquered Greece and took on its customs in the second century B.C., the Olympics became completely professionalized and slowly degenerated until Christian Emperor Theodosius stopped them in A.D. 393, when he banned all pagan practices.[9]

THE BRITISH ETHIC AND THE RISE OF THE MODERN OLYMPICS   By the 19th century, the Olympic Games of ancient Greece had been forgotten by all but a few historians and archeologists. However, as the British came to dominate the economics, politics, and culture of Europe, their brand of "muscular Christianity" assumed increasing importance. The British, more than any country, took Juvenal's claim *mens sana in corpore sano* ("a sound mind in a sound body") to heart. The Duke of Wellington found a practical application of this admonition when he attributed his victory over Napoleon at Waterloo to the sports his soldiers played at British public schools.[10]

For the rest of Europe, the impetus to develop sports programs sprang from defeat on the battlefield. Humiliated by Napoleon, the German states expressed their nationalism and combated the popular perception that they were physically inferior to the French through a mass gymnastics association known as the *Turnverein*, or Turner Movement.[11]

---

[6]Moses Finley and H. W. Pleket, *The Olympic Games* (1976), pp. 77–78; and University of Pennsylvania Museum of Anthropology and Archeology, "The Real Story of the Ancient Olympic Games," 1996, at http://www.upenn.edu/museum/Olympics/olympicathletes.html.

[7]Tony Perrotet, *The Naked Olympics* (New York: Random House, 2004), p. 53.

[8]Moses Finley and H. W. Pleket, *The Olympic Games* (1976), pp. 70–71; Francis Dealy, *Win at Any Cost* (1990), p. 60; and Lawrence Hatab, "The Greeks and the Meaning of Athletics" (1991), pp. 31–35.

[9]Lawrence Hatab, "The Greeks and the Meaning of Athletics" (1991), p. 35; Richard Mandell, *The Nazi Olympics* (New York: Ballantine Books, 1972), pp. 4–5; Lynn Poole and Gray Poole, *History of Ancient Greek Olympic Games* (1963), pp. 24–25 and 33; and Bruce Kidd, "The Myth of the Ancient Games" (1984), pp. 72–80.

[10]The Duke of Wellington is alleged to have said, "The Battle of Waterloo was won on the playing fields of Eton." See Richard Mandell, *The Nazi Olympics* (1972), p. 8–9.

[11]Richard Mandell, *The Nazi Olympics* (1972), pp. 12–13. Mass gymnastics survive to this day, as in the Czech *Sokol* movement.

When the German states turned the tables on the French in the Franco-Prussian War of 1870–1871, the French sought a model for national revival. Pierre de Coubertin, a wealthy young Frenchman, looked to England to find a way to restore French youth to the moral and physical vigor associated with the days of Napoleonic glory. Two particular items captured de Coubertin's attention: the British educational system's emphasis on athletics (probably a result of his lifelong fascination with the book *Tom Brown's School Days*) and the "Wenlock Olympic Games," a festival staged in the town of Wenlock by William P. Brookes, a physician and fitness advocate.

De Coubertin's 1892 proposal to revive the Olympic Games stems from an attempt to shame and inspire French youth to follow the example of superior athletes from elsewhere in the world, especially from England and the United States. De Coubertin's choice of the name "Olympic Games" was a mix of public relations gimmickry and his happening upon Dr. Brookes and his festival. De Coubertin found the name of Brookes's contest "more festive and potentially inspiring than any other at hand."[12]

Given the vital role of the Olympic Games in the history of competitive sports, it is worth noting that early sporting events were limited by gender. At the insistence of de Coubertin, women were prohibited from competing in early Olympic contests. Women did not compete in the Olympics at all until 1900, and did not compete in track and field events until the 1928 Olympic Games.[13]

De Coubertin's aristocratic upbringing, his indifference to the original Olympic Games, and his worship of the English system of education explain the central part that amateurism plays in the modern Olympic ideal. Since the English schools that de Coubertin visited drew from the upper strata of British society, when he developed the modern Olympic Games, he focused largely on attitudes held by the British upper class. As the next section describes, however, the British aristocracy was beginning to feel threatened by, and started to react to, the encroachments made by working-class athletes on the "gentlemen's" sporting world.

AMATEURISM IN AMERICAN COLLEGES Chapter 2 described how organized sports first took root among the well-to-do in the United States and England, spreading to other nations as they developed economically. As sports expanded geographically, they also expanded socially. Working-class people began to watch and participate in organized sports when the benefits of industrialization spread across all segments of these societies. The upper classes viewed the increasing participation—and then dominance—by the working-class teams with alarm because they felt that losing to teams drawn from "lesser" classes upset the natural order of society. In his classic *Theory of the Leisure Class*, Thorstein Veblen

---

[12]Richard Mandell, *The Nazi Olympics* (1972), pp. 12–24; Alan Tomlinson, "De Coubertin and the Modern Olympics," in *Five Ring Circus: Money, Power and Politics at the Olympic Games*, ed. by Alan Tomlinson and Garry Whannel (London: Pluto Press, 1984), pp. 88–90; and David Young, *The Modern Olympics: A Struggle for Revival* (Baltimore: Johns Hopkins University Press, 1996), pp. 24–80.

[13]Tony Perrotet, *The Naked Olympics* (2004), p. 160.

singled out sports as one of the "occupations" of a leisure class that studiously abstained from productive behavior. Their defeat at the hands of people whom they believed to be their social inferiors set dangerous social and political precedents, much as the competition between all-black and all-white teams would in generations to come.[14]

The reactions of the upper classes to this challenge varied. Harvard and Yale responded to losses in rowing competitions against "lesser" colleges, such as Massachusetts Agricultural College (later renamed the University of Massachusetts), by withdrawing from intercollegiate competition in 1875. This effectively ended crew's two-decade run as the dominant sport of intercollegiate athletics in the United States.[15] The British Rowing Association took a more proactive approach to limiting competition by lower classes.[16] It restricted competition to amateurs and defined an "amateur" as one who had never been "by trade or employment for wages a mechanic, artisan, or labourer or engaged in any menial duty."[17] This definition diverged dramatically from the notion held by the ancient Greeks, for whom "professional...meant a man who received proper training and devoted himself more or less full-time to an activity."[18] It also effectively excluded all competitors who were not independently wealthy.

British attitudes toward education and athletics took root in American universities. "Not only was the structure of educational instruction patterned after the English but the form of collegiate living, the collegiate way[,] was borrowed from the English."[19] Central to the "collegiate way" was a preoccupation with building the character of the students. The emphasis on character, which initially took the form of rigidly enforced religious devotions, often competed with intellectual concerns for primacy in American colleges.

While American society steadily moved away from strict religious adherence, colleges' preoccupation with character did not cease but was slowly replaced by the character-building force of athletics, epitomized in the 1940 film *Knute Rockne—All American*, a semibiographical film about the man who, as football coach at Notre Dame from 1918 to 1931, first brought the team to prominence. In the film, Rockne proclaims, "We [coaches] believe the finest work of man

---

[14]William Baker, *Sports in the Western World* (Totowa, N.J.: Rowman & Littlefield, 1982), p. 125; Robert Burk, *Never Just a Game: Players, Owners, and American Baseball to 1920* (Chapel Hill: University of North Carolina Press, 1994); and Thorstein Veblen, *Theory of the Leisure Class* (New York: The Viking Press, 1967), particularly Chapter 3, "Conspicuous Leisure."

[15]Ronald Smith, *Sports and Freedom: The Rise of Big-Time College Athletics* (New York: Oxford University Press, 1988), pp. 38–51.

[16]Allen Guttman, "The Anomaly of Intercollegiate Athletics," in *Rethinking College Athletics*, ed. by Judith Andre and David James (Philadelphia: Temple University Press, 1991), p. 18; and Ronald Smith, *Sports and Freedom* (1988), pp. 26–29.

[17]Quoted in Francis Dealy, *Win at Any Cost* (1990), p. 60; and Ronald Smith, *Sports and Freedom* (1988), p. 166. William Baker, *Sports in the Western World* (1982), p. 125, cites similar attitudes in the British Football Association. The class snobbery and ethnic prejudice that accompanied the code of amateurism is eloquently expressed in the 1981 film *Chariots of Fire*.

[18]Moses Finley and H. W. Pleket, *The Olympic Games* (1976), p. 71.

[19]Ronald Smith, *Sports and Freedom* (1988), p. 11.

is building the character of man. We have tried to build courage and initiative, tolerance and persistence—without which the most educated brain in the head of man is not worth very much."[20]

The NCAA manual reflects these ideals:

> Student-athletes shall be amateurs in an intercollegiate sport, and their participation should be motivated primarily by education and the physical, mental, and social benefits to be derived. Student participation in intercollegiate athletics is an avocation, and student-athletes should be protected from exploitation by professional and commercial enterprises.[21]

The manual goes on to define what aid a college athlete may receive:

> A grant-in-aid administered by an educational institution is not considered to be pay or the promise of pay for athletics skill provided it does not exceed the financial aid limitations set by the association's membership.[22]

The limits on scholarship levels have long been criticized as insufficient to meet the total cost of a college education. In February of 2006, three former college athletes filed suit against the NCAA. They sought a $2,500 increase (a figure that the NCAA itself agrees is an accurate measure of the shortfall in expenses) in scholarships in the form of a stipend designed to cover the "full cost of attendance."[23] The case was settled in 2008. Under the settlement, the NCAA will make $218 million available to Division I schools through the 2012–2013 year.[24] The increased funding will be available through preexisting funds (the special assistance fund, the student-athlete opportunity fund, and the academic enhancement fund), though the settlement increases access to the funds. These funds may be used for additional educational expenses, health and safety expenditures, travel and other personal or family expenses, and clothing. In 2008–2009, schools reported spending most of the student-athlete opportunity funds (over 60 percent) on educational activities, such as funding additional semesters of education. Much of the special assistance funds (almost 20 percent) were used for clothing.

---

[20]Quoted in Murray Sperber, *Onward to Victory: The Crises that Shaped College Sports* (New York: Henry Holt and Co., 1998), p. 18. Sperber makes an intriguing case for claiming that this movie is the most significant American film of the 20th century.

[21]NCAA, 2005–2006 *NCAA—Division I Manual,* at http://www.ncaa.org/library//_manual/2005-06/2005-06_d1_manual.pdf.p5.

[22]NCAA, *Division I Manual,* p. 69.

[23]Quote is from Mark Alesia, "Tourney Money Fuels Pay-to-Play Debate," at http://www.indystar.com/apps/pbcs.dll/article?Date=20060401&Category=SPORTS&ArtNo=604010509&SectionCat=&Template=printart, viewed August 22, 2006. See also Doug Lederman, "Court Challenge on Athletic Aid," *Inside Higher Ed,* at http://www.insidehighered.com/news/2006/02/23/antitrust, viewed August 22, 2006.

[24]Jack Carrey and Andy Gardiner, "NCAA Settlement Gives Aid to Athletes," *USA Today,* at http://www.usatoday.com/sports/college/2008-01-29-settlement-aid-details_N.htm, viewed August 17, 2009.

The academic enhancement funds were used for items such as tutorial services.[25] Together, these increases represent a significant rise in the funding directed to Division I athletes. Whether these increases bring the value that college athletes generate for their institutions in line with the benefits the athletes receive is unclear.

11.2   THE COSTS AND BENEFITS OF COLLEGE ATHLETICS

A persistent source of contention in intercollegiate athletics is the extent to which major university athletics programs can or should be a profit center. Technically, no athletic programs earn profits because they exist within not-for-profit colleges or universities. An athletic program that generates more revenue than cost creates a surplus, though as we describe later, whether a particular program creates a surplus may hinge in whether it receives transfers of revenue from elsewhere within the institution. In this chapter, we follow the common practice of referring to these surpluses as profits.

The argument surrounding profits demonstrates the peculiar position of athletics. After all, universities seldom debate the profitability of their physics or economics departments. The debate over athletics shows the discomfort that many feel with the role athletics plays in academe. At schools with unprofitable athletic departments, faculty members often complain that athletics drain resources away from "more deserving" activities. In the words of the late Myles Brand, then the President of the NCAA, "Athletics…has an obligation to conduct its revenue-generating activities in a productive and sound business-like manner. Anything less would be incompetence at best and malfeasance at worst."[26] At schools with highly profitable athletic departments, faculty members often claim that the profits show the misplaced values of the institution. Even if athletic departments do not make a profit, they might bring a variety of indirect benefits, such as increases in applications, donations, and state funding, that all help support the academic mission of the university. In this section, we examine the benefits and costs of university athletic programs and their profitability.

The Revenue from Intercollegiate Athletics

Most of an athletic department's revenue comes from football and, to a lesser extent, men's basketball. This is particularly true for schools in the Football Bowl Subdivision (FBS), which compete at the highest level of football. At the FBS level, revenue from football typically dwarfs even that from men's basketball. Table 11.1 shows *Forbes's* estimates of the revenue, profit, and market value of the 10 most valuable football programs in 2010.

---

[25]"Where the Money Goes," *NCAA Champion Magazine,* Spring 2010, at http://www.ncaachampion-magazine.org/Exclusives/WhereTheMoneyGoes.pdf, viewed September 19, 2012.

[26]Quoted in Chris Isidore, "College Sports' Fuzzy Math," *CNNMoney: SportsBiz,* November 10, 2006, at http://money.cnn.com/2006/11/10/commentary/sportsbiz/index.htm.

TABLE 11.1   Revenue, Profit, and Market Value of the Most Valuable Football Programs

University	Conference	Revenue[a]	Profit	Market Value
University of Texas	Big 12	96	71	129
University of Notre Dame	Independent	72	47	112
Penn State University	Big Ten	73	53	100
Louisiana State University	Southeastern Conference	69	47	96
University of Michigan	Big Ten	70	47	94
University of Alabama	Southeastern Conference	77	45	93
University of Georgia	Southeastern Conference	75	53	90
University of Arkansas	Southeastern Conference	61	37	89
Auburn University	Southeastern Conference	76	37	88
University of Oklahoma	Big 12	59	36	87

[a] All figures in millions of dollars.

Source: Chris Smith, "College Football's Most Valuable Teams," *Forbes.com*, December 22, 2011, at http://www.forbes.com/sites/chrissmith/2011/12/22/college-footballs-most-valuable-teams/.

Table 11.1 shows that, unlike the NFL, the distribution of revenue in college football is highly unequal. Five of the top 10 (and eight of the top 20) universities are from the Southeastern Conference, and only three conferences, plus Notre Dame, which remains unaffiliated in football, are represented in the top 10. Only one school from a different conference, the University of Southern California, ranks in the top 20.

GATE AND VENUE REVENUE   As is true for professional teams, gate revenue used to be the single most important source of income but has been steadily declining in importance (though not in dollar value) as revenue from television and other sources has risen. Charles T. Clotfelter estimates that 25 percent of all athletic department revenue for 98 state universities comes from ticket sales—almost all of that from football and men's basketball.[27]

Unlike professional franchises, intercollegiate athletic programs are inextricably linked to the universities that house them. While the NFL's Browns left Ohio for a better stadium deal in Baltimore, one could hardly imagine Ohio State's football team threatening to leave Columbus and move to Johns Hopkins University if the university did not build it a new facility. As we discuss later in the chapter, the NCAA discourages such moves by individual players, let alone entire teams. Still, many universities have followed their professional counterparts in enhancing their venue revenues. As noted in Chapter 3, an increasing number of schools have sold the naming rights to their athletic facilities. In addition, luxury boxes and club seating have become standard features of stadiums and arenas for

[27]Charles T. Clotfelter, *Big-Time Sports in American Universities* (Cambridge: Cambridge University Press: 2011), p. 96.

schools at the FBS level. Of the universities listed in Table 11.1, only Notre Dame does not have luxury suites in its football stadium. The University of Texas and the University of Alabama both have over 100.[28]

CONFERENCE DISTRIBUTIONS OF TELEVISION REVENUE   With notable exceptions—such as Notre Dame, which has a separate television deal with NBC, and the University of Texas, which has its own "Longhorn Network"—colleges do not receive the bulk of their broadcast revenue directly from televising their basketball or football games. Instead, they receive distributions from their conferences or the NCAA. Table 11.2 shows the television contracts for the six largest conferences in 2012.

As with TV revenue in the major professional sports, broadcast revenue from football has an equalizing influence on revenues, at least at the conference level. Vanderbilt University, for example, receives as much revenue as the University of Alabama from the Southeastern Conference's (SEC) contracts with ESPN and CBS, even if it rarely receives national TV exposure, while Alabama is on nearly every week.

Broadcast revenue is a major source of inequality *between* conferences. The Big East schools are not so big when it comes to TV revenue, earning less than one-fifth the revenue of schools in the other major conferences. Still they earn about three times what schools in lesser conferences make. Schools

TABLE 11.2   Major Conference Broadcast Revenue for Football

Conference	Revenue per School[a]	Term[b] (Expiration)	Network
ACC	16	15 (2027)	ESPN
Big East	3.18[c]	6 (2013)	ABC/ESPN
Big Ten	19.7–22	10 (2016); 25 (2032)[d]	ABC/ESPN; Big Ten Network
Big 12	20	13 (2025)	Fox; ABC/ESPN
Pac-12	20.2[e]	12 (2024)	Fox; ABC/ESPN
SEC	17.1	15 (2024)	ESPN; CBS

[a] In millions of dollars per year.

[b] In years.

[c] For football schools. Basketball-only schools receive $1.56 million per year.

[d] The Big Ten also has a six-year deal with Fox (expiring 2016) to broadcast the Big Ten Championship Game.

[e] Includes anticipated revenue from the Pac-12 Network, which was launched in 2012.

Source: Matt Peloquin, "2012 NCAA Television Revenue by Conference," *CollegeSportsInfo.com,* May 10, 2012, at http://collegesportsinfo.com/2012/05/10/2012-ncaa-television-revenue-by-conference/.

[28]Eric Dexheimer, "The Longhorn Economy," *Austin American-Statesman,* September 30, 2007, at http://www.statesman.com/sports/content/sports/stories/longhorns/09/30/0930utsportsmain.html; and Roll Tide, "Bryant-Denny Stadium," *Facilities,* at http://www.rolltide.com/facilities/bryant-denny.html, viewed, May 27, 2012.

in Conference-USA or the Mountain West Conference, for example, received only about $1 million each in 2012.

Schools also receive substantial revenues from the NCAA basketball tournament. In 2010, the NCAA signed a 14-year, $10.8 billion contract with CBS and Turner Sports. The $680 million the NCAA received from this agreement in 2011–2012 was expected to be about 87.5 percent of its total revenue for the year. The NCAA reports that roughly 60 percent of this total is distributed directly to member schools. Most of these grants are based on the number of scholarships a school provides or the number of sports that it sponsors.[29] In 2011, the NCAA also distributed about $180.5 million to conferences based on their member schools' performance in the basketball tournament. The payments are based on a six-year rolling period, with each game in which a team participates (except for the finals) resulting in a $250,000 payment to the school's conference. Hence, the University of Kentucky's 2012 championship run will bring the SEC over $1.25 million per year for the following six years.[30] Even Temple's first-round loss in the 2011 tournament is worth over $1.5 million to the Atlantic 10. The NCAA tournament thus brings far more revenue to powerful conferences, such as the Big East, which placed nine teams in the 2012 tournament than it does to the Missouri Valley Conference, which placed only two.

The Revenue from Bowl Games

While football is by far the greatest revenue source for college athletic departments, not all football programs have equal access to revenue. As the NCAA moves to a playoff system, a handful of games will pay their participants far more than others do. As Table 11.3 shows, this is similar to the BCS system. Placing teams in the playoffs will be vitally important to conferences, though—as we shall see—actually playing in a playoff game will not bring a large return for the teams that participate.

Of all the intercollegiate championships sponsored by the NCAA, FBS football was the last to institute a playoff system. The reason is a curious combination of tradition and profit maximization.[31] The college bowl game was born in 1902 as a way to bring tourists to Southern California. The game (a 49–0 drubbing of Stanford by Michigan) proved such a flop that local boosters turned to alternative attractions, including polo and chariot races, before finally returning to football in 1916.[32] During the Great Depression, a number of bowl games were created by other cities hoping to promote tourism and local business.

---

[29]Mark Schlabach, "NCAA: Where Does the Money Go?" *ESPN.com*, July 12, 2011, at http://espn.go.com/college-sports/story/_/id/6756472/following-ncaa-money.

[30]Because the annual payments have been rising, the figure is larger than $1.25 million. See Chris Smith, "Final Four Trip Worth $9.5 Million to Conference," *rivals.com*, March 15, 2012, at http://rivals.yahoo.com/ncaa/basketball/news?slug=ys-forbes-final_four_trip_worth_millions_031412.

[31]For an excellent analysis of the BCS Bowl system, see Andrew Zimbalist, "The BCS, Antitrust and Public Policy," *The Antitrust Bulletin*, vol. 54, no. 4 (Winter 2009), pp. 823–855.

[32]See, for example, Billy Reed, "Ben Hur Played the Rose Bowl," *SIVault*, December 23, 1968, at http://sportsillustrated.cnn.com/vault/article/magazine/MAG1081948/index.htm.

TABLE 11.3 Selected Bowl Payouts in 2011–2012

Name	First Played	Location	Payout
BCS			
Allstate BCS National Championship	2007[a]	Varies	$18,000,000
Rose Bowl presented by VIZIO	1902	Pasadena, CA	$17,000,000
Discover Orange Bowl	1934	Miami Gardens, FL	$17,000,000
Allstate Sugar Bowl	1934	New Orleans, LA	$17,000,000
Tostitos Fiesta Bowl	1971	Glendale, AZ	$17,000,000
Non-BCS (Highest-Paying)			
Capital One Bowl	1946	Orlando, FL	$ 4,600,000
Cotton Bowl Classic	1936	Dallas (Arlington), TX	$ 3,625,000
Outback Bowl	1986	Tampa, FL	$ 3,500,000
Non-BCS (Lowest-Paying)			
Armed Forces Bowl	2003	University Park, TX	$ 600,000
Poinsettia Bowl	2005	San Diego, CA	$ 500,000
New Orleans Bowl	2001	New Orleans, LA	$ 500,000

[a] From 1998 through 2006 the National Championship Game rotated among the other BCS Bowl Games.

Sources: Football Bowl Association, *2011–2012 Football Bowl Games,* at http://footballbowlassociation. com/bowls/index.php, viewed December 6, 2011; "2011–2012 College Football Season Bowl Results," *CollegeFootballPoll.com,* at http://www.collegefootballpoll.com/2011_archive_bowls.html, viewed May 28, 2012.

The typical structure of a bowl game was to match a popular local team with a powerful rival that was not from the area. That way, local fans and out-of-towners would be drawn to attend—and spend. To guarantee such a matchup, several of the bowls contracted with conferences to send representatives to their bowl games. Thus, the Cotton Bowl traditionally featured a team from the Southwest Conference, the Sugar Bowl invited a team from the Southeastern Conference, and the Rose Bowl brought Big Ten teams from the Midwest to play teams from the Pacific 8 (now the Pac-12). With such arrangements, it was only a coincidence for a postseason game to decide the national championship.

As with so much else in sports, television brought major changes to the bowl system. By broadcasting to a national audience, television vastly increased the payouts as well as the pressure on the bowls to provide a matchup that would appeal to a national audience. The need to guarantee highly ranked teams that would draw a large audience led the Orange, Sugar, and Fiesta Bowls to form the Bowl Alliance in 1994, with the Rose Bowl joining in 1996. These four bowls and—from 2007 to 2012—a separate national championship game constituted the "BCS Bowls" with payouts several times those of other postseason games. The BCS Bowls had an agreement with the six most powerful conferences—the ACC, Big East, Big Ten, Big 12, Pac-12, and SEC—and Notre Dame that guaranteed the champion of each conference a spot in one of the BCS games. With six of the 10 possible BCS slots taken by automatic qualifiers—seven if Notre Dame qualified for a bid[33]—only three slots remained for all other schools. One of these went automatically to a school from one of the five non-BCS conferences if it ranked in the top 12 or if it was in the top 16 and was ranked higher than the champion of one of the BCS conferences.[34]

As expected, this arrangement worked to the advantage of the BCS conferences. Table 11.4 shows the total bowl payouts for 2011–2012. The first six conferences listed in Table 11.4, the six BCS conferences, receive far more than the non-BCS conferences. Notre Dame alone earned more than the entire Sun Belt Conference.

While Alabama and Louisiana State University (LSU) played for the national championship in 2012, and six other SEC schools generated payments of over $1 million, the big winner in 2012, might well have been SEC also-rans like the University of Tennessee, which went 5–7 and did not play in a bowl game. The reason is that the Allstate National Championship Game did not pay $18 million each to Alabama and LSU. Instead, it paid $36 million to the Southeastern Conference. The SEC then provided some compensation to Alabama and LSU for expenses and divided the rest 13 ways (an equal share for each school and one share for the conference itself). After paying for transporting and housing bands,

TABLE 11.4   Bowl Payouts by Conference in 2011–2012

Conference	Total Payout
Southeastern Conference	$55,057,500
Big Ten	$52,537,500
Atlantic Coast Conference	$46,980,000
Pac-12	$43,262,500
Big 12	$33,950,000
Big East	$22,800,000
Conference USA	$ 5,387,500
Mid-American Conference	$ 3,862,500
Mountain West Conference	$ 3,212,500
Western Athletic Conference	$ 3,100,000
Notre Dame	$ 2,325,000
Sun Belt Conference	$ 1,750,000

Source: Figures calculated from revenues for individual bowl games in *CollegeFootballPoll.com* (2012).

---

[33]Notre Dame received a bid if it finished in the top eight of the BCS rankings or if it won at least nine games and ranked in the top fourteen. The BCS rankings were an arcane and constantly changing mixture of computer rankings and polls.

[34]If more than one school met this criteria, it had to compete for an at-large berth. The five non-BCS conferences were Conference-USA, the Mid-America Conference, the Mountain West Conference, The Sun Belt Conference, and the Western Athletic Conference.

cheerleaders, and college administrators and paying bonuses to coaches, the big winners on the field might wind up losers off it because they receive a share of the payout but do not bear the expense of playing in the game.[35] By one estimate, the University of Florida made a net profit of just $47,000 for winning the 2009 national championship game, and many teams that play in the lesser bowl games actually lose tens, even hundreds of thousands of dollars from participating in postseason games.[36]

In 2012, NCAA college presidents abandoned the BCS system in favor of a playoff, finally bringing major college football into line with all other intercollegiate sports. On December 31, 2014, and/or January 1, 2015, four teams chosen by a selection committee will meet in the national championship semifinals. These games will rotate among the four existing BCS Bowls and two more that will be added to the mix. The championship game will then be played on the first Monday in January that is at least six days later than the semifinal games.

On one level, this changes everything. The BCS is now history, as is the distinction between conferences that automatically qualify for the most prestigious—and most lucrative—bowl games. The distinction between the conferences that were automatic qualifiers (AQ) and those that were not had caused such dissatisfaction among the nonqualifiers that the state of Utah filed an antitrust lawsuit against the BCS. Avoiding this lawsuit might have been one motivation for the BCS Bowls and the AQ conferences to agree to a playoff system. Another motivation probably came from the fact that a playoff will probably bring in far more revenue. Estimates put the value of a playoff system at $360–$400 million, roughly double the value of the current BCS system.[37]

On another level, however, little is likely to change. In particular, the current BCS conference teams will likely benefit more from the new playoff system than will teams from other conferences. While at this writing the universities have yet to determine how they will divide the revenues, there is a good chance they will base the reward on past performance, such as number of top-25 finishes since 1998, the first year of the BCS system. According to such a system, in which a top finish is worth 25 points and a 25th-place finish is worth 1 point, the top two conferences would be the SEC with 1,054 points and the Big Ten with 860 points. The top conference among the current non-AQ conferences would be Conference USA with 49 points, 24 points behind Notre Dame. Such a system would only guarantee that the rich get richer.[38]

---

[35]Alabama coach Nick Saban alone received a $400,000 bonus for winning the championship game. Chris Smith, "BCS National Championship: Gameday Is Payday for Coaches," *Forbes,* January 9, 2012, at http://www.forbes.com/sites/chrissmith/2012/01/09/bcs-championship-game-day-is-pay-day-for-coaches/.

[36]Dan Wetzel, Josh Peter, and Jeff Passan, *Death to the BCS* (New York: Gotham Books, 2010).

[37]Brett McMurphy, "Power Conferences Likely to Receive Most of Playoff Revenue," *CBSSports.com*, June 18, 2012, at http://www.cbssports.com/collegefootball/story/19378895/power-conferences-likely-to-receive-most-of-playoff-revenue.

[38]Brett McMurphy, "Power Conferences Likely to Receive Most of Playoff Revenue" (2012).

The Cost of Intercollegiate Athletics

Athletic departments may resemble commercial enterprises, but they are unique in one key respect: they do not pay their labor force. As noted earlier in this chapter, athletes receive a maximum of little more than tuition and room and board. Despite their access to an ample supply of free labor, universities have been accused of engaging in an athletics arms race, with athletic budgets steadily rising, even as the rest of their budgets are being cut.[39] We now turn our attention to the costs facing athletic departments and the origins of the alleged arms race.

SCHOLARSHIPS   While athletic departments pay their athletes no salaries, grants-in-aid represent 14 percent of the average athletic department's budget because universities attribute the cost of scholarships to their athletic departments.[40] However, there is good reason to believe that this figure significantly overstates the "labor cost" of college athletics.

In standard economics, the price of an item reflects its opportunity cost. For example, spending $50 at a baseball game sacrifices $50 that could have been spent at a concert. The monetary value of a scholarship, however, does not necessarily come close to the opportunity cost it imposes.[41]

Awarding a basketball player a $20,000 scholarship imposes an opportunity cost of $20,000 only if the athlete would have paid full tuition to attend the university or if the university were operating at full capacity so that admitting the basketball player displaced another student who would have paid $20,000. It is highly unlikely that either of the above scenarios holds. It is more likely that the student would have gone elsewhere had she not received the scholarship, and universities seldom operate so close to full capacity that they cannot admit another student. (This argument may not hold for student housing.) It is far more likely that an athlete displaces another student who would have received some form of financial aid from the institution as well. It is even possible that athletes who receive a partial scholarship represent a net gain to the university, in that the university receives some tuition that it would not have received otherwise. In sum, athletic scholarships impose a significantly lower cost on the university than the official reports imply.

COACHES' SALARIES   If an athletics arms race exists, the most likely source of it lies in the salaries paid to coaches. According to the *USA Today* database, head football coaches at FBS schools had an average salary of over $1 million in 2011.

---

[39]See, for example, Robert Litan, Jonathan Orszag, and Peter Orszag, "The Empirical Effects of College Athletics: An Interim Report," *Sebago Associates*, 2003, at http://www.sc.edu/faculty/PDF/baseline.pdf.

[40]Charles T. Clotfelter notes, however, that some state universities do not charge athletics departments the added cost of scholarships for out-of-state students. Clotfelter, *Big-Time Sports in American Universities* (2011), pp. 96 and 107.

[41]For a good discussion of the slipperiness of scholarship costs, see Victor Matheson, Debra O'Connor, and Joseph Herberger, "The Bottom Line: Accounting for Revenues and Expenditures in Intercollegiate Athletics," *International Journal of Sport Finance*, vol. 7, no. 1 (February 2012), pp. 30–45.

Athletic Directors, the coaches' ostensible bosses, while highly paid, had average salaries that were about $400,000 lower.[42]

For star coaches, the sky is the limit. In addition to his $400,000 bonus for winning the 2012 national championship, Alabama coach Nick Saban received a contract extension that will pay him an average of $5.62 million per year through 2020. Basketball coach John Calipari was not far behind, receiving a $650,000 bonus on top of his $3.7 million salary for winning the NCAA basketball championship. Perhaps more surprising is the amount paid to the rest of the coaching staff. Alabama's assistant coaches are paid over $3.7 million in total, with the defensive coordinator earning close to $1 million and the defensive secondary coach, $260,000.[43]

Football and—to a lesser extent—basketball coaches have always been paid relatively high salaries. A 1929 report by the Carnegie Foundation for the Advancement of Teaching found that "on average football coaches at large institutions earned more than the highest-paid full professor on campus."[44] The gap between coaches and faculty has ballooned in recent years. Using data "for 44 public universities belonging to one of the five most established conferences," Charles T. Clotfelter finds that, between 1986 and 2010, the average salary of a full professor rose by 39 percent, the average salary of a university president rose by 90 percent, and the average salary of a head coach rose by 650 percent.[45]

Using revenue data from the 20 most valuable football programs and salary data from *USA Today* we find that the average head coach's salary in 2011 was almost 5.2 percent of the team's total revenue. If head football coaches in the NFL received a similar percentage of their team's revenue, then the average salary of an NFL coach would be $13.5 million. This is close to double what the *highest*-paid NFL coach (Bill Belichick—$7.5 million) earns.[46]

CAPITAL EXPENDITURES   The athletics arms race might also be expressed through expenditure on facilities. A study commissioned by the NCAA finds that the average annual expenditure on physical plant by an FBS university is $27 million,

---

[42]Numbers were compiled using Christopher Schnaars, Jodi Upton, and Kristin DeRamus, "USA Today College Football Head Coach Salary Database," *USA Today*, November 17, 2011, at http://www.usatoday.com/sports/college/football/story/2011-11-17/cover-college-football-coaches-salaries-rise/51242232/1; and Steve Berkowitz and Jodi Upton, "Athletic Director Salary Database for 2011," *USA Today*, October 6, 2011, at http://www.usatoday.com/sports/college/story/2011-athletics-director-salaries-database/50669958/1.

[43]Chris Low and Edward Aschoff, "Saban Gets Raise, Extension," *SEC Blog*, March 27, 2012, at http://espn.go.com/college-football/story/_/id/7740227/alabama-crimson-tide-grant-coach-nick-saban-raise-2-year-extension; and Jason Zengerle, "March Payday Madness," *Business Week*, March 25, 2010, at http://www.businessweek.com/magazine/content/10_14/b4172058546496.htm.

[44]Charles T. Clotfelter, *Big-Time Sports in American Colleges* (2011), p. 105.

[45]Charles T. Clotfelter, *Big-Time Sports in American Colleges* (2011), p. 106.

[46]Chris Smith, "College Football's Most Valuable Teams" (2012); Christopher Schnaars, Jodi Upton and Kristin DeRamus, "USAToday College Football Coach Salary Database: 2006-2011," *USA Today*, at http://www.usatoday.com/sports/college/football/story/2011-11-17/cover-college-football-coaches-salaries-rise/51242232/1, viewed May 26, 2012.

which actually exceeds the average operational expenditures (such as salaries).[47] Most of this expenditure is on football stadiums. Of the five most valuable football programs in Table 11.1, only Notre Dame has not undertaken a major stadium renovation since 2000. The total expenditures by these four universities alone exceeded $400 million, with Michigan's $226 million renovation of Michigan Stadium in 2010 topping the list.[48]

While colleges with major athletic programs do spend large amounts on sports, it is important to put these figures in context. The universities that house these athletic departments are huge enterprises. For example, official figures put Penn State's annual budget at over $4 billion.[49] As a result, expenditures by the average FBS athletic department constitute 3 to 3.5 percent of its university's budget.[50] This can be viewed in several ways. On the one hand, over 96 percent of the typical university with a big-time athletics department is devoted to nonathletic pursuits. On the other hand, athletics departments occupy a much more prominent place in the "economy" of a university than professional sports franchises do in a city's economy. Recall that all five sports franchises in Chicago comprise about half a percent of the local economy. Sports at the University of Illinois are about six times as prominent.

Do Colleges Profit from Athletics?

Asking whether colleges earn a profit from athletics might seem strange. Traditionally, colleges and universities are chartered as nonprofit organizations, which are prohibited from earning profits. Yet the NCAA's own reports on the economic status of intercollegiate sports frequently refer to surpluses or net revenues as profits. These reports reflect the fact that athletic departments are much more profit-oriented than most other divisions of the university. One analyst has referred to athletic departments as "commercial entertainment enterprises within a university."[51]

It is more difficult to measure profit for an athletic department than for other commercial enterprises. One reason, as noted above, is the ambiguity surrounding the true cost of scholarships. Another complication stems from the need to distinguish between generated revenue and allocated revenue. **Generated revenues** are brought in by the athletics department through ticket sales, radio and television contracts, alumni contributions to athletics, and other payments that are directly the result of the athletic endeavor. **Allocated revenues** are an internal transfer within the institution from sources outside athletics to the athletic department.

---

[47]Jonathan Orszag and Peter Orszag, "The Physical Capital Stock Used in College Athletics," *Compass*, April 2005. They find that average annual Division I-A operational expenditures are about $24 million.

[48]Two good sources for information on college football stadiums are Paul Munsey and Corey Suppes, *ballparks.com* (2012); and *collegegridirons.com*, at http://www.collegegridirons.com/, viewed May 28, 2012.

[49]Penn State University Budget Office, *Penn State Budget Primer*, at http://www.budget.psu.edu/openbudget/default.aspx, viewed May 30, 2012.

[50]Jonathan Orszag and Peter Orszag, "The Physical Capital Stock Used in College Athletics" (2005).

[51]Charles T. Clotfelter, *Big-Time Sports in American Universities* (2011) p. 33.

Allocated revenues consist of student activity fees, institutional support (direct budget transfers or payment of expenses), and government support. They are a substantial part of the athletic department's budget. Subsidies alone constitute about 18 percent of the typical FBS athletic department's revenues.[52] This distinction directly impacts the question of whether athletics programs are self-sustaining. If programs are "profitable" only after including institutional support, then they represent a net drain on the assets of the institution rather than a contribution.

A recent study by Victor Matheson, Debra O'Connor and Joseph Herberger of 166 state universities finds that profits depend crucially on how one defines revenues and costs. Because of the huge difference in bowl revenues, athletic department profits were much higher for universities belonging to BCS conferences. Counting all revenues and all costs, 72 percent of BCS departments were profitable in 2004–2005, with average profits of $1.9 million. When counting only generated revenues, less than 30 percent of BCS departments were profitable, with an average loss of over $2 million. After deleting scholarships from the cost figures, over 80 percent of BCS departments showed a profit, and average profits exceeded $4 million.

The figures for non-BCS schools were less favorable. Like BCS departments, about 72 percent of non-BCS departments show a profit when one includes all revenues and costs, though the average profit is much lower (about $209,000). Non-BCS schools, however, depend much more heavily on transfers. When one counts only generated revenues, no non-BCS departments show a profit, and average losses exceed $7.7 million. Discounting scholarships improves the figures only slightly, with less than 4 percent of the schools running a profit, with average losses of slightly less than $4.5 million.

Victor Matheson et al. also show how heavily athletic departments rely on their football and men's basketball programs. Depending on the specification, 88 to 96 percent of these sports show a profit at BCS schools, much higher than the overall athletic departments. For example, women's basketball, which is generally accepted to be the most profitable of women's sports, is profitable at only 3 to 3.5 percent of even BCS schools.[53]

Spillovers from Athletics to the University

Even if a college's athletic department loses money, a college might still want to subsidize it. As with cities, universities view sports more broadly than as a profit center. The public goods and financial spillovers play a major role in motivating all type of schools, from large state universities to small liberal arts colleges to support athletic programs.

SPORTS AS PUBLIC GOODS   As with professional teams and cities, college sports provide a public good to the broader college community. College teams give students a sense of identity and belonging beyond the classroom. Frequently, this

---

[52]Charles T. Clotfelter, *Big-Time Sports in American Universities* (2011), p. 96.

[53]All figures are from Victor Matheson et al. "The Bottom Line" (2012).

identification with a state university spills over from the students and alumni to the entire population of the state. Paul "Bear" Bryant, former football coach at the University of Alabama, justified the prominence of his program by claiming that "it was unlikely that 50,000 people would show up to watch an English professor give a final exam."[54]

The particularly rabid followings that football teams in the Midwest and South enjoy stem in part from the convergence of three historical forces. The first two—the rapid growth of state universities and the spread of football—occurred nationwide in the late 19th and early 20th centuries. The third force was the rise of professional sports in the Northeast. The presence of professional baseball teams— and, later, professional football teams—limited the growth of fan bases for college sports. With no professional teams farther west than St. Louis and none farther south than Washington, DC, states like Mississippi or Nebraska had no such competition.[55] With relatively few alternative activities, sports grew into a major social outlet. As a Nebraska fan told novelist James Michener, "'In this state, if you don't go for football, you're a pariah.'"[56]

ADMISSIONS   Numerous studies have shown that colleges with "big-time" athletic departments attract more and better students. Studies suggest, for example, that schools in major athletic conferences attract freshmen with higher SAT scores, and that the more successful a school's football program is, the higher the scores rise. Success on the football field expands a school's overall applicant pool (at least for FBS programs), allowing the school to generate more revenue by admitting more students or to generate greater prestige by being more selective in its admissions process.[57]

The studies, however, rely on data from a particular year. As a result, the way they identify athletic success might invalidate their conclusions. With only one year of data, one cannot say whether a school had a large applicant pool because its football team did well or because of some other underlying factor. For example, one study equates a big-time football program with one that belongs to a major athletic conference. That, however, includes many of the nation's premier state universities.[58] Finding that such programs attract more and better students

---

[54]Quoted in Andrew Zimbalist, *Unpaid Professionals* (1999), p. 223.

[55]See Charles T. Clotfelter, *Big-Time Sports in American Universities* (2011), pp. 46–51.

[56]James Michener, *Sports in America* (New York: Random House, 1976), p. 221. Many of these states still lack professional franchises.

[57]See Melvin Borland, Brian Goff, and Robert Pulsinelli, "College Athletics: Financial Burden or Boon?" in *Advances in the Economics of Sport*, vol. 1 (New York: JAI Press, 1992), p. 218; Robert McCormick and Maurice Tinsley, "Athletics versus Academics? Evidence from SAT Scores," *Journal of Political Economy*, vol. 95, no. 5 (October 1987), pp. 1103–1116; and Robert Murphy and Gregory Trandel, "The Relation between a University's Football Record and the Size of Its Applicant Pool," *Economics of Education Review*, vol. 13, no. 3 (September 1994), pp. 265–270.

[58]This opens the door to the question of what constitutes a "major" conference. Robert McCormick and Maurice Tinsley, "Athletics and Academics: A Model of University Contributions," in *Sportometics*, ed. by Brian Goff and Robert Tollison (College Station, Tex: Texas A&M University Press, 1990), pp. 193–204, used the Atlantic Coast, Southeastern, Southwest, Big 10, Big 8, and Pacific 10 conferences.

may reflect the impact of the school's position in the state rather than the prominence of its football team.

Two recent studies use **panel data**, data for a set of schools over time, to study the impact of athletic success on admissions. Panel data allow researchers to separate athletic success from other factors. Using the above example, one can ask whether a premier state university, such as the University of Kentucky, sees its applications rise in the wake of winning the NCAA basketball tournament.

The results of these studies are mixed. A study by Devin and Jaren Pope finds that applications to schools rise by about 3 percent if they reach the top 10 in football or the "Sweet 16" in the NCAA men's basketball tournament and by about 7 to 8 percent if their team wins the national championship in either sport. The study also finds that the added applications come from across the spectrum of SAT scores, so the school has the potential to increase the quality as well as the quantity of its incoming class. Randall Smith finds that success in basketball does not improve the profile of the student body. Progress through the NCAA tournament has no impact on class rank or grade-point average and only a marginal impact on SAT scores. These findings need not contradict each other, as it is possible that schools choose to increase the quantity of entering students rather than the test scores of the entering class. Testing that explanation, however, is a subject for future study.[59]

DONATIONS AND STATE FUNDING   Donations from proud alumni to their athletic teams constitute about 22 percent of a typical athletic department's revenue.[60] Many of these donations are probably less charitable donations than investments in stadium seating. At the University of Alabama, for example, one's priority for stadium tickets depends in part on one's membership in and donations to the Tide Pride booster group and on donations to the Crimson Tide Foundation.[61]

Donations by alumni and fans can have a broader benefit if they spill over to the rest of the university. Most studies of alumni donations analyze specific schools, which makes them difficult to generalize to different schools at different times. Moreover, the case studies provide contradictory evidence. Studies of Clemson University and Mississippi State University show that successful athletic teams lead to greater alumni giving, but a case study of Washington State University and a broader study by the Council for Financial Aid to Education show that athletic performance has no significant impact. A study commissioned by the NCAA also found no statistically significant relationship between either a school's expenditure on its football program or the success its football

---

[59]Devin Pope and Jaren Pope, "The Impact of College Sports Success on the Quantity and Quality of Student Applications," *Southern Economic Journal*, vol. 75, no. 3 (January 2009), pp. 750–780; and D. Randall Smith, "Big-Time Basketball and the Advertising Effect: Does Success Really Matter," *Journal of Sports Economics*, vol. 9, no. 4 (2008), pp. 387–406.

[60]Charles T. Clotfelter, *Big-Time Sports in American Universities* (2011), p. 96.

[61]Tide Pride, *Tide Totals*, 2012, at http://www.rolltide.com/boosters/tide-totals.html, viewed May 24, 2012.

program enjoyed and the amount of alumni giving.[62] A recent study by Brad Humphreys and Michael Mondello uses a sample of 320 institutions over a 20-year period to shed additional light on donations by separately analyzing how "restricted" (designated toward athletics) and "unrestricted" donations respond to performance by universities' athletic teams.[63] The study finds that restricted giving to public universities rises the year after a college's team appears in a post-season bowl game or the NCAA tournament but that unrestricted giving does not. Unrestricted giving to private schools is also insensitive to athletic performance and rises only in response to performance by the college's basketball team.

Jeffrey Stinson and Dennis Howard use data from the Voluntary Support of Education database to separate out donations to a college's athletic department.[64] This allows them to analyze movements in the percentage of total donations to a university that go to its athletic department. The study finds that the percentage of donations going to athletics has steadily risen over time and that the sensitivity of this percentage to athletic performance is lower for schools with stronger academic reputations. It thus appears likely that there are few if any spillovers from athletics to the rest of the university. It is much more likely that donations to athletic departments come at the expense of donations to the academic side of the university.

In addition to soliciting private donations, state universities try to leverage their success on the field into allocations from the state capital. In the 1940s, John Hannah, the President of what was then called Michigan State College of Agriculture and Applied Science, openly campaigned to have his institution replace the University of Chicago (which had abandoned big-time sports) in the Big Ten as a way to build the school from a small agricultural college into a major university.[65] More recently, the University of Connecticut used the success of its men's and women's basketball teams to the same effect.[66] Probably the most famous instance of using sports to solicit state funds came when George Lyn

---

[62]See, for example, Paul Grimes and George Chressanthis, "The Role of Intercollegiate Sports and NCAA Sanctions in Alumni Contributions," *American Journal of Economics and Sociology,* vol. 53, no. 1 (January 1994), pp. 27–40; Allen Guttman, "The Anomaly of Intercollegiate Athletics" (1991); Robert McCormick and Maurice Tinsley, "Athletics and Academics," (1990); Murray Sperber, *College Sports Inc.* (New York: Henry Holt and Co., 1990), pp. 70–81; James L. Shulman and William G. Bowen, *The Game of Life* (2001), pp. 220–226; Shannon Brownlee and Nancy Linnon, "The Myth of the Student-Athlete" (1990); Cletus C. Coughlin and O. Homer Erekson, "An Examination of Contributions to Support Intercollegiate Athletics," *Southern Economic Journal,* vol. 50, no. 1 (July 1984), pp. 180–195; and Lee Sigelman and Samuel Bookheimer, "Is It Whether You Win or Lose? Monetary Contributions to Big-Time College Athletic Programs," *Social Science Quarterly,* vol. 64, no. 2 (June 1983), pp. 347–359; and Robert E. Litan, Jonathan M. Orszag, and Peter R. Orszag, "The Empirical Effects of Collegiate Athletics: An Interim Report," (2003).

[63]Brad Humphreys and Michael Mondello, "Intercollegiate Athletic Success and Donations at NCAA Division I Institutions," *Journal of Sport Management,* vol. 21, no. 2 (April 2007), pp. 265–280.

[64]Jeffrey Stinson and Dennis Howard, "Athletic Success and Private Giving to Athletic and Academic Programs at NCAA Institutions," *Journal of Sport Management,* vol. 21, no. 2 (April 2007), pp. 235–264.

[65]Beth Shapiro, "John Hannah and the Growth of Big-Time Intercollegiate Athletics at Michigan State University," *Journal of Sports History,* vol. 10, no. 3 (Winter 1983), pp. 26–40.

[66]Charles T. Clotfelter, "Big-Time Athletics at American Universities" (2011), p. 126.

Cross, the president of the University of Oklahoma, pleaded for more state funds by stating, "We want to build a university our football team can be proud of."[67] Since then, Oklahoma has become more subtle in its lobbying. "[O]f all gifts that lobbyists in [Oklahoma] reported giving to legislators in a recent reporting period, more than half were for tickets to football games at Oklahoma or Oklahoma State."[68]

11.3 THE ROLE OF THE NCAA

One cannot analyze intercollegiate athletics without discussing the role of the NCAA. The NCAA is not the only regulatory body in intercollegiate athletics; for example, the National Association of Intercollegiate Athletics (NAIA) oversees about 300 colleges.[69] However, with about 1,200 schools, the NCAA is by far the largest and most prestigious organization of its kind in the United States. Despite its prominence, the NCAA's precise role and goals remain the subject of debate. As discussed in earlier chapters, the NCAA arose as a regulatory body, charged with establishing and enforcing rules of behavior for football. Today, it is often referred to as a cartel, albeit an incidental one, that maximizes the joint well-being of its members. We can also apply club theory to the NCAA, having previously applied it to individual athletic conferences, which have expanded and contracted as the marginal benefits and marginal costs of membership have changed.

One of the biggest problems in evaluating the NCAA is the fact that no single role fully captures the NCAA's behavior. Sometimes the NCAA acts like a high-minded guardian of academic principles, sometimes it acts like a profit-maximizing cartel, and sometimes it appears to be acting as both at once. In this section, we look more closely at each framework, how each arose, and how it colors our interpretations of NCAA policy.

The NCAA as Regulatory Agency

As in the early days of baseball, the athletes themselves ran intercollegiate sports during the late 19th century. Students operated sports clubs independent of—and sometimes in defiance of—faculty and administration. Most administrators were disdainful toward the growing popularity of football. In refusing to allow a group of students to travel to the University of Michigan to play a football game in 1873, Cornell President Andrew D. White proclaimed, "I will not permit thirty men to travel four hundred miles to agitate a bag of wind."[70] The size of football squads may have been determined by such hostility, as the Yale Football Association

---

[67]J. Robert Byrom, "ESPN Names Oklahoma Most Prestigious Program during AP/BCS Eras," *USC Trojans,* January 23, 2009, at http://bleacherreport.com/articles/114758-espn-names-ou-most-prestigous-school-during-apbcs-eras. At the time, Oklahoma was in the midst of a 47-game winning streak.

[68]Charles T. Clotfelter, *Big-Time Athletics in American Universities* (2010), p. 130.

[69]National Association of Intercollegiate Athletics, "About the NAIA" *NAIA,* at http://www.naia.org/ViewArticle.dbml?DB_OEM_ID=27900&ATCLID=205323019, viewed May 27, 2012.

[70]Ronald Smith, *Sports and Freedom* (1988), p. 74

pushed for team size to be limited to 11 players because it feared that the faculty would not allow a larger group of students to leave campus for away games.[71]

Control began to shift in the early 1880s, when many colleges established faculty oversight committees.[72] The rationale for such committees was concern over the growing violence in football. However, faculty, administrators, and alumni soon came to view sports teams as representatives of the entire school. Hence, once the NCAA had fulfilled its initial task of establishing safer rules of play for football, it was only natural for it to ensure that sports did not conflict with the central mission of the university.

One of the major challenges facing the NCAA was the "tramp athlete" of the early 20th century. Like the baseball players who jumped contracts in the days before the reserve clause, the tramp athlete was a mercenary who traveled from school to school, looking for the best deal. Carl Johanson, who spent eight years playing football at Williams, Harvard, and Cornell, may have set the record for such activity in the late 19th century. Some players never even bothered to enroll, as was the case for seven players on the 1893 University of Michigan football team.[73] Academic violations also date to the very beginning of the intercollegiate competition. In the first intercollegiate football game, an 1869 match between Rutgers and Princeton, the victorious Rutgers squad included three students who were failing algebra and a fourth who was failing geometry.[74]

Colleges needed an outside regulator because they continually faced a prisoner's dilemma. Table 11.5 shows a simplified version of the problem facing colleges that want to maintain academic standards but also want to win games. Suppose two schools—UCLA and USC—are evenly matched if both maintain standards or neither maintains standards. Each school realizes, however, that it can dominate a school that maintains academic standards by failing to maintain them itself. If both schools want to win badly enough, violating

TABLE 11.5 The Prisoners' Dilemma Leads Colleges to Violate Academic Standards

	UCLA Violates Standards	UCLA Maintains Standards
USC Violates Standards	Schools compete evenly Both have bad reputations	USC dominates rivalry USC's reputation suffers
USC Maintains Standards	UCLA dominates rivalry UCLA's reputation suffers	Schools recruit evenly Both have good reputations

---

[71]Ronald Smith, *Sports and Freedom* (1988), pp. 73–77.

[72]Princeton formed the first such committee in 1881. See Francis Dealy, *Win at Any Cost* (1990), p. 68.

[73]Ronald Smith, *Sports and Freedom* (1988), p. 177; and Lee Sigelman, "It's Academic—or Is It? Admissions Standards and Big-Time College Football," *Social Science Quarterly*, vol. 76, no. 2 (June 1995), p. 247.

[74]Andrew Zimbalist, *Unpaid Professionals* (1999), pp. 6–7 and 20; and Ronald Smith, *Sports and Freedom* (1988), pp. 30 and 71.

standards becomes a dominant strategy, and they occupy the upper left cell of Table 11.5. Both UCLA and USC betray their academic mission and fail to gain an advantage over the other. This leaves both schools worse off than if they had both maintained standards, in the lower right cell. The schools would again be evenly matched on the field, but they would both keep their academic reputations intact.

The NCAA can help UCLA and USC avoid the prisoners' dilemma by enforcing cooperation. This is accomplished by monitoring the schools' behavior and punishing anyone who deviates from the strategy that maximizes the group's well-being. In a cartel such as OPEC, an enforcer can be a large oil producer that threatens to increase production and drive down prices if the members do not obey their quotas. In college athletics, the NCAA can limit TV appearances, cut scholarships, or impose the "death penalty" to keep schools in line.

The NCAA as a Club

The NCAA has steadily redefined the structure of intercollegiate athletics by dividing schools into smaller, more homogeneous subgroups. When it was first formed, all members were equal partners.[75] In 1973, the schools split into Divisions I, II, and III. The main distinction between the divisions is in the rules governing recruiting and financial aid. Division III schools are typically small, private colleges that offer no athletic scholarships. Division II schools consist of private colleges and smaller state universities that offer some athletic scholarships. Division I represents mostly large state universities and private schools that place heavy emphasis on athletics, and allow athletes to receive full scholarships. Division I was initially synonymous with the big-time football powers, but the big-time was not big enough for some schools. In 1978, under pressure from the largest Division I football powers, the NCAA split Division I into Division I-A, since renamed the Football Bowl Subdivision (FBS), and Division I-AA, now called the Football Championship Subdivision (FCS). This distinction is made solely for football. There is no distinction among Division I schools for any other sport. Most of the criteria for FBS status relate to the school's commitment to big-time athletics. It must, for example, offer at least 16 varsity sports, including football, offer at least 200 athletic scholarships (or spend at least $4 million on scholarships), and have an average home attendance at its football games of at least 15,000 over a rolling two-year period.[76] The creation of the BCS coalition in 1998—an action taken by conferences and TV networks on their own—created yet another subdivision, albeit one outside the NCAA's jurisdiction.

The appearance of smaller, more elite groups within the NCAA resembles the changes that have occurred in British soccer. The Football Association (FA)

---

[75]For a good history of the subdivisions, see Joseph Crowley, *In the Arena: The NCAA's First Century* (Indianapolis: NCAA, 2006).

[76]National Collegiate Athletic Association, *Football Bowl Subdivision—Membership Requirements*, December 8, 2007, at http://fs.ncaa.org/Docs/AMA/Division%20I%20Forms/2010-11%20FBS%20 Forms/Football%20Bowl%20Subqa%2012%208%2010.pdf.

was established in 1863, with all soccer clubs as equal members. After 25 years, the top clubs formed a more select group within the FA known as the Football League (FL). Almost 100 years later, the best clubs in the FL split off to form the Premier League. In both British soccer and American football, the optimal size of the association changed as the market for the product changed.

According to the theory of clubs, the optimal club size occurs when the marginal benefit of admitting a new member equals the marginal cost of admitting that member. So far, we have assumed that all potential members are homogeneous, which means that each potential member brings the same added benefits and added costs. In the early years of college football, this might have been close to true. When the NCAA first formed in 1906, football powerhouses like Harvard and Yale were not much different from other members, such as Swarthmore College. By the 1970s, the growth of large state universities and the advent of television had significantly changed the value of membership.

For the football powers of the 1970s, such as Penn State and Notre Dame, the added TV revenue of joining with another big-time program, such as the University of Georgia, (MB_G) vastly outweighed the added costs of joining with Georgia (MC_G). Because $MB_G > MC_G$, it made sense for these schools to align themselves together. In contrast, the marginal benefit of adding a small liberal-arts college like Swarthmore was minuscule, so $MB_S < MC_S$. It made no economic sense to admit Swarthmore to the group. As the rewards have continued to change, so has the optimal size of the club that consists of the biggest programs.

The NCAA as a Cartel

Finally, as we describe in Chapter 4, one can view the NCAA as a cartel. Most cartels arise because a group of producers desire monopoly power over their output. The NCAA can also use its market power to exercise monopsony power over its inputs. The NCAA can thus drive up prices on the output market and drive down its costs on the input markets. We examine each in turn.

THE NCAA AS A MONOPOLY The basic model of monopoly behavior is inadequate for analyzing how cartels behave. In addition to determining what level of output maximizes profit, a cartel must allocate output and profit among its members. To see how a cartel operates, consider a simple cartel with only two members.

The output decision for a cartel with two members is identical to that facing a monopoly that must allocate its output between two plants. If the plants are identical, the decision is easy: Allocate half the output to each plant. This corresponds to equally dividing the monopoly profit between the two members of the cartel.

Generally, however, cartels consist of firms that are not identical. Figure 11.1 shows the marginal cost curves for two heterogeneous firms, A and B. Since the marginal cost curve for firm A lies below that for firm B, it is cheaper for firm A to increase its output a little bit than it is for firm B if both firms are producing the same level of output. Given the marginal cost curves for the individual firms, we

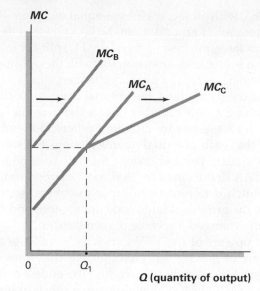

FIGURE 11.1 Cartels and Marginal Cost

The cartel's *MC* curve is the horizontal sum of the individual *MC* curves.

can construct the marginal cost curve for the cartel by computing the horizontal sum of the two individual curves, just as we computed the market demand curve from individual demand curves in Chapter 2. At very low levels of output, the cartel's marginal cost curve corresponds to the marginal cost curve for firm A alone (MC_A), since firm B can produce nothing at such low marginal cost. When firm A reaches output level Q_1, the cost of increasing its output by one unit is the same as firm B's cost of producing its first unit of output. At this point, it pays for both firms to produce, and the cartel's marginal cost curve (MC_C) lies to the right of the individual firms' curves.

If the two firms act like a single firm, then they face a single market demand curve. This effectively says that consumers do not care whether they make their purchases from firm A or firm B. As a result, the two firms also face common marginal revenue curve, as seen in Figure 11.2.

The optimal level of output for the cartel occurs where the cartel's marginal cost curve (MC_C) meets the marginal revenue curve (MR). The overall output of the cartel is thus Q_C^*, where $MR^* = MC_C^*$. The division of output that maximizes overall profit allocates production according to the individual firms' marginal costs so that $MC_A = MC_B = MR^*$. In Figure 11.2, this occurs at Q_A^* for firm A and Q_B^* for firm B. Because the marginal cost curve for the cartel is the horizontal sum of the individual marginal cost curves, $Q_A^* + Q_B^* = Q_C^*$.

A standard cartel therefore allocates a greater share of output and profit to the more efficient member. Thus, while it is possible for the continual restructuring of the NCAA to reflect the behavior of a club that shares the net benefits among its members, the restructuring could reflect an efficient cartel that allocates greater benefits to its most efficient members.

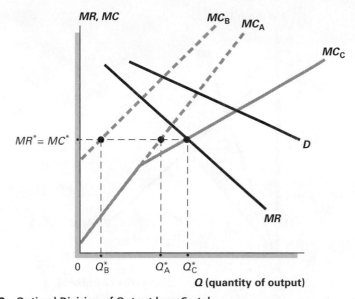

FIGURE 11.2   Optimal Division of Output by a Cartel

The cartel sets the optimal level of output, Q_C^*, by setting marginal revenue (*MR*) equal to the sum of the marginal cost curves (MC_C). Firm *A* produces Q_A^* and firm *B* produces Q_B^*.

THE NCAA AS A MONOPSONY   In addition to being a single seller in some of its output markets, the NCAA is a single buyer in some of its labor markets. Earlier in this chapter, we showed that the NCAA strictly limits the benefits that colleges can provide student-athletes. Some regard these limits as a vestige of the 19th-century British class system, while others see it as a staunch defense of academic integrity. We now see that the limits can also be the result of monopsony power. According to this view, "[a]mateurism is not a moral issue; it is an economic camouflage...."[77] The restrictions that the NCAA has placed on what colleges can pay a star quarterback or point guard have led many to conclude that the NCAA is acting like a cartel's enforcer.[78] Enforcers help cartels avert prisoners' dilemmas

---

[77]Walter Byers quoted in Ellen Staurowsky, "'Should College Athletes Be Paid?' Is the Wrong Question," *Atlantic Monthly*, September 19, 2011, at http://www.theatlantic.com/entertainment/archive/2011/09/should-college-athletes-get-paid-is-the-wrong-question/245312/.

[78]This view is forcefully expressed in Robert W. Brown, "An Estimate of the Rent Generated by a Premium College Football Player," *Economic Inquiry*, vol. 21, no. 4 (October 1993), pp. 671–684; Robert W. Brown, "Measuring Cartel Rents in the College Basketball Player Recruitment Market," *Applied Economics*, vol. 26, no. 1 (January 1994), pp. 27–34; Walter Byers with Charles Hammer, *Un-sportsmanlike Conduct: Exploiting College Athletes* (Ann Arbor: University of Michigan Press, 1995); Arthur Fleisher, Brian Goff, and Robert Tollison, *The National Collegiate Athletic Association: A Study in Cartel Behavior* (Chicago: University of Chicago Press, 1992); and Paul Lawrence, *Unsportsmanlike Conduct: The National Collegiate Athletic Association and the Business of College Football* (New York: Praeger, 1987). While we focus on the exploitation of athletes, the NCAA also depressed the pay of assistant coaches, for which it was successfully sued for $54.5 million (see, for example, Welch Suggs, "NCAA to Pay $55-Million to Settle Lawsuit by Assistant Coaches," *Chronicle of Higher Education*, March 19, 1999), p. A47.

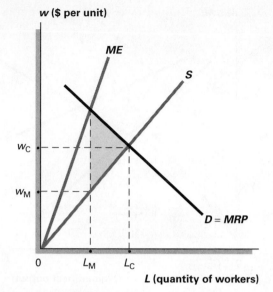

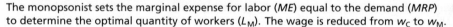

FIGURE 11.3   **College Sports as a Monopsony**

The monopsonist sets the marginal expense for labor (*ME*) equal to the demand (*MRP*) to determine the optimal quantity of workers (L_M). The wage is reduced from w_C to w_M.

like the one illustrated in Table 11.5. The only difference in this model is that the NCAA enforces low costs rather than academic integrity.[79]

By coordinating the actions of its members, the cartel can act like a monopsonist and minimize expenditures on athletes. This occurs where marginal expenditure on labor equals the marginal benefit of the last worker employed. Figure 11.3 shows the impact of a typical monopsony. The employer reduces both the number of workers and the level of pay below the competitive level, and a deadweight loss occurs.

The owners of professional teams relied on the reserve clause to ensure their monopsony power; college athletes face similar types of rules that bind them to colleges. With few exceptions, NCAA regulations require that collegiate athletes who have made a written commitment to a school must sit out a year and lose a year of eligibility if they want to play for another school. For example, when Todd O'Brien graduated from St. Joseph's University, he had a year of eligibility left as a basketball player. According to O'Brien, the "athletic department's academic advisers suggested that he delay graduation and fill his final year with courses like pottery."[80] Instead, O'Brien enrolled in a Masters of Public Policy program

---

[79]See, for example, Gary S. Becker, "College Athletes Should Get Paid What They're Worth," *Business Week*, September 30, 1985, p. 38; and Rick Telander, *The Hundred Yard Lie: The Corruption of College Football and What We Can Do to Stop It* (New York: Simon and Schuster, 1989).

[80]Joe Nocera, "More NCAA 'Justice'," *New York Times*, January 13, 2012, at http://www.nytimes.com/2012/01/14/opinion/nocera-more-ncaa-justice.html.

at the University of Alabama-Birmingham and tried to join the basketball team. However, he could not do so without the permission of St. Joseph's coach. Despite O'Brien's having graduated and playing relatively little, St. Joseph's refused to grant O'Brien permission to play, forcing him to sit out the 2011–2012 season. Clearly, Todd O'Brien was not moving from school to school as in the tramp athlete discussion above, and restricting his movements served no higher purpose. Such restrictions do, however, help enforce universities' monopsony power over their athletes.

Academic Standards: A Basis of Academic Integrity or Monopoly Power?

As we have seen, it is sometimes possible to give an action by the NCAA several different interpretations. One of the NCAA's most contentious policies is its attempt to set academic standards for student-athletes. This should come as no surprise, as standards are a double-edged sword in many areas. Doctors, lawyers, accountants, and many other professionals must meet a set of standards to practice their profession. Such standards may protect the public by winnowing out unqualified individuals and ensuring that capable students receive adequate training. In so doing, however, they limit the degree of competition in the market and inflate the pay of workers. Similarly, setting academic standards helps to defend the academic mission of universities. However, it could also protect the interests of established powers by reducing competition.

THE NCAA'S CURRENT ACADEMIC STANDARDS The NCAA's current standards are based on both students' readiness for college and their academic progress once they are admitted. Applicants must have completed 14 core courses while in high school. They must also satisfy a sliding scale of SAT scores and high school grades. Students are eligible to compete as freshmen if they have a cumulative SAT of 400 and a grade-point average of at least 3.55. Students with lower grades may compete only if their SAT scores are sufficiently higher. To maintain their eligibility, students must complete 40 percent of their work after two years of college, 60 percent after three years, and 80 percent after four years.

Although the sliding SAT and grade-point average increases fairness in the sense that it gives students who perform poorly on standardized tests a chance to qualify, there is evidence that it has created a new problem. Pete Thamel of the *New York Times* found that at some prep academies, eligibility, rather than academics, was the primary focus. He noted that "[t]hese athletes were trying to raise their grades to compensate for poor College Board scores or trying to gain attention from major-college coaches."[81] There was concern that students at these academies spent most of their time focusing on basketball and very little time on academics. According to Thamel, over 200 players attended such schools

---

[81]Pete Thamel, "Schools Where the Only Real Test Is Basketball," *New York Times*, February 25, 2006, at http://www.nytimes.com/2006/02/25/sports/ncaabasketball/25preps.html?pagewanted=1&ei=5088&en=b4408741cba1781f&ex=1298523600&partner=rssnyt&emc=rss, viewed August 22, 2006.

over a 10-year period, many going on to play in top Division I programs. Because the NCAA has not historically evaluated high schools, transcripts are not scrutinized for academic content. To address the problem, the NCAA created a task force to begin the process of reviewing high schools and their academic curricula.

In 2005, the NCAA introduced sweeping changes in how it would monitor student-athletes' academic performance in college. Division I institutions must now track academic progress rates and can be penalized if too few athletes are making adequate progress toward graduation.[82] **Academic Progress Rates (APRs)** are calculated by awarding student-athletes one point for remaining enrolled in the institution and one point for remaining academically eligible. For example, "[a] men's basketball team offering the full complement of 13 scholarships could accumulate a maximum of 52 points (13 × 2 points × 2 semesters) each year. Losing four points would lower its APR from 1,000 to 923 (92.3%)."[83] Scores are calculated and penalties are assessed on a team-by-team basis. Once a team's score falls below 925 (a standard that will rise to 930 in 2015–2016), it is subject to sanctions that increase with repeated violations:

- Stage 1: the program receives a public reprimand
- Stage 2: the program loses scholarships and/or practice time
- Stage 3: the program is banned from postseason play
- Stage 4: all the university's athletic programs lose membership in Division I[84]

In 2012, two programs received notable increases in sanctions. The University of Connecticut's men's basketball program, NCAA champions in 2011, moved to Stage 3 and lost the right to participate in the tournament scheduled for 2013. The situation at Grambling State was worse. It was informed that if it did not improve its performance sufficiently in 2012–2013, all Grambling State's programs could lose their NCAA Division I affiliation.[85]

ACADEMIC STANDARDS AS A BARRIER TO ENTRY As was the case for athletic scholarships, it is possible to view the restrictions put in place by the NCAA's reforms in one of two ways. Defenders of these standards fear that abolishing

---

[82]For institutions that do not offer scholarship athletes, the measure applies to recruited athletes. See Welch Suggs, "New Grades on Academic Progress Show Widespread Failings among Teams," *The Chronicle of Higher Education,* March 11, 2005, at http://chronicle.com/free/v51/i27/27a04001.htm, viewed August 6, 2006.

[83]Steve Wieberg, "Academic progress rates analyzed," *USA Today,* March 1, 2005, at http://www.usatoday.com/sports/college/2005-03-01-apr-analysis_x.htm, viewed August 6, 2006.

[84]National Collegiate Athletic Association, *Academic Progress Rate Penalties List,* April 15, 2010, at http://www.ncaa.org/wps/wcm/connect/public/NCAA/Academics/Division+I/APR+penalties+list.

[85]Associated Press, "NCAA Defends Connecticut Ban," *ESPN: Men's Basketball,* April 20, 2012, at http://espn.go.com/mens-college-basketball/story/_/id/7834136/ncaa-defends-connecticut-huskies-postseason-ban-stemming-apr; and Raphielle Johnson, "NCAA Hands Grambling More Sanctions Due to Low APR Scores," *NBC Sports: College Basketball Talk,* May 15, 2012, at http://collegebasketballtalk.nbcsports.com/2012/05/15/ncaa-hands-grambling-more-sanctions-due-to-low-apr-scores/.

them would create a "win at all costs" atmosphere.[86] Former NCAA Commissioner Walter Byers went further and questioned the motives of the schools opposing standards. He believed that administrators of these schools did not feel that they could compete with the major athletic programs for athletes if their schools were held to the same academic standard as the established athletic powers.[87]

Some opponents of the eligibility requirements claim that established athletic programs use academic standards as a barrier to entry. Unable to pay students more and unable to admit weaker students, less established athletic programs find it difficult to compete with traditional powers, which have an advantage recruiting athletes who meet the higher academic standards. A study of competitive balance and eligibility requirements by E. Woodrow Eckard has reported that, whatever their benefits, the restrictions on recruiting imposed by the NCAA have worsened competitive balance among the big-time football schools, with conference standings and national rankings becoming increasingly predictable.[88] A more recent study by Craig Depken and Dennis Wilson has found conflicting evidence regarding the effects of standards and enforcement. According to their study, while increases in enforcement efforts increase competitive balance, increases in penalties for violations of those standards decrease it.[89]

11.4   THE RETURNS TO THE ATHLETE

The late Joe Paterno once said that "[a]n athlete who does not graduate is grossly underpaid as an entertainer. One who graduates is overpaid."[90] In this section, we examine that claim from a number of standpoints. We begin by examining the payment granted to student-athletes and what the term "student-athlete" really means. We then examine how student-athletes invest in themselves as students and as athletes.

Pay for Play: The Grant-in-Aid

Today, sports fans across the country eagerly follow blogs to see to which high school sophomore running back has been offered a scholarship by their favorite college. They then spend the next two years learning every detail about him and agonizing on "signing day," as they wait to hear whether he has accepted the offer. It is hard to imagine that athletic scholarships were ever a subject of controversy, but, as recently as the late 1950s, many colleges refused to offer such payments for nonacademic talent.

---

[86]Joe Paterno, "Score on the SAT to Score on the Field," *Wall Street Journal,* March 16, 1999, p. A26.

[87]Walter Byers, *Unsportsmanlike Conduct* (1995), pp. 73–74.

[88]E. Woodrow Eckard, "The NCAA Cartel and Competitive Balance in College Football," *Review of Industrial Organization,* vol. 13, no. 3 (June 1998), pp. 347–369.

[89]Craig A. Depken, II and Dennis P. Wilson, "NCAA Enforcement and Competitive Balance in College Football," *Southern Economic Journal,* vol. 72, no. 4, pp. 826–845.

[90]Martin Kane, "Scorecard," *SIVault,* August 14, 1972, at http://sportsillustrated.cnn.com/vault/article/magazine/MAG1086398/4/index.htm.

Penn State offered the first athletic scholarship in 1900. Several schools quickly followed suit, while many others offered money under the table. Still, most schools frowned upon such practices.[91] In 1929, the Carnegie Foundation reported with horror that a "system of recruiting and subsidizing has grown up, under which boys are offered pecuniary and other inducements to enter a particular college." Prior to 1956, the NCAA forbade schools from making any distinction in the aid it offered athletes and non-athletes, though the Carnegie Foundation reported that as many as three-fourths of the NCAA's members disobeyed the rules they helped promulgate.[92] Officially, all students drew from the same pool of funds, which were awarded on the basis of a uniform set of criteria.

The defeat of the Sanity Code (detailed in Chapter 4) ended the attempt to treat athletes like other students. The code's defeat stemmed largely from its attempts to formalize the limits on financial aid and on the rampant unofficial support given to athletes by alumni and other boosters. In 1956, the NCAA membership voted to allow schools to provide scholarships to athletes regardless of their financial need or academic merit. The justification for athletic grants-in-aid was essentially that "Everyone is doing it anyway, so we may as well keep it all out in the open where we can regulate things." However, this assessment was not universal. The Big Ten conference tried for several years to hold athletes and non-athletes to the same standard for financial aid. Other schools questioned the sincerity of the Big Ten's stance and pointed out that, while the Big Ten schools did not give outright athletic scholarships, they did provide ample compensation for questionable on-campus employment.[93]

While the advent of grants-in-aid specifically targeted for athletes may have eliminated hypocrisy in recruiting, it created a number of philosophical and legal problems for colleges. Philosophically, schools now had to reconcile themselves to providing financial assistance to students for participating in activities that often forced them to miss classes.

More practically, schools had placed themselves in the position of being considered the athletes' employers. This relationship left colleges open to claims for workers' compensation insurance by athletes who were injured "on the job." Former NCAA Executive Director Walter Byers first coined the term *student-athlete* in an attempt to avoid such claims. In a Kafkaesque twist, athletes who wish to receive an athletic scholarship must now sign an agreement that explicitly rejects the notion that they are being paid for their performance as athletes.[94]

---

[91]Ronald Smith, *Sports and Freedom* (1988), p. 171. In the 1880s Yale supposedly had a secret $100,000 fund to pay its athletes. See Francis Dealy, *Win at Any Cost* (1990), p. 69; and Andrew Zimbalist, *Unpaid Professionals* (Princeton, N.J.: Princeton University Press, 1999), p. 7.

[92]Quote from Allen Guttman, "The Anomaly of Intercollegiate Athletics" (1991), p. 20. See also Andrew Zimbalist, *Unpaid Professionals* (1999), p. 8.

[93]See, for example, Walter Byers, *Unsportsmanlike Conduct* (1995), pp. 67–72; and Murray Sperber, *Onward to Victory* (1998), pp. 177–185 and 227–242.

[94]Andrew Zimbalist, *Unpaid Professionals* (1999), p. 37; and Walter Byers, *Unsportsmanlike Conduct* (1995), pp. 67–70.

Measuring the Net Value of Athletes to Colleges

By depressing athletes' pay, colleges can generate considerable economic rent. In this situation, economic rent is the difference between the marginal revenue product (*MRP*) of the athlete and the payment for tuition and fees. In 1993, Robert Brown estimated the *MRP* of premium players by assuming that a professional franchise drafts a player only if it regards that player as having the potential to be a professional. He then estimated how the number of players the college teams have sent to the professional draft (controlling for overall team quality) affects the teams' revenues. He found that a player with the potential to play in the NFL brought a college football team between $539,000 and $646,000 per year, more than $2 million over a four-year career.[95]

A simpler but more up-to-date formula can be computed using data from Table 11.1 and the *USA Today* NFL Salary database. The average revenue of the 20 most valuable college football teams is $62.25 million. If these teams were subject to the salary cap rules that apply in the NFL, they would have to pay 48 percent of this total to their players, yielding an average team payroll of $29.88 million. If we assume that the team pays only the 85 players on scholarship, then the average salary of a player would be approximately $355,000. To approximate the salary of a star player, we note from the *USA Today* data that Eli Manning is paid a little less than 15 percent of the New York Giants' total payroll. Assuming that a star college quarterback is worth as much to his team as Manning is to the Giants, we conclude that, in 2011, Andrew Luck and Robert Griffin III were worth about $4.4 million to Stanford and Baylor. Regardless of which methodology one uses, Stanford and Baylor profited handsomely from an annual commitment of perhaps $30,000 in scholarship money.

College as an Investment for the Student-Athlete

As explained in Chapter 8, the basic theory of human capital states that workers invest in skills in order to increase their future earnings. When workers invest in on-the-job training that will increase their earning power at competing employers, they "pay" for their training by receiving lower wages than they otherwise would. Therefore, looking solely at their wages or salaries understates the value of their total compensation. Even if they do not graduate, student-athletes who go on to professional sports careers may be making such a significant investment in their skills as athletes that their scholarships overcompensate them. While in college, student-athletes may invest in their athletic human capital and prepare for a career as a professional athlete or they may invest in their intellectual human capital and work toward a college degree. If one judges success in either area by the likelihood of receiving a degree or making the professional ranks, then playing

---

[95]Using a similar methodology, he estimated the *MRP* of a star basketball player to be close to $1 million annually. Robert Brown, "An Estimate of the Rent Generated by a Premium College Football Player" (1993), p. 679; and Robert Brown, "Measuring Cartel Rents in the College Basketball Recruitment Market" (1994), p. 32.

TABLE 11.6	The Probability of Signing with a Professional Team					
Student-athletes	Men's Basketball	Women's Basketball	Football	Baseball	Men's Ice Hockey	Men's Soccer
			(in percent)			
High School to NCAA	3.2	3.6	6.1	6.6	10.7	5.7
NCAA to Professional	1.2	0.9	1.7	11.6	1.3	1.0
High School to Professional	0.03	0.03	0.08	0.60	0.10	0.04

Source: National Collegiate Athletic Association, *Estimated Probability of Competing in Athletics beyond the High School Interscholastic Level,* 2012, at http://www.ncaa.org/wps/wcm/connect/public/Test/Issues/Recruiting/Probability+ of+Going+Pro, viewed May 30, 2012.

intercollegiate sports as a scholarship athlete appears to be a good investment only for a select few.

The data in Table 11.6 suggest that investing in a career in professional athletics resembles a winner-take-all environment in that the payoff to being a professional athlete is very high, but the odds of success are very low. The NCAA compiled the data in Table 11.6 using information obtained from the National Federation of State High School Associations and the NCAA's own 1982–2011 Participation Statistics Report. The table clearly shows that the chances of moving from the NCAA to the professional ranks in any of the major sports are very small. Other than baseball, which has an extensive minor league system (though it still counts as "professional" baseball), the chances of an NCAA senior athlete's being drafted by a professional team are less than 2 percent. While the NCAA does not break down these figures by division, even if a Division I basketball player was five times as likely to be drafted, his chances are still less than 1 in 20 of being selected (let alone playing).

A study by James Long and Steven Caudill suggests that athletics may be a good investment even if it does not lead to a professional career. According to the study, men who participate in intercollegiate athletics earn more in later life than men who do not. (They find no statistically significant differential for women.) The study, however, is hampered by limitations imposed by the data. Data sets that identify whether a person participated in interscholastic or intercollegiate athletics and follow his or her earnings history have only recently become available and are often imperfect. The data available to Long and Caudill did not permit them to control for either the sport the student played or the school attended. Their study thus treats squash players at Swarthmore and football players at Ohio State as one and the same.[96]

Because of the lack of detailed data, both researchers and the popular media have generally not tried to measure future earnings and have looked at the graduation rates of varsity athletes instead. Graduation rates are also imperfect

---

[96]James Long and Steven Caudill, "The Impact of Participation in Intercollegiate Athletics on Income and Graduation," *Review of Economics and Statistics,* vol. 73, no. 3 (August 1991), pp. 525–531. See also Zimbalist, *Unpaid Professionals* (1999), p. 51.

measures, as they do not account for many differences between athletes and non-athletes. They do not, for example, account for the fact that, unlike other students, scholarship athletes rarely have to leave school because they cannot pay their tuition bills. Conversely, athletes may leave college early for the (sometimes incorrectly) anticipated bonanza of a professional career.

Equating the graduation rates of athletes and non-athletes also fails to account for the millions of dollars spent on academic support facilities for athletes, a service mandated by the NCAA. The magnitude of such commitments was made clear by University of Michigan president emeritus James J. Duderstadt, who noted that "the Student Athlete Support Program consists of a director, 6 full-time advisors, 3 assistant advisors, 70 tutors, 10 specialized writing instructors, and 15 proctors for supervised study sessions."[97] Finally, aggregate statistics obscure the difference between major athletic powers and small, more recreational programs. Football players and basketball players at major programs are less likely to graduate than other athletes and are far less likely to graduate than the typical male undergraduate at their institution. Moreover, this gap is generally larger at the more successful programs.[98]

Tables 11.7 and 11.8 show average graduation success rates (GSR) for all of the men's and women's teams that reached the 2012 "Sweet 16" round of the NCAA basketball tournament. The **graduation success rate** modifies the federal graduation rate (all first-time full-time students who complete their degree within six years) by excluding students who leave the school in good academic standing from the denominator and including those who transfer in and graduate in the numerator. Thus, GSRs are typically higher than the federal rate.[99] The data show that most men's teams were more successful on the court than in the classroom.

Tables 11.7 and 11.8 show that the graduation success rates vary dramatically by gender when it comes to basketball. Half of the women's teams that reached the Sweet 16 had GSRs of 100 percent, and four more had GSRs over 90 percent. On the men's side, only Xavier University's GSR would have ranked among the top 10 women's scores, and half the men's teams ranked below the lowest women's team. Of the final four teams, only Kansas had a GSR higher than 70 on the men's side, while all of the women's teams had GSRs over 90.

Studies cite a variety of reasons for the low graduation rates of football and men's basketball players, such as the fact that athletes are less prepared for college

---

[97]James J. Duderstadt, *Intercollegiate Athletics and the American University: A University President's Perspective* (Ann Arbor, University of Michigan Press, 2000), p. 199.

[98]See, for example, Dean Purdy, D. Stanley Eitzen, and Rick Hufnagel, "Are Athletes Also Students? The Educational Attainment of College Athletes," in *Sports and Higher Education*, ed. by Donald Chu, Jeffrey Segrave, and Beverly Becker (Champaign, Ill.: Human Kinetics Publishers, 1985), pp. 231–234; and Louis Amato, John Gandar, Irvin Tucker, and Richard Zuber, "Bowls Versus Playoffs: The Impact on Football Player Graduation Rates in the National Collegiate Athletic Association," *Economics of Education Review*, vol. 15, no. 2 (April 1996), pp. 187–195. Louis Amato et al. have found that the graduation rate for players in Division I-A programs declines by 3 percent per bowl appearance. They find no statistically significant relationship for Division I-AA programs.

[99]"A New Way to Keep Score," *Inside Higher Ed,* at http://www.insidehighered.com/news/2005/12/20/grad, viewed August 17, 2009.

TABLE 11.7 Graduation Success Rates (GSRs) for Men's 2012 Sweet 16 Teams

School[a]	GSR
Xavier	93
Kansas	*91*
Marquette	91
North Carolina	89
Michigan State	82
North Carolina State	80
Ohio	79
***Kentucky*[b]**	*69*
Ohio State	*57*
Baylor	56
Cincinnati	56
Louisville	*56*
Syracuse	54
Wisconsin	50
Indiana	47
Florida	38

[a] Final Four teams appear in italics.

[b] National champion in bold.

Source: The Institute for Diversity and Ethics in Sport, *Keeping Score When It Counts: Academic Progress/Graduation Success Rate Study of 2012 NCAA Division I Women's and Men's Basketball Tournament Teams*, March 13, 2011, at http://www.tidesport.org/Grad%20Rates/2012%20Women%27s%20Basketball%20Tournament%20Teams%20Study.pdf.

than their fellow students. For example, Dean Purdy, D. Stanley Eitzen, and Rick Hufnagel conducted a case study of students at Colorado State University from 1970 through 1980 showed that athletes there had lower SAT scores, lower grades, and lower high school class rank than the typical Colorado State student. The shortfall in preparation was particularly large for male athletes, black athletes, and members of the football and men's basketball teams. A study by Lee Sigelman of FBS football programs showed that similar gaps existed at many schools well into the 1990s: The average entering student had SAT scores 165 points higher than the average entering student with a football scholarship, and coaches who try to build a team that resembles the student body at large may damage their chances of winning by "unduly" restricting their recruiting, as teams with larger gaps in SAT scores generally had better records.[100]

The poor performance of male athletes is not restricted to big-time programs like Florida or Connecticut. A study of schools in the Ivy League and the New England Small College Athletic Conference (home of such prestigious liberal arts colleges as Amherst, Hamilton, and Wesleyan) found a disturbingly

---

[100]See, for example, Dean Purdy et al., "Are Athletes Also Students?" (1985), pp. 221–234; and Lee Sigelman, "It's Academic—or Is It?" (1995), pp. 247–261.

TABLE 11.8   Graduation Success Rates (GSRs) for 2012 Women's Sweet 16 Teams

School[a]	GSR
Connecticut	*100*
Duke	100
Kentucky	100
Notre Dame	*100*
Penn State	100
St. John's	100
South Carolina	100
Tennessee	100
Gonzaga	94
Stanford	*93*
Baylor[b]	92
St. Bonaventure	91
Maryland	81
Georgia Tech	73
Texas A&M	70
Kansas	63

[a] Final Four teams appear in italics.

[b] National champion in bold.

Source: The Institute for Diversity and Ethics in Sport, *Keeping Score When It Counts: Academic Progress/Graduation Success Rate Study of 2012 NCAA Division I Women's and Men's Basketball Tournament Teams*, March 13, 2011, at http://www.tidesport.org/Grad%20Rates/2012%20 Women%27s%20Basketball%20Tournament%20Teams%20Study.pdf.

similar pattern. At these schools, young men who were recruited to play football, basketball, or ice hockey had SAT scores that averaged between 119 and 165 points below those of non-athletes. Worse still, the student-athletes underperformed relative to these predictors, so that three-quarters of recruited male athletes ranked in the bottom third of their class. Even students in lower-profile sports, such as track, did poorly, with two-thirds of them in the bottom third of the class. Consistent with Table 11.8, there was little evidence of similar problems for female athletes.[101]

In some cases, however, low graduation rates may be a sign of success rather than failure. One study claims that some college athletes choose to leave college as the result of rationally maximizing their utility. It points out that it makes more sense for a student-athlete to focus on his prospects as a football player at Notre Dame, which sent 76 players to the NFL from 1979 through 1993, than at Bucknell, which sent only 1 player during the same time period. In light of such differences in professional prospects, student-athletes might make their decisions to attend a specific college—and to become part of a specific athletic program—as part of their

---

[101]William Bowen and Sarah Levin, *Reclaiming the Game: College Sports and Educational Values* (Princeton: Princeton University Press, 2003).

broader career choices. It is therefore no more surprising for a football player from a traditional football power such as Tennessee to fail to make the NFL than it is for a premed student at a small liberal arts college to fail to get into medical school.[102]

BIOGRAPHICAL SKETCH

Anita Defrantz

Without Anita DeFrantz, the corruption and the image of corruption will run unabated. With her, I have a genuine hope for our Olympic athletes inspiring young people that they can all live within that one circle of humanity.

—*Richard E. Lapchick*[1]

One of the most powerful women in the sports industry had little intention of following a career in sports. Instead, she came to her position as the result of a couple of fortuitous coincidences. Born and raised in Indiana, Anita DeFrantz attended Connecticut College, a small school better known for its academics than for its Division III athletics. The first coincidence occurred when, as a sophomore, DeFrantz saw the school's crew coach carrying a boat and asked him what it was for. The coach noticed that DeFrantz, at 5'11", looked strong and athletic, and he soon had her on the water with the team. DeFrantz went on to be a six-time national champion, and, three years after her chance encounter with the crew coach, she captained the eight-woman boat to a bronze medal in the 1976 Summer Olympic Games in Montreal, the first Olympics to feature women's rowing.

The second coincidence led DeFrantz from athletic success to a career in sports administration. While preparing for the 1980 Games, DeFrantz earned a law degree from the University of Pennsylvania and passed the bar exam. Her hopes for a gold medal were dashed, however, when the United States boycotted the 1980 Moscow Games to protest the Soviet Union's invasion of Afghanistan. DeFrantz then took a step that set the future course of her career. She put her legal training to use by suing the United States Olympic Committee (USOC). Her lawsuit claimed that the government could not force individual athletes to boycott the Olympics.

DeFrantz's lawsuit proved politically unpopular—some critics suggested that she join the Communist Party—and, ultimately, unsuccessful. Although DeFrantz lost her suit, she caught the attention of the International Olympic Committee (IOC). It awarded her a medal for her effort to put Olympic competition above politics and helped her to begin a career in the Olympic movement. In 1984, DeFrantz was named vice-president of the Los Angeles Olympic Organizing Committee. She later joined the Amateur Athletic Foundation (AAF) and the USOC, rapidly rising in each to become the president of the AAF and a member of the executive committee of the USOC. Since 1993, she has been a vice-president of the international rowing association (FISA), the international rowing federation. Recognizing her talents, the IOC named her as a lifetime member.

---

[102]Lawrence DeBrock, Wallace Hendricks, and Roger Koenker, "The Economics of Persistence: Graduation Rates of Athletes as Labor Market Choice," *Journal of Human Resources,* vol. 31, no. 3 (Summer 1996), pp. 513–539.

DeFrantz's appointment again made her a pioneer. She became the first American woman and only the fifth woman ever invited to join the IOC. Since her appointment, DeFrantz has become an influential member of the IOC, especially in matters related to women's sports and developing countries. She was a member of the IOC Coordinating Committee for the 2012 London Olympics.

DeFrantz's reputation for integrity and fairness helped her become the first woman to be elected vice-president of the IOC's Executive Committee in 1997. After IOC president Juan Antonio Samaranch retired, DeFrantz ran unsuccessfully to succeed him. Despite this setback, she has continued to use her position to speak out as a voice for athletes.

---

[1]Richard Lapchick, "What IOC Needs, Anita DeFrantz Offers," *Street and Smith's Sports Business Journal*, March 12–18, 2001, at http://www.sportsbusinessdaily.com/Journal/Issues/2001/03/20010312/This-Weeks-Issue/What-IOC-Needs-Anita-Defrantz-Offers.aspx.

Summary

This chapter uses the tools of economics to analyze the behavior of the NCAA, its member schools, and the athletes who participate in collegiate sports. Amateurism lies at the heart of intercollegiate athletics. Though its origins and meanings are often misunderstood, its implications are clear: college athletes should not be paid.

Intercollegiate athletics brings a number of benefits and costs to a university. As with professional sports, ticket sales and television revenues are important revenue sources. Venue revenue from luxury boxes and club seating are also becoming increasingly important. Unlike professional athletics, many of these payments are filtered through the NCAA and conferences. The results often level revenues within conferences but exacerbate differences between them. While athletes are not paid, their scholarships are counted—perhaps incorrectly—as a major expense. College coaches and athletic directors are very well paid, earning more—relative to the revenue stream—than their professional counterparts. Whether a college profits from athletics can depend on how one defines revenues and costs. Even if a college does not profit financially, it might want to support athletics due to the other benefits that they bring. Applications and donations to the university rise with athletic success, though the impact on the quality of students and on donations to nonathletic parts of the university is small.

We can think of the NCAA in many ways. One can model it as a regulatory agency, as a club (using Buchanan's Theory of Clubs), and as a cartel that exercises monopoly and monopsony power. No one framework is always superior to the others, and which framework we choose can determine how we interpret a given action by the NCAA.

Although student-athletes are not paid, they can use their time in college to invest in academic and athletic skills. Evidence suggests that student-athletes in football and men's basketball do not have the same academic preparation as non-athletes and that male athletes in general underperform academically at both major sports powers and academically oriented institutions. Women show no such ill effects.

Discussion Questions

1. Discuss the viability of amateurism in the United States today. Is it possible, given the attention that elite athletes receive, to have "pure" amateurs?
2. Should college athletes be paid? If not, why not? If so, what is the appropriate payment scheme?
3. Does the athletic department at your college make a profit? Does it profit even when transfers—such as student fees—are deducted? If it lost money, what—if anything—should be done?
4. If your college were invited to the New Mexico Bowl, would you favor accepting the bid? Why or why not?
5. Are head football and basketball coaches worth the money they are paid?

Problems

11.1. Show, using supply and demand for labor diagrams for Divisions I and III, the effect of a new rule allowing Division III schools to pay athletes a one-time bonus for enrolling at their schools.
11.2. Use *MC* and *MR* curves to show why the BCS schools claimed a larger share of bowl and TV revenues than non-BCS schools.
11.3. Use human capital theory to explain why colleges might not pay students their full marginal product.
11.4. Assume that you are the newly appointed head of the NCAA. Construct a framework for a new scholarship program that would entirely replace the existing system. Describe what should be its fundamental tenets if
    a. The primary goal is to ensure that athletes were not exploited.
    b. The primary goal is to ensure that student-athletes receive degrees.
    c. The primary goal is to maximize profits.
11.5. What effect do the following have on a person's decision to invest in athletic training versus academic training? In each case, explain the direction and likely significance of the effect.
    a. Risk of career-ending injury
    b. The probability of success in athletics
    c. An increase in the cost of college tuition
    d. An increase in the demand for professional sports
11.6. Use game theory to describe how an effort by two universities to recruit a top basketball player might result in both committing NCAA recruiting violations.
11.7. What unselfish and selfish motives might be behind the attempts by some schools to set academic standards for student-athletes?
11.8. Use supply and demand analysis to show and describe the dramatic increase in "basketball academy" prep schools in response to higher academic standards.
11.9. How might failing to graduate from college be an optimal investment in one's human capital?
11.10. Use human capital theory to explain why graduation rates for women's basketball players are so much higher than those for men's basketball players.

WORKS CITED

"10 Highest Earning Players," *Forbes*, at http://www.forbes.com/pictures/mlh45eel/no-3-lionel-messi/#gallerycontent, viewed May 23, 2012.

2007–2011 Basic Agreement, at http://mlb.mlb.com/pa/pdf/cba_english.pdf.

"2011–2012 College Football Season Bowl Results," *CollegeFootballPoll.com*, at http://www.collegefootballpoll.com/2011_archive_bowls.html, viewed May 28, 2012.

Abrams, Roger. *Legal Bases: Baseball and the Law.* Philadelphia: Temple University Press, 1998.

Agence France Presse. "Previous FIFA Ballon d'Or Winners," *The Times of India*, January 10, 2012, at http://timesofindia.indiatimes.com/sports/football/top-stories/Previous-FIFA-Ballon-dOr-winners/articleshow/11430535.cms.

Aldrich, Eric M., Peter S. Arcidiacono, and Joseph L. Vigdor "Do People Value Racial Diversity? Evidence from Nielsen Ratings," *The B.E. Journal of Economic Analysis and Policy*, vol. 5, no. 1 (2005), Article 4.

Alesia, Mark. "Tourney Money Fuels Pay-to-Play Debate," *Indianapolis Star*, April 1, 2006, at http://www.indystar.com/apps/pbcs.dll/article?Date=20060401&Category=SPORTS&ArtNo=604010509&SectionCat=&Template=printart.

Amato, Louis, John Gandar, Irvin Tucker, and Richard Zuber. "Bowls versus Playoffs: The Impact on Football Player Graduation Rates in the National Collegiate Athletic Association," *Economics of Education Review*, vol. 15, no. 2 (April 1996), pp. 187–195.

Amick, Sam. "Inside the NBA: Summary of the Tentative NBA Deal," *SI.com*, November 26, 2011, at http://sportsillustrated.cnn.com/2011/writers/sam_amick/11/26/tentative.deal/index.html.

———. "Inside the NBA," *SI.com*, April 20, 2011, at http://sportsillustrated.cnn.com/2011/writers/sam_amick/04/20/sacramento.kings/index.html.

Anderson, Kelli. "Nine for IX," *Sports Illustrated*, May 7, 2012, p. 49.

Anderson, Torben, and Sumner J. La Croix. "Customer Discrimination in Major League Baseball," *Economic Inquiry*, vol. 29, no. 4 (October 1991), pp. 665–677.

Andreff, Wladimir, and Paul Staudohar. "European and U.S. Business Sports Models," in *Transatlantic Sport: The Comparative Economics of North American and European Sport*, ed. by C. Barros, M. Ibrahimo, and S. Szymanski. Cheltenham, U.K.: Edward Elgar, 2002, pp. 23-49.

Andrews, Geoff. *Not a Normal Country: Italy after Berlusconi*. London: Pluto Press, 2005.

Anonymous. "Allan H. 'Bud' Selig," *Commissioners*, at http://mlb.mlb.com/mlb/history/mlb_history_people.jsp?story=com_bio_9.

"Answers Please," *The Economist*, August 2, 2003, pp. 23–27.

Associated Press. "MLB Official Says 'Nothing Improper' about 1995 Loan," *ESPN Baseball*, January 9, 2002, at http://espn.go.com/mlb/news/2002/0108/1307601.html.

———. "Evans Takes Over As Acting Commish," *ESPN Golf*, July 13, 2009, at http://m.espn.go.com/golf/story?storyId=4323583.

———. "Barcelona Agree €150 Million Shirt Sponsor Deal with Qatar Foundation," *The Guardian*, December 10, 2010, at http://www.guardian.co.uk/football/2010/dec/10/barcelona-shirt-sponsor-qatar-foundation.

———. *Yanks, Red Sox Hit with Luxury Tax*, December 22, 2011, at http://espn.go.com/mlb/story/_/id/7381414/new-york-yankees-boston-red-sox-only-teams-hit-luxury-tax.

———. "NCAA Defends Connecticut Ban," *ESPN: Men's Basketball*, April 20, 2012, at http://espn.go.com/mens-college-basketball/story/_/id/7834136/ncaa-defends-connecticut-huskies-postseason-ban-stemming-apr.

ATP Tour, Inc. *The 2012 ATP Official Rulebook,* 2012, at http://www.atpworldtour.com/Corporate/Rulebook.aspx.

Austrian, Ziona, and Mark Rosentraub. "Cleveland's Gateway to the Future," in *Sports, Jobs, and Taxes,* ed. by Roger Noll and Andrew Zimbalist. Washington, D.C.: Brookings Institution Press, 1997, pp. 355–384.

Aynsworth, Hugh. "Owner of Dallas Cowboys Seeks $1 Billion in Tax Funds," *Washington Times,* February 2, 2004, at http://www.washington-times.com/national/20040202-120350-8901r.htm.

Baade, Robert. "Should Congress Stop the Bidding War for Sports Franchises?" *The Heartland Insitute,* August 1, 1996, at http://heartland.org/policy-documents/should-congress-stop-bidding-war-sports-franchises-baade.

Baade, Robert, and Richard Dye. "Sports Stadiums and Area Development: A Critical Review," *Economic Development Quarterly,* vol. 2, no. 3 (August 1988), pp. 265–275.

Baade, Robert, and Allen R. Sanderson. "The Employment Effect of Teams and Sports Facilities," in *Sports, Jobs, and Taxes*, ed. By Roger Noll and Andrew Zimbalist. Washington, D.C.: Brookings Institution Press, 1997, pp. 94–95.

Baade, Robert, and Victor Matheson. "Bidding for Fool's Gold?" in *Transatlantic Sport,* ed. by C. P. Barros, M. Ibrahimo, and S, Szymanski. Cheltenham, U.K.: Edward Elgar, 2002, pp. 127–251.

———. "Have Public Finance Principles Been Shut Out of Financing New Stadiums for the NFL?" *Public Finance and Management*, vol. 6, no. 3 (2006), pp. 284–320.

Badenhausen, Kurt, Michael K. Ozanian, and Christina Settimi. "The Business of Baseball," *Forbes,* April 7, 2010, at http://www.forbes.com/lists/2010/33/baseball-valuations-10_New-York-Yankees_334613.html.

———. "The Business of Baseball 2012," *Forbes,* March 21, 2012, at http://www.forbes.com/mlb-valuations/list.

———. "MLB Team Values," *Forbes,* March 22, 2011, at http://www.forbes.com/lists/2011/33/baseball-valuations-11_land.html.

———. "NFL Team Values," *Forbes,* at http://www.forbes.com/lists/2011/30/nfl-valuations-11_land.html.

———. "NBA Team Values," *Forbes,* at http://www.forbes.com/lists/2011/32/basketball-valuations-11_land.html.

———. "NHL Team Values," *Forbes,* at http://www.forbes.com/nhl-valuations/

Baker, William. *Sports in the Western World.* Totowa, N.J.: Rowman & Littlefield, 1982.

"Baltimore Orioles Attendance Analysis" and "Cleveland Indians Attendance Analysis," *Baseball Almanac,* copyright on 2000–2012, at www.baseball-almanac.com.

Baltzell, E. Digby. *Sporting Gentlemen: Men's Tennis form the Age of Honor to the Cult of the Superstar* New York: The Free Press, 1995.

Bamberger, Michael, and Don Yaeger. "Over the Edge," *Sports Illustrated,* April 14, 1997, pp. 61–70.

Baroncelli, Alessandro, and Umberto Lago. "Italian Football," *Journal of Sports Economics,* vol. 7, no. 1 (February 2006), pp. 13–28.

Barra, Allen. "In Anti-trust We Trust," *Salon Magazine,* May 19, 2000, at http://www.salon.com/news/feature/2000/05/19/antitrust/index.html.

———. *The Last Coach: A Life of Paul "Bear" Bryant.* New York: W. W. Norton, 2005.

Barry, Dave. *Dave Barry Turns Fifty.* New York: Random House, 1999.

Bartlett, Donald, and James Steele. "Snow Job," *Sports Illustrated*, December 10, 2001, pp. 79–97.

Basco, Dan, and Michael Davies. "The Many Flavors of DIPS: A History and an Overview," *Society for American Baseball Research,* Fall 2010, at http://sabr.org/research/many-flavors-dips-history-and-overview, viewed May 23, 2012.

Baseball Almanac, at http://www.baseball-almanc.com.

Becker, Gary S. *The Economics of Discrimination,* 2nd ed. Chicago: University of Chicago Press, 1971.

———. "De Gustibus Non Est Disputandum," *American Economic Review,* vol. 67, no. 1 (March 1977), pp. 76–90.

———. "A Theory of Competition Among Pressure Groups for Political Influence," *Quarterly Journal of Economics,* vol. 97, no. 3 (August 1983), pp. 371–400.

———. "College Athletes Should Get Paid What They're Worth," *Business Week,* September 30, 1985, p. 38.

———. *Human Capital,* 3rd ed. Chicago: University of Chicago Press, 1993.

Beckett Baseball, vol. 12, no. 3 (March 2012), p. 72.

Belson, Ken. "Tickets Cost Too Much? Check Back Tomorrow," *New York Times,* May 18, 2009, p. D-2.

———. "New Sponsor on WNBA Uniforms," *New York Times,* August 22, 2011, at http://www.nytimes.com/2011/08/22/sports/basketball/wnba-makes-sponsorship-deal-with-boost-mobile.html?_r=1.

Bell, Jarret. "NFL salaries: Top NFL QBs Could Be in Line for Contract Hikes," *USA Today,* March 9, 2010, at http://www.usatoday.com/sports/football/nfl/2010-03-09-nfl-salaries-story_N.htm.

———. "Freeman McNeil Sees History Repeating in NFL Labor Dispute," *USA Today*, April 3, 2011, at http://www.usatoday.com/sports/football/nfl/2011-03-31-freeman-mcneil-nfl-labor_N.htm.

Berkowitz, Steve, and Jodi Upton. "Athletic Director Salary Database for 2011," *USA Today,* October 6, 2011, at http://www.usatoday.com/sports/college/story/2011-athletics-director-salaries-database/50669958/1.

Berentsen, Aleksander. "The Economics of Doping," *European Journal of Political Economy,* vol. 18, no. 1 (March 2002), pp. 109–127.

Berman, Gabrielle, Robert Brooks, and Sinclair Davidson. "The Sydney Olympic Games Announcement and Australian Stock Market Reaction," *Applied Economics Letters,* vol. 7, no. 12 (December 2000), pp. 781–784.

Bernstein, Andy. "Inside the Complex NHL Deal," June 4, 2009, at http://www.sportsbusinessdaily.com/Journal/Issues/2005/08/20050801/Labor-Agents/Inside-The-Complex-NHL-Deal.aspx.

Berr, Jonathan. "New Stadiums Strike Out for Investors and Taxpayers," *DailyFinance,* September 20, 2010, at http://www.dailyfinance.com/2010/09/20/defaulting-new-stadiums/.

Berri, David J. "What Do Chris Paul, Dwight Howard, LeBron James, and Tim Duncan Have in Common" *The Wages of Wins Journal,* May 22, 2008, at http://dberri.wordpress.com/2008/05/22/what-do-chris-paul-dwight-howard-lebron-james-and-tim-duncan-have-in-common/.

Berri, David J., Stacey Brook, Bernd Frick, Aju Fenn, and Roberto Vicente-Mayoral. "The Short Supply of Tall People: Explaining Competitive Imbalance in the National Basketball Association," *Journal of Economic Issues,* vol. 39, no. 4 (December 2005), pp. 1029–1041.

Berri, David J., and Martin B. Schmidt, *Stumbling on Wins*, Upper Saddle River, N.J.: FT Press, 2010.

Berri, David J., Martin Schmidt, and Stacey Brook. *The Wages of Wins.* Stanford, Calif.: Stanford University Press, 2006.

Berri, David J., and Rob Simmons. "Race and the Evaluation of Signal Callers in the National Football League," *Journal of Sports Economics*, vol. 10, no. 1 (February 2009), pp. 23–43.

"Best Paid Athletes from 200 Countries," *ESPN The Magazine,* April 26, 2012, at http://espn.go.com/espn/story/_/id/7858737/floyd-mayweather-united-states-best-paid-athlete-espn-magazine.

Betzold, Michael, and Ethan Casey. *Queen of Diamonds: The Tiger Stadium Story.* West Bloomfield, Mich.: Northfield Publishing Co., 1992.

Bigman, Dan. "The World's Most Valuable Soccer Teams," *Forbes,* at http://www.forbes.com/2011/04/20/worlds-most-valuable-soccer-teams_slide.html.

Borland, Melvin, Brian Goff, and Robert Pulsinelli. "College Athletics: Financial Burden or Boon?" in *Advances in the Economics of Sport,* vol. 1, ed. by Gerald Scully. New York: JAI Press, 1992.

Borland, Jeffrey, and Robert MacDonald. "Demand for Sport," *Oxford Review of Economic Policy*, vol. 19, no. 4 (2003), pp. 478–502.

Bovarsson, Orn B. "A Test of Employer Discrimination in the NBA," *Contemporary Economic Policy*, vol. 17, no. 2 (April 1999), pp. 243–256.

Bowen, William, and Sarah Levin. *Reclaiming the Game: College Sports and Educational Values.* Princeton, N.J.: Princeton University Press, 2003.

Briggs, Lindsey Valaine. "UEFA v The European Community: Attempts of the Governing Body of European Soccer to Circumvent EU Freedom of Movement and Antidiscrimination Labor Law," *Chicago Journal of International Law,* vol. 6, no. 1 (Summer 2005), pp. 439–454.

Brown, Maury. "The Effect of Regional Sports Networks," *The Ledger Domain,* February 5, 2007, at http://www.baseballprospectus.com/article.php?articleid=5843.

———. "2009 MLB Salary Arbitration Vital Stats," *The Biz of Baseball,* February 20, 2009, at http://www.bizofbaseball.com/index.php?option=com_content&view=article&id=2974:2009-mlb-salary-arbitration-vital-stats&catid=66:free-agency-and-trades&Itemid=153.

———. "Average Salary for MLB in 2009," *The Biz of Baseball,* December 1, 2009, at http://bizofbaseball.com/index.php?option=com_content&view=article&id=3777:inside-the-numbers-average-salary-2009&catid=26:editorials&Itemid=39.

———. "Arbitration Figures," *The Biz of Baseball,* February 19, 2011, at http://bizofbaseball.com/index.php?option=com_content&view=article&id=599&Itemid=72.

———. "Inside MLB/s New 5-year Labor Agreement," *The Biz of Baseball,* November 22, 2011, at http://bizofbaseball.com/index.php?option=com_content&view=article&id=5521:inside-mlbs-new-5-year-labor-agreement&catid=30:mlb-news&Itemid=42.

———. "Yankees Surpass $200 Million in total Luxury Tax Payments," *The Biz of Baseball,* December 22, 2011, at http://bizofbaseball.com/index.php?option=com_content&view=article&id=5560:yankees-surpass-200-million-in-total-luxury-tax-payments&catid=26:editorials&Itemid=39.

Brown, Robert W. "An Estimate of the Rent Generated by a Premium College Football Player," *Economic Inquiry,* vol. 21, no. 4 (October 1993), pp. 671–684.

———. "Measuring Cartel Rents in the College Basketball Player Recruitment Market," *Applied Economics,* vol. 26, no. 1 (January 1994), pp. 27–34.

Brown, Robert W., and R. Todd Jewell. "Is There Customer Discrimination in College Basketball? The Premium Fans Pay for White Players," *Social Science Quarterly,* vol. 75, no. 2 (June 1994), pp. 401–412.

Brownlee, Shannon, and Nancy Linnon. "The Myth of the Student-Athlete," *U.S. News and World Report,* January 8, 1990, p. 50.

Brustein, Joshua. "Star Pitchers in a Duel? Tickets Will Cost More," *New York Times,* June 27, 2010, at http://www.nytimes.com/2010/06/28/technology/28tickets.html.

Bryant, Howard. "Angels, Rangers Join the Big Boys," *ESPN.com,* March 29, 2012, at http://espn.go.com/mlb/preview12/story/_/id/7750708/los-angeles-angels-texas-rangers-now-baseball-superpowers.

Buffalo Sabres. *Tickets: 2011–2012 Individual Game Tickets,* 2010, at http://sabres.nhl.com/club/page.htm?id=70166.

Buchanan, James. "An Economic Theory of Clubs," *Economica,* vol. 32, no. 125 (February 1965), pp. 1–14.

Buraimo, Babatunde, and Rob Simmons. "Do Sports Fans Really Value Uncertainty of Outcome? Evidence from the English Premier League," *International Journal of Sport Finance,* vol. 3, no. 3 (August 2008), pp. 146–155.

Bureau of Labor Statistics. *Economic News Release: Union Members Summary,* January 28, 2012, at http://www.bls.gov/news.release/union2.nr0.htm.

Burk, Robert. *Never Just a Game: Players, Owners, and American Baseball to 1920.* Chapel Hill: University of North Carolina Press, 1994.

Burke, Monte. "Is DeMaurice Smith the Most Important Man in Football," *Forbes,* October 28, 2010, at http://www.forbes/sites/monteburke/2010/10/28/is-demaurice-smith-the-most-important-man-in-football/.

Burns, Ken. "Bottom of the Sixth" episode, *Baseball* (film). Alexandria, Va.: PBS Video, 1994.

Byers, Walter, with Charles Hammer. *Unsportsmanlike Conduct: Exploiting College Athletes.* Ann Arbor: University of Michigan Press, 1995.

Byrne, Jim. *The $1 League: The Rise and Fall of the USFL.* New York: Prentice Hall, 1986.

Byrom, J. Robert. "ESPN Names Oklahoma Most Prestigious Program during AP/BCS Eras," *USC Trojans*, January 23, 2009, at http://bleacherreport.com/articles/114758-espn-names-ou-most-prestigous-school-during-apbcs-eras.

Cagan, Joanna, and Neil deMause. *Field of Schemes.* Monroe, Maine: Common Courage Press, 1998.

Calcaterra, Craig. "Yankees President Randy Levine Blasts Rangers Owner Chuck Greenberg," *Hardball Talk,* January 28, 2011, at http://hardballtalk.nbcsports.com/2011/01/28/yankees-president-randy-levine-blasts-rangers-owner-chuck-greenberg.

Campbell, Tim. "Jets Will Not Need NHL's Revenue-Sharing." *Winnipeg Free Press*, April 25, 2012, at http://www.winnipegfreepress.com/breakingnews/Jets-will-not-need-NHLs-revenue-sharing--146445605.html.

Canellos, Peter S. "In City with Short Memory, Astrodome May Become History," *Milwaukee Journal-Sentinel,* July 27, 1997, p. 26A, at http://news.google.com/newspapers?nid=1683&dat=19970727&id=q0MqAAAAIBAJ&sjid=Ky4EAAAAIBAJ&pg=6675,7160037.

Card, David, and Gordon B. Dahl. "Family Violence and Football: The Effect of Unexpected Emotional Cues on Violent Behavior," *Quarterly Journal of Economics,* vol. 126, no. 1 (February 2011), pp. 103–143.

Carlino, Gerald, and N. Edward Coulson. "Compensating Differentials and the Social Benefit of the NFL," *Journal of Urban Economics,* vol. 56, no. 1 (July 2004), pp. 25–50.

Carrey, Jack, and Andy Gardiner. "NCAA Settlement Gives Aid to Athletes," *USA Today,* January 29, 2008, at http://www.usatoday.com/sports/college/2008-01-29-settlement-aid-details_N.htm.

Cassing, James, and Richard Douglas. "Implications of the Auction Mechanism in Baseball's Free Agent Draft," *Southern Economic Journal,* vol. 47, no. 1 (July 1980), pp. 110–121.

Cayleff, Susan. *Babe: The Life and Legend of Babe Didrickson Zaharias.* Urbana: University of Illinois Press, 1995.

Center for Responsive Politics. "Annual Lobbying by the National Football League," *OpenSecrets.org*, March 26, 2012, at http://www.opensecrets.org/lobby/clientsum.php?id=D000027847&year=2011.

Che, XiaoGang, and Brad Humphreys. "Earnings and Performance in Women's Skiing," *The Handbook on the Economics of Women's Sports.* ed. by Eva Marikova Leeds and Michael A. Leeds. Cheltenham, U.K.: Edward Elgar, forthcoming.

Chema, Thomas. "When Professional Sports Justify the Subsidy," *Journal of Urban Affairs,* vol. 18, no. 1 (February 1996), pp. 19–22.

Clapp, Christopher M., and Jahn K. Hakes. "How Long a Honeymoon? The Effect of New Stadiums on Attendance in Major League Baseball," *Journal of Sports Economics,* vol. 6, no. 3 (August 2005), pp. 237–263.

Clotfelter, Charles T. *Big-Time Sports in American Universities.* Cambridge, U.K.: Cambridge University Press, 2011.

Coase, Ronald. "The Problem of Social Cost," *Journal of Law and Economics,* vol. 3, no. 1 (October 1960), pp. 1–44.

Coates, Dennis. "Stadiums and Arenas: Economic Development or Economic Redistribution?" *Contemporary Economic Policy,* vol. 25, no. 4 (October 2007), pp. 565–577.

Coates, Dennis, and Brad R. Humphreys. "The Effect of Professional Sports on Earnings and Employment in U.S. Cities," *Regional Science and Urban Economics,* vol. 33, no. 2 (March 2003), pp. 175–198.

———. "Professional Sports Facilities, Franchises, and Urban Economic Development," *Public Finance and Management,* vol. 3, no. 3 (September 2003), pp. 335–357.

Cobb, Nathan. "Baseball Border War: In Milford, Conn. Geography Brings Sox and Mets Fans Cheek to Jowl," *Boston Globe,* October 20, 1986, p. 8.

Collegegridirons.com, at http://www.collegegridirons.com/.

"Company Overview of Giants Stadium LLC," *Business Week,* August 31, 2012, at http://investing.businessweek.com/research/stocks/private/snapshot.asp?privcapId=36320464.

Conlin, Michael and Patrick M. Emerson. "Discrimination in Hiring versus Retention and Promotion: An Empirical Analysis of Within-Firm Treatment of Players in the NFL," *Journal of Law, Economics & Organization,* vol. 22, no. 1 (April 2006), pp. 115–136.

Conway, Russ. *Game Misconduct: Alan Eagleson and the Corruption of Hockey,* Buffalo: MacFarlane, Walter, and Ross, 1997.

Coon, Larry. *NBA Salary Cap FAQ,* copyright on 1999–2012, at http://www.cbafaq.com/salarycap.htm#Q13.

———. "Breaking down changes in the new CBA," *ESPN NBA,* December 3, 2011, at http://espn.go.com/nba/story/_/page/CBA-111128/how-new-nba-deal-compares-last-one.

Corbitt, Craig, and Jan Yi. "*American Needle, Inc.* v. *National Football League, et al.*: Amicus Curiae Brief of Economists in Support of Petitioner," at http://www.scribd.com/bigtkirk/d/20345483-Sports-Economics-Amicus-Brief-in-American-Needle-Case.

Coughlin, Cletus C., and O. Homer Erekson. "An Examination of Contributions to Support Intercollegiate Athletics," *Southern Economic Journal,* vol. 50, no. 1 (July 1984), pp. 180–195.

Covington, Robert N. "How Much Is the Law to Blame for Baseball's Turbulent Labor Relations?" *Journal of Sports Economics,* vol. 4, no. 4 (November 2003), pp. 357–361.

Croson, Rachel, and Uri Gneezy. "Gender Differences in Preferences," *Journal of Economic Literature,* vol. 47, no. 2 (Summer 2009), pp. 1–27.

Crowley, Joseph *In the Arena: The NCAA's First Century.* Indianapolis: NCAA, 2006.

Cubs.com, *Six Game Pack,* 2012, at http://chicago.cubs.mlb.com/chc/ticketing/sixpacks.jsp, viewed March 20, 2012.

Curme, Michael A. and Greg M. Dougherty. "Competition and Pay for National Hockey League Players Born in Quebec," *Journal of Sports Economics,* vol. 5, no. 2 (May 2004), pp. 186–205.

Danielson, Michael. *Home Team: Professional Sport and the American Metropolis.* Princeton, N.J.: Princeton University Press, 1997.

Davis, Nate. "NFL, Players Announce New 10-Year Labor Agreement," *USA Today,* July 25, 2011, at http://content.usatoday.com/communities/thehuddle/post/2011/07/reports-nfl-players-agree-to-new-collective-bargaining-agreement/1.

Dealy, Francis. *Win at Any Cost: The Sell Out of College Athletics.* New York: Birch Lane Press, 1990.

DeBrock, Lawrence, Wallace Hendricks, and Roger Koenker. "The Economics of Persistence: Graduation Rates of Athletes as Labor Market Choice," *Journal of Human Resources,* vol. 31, no. 3 (Summer 1996), pp. 513–539.

De Groote, Michael. "Games Not Over: Financial Principles That Saved the 2002 Olympic Games," *Deseret News,* February 5, 2012, at http://www.deseretnews.com/article/700222487/Games-not-over-Financial-principles-that-saved-the-2002-Olympic-Winter-Games.html?pg=all.

Delaney, Kevin. *Public Dollars, Private Stadiums,* New Brunswick: Rutgers University Press, 2003.

Depken, Craig A. II. "Free-Agency and the Competitiveness of Major League Baseball," *Review of Industrial Organization,* vol. 14, no. 3 (May 1999), pp. 205–217.

Depken, Craig A. II, and Dennis P. Wilson. "NCAA Enforcement and Competitive Balance in College Football," *Southern Economic Journal,* vol. 72, no. 4 (April 2005), pp. 826–845.

Depken, Craig A. II, David R. Kamerschen, and Arthur Snow. "Generic Advertising of Intermediate Goods: Theory and Evidence," *The Review of Industrial Organization,* vol. 20, no. 3 (May 2002), pp. 205–220.

Dexheimer, Eric. "The Longhorn Economy," *Austin American-Statesman*, September 30, 2007, at http://www.statesman.com/sports/content/sports/stories/longhorns/09/30/0930utsportsmain.html.

Dey, Matthew S. "Racial Differences in National Basketball Association Salaries: A New Look," *American Economist*, vol. 41, no. 2 (Fall 1997), pp. 84–90.

Dickey, Glenn. *Just Win, Baby: Al Davis and His Raiders.* New York: Harcourt, Brace, Jovanovich, 1991.

Dickey, Jack. "Melky Cabrera Tests Postive for Testosterone, Is Suspended 50 Games, Can Still Win the Batting Title," *Deadspin*, August 15, 2012, at http://deadspin.com/5935082/melky-cabrera-tests-positive-for-testosterone-suspended-50-games-can-still-win-the-batting-title.

Donadio, Rachel. "Berlusconi's Wife Says She Wants a Divorce," *New York Times*, 2009, at www.nytimes.com/2009/05/04/world/europe/04iht-italy.html.

Dorian, P. Owen, Michael Ryan, and Clayton R. Weatherston. "Measuring Competitive Balance in Professional Team Sports Using the Herfindahl-Hirschman Index," *Journal of Industrial Organization*, vol. 31, no. 4 (December 2007), pp. 289–302.

Dosh, Kristi. "MLB's Luxury and Tax and Revenue Sharing Are Not One and the Same," *The Biz of Baseball*, April 19, 2010, at http://bizofbaseball.com/index.php?option=com_content&view=article&id=4298:dosh-mlbs-revenue-sharing-and-the-luxury-tax-are-not-one-in-the-same&catid=29:articles-a-opinion&Itemid=41.

Duderstadt, James J. *Intercollegiate Athletics and the American University: A University President's Perspective.* Ann Arbor: University of Michigan Press, 2000.

Dworkin, James. *Owners versus Players: Baseball and Collective Bargaining.* Boston: Auburn House, 1981.

Ebert, Graydon. "MLSE Buy," *Offside: A Sports Law Blog*, at http://offsidesportsblog.blogspot.com/p/mlse-buy.html.

Eckard, E. Woodrow. "The NCAA Cartel and Competitive Balance in College Football," *Review of Industrial Organization*, vol. 13, no. 3 (June 1998), pp. 347–369.

———. "The ANOVA-Based Competitive Balance Measure: A Defense," *Journal of Sports Economics*, vol. 4, no. 1 (February 2003), pp. 74–80.

Ehrenberg, Ronald G. and Michael Bognanno. "Do Tournaments Have Incentive Effects?" *Journal of Political Economy*, vol. 98, no. 6 (December 1990), pp. 1307–1324.

Ehrenberg, Ronald G. and Robert Smith. *Modern Labor Economics: Theory and Public Policy*, 11th ed. Reading, Mass.: Prentice Hall, 2011.

El Clasico TV Ratings Break Record, December 13, 2011, at http://www.insidespanishfootball.com/el-clasico-tv-ratings-break-record/.

El-Hodiri, Mohamed, and James Quirk. "An Economic Model of a Professional Sports League," *Journal of Political Economy*, vol. 79, no. 6 (November–December 1971), pp. 1302–1319.

Euchner, Charles. *Playing the Field.* Baltimore: Johns Hopkins University Press, 1993.

Euston, Jeff. "Cots Baseball Contracts," *Baseball Prospectus*, February 4, 2005, at http://www.baseballprospectus.com/compensation/cots/?author=2.

Fainaru-Wade, Mark, and Lance Williams. *Game of Shadows: Barry Bonds, BALCO, and the Steroids Scandal That Rocked Professional Sports.* New York: Gotham Books, 2006.

Famous quotes and quotations: *Sports Quotes—Our List of Top Ten Favorites . . .*, at http://www.famous-quotes-and-quotations.com/sports-quotes.html.

Farber, Michael. "Giant Sucking Sound," *Sports Illustrated*, March 20, 1995, p. 104.

Farrar, Doug. "The NFL Loses American Needle: What It Means," *Shutdown Corner/Yahoo! Sports*, May 24, 2010, at http://sports.yahoo.com/nfl/blog/shutdown_corner/post/The-NFL-loses-American-Needle-What-it-means?urn=nfl,243282.

Feddersen, Arne, and Wolfgang Maenning. "Wages and Employment Effects of the Olympic Games in Atlanta 1996 Reconsidered," *IAASE/NAASE Working Paper 09-16*, November 2009.

"FIFA Thumbs-up for 'Six-Plus-Five' Player Rule," *ESPN.com*, May 30, 2008, at http://soccernet.espn.go.com/news/story?id=540901&cc=5901.

Finley, Moses, and H. W. Pleket. *The Olympic Games: The First Thousand Years.* New York: Viking Press, 1976.

Fitts, Robert. *Banzai Babe Ruth.* Lincoln: University of Nebraska Press, 2012.

Fleisher, Arthur Brian Goff, and Robert Tollison. *The National Collegiate Athletic Association: A Study in Cartel Behavior,* Chicago: University of Chicago Press, 1992.

Flint, Joe. "Time Warner Cable, Lakers Strike 20-year TV Deal," *Los Angeles Times,* February 14, 2011, at http://articles.latimes.com/2011/feb/14/sports/la-sp-0215-lakers-time-warner-20110215.

Foer, Franklin. *How Soccer Explains the World: An Unlikely Theory of Globalization.* New York: HarperCollins, 2004.

Football Bowl Association. *2011-2012 Football Bowl Games,* 2011, at http://footballbowlassociation.com/bowls/index.php, viewed December 6, 2011.

Forde, Pat. "Tressel's End Fits with Saga's Pattern," *ESPN College Football,* May 30, 2011, at http://sports.espn.go.com/ncf/columns/story?columnist=forde_pat&id=6607408, viewed May 26, 2012.

Forsyth, Jennifer S. "American Needle Throws Downfield in NFL Licensing Dispute" *Law Blog: The Wall Street Journal,* September 18, 2009, at http://blogs.wsj.com/law/2009/09/18/american-needle-throws-downfield-in-nfl-licensing-dispute/.

Fort, Rodney. "Owner Objectives and Competitive Balance," *Journal of Sports Economics,* vol. 5, no. 1 (February 2004), pp. 20–32.

Fort, Rodney, and Andrew Gill. "Race and Ethnicity Assessment in Baseball Card Markets," *Journal of Sports Economics,* vol. 1, no. 1 (February 2000), pp. 21–38.

Fort, Rodney and Robert Rosenman. "Streak Management," in *Sports Economic: Current Research,* ed. by J. Fizel, E. Gustafson, and L. Hadley. Westport, Conn.: Praeger, 1999.

"Fortune 500," *Fortune,* May 12, 2012, at http://money.cnn.com/magazines/fortune/fortune500/2011/full_list/index.html.

Foy, Paul. "Romney Just Glad Olympics Worked," *2002 Winter Olympic Games,* February 25, 2002, at http://www.olympics.hiasys.com/olympics_main/news/ap_olynewsscene02252002.htm.

Frank, Robert, and Philip Cook. *The Winner-Take-All Society.* New York: The Free Press, 1995.

"Freedom of the Press 2012: Breakthroughs and Pushback in the Middle East," *Freedom House,* at http://www.freedomhouse.org/article/freedom-press-2012-breakthroughs-and-pushback-middle-east.

Freeman, Richard, and James Medoff. *What Do Unions Do?* New York: Basic Books, 1984.

Frick, Bernd, and Brad Humphries. "Prize Structure and Performance: Evidence from NASCAR," *Working Paper,* August 2011–12, at http://www.economics.ualberta.ca/~/media/economics/FacultyAndStaff/WPs/WP2011-12-Humphreys.pdf.

Frick, Bernd, and Joachim Prinz. "Pay and Performance in Professional Road Running: The Case of City Marathons," *International Journal of Sport Finance,* vol. 2, no. 1 (February 2007), pp. 25–35.

Frommer, Harvey. *Rickey and Robinson.* New York: Macmillan, 1982.

Gabriel, Paul E., Curtis D. Johnson, and Timothy J. Stanton. "Customer Racial Discrimination for Baseball Memorabilia," *Applied Economics,* vol. 31, no. 11 (1999), pp. 1331–1335.

Gallagher, Dan. "Electronic Arts' Riccitiello Aims High," *MediaWatch.com,* January 17, 2012, at http://articles.marketwatch.com/2012-01-17/industries/30800220_1_mobile-games-elevation-partners-john-riccitiello/3.

Gavora, Jessica, *Tilting the Playing Field.* San Francisco: Encounter Books, 2002.

"Geekstats for NBA Players," *The NBA Geek,* at http://www.thenbageek.com/players, viewed May 15, 2012.

Gery, Ryne. "Mark Cuban Deserves a Chance in Baseball, the Pirates Need Him," *Call to the Pen*, August 7, 2010, at http://calltothepen.com/2010/08/07/mark-cuban-deserves-a-chance-in-baseball-the-pirates-need-him/.

Gilbert, Susan. "The Smallest Olympians Face the Biggest Risk," *New York Times*, July 28, 1996, p. E4.

"Gillette Stadium," *ESPN.com*, 2012, at http://espn.go.com/travel/stadium/_/s/nfl/id/17/gillette-stadium.

Gillis, Richard. "Soccer's Biggest Signings," *Wall Street Journal*, November 1, 2010, at http://online.wsj.com/article/SB10001424052748703708404575586162309028930.html.

Gilsdorf, Keith, and Vasant A. Sukhatme. "Tournament Incentives and Match Outcomes in Women's Professional Tennis," *Applied Economics*, vol. 40, no. 16–18 (September 2008), pp. 2405–2412.

Ginsborg, Paul. *Silvio Berlusconi: Television, Power and Patrimony.* London: Verso, 2004.

Gius, Mark, and Donn Johnson. "An Empirical Investigation of Wage Discrimination in Professional Basketball," *Applied Economics Letters*, vol. 5, no. 11 (November 1998), pp. 703–705.

Gneezy, Uri, and Aldo Rustichini. "Gender and Competition at a Young Age," *American Economic Review*, vol. 94, no. 2 (May 2004), pp. 377–381.

Goldblatt, David. *The Ball Is Round: A Global History of Soccer.* New York: Riverhead Books, 2006.

Goldman, William. *The Princess Bride.* New York: Ballantine Books, 1974.

"Governor Mitt Romney," *Massachusetts Office of the Governor*, at http://www.mass.gov/portal/index.jsp?pageID=agcc&agid=gov&agca=biographies&agcc=mittromneybiom.

Gramm, Cynthia, and John Schnell. "Difficult Choices: Crossing the Picket Line during the 1987 National Football League Strike," *Journal of Labor Economics*, vol. 12, no. 1 (January 1994), pp. 41–71.

Gary Graves. "Women are no strangers to drag racing success," *USA Today*, June 4, 2008, at http://www.usatoday.com/sports/motor/nhra/2008-06-04-women-drag-racing_N.htm.

Gregory, Sean, and Steve Goldberg. "Daytona Drag: NASCAR Tries to Outrace the Recession," *Time*, February 12, 2009, at http://www.time.com/time/business/article/0,8599,1879136,00.html.

Grimes, Paul, and George Chressanthis. "The Role of Intercollegiate Sports and NCAA Sanctions in Alumni Contributions," *American Journal of Economics and Sociology*, vol. 53, no. 1 (January 1994), pp. 27–40.

Groothuis, Peter, Bruce Johnson, and John Whitehead. "Public Funding of Professional Sports Stadiums: Public Choice or Civic Pride?" *Eastern Economic Journal*, vol. 30, no. 4 (Fall 2004), pp. 515–526.

Guttman, Allen. "The Anomaly of Intercollegiate Athletics," in *Rethinking College Athletics*, ed. by Judith Andre and David James. Philadelphia: Temple University Press, 1991, pp. 17–30.

Gwartney, James A., and Charles Haworth. "Employer Costs and Discrimination: The Case of Baseball," *Journal of Political Economy*, vol. 82, no. 4 (July/August 1974), pp. 873–881.

Hakes, Jahn, and Christopher Clapp. "The Edifice Complex: The Economics of Public Subsidization of Major League Baseball Facilities," *The International Journal of Sport Finance*, vol. 1, no. 2 (May 2006), pp. 77–95.

Hakes, Jahn, and Raymond Sauer. "An Economic Evaluation of the *Moneyball* Hypothesis," *Journal of Economic Perspectives*, vol. 20, no. 3 (Summer 2006), pp. 173–185.

Hamilton, Barton H. "Racial Discrimination and Professional Basketball Salaries in the 1990s," *Applied Economics*, vol. 29, no. 3 (March 1997), pp. 287–296.

Hamilton, Bruce, and Peter Kahn. "Baltimore's Camden Yards Ballparks," in *Sports, Jobs, and Taxes*, ed. by Roger Noll and Andrew Zimbalist. Washington, D.C.: Brookings Institution Press, 1997, pp. 245–281.

Hanssen, Andrew F., and Torben Anderson. "Has Discrimination Lessened over Time? A Test Using Baseball's All-Star Vote," *Economic Inquiry*, vol. 37, no. 2 (April 1999), pp. 326–352.

Harline, Andrew. "The NFL Lockout: The Current NFLPA Antitrust Strategy Lacks Staying Power," *Vanderbilt Journal of Entertainment and Technology Law,* March 19, 2011, at http://www.jetlaw.org/?p=5938

Harris, David. *The League: The Rise and Decline of the NFL.* New York: Bantam Books, 1986.

Hatab, Lawrence. "The Greeks and the Meaning of Athletics," in *Rethinking College Athletics,* ed. by Judith Andre and David James. Philadelphia: Temple University Press, 1991, pp. 31–42.

Haugen, Kjetil K. "The Performance Enhancing Drug Game," *Journal of Sports Economics*, vol. 5, no. 1 (February 2004), pp. 67–86.

Haupert, Michael J. "The Economic History of Major League Baseball," in *EH.Net Encyclopedia*, ed. by Robert Whaples, December 3, 2007, at http://eh.net/encyclopedia/article/haupert.mlb.

Hayes, Beth. "Unions and Strikes with Asymmetric Information," *Journal of Labor Economics*, vol. 2, no. 1 (January 1984), pp. 57–84.

Heintel, Robert. "The Need for an Alternative to Antitrust Regulation of the National Football League," *Case Western Reserve Law Review*, vol. 46, no. 4 (Summer 1996), pp. 1033–1069.

Helgeson, Baird, and Jennifer Brooks. "After Years of Dealing and Debate, Viking Get their Biggest Win," *Minnesota Star-Tribune*, May 11, 2012, at http://www.startribune.com/politics/statelocal/150960525.html.

Helyar, John. *Lords of the Realm.* New York: Villard Books, 1994.

Hepp, Christopher. "Near Fabled Park, Ambience a Lure," *Philadelphia Inquirer,* September 29, 1999, pp. A1 and A6.

"History of the NFL Salary Cap," *Business Insider*, at http://articles.businessinsider.com/2011-07-20/sports/30074982_1_nfl-salary-cap-nfl-lockout-history.

Hodgson, Andrew. "Blatter Bid to Limit on Foreign Players Wins FIFA Backing," May 30, 2008. *London Evening Standard (Standard.co.uk)*, at http://www.thisislondon.co.uk/standard-sport/article-23488572-details/Blatter+bid+to+put+limit+on+foreign+players+wins+FIFA+backing/article.do.

Hotchkiss, Julie, Robert Moore, and Stephanie Zobay. "Impact of the 1996 Summer Olympic Games on Employment and Wages in Georgia," *Southern Economic Journal,* vol. 69, no. 3 (January 2003), pp. 691–704.

Humphreys, Brad. "Alternative Measures of Competitive Balance," *Journal of Sports Economics,* vol. 3, no. 2 (May 2002), pp. 133–148.

———. "The ANOVA-Based Competitive Balance Measure: A Reply," *Journal of Sports Economics,* vol. 4, no. 1 (February, 2003), pp. 81–82.

Humphreys, Brad, and Xia Feng. "Assessing the Economic Impact of Sports Facilities on Housing Values: A Spatial Hedonic Approach," *IASE/NAASE Working Paper 08-12,* August 2008.

Humphreys, Brad, and Michael Mondello. "Intercollegiate Athletic Success and Donations at NCAA Division I Institutions," *Journal of Sport Management*, vol. 21, no. 2 (April 2007), pp. 265–280.

Humphreys, Brad, and Jane Ruseski. "Socio-Economic Determinants of Adolescent Use of Performance Enhancing Drugs: Evidence from the YRBSS," *The Journal of Socio-Economics*, vol. 40, no. 2 (April 2011), pp. 208–216.

Hurtado, Patricia, and Bob Van Voris. "Defunct Basketball Team Claims TV Revenue from Lawsuit Settlement in 1976," *Bloomberg.com,* November 22, 2011, at http://www.bloomberg.com/news/2011-11-22/decades-old-nba-antitrust-labor-case-filed-by-oscar-robertson-under-review.html.

Isidore, Chris. "College Sports' Fuzzy Math," *CNNMoney: SportsBiz,* November 10, 2006, at http://money.cnn.com/2006/11/10/commentary/sportsbiz/index.htm.

The Institute for Diversity and Ethics in Sport. *Keeping Score When It Counts: Academic Progress/Graduation Success Rate Study of 2012 NCAA Division I Women's and Men's Basketball Tournament Teams,* March 13, 2011, at http://www.tidesport.org/Grad%20Rates/2012%20Women%27s%20Basketball%20Tournament%20Teams%20Study.pdf.

Irani, Daraius. "Estimating Consumer Discrimination Using Panel Data: 1972–1991," in *Baseball Economics: Current Research,* ed. by John Fizel, Elizabeth Gustafson, and Lawrence Hadley. Westport, Conn.: Praeger, 1996.

"Japan's Earthquake and Tsunami Hit Parts Supplies," *Motor Trend,* June 2011, at http://www.motortrend.com/features/auto_news/2011/1106_japan_earthquake_tsunami_hit_parts_supplies/viewall.html.

Jenkins, Jeffrey A. "A Reexamination of Salary Determination in Professional Basketball," *Social Science Quarterly,* vol. 77, no. 3 (September 1996), pp. 594–608.

"Joe Louis (Barrow)," *Arlington National Cemetery Website,* April 13, 1981, at http://www.arlingtoncemetery.net/joelouis.htm.

Johnson, Bruce K. and John C. Whitehead. "Contingent Valuation of Sports," in *The Oxford Handbook of Sports Economics*, ed. by Stephen Shmanske and Leo Kahane. Oxford: Oxford University Press, 2012.

Johnson, John. "When a Professional Sport Is Not a Business: Baseball's Infamous Antitrust Exemption," in *Sports and the Law,* ed. by Charles Quirk. New York: Garland, 1996, pp. 149–165.

Johnson, Raphielle. "NCAA Hands Grambling More Sanctions Due to Low APR Scores," *NBC Sports: College Basketball Talk,* May 15, 2012, at http://collegebasketballtalk.nbcsports.com/2012/05/15/ncaa-hands-grambling-more-sanctions-due-to-low-apr-scores/.

Jones, J. C. H., and W. D. Walsh. "Salary Determination in the National Hockey League: The Effects of Skills, Franchise Characteristics, and Discrimination," *Industrial and Labor Relations Review,* vol. 41, no. 4 (July 1988), pp. 592–604.

———. "The World Hockey Association and Player Exploitation in the National Hockey League," *Quarterly Review of Economics and Business,* vol. 27, no. 2 (Summer 1987), pp. 87–101.

Jones, Richard, and Don Walker. "Packer Boss Warns of Move if Stadium Doesn't Get Upgrade," *Milwaukee Sentinel Journal,* March 1, 2000, at http://www.jsonline.com/packer/news/feb00/lambeau01022900.asp.

Kahn, Lawrence M. "Discrimination in Professional Sports: A Survey of the Literature," *Industrial and Labor Relations Review,* vol. 44, no. 3 (April 1991), pp. 395–418.

———. "The Effects of Race on Professional Football Players' Compensation," *Industrial Labor Relations Review,* vol. 45, no. 2 (January 1992), pp. 295–310.

———. "The Sports Business as a Labor Market Laboratory," *Journal of Economic Perspectives,* vol. 14, no. 3 (Summer 2000), pp. 75–94.

———. "Race, Performance, Pay, and Retention among National Basketball Association Head Coaches," *Journal of Sports Economics,* vol. 7, no. 2 (May 2006), pp. 119–149.

Kahn, Lawrence M., and Peter Sherer. "Racial Differences in Professional Basketball Players' Compensation," *Journal of Labor Economics,* vol. 6, no. 1 (January 1988), pp. 40–61.

Kahn, Roger. *The Era: 1947–1957.* New York: Ticknor and Fields, 1993.

Kanazawa, Mark T., and Jonas P. Funk. "Racial Discrimination in Professional Basketball: Evidence from Nielsen Ratings," *Economics Inquiry,* vol. 39, no. 4 (October 2001), pp. 599–608.

Kane, Martin. "Scorecard," *SIVault,* August 14, 1972, at http://sportsillustrated.cnn.com/vault/article/magazine/MAG1086398/4/index.htm.

Kaplan, Daniel. "NFL Labor Deal Paying Off," *Street and Smith's Sports Business Journal,* January 30, 2012, at http://m.sportsbusinessdaily.com/Journal/Issues/2012/01/30/Super-Bowl/Lead.aspx.

Késenne, Stefan. "The Win Maximization Model Reconsidered: Flexible Talent Supply and Efficient Wages," *Journal of Sports Economics,* vol. 7, no. 4 (November 2006), pp. 416–427.

Kidd, Bruce. "The Myth of the Ancient Games," in *Five Ring Circus: Money, Power and Politics at the Olympic Games,* ed. by Alan Tomlinson and Garry Whannel. London: Pluto Press, 1984, pp. 71–83.

Kindelain, Katie. "Kentucky Students Riot after NCAA Championship Win," *abcnews.com,*

April 3, 2012, at http://abcnews.go.com/blogs/headlines/2012/04/kentucky-students-riot-after-ncaa-championship-win

Klein, Eugene. *First Down and a Billion: The Funny Business of Pro Football.* New York: Morrow, 1987.

Knapple, Jeffrey S. "Naming Rights Industry," in *Naming Rights Deals.* Chicago: Team Marketing Report, 2001.

Knight Foundation Commission on Intercollegiate Athletics. *A Call to Action: Reconnecting College Sports and Higher Education.* Miami: John S. and James L. Knight Foundation, 2001, p. 13, at http://www.knightcommission.org/images/pdfs/2001_knight_report.pdf.

Knowles, Glenn, Keith Sherony, and Mike Haupert. "The Demand for Major League Baseball: A Test of the Uncertainty of Outcome Hypothesis," *American Economist,* vol. 36, no. 2 (Fall 1992), pp. 72–80.

Koch, James. "Intercollegiate Athletics: An Economic Explanation," *Social Science Quarterly,* vol. 64, no. 2 (June 1983), pp. 360–374.

Komisarchik, Mayya, and Aju Fenn. "Trends in Stadium and Arena Construction, 1995–2015," *Colorado College Working Paper 2010–03*, April 2010.

Korr, Charles. "Marvin Miller and the New Unionism in Baseball," in *The Business of Professional Sports,* ed. by Paul Staudohar and James Mangan. Urbana: University of Illinois Press, 1991, pp. 115–134.

Kramer, Staci D. "CES: NBA Digital Expands to More Connected TVs and Adds More Premium Live Games," *paidContent.org,* January 6, 2011, at http://paidcontent.org/2011/01/06/419-ces-nba-digital-expanda-to-more-connected-tvs-and-adds-premium-live-gam.

Krashinsky, Michael, and Harry D. Krashinsky. "Do English Canadian Hockey Teams Discriminate Against French Canadian Players?" *Canadian Public Policy,* vol. 23, no. 2 (June 1997), pp. 212–216.

Krautmann, Anthony. "What's Wrong with Scully Estimates of a Player's Marginal Revenue Product," *Economic Inquiry,* vol. 37, no. 2 (April 1999), pp. 369–381.

Krautmann, Anthony C., and David C. Berri. "Can We Find It in the Concessions: Understanding Price Elasticity in Professional Sports," *Journal of Sports Economics,* vol. 8, no. 2 (May 2007), pp. 183–191.

Krautmann, Anthony C., Peter von Allmen, and David Berri. "The Underpayment of Restricted Players in North American Sports Leagues," *International Journal of Sport Finance,* vol. 4, no. 3 (August 2009), pp. 75–93.

Kuklick, Bruce. *To Everything a Season: Shibe Park and Urban Philadelphia, 1909–1976.* Princeton, N.J.: Princeton University Press, 1991.

Lago, Umberto, Rob Simmons, and Stefan Szymanski. "The Financial Crisis in European Football," *Journal of Sports Economics,* vol. 7, no. 1 (February 2006), pp. 3–12.

Lambrinos, James, and Thomas D. Ashman. "Salary Determination in the National Hockey League: Is Arbitration Efficient?" *Journal of Sports Economics,* vol. 8, no. 2 (April 2007), pp. 192–201.

Lapchick, Richard E. "What IOC Needs, Anita DeFrantz Offers," *Street and Smith's Sports Business Journal,* March 12–18, 2001, at http://www.sportsbusinessdaily.com/Journal/Issues/2001/03/20010312/This-Weeks-Issue/What-IOC-Needs-Anita-Defrantz-Offers.aspx.

Lapchick, Richard E., Alejandra Diaz-Calderon, and Derek McMechan. "The 2011 Racial and Gender Report Card: Major League Baseball," *The Institute for Ethics and Diversity in Sport,* at http://www.tidesport.org.

Lapchick, Richard E., Cara-Lynn Lopresti, and Nathalie Reshard. "The 2011 Racial and Gender Report Card: Women's National Basketball Association," *The Institute for Ethics and Diversity in Sport,* at http://www.tidesport.org/.

Lapchick, Richard E., Eric Little, and Colleen Lerner. "The 2011 Racial and Gender Report Card: National Football League," *The Institute for Ethics and Diversity in Sport,* at http://www.tidesport.org/.

Lapchick, Richard E., Eric Little, Colleen Lerner, and Ray Mathew. "The 2011 Racial and Gender Report Card: College Sport," *The Institute for Ethics and Diversity in Sport,* at http://www.tidesport.org.

Lapchick, Richard E., Nicole Bowey, and Jessica Zahn. "The 2011 Racial and Gender Report Card: Major League Soccer," *The Institute for Ethics and Diversity in Sport*, at http://www.tidesport.org.

Lapchick, Richard E., Jessica Hanson, Charles Harless, and William Johnson. "The 2011 Racial and Gender Report Card: National Basketball Association," *The Institute for Ethics and Diversity in Sport*, at http://www.tidesport.org/.

Lavoie, Marc, Gilles Grenier, and Serge Columbe. "Discrimination and Performance Differentials in the National Hockey League," *Canadian Public Policy*, vol. 13, no. 4 (December 1987), pp. 407–422.

———. "Comment: Performance Differentials in the National Hockey League: Discrimination versus Style of Play Thesis," *Canadian Public Policy*, vol. 15, no. 1 (December 1989), pp. 461–469.

Lawrence, Paul. *Unsportsmanlike Conduct: The National Collegiate Athletic Association and the Business of College Football*. New York: Praeger, 1987.

Lazear, Edward, and Sherwin Rosen. "Rank Order Tournaments as Optimum Labor Contracts," *Journal of Political Economy*, vol. 89, no. 5 (October 1981), pp. 841–864.

Leadley, John C., and Zenon X. Zygmont. "When Is the Honeymoon Over? Major League Baseball Attendance 1970–2000," *Journal of Sport Management*, vol. 19, no. 3 (July 2005), pp. 278–299.

———. "When Is the Honeymoon Over? National Hockey League Attendance 1970–2003," *Canadian Public Policy*, vol. 32, no. 2 (June 2006), pp. 213–232.

———. "When Is the Honeymoon Over? National Basketball Association Attendance 1971–2000," *Journal of Sports Economics*, vol. 6, no. 2 (May 2005), pp. 203–221.

LeBrun, Pierre. "The State of CBA Negotiations," *ESPN: NHL*, September 6, 2012, at http://espn.go.com/nhl/story/_/id/8344702/state-discussions.

Lederman, Doug. "Court Challenge on Athletic Aid," *Inside Higher Ed*, at http://www.insidehighered.com/news/2006/02/23/antitrust.

Leeds, Eva Marikova and Michael A. Leeds. "Event Analysis" in *The Oxford Handbook of Sports Economics*, vol. 2, ed. by Stephen Shmanske and Leo Kahane. Oxford: Oxford University Press, 2012.

———. "Do Men and Women Respond Differently to Economic Contests? The Case of Men's and Ladies' Figure Skating," ed. by Eva Marikova Leeds and Michael A. Leeds. *The Handbook on the Economics of Women's Sports*. Cheltenham, U.K.: Edward Elgar, forthcoming.

Leeds, Eva Marikova, Michael A. Leeds, and Irina Pistolet. "A Stadium by Any Other Name," *Journal of Sports Economics*, vol. 8, no. 6 (December 2007), pp. 585–595.

Leeds, Michael A. "Bargaining as Search Behavior under Mutual Uncertainty," *Southern Economic Journal*, vol. 53, no. 3 (January 1987), pp. 677–684.

———. "Do Good Olympics Make Good Neighbors?" *Contemporary Economic Policy*, vol. 26, no. 3 (July 2008), pp. 460–467.

———. "Salary Caps and Luxury Taxes in Professional Sports Leagues," in *The Business of Sports*, vol. 2. ed. by Brad R. Humphreys and Dennis R. Howard. Westport, Conn.: Praeger, 2008, pp. 181–206.

Leeds, Michael, John Mirikitani, and Danna Tang. "Rational Exuberance? An Event Analysis of the 2008 Olympic Announcement," *International Journal of Sport Finance*, vol. 4, no. 1 (February 2009), pp. 5–15.

Legal Information Institute. *15 USC Chapter 1—Monopolies and Combinations in Restraint of Trade*, at http://www.law.cornell.edu/uscode/text/15/chapter-1

Leifer, Eric. *Making the Majors: The Transformation of Team Sports in America*. Cambridge, Mass.: Harvard University Press, 1995.

Lewis, Michael. *Moneyball*, New York: Norton, 2003.

———. *The Blind Side: Evolution of a Game*, New York: W.W. Norton, 2006.

Litan, Robert, Jonathan Orszag, and Peter Orszag. "The Empirical Effects of College Athletics: An Interim Report," *Sebago Associates*, 2003, at http://www.sc.edu/faculty/PDF/baseline.pdf.

Lo Franco, Robert. "Profits on Ice," *Forbes*, May 5, 1997, pp. 86–89.

Lombardo, John. "Inside NBA's Revenue Sharing: How Complex Plan Will Shift $140 Million to Needy Teams," *Street and Smith's Sports Business Journal*, January 23, 2012, at http://www.sportsbusinessdaily.com/Journal/Issues/2012/01/23/Leagues-and-Governing-Bodies/NBA-revenue.aspx.

Long, James, and Steven Caudill. "The Impact of Participation in Intercollegiate Athletics on Income and Graduation," *Review of Economics and Statistics,* vol. 73, no. 3 (August 1991), pp. 525–531.

Long, Judith Grant. "Public Funding for Major League Sports Facilities Data Series: A History of Public Funding, 1890 to 2005," *Edward J. Bloustein School of Planning and Public Policy Center for Urban Policy Research Working Paper Series,* 2004.

———. "Full Count: The Real Cost of Public Funding for Major League Sports Facilities," *Journal of Sports Economics,* vol. 6, no. 2 (May 2005), pp. 119–143.

Longley, Neil. "Salary Discrimination in the National Hockey League: The Effects of Location," *Canadian Public Policy*, vol. 21, no. 4 (December 1995), pp. 413–422.

———. "The Underrepresentation of French Canadians on English Canadian Teams," *Journal of Sports Economics,* vol. 1, no. 3 (August 2000), pp. 236–256.

Lopez, Steve. "They Got Next," *Sports Illustrated,* June 30, 1997, pp. 44–47.

Lorge, Barry. "Kroc Wanted to Give Padres to City," *San Diego Union-Tribune,* July 29, 1990, p. H1.

Low, Chris, and Edward Aschoff. "Saban Gets Raise, Extension," *SEC Blog,* March 27, 2012, at http://espn.go.com/college-football/story/_/id/7740227/alabama-crimson-tide-grant-coach-nick-saban-raise-2-year-extension.

MacCambridge, Michael. *America's Game.* New York: Random House, 2004.

Madden, Janice Fanning. "Differences in the Success of NFL Coaches by Race, 1990–2002: Evidence of Last Hire, First Fire," *Journal of Sports Economics,* vol. 5, no. 1 (February 2004), pp. 6–19.

Mandell, Richard. *The Nazi Olympics.* New York: Ballantine Books, 1972.

Margolick, David. *Beyond Glory: Joe Louis vs. Max Schmeling, and a World on the Brink.* New York: Alfred A. Knopf, 2005.

Marvez, Alex. *NFL Owners Lock Out Players,* March 12, 2011, at http://msn.foxsports.com/nfl/story/NFL-Players-Association-union-decertifies-labor-talks-owners-031111.

Matheson, Victor, Debra O'Connor, and Joseph Herberger. "The Bottom Line: Accounting for Revenues and Expenditures in Intercollegiate Athletics," *International Journal of Sport Finance,* vol. 7, no. 1 (February 2012), pp. 30–45.

Mathews, Karen. "Yankees Break Ground on New $1 Billion Stadium," *USA Today,* August 16, 2006, at http://www.usatoday.com/sports/baseball/al/yankees/2006-08-16-stadium-groundbreaking_x.htm.

McCormick, Robert, and Maurice Tinsley. "Athletics and Academics: A Model of University Contributions," in *Sportometrics,* ed. by Brian Goff and Robert Tollison. College Station: Texas A&M University Press, 1990, pp. 193–204.

———. "Athletics versus Academics? Evidence from SAT Scores," *Journal of Political Economy,* vol. 95, no. 5 (October 1987), pp. 1103–1116.

McGrath, Ben. "The Extortionist," *The New Yorker,* October 29, 2009, at http://www.newyorker.com/reporting/2007/10/29/071029fa_fact_mcgrath.

McGraw, Dan. "The Foreign Invasion of the American Game," *The Village Voice,* May 28–June 3, 2003, at http://www.villagevoice.com/news/0322,mcgraw,44409,1.html.

McLean, Alan, Archie Tse, and Lisa Waananen. "Top Finishers of the Tour de France Tainted by Doping," *New York Times,* August 24, 2012, at http://www.nytimes.com/interactive/2012/08/24/sports/top-finishers-of-the-tour-de-france-tainted-by-doping.html?smid=tw-nytimes.

McManimon, Kevin. "The House That Debt Built," *McManimon and Scotland, LLC,* May 29, 2006, at http://www.mandslaw.com/articles/ the-house-that-debt-built-will-the-irs-allow- cities-to-finance-construction-of-stadiums- on-a-tax-exempt-basis/.

McMurphy, Brett. "Power Conferences Likely to Receive Most of Playoff Revenue," *CBSSports. com,* June 18, 2012, at http://www.cbssports. com/collegefootball/story/19378895/power- conferences-likely-to-receive-most-of-playoff- revenue.

Mead, Chris. "Triumphs and Trials," *SIVault,* September 23, 1985, at http://vault. sportsillustrated.cnn.com/vault/article/ magazine/MAG1119926/4/index.htm.

Meyer, Joe. *The Roman Colosseum,* March 10, 2009, at http://www.synthreal.com/Colosseum.htm.

Michener, James. *Sports in America.* New York: Random House, 1976.

Mickle, Tripp, and Terry Lefton. "Several Leagues Later, Debate on Single Entity Model Still Lively," *SportsBusinessJournal.com,* June 8, 2009, at http:// www.sportsbusinessjournal.com/article59720.

Miller, James. *The Baseball Business: Pursuing Pennants and Profits in Baltimore.* Chapel Hill: University of North Carolina Press, 1990.

Miller, Marvin. *A Whole Different Ballgame: The Sport and Business of Baseball.* Secaucus, N.J.: Carol Publishing Group, 1991.

"MLB Attendance Report—2011," *ESPN.com,* at http:// espn.go.com/mlb/attendance/_/year/2011.

"MLB Confidential: The Financial Documents MLB Doesn't Want You to See, Part 1," *Deadspin,* at http://deadspin.com/5615096.

"MLB Confidential Part 2: Seattle Mariners," *Deadspin,* at http://deadspin.com/5619509.

"MLB, MLBPA Reach New Five-year Labor Agreement," *mlb.com,* November 22, 2011, at http://mlb.mlb.com/news/article.jsp?ymd= 20111122&content_id=26025138&vkey= pr_mlb&c_id=mlb.

"MLB Standings—2011," *ESPN.com,* at http:// espn.go.com/mlb/standings/_/year/2011/ seasontype/2.

Money and Company. "Yankee Stadiums Troubled Tax-Free Financing," *Los Angeles Times,* June 17, 2011, at http://latimesblogs.latimes.com/money_ co/2011/06/yankee-stadiums-troubled-tax-free- financing-.html.

Morgan, Jon. *Glory for Sale: Fans, Dollars, and the New NFL.* Baltimore: Bancroft Press, 1997.

MSC Sports. *New Park Financing: How the Deals Got Done,* 1999, at http://www.wcco.com/sports/ stadiums.html.

Munsey, Paul, and Corey Suppes. *Ballparks,* 2012, at http://www.ballparks.com.

Murphy, Robert, and Gregory Trandel. "The Relation between a University's Football Record and the Size of Its Applicant Pool," *Economics of Education Review,* vol. 13, no. 3 (September 1994), pp. 265–270.

Nack, William. "This Old House," *Sports Illustrated,* June 7, 1999, pp. 100–116.

"Naming Rights Deals," *Sports Business Journal Daily,* September 19, 2011, pp. 22–23, at http://www. sportsbusinessdaily.com/Journal/Issues/2011/ 09/19/In-Depth/Naming-rights-deals.aspx.

"Naming Rights Deals," *Street and Smith's Sports Business Journal,* at http://www.sportsbusiness daily.com/Journal/Issues/2011/09/19/In- Depth/Naming-rights-deals.aspx, September 19, 2011.

Nardinelli, Curtis, and Clark Simon. "Customer Discrimination in the Market for Memorabilia: The Case of Baseball," *Quarterly Journal of Economics,* vol. 105, no. 3 (August 1990), pp. 575–595.

National Association of Intercollegiate Athletics. "About the NAIA," *NAIA,* at http://www.naia. org/ViewArticle.dbml?DB_OEM_ID=27900& ATCLID=205323019, viewed May 27, 2012.

National Sports Law Institute. "Sports Facilities Reports," *Marquette University Law School,* vol. 13 (Summer 2012), at http://law.marquette.edu/ national-sports-law-institute/sports-facility- reports.

"NBA Lockout Timeline," *NBA.com,* December 9, 2011, at http://www.nba.com/2011/ news/09/09/labor-timeline/index.html.

"NBA Players in China Might Be Stuck," *Fox Sports*, December 1, 2011, at http://msn.foxsports.com/ nba/story/NBA-players-who-went-to-China-in-lockout-might-be-stuck-once-it-ends-113011.

NBPA 2005 Collective Bargaining Agreement: Article VII at http://www.nbpa.org/sites/default/files/ARTICLE%20VII.pdf.

NCAA, *Estimated Probability of Competing in Athletics beyond the High School Interscholastic Level*, at http://www.ncaa.org/wps/wcm/connect/public/Test/Issues/Recruiting/Probability+of+Going+Pro, viewed May 30, 2012.

———. *NCAA Division I, II, and III Membership Criteria*, 1999, at http://www.ncaa.org/about/div_criteria.html.

———. *2005–2006 NCAA Division I Manual*, at www.ncaa.org/library/1_manual/2005-06/2005-06_dl_manual.pdf.

———. *Football Bowl Subdivision—Membership Requirements*, December 8, 2007, at http://fs.ncaa.org/Docs/AMA/Division%20I%20Forms/2010-11%20FBS%20Forms/Football%20Bowl%20Subqa%2012%208%2010.pdf.

———. *Academic Progress Rate Penalties List*, April 15, 2010, at http://www.ncaa.org/wps/wcm/connect/public/NCAA/Academics/Division+I/APR+penalties+list

Neale, Walter. "The Peculiar Economics of Professional Sports," *Quarterly Journal of Economics*, vol. 78, no. 1 (February 1964), pp. 1–14.

"New York Yankees Attendance Data," *Baseball Almanac*, 2000–2012, at http://www.baseball-almanac.com/teams/yankatte.shtml.

NFL Clubs Approve Comprehensive Agreement, July 21, 2011, at http://www.nfl.com/news/story/09000d5d820e6311/article/nfl-clubs-approve-comprehensive-agreement-.

NFL Collective Bargaining Agreement, August 4, 2011, at http://images.nflplayers.com/mediaResources/files/PDFs/General/2011_Final_CBA_Searchable_Bookmarked.pdf.

"A New Way to Keep Score," *Inside Higher Ed*, December 20, 2005, at http://www.insidehighered.com/news/2005/12/20/grad, viewed August 17, 2009.

Nightengale, Bob. "Boras Is Baseball's Bigger Deal Man," *USA Today*, November 14, 2006, at http://www.usatoday.com/sports/baseball/2006-11-14-boras-cover_x.htm.

Nocera, Joe. "More NCAA 'Justice'," *New York Times*, January 13, 2012, at http://www.nytimes.com/2012/01/14/opinion/nocera-more-ncaa-justice.html.

Noden, Merrell. "Dying to Win," *Sports Illustrated*, August 8, 1994, pp. 52–59.

Noll, Roger G. "Attendance and Price Setting," in *Government and the Sports Business*, ed. by Roger Noll.Washington, D.C.: Brookings Institution, 1974.

———."The Economics of Sports Leagues," in *Law of Professional and Amateur Sports*, ed. by Gary A. Uberstine, K. R. Stratos, and R. J. Grad. Deerfield, Ill.: The West Group, 1989, pp. 17–20.

———. "The Economics of Intercollegiate Sports," in *Rethinking College Athletics*, ed. by Judith Andre and David James. Philadelphia: Temple University Press, 1992, pp. 197–209.

———. "The Organization of Sports Leagues," *Oxford Review of Economic Policy*, vol. 19, no. 4 (Winter 2003), pp. 530–551.

Noll, Roger G., and Andrew Zimbalist. "Build the Stadium—Create the Jobs!" in *Sports, Jobs, and Taxes*, ed. by Roger Noll and Andrew Zimbalist. Washington, D.C.: Brookings Institution Press, 1997, pp. 1–54.

———. "The Economic Impact of Sports Teams and Facilities," in *Sports, Jobs, and Taxes*, ed. by Roger Noll and Andrew Zimbalist. Washington, D.C.: Brookings Institution Press, 1997, pp. 55–91.

"Not About Money: HBO Declines to Renew Wimbledon Contract after 25 Years," *CNN/ SI*, June 28, 1999, at http://www.cnnsi.com/tennis/1999/wimbledon/news/1999/06/28/hbo_wimbledon/index.html.

O'Hara, Jane, et al. "In the Name of Greed," *Maclean's*, January 19, 1998, pp. 22–24.

"Open to All: Title IX at Thirty," *The Secretary of Education's Commission on Opportunity in Athletics*, February 2003, at http://www.gpo.gov/fdsys/pkg/ERIC-ED480939/pdf/ERIC-ED480939.pdf.

Orszag, Jonathan, and Peter Orszag. "The Physical Capital Stock Used in College Athletics," *Compass*, April 2005.

Parrish, Paula. "Leap of Faith: Mitt Romney Embraces Challenges, and This Might Be His Biggest One," *Rocky Mountain News*, February 4, 2002, p. 8S.

Pastier, John. "Diamonds in the Rough: Two Cheers for the New Baseball Palaces," *Slate*, July 31, 1996, at http://www.slate.msn.com/feature2/96-07-31/feature2.asp.

Paterno, Joe. "Score on the SAT to Score on the Field," *Wall Street Journal*, March 16, 1999, p. A26.

Patrick, Aaron O., and Dana Cimilluca. "English Soccer's Morning After," *Wall Street Journal*, June 5, 2009, at http://online.wsj.com/article/SB124346762522860417.html.

Pearlman, Jeff. "At Full Blast," *Sports Illustrated*, December 27, 1999–January 3, 2000, pp. 62–64.

Pedace, Roberto. "Earnings Performance, and Nationality Discrimination in a Highly Competitive Labor Market as an Analysis of the English Professional Soccer League," *Journal of Sports Economics*, vol. 9, no. 2 (April 2008), pp. 115–140.

Peloquin, Matt. "2012 NCAA Television Revenue by Conference," *CollegeSportsInfo.com*, May 10, 2012, at http://collegesportsinfo.com/2012/05/10/2012-ncaa-television-revenue-by-conference/.

Penn State University Budget Office. *Penn State Budget Primer*, at http://www.budget.psu.edu/openbudget/default.aspx, viewed May 30, 2012.

Perrotet, Tony. *The Naked Olympics*. New York: Random House, 2004.

Peterson, Robert. *Only the Ball Was White: A History of Legendary Black Players and All-Black Professional Teams*. New York: Gramercy Books, 1970.

Pirates Press Release. *Pirates to Introduce Dynamic Ticket Pricing for 2012 Season*, at http://pittsburgh.pirates.mlb.com/news/article.jsp?ymd=20111216&content_id=26182894&vkey=pr_pit&c_id=pit.

Pluto, Terry. *Loose Balls: The Short, Wild Life of the American Basketball Association*. Upper Saddle River, N.J.: Simon & Schuster, 1990.

Pomerantz, Dorothy. "The World's Most Powerful Celebrities," *Forbes*. May 16, 2011, at http://www.forbes.com/wealth/celebrities#p_2_s_dsalary.

Poole, Lynn, and Gray Poole. *History of Ancient Greek Olympic Games*. New York: Ivan Obolensky, Inc., 1963.

Pope, Devin, and Jaren Pope. "The Impact of College Sports Success on the Quantity and Quality of Student Applications," *Southern Economic Journal*, vol. 75, no. 3 (January 2009), pp. 750–780.

Porter, Philip. "Mega-Sporting Events as Municipal Investments: A Critique of Impact Analysis," in *Sports Economics: Current Research*, ed. by John Fizel, Elizabeth Gustafson, and Larry Hadley. Westport, Conn.: Praeger Publishers, 1999.

Posner, Richard. "The Social Costs of Monopoly and Regulation," *Journal of Political Economy*, vol. 83, no. 4 (August 1975), pp. 807–827.

Preston, Ian, and Stefan Szymanski. "Racial Discrimination in English Football," *Scottish Journal of Political Economy*, vol. 47, no. 4 (September 2000), pp. 342–363.

Price, Joseph, and Justin Wolfers. "Racial Discrimination among NBA Referees," *Quarterly Journal of Economics*, vol. 125, no. 4 (November 2010), pp. 1859–1887.

Price, Joseph, Brian Soebbing, David Berri, and Brad Humphreys. "Tournament Incentives, League Policy, and NBA Team Performance Revisited," *Journal of Sports Economics*, vol. 11, no. 2 (April 2010), pp. 117–135.

"Prize Money," *Wimbledon: The Official Site*, at http://aeltc.wimbledon.org/en_GB/about/history/prizemoney_history.html.

Purdy, Dean D., Stanley Eitzen, and Rick Hufnagel. "Are Athletes Also Students? The Educational Attainment of College Athletes," in *Sport and Higher Education*, ed. by Donald Chu, Jeffrey Segrave, and Beverly Becker. Champaign, Ill.: Human Kinetics Publishers, 1985, pp. 221–234.

Quinn, Kevin, Paul B. Bursik, Christopher Borick, and Lisa Raethz. "Do New Digs Mean More Wins? The Relationship between a New Venue and a Professional Sports Team's Success," *Journal of Sports Economics*, vol. 4, no.3 (August 2003), pp. 167–182.

Quirk, James, and Rodney Fort. *Hardball*. Princeton, N.J.: Princeton University Press, 1999.

———. *Pay Dirt*. Princeton, N.J.: Princeton University Press, 1992.

Rabin, Charles, Martha Brannigan, and Patricia Mazzei. "Feds Open SEC Probe into Miami Marlins Stadium Deal," *Miami Herald*, December 3, 2011, at http://www.miamiherald.com/2011/12/02/2529191/feds-open-sec-probe-into-miami.html.

Rascher, Daniel A. "Franchise Relocation, Expansions, and Mergers in Professional Sports Leagues," in *The Business of Sports, Volume 2: Economic Perspectives on Sport*, ed. by Brad H. Humphries and Dennis R. Howard. Westport, Conn.: Praeger, 2008.

Rascher, Daniel A., Chad McEvoy, Mark Nagel, and Matthew Brown. "Variable Ticket Pricing in Major League Baseball," *Journal of Sport Management*, vol. 21, no. 3 (July 2007), pp. 407–437.

Ray, Edgar W. *The Grand Huckster: Houston's Judge Roy Hofheinz, Genius of the Astrodome*. Memphis: Memphis State University Press, 1980.

Ray, Margaret A., and Paul W. Grimes. "Jockeying for Position: Winnings and Gender Discrimination on the Thoroughbred Track," *Social Science Quarterly*, vol. 74, no.1 (March 1993), pp. 46–61.

Reaves, Joseph A. *Taking in a Game: The History of Baseball in Asia*. Lincoln: University of Nebraska Press, 2002.

Reed, Billy. "Ben Hur Played the Rose Bowl," *SIVault*, December 23, 1968, at http://sportsillustrated.cnn.com/vault/article/magazine/MAG1081948/index.htm.

Revenues from Sports Venues, 2012, at http://www.sportsvenues.com/info.htm#Suites.

Ribowsky, Mark. *Slick: The Silver and Black Life of Al Davis*. New York: Macmillan, 1991.

Rice, Lewis. "Games Saver," *Harvard Law Bulletin*, Spring 2002, at http://www.law.harvard.edu/alumni/bulletin/2002/spring/feature_1-1.html.

Rieger, Carol and Charles Lloyd. "The Effect of *McNeil v. NFL* on Contract Negotiation in the NFL—That Was Then and This Is Now," *Marquette Sports Law Review*, vol. 3, no. 1 (Fall 1992), pp. 45–58.

Rishe, Patrick. "The Best and Worst NFL Teams Regarding Drafting Proficiency," *Forbes*, April 25, 2012, at http://www.forbes.com/sites/prishe/2012/04/25/the-best-and-worst-nfl-teams-in-drafting-collegiate-talent/.

———. "Dynamic Pricing: The Future of Ticket Pricing in Sports," *Forbes*, January 6, 2012, at http://www.forbes.com/sites/prishe/2012/01/06/dynamic-pricing-the-future-of-ticket-pricing-in-sports/.

Roberts, Gary. "Antitrust Issues in Professional Sports," in *Law of Professional and Amateur Sports*, ed. by Gary Uberstine. Deerfield, Ill.: Clark, Boardman, and Callaghan, 1992, pp. 19-1–19-45.

———. "Should Congress Stop the Bidding War for Sports Franchises?" Hearing before the Subcommittee on Antitrust, Business Rights, and Compensation, Senate Committee on the Judiciary. "Academics," *Heartland Policy*, vol. 4, November 29, 1995, at http://heartland.org/policy-documents/no-77-should-congress-stop-bidding-war-sports-franchises-volume-4-academics.

———. "*Brown* v. *Pro Football, Inc.:* The Supreme Court Gets It Right for the Wrong Reasons," *Antitrust Bulletin*, vol. 42, no. 3 (Fall 1997), pp. 595–639.

Roll Tide. "Bryant-Denny Stadium," *Facilities*, at http://www.rolltide.com/facilities/bryant-denny.html.

Rosen, Sherwin. "The Economics of Superstars," *American Economic Review*, vol. 71, no. 5 (December 1981), pp. 845–858.

Rosentraub, Mark. *Major League Losers: The Real Cost of Sports and Who'sPaying for it*. New York: Basic Books/Princeton University Press, 1997.

———. "Stadiums and Urban Space," in *Sports, Jobs, and Taxes*, ed. by Roger Noll and Andrew Zimbalist. Washington, D.C.: Brookings Institution Press, 1997, pp. 178–207.

Ross, Sonya. "Clinton Signs Bill Removing Baseball Antitrust Exemption for Labor Matters," *Associated Press,* October 28, 1998, at http://www.fl.milive.com/tigers/stories/19981028antitrust.html.

Rottenberg, Simon. "The Baseball Players Labor Market," *Journal of Political Economy,* vol. 64, no. 3 (June 1956), pp. 242–258.

Rovell, Darren. "Publication: MLB Will Beat NFL in Licensing Revenue in '10," *Sports.biz with Darren Rovell,* June 14, 2010, at http://www.cnbc.com/id/37692194/Publication_MLB_Will_Beat_NFL_In_Licensing_Revenue_In_10.

———. "Sports Fans Feel Pinch in Seat (Prices)," *ESPN Sports Business,* June 21, 2002, at http://espn.go.com/sportsbusiness/s/2002/0621/1397693.html.

Ryan, Joan. *Little Girls in Pretty Boxes.* New York: Doubleday, 1995.

Sando, Mike. "10 Things to Know About NFL Labor Situation," *ESPN NFL,* January 31, 2011, at http://espn.go.com/blog/nfcwest/post/_/id/32363/10-things-to-know-about-nfl-labor-situation.

Sandomir, Richard. "Yankees Slash the Price of Top Tickets," *The New York Times,* April 29, 2009, at http: www.nytimes.com/2009/04/29/sports/baseball/29tickts.html?_r=1&scp=4& sg=+%20yankees%20+%%22ticket%20prices%22&st=cse.

San Jose Redevelopment Agency. *Economic Impact Analysis: Proposed Major League Ballpark in San Jose, CA,* September 22, 2009, at http://www.sjredevelopment.org/ballpark/meetings/092409/SanJosePresentation092109.pdf.

Scahill, Edward. "Did Babe Ruth Have a Comparative Advantage as a Pitcher?" *Journal of Economic Education,* vol. 21, no. 4 (Fall 1990), pp. 402–410.

Schlabach, Mark. "NCAA: Where Does the Money Go?" *ESPN.com,* July 12, 2011, at http://espn.go.com/college-sports/story/_/id/6756472/following-ncaa-money.

Schmidt, Martin B., and David J. Berri. "Competitive Balance and Market Size in Major League Baseball," *Review of Industrial Organization,* vol. 21, no.1 (August 2002), pp. 41–54.

Schnaars, Christopher, Jodi Upton, and Kristin DeRamus. "USA Today College Football Head Coach Salary Database," *USA Today,* November 17, 2011, at http://www.usatoday.com/sports/college/football/story/2011-11-17/cover-college-football-coaches-salaries-rise/51242232/1, viewed May 26, 2012.

Schmuckler, Eric. "Is the NFL Still Worth It?" *Mediaweek,* September 28, 1998, pp. 26–32.

Scott, Matt. "Phil Jones's Deal Shows FIFA New Rule Drives Up the Price of English Talent," *The Guardian,* June 9, 2011, at http://www.guardian.co.uk/football/2011/jun/10/phil-jones-fifa-rules-price/print.

Scully, Gerald W. "Pay and Performance in Major League Baseball," *American Economic Review,* vol. 64, no. 5 (December 1974), pp. 915–930.

———. *The Business of Major League Baseball.* Chicago: University of Chicago Press, 1989.

———. *The Market Structure of Sports.* Chicago: University of Chicago Press, 1995.

Seiken, Eric. "The NCAA and the Courts: College Football on Television," in *Sports and the Law,* ed. by Charles Quirk. New York: Garland, 1996, pp. 56–62.

Seldon, Arthur. "Public Choice and the Choices of the Public," in *Democracy and Public Choice,* ed. by Charles Rowley. London: Basil Blackwell, 1987, pp. 122–134.

Seymour, Harold. *Baseball: The Early Years.* New York: Oxford University Press, 1960.

———. *Baseball: The Golden Years.* New York: Oxford University Press, 1971.

Shaikin, Bill, and Kevin Baxter. "Angels' Double-play: Pujols and Wilson; Money from TV Allows Team to Acquire Stars," *Los Angeles Times,* December 8, 2011, p. C1.

Shapiro, Beth. "John Hannah and the Growth of Big-Time Intercollegiate Athletics at Michigan State University," *Journal of Sports History,* vol. 10, no. 3 (Winter 1983), pp 26–40.

Sheehan, Joe. "Don't Blame the Pirates, Blame MLB's Revenue Sharing System," *SI.com,* August 25, 2010, at http://sportsillustrated.cnn.com/2010/

writers/joe_sheehan/08/25/pirates.finances/index.html.

Shingler, Ronald J. "Antitrust Law and the Sports League Relocation Rules," *Golden State University Law Review*, vol. 18, no. 1 (2010), article 5, at http://digitalcommons.law.ggu.edu/ggulrev/vol18/iss1/5, viewed April 4, 2012.

Shulman, James L., and William G. Bowen. *The Game of Life*. Princeton, N.J.: Princeton University Press, 2001.

Siegfried, John, and Andrew Zimbalist. "The Economics of Sports Facilities and Their Construction," *Journal of Economic Perspectives*, vol. 14, no. 3 (Summer 2000), pp. 95–114.

———. "A Note on the Local Economic Impact of Sports Expenditures," *Journal of Sports Economics*, vol. 3, no. 4 (November 2002), pp. 361–366.

Sigelman, Lee, and Samuel Bookheimer. "Is It Whether You Win or Lose? Monetary Contributions to Big-Time College Athletic Programs," *Social Science Quarterly*, vol. 64, no. 2 (June 1983), pp. 347–359.

"Silvio Berlusconi and Family," *The World's Billionaires*, March 2012, at http://www.forbes.com/profile/silvio-berlusconi/.

Simmons, Bill. "Welcome to the No Benjamins Association," *ESPN.com*, February 27, 2009, at http://espn.go.com.

Sirak, Ron. "LPGA Facing Economic Realities," *Golf Digest*, November 18, 2008, at http://www.golfdigest.com/golf-tours-news/2008-11/20081119sirak.Smith, Chris. "College Football's Most Valuable Teams," *Forbes*, December 22, 2011, at http://www.forbes.com/sites/chrissmith/2011/12/22/college-footballs-most-valuable-teams.

———. "BCS National Championship: Gameday Is Payday for Coaches," *Forbes*, January 9, 2012, at http://www.forbes.com/sites/chrissmith/2012/01/09/bcs-championship-game-day-is-pay-day-for-coaches/.

———. "Final Four Trip Worth $9.5 Million to Conference," *rivals.com*, March 15, 2012, at http://rivals.yahoo.com/ncaa/basketball/news?slug=ys-forbes-final_four_trip_worth_millions_031412.

———. "Baseball after Cable: Team Sales Prices Boosted by Cable Networks," *Forbes*, March 21, 2012, at http://www.forbes.com/sites/chrissmith/2012/03/21/baseball-after-cable-team-sale-prices-boosted-by-cable-networks.

Smith, Gary. "A New Life," *Sports Illustrated*, March 28, 1983, pp. 60–67.

Smith, D. Randall. "Big-Time Basketball and the Advertising Effect: Does Success Really Matter," *Journal of Sports Economics*, vol. 9, no.4 (2008), pp. 387–406.

Smith, Ronald. *Sports and Freedom: The Rise of Big-Time College Athletics*. New York: Oxford University Press, 1988.

SoccerEx. "Peace At Last as Serie A Clubs Agree Revenue Sharing Deal," *SoccerEx Business Daily*, 2009–2012, at http://www.soccerex.com/industry-news/peace-at-last-as-serie-a-clubs-agree-revenue-sharing-deal/.

Solow, John L. and Anthony C. Krautmann. "Leveling the Playing Field or Just Lowering Salaries? The Effects of Redistribution in Baseball," *Southern Economic Journal*, vol. 73, no. 4 (2007), pp. 947–958.

Spalding, Albert G. *America's National Game*. New York: American Sports Publishing Company, 1911, p. 302.

Spence, A. Michael. "Job Market Signaling," *Quarterly Journal of Economics*, vol. 87, no. 3 (August 1973), pp. 355–374.

Sperber, Murray. *College Sports Inc*. New York: Henry Holt and Co., 1990.

———. *Onward to Victory: The Crises That Shaped College Sports*. New York: Henry Holt, 1998.

"Sports Quotes—Another 'Top 10' List of Favorites…," at http://www.famous-quotes-and-quotations.com/sports-quotes.html.

Stark, Jayson. "How the new BCA Changes Baseball," *ESPN.com: Baseball*, November 22, 2011, at http://espn.go.com/espn/print?id=7270203&type=story.

Staudohar, Paul. *Playing for Dollars: Labor Relations and the Sports Business.* Ithaca, N.Y.: ILR Press, 1996.

———. "The Hockey Lockout of 2004–2005," *Monthly Labor Report,* December 2005, pp 23–29.

———. "Why No Baseball Work Stoppage?" *Journal of Sports Economics,* vol. 4, no. 4 (November 2003), pp. 362–366.

Staurowsky, Ellen. " 'Should College Athletes Be Paid?' Is the Wrong Question," *Atlantic Monthly,* September 19, 2011, at http://www.theatlantic.com/entertainment/archive/2011/09/should-college-athletes-get-paid-is-the-wrong-question/245312/.

Steptoe, Sonja, and E. M. Swift. "A Done Deal," *Sports Illustrated,* March 28, 1994, pp. 32–36.

"Steroid Suspensions," *Baseball Almanac.* 2000–2012, at http://www.baseball-almanac.com/legendary/steroids_baseball.shtml.

Stinson, Jeffrey, and Dennis Howard. "Athletic Success and Private Giving to Athletic and Academic Programs at NCAA Institutions," *Journal of Sport Management,* vol. 21, no. 2 (April 2007), pp. 235–264.

Stratmann, Thomas. "Logrolling," in *Perspectives on Public Choice: A Handbook,* ed. by Dennis Mueller. Cambridge, U.K.: Cambridge University Press, 1997, pp 322–341.

Suellentrop, Chris. "Mark Cuban: How to Meddle with Your Sports Team—The Right Way," *Slate magazine online,* December 4, 2002, at http://www.slate.com.

Suggs, Welch. "The Demise of the 'Amateur Ideal,' " *Chronicle of Higher Education,* October 29, 1999, pp. A75–A76.

———. "New Grades on Academic Progress Show Widespread Failings among Teams," *The Chronicle of Higher Education,* March 11, 2005, at http://chronicle.com/free/v51/i27/27a04001.htm.

———. "NCAA to Pay $55-Million to Settle Lawsuit by Assistant Coaches," *The Chronicle of Higher Education,* March 19, 1999, p. A47.

Sullivan, Neil J. *The Dodgers Move West.* New York: Oxford University Press, 1987.

"Summary of Major League Baseball Players Association—Major League Baseball Labor Agreement," *MLB.com,* at http://mlb.mlb.com/mlb/downloads/2011_CBA.pdf.

"Summary of the New NFL Collective Bargaining Agreement," *SI.com,* July 25, 2011, at http://sportsillustrated.cnn.com/2011/football/nfl/07/25/cba-settlement-summary/index.html.

Sunde, Uwe. "Heterogeneity and Performance in Tournaments: A Test for Incentive Effects Using Professional Tennis Data," *Applied Economics,* vol. 41, no. 25–27 (November–December 2009), pp. 3199–3208.

Swift, E. M. "Anatomy of a Plot: The Kerrigan Assault," *Sports Illustrated,* February 14, 1994, pp. 28–38.

Swindell, David, and Mark Rosentraub. "Who Benefits from the Presence of Professional Sports Teams? The Implications for Public Funding of Stadiums and Arenas," *Public Administration Review,* vol. 58, no. 1 (January/February 1998), pp. 11–20.

Szymanski, Stefan. "A Market Test for Discrimination in the English Professional Soccer Leagues," *Journal of Political Economy,* vol. 108, no. 3 (June 2000), pp. 590–603.

Szymanski, Stefan, and Andrew Zimbalist. *National Pastime: How Americans Play Baseball and the Rest of the World Plays Soccer.* Washington, D.C.: Brookings Institution Press, 2005.

Taibbi, Matt. "The Devil's Doorstep: A Visit with Scott Boras," *Men's Journal,* February 23, 2009, at http://www.mensjournal.com/the-devil%E2%80%99s-doorstep.

Taylor, Beck A., and Justin G. Trogdon. "Losing to Win: Tournament Incentives in the National Basketball Association," *Journal of Labor Economics,* vol. 20, no. 1 (January 2002), pp. 23–41.

"Team Marketing Research," *Team Marketing Report,* April 2011, at https://www.teammarketing.com/public/files/2011_mlb_fci.pdf.

Telander, Rick. *The Hundred-Yard Lie: The Corruption of College Football and What We Can Do to Stop It.* New York: Simon & Schuster, 1989.

"Terms of the Owners' Proposed CBA," *Fox Sports,* July 21, 2011, at http://msn.foxsports.com/nfl/story/Terms-of-NFL-owners-proposed-collective-bargaining-agreement-072111.

Thaler, Richard. "The Winner's Curse," *Journal of Economic Perspectives,* vol. 2, no. 1 (Winter 1988), pp. 191–202.

Thamel, Pete. "Schools Where the Only Real Test Is Basketball," *New York Times,* February 25, 2006, at http://www.nytimes.com/2006/02/25/sports/ncaabasketball/25preps.html?pagewanted=1&ei=5088&en=b4408741cbal781f&ex=1298523600&partner=rssnyt&emc=rss.

Thomas, G. Scott. "Surhoff Proves to Be '99s Best Investment," *Street & Smith's SportsBusiness Journal,* October 25–31, 1999, p. 1.

Thornley, Stew. *Land of the Giants: New York's Polo Grounds.* Philadelphia: Temple University Press, 2000.

Tide Pride, *Tide Totals,* 2012, at http://www.rolltide.com/boosters/tide-totals.html.

Tirone, Mike. "Top 25 Digital Media Companies, By Revenue," *Wealth Wire,* April 14, 2011, at http://www.wealthwire.com/news/economy/1005.

Title IX Legal Manual, U.S. Dept. of Justice, Civil Rights Division, January 11, 2001, at http://www.usdoj.gov/crt/cor/coord/ixlegal.htm.

Tofler, Ian, Barri Katz Stryer, Lyle J. Micheli, and Lisa Herman. "Physical and Emotional Problems of Elite Female Gymnasts," *New England Journal of Medicine,* vol. 335, no. 4 (July 25, 1996), pp. 281–283.

Tollison, Robert. "Rent Seeking," in *Perspectives on Public Choice: A Handbook,* ed. by Dennis Mueller. Cambridge, U.K.: Cambridge University Press, 1997, pp. 506–525.

Tomlinson, Alan. "De Coubertin and the Modern Olympics," in *Five Ring Circus: Money, Power and Politics at the Olympic Games,* ed. by Alan Tomlinson and Garry Whannel. London: Pluto Press, 1984, pp. 84–97.

Trumpbour, Robert. *The New Cathedrals,* Syracuse: Syracuse University Press, 2007.

Tu, Charles. "How Does a New Stadium Affect Housing Values? The Case of FedEx Field," *Land Economics,* vol. 81, no. 3 (August 2005), pp. 379–395.

UEFA. "Champions League Financial Distribution," *Management,* August 16, 2011, at http://www.uefa.com/uefa/management/finance/news/newsid=1661038.html.

Ungerleider, Steven. *Faust's Gold: Inside the East German Doping Machine.* New York: Thomas Dunne Books, 2001.

UPI International. "Average N.F.L. Salary is $90,102, Survey Says," *New York Times,* January 29, 1982, at http://www.nytimes.com/1982/01/29/sports/average-nfl-salary-is-90102-survey-says.html.

University of Pennsylvania Museum of Anthropology and Archeology. *The Real Story of the Ancient Olympic Games,* 1996, at http://www.upenn.edu/museum/Olympics/olympicathletes.html.

U.S. Census Bureau. "Population and Housing Occupancy Status: 2010—United States—Metropolitan Statistical Areas," *American FactFinder,* 2010, at http://factfinder2.census.gov/faces/tableservices/jsf/pages/productview.xhtml?pid=DEC_10_NSRD_GCTPL2.US24PR&prodType=table.

U.S. Department of Commerce. "Table CA1-3: Personal Income Summary," *Regional Data: GDP & Personal Income,* April 25, 2012, at http://www.bea.gov/iTable/iTable.cfm?reqid=70&step=1&isuri=1&acrdn=5, viewed April 27, 2012.

U.S. Supreme Court, *NCAA v. Board of Regents of Univ. of Okla.,* 468 U.S. 85 (1984), at http://caselaw.lp.findlaw.com/scrips/getcase.pl?court=us&vol=468&invol=85, viewed March 20, 2012.

"*USA Today* Salary Databases: MLB," *USA Today* at http://content.usatoday.com/sportsdata/baseball/mlb/salaries/team.

"*USA Today* Salary Databases: NBA," 2012, *USA Today* at http://content.usatoday.com/sportsdata/basketball/nba/salaries/team.

"*USA Today* Salary Databases: NFL," *USA Today* at http://content.usatoday.com/sportsdata/football/nfl/salaries/team.

"*USA Today* Salary Databases: NHL," *USA Today* at http://content.usatoday.com/sportsdata/hockey/nhl/salaries/team.

Vamplew, Wray. *Pay Up and Play the Game: Professional Sport in Britain, 1875–1914.* Cambridge, U.K.: Cambridge University Press, 1988.

van Riper, Tom. "Boxing's Last Golden Boy?" *Forbes,* January 15, 2009, at http://www.forbes.com/2009/01/14/boxing-oscar-de-la-hoya-biz-sports_cx_tvr_0115delahoya.html?partner=whiteglove_google.

————. "The NFL vs. American Needle," *Forbes,* January 7, 2010, at http://www.forbes.com/2010/01/06/american-needle-supreme-court-business-sports-nfl.html.

Veblen, Thorstein. *Theory of the Leisure Class.* New York: The Viking Press, 1967.

Veeck, Bill, with Ed Linn. *The Hustler's Handbook.* Durham, N.C.: Baseball America Classic Books, 1996.

————. *Veeck as in Wreck.* Chicago: University of Chicago Press, 1962.

Veraros, Nikolaos, Evangelia Kasimati, and Peter Dawson. "The 2004 Olympic Games Announcement and Its Effect on the Athens and Milan Stock Exchanges," *Applied Economics Letters,* vol. 11, no. 12 (October 2004), pp. 749–753.

von Allmen, Peter. "Is the Reward System in NASCAR Efficient?" *Journal of Sports Economics,* vol. 2, no. 1 (February 2000), pp. 62–79.

————. "Multiplier Effects and Local Economic Impact," in *The Oxford Handbook of Sports Economics,* vol. 2, ed. by Stephen Shmanske and Leo Kahane. Oxford: Oxford University Press, 2012.

————. "Coaching Women and Women Coaching: Pay Differentials in the Title IX Era," in *The Handbook on the Economics of Women's Sports,* ed. by Eva Marikova Leeds and Michael A. Leeds. Cheltenham, U.K.: Edward Elgar, forthcoming.

Vrooman, John. "Franchise Free Agency in Professional Sports Leagues," *Southern Journal of Economics,* vol. 64, no. 1 (July 1997), pp. 191–219.

————. "Theory of the Perfect Game: Competitive Balance in Monopoly Sports," *Review of Industrial Organization,* vol. 34, no. 5 (2009), pp. 5–44.

Walker, Mark, and John Wooders. "Minimax Play at Wimbledon," *American Economic Review,* vol. 91, no. 5 (December 2001), pp. 1521–1538.

Walker, Simone. "De la Hoya: Boxing's Future Is Golden," *SportsPro,* October 13, 2009, at http://www.sportspromedia.com/notes_and_insights/de_la_hoya_-_boxings_future_is_golden/.

Walsh, William D. "The Entry Problem of Francophones in the National Hockey League: A Systematic Interpretation," *Canadian Public Policy,* vol. 18, no. 4 (December 1992), pp. 443–460.

Ward, Geoffrey, and Kenneth Burns. *Baseball: An Illustrated History.* New York: Alfred A. Knopf, 1994.

Warren, Earl. Writing for the Majority. Cited in *United States* v. *International Boxing Club of NY, Inc.,* 348 US 236—Supreme Court 1955, at *FindLaw,* at http://caselaw.lp.findlaw.com/scripts/getcase.pl?court=us&vol=348&invol=236.

Weaver, Jane. "Steroid Addiction a Risk for Young Athletes," *MSNBC,* April 5, 2005, at http://www.msnbc.msn.com/id/7348758.

Westcott, Rich. *Philadelphia's Old Ballparks.* Philadelphia: Temple University Press, 1996.

Westhead, Rick. "Maple Leaf Sports Plans Broadcast Gamble," *TheStar.com,* November 27, 2011, at http://www.thestar.com/sports/article/1093199-maple-leaf-sports-plans-broadcast-gamble.

Wetzel, Dan, Josh Peter, and Jeff Passan, *Death to the BCS,* New York: Gotham Books, 2010.

"Where the Money Goes," *NCAA Champion Magazine,* Spring 2010, at http://www.ncaachampionmagazine.org/Exclusives/WhereTheMoneyGoes.pdf.

Whitney, Daisy. "Demand for Online Video Fuels Digital Revenue for Sports Programming," *ReelSEO.com,* 2012, at http://www.reelseo.com/digital-revenue-for-sports-programming.

Wieberg, Steve. "Academic Progress Rates Analyzed," *USA Today,* March 1, 2005, at http://www.usatoday.com/sports/college/2005-03-01-apr-analysis_x.htm.

"Wimbledon 2009 Prize Money," *The Tennis Times,* June 2009, at http://thetennistimes.com/here-are-prizemoney-breakdowns-for-wimbledon-2009/.

Will, George. *Bunts.* New York: Scribner, 1998.

Winfree, Jason, Jill McCluskey, Ron Mittelhammer, and Rodney Fort. "Location and Attendance in Major League Baseball," *Applied Economics,* vol. 36, no. 19 (October 2004), pp. 2117–2124.

Wong, Glenn. *Essentials of Sports Law Fourth Edition,* Santa Barbara: Praeger, 2010.

"World Series History: Recaps and Results," *World Series.com,* June 19, 2012, at http://mlb.mlb.com/mlb/history/postseason/mlb_ws.jsp?feature=recaps_index.

WTA Tour Incorporated. "WTA Prize Money Leaders," November 7, 2011, at http://www.wtatennis.com/SEWTATour-Archive/Rankings_Stats/prize_money_2011.pdf.

———. *WTA Women's Tennis Association 2012 Official Rulebook,* 2012, at http://www.wtatennis.com/SEWTATour-Archive/Archive/AboutTheTour/rules.pdf

Yahoo! Sport. "Ligue 1—France Fourth in Merchandise Sales," *EuroSport.com,* February 22, 2011, at http://uk.eurosport.yahoo.com/23022011/58/ligue-1-france-fourth-merchandise-sales.html.

Yang, Chih-Hai, and Hsuan-Y Lin. "Is There Salary Discrimination by Nationality in the NBA?: Foreign Talent or Foreign Market," *Journal of Sports Economics,* vol. 13, no. 1 (February 2012), pp. 53–75.

Young, David. *The Modern Olympics: A Struggle for Revival.* Baltimore: Johns Hopkins University Press, 1996.

Zacher, Elissa Michelle. *The Colosseum in Rome: Part One,* September 1, 2011, at http://socyberty.com/history/the-colosseum-in-rome-part-one/.

Zengerle, Jason. "March Payday Madness," *Business Week,* March 25, 2010, at http://www.businessweek.com/magazine/content/10_14/b4172058546496.htm.

Zimbalist, Andrew. *Baseball and Billions.* New York: Basic Books, 1992.

———. "Salaries and Performance: Beyond the Scully Model," in *Diamonds Are Forever: The Business of Baseball,* ed. by Paul M. Sommers. Washington, D.C.: The Brookings Institution, 1992, pp. 109–133.

———. "Labor Relations in Major League Baseball," *Journal of Sports Economics,* vol. 4, no. 4 (November 2003), pp. 332–355.

———. *May the Best Team Win: Baseball Economics and Public Policy.* Washington, D.C.: Brookings Institution Press, 2003, pp. 35–36.

———. Sport as Business," *Oxford Review of Economic Policy,* vol. 19, no. 4 (2003), pp. 503–511.

———. "The BCS, Antitrust and Public Policy," *The Antitrust Bulletin,* vol. 54, no. 4 (Winter 2009), pp. 823–855.

———. *Unpaid Professionals.* Princeton, N.J.: Princeton University Press, 1999.

Zimmerman, Dennis. "Subsidizing Stadiums: Who Benefits, Who Pays?" in *Sports, Jobs, and Taxes,* ed. by Roger G. Noll and Andrew Zimbalist. Washington, D.C.: Brookings Institution Press, 1997, pp. 119–147.

PHOTO CREDITS

INDEX

Note: Page numbers followed by the letters *f* and *t* refer to figures and tables, respectively.